CONTEMPORARY PROPERTY LAW

Contemporary Property Law

Lucy Marsh

Published by:

 Vandeplas Publishing, LLC – December 2018

801 International Parkway, 5th Floor
Lake Mary, FL. 32746
USA

www.vandeplaspublishing.com

ISBN 978-1-60042-302-4

# CONTEMPORARY PROPERTY LAW

LUCY MARSH

# INTRODUCTION

Property law includes a great diversity of topics - including Adverse Possession, Environmental Regulations, Water Rights, Landlord/Tenant Relationships, Future Interests, Oil & Gas, Buying Land, Zoning, and Wild Animals. That is what keeps it lively and interesting.

Cases in this book have been selected to illustrate the fundamentals of Property that every lawyer will be expected to understand. Most of the cases are also entertaining stories – which should make it easier to remember the law.

Although the cases have been extensively edited, enough has been left to illustrate the number of different issues involved in any fact situation, and to provide an understanding of how a judge reaches a decision. The "sub-plots," so to speak, are important. They cover additional materials that will help to provide a rich, well-rounded understanding of the basic rules of Property law, so that when you become a lawyer you will be able to start from a firm foundation in the law.

Issues change, and laws change. However, if you start with a good foundation you should be able to build effectively upon the vicarious experience you gain from reading the cases included in this book. The skills you develop by learning to read and understand somewhat complex cases will be of benefit to you throughout your career in the law.

Time to get started. Best wishes.

# TABLE OF CONTENTS

# CHAPTER ONE

# ADVERSE POSSESSION

## INTRODUCTION

The law of adverse possession is a way of gaining full legal title to a piece of land without paying for it. That comes as a surprise to most non-lawyers. But the concept has been part of the common law since at least 1235, and is available in virtually every state. The specific requirements for adverse possession vary a bit from state to state, but the basics are the same.

Note that consistent with the concept of governmental immunity, adverse possession is generally not permitted with regard to land owned by any governmental entity. You simply are not allowed to steal land from the government. But in conflicts between private landowners, the law of adverse possession is frequently used to determine who owns a particular parcel of land.

Now for some recent cases to illustrate some of the requirements for successfully gaining title by adverse possession.

The following case illustrates one of the situations in which adverse possession is used most frequently – to clear up boundary disputes. Note that because of the possibility of adverse possession, the buyer of land may not actually get all of the land described in the deed. What might the buyers in this case have done to protect themselves?

# SUPREME COURT OF NEW HAMPSHIRE
## BARBARA F. O'MALLEY & OTHERS.
## V.
## AARON LITTLE & OTHERS.

AUGUST 31, 2017

LYNN, J.

Defendants Aaron and Maryann Little (Littles) appeal an order of the Superior Court quieting title in the plaintiffs, Barbara F. O'Malley and her daughter Helen T. O'Malley, to a strip of land based upon adverse possession. We affirm.

## I

The pertinent facts are as follows. Barbara O'Malley and her husband, Joseph, acquired the property at 7 McKay Avenue in Hampton (McKay Lot) in 1963 for use as a summer home. Over the next 50 years, the couple lived there with their children, including their daughter Helen, during the summer months; they also used the property for week-long vacations in April, and intermittent weekend trips. The backyard of the McKay Lot abuts the backyard of the Littles' property at 6 Francis Street (Francis Lot).

In October 1993, Barbara contracted for the installation of a chain link fence between the McKay Lot and the Francis Lot after tenants from the latter began walking across the yard of the McKay Lot with beach chairs and scratching Helen's car. The fence was placed about three to five feet over the property line between the two lots. Between the fence and the property line (in the disputed area), there is a clothesline as well as an outdoor shower and grill, all of which were used frequently by the O'Malley family. The plaintiffs and their relatives and friends would occasionally park against the fence.

In 1996, following the death of her husband, Barbara deeded the McKay Lot to herself and her daughter Helen. Around this time, Helen planted three rose bushes in the disputed area against the fence, one of which still exists. Tenants of the Francis Lot and other individuals occasionally cut through a gap that existed between the fence and another fence that separated two other abutting properties, but few individuals walked across the disputed area. The individuals who did cross the disputed area did so on only a few occasions.

The Littles purchased the Francis Lot in December 2008. Upon acquiring the property, the Littles assumed that the actual property line was represented by the fence between the two properties. However, in the spring of 2010, Scott McCarthy, a prior owner of the Francis Lot, informed the Littles that the plaintiffs' fence encroached approximately three to five feet onto the Francis Lot from the actual property line. The Littles confirmed this statement by reviewing a survey plan and measuring the property line with a tape measure. They then called the plaintiffs in April 2010 to inform them of this discovery, before stating that the plaintiffs needed to move the fence. The plaintiffs refused. The Littles claimed that, during this conversation, they gave the plaintiffs permission to continue using the disputed area; the plaintiffs denied that such permission was given. Aaron Little testified that, around this time, he visited the O'Malley property and walked along the fence with Helen, asserting that the correct boundary between the two properties was represented by several pins from an earlier surveyor's plan. However, the location of those pins did not align with the property line depicted on the surveyor's plan.

Nothing more occurred until the fall of 2013, when the Littles once again e-mailed the plaintiffs and requested that the fence be moved. Although the Littles offered the plaintiffs a license to use the disputed area, the plaintiffs declined. In November, the Littles contacted the plaintiffs yet again and told them to remove the fence by the end of the year. The Littles threatened to take action to move the fence if the plaintiffs refused to relocate it. In December 2013, the plaintiffs instituted this suit to quiet title to the disputed area based upon adverse possession. After conducting a two-day bench trial in June 2016, the court found in favor of the plaintiffs. Specifically, the trial court found that the plaintiffs did not receive permission to use the disputed area in 2010, and that the Littles' statement to the plaintiffs that the fence needed to be moved "would not put a reasonably prudent person on notice that they had actually been ousted." This appeal followed.

II

On appeal, the Littles assert that they ousted the plaintiffs in 2010 and/or 2013, before the expiration of the 20–year statute of limitations applicable to adverse possession claims, by asserting their title to the disputed area and demanding that the fence be moved. The Littles further claim that they implicitly granted the plaintiffs permission by demanding the removal of the fence and then refraining from removing it.

## A

The Littles assert that the trial court erred by ruling that they did not interrupt the plaintiffs' possession of the disputed area. Specifically, they claim that a rightful owner, to oust an adverse possessor, need only assert title and demand that the adverse possessor leave. Consequently, they argue that the trial court erred by requiring them to demonstrate either a clear intent to retake possession of the property or actions sufficient to put a reasonably prudent person on notice that he or she actually has been ousted. The Littles rely primarily upon our decisions in *Locke v. Whitney*, 63 N.H. 597, 3 A. 920 (1886), and *Towle v. Ayer*, 8 N.H. 57 (1835), to support their view.

To acquire title to real property by adverse possession, the possessor must show twenty years of adverse, continuous, exclusive and uninterrupted use of the land claimed so as to give notice to the owner that an adverse claim is being made.

A review of our jurisprudence with regard to this question indicates that, contrary to the Littles' claim, ouster requires significantly more than mere verbal demands and assertions of title. In *Locke*, we held that a dispossessed owner of a lot retained title against an adverse possessor. In the course of reaching our decision we stated that the owner's "entry upon the land" and "claim of title" interrupted adverse possession. However, this statement was dicta; the decision in favor of the dispossessed owner was ultimately based upon the fact that the adverse possessor was not entitled to avail himself of the possession of prior possessors of the lot because he did not claim under them. Furthermore, we have recognized that entry upon the land does not necessarily interrupt adverse possession. *See Alukonis v. Kashulines*, (1952) (holding that a survey of a property did not interrupt the continuity of an adverse possession claim over that property).

Ouster of an adverse possessor requires conduct that puts a reasonably prudent person on notice that he or she actually has been ousted. A true owner's entry will toll the statute of limitations if his or her acts of dominion are such that they put a reasonably prudent person on notice that the true owner's purpose is to resume possession of the land and that such person actually has been ousted.

The Littles also rely on our decision in *Zivic v. Place*, (1982). However, we find that case distinguishable from this one. In *Zivic*, the record owner of a road sent a letter to the person claiming an easement by prescription that both asserted title to the road and gave the claimant explicit permission to use the road.We found that this letter ended the adversity of the claimant's use because he took no action after receiving the letter to put the rightful owner on notice that his use of the road was still adverse. Here, the Littles did not grant the plaintiffs explicit permission to use the area, and the plaintiffs ignored the Littles' demands to move the fence, plainly indicating that their use was still adverse. Thus, *Zivic* does not support the Littles' position.

Here, the Littles repeatedly claimed through telephone calls and e-mails that the fence encroached upon their property and had to be moved. Yet demands communicated over the telephone or by e-mail are no more effective at ousting an adverse possessor in the present day than demands shouted from a nearby property or delivered by letter would have been at the time of Locke. *See Brown v. Whitcomb*, 150 Vt. 106, (1988) ("Mere verbal protestations without action to reassert control or dominion over the disputed land does not interrupt the adverse possessor's interest in the property."). Although Aaron Little visited the McKay Lot and conducted a walk along the fence with Helen, he did so merely to reiterate his claim that the fence encroached on his property and had to be moved, and took no further action against the plaintiffs until repeating his demands in 2013. That action alone would not put a reasonably prudent person on notice that he or she has been ousted.

B

The Littles also claim that their assertions of title constituted implied permission to the plaintiffs to continue using the disputed area. In their view, "a demand to move the fence, followed by forbearance, is permission." Assuming without deciding that this argument is preserved for our review, we reject it.

A use of land is adverse when made under a claim of right where no right exists. To establish a prima facie case of adverse use, the plaintiff must first produce evidence of acts of such a character that they create an inference of non-permissive use. Once the plaintiff satisfies this initial burden, the burden shifts to the defendant to produce evidence that the plaintiff's use of the disputed area was permitted. The burden of persuasion remains at all times on the plaintiff.

The determination of whether the use of a property has been adverse or permissive is a matter of fact to be determined by the trial court. The nature of the use, whether adverse or permissive, may be inferred from the manner, character and frequency of the exercise of the right and the situation of the parties.

We agree with the Littles that permission in the context of adverse possession can be either explicit or implied. However, implied permission must be evidenced by the use of the property and the "situation of the parties," not by the Littles' failure to oust the plaintiffs after making a verbal assertion of title. Here, the trial court evaluated the evidence and concluded that there was insufficient evidence to find that the plaintiffs' control of the disputed area was either explicitly or implicitly permitted. Upon reviewing the record, we find ample evidence that the plaintiffs disputed the

Littles' assertion of title over the disputed area and continually defied their demands to move the fence. Consequently, we cannot say that the trial court's ruling was unsupported by the evidence or erroneous as a matter of law.[4]

Affirmed.

Note: The following case is considerably more complex, involving rights to the oil that is now being produced from the land. The Montana Supreme Court resolves the case by using the law of adverse possession.

First, some background. When someone dies without a will, (intestate), his or her property goes to the closest relatives – usually spouse and children – according to the laws of intestate succession in the state in which the land is located.

Second, it is possible to sever ownership of the surface of land from ownership of the underlying minerals. Until a specific severance, the owner of the surface of land owns everything directly below the surface, down "to the center of the earth."

Third, it is possible for several people to own a parcel of land at the same time. This is called concurrent ownership. For example, if A, B and C all chip in to buy a piece of land they would probably take title to the land as tenants in common, giving each of them a right to be anywhere on the land, at any time. Since each tenant in common has a right to enjoy possession of any part of the land, you can see that adverse possession against a cotenant might be very difficult. But it can happen.

In places where there may be valuable minerals, such as coal, copper, or uranium below the surface of the land it is not infrequent for a landowner when selling land to reserve all or some of the minerals below the surface of the land – in case valuable minerals are later discovered. For this purpose, oil and gas are considered to be minerals – part of the mineral estate.

When the owner of land sells the surface, but retains legal title to the minerals, that causes a severance. From then on, the ownership of the surface is treated separately from the ownership of the minerals. Adverse possession of the surface estate would not include adverse possession of the mineral estate. To gain title by adverse possession to the minerals there would have to be actual possession of the minerals – which basically means bringing the minerals to the surface – for example, beginning to produce oil.

---

4    We note the peculiar outcomes that would be produced by the Littles' construction of the concept of implied permission. Under their view, a rightful property owner could undertake two entirely opposing courses of action—granting permission to an adverse possessor or demanding that the adverse possessor vacate the property—and nevertheless realize the same outcome: permission. Furthermore, any property owner could end an adverse possession claim merely by verbally demanding that the adverse possessor leave, because his or her subsequent forbearance would constitute "implied" permission. Such an outcome would contradict our past cases, where we have held that verbal protests are insufficient to end an adverse possession claim. See, *e.g.*, *Gallo*, 166 N.H. at 739, 103 A.3d 1183

It is not infrequent that people do not pay much attention to ownership of the mineral interest – until oil is discovered. Then it becomes vitally important to determine who is entitled to the financial benefits from production of oil.

Note that in the following case there was no severance of the mineral and surface estates until 1997. But in order to find out who is entitled to the oil in 2018, the court has to check title to the land – going back 102 years, all the way back to 1916.

To bring this matter before the court, and get a final resolution of the rights of all possible claimants, one set of claimants, the Nelsons, brought a quiet title action, joining all the people with known claims, plus "all other persons unknown, claiming or who might claim any right, title, estate, or interest in the land." Thus, once the Montana Supreme Court reached a conclusion in this quiet title action the result became binding on everyone – whether or not the person had been personally named or served in this lawsuit.

# SUPREME COURT OF MONTANA
## MARK T. NELSON AND JO MARIE S. NELSON, PLAINTIFFS AND APPELLEES,
### V.
## LAYNE STUART DAVIS AND MARY JO DAVIS AS TRUSTEES OF THE LAYNE STUART DAVIS AND MARY JO DAVIS REVOCABLE TRUST DATED 8-2-2011; ANTHONY M. PALESE, JR.; AND CHRISTINA L. FISCHER, AND ALL OTHER PERSONS UNKNOWN, CLAIMING OR WHO MIGHT CLAIM ANY RIGHT, TITLE, ESTATE, OR INTEREST IN, OR LIEN OR ENCUMBRANCE UPON, THE REAL PROPERTY DESCRIBED IN THE COMPLAINT, OR, ANY PART THEREOF, ADVERSE TO PLAINTIFFS' OWNERSHIP, OR ANY COULD UPON PLAINTIFFS' TITLE THERETO, WHETHER SUCH CLAIM OR POSSIBLE CLAIM BE PRESENT OR CONTINGENT, INCHOATE OR ACCRUED, DEFENDANTS AND APPELLEES,
### AND
## GEORGE SALITURO, JR.; ROSE M. SALITURO; THE HEIRS AND DEVISEES, IF ANY, OF GEORGE SALITURO, DEFENDANTS AND APPELLANTS.

DECIDED: MAY 8, 2018

## Opinion

Justice Beth Baker delivered the Opinion of the Court.

Mark T. Nelson and Jo Marie S. Nelson (the Nelsons) purchased property from Mary Jo Davis and Anthony Palese, Jr., (Davis & Palese), in 1997. The deed purported to sell the Nelsons the property in its entirety save a portion of the mineral estate reserved in Davis & Palese. After years of farm use, the Nelsons and Davis & Palese leased the property for oil and gas development. In the ensuing title research, the Nelsons' counsel uncovered possible remote heirs with an interest in the property— George Salituro, Jr., and Rose M. Salituro, (the Salituros). The Nelsons brought a quiet title action, and the District Court ruled in their favor. The court quieted surface title and a one-half interest in the mineral estate in the Nelsons, with the remaining half interest in the mineral estate to Davis & Palese. The Salituros appeal. We affirm.

## PROCEDURAL AND FACTUAL BACKGROUND

For purposes of the issues involved in this case, title to the Property is traced back to Paul Bisceglia (Paul). Paul died in 1916, leaving behind his wife Louise and their five children. Under a recorded Decree of Distribution Louise received a one-third interest in the Property, and each of their five children received a two-fifteenths interest.

Three of the five children preceded Louise in death and died with no children or spouses. Under the laws of intestate succession, their interests in the Property passed to Louise. Louise died in 1965, survived by two of her children, Rose and Angelo. Under the laws of intestate succession, when Louise died, her interests in the Property passed equally to her two surviving children: Rose and Angelo. Thus, after the death of their mother, Rose and Angelo each owned a one-half interest in the Property.

Rose married twice. At her death Rose was survived by one child, Josephine from Rose's first marriage, and by Rose's second husband, George Salituro. When Rose died in 1987, her one-half interest in the Property passed in equal shares to her surviving daughter, Josephine, (who thus became the owner of a one-quarter interest), and to Rose's second husband, George Salituro, (who thus became the owner of a one-quarter interest). Angelo continued to own his one-half interest.

The parties to this action do not dispute that an interest in the Property passed to George Salituro upon Rose's death. However, an affidavit was mistakenly recorded saying that no interest passed to George Salituro. In 1988, Rose's daughter, Josephine, and Rose's son, Angelo issued a deed purporting to convey the entirety of the Property to Josephine's two children—Mary Jo Davis and Anthony Palese, Jr. (Davis & Palese). [At that time Angelo owned a one-half interest, Davis & Palese owned a one-quarter interest, and George Salituro owned a one-quarter interest, all as tenants in common. There had been no severance of the surface and mineral estates.]

From 1988 to 1997, Davis & Palese leased the Property to Tom Nelson for grazing and grain farming, and paid all of the property taxes. In 1997, they sold the Property to Mark T. Nelson and Jo Marie S. Nelson (the Nelsons), reserving "an undivided one-half of all Grantor's right, title and interest in and to all of the oil, gas and other minerals in and under" the Property. The Nelsons used the Property for grazing. Starting in 2006, the Nelsons began leasing the Property for oil and gas development.

At some point after mineral production started, a mineral developer sought confirmation of the Property's title. Upon investigation, the Nelsons' attorney discovered the overlooked one-quarter interest that vested in Rose's second husband, George Salituro. George Salituro died in 1991 and his one-quarter interest in the Property passed to his two children from a prior marriage, the Salituros. The Nelsons filed a quiet title action, naming George Salituro's children, and all other possible claimants, as defendants.

The District Court granted summary judgment in favor of the Nelsons and Davis & Palese, concluding in part that Davis & Palese had extinguished the Salituros' interest in the Property through adverse possession before transferring it to the Nelsons in 1997. The District Court quieted title in favor of the Nelsons, except for a fifty percent mineral reservation in favor of Davis & Palese.

## DISCUSSION

The Salituros argue that Davis & Palese never filed an adverse possession lawsuit against the Salituros and are now barred by the statute of limitations from doing so. The Salituros argue that the adverse possession claims of Davis & Palese also fail on the merits because to extinguish the interests of fellow cotenants, a cotenant not only must meet the elements of adverse possession, but also must "oust" fellow cotenants from the property. The Salituros maintain that no ouster occurred here because Davis & Palese never communicated to the Salituros that they were ousting them, nor did Davis & Palese take any other action that was beyond what a cotenant has the right to do.

For a claim of adverse possession to succeed, the claimant must prove that the property was claimed under color of title or by actual, visible, exclusive, hostile and continuous possession for the full statutory period of five years. In addition, the claimant must have paid all taxes due on the property during the statutory period. Section 70-19-407, MCA, governs adverse possession under color of title. It provides that a party may adversely possess property if he or she "entered into the possession of the property under claim of title, exclusive of other right" and continued in occupation and possession for five years. A person enters into possession under claim of title when the person holds land under "any instrument purporting to convey the land or the right to its possession, provided the claim is made thereunder in good faith." For a party to possess and occupy a property under § 70-19-407, MCA, the party must "usually cultivate or improve" the property, protect it "by a substantial enclosure," use it "for pasturage," or put it to "the ordinary use of the occupant." Section 70-19-408(1)(a)-(c), MCA.

Generally, when a cotenant is in possession of shared property, that cotenant's possession is not hostile to the rights of another cotenant, but is presumed to be the possession of his cotenants and himself. This Court has recognized the exception that one tenant in common may so enter and hold as to render the entry and possession adverse, and amount to an ouster of a cotenant. Although a cotenant claiming sole title must "oust" the other cotenants, this does not necessarily imply an actual physical ouster, but it is sufficient if the grantee claims exclusive ownership and by his conduct denies the right of others to any interest in the property. A cotenant can oust a fellow cotenant by providing notice that he or she is claiming an interest hostile and adverse to the fellow cotenant's interest.

Where one goes into possession of property under deed, or deeds, executed by a cotenant, and purporting to convey the entire property, such possession is hostile to that of the cotenant, and he is charged with knowledge of the hostile character thereof.

The Salituros argue that under our precedent a cotenant in possession must provide actual notice to the non-possessing cotenants of their ouster. But *YA Bar Livestock Company* did not change the rule established that an out-of-possession cotenant is charged with knowledge of the hostile character of a cotenant's possession if the cotenant in possession entered under color of title.[2] We held in *YA Bar Livestock* that a grantor could not create color of title by conveying land that he did not own to a corporation of which he was president and majority shareholder.

Under Montana law, an instrument which purports to convey land or the right to its possession is sufficient color of title as a basis for adverse possession *if the claim is made in good faith.*

Davis & Palese entered into possession under color of title. Upon Rose's death, Rose's daughter Josephine, and Rose's second husband, George Salituro were cotenants in the Property. Later one of the cotenants— Josephine —purported to convey the entirety of the Property to Davis & Palese, who were third parties to the cotenancy. Davis & Palese recorded this deed. Davis & Palese both stated in affidavits that they believed they received the entirety of the Property in the 1988 deed. These statements are uncontradicted in the record. The Salituros presented no evidence in the District Court and do not argue on appeal that Josephine had actual knowledge of George Salituro's interest. And the public record in Roosevelt County included an affidavit of heirship which did not mention George Salituro. On this record, we conclude that Davis & Palese had no actual or constructive knowledge that they were cotenants with anyone. Although the 1988 deed could not convey title to the entirety of the Property because Josephine Palese did not own the Property in its entirety, the deed gave Davis & Palese color of title to the entirety of the Property because the

---

2    The principles espoused herein are consistent with the clear weight of authority that ouster occurs when one cotenant purports to convey the entire property to a party that was not previously a cotenant, a deed of transfer is recorded, and the transferee takes possession of the property. Under such circumstances no additional direct notice is required. A minority of jurisdictions hold that a deed purporting to transfer the entire estate to a non-cotenant party does not meet the requirements of notice and ouster.

deed purported to convey the entirety of the Property, was not void on its face, and was made in good faith.

After the 1988 deed, Davis & Palese leased the Property to Tom Nelson, and paid all of the property taxes. These actions meet the requirements for possession and occupation of the Property under § 70-19-408, MCA. We agree with the Salituros that many of the acts upon which Davis & Palese rely to demonstrate possession and occupation would be consistent with holding an interest in a cotenancy if Davis & Palese's entry were not hostile. But because they entered under a recorded deed that purported to convey to them the entirety of the Property, Davis & Palese's initial entry of the Property was obviously consistent with the disclaimer and disavowal of other tenants' interests. Their entry under color of title constitutes ouster. Five years after the 1988 deed, Davis's and Palese's claims to the Property in its entirety ripened into good title.

When Davis & Palese conveyed the Property to the Nelsons in 1997, the Salituros' interests in the Property already had been extinguished. The District Court correctly quieted titled to the Property in favor of the Nelsons, except for and subject to Davis & Palese's combined fifty percent mineral reservation.

The District Court's judgment is affirmed.

Note: In the preceding case the Montana Supreme Court recognized that there might be some question as to the sufficiency of the ouster of a co-tenant. In the following case, there is no question about the sufficiency of the ouster. Does the result in the next case comply with the law? Does it seem like an appropriate result? What might you have done if you had been representing Charlie's siblings?

# COURT OF APPEALS OF ARKANSAS.
## HAZEL SUTTON, AS ADMINISTRATRIX OF THE ESTATE OF JENNIE FAYE ROLEN,
## DECEASED, AND BESSIE TILLERY, APPELLANTS
## V.
## CHARLIE GARDNER, APPELLEE

NOVEMBER 30, 2011

*one liner:*
*Family relation between co-tenants requires stronger evidence of adverse possession that is met by exclusive use of the property, w/ hostile intent that was understood by the co-tenants for more than 7 yrs.*

CLIFF HOOFMAN, Judge.

This case involves a long-running and sometimes violent family dispute over a tract of land in Van Buren and Stone Counties. [Appellant Bessie Tillery and appellee Charlie Gardner are two of the eight children of Thomas Gardner, who died in 1961, leaving a large tract of land, which included the disputed twenty-eight acres in Van Buren County, to pass by intestacy. [So after the death of Thomas' wife, all eight children became owners of the land, as tenants-in-common.]

Appellant appeals from the circuit court's order quieting title to a portion of the disputed property in appellee. We affirm the circuit court's decision.

The family has engaged in litigation over this property more than once. [But no final decision had been reached previously, because suits were dismissed without prejudice, etc.]

[In computing the period of adverse possession of land, the time of pendency of any dismissed, abandoned, or otherwise discontinued action in respect to the property is to be treated as though the action had never been instituted] [It is clear from the evidence presented by both parties that appellee established common-law adverse possession of the property, and we affirm on this basis.]

[To prove the common-law elements of adverse possession, a claimant must show that he has been in possession of the property continuously for more than seven years and that his possession has been visible, notorious, distinct, exclusive, hostile, and with the intent to hold against the true owner.] [It is ordinarily sufficient proof of adverse possession that the claimant's acts of ownership are of such a nature as one would exercise over his own property and would not exercise over the land of another.] Whether possession is adverse to the true owner is a question of fact.

Additional factors come into play when one co-tenant asserts adverse possession against the others, because the possession of one tenant-in-common is the possession of all. Because possession by a co-tenant is not ordinarily adverse to other co-tenants, each having an equal right to possession, a co-tenant must give actual notice to other co-tenants that his possession is adverse to their interests or commit sufficient acts of hostility so that their knowledge of his adverse claim may be presumed. The statutory period of time for an adverse-possession claim does not begin to run until such knowledge has been brought home to the other co-tenants. There is no hard-and-fast rule by which the sufficiency of an adverse claim may be determined; however, the court considers factors such as the relationship of the parties, their reasonable access to the property, kinship, and innumerable other factors to determine if non-possessory co-tenants have been given sufficient warning that the status of a co-tenant in possession has shifted from mutuality to hostility. When there is a family relation between co-tenants, stronger evidence of adverse possession is required.

Appellee met his burden of establishing adverse possession against his co-tenants. It is true, as appellants point out, that appellee did not personally live on this property for the entire period of time since his mother died. He and his wife built two houses in Stone County, where they still live. However, he and his daughters testified that everyone (family members and renters) who has lived on the property since that time has done so with appellee's permission. Kelly testified that she and her husband were the first persons to move there, about one or two years after her grandmother died. She said that appellee had rented the house to other people; Merlene, their sister Carolyn, and Wanda and Leonard Holly had also lived there. She said, "My dad ... let each one of us ... or, ... people in need that ... would take care of it ... and treat it right cause that was his place and everybody knows that...." Appellee testified that he had controlled the property over forty years and had used it as if it were his. He said that, except for a couple of years, he had paid taxes on the property from the 1970s through 2009. He stated that, over the years, he had added a bathroom and a new roof to the house; run livestock; cut and sold firewood; sold a few loads of rock; drilled a well; and built fences around the property. Kelly and Merlene corroborated appellee's testimony.

Appellants helped appellee establish his claim of adverse possession. Bessie stated, "Charlie ... used it like it was his. He didn't ask nobody. He didn't divide up the house stuff. He took it all." She said that appellee had threatened her and would not let her or the other siblings come onto the property after their mother died. "He said he'd shoot us," she stated. Hazel testified that she had heard appellee threaten her mother "to either leave the property alone and get out of the court system ... or he was going to kill her." She added that, in addition to Charlie, her mother and her mother's siblings claimed an interest in this property but had not possessed it because of "threats and actions that's been taken from him or members of his family. They're not allowed onto the property."

In light of this evidence, we hold that appellee established that he began exclusively using the property, with hostile intent that was thoroughly understood by his co-tenants, for more than seven years, and therefore, his claim vested.

Affirmed.

Note: The next case is a lovely contrast, and demonstrates lots of important rules with regard to adverse possession.

## SUPREME COURT, APPELLATE DIVISION, NEW YORK
## CHILDREN'S MAGICAL GARDEN, INC., PLAINTIFF–RESPONDENT,
## V.
## NORFOLK STREET DEVELOPMENT, LLC, ET AL., DEFENDANTS–APPELLANTS.

JULY 12, 2018

*One liner: A lot filled w/ needles across a school turned into a Garden establishes adverse possession when it is possessed continuously under a claim of right for at least 10 yrs, & was possessed in a hostile, actual, open, & obvious manner which was exclusive & continuous.*

**Opinion**

TOM, J.

This appeal involves what must be an extremely rare occurrence in Manhattan, to wit, a claim of adverse possession of prime real estate located in the Lower East Side neighborhood of Manhattan. Specifically, we are presented with a dispute over a vacant corner lot located at 157 Norfolk Street at its intersection with Stanton Street, one block south of East Houston Street in lower Manhattan. Plaintiff Children's Magical Garden (the Garden), a not-for-profit corporation incorporated in 2012, is a community garden founded by its members in 1985 on Lots 16, 18, and 19 in Block 154. The Garden was founded by activists outraged by the accumulation of garbage and used needles on the lots located across the street from an elementary school.

Defendants Norfolk Street Development (Norfolk), and Serge Hoyda (Hoyda) are alleged to have been the record owners of Lot 19 during the prescriptive period. Defendant 157, LLC is alleged to have purchased the property from Norfolk and Hoyda on or about January 6, 2014.

[The central issue presented by this appeal is whether plaintiff stated a claim for adverse possession of Lot 19 by sufficiently pleading the continuous possession element] [We find that the complaint sufficiently pleaded a cause of action for adverse possession.]

The complaint alleges that more than 30 years ago, in 1985, the Garden was founded by community activists who sought to improve their neighborhood. Because crime plagued the neighborhood at that time, and used needles and piles of garbage littered the abandoned corner lot in question—across the street from elementary school P.S. 20—these neighborhood activists decided to build what plaintiff describes as what is now a "neighborhood icon." Plaintiff also states that defendants and their predecessors abandoned Lot 19 as a "shameful eyesore" and that plaintiff and its members took possession and "by their tremendous efforts transformed the Premises into a vibrant community garden where generations of children have thrived."

Among other things, Garden members, starting in 1985, cleared garbage and debris, pulled weeds, and erected a chain-link fence to enclose the premises. They planted fruit, vegetables, plants, bushes and trees, including an apple tree and a dogwood tree, built a seesaw and other playground equipment, and added a stage used for concerts and to display art. Over the years, neighborhood children have used the stage to put on performances. At some point, members also built a fish pond and pathways throughout the Garden.

Plaintiff also alleged that the Garden has never been open to the general public, and that the premises can only be accessed by first unlocking the gate with a special key available only to members. Members keep the gates locked at night and any other time the Garden is not in use under the supervision of a member.

In addition, over many years the Garden hosted various schools, afterschool and camp programs for science, math, culinary arts, and community service activities. Each year, the Garden hosted local youth for the planting of a "pizza garden" and in the fall held a pizza-making party on the premises where children enjoyed the harvest of vegetables.

Plaintiff maintains that throughout all these years the Garden's members protected the Garden's claim of right, including against defendants. As an example, plaintiff alleges that in August 1999, defendants Hoyda and Norfolk or their agents cut through the Garden's exterior fence and entered the premises. They claim that a tree planted more than a decade earlier was chopped down and a children's clubhouse was damaged. A makeshift interior fence was also erected. However, Garden members immediately tore down the fence and removed it. Members also repaired the other damage.

According to plaintiff, in May 2013, a group of men with power tools and construction equipment accompanied by private security guards arrived at the Garden, and signaled their intention to breach the exterior fence. A standoff took place with Garden members blocking the gate. Ultimately, police officers ordered the group of men to be given access to the premises. Plaintiff alleged the men were defendants or their agents and that among them was an attorney purporting to represent defendant Hoyda.

The men "trampled, destroyed, and dug up plants, shrubs, trees" and erected a metal fence inside the Garden purporting to barricade Lot 19 from the remainder of the other two lots. Defendants also employed a private security firm to guard the premises.

Plaintiff states that despite requests from various public officials to remove the fence, the fence still cuts across the premises rendering certain vegetable beds, trees and a meditation area inaccessible.

In July 2013, the other lots that make up the Garden—16 and 18—were preserved under New York City's GreenThumb program after Manhattan Community Board 3 passed a resolution declaring that it "very strongly favors a proposal to the extent possible to preserve the whole community garden." Under that program, the New York City Department of Parks and Recreation enters into licensing agreements with community groups which create and maintain gardens on city-owned vacant property.

According to the record evidence, on or about December 15, 1998, a buyer entered into a contract to purchase 157 Norfolk Street, Lot 19, from the record owners. In the contract, Seller warranted that it would deliver Lot 19 "vacant and free of any occupancy and any claim of right of occupancy." In or about November 1999, Buyer brought an action against Seller for specific performance and a declaration that it must satisfy the vacancy condition of the contract. Buyer's complaint alleged that "a portion of the Premises, has been, and remains, *occupied by third parties claiming a right to use and occupy a portion of the Premises*." Seller, (including many of the current defendants) responded that "the occupancy was illegal and unauthorized."

After various transactions, on or about August 27, 2003, defendant Norfolk, (in which Hoyda is a member), became the record owner of Lot 19. By deed, dated January 9, 2014, Norfolk conveyed Lot 19 to defendant 157, LLC, allegedly for $3,350,000 and other consideration.

Plaintiff, (the Garden), commenced this action in 2014, alleging that defendants had filed an application to construct a six-story, 70–foot–tall residential building on Lot 19. The complaint asserts six causes of action, including one for declaratory judgment that plaintiff is the sole and exclusive legal and equitable owner of Lot

19, via adverse possession. With regard to that cause of action, plaintiff alleged that the Garden was surrounded by a fence and has been cultivated and improved and accessed by a locked gate since 1985. Plaintiff also alleged that it had possessed Lot 19 continuously under a claim of right for not less than 10 consecutive years, and had possessed it in a hostile, actual, open and obvious manner which was exclusive and continuous for that time period.

Defendants moved to dismiss the complaint for failure to state a cause of action, claiming that since the Garden, *as a corporation*, did not exist until December 2012, it could not have occupied the property for the requisite period. They also asserted that the complaint fails to allege any occupancy by plaintiff was done under a claim of right.

In opposition to the motion to dismiss, Kate Temple–West, the current president and director of the Garden, filed an affidavit in which she stated that when she moved to 153 Norfolk Street in 1997, she observed that the Garden, which was enclosed by a fence, had various trees and bushes planted in it and structures that were regularly maintained. Temple–West also observed children playing in the Garden, which was managed by members, who controlled access with a key and supervised visitors. Temple–West became involved with the Garden soon after moving to the neighborhood and has since helped others to excavate and demolish the burned-down remains of a building that once stood on Lot 19, using shovels, pick-axes, and wheelbarrows. Beginning in or about 2000, Temple–West hired trucks to haul away rubble and debris from the Garden and has since hired dumpsters and/or trucks approximately once per year for maintenance.

Since Temple–West's arrival in 1997, she and other members have installed chicken wire on the perimeter chain-link fence to keep rats and garbage out. They have laid down soil and compost, planted various types of trees and shrubs, constructed brick paths that run through the garden, built a swing set, and observed and/or overseen the installation of a second seesaw, concrete art sculptures, a traditional medicine plant bed, a youth meditation area, and a rain garden. In 2003, Temple–West became the Garden's co-director. She later became the director. In December 2012, the Garden incorporated and took title to Lot 19. Temple–West became the Garden's president and director.

Temple–West noted the Garden's role in the community since her arrival, including hosting various student groups, the Cub Scouts, pizza-making parties, concerts, poetry readings, and movie nights, and noted recent events, including the installation of a chicken coop in 2012. As of the time of submission of Temple–West's opposition to defendants' motion to dismiss, the Garden had over 20 active adult members and 30 children who used the Garden each week, and events hosted at the Garden are attended by hundreds of community members.

In his affidavit, Barden Prisant[1] explained he was a member of the Garden from about 1985 until 1991, during which time he, Carmen Rubio, and Alfredo Feliciano cultivated, improved, and maintained the Garden. In 1985, the Garden was filled with piles of garbage, discarded metal, and other debris. Prisant, Rubio, Feliciano, and others cleaned up the Garden, planted trees and bushes, and oversaw the installation of structures, including a seesaw, pond, and wooden stage. Prisant remained a member of the Garden until 1991, when he moved away. During his time as a member, Prisant, who contributed financially to the Garden, observed that no one was permitted access unless either he, Feliciano, or Rubio had opened the gates and was present, and that the Garden was enclosed by a chain-link fence, which was accessible by gates at Stanton and Norfolk Streets.

During Prisant's involvement with the Garden, members put on various programs, including a May Day festival at which a Maypole was erected in the Garden. At Christmas time each year, children would decorate a pine tree which he and Feliciano had planted. The wooden stage was used for painting and acting classes as well as for musical performances.

Prisant averred that since 1985 the Garden has been enclosed by a chain-link fence. After Prisant moved in 1991, he converted his wife's studio apartment at 151 Norfolk Street into his office and passed the Garden daily, on his way to and from work. For approximately eight years thereafter, on a daily basis he observed that the Garden, which had a steady growth of trees and plantings, remained enclosed by a chain-link fence, with gates that were kept locked unless the Garden was under supervised use. He also observed during that time period that Rubio, Feliciano and others he understood to be members continued the care and maintenance of the Garden.

The trial court denied the motions to dismiss. This appeal followed. We now affirm.

In order to establish a claim of adverse possession, a plaintiff must prove that the possession was: (1) hostile and under a claim of right; (2) actual; (3) open and notorious; (4) exclusive; and (5) continuous throughout the 10–year statutory period. The only elements in dispute here are the "claim of right" and "continuous" elements.

Defendants argue that plaintiff failed to plead sufficient facts evidencing continuous possession by its predecessor members for the statutory period, through an unbroken chain of privity, by tacking periods between anonymous possessors who are not alleged to have intended to transfer title to the incorporating members. This

---

1    In the summer of 2016 Barden Prisant, President of International Art Advisors, joined Ann Gray in an entertaining project to estimate a value for the White House. For the 132 rooms, 18 acres of land, and artifacts included they came up with a value of $250 million. Among the "comparables" used were 10 Downing Street, and Mar-A-Lago, which was once donated to the US by heiress Marjorie Merriweather Post as a presidential and diplomatic retreat, then given back to the family in 1980 when the US didn't want it, and then purchased by Donald Trump in 1985. See *"What would the White House bring on the open property market?"* The Washington Post, Aug 17, 2016.

argument is based on the fact that plaintiff was incorporated in 2012 and defendants' contention that there is no allegation that plaintiff had the necessary privity with Garden members prior to incorporation. This argument fails, particularly at the pleading stage of this litigation.

It is well settled that an unincorporated association may adversely possess property and later incorporate and take title to it because "although the unincorporated society could not acquire title by adverse possession, its officers could for its benefit, and when the corporation is duly organized *the prior possession may be tacked to its own to establish its title under the statute of limitations* "(*Reformed Church of Gallupville v Schoolcraft, (1875)*).

Here, the complaint sufficiently alleges possession by the Garden members for nearly 30 years before the Garden was incorporated. As set forth above, the allegations include significant work by the members to clean the abandoned lot and transform it into a treasured community resource containing a fish pond, playground equipment, trees, plants, and a stage, all of which has been fenced-off with access restricted by members. Such allegations, if proven, would establish adverse possession by the members for the statutory period.

Further, to the extent that the complaint alleges and the record evidence shows that there has been a succession of different individual Garden members, "all that is necessary in order to make an adverse possession effectual for the statutory period by successive persons is that such possession be continued by an unbroken chain of privity between the adverse possessors" (*Belotti v. Bickhardt, (1920)*).

Since it is alleged that the Garden members had adversely possessed the lot for the statutory period long before the Garden was incorporated, the question of tacking is not at issue here. Indeed, based on the allegations in the complaint, the members possessed the lot for more than 10 years and could transfer their interest in the lot to the corporation in 2012.

In particular, Prisant stated that he was a member of the Garden from 1985 to 1991 during which time he, Carmen Rubio, and Alfredo Feliciano cultivated, improved, and maintained the Garden. However, he also explained that from 1991 to 1999 he worked near and passed by the Garden daily and observed Rubio and Feliciano and other members continue to maintain and possess the Garden, and that it remained enclosed by a fence and locked gates. In addition, Temple–West also stated that from 1997 to 2013 she and other members continued to possess the Garden and keep it enclosed by the fence and locked gates. These statements, along with the complaint, adequately allege continuous possession of Lot 19 for more than the statutory period by the same individuals and members of the Garden.

157 LLC's reliance on cases involving transients seeking to adversely possess separate units in residential apartment buildings is unavailing. For example, in *East 13th St. Homesteaders' Coalition v. Lower E. Side Coalition Hous. Dev.*, (1996), we denied a coalition of homesteaders who sought adverse possession of an apartment building a preliminary injunction, finding that there was no evidence of privity between successive occupants of the apartments, or evidence of any intended transfers, with some apartments having remained vacant for extended periods, "such that the vacating occupant and the new occupant apparently had no contact at all." Unlike *East 13th St.*, here the allegations are that the same individual members of the Garden worked together, enclosed the property by a chain-link fence, limited access by locked gates, and improved the property.

Nor are defendants aided by referencing the 1999 effort allegedly by the Hoyda defendants to retake possession of the premises. The allegations in the complaint are that the statutory period had been met by 1995, and, in any event, the 1999 intrusion did not cause any disruption in the Garden's exclusive possession, as the members took swift action to repair the damage caused by the unidentified intruders. We also reject 157 LLC's contention that the post–2008 version of RPAPL 501, which requires the adverse possessor to have a "reasonable basis for the belief that the property belongs to the adverse possessor," has any bearing on this matter since there are no adverse possession claims alleged to have ripened after 2008.

Defendants also argue that plaintiff has not sufficiently pleaded the mandatory element of a claim of right. Specifically, defendants maintain that plaintiff must plead an initial claim in the land rooted in expectations that have an "objective basis in fact." This claim is without merit.

The "hostile and under a claim of right" element contains two parts that have been viewed as virtually synonymous. Both parts require that the possession be truly adverse to the rights of the party holding record title. In *Humbert v. Trinity Church*, (1840), the Court for the Correction of Errors, the predecessor to the Court of Appeals, held that ownership can be obtained by adverse possession even where the possessor claims title wrongfully, fraudulently and "with whatever degree of knowledge that he has no right." The present day Court of Appeals has cited *Humbert* approvingly, noting that "the fact that adverse possession will defeat a deed even if the adverse possessor has knowledge of the deed is not new" (*Walling*)

In *Estate of Becker*, the Court of Appeals further explained that the element of hostility is "satisfied where an individual asserts a right to the property that is adverse to the title owner and also in opposition to the rights of the true owner." The court noted that "a rebuttable presumption of hostility arises from possession accompanied by the usual acts of ownership, and this presumption continues until the possession is shown to be subservient to the title of another. The ultimate element in the rise of a title through adverse possession is the acquiescence of the real owner in the exercise of an obvious adverse or hostile ownership through the statutory period."

In *Walling*, the Court of Appeals noted that "an adverse possessor's actual knowledge of the true owner is not fatal to an adverse possession claim," absent an overt acknowledgment by the claimant during the prescription period. The issue is actual occupation, not subjective knowledge. Stated another way, conduct will prevail over knowledge, particularly when the true owners have acquiesced in the exercise of ownership rights by the adverse possessors. A presumption of hostility will not apply, however, where the use of disputed land is permissive.

Here, the complaint sufficiently alleges that plaintiff's predecessor members continuously occupied Lot 19, improved the land, restricted entry and kept out intruders, and thus actually occupied the land in a manner adverse to the true owner. Therefore, the complaint satisfies the "hostile and under a claim of right" element. Moreover, as neither plaintiff nor the predecessor members have overtly acknowledged any of defendants' rights to Lot 19, and there is no indication that the use was permissive, Supreme Court properly found that the claim of right element had been sufficiently asserted.

Moreover, unlike this case, in *All the Way E. Fourth St. Block Assn. v. Ryan–Nena Community Health Ctr.*, (2006), which also involved a community garden, the Block Association sought and received a month to month tenancy under Operation Greenthumb for the disputed parcel and from 1981 through 1994 sought to determine the true ownership of the lot so that it might receive the consent of the owner for the erection of a fence. No such allegations which demonstrate overt acknowledgement of the true owner's ownership are present in this case.

We conclude that plaintiff has adequately pleaded a cause of action for adverse possession. Affirmed.

Note: Technically speaking, the following case is not actually an adverse possession case. But the dissent is too good to miss. In what way, if any, might the rules of adverse possession now be applied to the dispute between the parties?

## COURT OF APPEALS OF KENTUCKY
## EDWARDS ET AL.
## V.
## SIMS, JUDGE

DECEMBER 3, 1929

*[handwritten note: One liner: The owner of property owns all of the property above & beneath his property, including a cave.]*

Original proceeding by L. P. Edwards and others for a writ of prohibition to N. P. Sims, Judge of the Edmonson Circuit Court. Writ denied.

STANLEY, C.

This case presents a novel question.

In the recent case of <u>Edwards v. Lee,</u> an appeal was dismissed which sought a review and reversal of an order of the Edmonson circuit court directing surveyors to enter upon and under the lands of Edwards and others and survey the Great Onyx Cave for the purpose of securing evidence on an issue as to whether or not a part of the cave being exploited and shown by the appellants runs under the ground of Lee. The nature of the litigation is stated in the opinion and the order set forth in full. It was held that the order was interlocutory and consequently one from which no appeal would lie.

Following that decision, this original proceeding was filed in this court by the appellants in that case (who were defendants below) against Hon. N. P. Sims, judge of the Edmonson circuit court, seeking a writ of prohibition to prevent him enforcing the order and punishing the petitioners for contempt for any disobedience of it. It is alleged by the petitioners that the lower court was without jurisdiction or authority to make the order, and that their cave property and their right of possession and privacy will be wrongfully and illegally invaded, and that they will be greatly and irreparably injured and damaged without having an adequate remedy, since the damage will have been suffered before there can be an adjudication of their rights on a final appeal.

1. There is no question as to the jurisdiction of the parties and the subject-matter. It is only whether the court is proceeding erroneously within its jurisdiction in entering and enforcing the order directing the survey of the subterranean premises of the petitioners. There is but little authority of particular and special application to caves and cave rights. In few places, if any, can be found similar works of nature

of such grandeur and of such unique and marvelous character as to give to caves a commercial value sufficient to cause litigation as those peculiar to Edmonson and other counties in Kentucky. The reader will find of interest the address on "The Legal Story of Mammoth Cave" by Hon. John B. Rodes, of Bowling Green, before the 1929 Session of the Kentucky State Bar Association, published in its proceedings. In Cox v. Colossal Cavern Co. the subject of cave rights was considered, and this court held there may be a severance of the estate in the property, that is, that one may own the surface and another the cave rights, the conditions being quite similar to but not exactly like those of mineral lands. But there is no such severance involved in this case, as it appears that the defendants are the owners of the land and have in it an absolute right.

Cujus est solum, ejus est usque ad coelum ad infernos (to whomsoever the soil belongs, he owns also to the sky and to the depths), is an old maxim and rule. It is that the owner of realty, unless there has been a division of the estate, is entitled to the free and unfettered control of his own land above, upon, and beneath the surface. So whatever is in a direct line between the surface of the land and the center of the earth belongs to the owner of the surface. Ordinarily that ownership cannot be interfered with or infringed by third persons. There are, however, certain limitations on the right of enjoyment of possession of all property, such as its use to the detriment or interference with a neighbor and burdens which it must bear in common with property of a like kind.

With this doctrine of ownership in mind, we approach the question as to whether a court of equity has a transcendent power to invade that right through its agents for the purpose of ascertaining the truth of a matter before it, which fact thus disclosed will determine certainly whether or not the owner is trespassing upon his neighbor's property. Our attention has not been called to any domestic case, nor have we found one, in which the question was determined either directly or by analogy. It seems to the court, however, that there can be little differentiation, so far as the matter now before us is concerned, between caves and mines. And as declared in 40 C. J. 947: "A court of equity, however, has the inherent power, independent of statute, to compel a mine owner to permit an inspection of his works at the suit of a party who can show reasonable ground for suspicion that his lands are being trespassed upon through them, and may issue an injunction to permit such inspection."

There is some limitation upon this inherent power, such as that the person applying for such an inspection must show a bona fide claim and allege facts showing a necessity for the inspection and examination of the adverse party's property; and, of course, the party whose property is to be inspected must have had an opportunity to be heard in relation thereto. In the instant case it appears that these conditions were met.

We can see no difference in principle between the invasion of a mine on adjoining property to ascertain whether or not the minerals are being extracted from under the applicant's property and an inspection of this respondent's property through his cave to ascertain whether or not he is trespassing under this applicant's property.

It appears that before making this order the court had before him surveys of the surface of both properties and the conflicting opinions of witnesses as to whether or not the Great Onyx Cave extended under the surface of the plaintiff's land. This opinion evidence was of comparatively little value, and as the chancellor (now respondent) suggested, the controversy can be quickly and accurately settled by surveying the cave; and "if defendants are correct in their contention this survey will establish it beyond all doubt and their title to this cave will be forever quieted. If the survey shows the Great Onyx Cave extends under the lands of plaintiffs, defendants should be glad to know this fact and should be just as glad to cease trespassing upon plaintiff's lands, if they are in fact doing so." The peculiar nature of these conditions, it seems to us, makes it imperative and necessary in the administration of justice that the survey should have been ordered and should be made.

It appearing that the circuit court is not exceeding its jurisdiction or proceeding erroneously, the claim of irreparable injury need not be given consideration. It is only when the inferior court is acting erroneously, *and* great or irreparable damage will result, *and* there is no adequate remedy by appeal, that a writ of prohibition will issue restraining the other tribunal, as held by authorities cited above.

The writ of prohibition is therefore denied.

LOGAN, J. (dissenting).

The majority opinion allows that to be done which will prove of incalculable injury to Edwards without benefiting Lee, who is asking that this injury be done. I must dissent from the majority opinion, confessing that I may not be able to show, by any legal precedent, that the opinion is wrong, yet having an abiding faith in my own judgment that it is wrong.

It deprives Edwards of rights which are valuable, and perhaps destroys the value of his property, upon the motion of one who may have no interest in that which it takes away, and who could not subject it to his dominion or make any use of it, if he should establish that which he seeks to establish in the new suit wherein the survey is sought.

It sounds well in the majority opinion to tritely say that he who owns the surface of real estate, without reservation, owns from the center of the earth to the outmost sentinel of the solar system. The age-old statement, adhered to in the majority opinion as the law, in truth and fact, is not true now and never has been. I can subscribe to no doctrine which makes the owner of the surface also the owner of the atmosphere filling illimitable space. Neither can I subscribe to the doctrine that he who owns the surface is also the owner of the vacant spaces in the bowels of the earth.

[The rule should be that he who owns the surface is the owner of everything that may be taken from the earth and used for his profit or happiness. Anything which he may take is thereby subjected to his dominion, and it may be well said that it belongs to him] I concede the soundness of that rule, which is supported by the cases cited in the majority opinion; but they have no application to the question before the court in this case. They relate mainly to mining rights; that is, to substances under the surface which the owner may subject to his dominion. But no man can bring up from the depths of the earth the Stygian darkness and make it serve his purposes; neither can he subject to his dominion the bottom of the ways in the caves on which visitors tread, and for these reasons the owner of the surface has no right in such a cave which the law should, or can, protect because he has nothing of value therein, unless, perchance, he owns an entrance into it and has subjected the subterranean passages to his dominion.

A cave or cavern should belong absolutely to him who owns its entrance, and this ownership should extend even to its utmost reaches if he has explored and connected these reaches with the entrance. When the surface owner has discovered a cave and prepared it for purposes of exhibition, no one ought to be allowed to disturb him in his dominion over that which he has conquered and subjected to his uses.

It is well enough to hang to our theories and ideas, but when there is an effort to apply old principles to present-day conditions, and they will not fit, then it becomes necessary for a readjustment, and principles and facts as they exist in this age must be made conformable. For these reasons the old sophistry that the owner of the surface of land is the owner of everything from zenith to nadir must be reformed, and the reason why a reformation is necessary is because the theory was never true in the past, but no occasion arose that required the testing of it. Man had no dominion over the air until recently, and, prior to his conquering the air, no one had any occasion to question the claim of the surface owner that the air above him was subject to his dominion. Naturally the air above him should be subject to his dominion in so far as the use of the space is necessary for his proper enjoyment of the surface, but further than that he has no right in it separate from that of the public at large. The true principle should be announced to the effect that a man who owns the surface, without reservation, owns not only the land itself, but everything upon, above, or under it which he may use for his profit or pleasure, and which he may subject to his dominion and control. But further than this his ownership cannot extend. It should not be held that he owns that which he cannot use and which is of no benefit to him, and which may be of benefit to others.

Shall a man be allowed to stop airplanes flying above his land because he owns the surface? He cannot subject the atmosphere through which they fly to his profit or pleasure; therefore, so long as airplanes do not injure him, or interfere with the use of his property, he should be helpless to prevent their flying above his dominion. Should the waves that transmit intelligible sound through the atmosphere be allowed to pass over the lands of surface-owners? If they take nothing from him and in no way interfere with his profit or pleasure, he should be powerless to prevent their passage?

If it be a trespass to enter on the premises of the landowner, ownership meaning what the majority opinion holds that it means, the aviator who flies over the land of one who owns the surface, without his consent, is guilty of a trespass as defined by the common law and is subject to fine or imprisonment, or both, in the discretion of a jury.

If he who owns the surface does not own and control the atmosphere above him, he does not own and control vacuity beneath the surface. He owns everything beneath the surface that he can subject to his profit or pleasure, but he owns nothing more. Therefore, let it be written that a man who owns land does, in truth and in fact, own everything from zenith to nadir, but only for the use that he can make of it for his profit or pleasure. He owns nothing which he cannot subject to his dominion.

In the light of these unannounced principles which ought to be the law in this modern age, let us give thought to the petitioner Edwards, his rights and his predicament, if that is done to him which the circuit judge has directed to be done. Edwards owns this cave through right of discovery, exploration, development, advertising, exhibition, and conquest. Men fought their way through the eternal darkness, into the mysterious and abysmal depths of the bowels of a groaning world to discover the theretofore unseen splendors of unknown natural scenic wonders. They were conquerors of fear, although now and then one of them, as did Floyd Collins, paid with his life, for his hardihood in adventuring into the regions where Charon with his boat had never before seen any but the spirits of the departed. They let themselves down by flimsy ropes into pits that seemed bottomless; they clung to scanty handholds as they skirted the brinks of precipices while the flickering flare of their flaming flambeaux disclosed no bottom to the yawning gulf beneath them; they waded through rushing torrents, not knowing what awaited them on the farther side; they climbed slippery steeps to find other levels; they wounded their bodies on stalagmites and stalactites and other curious and weird formations; they found chambers, star-studded and filled with scintillating light reflected by a phantasmagoria revealing fancied phantoms, and tapestry woven by the toiling gods in the dominion of Erebus; hunger and thirst, danger and deprivation could not stop them. Through days, weeks, months, and years—ever linking chamber with chamber, disclosing an underground land of enchantment, they continued their explorations; through the years they toiled connecting these wonders with the outside world through the entrance on the land of Edwards which he had discovered; through the years they toiled finding safe ways for those who might come to view what they had found and placed their seal upon. They knew nothing, and cared less, of who owned the surface above; they were in another world where no law forbade their footsteps. They created an underground kingdom where Gulliver's people may have lived or where Ayesha may have found the revolving column of fire in which to bathe meant eternal youth.

When the wonders were unfolded and the ways were made safe, then Edwards patiently, and again through the years, commenced the advertisement of his cave. First came one to see, then another, then two together, then small groups, then small crowds, then large crowds, and then the multitudes. Edwards had seen his faith justified. The cave was his because he had made it what it was, and without what he had done it was nothing of value. The value is not in the black vacuum that the uninitiated call a cave. That which Edwards owns is something intangible and indefinable. It is his vision translated into a reality.

Then came the horse leach's daughters crying: "Give me," "give me." Then came the "surface men" crying, "I think this cave may run under my lands." They do not know they only "guess," but they seek to discover the secrets of Edwards so that they may harass him and take from him that which he has made his own. They have come to a court of equity and have asked that Edwards be forced to open his doors and his ways to them so that they may go in and despoil him; that they may lay his secrets bare so that others may follow their example and dig into the wonders which Edwards has made his own. What may be the result if they stop his ways? They destroy the cave, because those who visit it are they who give it value, and none will visit it when the ways are barred so that it may not be exhibited as a whole.

It may be that the law is as stated in the majority opinion of the court, but equity, according to my judgment, should not destroy that which belongs to one man when he at whose behest the destruction is visited, although with some legal right, is not benefited thereby. Any ruling by a court which brings great and irreparable injury to a party is erroneous.

For these reasons I dissent from the majority opinion.

# CHAPTER TWO

# FORMS OF OWNERSHIP

## INTRODUCTION

There are four basic forms of concurrent ownership – ownership in which two or more people have a present right to possession of all of the land: Tenancy in Common, Joint Tenancy, Tenancy by the Entireties, and Community Property. Each form of tenancy has some important distinctions.

The first two forms of concurrent ownership - Tenancy in Common and Joint Tenancy are available to anyone. The second two forms of tenancy – Tenancy by the Entireties and Community Property are available only to married couples.

## A. Tenancy in Common.

Tenancy in common is available to any group of people, whether they are related or not. Each person may own a different percentage of the land held as tenants in common. When one tenant in common dies, his or her share goes into his or her estate – to be passed on in accordance with the terms of that person's will, or by the laws of intestacy.

For example, if three friends, A, B, and C decide to chip in to buy 10 acres of land near a lake, each may be able to contribute a different amount to the purchase price. If A contributes 50% of the purchase price, B contributes 30% of the purchase price, and C contributes 20% of the purchase price, they will likely provide in the deed that A has a 50% undivided interest; B has a 30% undivided interest; and C has a 20% undivided interest – all as tenants in common. All three of them will have a right to be anywhere on the land at any time, but A will own a larger percentage of the land because A has contributed more of the purchase price.

When A dies, A's 50% share will go into A's estate, and will be distributed as specified in A's will, or to A's closest relatives in accordance with the applicable statute of intestate succession. Unless otherwise specified, the new owners, A's successors, will become additional tenants in common, along with B and C.

At any time any tenant in common may bring an action for partition – asking a court to set aside his or her specific share, and take that part of the land out of tenancy in common. For example, at any time C, who owns a 20% interest, may decide that C would prefer not to share the land with the other tenants in common, so C may bring an action in partition, and have the court set aside 20% of the land for C's use alone. If the land is all about the same, then the court will probably grant a partition in kind – giving C a specific two acres (20% of the land), and leaving the remaining 8 acres held by A and B, who will still be tenants in common as to those 8 acres. Then C can build a fence around C's two acres – and keep A and B out.

If the land is not all about the same, for example if there is a big house on one part of the land, and some of the land has such a steep slope that it is almost unusable, then the court is likely to grant C's request for partition by granting partition by sale. The court will just order the sale of the entire 10 acres, including the house, and give the appropriate percentage of the proceeds to A, B, and C as individuals. So it is important, when people purchase land as tenants in common that they expect to be able to get along with each other.

Keep in mind, too, that the judgment creditors of any one of the three tenants in common may also force a partition – at any time the creditors need that interest in land in order to be paid what is owed to the creditors by any one of the three tenants in common.

In summary, any group of people may own land as tenants in common, and when one tenant in common dies, his or her share goes into his or her estate.

The rest of the land will remain in tenancy in common.

## B. Joint Tenants.

Joint tenancy, another form of concurrent ownership, is available to any group of people. It is frequent that married couples own property as joint tenants. But there is no requirement that joint tenants be related by blood or marriage, and there is no limit to the number of people who may own land as joint tenants.

The most important characteristic of joint tenancy is the *right of survivorship.* When one joint tenant dies, his or her interest in the land simply vanishes, and the shares of the remaining joint tenants automatically get larger. For example, if A, B, and C take title to land as joint tenants, when A dies there is no way that A can give A's share away by will. At the moment of A's death, (when A's will goes into effect), A simply has no remaining interest in the land. Instead, B and C automatically become the owners of the full parcel of land. Similarly, when B dies, no part of the land will be in B's estate. C will simply become the full owner of the full parcel of land, by right of survivorship. So the last surviving joint tenant takes all.

It is always important, when creating a joint tenancy, to specify that there is this right of survivorship. The usual words would be to A and B, "as joint tenants, with right of survivorship."

At common law it was also required that each of the joint tenants have an equal share, and that all of the tenants obtain their interests at exactly the same time. This was called the requirement of *the four unities.* The unities were described as the unities of *time, title, interest, and possession.* If all of the joint tenants got their interests by means of the same deed the four unities were present. If they did not all get their interests under the same deed, the four unities were not present, and a joint tenancy with right of survivorship was not created. Instead, the parties in that case would hold their interests as tenants in common. The requirements of the four unities have now been relaxed in a number of states. But it is still a good idea, in every conveyance intended to create a joint tenancy, to use one deed to create all of the interests, and to specify that the people involved take their interests *as joint tenants, with right of survivorship.*

You can see why joint tenancy is very popular with married couples. If Husband and Wife take title to the house as joint tenants, then when Husband dies, Wife automatically becomes the full owner of the house. No probate is necessary. It would happen automatically upon Husband's death. After Husband's death, Husband's individual creditors would have no claims against the house, because Husband would no longer have any ownership rights in the house.

It is important to keep in mind, however, that at any point while both Husband and Wife are alive, the creditors of either Husband or Wife could go after the house, and cause a severance. Once Husband's creditors take title to Husband's interest in the house the joint tenancy ends – because the four unities are no longer present between the owners of the land. Husband's creditors got their interest in the house at a different time from when Wife got her interest in the house, and under the provisions of a different document. So there is no longer a joint tenancy, and there is no longer any right of survivorship. Wife, now owns the house as a tenant in common with Husband's creditors – until the creditors bring an action in partition, and have the court order a sale of the entire house – followed by distribution of the proceeds.

Severance of a joint tenancy by the creditors of one of the joint tenants is called an involuntary severance. It is always possible at any time during a joint tenancy.

A voluntary severance by any joint tenant is also possible – at any time.

For example, if Wife gets annoyed with Husband, and decides to leave, Wife can sell her part of the joint tenancy to a stranger – thus causing a severance of the joint tenancy. Wife doesn't have to give any advance notice to Husband, and there is nothing Husband could do to prevent the severance. Any joint tenant, at any time, has the right to sell or give away his or her share of the joint tenancy. At that moment, the joint tenancy will end, as to that part of the land, and there will no longer be any right of survivorship.

For example, if A, B and C take title to land as joint tenants with right of survivorship, and C wants out of the deal, C does not have to get any permission from A or B, and does not have to go to court. C simply sells C's share to X, and that will sever the joint tenancy as to C's share. X will then own one-third of the land, as a tenant in common with A & B. A and B will continue to own the other two-thirds of the land as joint tenants, with right of survivorship. So when A dies, B will automatically become the owner of two-thirds of the land, and X will continue to be the owner of one-third of the land. When X dies, his ownership, (because he holds as a tenant in common), will go into X's estate, to be distributed under the terms of X's will, or by the provisions of the intestate statute if X did not have a will. Neither A nor B would have any rights to X's one-third of the land.

Because land held as joint tenants with right of survivorship automatically goes to the surviving owner(s), without the need for any court action, it is a very popular form of ownership for husband and wife. Sometimes, an elderly couple will decide to add their son as another joint tenant on the family home. This would be done by conveying the home to a third-party, called a strawman, and having the strawman then convey the home back to husband, wife and son, as joint tenants with right of survivorship, in order to comply with the requirements of *the four unities*. Husband, wife, and son then become joint tenants, with right of survivorship - so whoever lives longest will end up with the home.

But remember, the creditors of husband, wife, *or son,* can cause a severance at any time. Or the son's property may become subject to distribution in a divorce. If any of that happens, the home will be partitioned, by sale, and the elderly couple will be out of their home.

## C. Tenancy by the Entireties (also called Tenants by the Entirety)

The third form of concurrent ownership is Tenancy by the Entireties, which is available *only* to *husband and wife.* Remember, state and federal law recently may have expanded the definition of husband and wife. So it may be more accurate to say that tenancy by the entireties is available only to spouses. In any case, there can never be more than two tenants by the entirety, and those two tenants must be related by marriage. Tenancy by the entireties automatically includes a right of survivorship and it *cannot* be severed unilaterally at any time by either owner or by the creditors of just one of the owners.

The following case illustrates the characteristics of tenancy by the entireties.

## DISTRICT COURT OF APPEAL OF FLORIDA
## JAMES J. GIBSON AND LORI G. GIBSON, APPELLANTS,
## V.
## WELLS FARGO BANK, N.A., AS SUCCESSOR BY MERGER TO WACHOVIA BANK, APPELLEE.

### JULY 13, 2018

### Opinion

LaROSE, Chief Judge.

Dr. Lori and James Gibson appeal the final summary judgment entered in favor of judgment creditor, Wells Fargo Bank. We must determine whether, under Florida law, a creditor may satisfy a debt incurred by one spouse by garnishing a federal tax refund issued in both spouses' names and deposited in their joint checking account. Florida law compels us to conclude that the joint tax refund is tenancy by the entirety (TBE) property not subject to garnishment. Thus, we reverse.

### Background

In December 2009, Wachovia Bank sued Mr. Gibson for breach of a promissory note that he, alone, executed in March 2008. The parties stipulated to the entry of a final judgment in favor of Wachovia for over one million dollars.

Following entry of final judgment, the Gibsons filed amended joint federal tax returns for tax years 2003 through 2006, seeking retroactive reduction in their tax burden. See American Recovery and Reinvestment Act of 2009, extending the carryback period to up to five years for 2008 net operating losses incurred by an eligible small business). Based upon these returns, the Internal Revenue Service issued two tax refund checks; one in June 2011 and the other in April 2014. Each check was payable to both Mr. Gibson and his wife, Dr. Gibson. The refund checks totaled over two million dollars. The Gibsons deposited both checks into their joint account at SunTrust Bank. The parties agree that the Gibsons held the SunTrust account as TBE property.

In October 2014, Wells Fargo Bank, as successor by merger to Wachovia, moved to garnish the SunTrust account.

The trial court granted Wells Fargo's motion. The trial court entered a final summary judgment providing that Wells Fargo could recover from Dr. and Mr. Gibson "jointly and severally and as tenants by the entireties, the sum of $1,310,491.78" from the SunTrust Account.

## Analysis

On appeal, the Gibsons argue that the joint tax refunds, issued in both of their names and deposited in their joint bank account, are TBE property. Therefore, Wells Fargo, a creditor to only Mr. Gibson, cannot reach those funds to satisfy his individual debt. Although they acknowledge that the IRS has statutory authority to attach TBE property in certain circumstances, the Gibsons contend that third-party creditors, such as Wells Fargo, lack such authority. The trial court, in their view, erred in ruling for Wells Fargo.

Finding its origins in paternalistic ideas of property ownership, ("The historic basis for the [TBE] was the assumed incapacity of married women to hold property individually,"), TBE's theoretical underpinnings suit a contemporary ethos. Indeed, "the distinctive feature of a tenancy by the entireties, that husband and wife hold property as an indivisible unit, renders this form of ownership equally well-suited to the concept of modern-day marriage as a partnership between equals." See *Beal Bank, SSB v. Almand & Assocs.*, (Fla. 2001).

In *Beal Bank*, the Florida Supreme Court answered the following rephrased certified question in the affirmative:

> In an action by the creditor of one spouse seeking to garnish a joint bank account titled in the name of both spouses, if the unities required to establish ownership as a tenancy by the entireties exist, should a presumption arise that shifts the burden to the creditor to prove that the subject account was not held as a tenancy by the entireties?

In so doing, the court eliminated any lingering distinctions between real property and personal property held jointly by wife and husband. And, the court adopted a presumption "shifting the burden to the creditor to prove by a preponderance of evidence that a tenancy by the entireties was not created." *Beal Bank*. Significantly,

*Beal Bank* affirmed that "property held by husband and wife as tenants by the entireties belongs to neither spouse individually, but each spouse is seized of the whole."

The court spoke broadly, finding strong policy considerations supporting a tenancy-by-the-entireties presumption when "a married couple jointly owns personal property."

*Beal Bank* noted that TBE property enjoys six unities:

> (1) unity of possession (joint ownership and control); (2) unity of interest (the interests in the account must be identical); (3) unity of title (the interests must have originated in the same instrument); (4) unity of time (the interests must have commenced simultaneously); (5) survivorship; and (6) unity of marriage (the parties must be married at the time the property became titled in their joint names).

The unity of marriage is the unique quality of TBE property. Because of the sixth characteristic—unity of marriage—a tenancy by the entireties is a form of ownership unique to married couples.

State law creates and defines property interests. Federal tax law, on the other hand, creates no property rights but merely attaches consequences, federally defined, to rights created under state law. Under Florida law, special protections assigned to TBE property which are not afforded to other forms of property ownership underscore the distinctiveness of TBE property. For example, and particularly relevant for us, funds owned by a husband and wife as tenants by the entireties are beyond the reach of a creditor of either one of the tenants. Such funds are immune from garnishment except where the debt was incurred by both spouses.

> If property is held as a joint tenancy with right of survivorship, a creditor of one of the joint tenants may attach the joint tenant's portion of the property to recover that joint tenant's individual debt. However, when property is held as a tenancy by the entireties, only the creditors of both the husband and wife, jointly, may attach the tenancy by the entireties property; the property is not divisible on behalf of one spouse alone, and therefore it cannot be reached to satisfy the obligation of only one spouse. *Beal Bank,* (emphasis added).

The Gibsons filed their tax returns jointly as husband and wife. They argue that "once the check was issued, both Dr. Gibson and her husband possessed the six unities of TBE property." We agree. It is important, however, to focus on the antecedent act of filing joint returns. We assess, initially, whether TBE status can attach to the anticipated receipt of a tax refund.

The field of bankruptcy law provides the key. "While a debtor may not obtain a refund until the tax year closes, the predicates for receiving the refund may occur prior to filing the bankruptcy petition." *In re Uttermohlen.* Thus, a debtor possesses an existing interest in the refund at the time of filing even though his enjoyment of that interest was postponed. Naturally, therefore, by filing jointly, the Gibsons had an expectation of a refund that satisfied the requisite unities of TBE property.

We are not persuaded by Wells Fargo's efforts to draw the line between the issuance of the refund checks, in the first instance, and their subsequent deposits in the Gibsons' joint account. This temporal legerdemain is insufficient to undermine our determination that the refunds were TBE property. When TBE property is established, its subsequent transfer to another asset does not terminate the unities of title or possession. The Gibsons possessed an interest in their prospective refunds as TBE property at the time they filed their amended joint returns. That interest continued intact following issuance of the checks and their deposits into their joint back account.[1]

Under Florida law, the Gibsons were entitled to a rebuttable presumption that the tax refunds were TBE property. They demonstrated their intent to receive the refunds as TBE property by filing amended joint tax returns and receiving joint refund checks. Whether the refunds were related to Mr. Gibson's economic activity, alone, is irrelevant. They then deposited the checks into their joint bank account. In our view, their actions created a rebuttable presumption. Wells Fargo failed to rebut the presumption.

## Conclusion

We reverse the trial court's entry of summary judgment in favor of Wells Fargo and remand for further proceedings consistent with this opinion.

Reversed and remanded.

## D. Community Property

The fourth form of concurrent ownership is Community Property. Roughly one-fourth of the people in the United States live in states that are community property states. Many, but not all, of those states have laws derived from French or Spanish legal systems. Many, but not all, of the community property states are "Sunbelt" states, where

---

[1]   As underscored by Florida law, "[a]ny deposit or account made in the name of two persons who are husband and wife shall be considered a tenancy by the entirety unless otherwise specified in writing." § 655.79(1), Fla. Stat. (2014). Our record is devoid of a writing specifying otherwise.

people from other parts of the country go to retire. The community property states are: Louisiana, Texas, New Mexico, Arizona, Nevada, California, Washington, Idaho, Wisconsin, and sometimes Alaska. What does that mean – *sometimes* Alaska?! The fact is that in Alaska, by statute, the presumption is against community property. But people living in Alaska, *or elsewhere,* may elect to hold property, *located anywhere,* in an Alaska Community Property Trust – primarily for some complex, and perhaps not effective tax reasons.

For now, we will concentrate on the standard community property rules of Louisiana, Texas, New Mexico, Arizona, Nevada, California, Washington, Idaho and Wisconsin. And remember, each of these nine community property states has slightly different rules regarding community property. But the fundamentals are the same.

In a community property state, husband and wife are considered to be one community, and the earnings of each spouse automatically become community property, as soon as the paycheck is issued to either of them. Each spouse is automatically entitled to one-half of the community property. For example, when wife receives a paycheck from the law firm for which she is working, husband automatically, immediately, owns one-half of that paycheck. The same thing is true with regard to any of husband's earnings during the marriage – with some of the exceptions illustrated by the cases that follow.

## SUPREME COURT OF IDAHO
## LINDA DUNN, INDIVIDUALLY, AND AS SURVIVING SPOUSE OF BARRY DUNN, DECEASED, PLAINTIFF-APPELLANT,
## V.
## IDAHO STATE TAX COMMISSION, DEFENDANT-RESPONDENT.

### SEPTEMBER 25, 2017

JONES, Justice

### NATURE OF THE CASE

Linda Dunn ("Linda") appeals from a district court's judgment affirming the Idaho State Tax Commission's (the "Commission") deficiency determination. The Commission issued a deficiency against Linda after determining that her one-half community interest in her husband's, Barry Dunn ("Husband"), out-of-state earnings should have been included as Idaho taxable income for 2000–01, 2003–05, and 2007–10 (the "Taxable Years").

## FACTUAL AND PROCEDURAL BACKGROUND

The crux of this appeal concerns the proper tax treatment of Linda's one-half community interest in Husband's out-of-state earnings. The facts are uncontested. Linda was married to Husband during the Taxable Years. During the Taxable Years, Husband lived primarily in Texas and was employed by a Texas offshore drilling company. All of the earnings at issue were earned by Husband personally as a wage earner in Texas, Alaska, or Washington and were directly deposited into his bank account in Tomball, Texas. Husband never worked or was domiciled in Idaho during the Taxable Years. Throughout the Taxable Years, Linda temporarily lived with Husband at his work location, but always returned to Idaho to operate a horse farm. She was a resident of Idaho for all of the Taxable Years. Linda and Husband's tax filing status was "married filing jointly."

On April 13, 2012, the Commission issued a Notice of Deficiency Determination. The Commission's deficiency was only addressed to income attributed to Linda. Linda appealed the decision to the Idaho Board of Tax Appeals, and the Board affirmed the Commission's decision. On May 11, 2015, Linda petitioned a district court for review of the Commission's decision.

On June 8, 2016, the district court issued a memorandum decision and order affirming the Commission's decision wherein it held that: (1) Linda owned a one-half undivided interest in the Texas earnings of Husband, and, because she was domiciled in Idaho at the time she acquired the interest in Husband's wages, her interest was subject to the tax laws of Idaho; (2) Linda owned a vested interest in the community property wages earned by Husband in Washington, which were subject to taxation under the laws of Idaho as the domicile of Linda; and (3) Idaho's personal income tax scheme did not violate the dormant Commerce Clause or the Privileges and Immunities Clause of the United States Constitution because Linda failed to show a substantial effect on an identifiable interstate economic activity or market. The district court denied the Commission's request for costs and attorney fees because, although Linda's argument was ultimately failing, it was not devoid of merit. A corresponding judgment was issued on August 3, 2016.

Linda appeals.

## ANALYSIS

Throughout her briefing, Linda focuses solely on Husband's Texas earnings and Texas law. She does not proffer an argument related to Husband's Washington earnings or Washington law. Accordingly, we only consider Linda's appeal as it relates to her one-half community interest in Husband's Texas earnings.

Idaho's income tax scheme does not, as Linda claims "flunk the internal consistency test." Linda asserts that there is no internal consistency because "Idaho seeks an income tax on Linda's presumed community half that would not be taxed in Texas." Linda clearly misunderstands the internal consistency test. For purposes of the internal consistency test, whether or not Texas would tax Linda's one-half community interest in Husband's earnings is irrelevant. Indeed, comparing Texas and Idaho tax law merely demonstrates that the differences create disparate incentives to engage in interstate commerce (and sometimes result in double taxation) only as a result of the interaction of two different but nondiscriminatory and internally consistent schemes. The United States Supreme Court held that such a result is not unconstitutional.

To apply the internal consistency test, we must first examine Idaho's tax statutes. Idaho taxes its residents on income, "wherever derived," and taxes nonresidents on income "which is the result of activity within or derived from sources within the state." However, Idaho grants residents "a credit against the tax otherwise due under this chapter for the amount of any income tax imposed on the individual by another state on income derived from sources therein while domiciled in Idaho and that is also subject to tax under Idaho law. Idaho's tax scheme is not inherently discriminatory because, if adopted by every state, interstate commerce would not be at a disadvantage as compared to intrastate commerce. As acknowledged by the United States Supreme Court in _Wynne_, a tax credit may cure an otherwise discriminatory tax scheme. Accordingly, Linda's argument—that Idaho's tax scheme fails the internal consistency test—is meritless.

Lastly, the Privileges and Immunities Clause is not violated by the Commission's taxing of Linda's one-half community interest in Husband's earnings. Linda's suggestion that the holding from _Lunding v. New York Tax Appeals Tribunal_ is applicable here is meritless. In _Lunding_, the United States Supreme Court analyzed a tax law that treated nonresidents differently from residents. That is not the case here. The Commission is taxing Linda, a resident of Idaho. The Commission is not seeking to tax Husband. Therefore, the Privileges and Immunities Clause is not implicated because Linda has failed to demonstrate that Idaho, without substantial reason, is taxing nonresidents differently than residents.

**B. The district court did not err by holding that Linda's one-half community interest in Husband's Texas earnings was subject to the tax laws of Idaho.**

Linda submits that if *Wynne* is not binding, Texas tax law applies and the community property at issue is not subject to Idaho's income tax.

It appears that the conflict of law analysis regarding the characterization of Husband's Texas earnings is an issue of first impression for this Court. We decline to address the issue because the Commission concedes that Texas community property law applies.

Turning to Texas community property law:

> With limited exceptions, community property under Texas law consists of all property either spouse acquired during the marriage "other than separate property." Texas recognizes both sole and joint-management community property.... Sole-management community property is that property which, though acquired during the marriage, would have belonged to that spouse if single.
>
> The characterization of property as either community or separate is determined by the inception of title to the property. Inception of title occurs when a party first has a right of claim to the property by virtue of which title is finally vested.

However, there is a unique feature of Texas community property law:

> (a) During marriage, each spouse has the sole management, control, and disposition of the community property that the spouse would have owned if single, including:
>
> (1) personal earnings....

Tex. Family Code § 3.102. Property that is under the sole management of one spouse is known as "special community property." While personal earnings may be controlled or managed by one spouse, this characterization does not render them immune from the non-earning spouse's community property interest.

Texas Family Code section 3.202(b) protects special community property from non-tortious liabilities incurred by the other spouse. However, in Kimsey, the Texas Court of Appeals held that "both spouses are jointly and severally liable for the tax due on a joint return.... Thus, a spouse may be liable for the entire tax liability although the income was totally earned by the other spouse." It stands to reason, then, that Texas

Family Code section 3.202(b) does not immunize special community property from the tax liability of the non-controlling spouse.]

[Idaho Code section 63-3002 provides that Idaho imposes "a tax on residents of this state measured by Idaho taxable income *wherever derived*." The Supreme Court of the United States has made it clear that a state has the power to tax in relation to a resident's income derived from sources outside the State and that there is nothing in the Federal Constitution to prevent the exercise of such power.] The rationale for allowing a state to compute a tax on income earned elsewhere is based on the premise that inhabitants are supplied many services by their state of residence and should contribute toward the support of the state, no matter where their income is earned.

→ Important

It is true that this is a two-step analysis, but the steps must not be confused. [First, we will apply Texas community property law to characterize Husband's Texas earnings as either community or separate property.] This step determines whether Linda owns a one-half community interest in Husband's Texas earnings. [Second, we will apply Idaho tax law to Linda, an Idaho resident.] Crucially, Idaho tax law is not applied to Husband.

Texas community property law is applied to characterize Husband's Texas earnings as either separate or community property and to determine Linda's interest in those earnings. [But, Texas *tax* law is not applied because Idaho is taxing Linda, a resident of Idaho. Applying Texas community property law makes clear that Linda owns a one-half community interest in Husband's Texas earnings.] Linda is correct in pointing out that community property may be classified as special community property, [but the Texas court in *Massey* demonstrated that the sole-management aspect of special community property does not render it immune from the non-earning spouse's community property interest.] ["Each spouse owns an undivided one-half interest in all community assets and funds regardless of which spouse has management and control."] Therefore, [according to Texas community property law, Linda owns a one-half community interest in Husband's Texas earnings because they are community property.]

Linda's claim that Texas Family Code section 3.202(b) exempts her interest in Husband's sole-management special community property from Idaho's income tax is unpersuasive. [The Texas court in *Kimsey* provided that both spouses are jointly and severally liable for tax due on a joint return. The parties' stipulated facts indicate that Linda and Husband's filing status was "married filing jointly" during the Taxable Years. Therefore, Texas Family Code section 3.202(b) does not exempt Linda's one-half community interest in Husband's special community property from Idaho's income tax.]

In sum: Texas community property law characterizes Husband's earnings as community property; Linda owns a one-half community interest in said property; and, [because Linda was domiciled in Idaho during the Taxable Years, her one-half community interest is subject to Idaho income tax.]

[We affirm the district court's judgment.]

Note: In theory, it should be easy to divide community property when there is a divorce between spouses, because each has automatically become owner of half of the earnings of either of them during the marriage. But it turns out not to be that easy, as illustrated by the following two cases.

## COURT OF APPEALS OF WASHINGTON
### IN RE THE MARRIAGE OF: PAMELA R. FLAGELLA, RESPONDENT, AND ROBERT N. FLAGELLA, APPELLANT.

OCTOBER 17, 2017

Melnick, J.

Robert N. Flagella appeals the trial court's distribution of property and award of maintenance to his former wife, Pamela R. Flagella. [He asserts that the trial court erred when it mischaracterized property and when it failed to modify his maintenance because of his subsequent job loss.] We affirm.

## FACTS

The parties married in September 1995 and separated in June 2014. At the time of marriage Pamela had two children. Robert did not have any children and no children were born during the marriage. At the time of separation, Robert was 62 years old and Pamela was 57 years old.

## I. OCCUPATIONS

At the time the parties married, Robert worked as a chemical engineer for Union Carbide Corporation. He worked for Union Carbide for 20 years prior to his marriage to Pamela. Robert continued to work for Union Carbide for two more years after the parties married. Union Carbide subsequently merged with Dow Chemical and it laid off Robert in 1997.

Robert then worked for two years at Aluminum Oxide Laboratories, and then a year at Honeywell Electronic Materials. From 2000 to 2013, Robert worked for CH2M Hill/I & AT. At the time of trial, Robert earned $170,000 per year as a senior project manager for Glumac.

Pamela earned an associate's degree in 1978 and began working as an administrative assistant at Arthur Anderson, an accounting firm. Pamela left her job in 1995, soon after the parties married, to stay home with her children.

Pamela worked for a short period of time as an administrative assistant when Union Carbide laid off Robert, but did not return full time to the workforce until 2002. She then worked for eight years with a family-owned business until the company was bought out in 2010. At that time, Pamela and Robert agreed she would stop working. After the parties separated, Pamela enrolled at a community college to earn a Microsoft certificate to allow her to reenter the workforce as a clerical administrative assistant.

## II. DISSOLUTION

In August 2014, Pamela petitioned for legal separation.

## III. TRIAL

During the parties' March 2016 dissolution trial, Robert and Pamela disputed the character and distribution of various assets relevant to this appeal.

## ANALYSIS

### APPLICABLE LAW

All property is before the court for distribution in a marriage dissolution. The character of property, whether separate or community, is determined at the time of acquisition. An asset is separate property if acquired before marriage; acquired during marriage by gift or inheritance; acquired during marriage with the traceable proceeds of separate property; or, in the case of earnings or accumulations, acquired during permanent separation. Property acquired during marriage is presumptively community property. A party may rebut this presumption by offering clear and convincing evidence that the property was acquired with separate funds. Commingling of separate and community funds may give rise to a presumption that all are community property. This is not commingling in the ordinary sense, however; it must be hopeless commingling. Only if community and separate funds are so commingled that they may not be distinguished or apportioned is the entire amount rendered community property. If the sources of the deposits can be traced and identified, the separate identity of the funds is preserved.

## DOW 401(K) FUND

Robert argues the trial court erroneously characterized the majority of the 401(k) fund as community property. As previously stated, an asset is separate property if acquired before marriage; acquired during marriage by gift or inheritance; or acquired during marriage with the traceable proceeds of separate property.

Here, part of the 401(k) fund was acquired before marriage and part was acquired after. Commingling of separate and community funds may give rise to a presumption that all are community property.

Here, the trial court found that Robert provided no statements showing the value of the property before the marriage, during the marriage or at date of separation. Robert continued to work for Union Carbide after the parties were married and continued to contribute to the 401(k) fund.

Here there were no detailed records tracing the commingling of separate property and community property. Indeed, there are no records indicating the exact date that Robert began contributing to the 401(k) fund given that he started working for Union Carbide in 1975 and it was not until 1978 that congress originally established the Revenue Act of 1978, which included section 401(k) that gave employees a tax-free way to defer compensation for retirement. The law went into effect on January 1, 1980. We also do not know the amounts Robert contributed. For all of these reasons, it was not possible to distinguish or apportion the funds, rendering them hopelessly commingled and raising the presumption that the Dow 401(k) should be characterized as community property.

## AMERICAN CENTURY IRAS

Robert next argues the trial court erred in characterizing the two American Century IRAs as community property. We disagree.

Prior to marriage, Robert established two American Century IRA accounts. At the time of marriage, the value of the IRAs was $12,473.24. At the time of trial, value of the IRAs was $51,718.31. During trial, numerous checks were admitted that were written to American Century.

The IRAs were initially Robert's separate property. The parties, however, contributed to the IRAs during marriage, commingling separate funds with community funds. This gives rise to a presumption that all are community property. Accordingly, the trial court did not err in characterizing the IRAs as community property.

## BUSINESS VENTURE

When distributing property in a dissolution, a trial court may properly consider one spouse's waste or concealment of assets. Waste has also been characterized as gross fiscal improvidence or the squandering of marital assets.

Just prior to separation, Robert invested community assets of approximately $85,000 in a business venture involving sapphires. Pamela claims she did not know about the investment and when she discovered the missing funds, she asked Robert to stop investing in the business. He continued to do so even after the parties separated in June 2014. In its oral ruling, the trial court found:

> Under the gem-polishing Crystalent $85,000 represents moneys that Mr. Flagella gave to Amy Judson beginning in the last quarter of 2013 until discovered by Mrs. Flagella in August of 2014, just prior to their separation.
>
> The money was given to Ms. Judson in $5,000–a-month increments for the development and marketing of a new business. Money was also either given to, or credit card expenses were incurred for, Ms. Judson and her daughter. All of this transpired without the knowledge or consent of Ms. Flagella and, further, Mr. Flagella failed to produce any documentation to support his reasons for the expenditure of the party's community funds.

Because Robert failed to provide documentation showing that Pamela was aware of the business investment or documentation showing that the investment was not gross fiscal improvidence, and because we leave credibility determinations to the trier of fact, the trial court did not err in deducting $85,000 from Robert's share of the property distribution.⌉

We affirm the rulings made by the trial court.

Note: Divorce in a community property state may prove exciting.

## COURT OF APPEALS OF NEW MEXICO
## JEFFREY MARTINEZ, PETITIONER-APPELLANT/CROSS-APPELLEE,
### V.
## ANGELA MARTINEZ, RESPONDENT-APPELLEE/CROSS-APPELLANT.

DECEMBER 29, 2016

**APPEAL FROM THE DISTRICT COURT OF SANTA FE COUNTY**

OPINION

SUTIN, Judge.

Husband filed for divorce from Wife in April 2010. In the months following Husband's filing, the parties made numerous allegations against each other. Husband alleged, among other averments, that Wife violated the temporary domestic order (1) when she took Husband's clothes to Goodwill, (2) when Wife and the parties' son allegedly assaulted Husband's parents, and (3) when Wife and their children broke a television and left it outside of the marital residence. Wife alleged, among other averments, that Husband (1) abused her and their children, (2) removed community property from the marital home while she and the children were not present, and (3) misconstrued the altercation between their son and Husband's parents and that, in fact, their son was defending himself and Wife.

During this same tumultuous time frame, in June 2010, Husband's truck, which was community property, was destroyed in a fire. Husband made a claim with Allstate Insurance Company, which was denied. Thereafter, Husband filed a bad faith claim against Allstate, which ultimately settled on September 7, 2011.

After a hearing in May 2011, the district court entered a decree of dissolution of marriage and entered an order on the distribution of community assets, community personal property, child support, and spousal support.

In July 2012 Wife filed a motion to impose a constructive trust on insurance proceeds. In the motion, Wife addressed a $250,000 insurance check from Allstate in settlement of Husband's bad faith claim and for damage to his truck. Wife argued that the truck was community property, that the settlement proceeds were community property, and that one-half of those proceeds should have been awarded to her. She sought a constructive trust for one-half of the insurance proceeds, minus attorney fees, and requested that those funds be placed in the court registry.

In response to Wife's motion, Husband argued that Wife "actively conspired with Allstate and, as a result, her conduct, in part, played a significant part in the decision by Allstate to wrongfully deny Husband's property damage claim under his Allstate automobile policy." Husband accused Wife of committing "deceptive actions against the community" as evidenced by a letter from Allstate to Wife regarding Husband's claim. In the letter, Allstate employee Bruce Zinzer sent Wife a copy of an inventory submitted by Husband with a note to Wife that stated, "Let me know what you think." Husband also asserted that Wife, when interviewed by Allstate's counsel regarding Husband's insurance claim, stated that Husband was making a fraudulent claim for personal property damages. Husband argued that Wife's conduct was aimed at denying the community the benefit of insurance coverage under the Allstate policy, and thus she should not be rewarded with any interest in the proceeds.

Husband's arguments related to the insurance proceeds dispute rested primarily on *Delph v. Potomac Insurance Co.* In *Delph*, the husband and the wife owned a residence as community property. The residence was insured, and both the husband and the wife were named on the policy. The wife moved out of the residence and sought a dissolution of marriage. The wife was granted a divorce and was awarded the residence. However, prior to entry of the divorce decree, the husband intentionally set fire to the residence. The wife sought to recover proceeds under the insurance policy for damages caused by the fire, but the insurer refused to pay her, contending that "the husband's arson constituted 'fraud' by the 'insured' and that the policy coverage was vitiated by the fraud." The wife brought suit against the insurer, the district court granted summary judgment in favor of the insurer, and the wife appealed. On appeal, our Supreme Court considered "whether the intentional burning of a community residence by one spouse will bar recovery by an innocent spouse under a fire insurance policy issued to the community."

In resolving the question on appeal, the Court in *Delph* first held that the residence as well as the insurance policy were community property. The Court, however, noted that "New Mexico courts have segregated out the interests of spouses in community property when it has been necessary to do so in order to avoid injustice." Because the parties' interests were capable of being segregated, the Court held that "both logic and justice mandated that the wife should be entitled to recover up to one-half of the policy limits in order to compensate for the damages resulting from the fire." The Court stated that in New Mexico a "spouse who commits a separate tort is individually liable for damages arising out of the tort and that the separate (or segregable) assets of the innocent spouse may not be reached to satisfy the liability arising out of the tort." In deciding whether the husband's act of arson was a "community" or "separate" tort, the *Delph* Court considered "whether the act in which the spouse was engaged at the time of the tort was one which was of actual or potential benefit to the community." According to the Court, "if it was of benefit, the tort is a 'community' tort, and thus a community debt. If the activity in which the tortfeasor spouse was engaged was of no benefit to the community, the tort is a 'separate' tort and thus a separate debt." Ultimately, the Court held that the husband did not engage in an act that could be of benefit to the community, and thus his responsibility for the fraud was separate. While the husband's actions could void his own interest in the policy, his fraud "did not void the policy as to the wife."

Wife admitted that she informed Allstate of Husband's practice of forging documents, but also asserted that Husband had initially told authorities that Wife and/or the parties' sons were responsible for having damaged the truck. She argued that because neither party was ultimately found to have caused the loss to the property and because Wife did not commit a tort, *Delph* did not apply.

In May 2013, Wife filed a motion for summary judgment on division of the Allstate settlement funds. Wife set out fifty-four statements of fact. Among those facts were the following. The truck was bought with community funds, was insured with community funds, and both Husband and Wife were named insureds. Bruce Zinzer, the Allstate employee who handled the personal property damage aspect of the claim, reached out to Wife because she was a named insured. When asked about Husband's reputation for honesty, Wife gave her "candid opinion of Husband's historical lack of truthfulness, based on examples from her life with Husband." Allstate provided Wife with Husband's inventory of items in the truck, and Wife informed Allstate that some of the items would not have been in the truck and that others did not have the value claimed by Husband. When asked by Allstate's attorney, Mark Klecan, during an examination under oath about Husband's reputation for honesty, Wife answered the question by referencing "police reports and an event involving Husband's lying to his probation officer." When asked for any other examples or instances of Husband's reputation for honesty or truthfulness, Wife referenced instances where Husband allegedly stole inventory from his employers. Although Klecan stated under oath that Wife's position was the primary reason for the delay in payment, Zinzer did not believe that Wife's input caused the denial of the claim.

Wife also highlighted a number of other errors and omissions by Allstate in handling the claim, including Allstate's failure to hire a fire investigator, failure to independently obtain the police report, and failure to respond to Husband's attorney's letters.

Husband contends the settlement funds are his separate property under Section 40-3-8(A) but that, even if the funds are community property, community property is subject to equitable division.

As to his "equitable division" point, Husband argues that should we determine that the Allstate proceeds are community property, equity must be taken into account, and we must determine that, based on equitable considerations, Wife is not entitled to any part of the beneficial resolution of the insurance claim. He relies on *Delph* and the equitable underpinnings of *Delph* to support his assertion that to permit Wife to benefit from her wrongdoing and receive a share of the settlement funds in any form of an award in the divorce action would be contrary to and thwarts New Mexico public policy. He also responds to Wife's no-fault divorce argument by arguing that no-fault divorce is unrelated to post-petition spousal behavior. According to Husband, Wife conflated the "fault" of the parties in the dissolution of the marriage and the equitable fault the district court assigned to Wife for her post-petition role in defeating Husband's insurance claim.

## B. Analysis

We agree with Wife that the law regarding community property supports her assertion that the settlement proceeds are community property. In determining whether Wife is entitled to a portion of the settlement proceeds as community property, it is useful to begin by establishing that the settlement proceeds are presumptively community property and that the statutes do not support Husband's argument that the proceeds are separate property.

"Community property" is defined as "property acquired by either or both spouses during marriage which is not separate property." "Separate property" is defined, in relevant part, as "property acquired by either spouse before marriage or after entry of a decree of dissolution of marriage." In New Mexico, property acquired during marriage by either husband or wife, or both, is presumed to be community property. The party asserting that property acquired during marriage is separate bears the burden of presenting evidence that would rebut the presumption by a preponderance of the evidence.

Allstate's alleged bad-faith-claim handling occurred while the parties were married and impacted both parties, who undisputedly had a community interest in the truck.] [Thus, the settlement proceeds are presumptively community property.] With the understanding that the settlement proceeds are presumptively community property, we turn our focus to Husband's position that, regardless of our interpretation of the property as community or separate property under the statutes, [the settlement proceeds are nevertheless separate under *Delph*.] [Husband argues that, per *Delph*, Wife is not entitled to any portion of the settlement proceeds because she did not act to benefit the community when she told Allstate that Husband was dishonest.] [We hold that *Delph* is distinguishable from the present case and does not form a basis for overcoming New Mexico's presumption in favor of community property. And we hold that the district court erred in denying Wife's community property interest in the settlement proceeds.]

The holding in *Delph* cannot be used to deny Wife's community interest in the settlement proceeds because the circumstances here are entirely different from the circumstances in *Delph*. In *Delph*, the Court considered the impact of an intentional tort on an innocent spouse. [In this case, there was no ruling that Wife committed an intentional tort, or for that matter, any tort.] Although the district court opined in a hearing that Wife's actions "may be tantamount to" the tort of interference with contractual relations, there was never an argument or ruling that Wife actually tortiously interfered with Husband's contract. [In fact, Husband failed to present evidence or elicit necessary findings that would support a tortious interference with contract claim, which would require proof in relevant part that there be some voluntary conduct on the part of Wife, and that the contract interference was without justification or privilege.] [There is also no finding by the district court that Wife acted "either with an improper motive or by use of improper means," as required for a tortious interference with contract claim.] To the contrary, the evidence presented indicated that, in expressing her opinion as to Husband's dishonesty, Wife was responding to questions posed by Allstate about Husband's credibility and reputation for honesty and truthfulness. Allstate also sent a copy of Husband's inventory to Wife, and she was specifically told to let Allstate know what she thought about the inventory. She was correct to answer those questions as a co-insured and was required to give her honest and accurate answers as an individual who was duly sworn under oath.

Additionally, despite Husband's assertions that Wife's accusations were false, there was no evidence or finding by the district court that her responses to Allstate's questions were dishonest or inaccurate. There is no evidence in the record that Wife volunteered information that was harmful to Husband before she was asked to give information, as a co-insured. There is no evidence from which the district court could reasonably infer, find, or conclude that Wife did anything more than cooperate, as she was required to do, or that she gave information beyond the information required in response to Allstate's questions in connection with its investigation of possible fraud.

We do not approve of an expansion of *Delph* which would allow a party to generally allege that a spouse behaved badly, absent proof of an intentional tort, and then use those allegations to effectively void the spouse's interest in community property. To affirm and approve of such a broad use of *Delph* would almost certainly, in the oft-quoted words of former New Mexico Governor Bruce King, "open up a whole box of Pandoras."

Because neither the statutes nor *Delph* provides a basis under which to deny Wife's community interest in the settlement proceeds, Husband has failed to overcome the presumption in favor of community property.

We therefore hold that the district court erred in denying Wife's community share of the settlement proceeds.

# CHAPTER THREE

# FUTURE INTERESTS

## INTRODUCTION

This chapter, on Future Interests, should be a fun topic for those who enjoy certainty, definite rules, and an intellectual challenge. It is somewhat like a good game of chess – or checkers. The rules stay the same, and the skill comes in learning how to use the rules most effectively. Most of the rules have been part of the common law for centuries, and most of them are applied in the same way in nearly all jurisdictions. So there is excellent predictability in this area of the law – once you know and understand the rules.

Future interests are created frequently – in both deeds and wills. Here's an easy example: Wife, in her will, says, "I give my house to my husband for life, then to my daughter." When Wife's will goes into effect, at Wife's death, her husband would then have a life estate, (a present interest), and the daughter would have a remainder, (a future interest). Both husband and daughter would have legal interests in the house, but husband would have the exclusive right to possession for his life. Then daughter would become the owner. So future interests are just ownership interests that are not yet possessory.

There are only five kinds of future interests: Remainders, (like the daughter's interest above); Executory Interests; Reversions; Possibilities of Reverter; and Rights of Entry. There are definitions for each of these at the end of the chapter.

But it will probably be much easier and faster just to start reading some cases. Notice that the oldest of the first five cases in this chapter was decided in 2016. The rules of future interests are old – but still very much in use. Skillfully used, documents applying the rules of future interests can create provisions that control the use and ownership of property for a very long time.

## A. The Rule Against Perpetuities

The common law Rule against Perpetuities was first announced by Lord
Nottingham in *the Duke of Norfolk's case,* in 1682. The rule is designed to prevent anyone from tying up the ownership of land for too long a period. The classic statement of the rule is:

> *"No interest is good, unless it must vest, if at all, not later than 21 years after some life in being at the creation of the interest."*

As you read the following cases you will begin to get a feel for how the Rule Against Perpetuities (RAP) is applied.

The following case, *Neal v. Nicholson* (2016), involves Osage headrights, the property interests owned by members of the Osage Tribe, which were at the heart of the book, *Killers of the Flower Moon*, by David Sedaris. The book has been on the Best Seller list for more than 60 weeks. Without giving away the story, it is enough to say that the book involves the nefarious attempts by white men to become the owners of various Osage headrights - the rights members of the Osage tribe have to huge profits derived from the production of oil.

### UNITED STATES DISTRICT COURT
### N.D. OKLAHOMA
### EDITH DOLORES NEAL, A/K/A/ EDITH DOLORES TAYRIEN
### LEE, PLAINTIFF,
### V.
### HELEN ANN NICHOLSON, THE ESTATE OF ELMER C.
### TAYRIEN, AND ROBIN PHILLIPS, SUPERINTENDENT OF
### THE BUREAU OF INDIAN AFFAIRS FOR THE OSAGE TRIBE
### BY AND THROUGH THE DEPARTMENT OF THE INTERIOR,
### DEFENDANTS.

OCTOBER 7, 2016

**OPINION AND ORDER**

CLAIRE V. EAGAN, UNITED STATES DISTRICT JUDGE

## I.

Plaintiff originally filed this action in Osage County District Court, seeking a declaratory judgment that the devise of property pursuant to an Osage Tribe member's will, probated in 1982, violates the rule against perpetuities. In 1981, the decedent, Elmer C. Tayrien, died. At the time of his death, Elmer owned an Osage headright, which is "an interest in the income from oil wells held in trust for the Osage Indian Tribe by the United States." Elmer's will provided for the disposition of this headright, leaving a life estate to his widow, Gladys Tayrien, and upon Gladys's death, leaving a life estate to plaintiff. Upon plaintiff's death, the headright would vest in defendant Nicholson, plaintiff's daughter. Pursuant to Pub. L. No. 95–496 the Superintendent of the Bureau of Indian Affairs for the Osage Tribe (Superintendent) conducted a will approval proceeding and approved the will. Plaintiff filed this action asserting that the devise to Nicholson violates the rule against perpetuities and seeking modification of the will to eliminate Nicholson's vested remainder.

The United States, on behalf of defendant Robin Phillips, the current Superintendent, removed the action to this Court. The United States argues that the statute of limitations bars plaintiff's action, that plaintiff failed to exhaust her administrative remedies, and that the state court had no jurisdiction to grant plaintiff relief.

The United States asserts that this action is barred by the statute of limitations, arguing that a six-year statute of limitations applies to plaintiff's claim, and began to run when the will was probated in 1982.

Perpetuities are barred under the Oklahoma Constitution. The common law rule against perpetuities is most often defined as stating that "no interest (in property) is good unless it must vest, if at all, not later than twenty-one years after some life in being at the creation of the interest." When considering possible perpetuities issues in a will, if under any possible contingency a future interest will not vest until after twenty-one years after the death of a measuring life, the attempted conveyance or disposition is invalid.

Plaintiff argues that the statute of limitations began running twenty-one years after Gladys's death when the rule against perpetuities was violated because the property had not vested in Nicholson at that time. Plaintiff asserts that because no one knew whether the property would vest in Nicholson within twenty-one years of Gladys's death, she could not have known about the perpetuities problem before 2013, meaning the statute of limitations did not begin running until that time. Plaintiff's claim relies on several misunderstandings about the rule against perpetuities. First, the measuring life can be anyone alive at the time of the testator's death. See generally Jesse Dukeminier, Perpetuities: The Measuring Lives, 85 Colum. L. Rev. 1648

(1985). There is no reason that the measuring life has to be Gladys. Because Nicholson was alive at the time the interest was created, she could be used as a measuring life. Second, vested is not a synonym for possession. A vested interest does not necessarily include a right to possession. The general rule is that where the uncertainty is as to the event, and the persons are ascertained, there is a vested interest. Nicholson was specifically named in the will; there was never any uncertainty as to who had a right to her interest. Third, even if there were a perpetuities issue, it would have been a problem when the will was probated. The rule is concerned with interests that could vest after the required period. Thus, any disposition that fails to vest within the required time must have had a perpetuities problem when the will was probated because it must have been possible from the beginning to vest outside the required time if that eventually occurred. Therefore, the statute of limitations began running when the will was probated in 1982, and there is no basis for tolling the limitations period.

An action for the recovery of real property must be brought within fifteen years. Thus, plaintiff's claim is barred by the statutes of limitations.

**IT IS THEREFORE ORDERED** that Defendant the United States of America's Motion to Dismiss is **granted.**

Note: In the following case, note how easy it was to violate the Rule Against Perpetuities – and how complex it turned out to be to correct the original error. What wording should have been used in the first deed, to avoid all of these problems?

## COURT OF APPEALS OF OREGON
## BRYAN KERR AND KERWIN KERR, PLAINTIFFS-APPELLANTS,
## V.
## DONALD R. BAUER, TRUSTEE OF THE KERR HOMESTEAD TRUST, DEFENDANT–RESPONDENT,

MAY 11, 2016.

Opinion

SERCOMBE, P.J.

In 1956, Sylva Kerr deeded property in trust to two of her children as trustees for the benefit of all of her descendants. That deed was inconsistent with the common-law rule against perpetuities. The trustees attempted to reconvey the property to Kerr by deed. Kerr then deeded the property outright to three of her children. The property was later conveyed to a family trust. Three of Kerr's grandchildren brought suit to cancel the later deeds and quiet title to the property in the original trustees. The trial court granted that relief and modified the 1956 deed to correct the rule against perpetuities violation. *Kerr I*

We restate the underlying facts from *Kerr I*:

The land at issue was once owned by Sylva Kerr. Sylva had eight children.

The property at issue, according to plaintiff Bryan, (one of Sylva's grandchildren), "was the homestead of my grandparents, the childhood home of their children, a 40–acre retreat in the Coast Range, and through several generations has been a special and unique place of rest and recreation for their descendants. Annual family reunions were held on the property for 35 years, as well as other family recreational activities."

In 1956 Sylva executed a warranty deed (Deed # 1) transferring the property to her sons Senior and J.M., in trust. Deed # 1 provides, in part:

"This grant is made for the purpose of creating a place of rest, recreation and recuperation for each and all of the children, grandchildren and descendants of Sylva Leona Kerr and Henry Allen Kerr, including the grantees specifically named herein, to hold in trust as herein designated, grantees to pay all taxes and care for the property."

After Sylva executed Deed # 1, attorneys told two of Sylva's children that the deed violated the rule against perpetuities. In 1968, Senior and J.M., as trustees, executed a deed (Deed # 2) conveying the property back to Sylva. Deed # 2 provides that the conveyance was made "for the reason that the trust created by Deed # 1 is invalid in that it violates the rule against perpetuities and in order that said grantee may reconvey said premises to the grantee's children, Senior, J.M., and Marjorie, as tenants in common, for their use and benefit." Two days later, Sylva executed a bargain and sale deed (Deed # 3) conveying the property to Senior, J.M., and Marjorie.

In 1989, Senior executed a bargain and sale deed (Deed # 3.5) conveying his interest in the property to Marjorie and J.M. Later that year, Marjorie and J.M. executed a bargain and sale deed (Deed # 4) that conveyed the property to the Kerr Homestead Trust. Marjorie and J.M. also executed a trust agreement for the Kerr Homestead Trust.

The trial court in *Kerr I* quieted title in the two trustees named in Deed #1 and ordered all subsequent deeds of the real property cancelled. The trial court acknowledged that Deed # 1 violated the common-law rule against perpetuities but held that the interests of the grandchildren and descendants could be severed from the interests of the children, so as to change the deed to cure the rule against perpetuities defect. The trial court also concluded that the trustees under Deed # 1 did not have the power to convey the property to Sylva in Deed # 2, and, therefore, all deeds that followed that conveyance were void as a matter of law.

In *Kerr I*, we concluded that the rule against perpetuities violation could not be cured by severance. We explained that the doctrine of severance can be applied only when "severing invalid provisions from the remainder of the trust" would not be "contrary to the settlor's purpose of plan" and interpreted Deed # 1 to "evidence Sylva's intent to benefit her children, grandchildren, and descendants by preserving the property as a place of rest and recreation for all of them equally, with no end date and no provision for the final disposition of the property to any individual." Thus, Deed # 1 was "one entire scheme from which interests cannot be severed without defeating Sylva's manifest purpose to benefit 'each and all' of the beneficiaries." Accordingly, we reversed and remanded.

On appeal from the decision on that remand Appellants now contend that no deed can be void for violating the rule against perpetuities unless it is determined to be void by a court, and, until a court voids a deed, it is effective. Thus, on appellants' reasoning, Deed # 1 was valid and effective to pass title to the property to the trustees that it names. Appellants further assert that Deed # 2 was void (and ineffective to convey title through the subsequent deeds) because the trustees lacked authority to convey the property under the terms of the trust created by Deed # 1. Donald, (a grandchild who wants to see the Kerr Homestead Trust held to be valid), answers that Deed # 1 was void *ab initio* and, therefore, Deed # 3 was valid because Sylva retained title to the property until she conveyed it through Deed # 3. We agree with Donald.

At the time Deed # 1 was made, the law was clear: An instrument that violated the rule against perpetuities was void *ab initio* and could not pass title to the property at issue. An instrument that violated the rule was void unless the invalid interests could be severed from the valid interests, and, as we held in *Kerr I*, that severance could not be made in Deed # 1. Thus, the conveyance to the trustees in Deed # 1 failed altogether.

Since Deed # 1 was void and did not create a trust, Sylva retained title to the property. The trial court was therefore correct that Deed # 2 had no effect, because J.M. and Senior, the grantors in Deed # 2, never received title to the property. Because Sylva retained title, she was free to convey the property to her children in Deed # 3. It follows that the conveyances that followed, (Deed #3.5 and Deed #4), culminating in the creation of the Kerr Homestead Trust, were also valid.

In sum, we conclude that the trial court did not abuse its discretion in declining to reform Deed # 1 and that no genuine issues of material fact precluded the grant of summary judgment in Donald's favor, upholding the trust established in 1989 as the Kerr Homestead Trust.

Affirmed.

Note: First a bit of background for the next two cases, both of which involve revocable trusts. A *trust* is a legal entity – somewhat like a box – into which a person, (called the *settlor*), puts assets to be managed in accordance with the provisions set out in the instrument creating the trust. The person or entity that manages the trust assets is called the *trustee*. The persons for whose benefit the assets are to be managed are called the *beneficiaries*. During life, a settlor may establish a *revocable* trust, retaining the right to revoke or amend the trust at any time, and usually naming the settlor to serve as the trustee until the death or incapacity of the settlor. When establishing a revocable trust the settlor also names another person, (or bank) to take over as trustee upon the death or incapacity of the settlor. As long as the trust is revocable, the Rule Against Perpetuities is of no concern. No real gift has yet been made. But when the trust becomes irrevocable, then the Rule Against Perpetuities applies to the provisions of the trust.

Remember that under the common law Rule Against Perpetuities, "No interest is good, unless it must vest, if at all, not later than 21 years after some life in being at the creation of the interest." All that is required is *vesting*. A gift is *valid* under RAP if it must *vest*, if at all, within the specified time. Once a gift is *vested* actual enjoyment of the gift, including the right to possession, may be postponed until a much later time. RAP is concerned only with *vesting*.

The following case is a remarkable case. The landowners, operating under the common law Rule Against Perpetuities, set out to restrict use of their Wyoming ranch to agricultural purposes until the year 2100! Did they get away with it? What would Lord Nottingham have said?

# SUPREME COURT OF WYOMING
## SHRINERS HOSPITALS FOR CHILDREN, IN ITS CAPACITY AS BENEFICIARY OF THE ALFRED J. AND PEGGE A. COOKSLEY TRUST, APPELLANT (PLAINTIFF),
### V.
## FIRST NORTHERN BANK OF WYOMING, IN ITS CAPACITY AS TRUSTEE OF THE ALFRED J. AND PEGGE A. COOKSLEY TRUST, APPELLEE (DEFENDANT).

MAY 18, 2016.

**Opinion**

HILL, Justice.

Alfred "Jack" Cooksley and Pegge Cooksley placed their ranch and other property in a revocable trust entitled the Alfred J. and Pegge A. Cooksley Trust (Trust). The Trust named Shriners Hospitals for Children (Shriners) and the Kalif Children's Travel Fund (Kalif) as beneficiaries, and First Northern Bank of Wyoming as the successor trustee. The Trust specified the year 2100 as its termination date, and it directed First Northern Bank to hold the ranch and other property in the Trust until that date. Upon termination of the Trust, First Northern Bank was to distribute the Trust assets to the beneficiaries, and, until then, the Bank was to distribute to the beneficiaries any Trust income not otherwise required to maintain and operate the ranch.

Pegge Cooksley died in 2007, and Jack Cooksley died in 2011. After Jack Cooksley's death, Shriners filed a petition seeking termination of the Trust and an immediate distribution of the Trust assets. In a separate action, Shriners filed a complaint against First Northern Bank alleging it had breached its fiduciary duty to the Trust beneficiaries and seeking the Bank's removal as trustee, an award of damages, and a disgorgement of any fees paid to the Bank. Shriners' actions were consolidated, and following a bench trial the district court ruled against Shriners and issued a judgment denying all of its claims. The court thereafter entered an order directing Shriners to pay First Northern Bank its attorney fees and costs in the amount of $48,343.74. Shriners appeals both the judgment denying its claims and the order awarding fees and costs. We affirm both.

## FACTS

The principal asset of the Trust is an approximately 1,620–acre ranch that the Cooksleys purchased in 1951. The ranch is located in Sheridan County, Wyoming, about twenty-five miles southeast of Sheridan, and is accessible by U.S. Highway 14. The ranch appraised at a value of $2,000,000.00 in 2011 and, with over a mile of frontage on Piney Creek, was described in that property appraisal as being located in "a highly sought after area situated along the year-round flowing Piney Creek." The property appraiser observed: "The meadows/creek bottom land, located along Piney Creek, are not only highly productive (providing a good hay base for the ranching operation) but also esthetically pleasing and valued for their recreational amenities."

The Trust provided that while both Jack and Pegge Cooksley were living, the trustee was to pay the net income and principal (up to the entire amount) of the Trust to or for their benefit, in such amounts and at such times as either might direct. Such payments were to continue until the death of the survivor of them.

After the deaths of both Jack and Pegge, the Trust directed the following disposition of the Trust property:

> 2.2 *Disposition After Death of Both Settlors.* Upon the death of the survivor of us, the Trustee shall administer, dispose of and distribute the then remainder of this trust, including income accruing after the date of death of the survivor of us, as follows:
>
> A. [distribution of personal property per any separate writing]
>
> B. [distribution of rocks, minerals, and historical artifacts to Jim Gatchell Museum]
>
> C. The Trustee may make distribution or disposition of any other tangible personal property as the Trustee, in its sole discretion, shall deem appropriate, including but not limited to private sale, auction and charitable donation. We intend that the trust continue for some years, and direct the Trustee to dispose of tangible personal property so that it is not a burden on the trust.
>
> Notwithstanding the foregoing, the Trustee is authorized to retain such tangible personal property as it deems appropriate or necessary to the management of the ranch land, buildings and residence.
>
> D. The Trustee shall thereafter hold, manage, invest, reinvest and distribute the remaining trust estate for the benefit of the **SHRINERS HOSPITAL FOR CRIPPLED CHILDREN—INTERMOUNTAIN,** or its successor, ("**SHRINERS HOSPITAL**") as follows:

(i) The Trustee shall distribute to or apply for the benefit of the **SHRINERS HOSPITAL,** at least semi-annually, all of the net income of the trust. We specifically direct that any and all accumulation of funds, whether from depletion, depreciation, and/or any other non-distributable source, be managed by the Trustee and used to the extent that the Trustee deems appropriate or necessary, to maintain the real property. In the event that there are insufficient funds to pay such expenses, then the Trustee is authorized to withhold so much of the net income otherwise distributable as is necessary or advisable, in the Trustee's sole discretion, to provide for such expenses.

(ii) As soon as practical after the year 2100, the Trustee shall distribute outright to the **SHRINERS HOSPITAL** all of the then-remaining principal together with any undistributed income, free and clear from the restrictions of these Trust provisions, and when all funds have been distributed, the Trust shall terminate.

(iii) If **SHRINERS HOSPITAL** shall cease to exist, without a successor qualified as an IRC Section 501(c)(3), as amended, then the Trustee shall designate one or more qualified IRC Section 501(c)(3) recipient(s), upon application to and approval of a court of competent jurisdiction, such qualified recipient(s) to be chosen according to the criteria of assisting and promoting the medical diagnosis, care and treatment of children in Wyoming and the greater intermountain region.

## First Amendment to Trust

On January 15, 2007, the Cooksleys executed the first amendment to the Trust, to provide for distribution of the Trust assets to Shriners as soon as practical after the year 2050 and to provide for the Trust's termination after that 2050 distribution.

Just over a month after the first amendment to the Trust was executed, on February 21, 2007, Pegge Cooksley died.

## Second Amendment to the Trust

On November 13, 2007, Jack Cooksley executed a second amendment to the Trust. The changes included: 1) the addition of Kalif Children's Travel Fund (Kalif) as an additional beneficiary; and 2) an extension of the Trust's termination date back to the year 2100.

When First Northern Bank received a copy of the second amendment to the Trust, it requested confirmation that Mr. Cooksley did in fact intend to extend the Trust's termination date from the Year 2050 to the Year 2100. Mr. Cooksley's attorney, Darlene Reiter, responded in a letter dated January 17, 2008:

I discussed the term of the Cooksley Trust with Jack when we met earlier this week. Jack confirmed that the Trust is intended to continue to the year 2100, unless earlier terminated by exercise of the very limited provision for sale of the surface.

Shriners' Challenge to Trust following Jack Cooksley's Death

Jack Cooksley died on March 17, 2011. On April 28, 2011, Wendy Martin, a trust officer at First Northern Bank, sent a letter to Patricia Dockery in Shriners' legal department informing her of Mr. Cooksley's death and providing copies of the Trust and the amendments to the Trust. On May 20, 2011, Ms. Dockery notified Ms. Martin of concerns Shriners had with the Trust and its amendments. Ms. Dockery cited various concerns: she suggested the Trust's year 2100 termination date would appear to violate Wyoming's statutory rule against perpetuities; and she indicated that she had received information that Mr. Cooksley renegotiated an agricultural lease on the ranch, prior to the lease's expiration, resulting in terms less favorable to the Trust and she expressed concerns regarding Mr. Cooksely's motivation and his mental and physical status when the lease was renegotiated.

On September 1, 2011, Patricia Dockery sent another letter to First Northern Bank again raising her concern that the Trust violated the statutory rule against perpetuities. Ms. Dockery wrote:

> Shriners Hospitals for Children would be interested in the early termination of the trust and outright distribution of the trust assets. If court action is necessary to terminate the trust, we would suggest that perhaps Mr. Cooksley's attorney, Darlene Reiter, should absorb those costs as the effective date of W.S. § 34–1–139 is some three years prior to the execution of the Cooksley's trust and Ms. Reiter had a duty to be familiar with the statutes of the state in which she practices.

On October 6, 2011, First Northern Bank acted on Shriners' concerns regarding the rule against perpetuities by filing a Petition to Amend Trust in the Fourth Judicial District Court, Johnson County. The petition alleged that the Trust violated the rule against perpetuities and asked that the court enter an order amending the Trust to provide a termination date of not later than twenty-one years after the last to die of Jack and Pegge Cooksley.

On May 14, 2012, Shriners filed its own petition requesting an order terminating the Trust. Shriners alleged that the Trust could not be modified without consent of the beneficiaries and because Shriners objected to any modification, the Bank's petition to amend should be denied. Shriners further alleged that continuation of the

Trust was not economical or necessary to achieve a material purpose of the Trust and its termination was therefore proper.

On June 18, 2012, the district court held a hearing on First Northern Bank's petition to amend the Trust and Shriners' petition to terminate the Trust. Following that hearing, First Northern Bank moved to amend its petition, arguing:

> 3. First Northern Bank's original Petition inadvertently alleged that the Trust violated the rule against perpetuities. Evidence was presented at the hearing alleging the Trust is a charitable trust in which case there is no violation of the Rule Against Perpetuities. Justice requires allowing First Northern Bank to amend the Petition in order to conform the pleadings to the evidence presented at the hearing in this matter.

On August 20, 2012, Shriners filed a new and separate action against First Northern Bank, this time alleging that First Northern Bank breached its fiduciary duty to the Trust beneficiaries by failing to diversify the Trust's investments and failing to prudently invest and manage the Trust's assets, and that First Northern Bank breached its duty of loyalty to the beneficiaries, its duty of prudent administration, its duty of good faith, and its duty to minimize the costs of administering the Trust. For its relief, Shriners sought removal of First Northern Bank as trustee, an order compelling diversification and sale of the Cooksley ranch, and an order denying any further compensation to the Bank, imposing a surcharge against the Bank, and a disgorgement of any and all fees the Bank had received from the Trust.

A two-day bench trial was held on March 17–18, 2015. The court found:

> The Trust has two valid material charitable purposes: (1) to keep the Ranch open and used for agricultural purposes or preservation until 2100, and (2) to benefit Shriners and Kalif. This Court further holds that, according to the Trust terms, the material charitable purpose of keeping the Ranch open takes precedence.

The district court concluded that termination of the Trust would defeat the Trust's dominant material purpose of retaining the ranch until the year 2100 and that First Northern Bank did not breach any of its fiduciary obligations. The court found Shriners filed its litigation in bad faith and would therefore be responsible for payment of the Bank's fees and costs in the amount of $48,343.74.

# DISCUSSION

## A. Rule against Perpetuities

The district court ruled as a matter of law that the rule against perpetuities did not apply to the Trust because the Trust is a charitable trust. On appeal, Shriners contends that the Trust is not a charitable trust, at least not the portion of the Trust devoted to retention of the Cooksley ranch. We conclude that rule against perpetuities does not apply here.

Article 1, § 30 of the Wyoming Constitution states: "Perpetuities and monopolies are contrary to the genius of a free state, and shall not be allowed." Wyoming's rule against perpetuities has been codified and provides, in relevant part:

> No interest in real or personal property shall be good unless it must vest not later than twenty-one (21) years after some life in being at the creation of the interest and any period of gestation involved in the situation to which the limitation applies. The lives selected to govern the time of vesting must not be so numerous nor so situated that evidence of their deaths is likely to be unreasonably difficult to obtain. It is intended by the enactment of this statute to make effective in this state the American common-law rule against perpetuities.

Wyo. Stat. Ann. § 34–1–139(a) (LexisNexis 2015).

Wyoming's rule against perpetuities encourages the constitutional goal of alienability of property by voiding property interests that will not vest within the statutory term. The rule against perpetuities does not apply to a property interest that has already vested. A property interest vests at the point when no contingency can defeat the interest. We have distinguished vested and contingent interests as follows:

> The broad distinction between vested and contingent remainders is this: In the first, there is some person in esse known and ascertained, who, by the will or deed creating the estate, is to take and enjoy the estate, and whose right to such remainder no contingency can defeat. In the second, it depends upon the happening of a contingent event, whether the estate limited as a remainder shall ever take effect at all. The event may either never happen, or it may not happen until after the particular estate upon which it depended shall have been determined, so that the estate in remainder will never take effect.

Pursuant to the Trust terms, the beneficiaries, Shriners and Kalif, do not take possession of the Trust property until the year 2100. Their interest in that property, however, vested upon Jack Cooksley's death. There is no contingency that can defeat the beneficiaries' interest in the property, and it is certain that when the Trust terminates in the year 2100, the beneficiaries will receive possession of the Trust property. This result is not affected by the risk that the Trust property may be diminished in some respect before the beneficiaries take possession. We have explained:

> Although it may be uncertain whether a remainder will ever take effect in possession, it will nevertheless be a vested remainder if the interest is fixed. It is the uncertainty of the right of enjoyment, and not the uncertainty of its actual enjoyment, which renders a remainder contingent and distinguishes it from a vested remainder.

Shriners and Kalif have a fixed and vested interest to which the rule of perpetuities does not apply. This conclusion is captured in the following explanation:

> The rule against perpetuities requires a creator of a contingent interest to ensure that any contingent interest will vest or fail within 21 years of the death of a life or lives in being at creation. It is concerned with vesting in interest or ownership, and not with vesting in possession (the right to occupy or enjoy the subject matter of the transfer). Thus if a fee owner dies leaving a will by which he creates a trust for A and A's successors to last for 25 years, remainder to B (a person living at that time), the Rule is not involved because the interest of B is vested at once as far as ownership is concerned, and the fact that B will not come into the enjoyment of the property until the lapse of 25 years is immaterial to the Rule, because no contingent interest is involved.
> George Gleason Bogert & Helen S. Shapo, *The Law of Trusts and Trustees* § 213, p. 170 (3d ed. 2007).

Because the interest of Shriners and Kalif in the Trust property was fixed and vested upon Jack Cooksley's death, the Trust does not violate the rule against perpetuities. We therefore uphold the district court's ruling on First Northern Bank's petition to amend the Trust.

## B. Termination of the Trust

The district court rejected Shriners' petition to terminate the Trust based on its findings that holding the ranch in the Trust until the year 2100 was the Trust's dominant material purpose and termination of the Trust would defeat that material purpose.

Shriners contends that the district court erred in finding that retention of the ranch was a material purpose of the Trust. It further contends that the Trust's only remaining material purpose is that of benefitting Shriners and Kalif, which purpose it asserts is better served by termination of the Trust. We disagree and find the district court's ruling supported by both the Trust's plain terms and Wyoming law.

Section 411 of Wyoming's Uniform Trust Code (UTC) provides for termination of a trust if "no material purpose of the trust remains to be achieved or the purposes of the trust have become unlawful, contrary to public policy or impossible to achieve."

This Court has also adopted the Restatement (Second) of Trusts § 337, which, consistent with the UTC, allows beneficiaries to compel the early termination of a trust as follows:

> (1) Except as stated in Subsection (2), if all of the beneficiaries of a trust consent and none of them is under an incapacity, they can compel the termination of the trust.

> (2) If the continuance of the trust is necessary to carry out a material purpose of the trust, the beneficiaries cannot compel its termination.
> American Nat'l Bank v. Miller, 899 P.2d 1337, 1340 (Wyo.1995).

In adopting this Restatement provision, we observed:

> This rule balances between protecting and enforcing a grantor's instructions regarding a trust, and providing for distribution to beneficiaries at the earliest time after all the grantor's material purposes have been fulfilled. The law should guard and enforce a grantor's wishes and purposes, so long as they remain unfulfilled. When those purposes have been fulfilled, however, the law should provide for the most expeditious termination and distribution of the trust estate.
> American Nat'l Bank, 899 P.2d at 1340.

Shriners does not contend that unanticipated circumstances have arisen, or that retention of the Cooksley ranch has become unlawful, contrary to public policy or impossible to achieve.

### 1. Interpretation of the Trust

Shriners argues that the material purpose of the Trust was established in the Cooksley's Declaration of Trust with the Declaration's statement: "The purpose of this agreement is to create the trust as described in Exhibit A for our benefit and

the other beneficiaries designated there." Shriners points out that the other designated beneficiaries are Shriners and Kalif and that each amendment to the Trust reaffirmed all unaltered provisions of the Declaration and Trust. To say that it is the only
remaining material purpose, however, requires that we ignore other clear statements
of the settlors' intent, contrary to our rules of interpretation. The settlors' intent
was clear from the outset that the ranch was to be retained, and its operation and
maintenance trumped payment of income to Shriners and Kalif. Given this clear and
continuing expression of the settlors' intent, we must agree with the district court's
conclusion that retention of the ranch was at least a material purpose of the Trust, if
not its paramount purpose.

### 2. Retention of Trust Asset as Material Purpose

Under the Uniform Trust Code, a trust may be created for any purpose that is
lawful, not contrary to public policy, and possible to achieve.

Retention of the ranch is not unlawful, contrary to public policy, or impossible.
That said, we recognize that the Trust's retention of the ranch is not necessarily a
term directed to the benefit of Shriners and Kalif, given that it delays their immediate possession of the asset and consumes income that would otherwise be available
to them. As the comments to the Uniform Trust Code explain, though, this does not
place the Trust crosswise with section 405. A trust may have more than one purpose,
and its purposes can be a mix of charitable and noncharitable. As one court explained:

> If a trust satisfies all of the requirements for a valid charitable trust and all of the
> requirements of a valid private trust, there is no good reason why the courts should
> not carry out the intentions of the settlor by enforcing the trust. <u>Bogert, Law of Trusts,</u>
> <u>§ 65 (Fifth Edition 1973)</u>

The Trust has two distinct material purposes: 1) retention of the ranch; and 2) providing a benefit to Shriners and Kalif. We need not decide whether the purpose
served by retention of the ranch is a charitable purpose or a noncharitable purpose.
The Code allows for either, and we resolved the Trust's alleged violation of the rule
against perpetuities without regard to the Trust's charitable status.

For all the reasons stated above, we find no error in the district court's denial of
Shriners' petition to terminate the Trust.

We agree with the district court's observation that Shriners' actions against the
Bank and the Trust were taken with utter disregard for the Cooksleys' intentions, a
position contrary to the paramount importance Wyoming law places on a settler's

intentions. We therefore find no abuse of discretion in the district court's determination that Shriners should be responsible for payment of the attorney fees and costs awarded in this matter.

## CONCLUSION

We affirm the district court's ruling that the Trust does not violate the rule against perpetuities. We also affirm the district court's judgment denying Shriners' claims against First Northern Bank and its order awarding attorney fees and costs.

Note: OK, in the following 2018 case, whoever drafted the trust seems to have made an attempt to create a trust that screams out that it violates the Rule Against Perpetuities. Was that designed as a way to tempt the children to sue, and thus trigger the provision that would give each of the children only $1? Who is going to keep an eye on the trustees of this trust until payments are finally made? Who will be in a position to object if the trustees start paying themselves exorbitant fees for managing the trust assets?

**COURT OF APPEALS OF KANSAS**
**LARRY SELL AND PATRICIA G. COYER, AS THE COTRUSTEES**
**OF THE WILLIAM L. GRAHAM REVOCABLE TRUST,**
**APPELLEES,**
**V.**
**REBECCA JOY (GRAHAM) DORIAN, ET AL., APPELLANTS.**

JULY 6, 2018.

**MEMORANDUM OPINION**

Per Curiam:

This appeal arises from a dispute over the administration of the William L. Graham Revocable Trust. The cotrustees, Larry Sell and Patricia G. Coyer, filed a petition for declaratory judgment asking the district court to determine the validity of a provision of the trust agreement relating to the future distribution of certain assets set aside for the benefit of William Graham's great-great-great-grandchildren. In response, some of William's descendants filed counterclaims asserting that this provision of the trust agreement is invalid because it violates the rule against perpetuities. Moreover, some of the descendants sought an accounting of the trust estate and some sought a determination regarding the validity of a provision of the trust agreement purport-edly excluding potential beneficiaries who are born out of wedlock. The district court granted summary judgment as a matter of law to the cotrustees but did not address the issue relating to potential beneficiaries who are born out of wedlock. The district court also determined that the descendants were not entitled to an accounting and that it lacked the power to order periodic accountings to a neutral representative of the yet-to-be-born beneficiaries.

## FACTUAL AND PROCEDURAL BACKGROUND
### Creation of the William L. Graham Revocable Trust

On August 1, 1978, William L. Graham (William) and Betty Harrison Graham (Betty)—who were husband and wife—executed the William L. Graham Revocable Trust Agreement. Two days later, William executed his Last Will and Testament, directing that his personal effects go to Betty—if she survived him—and that the resi-due of his probate estate flow to the William L. Graham Revocable Trust.

In his Last Will and Testament, William also included the following provision:

"I am not unmindful of four of my children, Marjorie March Stevens, Theodore Lyman Graham, Constance Kay Culley, and Jack Lyman Graham, their respective spouses and descendants; however, I consider that the provisions which I have made for them by gifts during my lifetime are adequate to provide for their needs and the needs of their spouses and descendants, and accordingly I make no further provisions for them.

"In the event any of such four of my children, their spouses, or their descendants should contest my Will or any Trust established by me, and be successful in such contest, then and in that event I give and bequeath to each of my children, each of their spouses and each of their descendants, the sum of One Dollar ($1.00) and no more."

ARTICLE SIXTH of the trust agreement—which is at the center of this dispute—states:

"1. If at the time of the Grantor's death, Grantor's spouse, Betty H. Graham, survives Grantor, the Trustee shall: ...

G. l. Retain an amount equal to ten percent (10%) of the Grantor's adjusted gross estate to be held and administered for the benefit of the great-great-great-grandchildren of Grantor. As each such great-great-great-grandchild of Grantor attains the age of twenty-seven and one/half (27-1/2) years there shall be distributed to such great-great-great-grandchild the portion of the Trust Estate equal to a fraction, the numerator of which is one, and the denominator being one plus the number of the then-living great-great-great-grandchildren of Grantor who have not yet attained the age of twenty-seven and one/half (27-1/2) years. In the event all of the assets of the Trust Estate have not been distributed, and there are no great-great-great-grandchildren of Grantor who have not attained the age of twenty-seven and one/half (27-1/2) years and all the great-great-grandchildren of Grantor are deceased, then the remaining Trust assets shall be distributed equally among the great-great-great-grandchildren of Grantor who had previously received distributions, per stirpes.]

"2. Anything contained herein to the contrary notwithstanding, the Trust for the benefit of Grantor's great-great-great-grandchildren shall terminate not later than twenty (20) years after the death of the last survivor of the following:

William L. Graham III
Susan Rebecca Graham
Pamela Rae Dorian        *savings*
Marjorie Ellen Dorian     *clause*
James Graham Dorian
Sarah Joy Dorian"

[It is undisputed that William L. Graham III, Susan Rebecca Graham, Pamela Rae Dorian, Marjorie Ellen Dorian, James Graham Dorian, and Sarah Joy Dorian are six of William and Betty's grandchildren—each of whom was alive at the time the trust agreement and will were executed.]

*Death of William L. Graham*

On February 4, 1981, William died and Betty survived him. A probate proceeding was filed in Butler County and the four children identified in William's will made inquiry regarding the terms of the trust agreement. On March 13, 1981, the district court entered an order requiring that a copy of the trust agreement be immediately provided to the children. The order also set a deadline for the filing of pleadings to contest the will. However, the deadline passed and no pleadings contesting the will were filed. Thereafter, the district court entered an order admitting the will to probate on April 21, 1981.

We note that at the time of his death, William had no great-grandchildren, great-great-grandchildren, or great-great-great-grandchildren. There are currently several great-grandchildren and at least two great-great-grandchildren. Both of the great-great-grandchildren are minors and are potentially beneficiaries under the terms of the trust agreement. Even so, [there is a question regarding whether these great-great-grandchildren are eligible to be beneficiaries under the terms of the trust agreement because they were born out of wedlock.]

*Declaratory Judgment Action*

In September 2014, one of William and Betty's daughters—Rebecca Dorian—retained legal counsel who sent a letter to counsel for the cotrustees raising questions about the trust. It was alleged that the provision of the trust agreement for the benefit of the great-great-great-grandchildren was now invalid because William died more than 21 years ago. Accordingly, it was suggested that the remaining trust assets should be distributed to William's heirs-at-law. However, the cotrustees disagreed with this suggestion.

On November 18, 2015, the cotrustees filed a petition for declaratory judgment seeking an order from the district court regarding "the interpretation and application of the trust agreement." The petition named more than 60 defendants as well as unknown individuals who may become beneficiaries of the William L. Graham Revocable Trust. In the petition, the cotrustees asked that the district court issue a declaratory judgment that the provision of the trust relating to the great-great-great-grandchildren is valid under Kansas law.

A guardian ad litem—who was evidently appointed by the cotrustees—filed an answer on behalf of the unknown and unborn individuals who may become beneficiaries under the terms of the trust agreement. Yet it does not appear that a guardian ad litem was appointed to represent the interests of the two minor great-great-grand-children who were born out of wedlock. Moreover, the district court did not decide the issue of whether they could be beneficiaries under the terms of the trust agreement as interpreted given the current status of Kansas law.

[The district court determined that the trust did not violate the rule against perpetuities, that the defendants were not entitled to an accounting of the trust estate, and that it had no authority to enter an order requiring periodic accountings to a neutral representative of beneficiaries who are not yet born.]

## ANALYSIS

*Common-Law Rule Against Perpetuities*

At the outset, we note that the parties agree that the William L. Graham Revocable Trust was created several years before the Kansas Legislature adopted the Uniform Statutory Rule Against Perpetuities. As a result, the Uniform Statutory Rule Against Perpetuities does not apply to the future or nonvested interests created by the trust agreement in this case. Instead, we must apply the common-law rule against perpetuities.

The common-law rule against perpetuities "precludes the creation of any future interest in property which does not necessarily vest within twenty-one years after a life or lives presently in being, plus the period of gestation, where gestation is in fact taking place." In other words, any future or nonvested property interest that does not vest within 21 years after the termination of a life in being is void. Although Kansas courts have long recognized that the creation of property interests is subject to the rule against perpetuities, modern courts have acknowledged that the rule bears little relation to modern business practices and have limited application of the rule. Thus, a document granting a future interest in property should be interpreted where possible to avoid the conclusion that it violates the rule against perpetuities.

Here, based on our review of the trust agreement in its entirety, we find that ARTICLE SIXTH, Section 1.G does not violate the common-law rule against perpetuities. In particular, ARTICLE SIXTH, Section 1.G.1. and Section 1.G.2 must be read together. Although standing alone there is a possibility that ARTICLE SIXTH, Section 1.G.1 could violate the common-law rule against perpetuities, the plain and unambiguous language of ARTICLE SIXTH, Section 1.G.2 prevents this from happening.

ARTICLE SIXTH, Section 1.G.2 explicitly states:

> "2. Anything contained herein to the contrary notwithstanding, the Trust for the benefit of Grantor's great-great-great-grandchildren shall terminate not later than twenty (20) years after the death of the following:
>
> William L. Graham III
> Susan Rebecca Graham
> Pamela Rae Dorian
> Marjorie Ellen Dorian
> James Graham Dorian
> Sarah Joy Dorian"

It is undisputed that each of the persons listed in ARTICLE SIXTH, Section 1.G.2 were William's living grandchildren at the time this provision of the trust agreement was written. Under this provision—often referred to as a savings clause—the assets held in trust for the benefit of William's great-great-great-grandchildren must be distributed within 21 years of a life in being. One way or the other, the provision setting aside 10% of the adjusted gross trust estate to be held and administered for the benefit of William's great-great-great-grandchildren will terminate no later than 20 years after the death of his last surviving grandchild named in ARTICLE SIXTH, Section 1.G.2.

Although it is possible that there will never be any great-great-great-grandchildren or great-great-grandchildren, this does not mean that the provisions of ARTICLE SIXTH, Section 1.G violates the common-law rule against perpetuities. As the Kansas Supreme Court has held: " 'No interest is good unless it must vest, *if at all*, not later than 21 years after some life in being at the creation of the interest.' " (Emphasis added.) *Beverlin v. First National Bank* (1940). As indicated above, regardless of where the trust assets held for the benefit of the great-great-great-grandchildren ultimately end up—which is a question that we find to be purely speculative at this point—they will be distributed within the period prescribed by the common-law rule against perpetuities. Thus, we conclude that the district court did not err in determining that the provisions of ARTICLE SIXTH, Section 1.G. do not violate the common-law rule against perpetuities.

*Accounting of Trust Estate*

Under K.S.A. 59-2254, "any beneficiary who is under legal disability, and also all possible unborn or unascertained beneficiaries may be represented in a trust accounting by living competent members of the class to which they do or would belong, or by a guardian *ad litem*, as the court deems best."

Likewise, K.S.A. 58a-305(a) grants the district court—as well as a trustee—authority to appoint "a representative to receive notice, give consent, and otherwise represent, bind, and act on behalf of a minor, incapacitated, or unborn individual, or a person whose identity or location is unknown." It is important to recognize that under K.S.A. 58a-305(b), the district court may appoint such a representative "whether or not a judicial proceeding concerning the trust is pending." Thus, we conclude that the district court has the authority to appoint a guardian ad litem or other neutral representative to protect the rights of possible trust beneficiaries who are under legal disability, who are not yet born, or who are otherwise unknown.

## CONCLUSION

In summary, we conclude that the district court properly determined that the provisions of ARTICLE SIXTH, Section 1.G. do not violate the common-law rule against perpetuities. We also conclude that the district court properly determined that William's children, grandchildren, and great-grandchildren are not entitled to an accounting of the trust estate. However, we conclude that the district court erred in finding that it did not have the authority to appoint a guardian ad litem or other neutral representative to protect the rights of possible trust beneficiaries who are under legal disability, who are not yet born, or who are otherwise unknown.

Finally, we conclude that the issue of whether William's great-great-grandchildren who were born out of wedlock are also potential beneficiaries of the trust based on the language of the trust agreement as interpreted in light of current status of Kansas law should be remanded to the district court for ruling. We find this issue to be significant because if these great-great-grandchildren are found to be potential beneficiaries, they may ultimately receive some or all of the assets set aside by William in ARTICLE SIXTH, Section G.1., and would have the right to review the books of account showing all of the transactions pertaining to the trust estate. Furthermore, if the district court determines that there is not a parent who can adequately represent the interests of the minor great-great-grandchildren born out of wedlock, then it should appoint a guardian ad litem or other neutral representative to represent their interests as this issue is being considered.

Affirmed in part, reversed in part, and remanded with directions for further proceedings.

Note: The following case is a brief illustration of one of the most common situations in which the Rule Against Perpetuities comes up in commercial transactions - a right of first refusal. It is so easy, and sensible, to draft a right of first refusal which is totally compliant with common law RAP. But for some reason non-expert drafters seem to love to throw in the phrase that the right of first refusal is binding on the "heirs and assigns" of the parties. And those few words, which are both unnecessary and unwise, may cause the whole right of first refusal to be void. Just limit any right of first refusal to the lives of the parties involved – or to a set number of years, less than 21 years – or to the lives of the parties involved *plus* 21 years. That should provide more than enough time for a right of first refusal – and it will prevent the whole thing from being void from the beginning! Yet there are a great many current cases in which an attempted right of first refusal is held to have been void from the beginning, because of a violation of RAP.

# SUPREME COURT, APPELLATE DIVISION, NEW YORK
## JAMES KOZAK ET AL., APPELLANTS,
### V
## KEITH PORADA ET AL., RESPONDENTS, ET AL., DEFENDANT.

OCTOBER 26, 2017

Garry, J.

In 1968, plaintiffs James Kozak, Lawrence Porada and three other individuals (hereinafter collectively referred to as the original tenants in common) purchased approximately 85 acres of rural land in the Town of Smithville, Chenango County. In connection with this purchase, they executed a contract in which, as pertinent here, they agreed that if any of them decided to sell his interest in the property, he would be required to offer it first to the remaining tenants in common upon 60 days' notice (hereinafter the divestiture agreement). Two of the original tenants in common later sold their interests in the property to the others in accord with the divestiture agreement. A third tenant in common died, and his wife, plaintiff Joan Zopp, became the executor of his estate. In December 2008, Lawrence Porada executed and recorded a quitclaim deed—drafted by defendant Brian Gallagher, an attorney—transferring his interest in the property to his son, defendant Keith Porada. No notice or offer of sale was given to plaintiffs. Lawrence Porada later passed away, and defendant Barbara Porada became the executor of his estate.

In December 2011, plaintiffs commenced this action seeking to enforce the terms of the divestiture agreement and to set aside the conveyance to Keith Porada. Gallagher moved to dismiss the complaint against him. The Supreme Court, Trial Division, granted the motion and dismissed the complaint upon grounds that included a finding that the divestiture agreement violated the rule against perpetuities and was therefore invalid. Plaintiffs appeal.

We note initially that all of the causes of action depend upon the validity of the divestiture agreement. Although Gallagher moved for relief only on his own behalf, the action cannot succeed against any defendant if the agreement is unenforceable. Thus, dismissal as to Gallagher upon this ground results in dismissal of the complaint in its entirety. As to the substance of the parties' claims, we agree with the Supreme Court, Trial Division, that the divestiture agreement is invalid in that it violates the rule against perpetuities prohibiting remote vesting.

As codified in <u>EPTL 9-1.1 (b)</u>, this rule provides that "no estate in property shall be valid unless it must vest, if at all, not later than 21 years after one or more lives in being at the creation of the estate and any period of gestation involved." Here, although the divestiture agreement describes the future interests it creates as "options to purchase," they are more properly termed rights of first refusal, as they do not create a power to compel an unwilling seller to convey the interest, but instead restrict a *willing* seller's power to do so without first offering the property to the other tenants in common "upon the happening of a contingency: the seller's decision to sell to a third party." The future interest created by such a right of first refusal vests if and when that contingency occurs.

In general, rights of first refusal are subject to the rule against perpetuities and are thus invalid if it is possible for the future interests they represent to vest outside the prescribed time period.

We further reject plaintiffs' contention that the rights of first refusal created by the divestiture agreement cannot vest outside the time period established by <u>EPTL 9-1.1 (b)</u> because they were intended to be personal to the original tenants in common and to terminate upon their deaths. Nothing in the unambiguous contractual language supports such a construction. On the contrary, the divestiture agreement expressly provides that it "shall not be abrogated or affected by the death of any of the original tenants in common, and the heirs, executors, administrators, successors and assigns of the original tenants in common shall be bound by its provisions."

This same language compels the conclusion that the divestiture agreement violates the rule against remote vesting. The inclusion of a contractual provision that makes a restraint on alienation binding upon heirs, assigns and other such successors in interest, with no limiting time period, "is significant and shows the parties' understanding that the restraint is to extend in duration for an indefinite period of time." The rights of first refusal created by the divestiture agreement may be exercised more than 21 years after lives that were in being when the rights were created, and therefore they violate the rule against perpetuities. Accordingly, the Supreme Court, Trial Division, properly determined that the divestiture agreement was invalid and dismissed the complaint. The parties' remaining contentions are rendered academic by this determination.

McCarthy, J.P., Clark, Mulvey and Rumsey, JJ., concur. The order is affirmed, with one bill of costs.

## The Uniform Statutory Rule Against Perpetuities (USRAP)

In *Sell v. Dorian* the Kansas court mentioned that even though the Uniform Statutory Rule Against Perpetuities (USRAP) had been adopted in Kansas in 1991, it was not applicable to the litigation taking place in 2018, because the document at issue went into effect in 1981, prior to the state's adoption of USRAP. That is likely to be the situation in many of the states that have adopted USRAP – for about a generation. Frequently, it is when the life estate ends that questions arise as to whether the intended remainder is valid – or void.

USRAP is anything but uniform in the 27 states which have adopted it as of 2018. There is uncertainty as to whether USRAP applies to commercial transactions or not.[1] If USRAP does not apply to commercial transactions, then are those transactions, such as rights of first refusal, subject to the common law Rule Against Perpetuities? Or not subject to any restrictions on the length of time for which they may endure? Is it a commercial transaction, or a donative transfer, if Mom sells her $100,000 parcel of land to Son for $5? Or to the neighbor for $10? Where is the line that distinguishes a commercial transaction from a donative transfer?

There have been some unintended adverse tax consequences caused by the adoption of USRAP.[2] There are some potentially very serious adverse consequences in the states which have adopted a newer version of USRAP which specifically allows a private trust to continue for 500 – or 1,000 years! One thousand years?! That would be about as far into the future as the year *1019* is in the past! Do you remember learning in History class what happened in the year 1019? Does anyone really have any business trying to tie up ownership and use of land that far into the future? In a country that has only been in existence for less than 250 years? Have things changed a bit since the founding of our country? And who, if anyone, would supervise the bank trustees during that 1,000 years? Needless to say, it was the banks that lobbied heavily for this provision, allowing individuals to set up what are called Dynasty trusts.

USRAP has been remarkably ineffective in clearing up potential difficulties with the common law Rule Against Perpetuities. But it has created lots of new headaches

---

1    *See Walters v. Sporer, 298 Neb. 536* (2017).

2    The most serious was the "Delaware Tax Trap," which the drafters of USRAP later tried to correct with the spectacularly obtuse provision which stated, "If, in measuring a period from the creation of a trust or other property arrangement for purposes of interests, powers, and trusts subject to this paragraph (b), language in a governing instrument seeks to disallow the vesting or termination of any interest or trust beyond, seeks to postpone the vesting or termination of any interest or trust until, or seeks to operate in effect in any similar fashion upon the later of the expiration of a period of time not exceeding twenty-one years after the death of the survivor of specified lives in being at the creation of the trust or other property arrangement or the expiration of a period of time that exceeds or might exceed twenty-one years after the death of the survivor of lives in being at the creation of the trust or other property arrangement, that language is inoperative to the extent it produces a period of time that exceeds twenty-one years after the death of the survivor of the specified lives."

for lawyers. In Colorado, for example, thanks to USRAP, there are now three different versions of RAP – the common law version, the 1991 version, and the 2001 version.

But take heart – anything that complies with common law RAP will be valid in any state. Yet that still might not protect you from being sued. The following case, *Buell v. Holland & Hart,* is probably the most frightening case in this chapter.

## COLORADO COURT OF APPEALS
## THE TEMPLE HOYNE BUELL FOUNDATION, A COLORADO NONPROFIT CORPORATION, AND BUELL DEVELOPMENT CORPORATION, A COLORADO CORPORATION, PLAINTIFFS-APPELLEES AND CROSS-APPELLANTS,
### V.
## HOLLAND & HART, A PARTNERSHIP AND BRUCE T. BUELL, DEFENDANTS-APPELLANTS AND CROSS-APPELLEES.

AUGUST 27, 1992. CERTIORARI DENIED MAY 10, 1993.

**Opinion by Judge SMITH.**

In this legal malpractice action, defendants, Holland & Hart and Bruce Buell, appeal the final judgment entered on a jury verdict awarding plaintiffs, Buell Development Corporation, $3,364,011 in damages and $2,125,195 in pre-judgment interest. Plaintiffs cross-appeal the portion of the trial court's judgment denying various costs. We reverse the judgment and remand for a new trial.

⌈The judgment at issue here arose from defendants' representation of plaintiffs in connection with the sale of stock in Kings County Development Corporation (KCDC), a California corporation, to John Rocovich. As part of the transaction, defendants drafted an option contract which provided that part of the consideration for the stock sale was an option in favor of plaintiffs to acquire from Rocovich a percentage of KCDC's minerals underlying its California farmland should KCDC ever distribute these interests to its shareholders.⌉

After this contract was signed, KCDC instituted two lawsuits against various defendants, including plaintiffs and Rocovich. The lawsuit asserted, among other things, that plaintiffs and Rocovich had breached their fiduciary duties by entering into the foregoing stock transaction.

In 1982, KCDC settled with Rocovich, and, as part of that settlement, Rocovich conveyed all of his KCDC stock to the corporation. KCDC, meanwhile, decided to distribute its mineral interest to the corporation's shareholders within the year 1982.

While the KCDC lawsuits were pending, plaintiffs attempted to exercise their option under the contract executed with Rocovich. KCDC refused to honor the agreement between plaintiffs and Rocovich and to transfer the mineral interests, asserting that the option violated the Rule against Perpetuities and was therefore unenforceable.

In 1984, plaintiffs, who had discharged defendants as counsel in 1981, during the KCDC lawsuits, settled their dispute with the corporation. Under the terms of this settlement, plaintiffs received one-half of the mineral interests that they would have been entitled to under the option.

In 1989, plaintiffs initiated this lawsuit against defendants, asserting claims of negligence and breach of contract relating to the option contract with Rocovich. Soon after the litigation commenced, defendants sought a determination from the trial court that the option did not violate the Rule against Perpetuities.

At the evidentiary hearing on this issue, defendants attempted to establish that the option was exclusively contractual in nature and, thus, outside the Rule. The trial court disagreed, concluding that the option was subject to, and in violation of, the Rule. Moreover, the court ruled that there were no public policy reasons to allow the enforcement of the option in spite of the violation. Finally, the trial court ruled that no testimony on this particular issue would be admissible at trial.

Numerous expert witnesses for both parties testified at trial concerning the effects of the Rule against Perpetuities violation as it related to the rights of the parties under the option contract. At the conclusion of the evidence, the jury was instructed that plaintiffs had to prove two conjectural "cases within a case": (1) That plaintiffs would have lost a lawsuit brought to enforce the option as drafted by defendants; and (2) that plaintiffs would have won a lawsuit to enforce the option if defendants had not drafted it negligently.

The jury returned a verdict that plaintiffs' losses were caused solely by defendants' negligence.

I.

Defendants contend that the jury verdict in favor of plaintiffs on their claim for legal malpractice is erroneous as a matter of law. The crux of defendants' argument is the trial court's pre-trial ruling that the option contract violated the Rule against Perpetuities. Defendants argue that the trial court's ruling was erroneous, tainted the entire trial, and justifies entry of judgment in their favor. We agree that the trial court's ruling was in error and that such error did, indeed, pervade the trial proceedings. We disagree, however, that these conclusions dispose of plaintiffs' claim of legal malpractice.

As relevant here, the option provided:

In further consideration of the mutual promises of the parties as herein provided, we agree as follows with respect to the mineral interests *owned by KCDC:*

2. I, Rocovich, will use my best efforts to have the mineral interests distributed or made available to shareholders of KCDC as soon as possible.

3. From and after the time of distribution, plaintiffs will have *six months to purchase, at its option,* 31.73576% of *the mineral interests now owned by KCDC,* and I, Rocovich, agree to sell to plaintiffs said interest for the sum of $305,500; if plaintiffs should not exercise its option, I, Rocovich, will, nevertheless, have the option, at any time during said six-month period, to offer plaintiffs the said 31.73576% of KCDC mineral interests which plaintiffs shall be required to purchase for the sum of $305,500.00.

This agreement will bind and enure to the benefit of the heirs, successors and assigns of the respective parties.

A. The Rule Issue

The Rule against Perpetuities is a rule of property law, the fundamental purpose of which is to keep property "unfettered," that is, free from inconvenient limitations. As such, the Rule operates to invalidate future interests in property, real or personal, legal or equitable, which vest too remotely, specifically, "later than twenty-one years after some life in being at the creation of the interest."

An option to purchase, such as that at issue here, may or may not be subject to the Rule. If the option may continue for a period longer than 21 years *and* it creates an interest in a specific parcel of land or in any "specific identifiable thing," the option is required to comply with the Rule. In such instances, the option, because it is specifically enforceable, "fetters" the property which is the subject matter of the option by imposing upon it an unfulfilled condition precedent for too long a time.

If the option is determined *not* to create an enforceable interest in a specific parcel of land or in any "specific identifiable thing," then no specific property is "fettered" or chargeable with performance under the option. Nor is any particular property subject to a potentially objectionable unfulfilled condition precedent. [Such option, therefore, while creating enforceable contract rights between the parties, involves no fettering of any property and hence, presents no occasion for applying the Rule.]

In analyzing the option here, the trial court rejected defendants' argument that the option was of this latter character, that is, "exclusively contractual." The trial court concluded, instead, that the option did implicate a specific property interest thereby subjecting it to the Rule. The crux of the trial court's conclusion was its determination that:

> The option does concern *specific land.* The option concerns the mineral interest which was then owned by KCDC. A clearly identifiable mineral interest is involved in the option which can be stated with particularity and identified at the time of the option execution. The option binds the parties to obligations regarding a particular piece of property to the exclusion of any other property.

Having found the Rule applied, the trial court turned to the question of whether the option was in violation of the Rule's terms. The trial court answered the question in the affirmative, noting that when the mineral interests would be distributed was uncertain and, hence, that "there are numerous possibilities which would result in plaintiffs' interest not vesting within the period of 21 years after Rocovich, (the measuring life), dies."

Defendants contend that the uncertainty created by the unknown date of the mineral distribution, if any, was an irrelevant circumstance because the Rule had no applicability to the option. The essence of defendants' argument is, thus, that the trial court erred in its initial conclusion that the option concerned specific property.

A cursory review of the terms of the option reveals that the parties clearly *identified* a specific property interest as the subject matter of the option. [However, based on the following principles of property and corporate law, we conclude that the terms were insufficient to *create an interest* in the property described.]

[It is fundamental that a grantor can convey no more rights in property than he himself owns.] Accordingly, for the option here to have created an interest in a specific property, to wit, the mineral property identified in the option, Rocovich, the "grantor," would have to have had, at the time the option was executed, an interest, legal or equitable, in this property.

The record discloses, however, that, at the pertinent time, Rocovich's status was only that of a shareholder in KCDC. As a shareholder, Rocovich was entitled to an interest in the minerals only *if and when* they were *distributed.* [However, until such time, he held no interest in specific property of the corporation.]

As succinctly stated by the United States Supreme Court in _Rhode Island Hospital Trust Co. v. Doughton_, (1925):

> The owner of the shares of stock in a company is not the owner of the corporation's property. He has a right to his share in the earnings of the corporation, as they may be declared in dividends, arising from the use of all its property. In the dissolution of the corporation he may take his proportionate share in what is left, after all the debts of the corporation have been paid and the assets are divided in accordance with the law of its creation. _But he does not own the corporate property._

Thus, when the parties executed their contract, Rocovich's rights and interests, while, indeed, valuable and enforceable, were in KCDC's earnings and profits not in its _divisible assets_, such as the mineral interests.

At most, Rocovich held only a hope or chance of acquiring _specific_ corporate property. Neither a hope or a chance, however, are sufficient to create an interest in property.

Hence, until the mineral interests were _distributed_, Rocovich had no rights in the mineral interests which he could convey or "fetter." The option contract could not, thus, subject this particular property to an unfulfilled condition precedent. Indeed, KCDC was equally free, both before and after the parties executed the option, to dispose of the mineral interests at issue in any particular manner it chose and to any particular person or entity.

The option contract, in sum, involved no fettering of a specific parcel of property or of any specific identifiable thing and, hence, presented no opportunity to invoke the Rule.

This is not to say that the option was unenforceable. Indeed, between plaintiffs and Rocovich, the contract created rights and obligations enforceable by one against the other, their heirs, successors, and assigns. Of critical significance, however, the contract, in the words of defendants' expert, did "nothing whatsoever to the subject matter of their contract - property owned by a stranger to that contract."

Under the provisions of the contract at issue here, no interest in the minerals could arise in Rocovich or in plaintiffs _unless and until_ the mineral interests were distributed by KCDC to its shareholders. Once the interest was created by distribution, moreover, the option to purchase it was to be exercised promptly, specifically, six months "from and after the time of distribution" or it would lapse. Hence, there was no "mathematical possibility" that once created, the interest would vest beyond the period of perpetuities.

Next, plaintiffs argue that Rocovich's sale of his stock to KCDC as part of their settlement agreement "created" an interest in the minerals which triggered Rocovich's obligations under the contract and the applicability of the Rule. This argument is without merit.

Rocovich could assign his obligations to KCDC only if such assignment would not impair plaintiffs' rights. Such is clearly not the case here where the assignment, in triggering the Rule, would operate to destroy plaintiffs' rights.

In conclusion, we hold that the trial court erred in ruling that the option contract violated the Rule against Perpetuities.

## B. Effect of the Erroneous Ruling

Defendants argue that the trial court's erroneous pre-trial ruling tainted the entire trial and thus constituted prejudicial error. Under the particular circumstances here, we agree.

The record reveals that, prior to trial, the trial court ruled that all testimony by defendants' experts or other witnesses concerning *whether* the contract violated the Rule against Perpetuities was inadmissible. Moreover, at trial the jury was instructed that:

> Plaintiffs must prove that if had it sued to enforce the option it would have lost that court action solely because of defendant's negligence.

Later, in instructing the jury as to the plaintiffs' burden in this regard, the trial court further instructed the jury:

> The court has ruled as a matter of law that the option violated the Rule against Perpetuities and there is no public policy reason for not applying the rule.

This latter instruction states, unequivocally, that, in drafting the option contract, defendants committed an error. When read in conjunction with the former instruction, these directives indicate that the error is significant in proving the plaintiffs' "case within a case."

Moreover, the transcript discloses that extensive reference was made to the option's "unenforceability" by both the trial court and plaintiffs' counsel. Indeed, as pointed out by defendants in their brief, mention of this matter was made "10 times by the court, 56 times by the plaintiffs' counsel and 7 times by witnesses."

Although oftentimes these references were couched in the broader claim that defendants had not been "reasonably careful" in drafting the option, the trial court's erroneous ruling, nonetheless, as evidenced above, pervaded the trial proceedings and, most critically, influenced the instructions given to the jury. Accordingly, we conclude that defendants are entitled to a new trial on plaintiffs' claim of legal malpractice.

Defendants argue, however, that if the option is valid and enforceable, there can be no malpractice claim as a matter of law, thus entitling them to entry of judgment in their favor. We disagree.

[An attorney owes a duty to his client to employ that degree of knowledge, skill, and judgment ordinarily possessed by members of the legal profession in carrying out the services for his client. One of these obligations is anticipating *reasonably foreseeable risks.*]

might be malpractice

[Thus, although we hold here that the option did not violate the Rule against Perpetuities, the question remains whether defendants, as reasonably prudent attorneys, should have foreseen that the option, as drafted, was likely to result in litigation and whether other attorneys, in similar circumstances, would have taken steps to prevent such a result.]

Plaintiffs argued at trial, and presented expert testimony in support of their assertion, that the principal negligence of defendants was their not protecting plaintiffs from loss by failing to research and analyze the Rule's applicability in the option, to recognize the likelihood that a good faith dispute could occur over the enforceability of the option because of the Rule, and to take the simple step of either adding a time limitation or "savings clause" or recommending the deletion of the provision that made the option binding on heirs, successors, and assigns.

Bruce Buell testified that he had given no specific consideration to the Rule in drafting the Letter Agreement. Nor did he perform any legal research, consider the choice of law, consult with experts, or even consult with other members of his own firm on the question of whether the Rule could apply to the option. He concluded that he had no duty to do any of these things because he "was an experienced business transactions lawyer" who "knew the rule against perpetuities" and "knew when it applied," and could "spot issues like that." As a result, plaintiffs argue, Buell did not advise his clients of the real likelihood that a good faith dispute could arise over the enforceability of the option under the Rule.

On the issue of defendant's negligence, one expert attorney-witness testified that a reasonable attorney would have no reason to include a savings clause in the option and concluded that defendants met the standard of care in drafting it. However, conflicting testimony was offered by two other attorney-experts who testified that defendants had failed to meet the standard of care and should have considered the possibility that the Rule might apply to the option and should have protected it against a Rule challenge.

Perhaps the strongest testimony on this issue was that of defendant's own attorney-expert. On cross-examination, he unequivocally testified that, in his opinion, an attorney would be guilty of malpractice if he: (a) did not research the issue of the Rule in the context of this transaction, (b) failed to consider the potential for a dispute over the applicability of the Rule to the option, and (c) failed to utilize a savings clause to protect against that potential dispute.

Thus, although there was a conflict in the expert testimony as to attorney negligence in drafting the option, no witness disagreed with the premise that the option would have been protected from any Rule dispute if defendants had considered the Rule, had recognized the clear potential for dispute, and had either included a savings clause or excluded the language making the option binding on heirs, successors, and assigns.

In short, resolution of the Rule of Perpetuities issue does not conclusively resolve the issue of whether defendants met the applicable standard of care in preparing the option contract. Hence, we reject defendant's argument that judgment be entered in their favor.

## II.

In light of our resolution of the foregoing issue, it is unnecessary for us to address either defendants' remaining contention regarding prejudgment interest or plaintiffs' contention on cross-appeal regarding costs.

The judgment is reversed, and the cause is remanded for a new trial on plaintiffs' claims for legal malpractice consistent with the views expressed in this opinion.

## B. Possibility of Reverter Compared to Right of Entry

Time now to turn to two types of future interests that simply are not subject to the Rule Against Perpetuities – namely, the Possibility of Reverter, and the Right of Entry. Both the Possibility of Reverter and the Right of Entry are created when a grantor gives away less than the grantor owns, and retains either a Possibility of Reverter or a Right of Entry. The particular wording for each of these interest is vital.

A Possibility of Reverter should be created by saying something such as, "to A so long as the land is used for agricultural purposes, and when the land is no longer used for agricultural purposes then to revert to me." The key words are "so long as" and "then to revert." This clearly indicates that whenever the specified condition is broken, the land will automatically revert to the grantor. No action is necessary on the part of the grantor. The grantee would have an interest that is called a fee simple determinable, and the grantor would retain a Possibility of Reverter. Because the Possibility of Reverter is not subject to the Rule Against Perpetuities, this could create a land use restriction that would continue for a very long time.

A Right of Entry is created by using very similar words, but the legal differences between a Right of Entry and a Possibility of Reverter are dramatic! Most importantly, at common law a Possibility of Reverter could be conveyed, but at common law even the *attempt* to convey a Right of Entry would *destroy* the Right of Entry. So, clearly, never buy a *Right of Entry* from anyone!

Another difference between a Right of Entry and a Possibility of Reverter is that while the Possibility of Reverter is automatic, the holder of a Right of Entry has to assert the Right of Entry within a reasonable time, or it will be too late.

The appropriate wording to create a Right of Entry is: "to A, but if alcohol is ever sold on the land I have a right to reenter." These words would create a fee simple subject to condition subsequent in the grantee, and leave a Right of Entry in the grantor.

A few recent cases will make it easier to understand these concepts.

Note: In the following case, decided in 2016, the court found that a possibility of reverter created in a deed in 1940 was still in effect, so the land automatically reverts to the donor.

### SUPREME COURT OF GEORGIA
### ATLANTA DEVELOPMENT AUTHORITY
### V.
### CLARK ATLANTA UNIVERSITY, INC.

MARCH 7, 2016

**Opinion**

HINES, Presiding Justice.

This Court granted defendant Atlanta Development Authority d/ b/a Invest Atlanta (Invest Atlanta) an interlocutory appeal of the superior court's denial of its motion to dismiss plaintiff Clark Atlanta University, Inc.'s (CAU) complaint for declaratory judgment For the reasons that follow, we affirm the judgment of the superior court.

On February 10, 1940, for the nominal consideration of $1.00, CAU executed a deed ("Deed") for the Property, which was composed of three adjoining parcels totaling approximately 13 acres, to Morris Brown College (MBC). At the time the Property was donated, MBC was experiencing financial difficulties and was at risk of losing its campus. The one-page Deed conveyed all three parcels, which will hereinafter be referred to as Parcel 1, Parcel 2, and Parcel 3, and was structured, as follows.

The sole granting clause ("Granting Clause") appears at the top of the Deed and states, in relevant part:

> WITNESSETH: That the said party of the first part, for and in consideration of the sum of One Dollar, and for the purposes herein set forth, in hand paid at and before the sealing and delivery of these presents, the receipt whereof is hereby acknowledged, has granted, bargained, sold and conveyed and by those presents does grant, bargain, sell and convey unto the said party of the second part....
> [Property description for each parcel]
>
> The above property is conveyed subject to the condition that [MBC] shall use the same for educational purposes, to wit: Undergraduate work in the fields of the Arts and Sciences, except that nothing in this clause is to be construed as prohibiting [MBC] from offering a graduate course in Theology, if it chooses to do so.
>
> If at any time the said [MBC] shall cease to use said property for the particular educational purposes above set forth, the title to said property shall revert to and become vested in the Grantor or its successors.
>
> TO HAVE AND TO HOLD the said bargained premises, together with all and singular the rights, members and appurtenances thereof, to the same being, belonging or in any wise appertaining to the only proper use, benefit and behoof of it, the said party of the second part, IN FEE SIMPLE.

In August 2012, MBC filed for Chapter 11 bankruptcy relief in an attempt to prevent the foreclosure and sale at auction of its campus. As a result of the Bankruptcy, in May 2014, MBC requested that the bankruptcy court approve the sale of a large portion of its campus, including the Property at issue here, to Invest Atlanta. In June 2014, the bankruptcy court held a hearing in the matter at which it noted that it was " clear that MBC can only sell whatever interest in the property it has" and that it was "not making any findings regarding the extent of MBC's interest in the reversionary property." The court further stated, "All that is being authorized is that MBC can sell whatever interest it has." On June 23, 2014, the bankruptcy court issued an order authorizing and approving the sale of the Property to Invest Atlanta; the order expressly provided that Invest Atlanta was "accepting the title subject to any alleged and recorded interest held by CAU."

On September 5, 2014, CAU filed the present complaint for declaratory judgment, seeking, inter alia, a declaration and judgment that the 1940 Deed transferred the Property in the form of a fee simple determinable estate or a fee simple estate subject to a limitation, that CAU therefore had a valid automatic reversionary interest in the Property, and that such reversionary interest was triggered when MBC stopped using the Property for educational purposes and sold it to Invest Atlanta; alternatively, CAU asked for a declaration and judgment that with respect to any portions of the Property that were then being used for educational purposes by MBC, if at any time MBC ceased to so use such portions of the Property, title to such property would immediately and automatically revert to CAU.

On February 20, 2015, the superior court determined that the Restriction is valid as falling within the "charitable purposes" exemption to the general rule against restraints on alienation, that the Restriction applies to all three parcels of the Property, that MBC's sale of the Property to Invest Atlanta did not constitute a "use" for educational purposes, and that the 1940 Deed from CAU conveyed a fee simple determinable estate.

The superior court determined that the Restriction applies to all three parcels, and so it does. The Restriction and the Reverter create a limitation upon the estate conveyed by the Deed, that is, that the estate is vested in the grantee, MBC, so long as the Property is used for the specified educational purposes; this limitation on the conveyed estate creates a fee simple determinable estate. The hallmark of a fee simple determinable estate is that it provides for automatic reversion of the estate upon the occurrence of the limitation. That is precisely the situation in this case.

The remaining question is whether MBC's sale of the Property to Invest Atlanta constitutes "use" of the Property for the purpose of the application of the Reverter.

The Restriction and the Reverter are legally enforceable. The express "use" for the donated Property is that of "educational purposes" as specified in the Deed. Certainly, as a general proposition, real property may be "used" for educational purposes in many ways, which might in another context include being sold to raise money for educational purposes. But, the very specific language of the Restriction and the Reverter militate against such a broad construction of use. As noted, the Restriction provides not only that the Property be used for "educational purposes" but then lists the fields of study which qualify as such "educational purposes." What is more, the Reverter is triggered when grantee MBC itself ceases to use the Property "for the particular educational purposes above set forth" in the Deed. Thus, even if MBC's utilization of the proceeds from the sale of the Property could qualify as its "use" of the Property generally for educational purposes, this does not address the particularity of educational purpose set forth in the Deed. Moreover, once the Property is alienated, MBC loses control over it for any purpose, and as to the sale proceeds, their use and eventual exhaustion would be pragmatically impossible to monitor in regard to any question of application of the Restriction and the Reverter. Consequently, in the present circumstances, sale of the Property to Invest Atlanta does not qualify as MBC's "use" of the Property as contemplated in the Deed.

Conclusion

The Deed transferred the property from CAU to MBC in the form of a fee simple determinable estate. Therefore, CAU has a valid reversionary interest in the Property, which was triggered when MBC sold the Property to Invest Atlanta. Accordingly, the judgment of the superior court is properly affirmed.

*Judgment affirmed.*

Note: In the following case, a grandmother, appearing pro se, prevails against a major lending institution, because the grandmother understands the characteristics of a possibility of reverter, and the bank loan officer who made the loan evidently did not understand future interests. Or did not take the time to read the actual provisions of the deed for the land on which the bank lent money. Cheers for Grandma!

GREEN TREE SERVICING, LLC AS SUCCESSOR IN INTEREST
TO CONSECO FINANCE SERVICING CORP. AS INTEREST
TO GREEN TREE FINANCIAL SERVICING CORPORATION,
PLAINTIFF
V.
RENIATA L. WILLIAMS A/K/A RENIATA GARVIN WILLIAMS;
SCOTT L. WILLIAMS, BB&T BANKCARD CORPORATION; THE
SOUTH CAROLINA DEPARTMENT OF MOTOR VEHICLES,
DEFENDANTS,
AND
GREEN TREE SERVICING, LLC AS SUCCESSOR IN INTEREST
TO CONSECO FINANCE SERVICING CORP. AS INTEREST
TO GREEN TREE FINANCIAL SERVICING CORPORATION,
RESPONDENTS,
V.
LUEVEANIA GARVIN, APPELLANT, PRO SE.

FEBRUARY 20, 2008. CERTIORARI DENIED JULY 23, 2009.

HUFF, J.:

Lueveania Garvin appeals the order of the special referee holding her interest in certain property was subject and junior to Green Tree's mortgages and that she was not entitled to damages for trespass. We reverse and remand.

## FACTUAL/PROCEDURAL BACKGROUND

In September of 1995, Garvin deeded .23 acres of property to her granddaughter, Reniata Williams. The deed provided the property was to be used for residential purposes and further provided:

> In the event Reniata L. Garvin Williams shall fail to use said property for residential purposes for a consecutive period of sixty (60) days or more, the aforementioned property shall revert back to Grantor or Grantor's heirs and assigns, in fee simple.

Thus, the interest Garvin transferred to Williams was a fee simple determinable while she retained a possibility of reverter.

Williams subsequently obtained two loans secured by mortgages on the property. Garvin was not a party to these mortgages. Williams had a mobile home placed on the property. The mobile home encroached onto Garvin's property by six feet.

On June 1, 2004, Williams wrote to Garvin that she no longer resided on the property and in recognition of the condition in the deed, she wished to return the property to Garvin.

Green Tree then brought this action for foreclosure of the mortgages in August of 2004. In an order filed December 30, 2004, the special referee ordered foreclosure of the mortgages. Garvin was not named a party to the action at this time. In April of 2005 Garvin wrote to Green Tree stating she would charge it $25.00 a day storage fee effective June 1, 2004 for the mobile home on her property. She explained $10.00 a day was for the part of the mobile home on the far end of her yard previously deeded to Williams and $15.00 a day was for the part of the mobile home that extended into her front yard.

Green Tree subsequently filed a petition for a rule to show cause requesting the court order Garvin to show cause why she should not be bound by the previous order and determine whether Garvin's interest was junior to Green Tree's mortgages. The court issued the rule as requested. Garvin answered asserting that Green Tree executed the mortgages with knowledge of the possibility of reverter. Garvin also asserted a claim for trespass.

After a hearing on the matter, the special referee held Garvin had no estate in the property until the possibility of reverter was triggered, which was after Green Tree had perfected its mortgage. Thus, the referee held Garvin's interest in the property was subject and junior to Green Tree's mortgage that was already in place when she acquired an estate in the property. In addition, the referee held that as Garvin had submitted no evidence of any diminution in the market value of her property due to the mobile home's presence on her property, she was not entitled to damages for trespass. However, the referee did order Green Tree to remove the trailer from Garvin's property. This appeal followed.

**LAW/ANALYSIS**

1. Mortgages

Garvin argues the special referee erred in holding that Garvin's interest in the property was subject to and junior to Green Tree's mortgages. We agree.

A fee simple determinable is a grant that can be cut short when a given term expires. "It is an estate in fee with a qualification annexed to it by which it is provided that it must determine whenever that qualification is at an end." The wording of the grant allows for defeasance of the grantee upon the terms, covenants and conditions of the grant. A possibility of reverter is the future interest that accompanies a fee simple determinable. In the case of a possibility of reverter, the possessory estate vests immediately and automatically upon the happening of the event whereby the determinable or conditional fee is terminated.

Although the grantee of a fee simple determinable may transfer or assign the estate, the determinable quality of the estate follows the transfer or assignment. The determinable fee may be mortgaged, subject to the qualification. The creator of the estate would have to join in the mortgage to subject the entire fee interest to the lien.

The deed granting Williams the fee simple determinable estate was duly recorded and was referred to in the mortgage. Green Tree was on notice of the nature of the estate. *See* S.C.Code Ann. § 30-9-30 (2007) (stating recording of instrument is notice to all persons, sufficient to put them upon inquiry of the purport of the filed instrument and the property affected by the instrument) *Binkley v. Rabon Creek Watershed Conservation Dist.*, (Ct.App.2001) (stating notice of a deed is notice of its whole contents) Garvin never joined in the mortgages and the mortgages were subject to the determinable quality of the estate. When the determinable fee was terminated, Green Tree's interest in the property terminated. Therefore, the special referee erred in holding Garvin's interest in the property was subject to Green Tree's mortgages.

Very important →

2. Trespass

Garvin argues the special referee erred in holding her claim for trespass failed as she had not established a diminution in the market value of the property due to placement of the mobile home on her property. We agree.

If a plaintiff establishes a willful trespass, the damages from invasion of the plaintiff's legal rights will be presumed sufficient to sustain the action even though such damages may be only nominal and not capable of measurement. Thus, Garvin did not need to establish a diminution in value to her property to maintain her claim for trespass. We reverse the order of the special referee and remand the trespass claim for further proceedings.

CONCLUSION

We reverse the special referee's holding that Garvin's interest in the property was subject and junior to Green Tree's mortgages. We further reverse the special referee's ruling on Garvin's trespass claim and remand for further proceedings consistent with this opinion.]

**REVERSED AND REMANDED**

Note: As you read the following case involving a possibility of reverter, are you able to figure out why Reginald was treated so differently? What should have been done to insure that Melba's other children were able to inherit the land from Melba?

### SUPREME COURT OF VIRGINIA
### EDWARD L. HAMM, JR.
### V.
### CHARLES W. HAZELWOOD, JR., ADMINISTRATOR DBN FOR THE ESTATE OF MELBA BIGELOW CLARKE, DECEASED, ET AL.

JUNE 23, 2016

Opinion [Most, but not all of the footnotes in the opinion have been omitted.]

BY JUSTICE D. ARTHUR KELSEY

I.

In 1989, Dorothy Bigelow Hamm executed and recorded a deed of gift transferring her one-half interest in a parcel of property to her sister, Melba Clarke. The deed of gift reserved a life estate for Dorothy for the duration of her life. She died in 2004, thereby extinguishing the life estate. In her will, Dorothy left any interest she had in the property to her son, Edward. Dorothy's sister, Melba, had children, including a son, Reginald Wayne Clarke, at the time of Dorothy's deed of gift in 1989. In the deed of gift, Dorothy included a provision that specifically mentioned Reginald:

> The PROPERTY hereby conveyed shall AUTOMATICALLY REVERT to Dorothy
> Bigelow Hamm, in the event Reginald Wayne Clarke, son of Melba Clarke, ever
> acquires any interest therein by grant, inheritance or otherwise or is otherwise permit-
> ted to occupy, even temporarily, any portion of said property.]

Nothing in the record explains Dorothy's reasons for including this provision in the deed.

Melba died intestate in 2012, eight years after her sister.[3] Melba's heirs included six children, including Reginald, and Melba's three grandchildren. The administrator of Melba's estate, Charles W. Hazelwood, Jr., filed a petition for aid and direction seeking a judicial order declaring that the possibility-of-reverter provision in the deed was void as an impermissible restraint on alienation. Edward, (Dorothy's son), countered that the provision was a lawful possibility of reverter limited in scope and in time to the life of a single person, Reginald. Rejecting Edward's view, the circuit court held that "the possibility of reverter contained in the Deed of Gift is void and unenforceable under Virginia law" and, thus, would be "hereby stricken from the conveyance."

## II.

On appeal, Edward argues that nothing in either Virginia law or any background principle of English common law forbids a landowner from conveying property subject to this type of contingent reversionary interest. We agree.

### A.

The first premise of property law is that a lawful owner, as a general rule, has the power to convey his real property to whomever he wishes under whatever conditions they agree to. "The exclusive right of using and transferring property," Chancellor Kent explained, "follows as a natural consequence, from the perception and admission of the right itself." 2 James Kent, Commentaries on American Law (1827). At common law, a lawful owner's right to property "consists in the free use, enjoyment, and disposal of all his acquisitions, without any control or diminution, save only by the laws of the land." 1 William Blackstone, Commentaries.

When a deed of conveyance uses no "words of limitation," Virginia law treats it as a transfer of a fee simple interest "unless a contrary intention shall appear." Such "contrary intention," could include an express reservation of a contingent reversionary interest. The grantor's right to impose such a condition, however, is not absolute.

---

3    Shortly after Melba's death, Reginald admitted a will to probate. Two of his siblings filed suit to challenge the will proffered by Reginald, claiming it was not in fact their mother's last will and testament. In a consent order, the circuit court vacated its earlier order admitting the will to probate. Deeming the proffered will to have "no force and effect whatsoever," the court vacated an order appointing another son of Melba, Victor Dale Clarke, as administrator and appointed Charles Hazelwood, an "independent third-party," to serve as an administrator d.b.n. of Melba's estate.

Centuries of common-law jurisprudence have marked off the legal boundaries of this presumptive right.

Perhaps the best-known boundary is the historic maxim against unreasonable restraints on alienation. In the late 1400s, Judge Littleton declared void as "against reason" conveyance conditions that denied a grantee the power to "alien" the property conveyed "to any person." Lord Coke confirmed this view, stating that under English common law such conditions are "repugnant and against law."

[This prohibition, however, did not apply to a condition against alienating to a particular person, "naming his name, or to any of his heirs, or of the issue" of such person, because such a condition "does not take away *all* power of alienation from the feoffee."] "Similar statements may be found in Year Book cases dating from the 15th century." Restatement (Second) of Property: Donative Transfers.

[Most modern courts continue to hold to the ancient view that "a condition in restraint of alienation general as to time and person is void."] 3 Thompson on Real Property. We, too, follow this common-law principle and have applied it in various contexts.

We are unaware of precedent, however, holding that all lesser forms of restraint—no matter their scope or duration—are per se repugnant. To the contrary, [courts generally uphold conditions that affect later alienation rights if, under all the circumstances of the case, the restraint is found to be reasonable.]

[Among the circumstances determining reasonableness is whether the restraint on alienation is limited in duration and limited as to the number of persons to whom transfer is prohibited.]

B.

The administrator of Melba's estate contends the contested provision in Dorothy's deed of gift should be analogized to a will provision we rejected in <u>Dunlop v. Dunlop's Ex'rs</u>, (1926). In that case, after giving the son a fee simple absolute in the land, another provision of the will stated that if the son sold the father's business as an entirety the son would forfeit three-fourths of his inheritance. The forfeiture provision thus punished the son if he sold the inherited property to anyone at any time.

For several reasons, we find the analogy to <u>Dunlop</u> unpersuasive.

1. The conveyance clause said only that Melba received the property "as and for her sole and separate equitable estate." The subsequent habendum clause clarified this phrase, stating that Melba was "TO HAVE AND TO HOLD" the property "for her sole and separate equitable estate, free from the control and marital rights of her

present or any future husband and free from any curtesy rights or inchoate curtesy rights of the present husband or any future husband."

These provisions make clear that the conveyance was to be free of any claim of right, including dower rights, from Melba's husband—which were standard provisions in some deeds prior to the statutory abolishment of dower and curtesy interests in 1991.

In Virginia, all rules of construction have but one object, and that is to ascertain the intent of the parties to the instrument to be construed, and that intent when ascertained, if it controverts no rule of law or of public policy, becomes the law of the case, and full effect must be given to it. From this perspective, all clauses of Dorothy's deed of gift point to a single conclusion: She intended to convey a fee simple defeasible upon a condition subsequent not a fee simple absolute.[7]

2. In our opinion, the contested provision in Dorothy's deed of gift was reasonably limited in duration and scope. It was directed at a single individual, Reginald, for the limited period of his life.[8]

3. Finally, the contested provision in Dorothy's deed of gift is best understood not as an overreaching restraint on alienation but rather as a mere possibility of reverter.[9]

At common law, reversionary interests were classified as either a reversion or a possibility of reverter. A true reversion is a vested estate *in praesenti*, with enjoyment *in futuro*. In this respect, a reversion is the remnant of an estate *continuing in the grantor*, undisposed of, after the grant of a part of his interest." Reversions, therefore, are "always *vested* estates," not contingent or conditional future interests.

In contrast, a possibility of reverter is a future interest that is always contingent and corresponds to a contingent limitation. In this respect, a possibility of reverter at common law is not an estate, present or future, but a possibility of having an estate. Even so, while a possibility of reverter is not a vested interest in real property, it is a

---

7   "The modern estate in fee simple can be either an estate in fee simple absolute or an estate in fee simple defeasible. When it is defeasible, it can end by virtue of a special limitation, a condition subsequent, or an executory limitation." 1 Powell, supra, § 13.02, at 13–9 (footnotes omitted) (citing 1 Restatement (First) of Property §§ 14–16 (1936)); see, e.g., Hermitage Methodist Homes of Va., Inc. v. Dominion Tr. Co., 239 Va. 46, 55–56, 387 S.E.2d 740, 745 (1990).

8   The rule against perpetuities is not at issue in this case because possibilities of reverter are excluded from the rule against perpetuities as "[a] property interest ... that was not subject to the common-law rule against perpetuities." Code § 55–12.4(A)(7); see Scott Cty. Sch. Bd. v.Dowell, 190 Va. 676, 688, 58 S.E.2d 38, 43–44 (1950) ("At common law the possibility of reverter was not an estate subject to grant" and, as such, "was not void as violative of the rule against perpetuities.").

9   See generally 3 Thompson, supra, § 24.02, at 455–57 ("The interest that remains in a grantor, testator or settlor of a trust after creating a fee simple determinable is called a possibility of reverter. ... The 'possibility of reverter' is created by the conveyance of a limited fee."); 1 Restatement (First) of Property § 154 cmt. g ("When the owner of an estate in fee simple absolute transfers an estate in fee simple determinable, the transferor has a possibility of reverter.").

property interest. Consequently, it is a right inheritable at common law and by statute may be transmitted also by deed or will.]

In Dorothy's deed of gift,[the disputed provision stated that the fee conveyed shall AUTOMATICALLY REVERT to the grantor if Reginald, ever acquired *any* interest in the property. This language created a possibility of reverter in Dorothy and her heirs upon the happening of the condition subsequent. It is true that the provision had the practical effect of precluding Melba or her successors in interest from ever selling or devising the property to Reginald, for the very act of doing so would trigger the possibility of reverter.]

[That said, in this case, Dorothy very clearly expressed her intention that the conveyance would revert if Reginald ever acquired any interest in the property. We know of no rule of law or equity that forbade Dorothy from making her conveyance subject to that condition or which authorizes us to declare it void.]For this reason, the circuit court erred in declaring the possibility-of-reverter provision to be void.

III.

We reverse the circuit court's holding that the possibility-of-reverter provision in the 1989 deed of gift was void.

Reversed and remanded.

Note: Frequently Possibilities of Reverter are used to protect continued use for educational or religious purposes. In the following case, golf is the protected activity.

**SUPREME COURT, APPELLATE DIVISION, NEW YORK**
**NJCB SPEC-1, LLC, APPELLANT,**
**V**
**THEODORA BUDNIK ET AL., RESPONDENTS, ET AL.,**
**DEFENDANTS.**

MAY 9, 2018

DECISION AND ORDER

[The plaintiff acquired title to premises being used as a golf club by deed in lieu of foreclosure in 2013. The premises comprises four plots of land subject to use restrictions, two of which are at issue on this appeal. Two deeds, dated August 19, 1941, and January 14, 1953, transferred their respective lots "for so long as" each was used "for golf club purposes, and for no other purposes." Should either lot "ever cease to be used for golf club purposes, then the estate granted shall thereupon become void, and title to said lands shall revert back to the grantors or the grantors' successors in interest, who thereupon may enter said lands as if this conveyance had never been made."

The defendants Theodora Budnik and Elizabeth Shafer are heirs to the grantors of the 1941 deed. On November 2, 1964, the grantor of the 1953 deed conveyed her future interest to Edward and Elizabeth Kearney (the Kearneys), and their successors in interest are defendants here.

In September 2013, the plaintiff commenced this action against the defendants for a judgment declaring that the use restrictions on the four plots of land are void and unenforceable. The plaintiff argued that the 1941 deed did not allow for the transfer of its future interest through inheritance, and that the future interest created by the 1953 deed terminated when the grantor transferred it in 1964 to the Kearneys. The trial court entered judgment for the defendants. The plaintiff appeals.

Contrary to the plaintiff's contention, the 1941 deed and the 1953 deed created possibilities of reverter. Every instrument creating or transferring an estate or interest in real property must be construed according to the intent of the parties, so far as such intent can be gathered from the whole instrument, and is consistent with the rules of law. No precise language is necessary to create a possibility of reverter, but a characteristic of the type of expression which works automatic expiration of the grantee's fee seems to be one in which time is an important factor, such as use of the words "until," "so long as," or "during." Here, the 1941 deed and the 1953 deed unequivocally called for automatic forfeiture of the estate upon breach and thereby created for their respective grantors possibilities of reverter.

The plaintiff's contention that the conveyance in 1964 of the future interest of the grantor of the 1953 deed invalidated the Kearney defendants' possibility of reverter is without merit. Although no statute in effect in 1964 explicitly provided the grantor of the 1953 deed with a right to convey her possibility of reverter, under the applicable rules of the common law, a possibility of reverter could be freely assigned and alienated. The cases cited by the plaintiff are inapposite, as they concern the right of reentry, which is a future estate left in the creator or in his or her successors in interest upon the simultaneous creation of an estate on a condition subsequent. Unlike a possibility of reverter, a right of reentry was rendered void at common law if an attempt was made to assign it. But that rule did not apply to possibilities of reverter. The 1964 conveyance to the Kearneys therefore did not invalidate the possibility of reverter now held by the Kearney defendants. Accordingly, the Supreme

Court properly declared that the Kearney defendants' possibility of reverter is valid and enforceable.

So ordered.

Note: Remember that a legislature always has the power, by statute, to change the rules that apply to various kinds of future interests, as illustrated in the following case.

## MASSACHUSETTS LAND COURT, DEPARTMENT OF THE TRIAL COURT
## TOWN OF WINCHENDON, BY AND THROUGH ITS BOARD OF SELECTMEN, PLAINTIFF,
## V.
## BRANDYWINE FARMS INC., DEFENDANT

MAY 18, 2018

MEMORANDUM AND ORDER: By the Court (Foster, J.)

Land may last forever, but many interests in land do not. Restrictions, for example, are often limited to a duration of 30 years. Leases by definition grant rights of possession for a fixed or monthly term. And the rule against perpetuities, the bane of law students and currently codified in G.L. c. 184A, places time limits on the vesting of certain reversionary interests. This case concerns the application of G.L. c. 184A, § 7, to such an interest.

In 1958, White Brothers, Inc. (White Brothers) conveyed certain flowage rights of Lake Monomonoc (the Lake), which straddles the Massachusetts–New Hampshire border, and usage rights of the Lake's appurtenant facilities to Monomonoc Lake Shores, Inc. (Monomonoc). These rights were subject to a reversionary interest in favor of White Brothers, its successors, and assigns. If Monomonoc, its successors, or assigns failed to maintain the dams or impound the waters of the Lake as agreed in the 1958 conveyance, White Brothers, its successors, or assigns could, at their option, record written declarations to effectuate their reversionary interest.

In 1972 Monomonoc conveyed its rights to the Town of Winchendon (Town). In 2016, Brandywine Farms, Inc. (Brandywine), the successor in interest to White Brothers, recorded a document entitled "Instrument of Reversal of Quitclaim Deed" which purported to effectuate its reversionary interest in the rights conveyed to Monomonoc in 1958. The Town seeks to quiet its title to the flowage and usage rights it obtained by the Deed from Monomonoc in 1972.

For the purposes of this motion the Town concedes that it has not maintained the dams and impounded the waters of the Lake but argues that under G.L. c. 184A, § 7, White Brothers or its successors had 30 years—until 1988—to make the necessary recording to effectuate its reversionary interest, after which time the Town's interest became a fee simple absolute. Brandywine argues that the failure of the town to maintain the dams and impound the waters of the Lake gave rise to a right of entry or an appurtenant option, either of which survives beyond the 30–year limitation of G.L. c. 184A, § 7.

As set forth below, the motion for judgment on the pleadings is allowed because White Brothers and its successors, under G.L. c. 184A, § 7, had 30 years from the creation of the reversionary interest in 1958 to effectuate such interest by recording the necessary declaration, and no such declaration was recorded prior to the lapse of the 30 period in 1988.

The Town filed its Complaint in this action on June 14, 2017.

The following facts are undisputed:

1. White Brothers conveyed certain flowage rights of the Lake and usage rights of the Lake's appurtenant facilities to Monomonoc by a deed dated October 2, 1958, and recorded in the Worcester South District Registry of Deeds.

2. The 1958 Deed included an agreement that Monomonoc and its successors impound the water of the Lake to certain heights and maintain certain dams.

3. The 1958 Deed contained a reversionary interest in favor of White Brothers, its successors and assigns, as follows:

(p) In the event that the Grantee, its successors or assigns, fails to keep and maintain the Main Dam and the Stump Pond Dam or fails to impound the waters of Lake Monomonoc as agreed, then in that event the Grantor, its successors and assigns, shall have the right, at its option, to keep and maintain said dams and impound said waters. If the Grantor, its successors and assigns, exercises said option, by recording a written declaration of the same in the proper registries in Worcester County, Massachusetts and in Cheshire County, New Hampshire, then said dams, contiguous areas thereto, and the rights in connection therewith, including all flowage rights, shall revert to the Grantor, its successors and assigns, without further action

on the part of the Grantor or its successors and assigns to effectuate this reversionary interest.]

4. The Town is Monomonoc's successor in interest, having acquired Monomonoc's
flowage and usage rights by a deed dated August 24, 1972, and recorded.

5. Brandywine is White Brothers' successor in interest by a deed from Mill–Winn, Inc.
dated January 29, 2014, and recorded.

6. Brandywine purported to effectuate the reversionary interest created in the 1958
Deed by recording a document entitled "Instrument of Reversal of Quitclaim Deed,"
dated October 11, 2016 in the Worcester , Massachusetts registry, and in the Registry of
Deeds for Cheshire County, New Hampshire.

## Discussion

A property owner has the right to impose limitations or conditions on an estate that
is conveyed to another, such that the conveyance is not one of fee simple absolute. A
property owner who imposes such limitations or conditions has conveyed a defeasible estate, one that may last forever, but may also terminate, either automatically
or by some affirmative step of the conveyor, on the occurrence of a stated event. A
defeasible estate may be a fee simple determinable or a fee simple subject to a condition subsequent, also known as a fee simple subject to a right of entry for condition
broken. [A fee simple determinable is created by a conveyance which contains words
effective to create a fee simple and in addition a provision for automatic expiration
of the estate on the occurrence of a stated event] [A fee simple subject to a condition
subsequent differs from a fee simple determinable in that a fee simple subject to a
condition subsequent is made defeasible upon the occurrence of the condition, followed by an entry which is necessary to terminate the fee] [The mere recital of the
purpose for which land conveyed was to be used is not in itself sufficient to impose
any limitation or restriction on the estate granted.]
   [The conveyance of a fee simple determinable estate is usually created by "words
of limitation, such as 'during,' 'as long as,' 'until,' and the like. Such technical words
are not, however, essential for such creation.]
   The 1958 Deed conveyed a defeasible fee which expressly provided for reversion
of the fee to the grantor if (1) the grantee failed to comply with the Conditions and
(2) the grantor recorded a declaration effectuating the reversionary interest at the

Worcester and Cheshire registries. The defeasible fee created by the 1958 Deed has characteristics which could be attributable to either a fee simple determinable or a fee simple subject to a condition subsequent. On one hand, the language used to describe the reversionary interest provides for the *automatic* reversion of the fee interest upon the recording of the contemplated declaration by the grantor, its successors, or assigns. The language of the 1958 Deed could be understood as conveying a fee simple determinable interest with two contingencies necessary to trigger the automatic expiration of the estate. On the other hand, the conveyance could be interpreted as a fee simple subject to a condition subsequent with only one contingency and a modified form of entry. The recording requirement could be read as a modification of the entry provision that is characteristic of a fee simple subject to a condition subsequent. Entry has traditionally been defined in real property law as the act of going peaceably upon a piece of land which is claimed as one's own, but is held by another person, with the intention and purpose of taking possession of it. However, notwithstanding the requirements of the early common law with respect to the necessity of entry to put an end to an estate upon breach of a condition subsequent the prevailing modern view as reflected both in decisions and statutes is to dispense with the ceremony of entry, and the grantor may terminate the estate by any appropriate manifestation of his intent.

Both types of defeasible fee are subject to the statutory rule against perpetuities found in <u>G.L. c. 184A, § 7</u>, which provides in part:

> A fee simple determinable in land or a fee simple in land subject to a right of entry for condition broken shall become a fee simple absolute if the specified contingency does not occur within thirty years from the date when such fee simple determinable or such fee simple subject to a right of entry becomes possessory. If such contingency occurs within said thirty years the succeeding interest, which may be an interest in a person other than the person creating the interest or his heirs, shall become possessory or the right of entry exercisable notwithstanding the rule against perpetuities.

*limiting →*

Prior to the enactment of Chapter 184A in 1954, the unexercised right to re-entry for condition broken could pass from the original grantors by descent or devise. But it could not pass from the original grantors to a third person by conveyance intervivos. An attempt to pass it, either before or after breach, would merely discharge the condition, and make unconditional the title of the original grantee. Chapter 184A had the effect of validating executory interests of the type described, which would otherwise be held void under the rule against perpetuities, but limited them to thirty years duration; while as to rights of entry and possibilities of reverter, traditionally exempt from the application of the rule, the new statute had the effect of limiting their possible duration, in effect leaving them indistinguishable in operation from executory interests created by analogous language. Whether the interest retained by White Brothers was a possibility of reverter or a right of entry, such right was transferrable to its successors and assigns under Chapter 184A.

Under Chapter 184A, the reversionary rights retained by White Brothers in the 1958 Deed were limited to a duration of 30 years. Construing the 1958 Deed as conveying a fee simple determinable would mean that the possibility of reverter expired, 30 years after 1958, on October 2, 1988, because even if the Town had at that time failed to comply with the Conditions, no declaration had been recorded by White Brothers or their successors by that date. Alternatively, construing the 1958 Deed as conveying a fee simple subject to a condition subsequent would mean that upon failure of the Town to comply with the Conditions, White Brothers or their successors possessed a right of entry that was exercisable until October 2, 1988. Accepting that Brandywine intended the recording of the declaration in the Worcester and Cheshire registries to be a substitute for physical entry as a means of effectuating the reversionary interest, that right of entry expired in 1988, as no such declaration had been recorded at that time. Under either theory of fee ownership, Brandywine's reversionary interest terminated in 1988 and the Town's interest in the rights conveyed in the 1958 Deed became a fee simple absolute.

Brandywine argues that the language of Chapter 184A only requires the contingency giving rise to the right of entry to occur within 30 years, and that a right of entry survives beyond that window if the contingency occurs before the running of 30 years. The suggestion that the right of entry survives beyond the statutory period defeats the purpose of Chapter 184A. The Legislature enacted Chapter 184A in order to limit the duration of possibilities of reverter or rights of entry created after January 1, 1955, with certain exceptions, to a maximum of thirty years. The intent of Chapter 184A was to clear titles, frequently in churches, where a fee is encumbered by a right of entry for condition broken or possibility of reverter. The period of 30 years is chosen because that is the duration permitted by the Massachusetts statute as to restrictions on land where the period is not otherwise specified. Chapter 184A, which seeks to clear titles, cannot be interpreted to leave open a window which would allow a right of entry that has become exercisable within 30 years to remain exercisable forever. That is precisely the kind of cloud on title that Chapter 184A was intended to forestall.

Even if, as Brandywine argues, a right of entry could exist beyond the 30-year period prescribed by Chapter 184A, that right of entry must be exercised within 20 years from the date it accrues pursuant to G.L. c. 260, (Chapter 260), which provides:

An action for the recovery of land shall be commenced, or an entry made thereon, only within twenty years after the right of action or of entry first accrued, or within twenty years after the demandant or the person making the entry, or those under whom they claim, have been seized or possessed of the premises; provided, however, that this section shall not bar an action by or on behalf of a nonprofit land conservation corporation or trust for the recovery of land or interests in land held for conservation, parks, recreation, water protection or wildlife protection purposes.

Under Brandywine's theory, its right of entry had accrued by October 2, 1988, at the latest. This means that White Brothers or its successors had until October 2, 2008, to make such entry before it became barred by Chapter 260. Thus, even accepting that (1) the Town failed to comply with the Condition of the 1958 Deed prior to October 2, 1988; (2) the 1958 Deed conveyed a fee simple subject to a condition subsequent rather than a fee simple determinable; (3) the right of entry may be exercised by recording the declaration described in the 1958 Deed alone; and (4) a right of entry subject to Chapter 184A is exercisable beyond 30 years as long as the contingency it is dependent on occurs within that time; Brandywine cannot overcome the fact that it did not record the declaration to effectuate its reversionary interest until October 11, 2016, more than eight years after its right of entry would have expired pursuant to Chapter 260.

As the Town argues, its possession and maintenance of the subject dams was uninterrupted and uncontested from 1972 to 2016—approximately 44 years. Even assuming that on October 2, 1988, the Town's interest reverted to Brandywine's predecessor, the successive 28 years of uninterrupted possession and maintenance before the recording of the declaration exceeds the time requirements of the prescriptive period for adverse possession, as set forth in Chapter 260, title by adverse possession can be acquired only by proof of nonpermissive use which is actual, open, notorious, exclusive and adverse for twenty years. Even under Brandywine's interpretation of the rights conveyed by the 1958 Deed, the Town is able to clear its title to those rights by its having shown a 20 continuous years of open, notorious, adverse, and exclusive use running from 1988 to 2008.

The Town has established that it holds title to the interests conveyed in the 1958 Deed in fee simple absolute. In each of the interpretations of the 1958 Deed and the applicable statutes discussed above, the reversionary interest claimed by Brandywine has expired, likely in 1988, but by 2008 at the latest. Brandywine, having taken no action to effectuate the reversionary interest prior to 2008 was barred from doing so thereafter by the statutory rule against perpetuities in Chapter 184A and the statute of limitations in Chapter 260. As such, the declaration recorded in 2016 by Brandywine had no effect on the Town's title.

## Conclusion

For the foregoing reasons, the Plaintiff's Motion for Judgment on the Pleadings is **ALLOWED**. Judgment shall enter declaring that the document entitled "Instrument of Reversal of Quitclaim Deed," dated October 11, 2016, is invalid, and the Town holds title to the rights conveyed in the 1958 Deed in fee simple absolute.

**SO ORDERED.**

Note: What if New Hampshire does not have the same limits on Possibilities of Reverter that are imposed by the Massachusetts statutes? Is it possible that the Possibility of Reverter would still be considered to be valid in New Hampshire, for the part of the lake that is located in New Hampshire?

## C. Executory Interests

If a grantor creates a fee simple determinable, providing for possible automatic termination of the estate of the grantee, but provides that on termination of the fee simple determinable the ownership of the land shall go directly to a third party, not to the grantor, then the grantor will have created a fee simple determinable followed by an *executory interest*. A Possibility of Reverter must always be an interest retained by the grantor. An *executory interest* may be created in a third party.

Example: Grantor provides: "I grant this land to ABC College, to be used for educational purposes, and when the land is no longer used for educational purposes, ownership of the land shall automatically go to the town of Springfield."

When the deed goes into effect ABC will have a fee simple determinable, and Springfield will have a shifting executory interest. Both interests are valid, because all educational institutions, (public or private), and all governments are considered to be charities, for purposes of the Rule Against Perpetuities. And RAP does not apply to a solid line of charities.

Wait! How did RAP get back into this? That is because all *executory interests* are subject to the RAP, even though Possibilities of Reverter and Rights of Entry are *not* subject to RAP. Why is that the rule? The answer is "history." But don't worry about it. For now, it is sufficient just to learn the rules of the chess game, (future interests), so that you can become skilled in this field.

Because it is uncertain when, if ever, a fee simple determinable may end, the Rule Against Perpetuities requires that it must be certain, when the executory interest is created, that the executory interest will become *possessory, if it ever does,* within the time allowed by RAP. The following case illustrates that point.

## COURT OF APPEALS OF OREGON
## THE CITY OF KLAMATH FALLS, OREGON, A MUNICIPAL CORPORATION, RESPONDENT,
### V.
## CONSTANCE F. BELL, A WIDOW, ET AL., DEFENDANTS, MARIJANE FLITCRAFT AND GEORGE C. FLITCRAFT, HER HUSBAND, APPELLANTS.

NOVEMBER 5, 1971

**Opinion [Some, but not all of the footnotes in the opinion have been omitted.]**

SCHWAB, Chief Judge.

In 1925, a corporation conveyed certain land to the city of Klamath Falls as a gift for use as the site for a city library. The deed provided, among other things, that the city should hold the land 'so long as' it complied with that condition with regard to its use.

In 1969, the city terminated the use of the land for a library, and the question presented by this appeal is, "Does the title to the land remain in the city or did the termination of use as a library cause title to pass to the descendants of the shareholders of the donor-corporation (now dissolved)?"

The issue was presented to the trial court in the form of an agreed narrative statement, pertinent portions of which, in addition to the facts set forth above, are: the donor-corporation was known as the Daggett-Schallock Investment Company; the corporate deed provided that if at any time the city ceased to use the land for library purposes, title to the land should pass to Fred Schallock and Floy R. Daggett, their heirs and assigns; on September 19, 1927, the corporation was voluntarily dissolved, all creditors paid, and all assets (which we interpret as including the rights of the corporation, if any, in the land in question) were distributed in accordance with law to the sole shareholders Schallock and Daggett.

The city of Klamath Falls built a library on the land in 1929 in compliance with the conditions set out in the deed. The library continued in use from that date until July 1, 1969, when the books were moved to the County Library Building. Since that time, the city library services have been provided by Klamath County on a contract basis. The City Library building has not been used for any other purpose and now stands vacant.

After the library closure, the city of Klamath Falls filed a complaint against all the heirs of Schallock and Daggett for declaratory judgment pursuant to ORS ch. 28, asking the court to adjudicate the respective rights of the parties under the deed. The city joined Constance F. Bell, the sole heir of Fred Schallock, and Marijane Flitcraft and Caroline Crapo, the sole heirs of Floy R. Daggett, along with George C. Flitcraft, the husband of Marijane Flitcraft, and Paul Crapo, the husband of Caroline Crapo, as all the necessary parties to the suit.

The defendants Constance F. Bell, Caroline Crapo, and Paul Crapo conveyed their interests in the real property to the defendant Marijane Flitcraft in May and June 1970.

The trial court found that title to the real property was vested in the city of Klamath Falls. Its decision was based on a finding that the gift over to Fred Schallock and Floy R. Daggett was void under the rule against perpetuities.

The deed, in pertinent part, is as follows:

> "KNOW ALL MEN BY THESE PRESENTS That Daggett-Schallock Investment
> Company a corporation organized and existing under the laws of the State of Oregon,
> for and as a gift and without any consideration, does hereby give, grant and convey
> unto the City of Klamath Falls, Oregon, so long as it complies with the conditions here-
> inafter set forth, and thereafter unto Fred Schallock and Floy R. Daggett, their heirs
> and assigns, the following described parcel of real estate, in Klamath County Oregon,
> to-wit * * * To have and to hold the same unto the said City of Klamath Falls, Oregon
> (and to any other municipal corporation which may lawfully succeed it) so long as it
> complies with the conditions above set forth, and thereafter unto Fred Schallock and
> Floy R. Daggett, their heirs and assigns forever."

I

We conclude that the estate that passed to the city under this deed was a fee simple on a special limitation, which is also known as a fee simple determinable, or a base or qualified fee.

The 'magic' words 'so long as' have generally been held to create such an estate. Simes and Smith, The Law of Future Interests 345, s 287 (2d ed. 1956), states:

> "The words of duration 'so long as' will almost certainly be judicially recognized as the distinctive insignia of such an estate, and, if coupled with a provision which clearly calls for an automatic termination of the estate granted, there is little room for construction."

O'Connell, Estates on Condition Subsequent and Estates on Special Limitation in Oregon, 18 Or.L.Rev. 63, 73 (1939), stresses the use of words:

> "The creation of an estate on a special limitation is characterized generally by the use of certain words. Typical words are 'so long as,' 'until,' or 'during.' However, any language in the instrument indicating an intent that the estate shall automatically end upon the occurrence of a designated event will be sufficient."

One of the features of the fee simple on a special limitation thus created is that it terminates automatically upon breach of condition.[2]

## II

Upon breach of the condition, the deed provided for a gift over to Fred Schallock and Floy R. Daggett or their heirs and assigns. This gift over was an attempt to grant an executory interest since only an executory interest can follow an earlier grant in fee simple. The rule against perpetuities applies to executory interests.
Gray's classic statement of the rule is as follows:

> "NO INTEREST IS GOOD UNLESS IT MUST VEST, IF AT ALL, NOT LATER THAN TWENTY-ONE YEARS AFTER SOME LIFE IN BEING AT THE CREATION OF THE INTEREST." Gray, The Rule Against Perpetuities 191, s 201 (4th ed. 1942).

One of the main characteristics of a defeasible fee simple estate is that the first grantee might continue in possession in perpetuity. The city of Klamath Falls could have maintained a library on the site for an indefinite time in the future, or even forever. Therefore, the trial judge correctly found that the gift over to Fred Schallock

---

2    There would be a different result if the interests of the city of Klamath Falls were characterized as a fee simple on a condition subsequent, which is also known as a fee simple conditional. When such an estate is created, there is no forfeiture until the grantor exercises his right of re-entry.

and Floy R. Daggett, their heirs and assigns, was void Ab initio under the rule against perpetuities.

## III

The trial court's conclusion does not, however, dispose of the case at bar. Just because the gift over is invalid, it does not follow that the city of Klamath Falls now has an absolute interest in the property in question. There remains the question of whether under the deed a possibility of reverter remained in the grantor corporation.

When a deed reveals an unquestionable intent to limit the interest of the first grantee (here the city of Klamath Falls) to a fee simple on a special limitation, the courts of the United States do not create an indefeasible estate in the first grantee when a subsequent executory interest (here that of Schallock and Daggett) is void under the rule against perpetuities. Instead, the grantor (here the corporation) retains an interest known as a possibility of reverter.[3]

The general rule has been stated to be:

> "When an executory interest, following a fee simple interest in land is void under
> the rule against perpetuities, the prior interest becomes absolute unless the language
> of the creating instrument makes it very clear that the prior interest is to terminate
> whether the executory interest takes effect or not." Simes and Smith, The Law of Future
> Interests (2d ed. 1956).

All the jurisdictions in the United States which have dealt with a determinable fee and an executory interest void under the rule against perpetuities have followed this rule.

---

3    It is well settled that the rule against perpetuities does not apply to possibilities of reverter. Gray, The Rule Against Perpetuities 46, 348, 349, ss 41, 313, 314 (4th ed. 1942); Simes and Smith, The Law of Future Interests 311, s 825 (2d ed. 1956); Tiffany, Real Property 167, s 404 (3d ed. 1939). This historical anomaly has been criticized for allowing 'dead hand rule' and creating 'appalling practical results' when a possibility of reverter does fall in many years after the original grant. Leach, Perpetuities in Perspective: Ending the Rule's Reign of Terror, 65 Harv.L.Rev. 721, 739 (1952); Leach, Perpetuities: The Nutshell Revisited, 78 Harv.L.Rev. 973, 980 (1965). However, as pointed out in 18 Or.L.Rev. supra, at 79: "(A) rule restricting the alienation of such interests will tend to avoid a long-outstanding 'contingent' interest and thereby effectuate the policy behind the rule against perpetuities, it would be far more desirable to expressly make rights of entry and possibilities of reverter subject to the rule against perpetuities rather than accomplish the same result by indirection." Where the rule against perpetuities has been applied to possibilities of reverter, it has always been done by legislative action.

## IV

However, before this conclusion can be reached, an unusual Oregon rule must be considered. Oregon is one of a small minority of states that holds that a possibility of reverter cannot be alienated, but the Oregon Supreme Court has never held that an attempt to alienate a possibility of reverter destroys it. In the case at bar, the grantor-corporation did attempt to alienate the possibility of reverter with its abortive gift over to Schallock and Daggett. Thus, the question of whether an attempt to alienate a possibility of reverter destroys it is presented to an Oregon appellate court for the first time.

The Oregon Supreme Court has dealt with the consequences that follow a grantor's attempt to transfer the interest that remains in him when he grants a defeasible fee. *Wagner v. Wallowa County* involved a fee simple estate on a condition subsequent. The grantors gave land to the county for a high school. The county had taken possession of the land and had built and operated a high school on the property until the electorate voted to abolish the school. The election was held November 5, 1912. Prior to the election, during October 1912, the plaintiff and his wife had executed a deed to a (different)Wallowa County school district. The court there applied a strict rule of construction and found that the grantors destroyed their right to re-enter when they attempted to convey it before the breach of the condition.

Nothing in *Wagner* is conclusive in determining whether an attempt to alienate a possibility of reverter destroys it, so we turn to cases from other jurisdictions.

In *Pure Oil Co. v. Miller-McFarland Drilling Co.*, (1941), the Illinois court held that a possibility of reverter is not destroyed when the grantor tries to transfer it, even though the possibility of reverter is not alienable under Illinois law. In *Reichard v. Chicago, B. & Q. R. Co.*, (1942), in a case which involved a conveyance after termination of a fee simple subject to a special limitation, the Iowa court said: "It seems rather fantastic to us, that a conveyance which is ineffective to convey what it attempts to convey is nevertheless an effective means of destroying it."

We hold that an attmept by a grantor to transfer his possibility of reverter does not destroy it.

## V

The remaining issue is the city's contention that upon dissolution of the corporation in 1927, or at the latest, upon the post-dissolution, winding-up period, the corporation was civilly dead and without a successor to whom the possibility of reverter could descend. As is pointed out by a Delaware court in *Addy and Errett v. Short et al.*,(1952), the statutory provision for distribution of corporate assets upon dissolution,

> "is in effect a statutory expansion of the equitable doctrine that upon dissolution of a corporation its property, notwithstanding the technical rules of the early common law, does not escheat to the sovereign or revert to the original grantor, and will be administered for the purpose of winding up the corporate affairs and distributing the assets to those equitably entitled to them."

In *Addy*, the corporation owning a possibility of reverter was dissolved and five years later the event (the abandonment of the use upon which the deed was conditioned) occurred. Delaware had only a three-year corporate dissolution winding-up period. The Delaware statutes did contain a provision that even after the three-year period, upon application of creditors or shareholders of a dissolved corporation, the court could appoint a receiver to take charge of the estate of the corporation and to collect debts and property due and belonging to the company. *Addy* held that neither the dissolution of the corporation nor the expiration of the three-year dissolution period worked an extinguishment of the possibility of reverter retained by the deed in question, and that upon the abandonment of the land by the grantee, the possibility of reverter was enlarged to a fee simple title. It further held that as statutory successors to the rights and powers of the corporation the receivers were entitled to the land.

Oregon has no such receivership statute, but the Oregon statutes make it clear that corporate assets no longer escheat or revert to the original grantor upon dissolution. In this case, the parties agree that the corporation was lawfully dissolved, all the creditors paid, and that Daggett and Schallock, the sole shareholders of the corporation, were statutorily entitled to and did receive all of the remaining assets of the corporation. One such asset was the possibility of reverter of the land in question.

The parties further agree that the defendants in this case were all of the heirs of Daggett and Schallock. As is pointed out in 18 Or.L.Rev. 63, there is no Oregon decision on the issue of the descendability of the possibility of reverter. However, the weight of authority recognizes that such an interest is descendable. We discern no sound policy considerations which lead us to a contrary conclusion.

Marijane Flitcraft acquired all rights to the property when the other defendants conveyed their interests to her in 1970.

Reversed.

## D. SUMMARY OF FUTURE INTERESTS

Here is a brief description of the five kinds of future interests – with examples.
There are five kinds of future interests:

Reversions
Possibilities of Reverter
Rights of Entry
Remainders: Four kinds - contingent, vested, vested subject to open, and vested subject
to divestment
Executory Interests: Two kinds – shifting and springing

The first three interests – Reversions, Possibilities of Reverter, and Rights of Entry,
can <u>only be created in the Grantor</u>, (and are NOT subject to the Rule Against
Perpetuities). The last two interests – Remainders and Executory Interests – can
<u>only be created in someone OTHER than the Grantor</u>, (and ARE subject to the Rule
Against Perpetuities).

**1. REVERSION:** A reversion is just what is left in the grantor after he has given
away less than he had – (as long as the interest left in the grantor doesn't meet the
special requirements of a Possibility of Reverter or Right of Entry).

EXAMPLE: Grantor gives land "to A for life."

Under this example A will have a life estate, and the grantor will have a reversion.
When A dies, the grantor will have full ownership of the land again. While A is still
alive, the grantor could sell his reversion to B. Then, when A died, B would own the
land. A reversion is an interest which is created – (or remains) – in the grantor. But
once the reversion has been created, it can be sold or given to another person – and
it will still be a reversion. The reversion just has to start off in the grantor.

**2. POSSIBILITY OF REVERTER:** A possibility of Reverter is an interest which
remains in the grantor after he has given away a "fee simple determinable."

EXAMPLE: Grantor gives land, "to the University of Denver <u>so long as</u> used for law
school purposes, and when no longer used for law school purposes, <u>then to revert</u> to
me."

The grantor has created a "fee simple determinable" in D.U., and the grantor has retained a *possibility of reverter*.

The interest D.U. has is some kind of a fee simple, because it MIGHT last forever. It is a fee simple determinable, because it will end, or "determine", whenever D.U. stops using the land for law school purposes. So the interest created in D.U. is a fee simple determinable. And the interest that is left in the grantor – the possibility of getting the land back when it is no longer used for law school purposes – is called a *Possibility of Reverter*.

In most states, the grantor, after creating a possibility of reverter, could convey the possibility of reverter to another person, and it would remain a possibility of reverter because it was originally created in the grantor. Even when the possibility of reverter is conveyed to a third person, it still remains a possibility of reverter – because it was originally created in the grantor.

If a state does not allow a possibility of reverter to be conveyed, nothing serious happens if the grantor attempts to convey the possibility of reverter. The courts would just hold that the grantor still had the possibility of reverter.

In any case, when the specified event happens, such as D.U. no longer using the land for law school purposes, the land will **automatically** revert to the person who then owns the possibility of reverter.

**3. RIGHT OF ENTRY** – (also called a POWER OF TERMINATION): This looks a lot like a possibility of reverter, but it works differently.

> EXAMPLE: Grantor gives land, "to A, <u>but if</u> liquor is ever sold on the land, then I have a <u>right to reenter</u> and take the land back."

By this provision the grantor has created a "fee simple subject to condition subsequent" in A, and has retained a Right of Entry in herself.

The interest A has in this example MIGHT last forever, and that is why it is some sort of a fee simple. But since it may be ended, if anyone ever sells liquor on the land, the interest created in A is called a "fee simple subject to a condition subsequent."

Notice that with a right of entry, the grantor has to <u>do</u> something to get the land back. It will <u>not</u> come back to the grantor automatically. This may be a good thing, for the grantor, if it turns out that the land is filled with hazardous substances when A sells that bottle of liquor. At that time, the grantor might decide that she didn't want the land back, with all the possible expenses under CERCLA. So the grantor might just decide <u>not</u> to assert her right of entry – and thus leave A with ownership of the land. Usually, under the applicable statute of limitations, the grantor has about two years to decide whether or not to assert the right of entry.

Another important thing to remember about a right of entry is that at common law **any attempt to convey a right of entry will DESTROY it!** So if a grantor, after retaining a right of entry in herself, tries to sell the right of entry to B, the whole right of entry is DESTROYED – and A will then have full ownership of the land, (a fee simple absolute), instead of just a fee simple subject to condition subsequent.

**4. REMAINDERS:** A Remainder is an interest created in a third person – and is almost always the interest that directly follows a life estate.

EXAMPLE: Grantor gives land, "to A for life, then to B."

The grantor has thus created a life estate in A, and a remainder in B."

THERE ARE FOUR KINDS OF REMAINDERS: Contingent; Vested; Vested Subject to Open; and Vested Subject to Divestment. Here are some samples:

A. CONTINGENT REMAINDER

EXAMPLE: "To A for life, then to A's children." – IF A does not yet have any children.

If A does not yet have any children, then the remainder in A's children will be contingent – contingent on the children being born. Any remainder in unborn, or unascertained persons will always be a contingent remainder.

You can also have a contingent remainder if there is some condition which has to be met before the person can get the remainder – some condition OTHER than just the death of the person who has the life estate.

For example, if the grantor says, **"to A for life, then if B graduates from law school, to B"** that would create a life estate in A, and a contingent remainder in B – (if B hasn't yet graduated from law school). B has to graduate from law school before she can get the gift. So B has a contingent remainder – contingent on graduating from law school.

A contingent remainder is subject to the Rule Against Perpetuities, (RAP). And whenever there is a contingent remainder the grantor also has a reversion – in case B never graduates from law school, for example.

## B. VESTED REMAINDER

EXAMPLE: "To A for life, then to B."

This remainder in B is called a vested remainder. B doesn't have to do anything to get the remainder – except wait for A to die. Even if B dies before A dies, it will be OK. The reminder will just go into B's estate, and be part of the property B could give to someone by her will, when she dies. So B has a vested remainder. We know who B is, and B doesn't have to do anything but wait for A to die.

If a remainder is certain to vest *if at all*, within the time allowed by RAP, it is OK under RAP.

## C. REMAINDER WHICH IS VESTED SUBJECT TO OPEN

EXAMPLE: "To A for life, then to A's children." – IF A already has one or more children alive.

Since all A's children have to do to be entitled to the remainder is to be A's children, then as soon as each child is born to A, that child has a vested remainder. But since more and more children may be born to A, the remainder is considered to be *vested subject to open* – subject to letting in more children, as each new child is born.

Somewhat surprisingly, a remainder which is vested subject to open still has not compiled with RAP. In order to comply with RAP, it must be certain that the remainder will have vested, *if at all*, in <u>everyone</u> who may be entitled to share in the remainder, within the time allowed by RAP.

## D. REMAINDER WHICH IS VESTED SUBJECT TO DIVESTMENT

EXAMPLE: "To A for life, then to B, <u>but if</u> B ever goes skiing on a Friday afternoon when he should be in Property class, <u>then to C</u>."

This creates a life estate in A; a remainder in B which is vested subject to divestment; and an executory interest in C. B's interest is vested, because we know who he is, and he doesn't have to do anything before he gets the gift – BUT IF he goes skiing when he shouldn't then the remainder will be taken away from him – it will be divested. So B has a vested remainder, subject to divestment.

A vested remainder subject to divestment has complied with RAP as soon as it has become vested.

The interest C has in the example above is called a SHIFTING EXECUTORY INTEREST – because it will SHIFT from B to C if B cuts class to go skiing. An executory interest is the ONLY interest that can follow a vested remainder. An executory interest is subject to RAP.

**5. EXECUTORY INTEREST**. There are two kinds of executory interests – shifting and springing. A SHIFTING executory interest shifts from one grantee to another. A SPRINGING executory interest SPRINGS from the grantor, over an interval of time, to a grantee. It is very unlikely that a springing executory interest will be created on purpose – but there are lots of shifting executory interests.

A. SHIFTING EXECUTORY INTEREST

> EXAMPLE: Grantor says, "To D.U. so long as used for law school purposes, and when no longer used for law school purposes, then to C.U."

By the provision above, the grantor will have created a fee simple determinable in D.U., and a shifting executory interest in C.U. The interest in D.U. MIGHT last forever, so it is a fee simple determinable. But if D.U. stops using the land for law school purposes, ownership will automatically shift over to C.U. So C.U. has a shifting executory interest. Both interests are good under RAP, because both D.U. (a private university), and C.U. (a public university), are considered to be charities – for the purposes of the Rule Against Perpetuities.

HOWEVER, if the grantor attempted to create a shifting executory interest in a non-charity, the attempted executory interest would be <u>void</u> under RAP – <u>unless</u> the condition that would cause the shift had been carefully limited to occur, *if at all,* within the time allowed by RAP.

When an executory interest is created, it will be <u>void</u> under RAP unless at the time that it is first created it is certain that the executory interest will vest, *if at all,* within the time allowed by RAP – and to comply with RAP it must be clear that the executory interest will vest IN POSSESSION, (if at all), within the time allowed by RAP.

An executory interest following a remainder that is vested subject to divestment, an executory interest following a fee simple determinable, and an executory interest following a fee simple subject to condition would all be subject to the same rules.

## B. SPRINGING EXECUTORY INTEREST

EXAMPLE: Grantor signs a document that says "I give my farm to my son, A, <u>when I die</u>."

The document cannot be recognized to be a valid will if it was not signed by two witnesses, as required for a formal will, or if it is not all in the handwriting of the grantor, which might make it valid as a holographic will in some jurisdictions. Clearly, the grantor does not intend for the son to own the land until the grantor dies. So the document will probably be held to be totally ineffective.

However, if a court wants to find a way of getting the farm to the son, the court may declare that the document created a *springing executory interest* in the son as soon as the document was signed. When the grantor dies, the ownership of the land will *spring* across the interval of time between when the document was signed and the time that the grantor died, and the son will then become the owner of the farm.

Needless to say, it would have been far better for the grantor just to write a formal will, which would go into effect at the death of the grantor. There are very few situations in which a person intentionally creates a springing executory interest.

But deciding that a document which is not valid as a will actually created a *springing executory interest* is a technique that some courts have used to carry out the grantor's intent that the grantor's son should have the farm.

# CHAPTER FOUR

# INHERITING PROPERTY

## INTRODUCTION

### A. Intestate Succession and Wills

This chapter is about inheritance. When a person dies, the statutes of the state where the person was domiciled at death provide how the person's property is to be distributed. State statutes vary, of course, but the basic pattern is that the property of the person who has died, (called the *decedent*), will be distributed to the decedent's closest relatives, usually some to the surviving spouse, if any, and the rest to the surviving children, if any. Anyone, (of sound mind and over the age of eighteen), may write a will if the person would prefer a pattern of distribution which is different from the one provided by statute.

There are certain technical terms that are used frequently in both wills and statutes on intestate succession. Each state, of course, has authority to define the meaning of the technical terms as seems most appropriate. So sometimes a technical phrase, such as "per stirpes" will mean one thing in one state, and a slightly different thing in another state, but the basics are usually about the same.

The following case illustrates the importance of using exactly the right word or phrase to describe the intent of the testator, (the person who signs the will).

# SUPREME COURT OF GEORGIA
## PICCIONE ET AL.
## V.
## ARP ET AL.

OCTOBER 16, 2017

**Opinion**

HINES, Chief Justice.

Gregory and Adam Piccione ("the Picciones"), grandchildren of testator Virginia Arp ("Virginia") and children of Donna Piccione ("Donna"), appeal from the superior court's denial of their motion for summary judgment in this action against their three uncles, Sam, Dwayne, and David Arp. For the reasons that follow, we affirm.

Virginia executed a will in 2002. It provides for her burial and the payment of her debts, and the sole paragraph that sets forth the disposition of her property states in toto: "I give, bequeath and devise unto my children, Sam Arp, Donna Piccione, David Arp and Dwayne Arp, all of the property that I may own at the time of my death, both real and personal, of every kind and description and wherever located, PER CAPITA." (Emphasis in original.) Virginia's daughter Donna died in 2006, and Virginia died in 2013. The executors of Virginia's estate, (the uncles), divided Virginia's estate among Virginia's three surviving children (i.e., themselves.). Donna's children, the Picciones, contending that they had a combined one-fourth interest in the property that comprised Virginia's estate, sued in superior court, asserting actions for conversion, fraud, and trespass regarding those property interests, and moved for summary judgement, which the trial court denied, concluding that Virginia's use of the words "PER CAPITA" was a "limitation" under the anti-lapse statute, OCGA § 53-4-64 (a); the anti-lapse provisions of the statute therefore did not apply to the gifts to Virginia's children; as Donna predeceased Virginia, the testamentary gift to Donna lapsed; and thus, the Picciones had no property interest upon which to base their claims. The trial court issued a certificate of immediate review, and this Court granted the Picciones' application for interlocutory appeal.

The trial court was correct that Donna's predeceasing Virginia caused the gift to Donna to lapse.

> At common law, and under the law of this State before the act of 1836, if the legatee
> died before the death of the testator the legacy lapsed, whether the legatee left issue or

not. Since 1836, if there be issue, it takes as substituting legatee under the provisions of the anti-lapse statute.

*Sanders v. First Nat. Bank,* (1939).

The trial court was correct in determining that the bequests in Virginia's will constituted individual gifts to her four named children.

Of course, the primary objective in will interpretation is to ascertain the testator's intent. To discover that intent, the court must look first to the "four corners' of the will," and where the language of a will is clear and can be given legal effect as it stands, the court will not, by construction, give the will a different effect.

Georgia's statutory scheme governing intestacy provides that the heirs in the first degree of one who dies without a will, and who is not survived by a spouse, shall be the children of the decedent, "with the descendants of any deceased child taking, per stirpes, the share that child would have taken if in life."

In the absence of anything in the will indicating a contrary intent it will be presumed that the testator intended a per stirpes distribution as would occur by law in the event of intestacy. Thus, there must be "plain language in Virginia's will to overcome the presumption that she intended a per stirpes distribution. Here, there is such language.

As the trial court noted, Virginia wrote the will with the words "PER CAPITA" in all capital letters; no other substantive portion of the will was so emphasized. "Per capita" is Latin for "by the head," and is stated in Black's Law Dictionary to mean "divided equally among all individuals, usually in the same class." By contrast, "per stirpes" which is also from Latin, means "by roots or stocks," and is defined as "proportionally divided between beneficiaries according to their *deceased ancestor's* share." As our precedent has stated:

> "Per capita" is defined: "By the heads or polls; according to the number of individuals; share and share alike." "When descendants take as individuals they are said to take *per capita.*"

> By contrast, when issue are said to take *per stirpes* it is meant that the *descendants* of a deceased person take the property to which he was entitled or would have been entitled if living, by or according to stock or root.

> Further, the terms "per capita" and "per stirpes" have a definite meaning in law and are presumed always to be used in their technical sense unless a contrary intention appears in the context of the will. "Per capita" means "by the head" or share and share

alike, according to the number of individuals. "Per stirpes" means "by the roots" or "stocks," or by representation. It denotes that method of distribution where a class or group of individuals or distributees take the share which their "stock" (deceased ancestor) would have been able to take in per capita distribution. The technical meaning of these words may be changed or even reversed by the manner in which the testator uses them in the will, as the testator's intention always controls.

As noted, in Virginia's will the only individuals named as recipients of the testamentary gifts are her four children; they alone take as individuals, and if their children took the gifts in their stead, it would be by representation.

The Picciones contend that in the will, "per capita" simply means "equally," i.e., that the bequests to the four named children were to be in equal amounts, and thus, as the legacy to Donna would ordinarily be considered to have lapsed, the anti-lapse provision of OCGA § 53-4-64 (a) requires that the testamentary gift to Donna does not lapse, but rather vests in them as Donna's descendants. Certainly, if Virginia had used the term "equally," that would be the case; the gift to Donna would be considered to have lapsed, and under OCGA § 53-4-64 (a), the Picciones would have taken her gift by representation. And, of course, if Virginia had designated the gifts for her named children "per stirpes," the Picciones would also receive the bequest made to Donna, although not by operation of OCGA § 53-4-64 (a), but by the specifics of the gift itself, as the descendants of a primary legatee. But, Virginia did not use either of those terms; she stated that her testamentary gifts to her children were to be "PER CAPITA," and that language must be given effect.

The plain language of the will indicates that Virginia *did not* intend that her bequests follow the law of intestacy, and the presumption in favor of a per stirpes distribution is thus overcome. The choice of "PER CAPITA" in this circumstance imposes a requirement that the individuals named take the bequests in their own stead, that those bequests not pass through representation, and accordingly, that the named individuals must survive Virginia.

Accordingly, the trial court did not err in denying the Picciones' motion for summary judgment.

Judgment affirmed.

## B. Standard Definitions of Some Basic Patterns of Distribution

**1. Per Stirpes**. *Per stirpes* is the Latin phrase meaning "by the root."

If a testator provides that the property is to be distributed to the testator's descendants *per stirpes*, then each of the testator's children who survives the testator would be given one share, and the descendants of any child who did not survive the testator would divide the share that would otherwise have gone to the testator's child who predeceased the testator. If one of the testator's children predeceases the testator leaving no issue (children, grandchildren, etc.) surviving, then no share is cut for that deceased child, and the shares for the other children, (or their descendents), will be larger.

For example: Assume that when T (the testator) dies, he has three children, A, B and C who survive T. T also had two other children, D and E, who did not survive T. A, B, and C each have two children. D had three children, all of whom survived T. E never had any children.

In that situation four shares would be cut. A, B, and C would each get one share, and D's surviving three children would divide the share D would otherwise have taken. No share would be cut for E's branch of the family, because there is no one alive to take it. The children of A, B and C would not get anything, because their respective parents are alive to take the share for that branch of the family.

If it happened that all five of T's children, A, B, C, D and E had all died before T died, then the property would still be cut into four shares, because there would be someone alive to take A's share, (A's two children); there would be someone alive to take B's share, (B's two children); there would be someone alive to take C's share, (C's two children); and there would be someone alive to take D's share, (D's three children). No share would be cut for E's branch of the family, because there would be no one alive to take that share.

The major thing to remember is that if T specifies that T's property is to be divided among his descendants *per stirpes*, then T's *children* are always the "roots" of their respective branches of the family, whether T's children survive T or not.

**2. By Representation:** If a testator directs that the testator's property shall go to the testator's descendants *by representation*, the important thing is that the shares will not automatically be cut at the generation closest to the testator (the testator's children). Instead, the shares will be cut at the closest generation to the testator *at which there is one person still alive*. So, if all of T's *children* have died before T, then the shares will be cut based on the number of T's *grandchildren* still living, plus deceased grandchildren who left some descendant surviving.

Example: If all five of T's children, A, B, C, D, and E have all died before T, but A, B and C each have two children who are surviving, and D has three children who are surviving, (and E has no surviving children), then T's property will be cut into 9 equal shares, and each of T's grandchildren will get an equal share. This will mean three shares for D's branch of the family, since D left more children surviving. So D's family comes out a little ahead, and each of the grandchildren is treated equally.

**3. Per Capita at Each Generation.** This is a slightly more complex form of distribution, but may appeal to some clients. Under this pattern, the shares that cannot be distributed to the closest level of descendants are *combined*, and distributed equally among those in the second generation who do not have a parent who has taken a share.

For example: If T had five children, (A, B, C, D, and E), and only A and E survived T, then the shares of B, C, and D would be *combined* and sent down to the next level. Since A and E both survived T, then A and E would each get one share – one fifth each. If B, C, and D did not survive T, but B left two children surviving, C left three children surviving, and D left four children surviving, then there would be a total of nine grandchildren in families that had not yet gotten any share of T's estate. So the shares of the T's deceased children, (B, C, and D) would be *combined*, and that three-fifths would be sent down to the level of the grandchildren. Then each of the nine grandchildren would get an equal share, specifically one-fifteenth for each grandchild. So the grandchildren are treated equally, but the families with more children get a larger percentage of the estate.

It is totally up to the client as to which form of distribution the client prefers. The lawyer just needs to be able to explain the differences to the client. Drawing pictures to illustrate the different forms of distribution frequently helps.

## C. Special Protections for a Surviving Spouse – The Augmented Estate

One thing that is *not* left up to the client is the choice as to whether or not to leave anything to the surviving spouse. Unless there is an effective pre-nuptial agreement, the law requires that every spouse leave something to his or her surviving spouse. The exact amount is specified in state statutes. At common law this issue was handled by the laws of dower and curtesy – giving each spouse a right to some ownership in land held by either spouse during the marriage. Now, statutory elective share amounts have replaced dower and curtesy – and in many states the elective share amount may even include property that a spouse no longer owns at death! For example, if wife, shortly before death, gave most her assets to her daughter from a prior marriage, those gifts would nevertheless be pulled back into the augmented estate, to be included when determining the size of husband's elective share. Husband would be entitled to the elective share provided by statute – no matter what wife's will might say. It is simply a matter of public policy – as set forth in the applicable legislation.

In community property states, where the earnings of husband and wife have been equally divided throughout the marriage, there may be less need for an elective share. Yet a few community property states, such as California and Idaho provide for an elective share, anyway, to protect couples who may have spent most of their married life in a state other than a community property state.

Note: The next two cases are rather entertaining cases which may help to clarify the concept of the augmented estate.

## SUPREME COURT OF MONTANA
## IN THE MATTER OF THE ESTATE OF FRED ALCORN

FEBRUARY 11, 1994

**OPINION BY: HARRISON**

This is an appeal from the Eighth Judicial District Court, Cascade County. Appellant Robert A. Alcorn (Robert), as personal representative of his father's estate, appeals the District Court's determination that a common-law marriage existed between respondent Kathee Melinda Young (Kathee) and Fred "Fritz" Alcorn (Fred), the decedent. In this matter of probate, Kathee asserted rights to an elective share of the augmented estate, a homestead allowance, an exempt property allowance and a family allowance. Robert appeals.

Fred and Kathee met on August 27, 1981, at Metra Park, a horse racetrack in Billings, Montana. At the time of their meeting, Kathee was separated from her husband, Fred Young (Young). Kathee's divorce from Young was complete in May 1985. From the day they met in August 1981, Fred and Kathee cohabited until Fred died on May 10, 1991. The couple first lived together in Great Falls, but soon moved to Fred's ranch house in Vaughn, Montana.

Kathee, 46, has been a Delta Airlines flight attendant for seventeen years. Fred, who died at age 59, owned and operated an automobile dealership in Great Falls. The couple shared a common interest in horses and in horse racing. In fact, they jointly owned race horses and regularly attended horse races together. Throughout her relationship with Fred, Kathee retained her last name and filed her tax returns as a single person; however, the couple did share joint bank accounts at First Liberty Credit Union in Great Falls.

During the time Kathee and Fred were together, Fred was plagued with physical ailments -- including heart problems, back problems which required surgery, throat cancer which required surgery, and a lung removal which required related surgeries. Fred died of a heart attack on May 10, 1991.

In his will, Fred designated his son, Robert, as the personal representative of his estate. On October 1, 1991, Kathee filed a Notice of Election Against Will by Surviving Spouse. Kathee contends that she and Fred had a common-law marriage from the day they met until the day Fred died. Robert challenges this assertion.

By will, Fred devised to Kathee one-half of the net value of his ranch and all of his household furniture and household goods. Kathee additionally sought the following entitlements: one third of the augmented estate, pursuant to § 72-2-223, MCA; a homestead allowance of $ 20,000, pursuant to § 72-2-412, MCA; an exempt property allowance not to exceed $ 3,500, pursuant to § 72-2-413, MCA; and a family allowance, pursuant to § 72-2-414, MCA.

The District Court conducted a non-jury trial in July and August 1992, and entered its findings of fact, conclusions of law and judgment on February 22, 1993. The District Court concluded that Kathee was Fred's common-law wife and, therefore, granted her the entitlements she sought as Fred's surviving spouse.

The sole issue before this Court is whether the District Court properly determined that a common-law marriage was established by Kathee Young.

Montana recognizes the validity of common-law marriages. Section 40-1-403, MCA. A rebuttable presumption exists in favor of a valid marriage when "a man and a woman deporting themselves as husband and wife have entered into a lawful contract of marriage." Section 26-1-602(30), MCA.

> In order to establish the existence of a common law marriage, the party asserting the marriage must show 1) the parties are competent to enter into a marriage; 2) assumption of such a relationship by mutual consent and agreement; and 3) cohabitation and repute.

Robert argues that Kathee failed to prove that she and Fred were ever married. Robert contends that Kathee was not competent to marry Fred until May 1, 1985, when her divorce with Young was finalized. According to Robert, Kathee failed to introduce evidence that she and Fred agreed to marry one another after her divorce in 1985. Robert asserts that "marriage cannot occur in a piecemeal fashion, but rather comes instantly into being or does not come at all." This Court addressed the same issue in *Estate of Murnion* (1984). In deciding that this concept was not determinative, we stated:

In addition to the consent required for a valid common-law marriage, there must be cohabitation and public repute of the marriage. The latter two factors do not take place instantly, but are continuing factors that extend through the life of the marriage.

The following exchange occurred at the August 17, 1992, hearing:

Q. [By Donald Ostrem, Kathee's attorney] Okay. Now there are several items that you and I have talked about involving common law marriage. Did you feel that you were married to Fritz Alcorn?
A. Yes, I did.
Q. And did you during the entirety of your relationship feel that you were married to Fritz Alcorn?
A. Yes, I did.
Q. Now, did you state that you -- when you first started living together, you were in the process of getting a divorce from your previous husband. And you did get that divorce?
A. Yes.
Q. So you also had the capability of consent at the time that you got that divorce is that correct?
A. Yes.

Kathee testified that she and Fred were capable to consent to marriage. She also testified that neither she nor Fred were incompetent or suffering from any disabilities.

We determine, as a matter of law, that Kathee and Fred were incapable of consenting to marriage until Kathee's divorce with Young became final on May 1, 1985. However, persons who cohabit after the removal of the impediment may become lawfully married as of the date of the removal of the impediment. Therefore, when Kathee's divorce to Young became final, the impediment to her common-law marriage to Fred was removed.

Having determined that Kathee and Fred were competent to marry after May 1, 1985, we turn our discussion to whether Kathee and Fred assumed a common-law marriage by mutual consent and agreement. In support of her contention that she and Fred mutually consented and agreed to marriage, Kathee claims to have a wedding ring given to her by Fred. The ring, which she wore to the August 17, 1992, hearing, contains two intertwining horseshoes made with Yogo sapphires. According to Kathee, "Fritz had it designed and had it made. And the bracelet -- he got a bracelet for me to match." In addition to the ring and bracelet, Kathee and Fred incorporated the intertwining horseshoe design into their home in Vaughn. The couple had horseshoes cemented into the concrete walkway leading to their house, with their names etched into the concrete beneath the horseshoes.

At the August 17th hearing, the following question was asked: "Did you both agree that you were married, that you were husband and wife?" Kathee responded, "Yes, we did." The combination of Kathee's wedding ring, the concrete design at the couple's home in Vaughn, and Kathee's testimony indicates that Kathee and Fred mutually consented and agreed to a common-law marriage.

We look finally to cohabitation and repute. It is clear from the record, and Robert agrees, that Kathee and Fred cohabited for about nine years -- from the day they met until the day Fred passed away. They lived together for a short time in Great Falls before moving to Fred's house in Vaughn. In fact, it is apparent that the couple invested a great deal of time and money in decorating and refurbishing their home. However, as Robert correctly asserts, marriage "does not result from mere cohabitation alone." Therefore, we now turn our attention to repute.

Robert contends that Kathee and Fred admitted in writing that they were not married after May 1, 1985. In support of his contention, Robert presented evidence that Kathee: 1) never changed her last name from "Young" to "Alcorn;" 2) did not list Fred as a beneficiary on her employee life insurance, health insurance or retirement forms; and 3) filed her tax returns as a single person throughout her entire relationship with Fred. Moreover, *Fred stated in his will that he was a single man.*

Kathee testified that she chose to keep the last name "Young" for professional reasons. Kathee testified that her mother was listed as beneficiary on her insurance, health and retirement forms. Kathee also testified that she filed her tax returns as a single person because she thought she could not file as "married" unless the marriage was a matter of record and because her accountants "told her to file it that way."

This Court is unaware of any legal requirement that a wife assume the last name of her husband or that she list her husband as beneficiary on her insurance, retirement or health forms. The District Court accepted Kathee's explanations -- including her rationale for filing her tax returns individually rather than as a married person -- as valid. The District Court was in the best position to observe Kathee and her demeanor. We determine that the District Court's finding as to this issue is not clearly erroneous.

Robert next contends that each witness testified either that Fred and Kathee were not married or that they merely assumed or considered the couple as married. According to Robert, the fact that people assumed or considered the couple as married does not demonstrate that Kathee ever held herself out to be Fred's wife.

The record, however, is replete with evidence and testimony that Kathee and Fred held themselves out to be husband and wife. Kathee and Fred shared joint checking accounts at First Liberty Credit Union. Kathee wore a wedding ring designed and made especially for her, compliments of Fred. The record indicates that Kathee and Fred spent all of their time -- excepting work -- together for nine years. Because the couple had a large home, they regularly hosted members from both Fred and Kathee's families for holidays. Christmas at the Vaughn ranch became a tradition. The couple hosted barbecues and pool parties in the summer for family and friends. Kathee's family members referred to Fred as "Uncle Fritz."

Fred spent about eight years of his time with Kathee in poor health. Throughout Fred's illnesses, Kathee was by his side. The record indicates that Kathee cared for Fred through chemotherapy and through visits to Seattle for treatment.

Robert's daughter and Fred's granddaughter, Kara Alcorn, testified that she and her brother, Robert, who live in Washington, would visit Fred and Kathee in Vaughn. Kara testified that she considered Kathee and Fred to be married, that she received Christmas cards from the couple, and that she received information concerning changes in Fred's medical condition from Kathee.

Robert Layton, Kara's brother and Fred's grandson, testified that the relationship between Kathee and Fred was always portrayed to him as that of husband and wife. He further testified that he visited them every summer, that they "always were together" and that he considered them to be married. On occasion, Robert would go to the horse racetrack with Fred, who would introduce Robert as his "grandson" and Kathee as his "wife."

Judge John McCarvel, a district court judge in Cascade County, was a long-time friend of Fred's. Judge McCarvel used to see Fred run his horses at racetracks in Spokane, Billings and Great Falls. The Judge testified that he considered Fred and Kathee to be married, that Fred always introduced Kathee as his wife, and that he "thought they were married all the time." On one occasion, as he left the Great Falls Airport, Kathee was waiting in the truck to pick up Fred. The Judge testified that "Kathee hollered to me, 'Is my husband on that plane?'"

Janice Mountan, Kathee's sister, testified that "Fritz introduced us as his in-laws. Everyone knew Fritz as being Kathee's husband and Kathee as Fritz's wife." We need not belabor the record. It is abundantly clear that Kathee and Fred cohabited and held themselves out to the community as being husband and wife.

Robert challenges the District Court's findings of fact as erroneous and contradicted by the record. Robert contends that the court omitted from its findings references to testimony which indicated that Fred and Kathee were not married. Specifically, Robert points to the testimony of Donna and Chuck Plant -- friends of Fred -- who stated that Fred had told them after 1985 that he was not married to Kathee. Robert also notes the absence of Robert Emmons' testimony from the findings. *Emmons, an attorney, testified that Fred represented that he was a single man in each of the three wills Emmons drafted for Fred.*

It cannot be said that the District Court failed to consider all the testimony merely because it chose not to reference all the testimony it heard in its findings of fact and conclusions of law. The court heard testimony from fifteen witnesses. It found capability of consent to a common-law marriage between Fred and Kathee, mutual assent and agreement to a common-law marriage, cohabitation, and repute in the community as husband and wife.

The court was in the best position to judge the credibility of the witnesses. We will not substitute our judgment for that of the District Court even where there is evidence in the record to support contrary findings.

After a careful review of the record, we determine that the District Court's findings of fact were not clearly erroneous. We hold that the District Court correctly interpreted the law when it concluded 1) that the relationship between Kathee Young and Fred Alcorn constituted a valid common-law marriage; and 2) that Kathee is entitled to claim the elections set forth in her Notice of Election Against the Will filed with the District Court on October 1, 1991.

Affirmed.

Note: If Fred believed that he and Kathee were *not* married, but were just living together, was there a valid common law marriage? Is there some way that Fred could have protected himself from having it determined – after his death – that he had been married to Kathee?

In the following case, what could have been done to prevent this outcome?

# SUPREME COURT OF ALASKA
# ROBERT J. RIDDELL, APPELLANT,
# V.
# IRVIN H. EDWARDS, APPELEE.

SEPTEMBER 5, 2003

OPINION BY: BRYNER

## INTRODUCTION

In a probate proceeding involving the estate of his deceased wife, Robert J. Riddell petitioned as a surviving spouse to receive his statutory homestead allowance, family allowance, and elective share. Despite finding that Riddell had "ingratiated himself" to his wife before their marriage "for the purpose of obtaining her assets" and that his wife had suffered from dementia for the majority of their relationship, the superior court ruled that Riddell and his wife had been validly married and that the estate had no standing to argue that the marriage was voidable. The court nonetheless concluded that Riddell's unconscionable conduct warranted establishing a constructive trust to give the estate Riddell's statutory benefits. Because the superior court's finding that the marriage was valid is not disputed and because Alaska law unconditionally gives the surviving spouse of a valid marriage the right to marital allowances and a share of the estate based solely on the existence of a valid marriage, we hold that the necessary elements for a constructive trust are lacking and that establishing the trust exceeded the court's equitable powers. We thus vacate the trust and remand with directions to fix the amount of Riddell's statutory benefits.

## FACTS AND PROCEEDINGS

In December 1993 Lillie Rahm-Riddell, who was in her early nineties, met Robert J. Riddell, who was in his mid-sixties. Riddell ingratiated himself to Lillie and became her handyman. He soon moved in with her and started to isolate her from her family and friends. Riddell married Lillie in Ketchikan in May 1995, while guardianship proceedings were pending to determine Lillie's competency to manage her personal and financial affairs. Those proceedings resulted in the appointment of the Public Guardian as Lillie's primary conservator; several months later, prompted by reports of domestic violence, the superior court entered an order restraining Riddell from contacting Lillie. Lillie moved to an assisted-living home in Washington state. Riddell spirited her away from the home and took her to Oregon, where they lived together until Lillie died in September 1997. The entire time that Lillie knew Riddell, she suffered from Alzheimer's disease and/or senile dementia.

Lillie's brother, Irvin H. Edwards, accepted the superior court's appointment as personal representative of her estate. Ensuing litigation between the estate and Riddell generated three appeals. In the first appeal, we affirmed the superior court's order invalidating for lack of testamentary capacity a will that Lillie executed shortly before her death leaving her entire estate to Riddell. In the second, we affirmed the superior court's order denying creditor claims that Riddell filed against the estate seeking compensation for alleged premarital and marital services to Lillie.

The third appeal, which we now consider, arises from two related superior court orders: (1) an order declaring Lillie's marriage to Riddell valid and finding Riddell eligible as Lillie's surviving spouse to claim his statutory rights to allowances and share; and (2) a subsequent order, based on a finding of fraudulent conduct by Riddell toward Lillie, establishing a constructive trust in the estate's favor to receive Riddell's payments of allowances and share. Our decision requires us to describe these orders in considerable detail.

In the course of the probate proceedings, after Riddell petitioned for his statutory allowances and share, the superior court ordered briefing and conducted a hearing to determine the validity of the marriage. The estate sought to invalidate the marriage, arguing that it was voidable because Lillie had been incompetent and Riddell had fraudulently induced her to enter into the marriage. Following the hearing, the court issued a thoughtful and carefully reasoned decision that found clear and convincing evidence of Riddell's fraudulent conduct toward Lillie but nevertheless rejected the estate's challenge to the marriage and declared Riddell eligible to claim allowances and share.

The superior court began its decision by unequivocally recognizing the compelling evidence of Riddell's misconduct toward Lillie:

> "A review of the prior evidence and the new evidence leaves no question to any objective observer by clear and convincing evidence Mr. Riddell ingratiated himself to Lillie for the purposes of obtaining her assets. She was suffering from dementia, was alone and lonely and he did small things for her in a way that kept her from making decisions that she would have made when she was fully competent. He isolated her by changing her phone, bullying family and friends that were old and frail themselves in such a way that they were not able to be supportive of her."

Three separate court actions involving injunctions under the Domestic Violence law, a conservatorship and a guardianship were filed. Lawyers, a conservator, a temporary guardian and a guardian ad litem were appointed for Lillie. Mr. Riddell defeated them all. In his own words, he and Lillie sneaked to Juneau to get a marriage license and got married secretly in Ketchikan while conservator proceedings were pending.

Mr. Riddell physically intimidated friends, family, lawyers and caregivers. He spirited Lillie away from the nursing home in Washington and kept her from authorities despite attempts to locate her by lawyers, a private investigator and court orders that he disclose her whereabouts.

Mr. Riddell provided Lillie with the attention she craved and did small things for her that made her life better. He also abused her physically and cut her off from her friends and family so that she was utterly dependent upon him for all her needs.

But the court also recognized that this evidence did not necessarily render Lillie's marriage invalid. Noting that "persons suffering from dementia have fluctuating periods of more contact with reality and ability to cope," the court reviewed the evidence and found credible testimony indicating that Lillie was competent and understood the consequences of her actions at the time that she married Riddell. In the court's view, then, the evidence did not convincingly prove Lillie's incompetence when she entered into the marriage: "this court cannot say that at the time she applied for the marriage license or when she actually participated in the ceremony she did not understand that she was getting married."

The superior court then proceeded to consider the legal significance of this finding; in so doing, it drew an important distinction between marriages that are void and those that are merely voidable. The court noted that, in AS 25.24.020, the Alaska Legislature defined a narrow class of marriages as legally void. That statute provides:

> A marriage which is prohibited by law on account of consanguinity between the persons, or a subsequent marriage contracted by a person during the life of a former husband or wife which marriage has not been annulled or dissolved is void.

In contrast, the court pointed out, AS 25.24.030 defines a broader class of marriages as voidable. Alaska Statute 25.24.030 provides:

> A marriage may be *declared* void for any of the following causes existing at the time of the marriage:
> (1) under the age of legal consent;
> (2) that either party was of unsound mind, unless that party, after coming to reason, freely cohabited with the other as husband and wife;

(3) that the consent of either party was obtained by fraud, unless that party afterwards, with full knowledge of the facts constituting the fraud, freely cohabited with the other as husband and wife;

(4) that the consent of either party was obtained by force, unless that party afterwards freely cohabited with the other as husband and wife;

(5) failure to consummate.

After surveying cases from other jurisdictions, the superior court further determined that Alaska's statutory scheme reflects the majority view, which the court characterized as precluding the personal representative of a deceased spouse from challenging the validity of the spouse's marriage in the absence of either an express statutory provision allowing post-mortem challenges or gross fraud coupled with mental disability.

Applying this analysis, then, the superior court declined to find the marriage void. The court went on to consider whether the case fell within the gross-fraud exception, which allows post-mortem challenges to a valid marriage upon proof of gross fraud arising from "a combination of incompetence and egregious behavior." Though it noted that "Mr. Riddell did isolate Lillie from her family and friends and he may have married her to obtain her property," the court found that "his conduct did not rise to the level of gross fraud."

Accordingly, the superior court's order declared the marriage valid. The court ruled that Riddell was Lillie's surviving spouse and was therefore eligible to claim a surviving spouse's statutory allowances and share.

After receiving the order declaring him eligible to receive the statutory marital allowances and share, Riddell filed a motion seeking to enforce that order. In response, the estate cross-moved to establish a constructive trust requiring Riddell's allowances and share to be paid to the estate.

The court ruled that, "because of the previous factual findings by the court, this court finds clear and convincing evidence that a constructive trust is warranted."

Riddell appeals.

## DISCUSSION

By ruling that Riddell's marriage was valid and could not be set aside by the estate, the superior court effectively determined that Riddell's statutory entitlements to allowances and share had vested upon Lillie's death -- before Lillie's estate ever received any cognizable interest or right to the portion of Lillie's estate that vested in Riddell. As a matter of law, then, the court's order validating the marriage ruled out the existence of an element necessary to support the court's subsequent decision to impose a constructive trust: a finding that the portion of Lillie's estate passing to Riddell "justly belonged" to the estate.

Moreover, even if we assume that the estate had a cognizable interest in these funds, the superior court's declaration of a valid marriage would still rule out the second prerequisite for a constructive trust: a finding that Riddell obtained his statutory rights "by reason of unjust, unconscionable, or unlawful means." As already explained, Riddell acquired his statutory right to allotments and share solely because he married Lillie and survived her with their marriage intact. For reasons we address below, we conclude that the superior court's order declaring the marriage to be valid *despite* Riddell's unconscionable premarital conduct precludes a finding that he acquired his statutory rights because of that conduct.

The absence of a causal link between Riddell's unconscionable postmarital conduct and his right to receive the statutory benefits of marriage thus readily distinguishes his case from cases involving constructive trusts imposed against murderers -- a category that the dissent mistakenly describes as being similar to the one before us. For as the dissent itself acknowledges, the constructive trust principle applies in those cases because "the title to property *is acquired by* murder." Thus, in the present case, the causal link that justifies imposing a constructive trust in cases of spousal murder -- and that certainly would have justified a constructive trust had it been found to exist here -- is missing.

### General Principles Governing Equitable Relief

A consideration of generally recognized principles governing equitable relief confirms the conclusion that a constructive trust was improper under these circumstances. Two equitable principles are relevant here.

First, a court acting in equity ordinarily cannot intrude in matters that are plain and fully covered by a statute. Here, the Alaska Legislature has explicitly set out the property interests that vest upon death in a surviving spouse: homestead allowance, family allowance, and elective share; the legislature has specified the circumstance that makes them vest: the existence of a "surviving spouse" -- that is, a spouse who remained legally married at the time of death; and the legislature has attached no other prerequisite to the surviving spouse's statutory right. Similarly, by specifying the requirements for a valid marriage and limiting the ways in which a marriage may be invalidated, the legislature has fully covered the manner in which courts may determine whether a person qualifies as a "surviving spouse" for purposes of acquiring a vested statutory right to allowances and share. As the superior court recognized in upholding the validity of Riddell's marriage, the legislature deliberately limited the right to challenge the validity of a marriage that is voidable on grounds of disability, force, or fraud, extending that right exclusively to "the party under the disability or upon whom the force or fraud is imposed." Given the superior court's findings that Riddell's marriage was neither void ab initio because of Lillie's incapacity nor voidable after her death for gross fraud arising from "a combination of Lillie's incompetence and Riddell's egregious behavior," it follows that the statutory provisions governing a surviving spouse's automatic entitlements to allotments and share "fully covered" Riddell's situation.

A second, closely related equitable principle that controls these circumstances is that a court must not apply equity to do indirectly what the law or its clearly defined policy forbids to be done directly. Here, the superior court recognized that Lillie, despite her incapacity, understood the consequences of her actions when she accepted Riddell in marriage; the court further held that, even when combined with Lillie's incapacity, Riddell's fraudulent actions were not sufficiently gross to allow a post-mortem claim that the marriage was voidable. In consequence, as we have seen, the law required the court to declare Riddell eligible to receive the statutory benefits of a surviving spouse; indeed, the court's first order recognized that requirement. Yet by subsequently invoking the same factual findings of fraud and incompetence to trigger the equitable mechanism of a constructive trust, the court did indirectly what the law specifically forbade it to do directly: in nullifying Riddell's already vested right to allotments and share and awarding the money to the estate, the court effectively allowed the estate to avoid on equitable grounds the direct legal consequences of the court's earlier legal conclusion that Lillie had made "a competent decision about her marriage" and had "understood the nature of her decision to marry Mr. Riddell."

## Other Considerations

The facts in this case obviously make it tempting to deny Riddell any benefit from his fraudulent conduct; this makes the recourse of a constructive trust seem alluringly sensible. But allowing offensive factual circumstances to dictate an unauthorized legal remedy can have a pernicious effect in the long-run by upsetting the complex and delicate balance that our system of government strives to maintain between the legislature's lawmaking powers and the courts' traditional equitable powers. The superior court here carefully examined all relevant evidence and declared Riddell to be the surviving spouse of a valid marriage. The legislature has spelled out the rights that Riddell acquires by virtue of his status. To dilute these plain and complete legislative directives with a legally inappropriate equitable remedy would impermissibly expand the court's equitable powers at the expense of established positive law.

We must therefore vacate the order imposing a constructive trust and remand this case to allow the superior court to determine the amount of Riddell's allowances and share. In remanding the case, however, we note that the applicable statutes specify the amount of both the homestead allowance and elective share but leave the amount of the family allowance in the court's discretion. To this extent, the statutes allow the superior court to factor equitable considerations into its decision on remand.

## CONCLUSION

We REVERSE the order imposing a constructive trust and REMAND for further proceedings to establish the amount of the statutory allowances and share.

# CHAPTER FIVE

# BUYING LAND

## INTRODUCTION

The standard way to become the owner of land is to buy it. Once a buyer and seller have agreed on the terms for purchase they both sign a contract specifying the terms of the sale, and specifying the date for the *closing* – the time when title will actually pass from seller to buyer. There will usually be several weeks between the date the contract is signed and the date of the actual closing. That period of time is called the gap, or the executory period.

It is during the executory period that the buyer's lawyer will go to work – checking title, to be sure that the seller actually owns the interest the seller has agreed to convey, and arranging for various inspections by experts – to be sure that any structures on the property are sound. During this time the buyer will also arrange the necessary financing, which usually entails getting a loan from a bank, and giving the bank a mortgage or deed of trust on the land – to secure repayment of the loan.

Here is a sample of some of the provisions of a basic contract for sale. The full contract goes on for 17 pages. Note the provisions for what happens if it turns out that either the seller or the buyer is unable to perform the provisions of the contract.

# CONTRACT TO BUY AND SELL REAL ESTATE
## (RESIDENTIAL)

Date: _____

## AGREEMENT

**1. AGREEMENT.** Buyer agrees to buy and Seller agrees to sell, the Property described below on the terms and conditions set forth in this contract (Contract).

## 2. PARTIES AND PROPERTY.

**2.1. Buyer.** Buyer, _____,
will take title to the Property described below as

**Joint Tenants**          **Tenants In Common**          **Other** _____.

**2.2. No Assignability.** This Contract **Is Not** assignable by Buyer unless otherwise specified in **Additional Provisions**.

**2.3. Seller.** Seller, _____, is
the current owner of the Property described below.

**2.4. Property.** The Property is the following legally described real estate in the
County of _____, Colorado: known as
No._____,

Street Address          City          State          Zip

together with the interests, easements, rights, benefits, improvements and attached fixtures appurtenant thereto, and all interest of Seller in vacated streets and alleys adjacent thereto, except as herein excluded (Property).

**2.5. Inclusions.** The Purchase Price includes the following items (Inclusions):

**2.5.1. Inclusions - Attached.** If attached to the Property on the date of this Contract, the following items are included unless excluded under **Exclusions**: lighting, heating, plumbing, ventilating and air conditioning units, TV antennas, inside telephone, network and coaxial (cable) wiring and connecting blocks/jacks, plants, mirrors, floor coverings, intercom systems , built-in kitchen appliances, sprinkler systems and controls, built-in vacuum systems (including accessories), garage door openers

**7. OWNERS' ASSOCIATION. This Section is applicable if the Property is located within a Common Interest Community and subject to such declaration.**

**7.1. Common Interest Community Disclosure.** THE PROPERTY IS LOCATED WITHIN A COMMON INTEREST COMMUNITY AND IS SUBJECT TO THE DECLARATION FOR THE COMMUNITY. THE OWNER OF THE PROPERTY WILL BE REQUIRED TO BE A MEMBER OF THE OWNERS' ASSOCIATION FOR THE COMMUNITY AND WILL BE SUBJECT TO THE BYLAWS AND RULES AND REGULATIONS OF THE ASSOCIATION. THE DECLARATION, BYLAWS, AND RULES AND REGULATIONS WILL IMPOSE FINANCIAL OBLIGATIONS UPON THE OWNER OF THE PROPERTY, INCLUDING AN OBLIGATION TO PAY ASSESSMENTS OF THE ASSOCIATION. IF THE OWNER DOES NOT PAY THESE ASSESSMENTS, THE ASSOCIATION COULD PLACE A LIEN ON THE PROPERTY AND POSSIBLY SELL IT TO PAY THE DEBT. THE DECLARATION, BYLAWS, AND RULES AND REGULATIONS OF THE COMMUNITY MAY PROHIBIT THE OWNER FROM MAKING CHANGES TO THE PROPERTY WITHOUT AN ARCHITECTURAL REVIEW BY THE ASSOCIATION (OR A COMMITTEE OF THE ASSOCIATION) AND THE APPROVAL OF THE ASSOCIATION. PURCHASERS OF PROPERTY WITHIN THE COMMON INTEREST COMMUNITY SHOULD INVESTIGATE THE FINANCIAL OBLIGATIONS OF MEMBERS OF THE ASSOCIATION. PURCHASERS SHOULD CAREFULLY READ THE DECLARATION FOR THE COMMUNITY AND THE BYLAWS AND RULES AND REGULATIONS OF THE ASSOCIATION.

**19.1. Causes of Loss, Insurance.** In the event the Property or Inclusions are damaged by fire, other perils or causes of loss prior to Closing in an amount of not more than ten percent of the total Purchase Price (Property Damage), and if the repair of the damage will be paid by insurance (other than the deductible to be paid by Seller), then Seller, upon receipt of the insurance proceeds, will use Seller's reasonable efforts to repair the Property before **Closing Date**. Buyer has the Right to Terminate under § 25.1, on or before **Closing Date** if the Property is not repaired before **Closing Date** or if the damage exceeds such sum. Should Buyer elect to carry out this Contract despite such Property Damage, Buyer is entitled to a credit at Closing for all insurance proceeds that were received by Seller (but not the Association, if any) resulting from damage to the Property and Inclusions, plus the amount of any deductible provided for in the insurance policy. This credit may not exceed the Purchase Price. In the event Seller has not received the insurance proceeds prior to Closing, the parties may agree to extend the **Closing Date** to have the Property repaired prior to Closing or, at the option of Buyer, (1) Seller must assign to Buyer the right to the proceeds at Closing, if acceptable to Seller's insurance company and Buyer's lender; or (2) the parties may enter into a written agreement prepared by the parties or their attorney requiring the Seller to escrow at Closing from Seller's sale proceeds the amount Seller has received and will receive due to such damage, not exceeding the total Purchase Price, plus the amount of any deductible that applies to the insurance claim.

**25.1. Right to Terminate.** If a party has a right to terminate, as provided in this Contract (Right to Terminate), the termination is effective upon the other party's receipt of a written notice to terminate (Notice to Terminate), provided such written notice was received on or before the applicable deadline specified in this Contract. If the Notice to Terminate is not received on or before the specified deadline, the party with the Right to Terminate accepts the specified matter, document or condition as satisfactory and waives the Right to Terminate under such provision.

**25.2. Effect of Termination.** In the event this Contract is terminated, all Earnest Money received hereunder will be returned and the parties are relieved of all obligations hereunder, subject to §§ 10.4, 22, 23 and 24.

Buyer's Name:_____ Buyer's Name: _____

_____

| Buyer's Signature | Date | | Buyer's Signature | Date |

Address:                                    Address:

Phone No.:                                  Phone No.:

Fax No.:                                    Fax No.:

Email Address:                              Email Address:



Phone No.:                                  Phone No.: Fax No.: Fax No.:

Email Address:                             Email Address:

If all goes well, the closing will take place on the date specified in the contract, and at that time the buyer will deliver the money to the seller, and the seller will deliver to the buyer a deed to the property. Then the buyer will promptly record that deed at the county clerk's office, to provide notice "to all the world" that the buyer is now the owner of the land.

The time when title actually passes to the buyer is when the deed is delivered to the buyer.

## A. Deeds and Warranties

### 1. Warranty Deed

Here is a sample deed, from the Colorado statutes. Many states have similar statutory forms for deeds. Note that the statute itself defines what is meant when the term "warranty" is used. By using this sort of deed the seller warrants that the seller is conveying good title to the land. If the title turns out not to be good, the buyer can sue the seller. The doctrine of after-acquired title also applies. If the person who sold the land by warranty deed did not actually have title at that time, but later acquires title, (by inheritance, for example), then that after-acquired title passes immediately to the purchaser under the prior warranty deed.

> § 38-30-113. Deeds--short form--acknowledgment--effect
>
> (1)(a) A deed for the conveyance of real property may be substantially in the following form:
> ...................., whose street address is ........................., City or Town of ........................., County of ......................... and State of ........................, for the consideration of ............. dollars, in hand paid, hereby sell(s) and convey(s) to .................... whose street address is ....................., City or Town of ...................., County of .................... and State of ...................., the following real property in the County of ........................ and State of Colorado, to wit: ......................... with all its appurtenances and warrant(s) the title to the same, subject to ......................
>
> Signed this ...................... day of ...................., 20......
>
> (b) Such deed may be acknowledged in accordance with section 38-35-101.
>
> (2) The words "warrant(s) the title" in a warranty deed as described in subsection (1)(a) of this section or in a mortgage as described in section 38-30-117 mean that the grantor covenants:
>
> (a) That at the time of the making of such instrument he was lawfully seized of an indefeasible estate in fee simple in and to the property therein described and has good right and full power to convey the same;

(b) That the same was free and clear from all encumbrances, except as stated in the instrument; and

(c) That he warrants to the grantee and his heirs and assigns the quiet and peaceable possession of such property and will defend the title thereto against all persons who may lawfully claim the same.

(3) Such covenants shall be binding upon any grantor and his heirs and personal representatives as fully as if written at length in said instrument.

Note: The following case illustrates the important distinctions between the various warranties included in a warranty deed.

## SUPREME COURT OF ILLINOIS
### JAMES R. BROWN ET AL., APPELLEES,
### V.
### MAUREEN M. LOBER, EX'R, APPELLANT

MAY 18, 1979

**Opinion**

UNDERWOOD, Justice:

Plaintiffs instituted this action in the Montgomery County circuit court based on an alleged breach of the covenant of seisin in their warranty deed. The trial court held that although there had been a breach of the covenant of seisin, the suit was barred by the 10-year statute of limitations. Plaintiffs' post-trial motion, which was based on an alleged breach of the covenant of quiet enjoyment, was also denied. A divided Fifth District Appellate Court reversed and remanded. We allowed the defendant's petition for leave to appeal.

The parties submitted an agreed statement of facts which sets forth the relevant history of this controversy. Plaintiffs purchased 80 acres of Montgomery County real estate from William and Faith Bost and received a statutory warranty deed, containing no exceptions, dated December 21, 1957. Subsequently, plaintiffs took possession of the land and recorded their deed.

On May 8, 1974, plaintiffs granted a coal option to Consolidated Coal Company (Consolidated) for the coal rights on the 80-acre tract for the sum of $6,000. Approximately two years later, however, plaintiffs "discovered" that they, in fact, owned only a one-third interest in the subsurface coal rights. It is a matter of public record that, in 1947, a prior grantor had reserved a two-thirds interest in the mineral rights on the property. Although plaintiffs had their abstract of title examined in 1958 and 1968 for loan purposes, they contend that until May 4, 1976, they believed that they were the sole owners of the surface and subsurface rights on the 80-acre tract. Upon discovering that a prior grantor had reserved a two-thirds interest in the coal rights, plaintiffs and Consolidated renegotiated their agreement to provide for payment of $2,000 in exchange for a one-third interest in the subsurface coal rights. On May 25, 1976, plaintiffs filed this action against the executor of the estate of Faith Bost, seeking damages in the amount of $4,000.

The deed which plaintiffs received from the Bosts was a general statutory form warranty deed meeting the requirements of section 9. That section provides:

> "Every deed in substance in the above form, when otherwise duly executed, shall be deemed and held a conveyance in fee simple, to the grantee, his heirs or assigns, with covenants on the part of the grantor, (1) that at the time of the making and delivery of such deed he was lawfully seized of an indefeasible estate in fee simple, in and to the premises therein described, and had good right and full power to convey the same; (2) that the same were then free from all incumbrances; and (3) that he warrants to the grantee, his heirs and assigns, the quiet and peaceable possession of such premises, and will defend the title thereto against all persons who may lawfully claim the same. And such covenants shall be obligatory upon any grantor, his heirs and personal representatives, as fully and with like effect as if written at length in such deed."

The effect of this provision is that certain covenants of title are implied in every statutory form warranty deed. Subsection 1 contains the covenant of seisin and the covenant of good right to convey. These covenants, which are considered synonymous, assure the grantee that the grantor is, at the time of the conveyance, lawfully seized and has the power to convey an estate of the quality and quantity which he professes to convey.

Subsection 2 represents the covenant against incumbrances. An incumbrance is any right to, or interest in, land which may subsist in a third party to the diminution of the value of the estate, but consistent with the passing of the fee by conveyance.

Subsection 3 sets forth the covenant of quiet enjoyment, which is synonymous with the covenant of warranty in Illinois. By this covenant, the grantor warrants to the grantee, his heirs and assigns, the possession of the premises and that he will defend the title granted by the terms of the deed against persons who may lawfully claim the same, and that such covenant shall be obligatory upon the grantor, his heirs, personal representatives, and assigns.

Plaintiffs' complaint is premised upon the fact that "William Roy Bost and Faith Bost covenanted that they were the owners in fee simple of the above described property at the time of the conveyance to the plaintiffs." While the complaint could be more explicit, it appears that plaintiffs were alleging a cause of action for breach of the covenant of seisin. This court has stated repeatedly that the covenant of seisin is a covenant In praesenti and, therefore, if broken at all, is broken at the time of delivery of the deed.

Since the deed was delivered to the plaintiffs on December 21, 1957, any cause of action for breach of the covenant of seisin would have accrued on that date. The trial court held that this cause of action was barred by the statute of limitations. No question is raised as to the applicability of the 10-year statute of limitations. We conclude, therefore, that the cause of action for breach of the covenant of seisin was properly determined by the trial court to be barred by the statute of limitations since plaintiffs did not file their complaint until May 25, 1976, nearly 20 years after their alleged cause of action accrued.

In their post-trial motion, plaintiffs set forth as an additional theory of recovery an alleged breach of the covenant of quiet enjoyment. The trial court, without explanation, denied the motion. The appellate court reversed, holding that the cause of action on the covenant of quiet enjoyment was not barred by the statute of limitations. The appellate court theorized that plaintiffs' cause of action did not accrue until 1976, when plaintiffs discovered that they only had a one-third interest in the subsurface coal rights and renegotiated their contract with the coal company for one-third of the previous contract price. The primary issue before us, therefore, is when, if at all, the plaintiffs' cause of action for breach of the covenant of quiet enjoyment is deemed to have accrued.

This court has stated on numerous occasions that, in contrast to the covenant of seisin, the covenant of warranty or quiet enjoyment is prospective in nature and is breached only when there is an actual or constructive eviction of the covenantee by the paramount titleholder.

The cases are also replete with statements to the effect that the mere existence of paramount title in one other than the covenantee is not sufficient to constitute a breach of the covenant of warranty or quiet enjoyment: There must be a union of acts of disturbance and lawful title, to constitute a breach of the covenant for quiet enjoyment, or warranty. There is a general concurrence that something more than the mere existence of a paramount title is necessary to constitute a breach of the covenant of warranty. *Scott v. Kirkendall* (1878). A mere want of title is no breach of this covenant. There must not only be a want of title, but there must be an ouster under a paramount title.

The question is whether plaintiffs have alleged facts sufficient to constitute a constructive eviction. They argue that if a covenantee fails in his effort to sell an interest in land because he discovers that he does not own what his warranty deed purported to convey, he has suffered a constructive eviction and is thereby entitled to bring an action against his grantor for breach of the covenant of quiet enjoyment. We think that the decision of this court in *Scott v. Kirkendall* is controlling on this issue and compels us to reject plaintiffs' argument.

In *Scott*, an action was brought for breach of the covenant of warranty by a grantee who discovered that other parties had paramount title to the land in question. The land was vacant and unoccupied at all relevant times. This court, in rejecting the grantee's claim that there was a breach of the covenant of quiet enjoyment, quoted the earlier decision in *Moore v. Vail* (1855):

> "Until that time, (the taking possession by the owner of the paramount title,) he might peaceably have entered upon and enjoyed the premises, without resistance or molestation, which was all his grantors covenanted he should do. They did not guarantee to him a perfect title, but the possession and enjoyment of the premises."

Relying on this language in *Moore*, the *Scott* court concluded: "We do not see but what this fully decides the present case against the appellant. It holds that the mere existence of a paramount title does not constitute a breach of the covenant. That is all there is here. There has been no assertion of the adverse title. The land has always been vacant. Appellant could at any time have taken peaceable possession of it. He has in no way been prevented or hindered from the enjoyment of the possession by any one having a better right. It was but the possession and enjoyment of the premises which was assured to him, and there has been no disturbance or interference in that respect. True, there is a superior title in another, but appellant has never 'felt its pressure upon him.'"

Admittedly, *Scott* dealt with surface rights while the case before us concerns subsurface mineral rights. We are, nevertheless, convinced that the reasoning employed in *Scott* is applicable to the present case. While plaintiffs went into possession of the surface area, they cannot be said to have possessed the subsurface minerals.

"Possession of the surface does not carry possession of the minerals. To possess the mineral estate, one must undertake the actual removal thereof from the ground or do such other act as will apprise the community that such interest is in the exclusive use and enjoyment of the claiming party."

Since no one has, as yet, undertaken to remove the coal or otherwise manifested a clear intent to exclusively "possess" the mineral estate, it must be concluded that the subsurface estate is "vacant." As in *Scott*, plaintiffs could at any time have taken peaceable possession of it. They have in no way been prevented or hindered from the enjoyment of the possession by any one having a better right. Accordingly, until such time as one holding paramount title interferes with plaintiffs' right of possession (E. g., by beginning to mine the coal), there can be no constructive eviction and, therefore, no breach of the covenant of quiet enjoyment.

What plaintiffs are apparently attempting to do on this appeal is to extend the protection afforded by the covenant of quiet enjoyment. However, we decline to expand the historical scope of this covenant to provide a remedy where another of the covenants of title is so clearly applicable. As this court stated in <u>Scott v. Kirkendall</u>:

> "To sustain the present action would be to confound all distinction between the covenant of warranty and that of seizin, or of right to convey. They are not equivalent covenants. An action will lie upon the latter, though there be no disturbance of possession. A defect of title will suffice. Not so with the covenant of warranty, or for quiet enjoyment, as has always been held by the prevailing authority."

The covenant of seisin, unquestionably, was breached when the Bosts delivered the deed to plaintiffs, and plaintiffs then had a cause of action. However, despite the fact that it was a matter of public record that there was a reservation of a two-thirds interest in the mineral rights in the earlier deed, plaintiffs failed to bring an action for breach of the covenant of seisin within the 10-year period following delivery of the deed. The likely explanation is that plaintiffs had not secured a title opinion at the time they purchased the property, and the subsequent examiners for the lenders were not concerned with the mineral rights. Plaintiffs' oversight, however, does not justify us in overruling earlier decisions in order to recognize an otherwise premature cause of action. The mere fact that plaintiffs' original contract with Consolidated had to be modified due to their discovery that paramount title to two-thirds of the subsurface minerals belonged to another is not sufficient to constitute the constructive eviction necessary to a breach of the covenant of quiet enjoyment.

Accordingly, the judgment of the appellate court is reversed, and the judgment of the circuit court of Montgomery County is affirmed.

## 2. Quitclaim Deed

Another form of deed is called a quitclaim deed – in which the seller conveys any interest the seller has in the land, but does not promise that the seller has any interest. If it turns out that the seller who used a quitclaim deed did not actually own the land, the buyer has no right to sue the seller. The buyer just takes the loss. The most appropriate use for quitclaim deeds is when there are some serious issues as to who actually owns the land, but no one wants to go to the expense of litigation. This frequently happens in family situations in which various people may have inherited various fractions of the title. Instead of going to the expense and delay of bringing an action to quiet title, all the potential owners just get together and quitclaim their various interests to one person. Then it is clear that that person owns the land – and the expense of litigation is avoided.

The doctrine of after-acquired title does not apply to quitclaim deeds.

Obviously, it is always important for a buyer's lawyer to check the title to the land before closing, to be sure that the buyer is getting the title for which the buyer has contracted.

The following sections of this chapter will illustrate some of the most important issues that may come up with regard to the sale of land.

## B. Boundaries – Accretion and Avulsion

The deed must accurately describe the boundaries of the land being conveyed. Usually this is a fairly straight-forward matter – just being careful to copy the legal description exactly from a prior deed, or from a survey, or from a plat (map) which will frequently be recorded when a developer takes a large piece of land, and divides it into many small parcels for individual home sites.

Yet there are forces of nature that may change these boundaries – without any human input - under some circumstances. If the land involved is bordered by water, then the doctrines of accretion and avulsion will probably apply.

A recent U.S. Supreme Court case describes these doctrines.

# SUPREME COURT OF THE UNITED STATES
# STOP THE BEACH RENOURISHMENT, INC.
## V.
# FLORIDA DEPARTMENT OF ENVIRONMENTAL PROTECTION
## ET AL.

JUNE 17, 2010

Justice SCALIA announced the judgment of the Court and delivered the opinion of the Court with respect to Parts I, IV, and V, and an opinion with respect to Parts II and III, in which THE CHIEF JUSTICE, Justice THOMAS, and Justice ALITO join.

We consider a claim that the decision of a State's court of last resort took property without just compensation in violation of the Takings Clause of the Fifth Amendment, as applied against the States through the Fourteenth, see *Dolan v. City of Tigard.*

## I

### A

Generally speaking, state law defines property interests, including property rights in navigable waters and the lands underneath them. In Florida, the State owns in trust for the public the land permanently submerged beneath navigable waters and the foreshore (the land between the low-tide line and the mean high-water line). Thus, the mean high-water line (the average reach of high tide over the preceding 19 years) is the ordinary boundary between private beachfront, or littoral [FN1] property, and state-owned land.

> FN1. Many cases and statutes use "riparian" to mean abutting any body of water. The Florida Supreme Court, however, has adopted a more precise usage whereby "riparian" means abutting a river or stream and "littoral" means abutting an ocean, sea, or lake. When speaking of the Florida law applicable to this case, we follow the Florida Supreme Court's terminology.

Littoral owners have, in addition to the rights of the public, certain "special rights" with regard to the water and the foreshore, rights which Florida considers to be property. These include the right of access to the water, the right to use the water for certain purposes, the right to an unobstructed view of the water, and the right to receive accretions and relictions to the littoral property. This is generally in accord with well-established common law, although the precise property rights vary among jurisdictions.

At the center of this case is the right to accretions and relictions. Accretions are additions of alluvion (sand, sediment, or other deposits) to waterfront land; relictions are lands once covered by water that become dry when the water recedes. (For simplicity's sake, we shall refer to accretions and relictions collectively as accretions, and the process whereby they occur as accretion.) In order for an addition to dry land to qualify as an accretion, it must have occurred gradually and imperceptibly-that is, so slowly that one could not see the change occurring, though over time the difference became apparent. When, on the other hand, there is a "sudden or perceptible loss of or addition to land by the action of the water or a sudden change in the bed of a lake or the course of a stream," the change is called an avulsion.

In Florida, as at common law, the littoral owner automatically takes title to dry land added to his property by accretion; but formerly submerged land that has become dry land by avulsion continues to belong to the owner of the seabed (usually the State). Thus, regardless of whether an avulsive event exposes land previously submerged or submerges land previously exposed, the boundary between littoral property and sovereign land does not change; it remains (ordinarily) what was the mean high-water line before the event. It follows from this that, when a new strip of land has been added to the shore by avulsion, the littoral owner has no right to subsequent accretions. Those accretions no longer add to *his* property, since the property abutting the water belongs not to him but to the State.

B

In 1961, Florida's Legislature passed the Beach and Shore Preservation Act. The Act establishes procedures for "beach restoration and nourishment projects," designed to deposit sand on eroded beaches (restoration) and to maintain the deposited sand (nourishment). A local government may apply to the Department of Environmental Protection for the funds and the necessary permits to restore a beach. When the project involves placing fill on the State's submerged lands, authorization is required from the Board of Trustees of the Internal Improvement Trust Fund, which holds title to those lands.

Once a beach restoration "is determined to be undertaken," the Board sets what is called "an erosion control line." It must be set by reference to the existing mean high-water line, though in theory it can be located seaward or landward of that. Much of the project work occurs seaward of the erosion-control line, as sand is dumped on what was once submerged land. The fixed erosion-control line replaces the fluctuating mean high-water line as the boundary between privately owned littoral property and state property. Once the erosion-control line is recorded, the common law ceases to increase upland property by accretion (or decrease it by erosion). Thus, when accretion to the shore moves the mean high-water line seaward, the property of beachfront landowners is not extended to that line (as the prior law provided), but remains bounded by the permanent erosion-control line. Those landowners "continue to be entitled," however, "to all common-law riparian rights" other than the right to accretions. If the beach erodes back landward of the erosion-control line over a substantial portion of the shoreline covered by the project, the Board may, on its own initiative, or must, if asked by the owners or lessees of a majority of the property affected, direct the agency responsible for maintaining the beach to return the beach to the condition contemplated by the project. If that is not done within a year, the project is canceled and the erosion-control line is null and void. Finally, by regulation, if the use of submerged land would "unreasonably infringe on riparian rights," the project cannot proceed unless the local governments show that they own or have a property interest in the upland property adjacent to the project site.

C

In 2003, the city of Destin, and Walton County, applied for the necessary permits to restore 6.9 miles of beach within their jurisdictions that had been eroded by several hurricanes. The project envisioned depositing along that shore sand dredged from further out. It would add about 75 feet of dry sand seaward of the mean high-water line (to be denominated the erosion-control line). The Department issued a notice of intent to award the permits, and the Board approved the erosion-control line.

The petitioner here, Stop the Beach Renourishment, Inc., is a nonprofit corporation formed by people who own beachfront property bordering the project area (we shall refer to them as the Members). It brought an administrative challenge to the proposed project, which was unsuccessful; the Department approved the permits. Petitioner then challenged that action in state court under the Florida Administrative Procedure Act. The District Court of Appeal for the First District concluded that, contrary to the Act's preservation of "all common-law riparian rights," the order had eliminated two of the Members' littoral rights: (1) the right to receive accretions to their property; and (2) the right to have the contact of their property with the water remain intact. This, it believed, would be an unconstitutional taking, which would "unreasonably infringe on riparian rights," and therefore require the showing under Fla. Admin. Code Rule 18-21.004(3)(b) that the local governments owned or had a property interest in the upland property. It set aside the Department's final order approving the permits and remanded for that showing to be made. It also certified to the Florida Supreme Court the following question (as rephrased by the latter court):

> "On its face, does the Beach and Shore Preservation Act unconstitutionally deprive upland owners of littoral rights without just compensation?"

The Florida Supreme Court answered the certified question in the negative, and quashed the First District's remand. It faulted the Court of Appeal for not considering the doctrine of avulsion, which it concluded permitted the State to reclaim the restored beach on behalf of the public. It described the right to accretions as a future contingent interest, not a vested property right, and held that there is no littoral right to contact with the water independent of the littoral right of access, which the Act does not infringe. We granted certiorari.

**[II & III are omitted – not enough votes]**

**IV**

We come at last to petitioner's takings attack on the decision below. At the outset, respondents raise two preliminary points which need not detain us long. The city and the county argue that petitioner cannot state a cause of action for a taking because, though the Members own private property, petitioner itself does not; and that the claim is unripe because petitioner has not sought just compensation. Neither objection appeared in the briefs in opposition to the petition for writ of certiorari, and since neither is jurisdictional, we deem both waived.

Petitioner argues that the Florida Supreme Court took two of the property rights of the Members by declaring that those rights did not exist: the right to accretions, and the right to have littoral property touch the water (which petitioner distinguishes from the mere right of access to the water). There is no taking unless petitioner can show that, before the Florida Supreme Court's decision, littoral-property owners had rights to future accretions and contact with the water superior to the State's right to fill in its submerged land. Though some may think the question close, in our view the showing cannot be made.

Two core principles of Florida property law intersect in this case. First, the State as owner of the submerged land adjacent to littoral property has the right to fill that land, so long as it does not interfere with the rights of the public and the rights of littoral landowners. Second, as we described *supra*, if an avulsion exposes land seaward of littoral property that had previously been submerged, that land belongs to the

State even if it interrupts the littoral owner's contact with the water. The issue here is whether there is an exception to this rule when the State is the cause of the avulsion. Prior law suggests there is not. In *Martin v. Busch*, (1927), the Florida Supreme Court held that when the State drained water from a lakebed belonging to the State, causing land that was formerly below the mean high-water line to become dry land, that land continued to belong to the State. This is not surprising, as there can be no accretions to land that no longer abuts the water.

Thus, Florida law as it stood before the decision below allowed the State to fill in its own seabed, and the resulting sudden exposure of previously submerged land was treated like an avulsion for purposes of ownership. The right to accretions was therefore subordinate to the State's right to fill.

The Florida Supreme Court decision before us is consistent with these background principles of state property law. Cf. *Lucas.* It did not abolish the Members' right to future accretions, but merely held that the right was not implicated by the beach-restoration project, because the doctrine of avulsion applied.

The result under Florida law may seem counter-intuitive. After all, the Members' property has been deprived of its character (and value) as oceanfront property by the State's artificial creation of an avulsion. Perhaps state-created avulsions ought to be treated differently from other avulsions insofar as the property right to accretion is concerned. But nothing in prior Florida law makes such a distinction. Even if there might be different interpretations of *Martin* and other Florida property-law cases that would prevent this arguably odd result, we are not free to adopt them. The Takings Clause only protects property rights as they are established under state law, not as they might have been established or ought to have been established. We cannot say that the Florida Supreme Court's decision eliminated a right of accretion established under Florida law.

Petitioner also contends that the State took the Members' littoral right to have their property continually maintain contact with the water. To be clear, petitioner does not allege that the State relocated the property line, as would have happened if the erosion-control line were *landward* of the old mean high-water line (instead of identical to it). Petitioner argues instead that the Members have a separate right for the boundary of their property to be always the mean high-water line. Petitioner points to dicta in *Sand Key* that refers to "the right to have the property's contact with the water remain intact." Even there, the right was included in the definition of the right to access, which is consistent with the Florida Supreme Court's later description that "there is no independent right of contact with the water" but it "exists to preserve the upland owner's core littoral right of access to the water." Petitioner's expansive interpretation of the dictum in *Sand Key* would cause it to contradict the clear Florida law governing avulsion. One cannot say that the Florida Supreme Court contravened established property law by rejecting it.[FN12]

> FN12. Petitioner also argues that the Members' other littoral rights have been infringed because the Act replaces their common-law rights with inferior statutory versions. Petitioner has not established that the statutory versions are inferior; and whether the source of a property right is the common law or a statute makes no difference, so long as the property owner continues to have what he previously had.

# V

Because the Florida Supreme Court's decision did not contravene the established property rights of petitioner's Members, Florida has not violated the Fifth and Fourteenth Amendments. The judgment of the Florida Supreme Court is therefore affirmed.

*It is so ordered.*

## C. Recording Acts

There are three basic types of recording acts in use in the United States – each designed to make it easier for a potential buyer to find out whether or not the potential seller actually has title to the land. Each type of recording act is designed to encourage a purchaser of land to record the deed promptly, in the public records. It is easiest to understand how the recording acts work if you imagine that a dishonest seller, O, sells the land three different times to three different purchasers, A, B, and C. Then the dishonest seller takes off for Argentina. So the problem becomes, who actually owns the land? One purchaser will be protected by the recording act. The other two purchasers will simply be out a great deal of money – with no recourse - unless they can somehow track down O and sue O successfully.

### 1. Pure Race Recording Acts.

The easiest, clearest form of recording act is the *Pure Race* recording Act. As between the three innocent purchasers, A, B, and C, the first buyer to *record* his or her deed owns the land. Unfortunately, only a very few states in the southeast have Pure Race recording acts. The other states are about equally divided between the other two forms of recording acts – *Notice*, and *Race-Notice*.

## 2. Notice Recording Acts

Under a *Notice* recording act, the *last* buyer who buys without notice of any prior buyer from the same grantor, wins against all other buyers – as soon as that purchaser gets the deed. If the first purchaser, A, does not record the deed, and then the second buyer, B, buys the same land from the same seller, and B buys without notice of the deed to A, then B will beat A - immediately - because B was the last one to buy without notice of any prior deed. Then B needs to get down to the clerk's office *promptly* to record his deed - or C, the third purchaser, will take title away from B. Once B has recorded, B is safe, because no subsequent buyer can buy without notice of B's deed, which has been properly recorded. It does not matter which deed was delivered to a purchaser first. The *last* of the several purchasers who *buys without notice* of any prior deed wins the land under a *Notice* recording act.

## 3. Race-Notice Recording Acts

The third standard form of recording act is the *Race-Notice* recording act. Under this type of recording act a buyer must take two steps to be protected by the recording act. First, the buyer must buy without notice of any prior deed from the same grantor. Second, the buyer must win the race to the clerk's office, and record the deed prior to any other deed from the same grantor being recorded. If B buys without notice of A's prior deed, but then A is the first to record, then B will not be protected by the recording act, because B did not complete the *two* steps necessary – buying without notice *and* being the first to record.

So once again, it is very important for any purchaser of land to record the deed promptly.

In a situation where a state's recording act does not cover the exact situation involved – for example, in a Race-Notice state when B buys without notice, but A records before B records, then the default provision is simply "first in time, first in right," so the first purchaser, A, would win, because B did not successfully complete the two steps necessary under a *Race-Notice* statute – buying without notice *and* recording first.

Note: The next case illustrates how important it is to check the records!

O

A —> ✗ in 1899     *doesn't show
1900                    in title search*
B —> 2000  Z owns by AP

C

D

## SUPREME COURT OF NEBRASKA
# JEREMY L. KLEIN AND KIMBERLY J. KLEIN, HUSBAND AND WIFE, AND ROBERT D. LYNCH AND ELAINE M. LYNCH, HUSBAND AND WIFE, APPELLEES,
## V.
# OAKLAND/RED OAK HOLDINGS, LLC, APPELLANT

### AUGUST 26, 2016

[Background facts for this case: Evidently the original landowner was having financial difficulties, and therefore had not made the necessary tax payments or mortgage
payments. So because of the non-payment of taxes the land was sold by the appropriate governmental entity, and on July 25, 2013 a _Treasurer's tax deed_ was issued, and
Vandelay investments became the owner of the land. That _Treasurer's tax deed_ was
properly recorded on August 1, 2013.

Thereafter, foreclosure on the mortgage took place, resulting in the sale of the land for
the benefit of the lender, Oakland. That sale resulted in a _Trustee's_ deed being issued to
plaintiffs, after they had paid $40,001.00 for the _Trustee's_ deed.

When plaintiffs discovered that in fact no title passed by means of the _Trustee's_ deed,
they sued to get their $40,0001.00 back from Oakland.]

Miller–Lerman, J.

Plaintiffs filed their complaint against Oakland on January 21, 2014. They alleged
that at the time of the trustee's sale, Oakland had no interest in the land described
in _trustee's_ deed and, therefore, no interest in the real property. The plaintiffs alleged
that they were owed $40,001 plus interest. They did not allege in their complaint a
specific basis for recovery, such as rescission due to mistake or unjust enrichment
because of a failure of consideration; accident; inadvertence; mutual mistake; relief
from caveat emptor based on fraud, misrepresentation, or mistake; or constructive
fraud.

On April 3, 2015, the district court filed an order in which it found in favor of the
plaintiffs and against Oakland. Oakland appeals.

## ANALYSIS

Oakland argues that the district court erred when it determined that the trustee's
sale was void and ordered Oakland to return the $40,001 purchase price to the plain-
tiffs. Oakland generally argues that caveat emptor should apply and that when the

plaintiffs purchased the *trustee's* deed, they were on record notice of the *treasurer's tax deed* that was issued to Vandelay Investments and recorded prior to the trustee's sale. We agree, and we reverse the decision of the district court.

We have noted that Nebraska's recording act, set forth in <u>Neb. Rev. Stat. § 76–238</u>, is intended to impart to a prospective purchaser notice of instruments which affect the title of land in which such a purchaser is interested. <u>Section 76–238(1)</u> provides:

> Except as otherwise provided in sections 76–3413 to 76–3415, all deeds, mortgages, and other instruments of writing which are required to be or which under the laws of this state may be recorded, shall take effect and be in force from and after the time of delivering such instruments to the register of deeds for recording, and not before, as to all creditors and subsequent purchasers in good faith without notice. All such instruments are void as to all creditors and subsequent purchasers without notice whose deeds, mortgages, or other instruments are recorded prior to such instruments. However, such instruments are valid between the parties to the instrument.

<u>Section 76–238(1)</u> is a "race-notice recording statute."

We have stated that "a purchaser of real estate is required to take notice of instruments properly placed of record in the office of the register of deeds. Increased diligence, alertness, and scrutiny in searching for the facts are expected of a purchaser who accepts a deed that is less than a general warranty with full covenants of ownership and title."

In Nebraska, we have long held that the doctrine of caveat emptor applies to judicial sales. With respect to the application of caveat emptor to judicial sales, we have stated:

> "It is a well-settled rule that the doctrine of *caveat emptor* applies to all judicial sales, subject to the qualification that the purchaser is entitled to relief on the ground of after-discovered mistake of material facts or fraud, where he is free from negligence. He is bound to examine the title, and not rely upon statements made by the officer conducting the sale, as to its condition. If he buys without such examination, he does so at his peril, and must suffer the loss occasioned by his neglect."

We have not previously stated that the doctrine of caveat emptor applies to nonjudicial sales, such as a trustee's sale. However, other jurisdictions have applied caveat emptor in nonjudicial sales. Regarding the application of caveat emptor in the context of trustee's sales, it has been recognized that:

"many courts apply a *caveat emptor* approach to title or physical defects in the real estate. As one court stated: "To the bidders the trustee owes no duty except to refrain from doing anything to hamper them in their search for information or to prevent the discovery of defects by inspection. He is under no duty to make representations or to answer questions; but if questions are asked and he undertakes to answer, then such answers must be full and accurate—nothing must then be concealed."1 Grant S. Nelson et al., *Real Estate Finance Law* § 7.22 at 979 (6th ed. 2014).

In *Michie v. National Bank of Caruthersville,* the court stated in a trustee's deed case that "a purchaser at a foreclosure sale buys under the doctrine of caveat emptor ... and the purchaser- is required to take notice of everything in the recorded chain of title." In discussing caveat emptor, the U.S. Supreme Court has stated:

"The doctrine of caveat emptor, substantially as we have stated it, is laid down in numerous adjudications. Where the means of information are at hand and equally open to both parties, and no concealment is made or attempted, the language of the cases is, that there is no ground for a court of equity to refuse to enforce the contract of the parties. The neglect of the purchaser to avail himself, in all such cases, of the means of information, whether attributable to his indolence or credulity, takes from him all just claim for relief." *Slaughter's Administrator v. Gerson,* (1871).

In accordance with these other jurisdictions and authorities noted above, just as we have applied the doctrine of caveat emptor in judicial sales, we now hold that the doctrine of caveat emptor applies in trustee's sales.

The parties in this case stipulated that they "do not dispute the validity of" the *treasurer's tax deed* that was issued to Vandelay Investments. Accordingly, pursuant to *Knosp,* the *treasurer's tax deed* that was issued to Vandelay Investments passed title free and clear of all previous liens and encumbrances, including the *trust* deed at issue in this case. Therefore, at the time of the trustee's sale on October 2, 2013, the *trust* deed conveyed no title due to the prior issuance of the *treasurer's tax deed.*

As set forth above, the record shows that the *treasurer's tax deed* issued to Vandelay Investments was recorded prior to the trustee's sale. The parties stipulated that neither party had "received actual knowledge" of the issuance of the *treasurer's tax deed*; however, the parties further agreed that the *treasurer's tax deed* "was a matter of public record at the time of the trustee's sale of the real estate." Because the *treasurer's tax deed* was recorded before the trustee's sale was held, the plaintiffs were on record notice of the *treasurer's tax deed.*

The plaintiffs in this case sought relief from entering into a deal with an unfavorable outcome. We have determined that the doctrine of caveat emptor applies in this case. [Under the doctrine of caveat emptor, the purchaser "is bound to examine the title" and if the purchaser buys without such examination, he does so at his peril, and must suffer the loss occasioned by his neglect.] In this case, had the plaintiffs examined the title, they would have realized that the treasurer's tax deeds had been issued and that the trust deed therefore could convey no title. In taking such steps to examine the chain of title, the plaintiffs would have protected themselves from entering into an unfortunate deal. We have stated that a purchaser of real estate is required to take notice of instruments properly placed of record in the office of the register of deeds. Because the plaintiffs failed to examine title before bidding at the trustee's sale, they must suffer the loss occasioned by their own inattention.

We have stated that equity will not relieve a purchaser of his own negligence, stating that ["a court of equity will not undertake, any more than a court of law, to relieve a party from the consequences of his own inattention and carelessness.] Therefore, we determine that the district court erred when it relieved the plaintiffs of the consequences of their inattention. We reverse the decision of the district court and remand the cause with directions that the district court enter judgment in favor of Oakland and dismiss the plaintiffs' complaint.

REVERSED AND REMANDED WITH DIRECTIONS.

### Lis Pendens

Note: As soon as litigation over the ownership of land begins, it is important to record a *notice of lis pendens* – to put any potential buyer on notice that ownership of the land is in dispute. The following case illustrates some of the rules with regard to a notice of lis pendens.

# RON SOMMERS, AS CHAPTER 7 TRUSTEE FOR ALABAMA AND DUNLAVY, LTD., FLAT STONE II, LTD., AND FLAT STONE, LTD., AND AS SUCCESSOR IN INTEREST TO JAY COHEN, INDIVIDUALLY AND AS TRUSTEE OF THE JHC TRUSTS I AND II, PETITIONER,
## V.
# SANDCASTLE HOMES, INC., AND NEWBISS, RESPONDENTS

JUNE 16, 2017

## Opinion

Justice Brown delivered the opinion of the Court.

Today we must decide just how much notice is "erased" or "destroyed" when a statute expunges a notice of pending litigation, or lis pendens. Sandcastle Homes, Inc., and NewBiss Property, LP, each bought real property involved in a title dispute.

Pending the outcome of an action involving proper title to, establishing an interest in, or enforcing an encumbrance against real property, the party seeking relief may file a notice of lis pendens in the county's real-property records. A notice of lis pendens broadcasts "to the world" the existence of ongoing litigation regarding ownership of the property. When the notice is properly filed, even a subsequent purchaser for value does not take the property free and clear.

We have explained that a lis pendens functions to provide constructive notice, avoid undue alienation of property, and facilitate an end to litigation. The latter two purposes are particularly implicated when we address the court's ability to *expunge* a notice of lis pendens. The trial court may expunge a notice of lis pendens if (1) the pleading on which the original order rests does not include a real-property claim; (2) the claimant does not appropriately establish the probable validity of his real-property claim; or (3) the claimant fails to serve a copy of the record notice on all entitled to receive it. Here, Sandcastle obtained the first expunction order because the trial court found Cohen's pleadings did not include a real-property claim, while the second order was based on Cohen's inability to establish the probable validity of his claim.

This case is a question of first impression for this Court—one of statutory interpretation.

Today the parties ask us to decide one basic question: When a notice of lis pendens is expunged, is all notice—no matter the sort and no matter its source—extinguished with the expunction order?

Property Code section 12.0071 allows a lis pendens to be expunged and details the expunction's effects:

After a certified copy of an order expunging a notice of lis pendens has been recorded, the notice of lis pendens and any information derived from the notice:

> (1) does not:
>> (A) constitute constructive or actual notice of any matter contained in the notice or of any matter relating to the proceeding;
>> (B) create any duty of inquiry in a person with respect to the property described in the notice; or
>> (C) affect the validity of a conveyance to a purchaser for value or of a mortgage to a lender for value; and
>
> (2) is not enforceable against a purchaser or lender described by Subdivision (1)(C), regardless of whether the purchaser or lender knew of the lis pendens action.

TEX. PROP. CODE § 12.0071(f)(1)–(2).

Cohen's primary contention before the court of appeals was that Sandcastle and NewBiss could not conclusively establish their bona-fide-purchaser affirmative defense because they had separate notice of the claim on the property—disqualifying knowledge obtained by means independent of the lis pendens filing. Such knowledge, Cohen urged, could not be effectively undermined by the expunction statute because independent actual notice does not constitute information contained in "the notice of lis pendens" or "any information derived from the notice."

The court of appeals rejected what it saw as a narrow view of the statute and instead advanced a bright-line rule that the expunction of notice includes *any notice* of the claims involved in the underlying suit covered by the lis pendens. But the court of appeals reads the plain text of the statute too broadly. We agree with the dissenting justice that "the statute simply doesn't address the circumstance of a purchaser who receives notice of a third-party claim by some means other than a recorded notice of lis pendens."

Property Code section 12.0071(f) provides that a purchaser cannot be charged with record notice, actual or constructive, following a proper expungement. But the extent of that protection is expressly limited to "the notice of lis pendens" and "any information derived from the notice." By negative implication, expunction is given no effect with respect to the universe of other information, not included in the scope of section 12.0071(f), that is neither (a) the notice of lis pendens itself nor (b) information derived from the notice of lis pendens.

The expunction statute specifically instructs that the recorded notice is expunged.

The fact that subpart (f) of section 12.0071 expressly precludes enforcement of the notice and information derived from the notice against a purchaser or lender "regardless of whether the purchaser or lender knew of the lis pendens action" merely confirms that the Legislature meant to address both actual and constructive notice arising from the lis pendens filing and the information contained in that notice. We decline to construe the provision to mean that *any* information coextensive with the information contained in the notice or the underlying litigation that may be obtained independently is also legally eradicated. Such separate means of notice is necessarily unrelated to the actual expungement and exceeds the reach expressed by the statutory language.

Accordingly, to the extent the recorded lis pendens puts a potential buyer on inquiry notice to look to the actual lawsuit before the notice's expunction, that buyer could claim protection under the statute. Any actual awareness obtained by review of the facts referred to in the lis pendens cannot be used to rebut that purchaser's status as a bona-fide purchaser or to continue to burden the property. But that does not mean the expunction statute can be read so far as to eradicate notice arising independently of the recorded instrument expunged.

Expunction of the lis pendens is a restoration of the chain of title free of the record notice of a potential claim of interest associated with the lis pendens. It is not an adjudication of a later purchaser's status as a bona-fide purchaser under any set of circumstances.

Cohen alleges that both Sandcastle and NewBiss had actual, independent knowledge of the issues covered by the lis pendens notice. Whether that is true is an unresolved fact issue precluding summary judgment. In light of Cohen's allegation, Sandcastle and NewBiss have not established bona-fide-purchaser status simply by relying on the expungement order.

We reverse the court of appeals' judgment and remand to the trial court for further proceedings consistent with this opinion.

Note: The *Shelter Rule*, illustrated by the following case, is an important limitation on the efficacy of a properly recorded *notice of lis pendens*.

# COURT OF APPEALS OF COLORADO
## JOHN STREKAL, PLAINTIFF-APPELLANT
## V.
## DWIGHT E. ESPE AND DOROTHY B. ESPE, DEFENDANTS-APPELLEES

DECEMBER 16, 2004

OPINION BY: RUSSEL

OPINION

Plaintiff, John Strekal, appeals the trial court's order granting summary judgment in favor of defendants, Dwight E. and Dorothy B. Espe. We affirm, although on grounds different from those relied on by the trial court.

According to the complaint, Strekal and his wife bought a house from Lee Crow in 1994, taking title in joint tenancy. In January 1996, Strekal's wife died, leaving Strekal the sole owner. In November 1996, Crow convinced Strekal to convey the property to her, promising that she would correct defects in the title and then reconvey the property to Strekal.

Crow did not reconvey the property. Instead, she forcibly evicted Strekal and kept his personal belongings. Crow later conveyed the house to David Masters.

In March 1999, Strekal filed suit against Crow, seeking money damages for fraud. Strekal did not name Masters, who then owned the property, as a defendant. The court entered default judgment against Crow, awarding Strekal $ 84,000 as compensation for the loss of the house and an additional sum for the loss of his personal property.

In October 1999, Strekal filed the present action, seeking the return of the house. As defendants, Strekal named Crow, Masters, and two lenders: Pacific Rim Financial Service, which had acquired a deed of trust from Masters, and Utah Mortgage Center, Inc., which later acquired the assets of Pacific Rim. Strekal also recorded a notice of lis pendens on the property.

In November 1999, Utah Mortgage acquired title by foreclosing on the Masters deed of trust.

In May 2000, Utah Mortgage sold the house to Dwight and Dorothy Espe. The court allowed Strekal to amend his complaint to name the Espes as defendants.

In November 2000, the court dismissed Strekal's action against the lenders for failure to state a claim and awarded attorney fees against Strekal and his lawyers.

A division of this court affirmed the award of attorney fees against the lawyers. Another division affirmed the judgment in favor of the lenders and the award of attorney fees against Strekal.

After the dismissal of Strekal's claims against the lenders, this action proceeded against the Espes. Strekal claimed that he could recover the house under Colorado's stolen property statute, § 18-4-405, C.R.S. 2004. The Espes moved for summary judgment, arguing that Strekal's claim was barred by res judicata and the statute of limitations. In a separate motion, the Espes argued that Strekal could not recover the house because the stolen property statute does not apply when the underlying theft is accomplished by fraud or deception.

The trial court granted summary judgment on the basis of res judicata. It did not address the statute of limitations or the scope of the stolen property statute.

Strekal now appeals from the order granting summary judgment.

## Part I. Res Judicata

Strekal contends that res judicata does not bar the present action. We agree.

Res judicata is the doctrine of claim preclusion. The doctrine bars claims that were litigated, or could have been litigated, in an earlier action that resulted in a final judgment on the merits. Under this doctrine, a final judgment is considered conclusive in any subsequent litigation that involves (1) the same claim for relief, (2) the same subject matter, and (3) the same parties or those in privity with them.

Strekal resists claim preclusion on the ground that the Espes were not parties to the first action. This argument requires us to consider the concept of privity, for claim preclusion is not limited to cases in which the parties are identical; it also may be invoked by and against those in privity with the parties.

"Privity" means that a nonparty is related to a case in such a way that he or she should be regarded as a party.

After examining the record, we find no support for the trial court's conclusion that the Espes are in privity with Crow. The Espes are not in privity as Crow's successors because Crow sold the house before Strekal commenced his first lawsuit.

We therefore conclude that the trial court erred in granting summary judgment on the basis of res judicata.

## Part II. Stolen Property and the *Recording Act*

Arguing in the alternative, the Espes contend that summary judgment was proper because one cannot bring an action to recover property under § 18-4-405 when the underlying theft was accomplished by fraud or deception.

Although the Espes raised this argument in the trial court, they did so only shortly before the court ruled on summary judgment. Consequently, Strekal did not respond to this argument in the trial court, and the court did not consider it. Nevertheless, we may address it here.

Both parties briefed this issue on appeal. And, at our request, both sides filed supplemental briefs addressing these related questions:

> Assuming that § 18-4-405 generally authorizes actions to recover property obtained by fraud, (1) does § 18-4-405 negate the protections accorded to good faith buyers of real estate under Colorado's *recording act*; and (2) are the Espes protected as good faith buyers under the recording act?

We now affirm the summary judgment on this alternative ground. Assuming, without deciding, that § 18-4-405 permits recovery of property obtained by fraud or deception in some circumstances, it does not permit recovery of real property so obtained when record title is held by a good faith purchaser. And we conclude that the Espes are good faith purchasers protected by *Colorado's recording act.*

### Part A. Pertinent Statutes

Rights in Stolen Property

Since 1861, Colorado has had a stolen property statute similar to § 18-4-405. Until 1967, that statute authorized recovery of property taken only by larceny, robbery, or burglary:

> All property obtained by larceny, robbery, or burglary shall be restored to the owner, and no sale, whether in good faith on the part of the purchaser or not, shall divest the owner of his right to such property. Such owner may maintain his action not only against the felon, but against any person in whose possession he may find the same.
> Colo. Sess. Laws 1967, ch. 312, § 40-5-12 at 575.

In 1967, the legislature introduced the crime of theft into the criminal code. The new crime merged larceny with other offenses, including false pretenses:

> Wherever any law of this state refers to or mentions larceny, stealing, embezzlement (except embezzlement of public moneys), false pretenses, confidence game, or shoplifting, said law shall be interpreted as if the word "theft" were substituted therefor.
> Colo. Sess. Laws 1967, ch. 312, § 40-5-2(4).

The purpose of this change was to remove technical distinctions that had frustrated the prosecution of property crimes.

At the same time, the legislature made conforming amendments to many related statutes. In the stolen property statute, the legislature changed the word "larceny" to "theft." The current version of the statute reflects this change:

> "All property obtained by theft, robbery, or burglary shall be restored to the owner, and no sale, whether in good faith on the part of the purchaser or not, shall divest the owner of his right to such property. The owner may maintain an action not only against the taker thereof, but also against any person in whose possession he finds the property."
> *Section 18-4-405.*

### Recording Act

Colorado has had a *recording act* ever since the first territorial legislature met in 1861. Although it has evolved over the years, the act has retained this essential feature: it will protect a good faith purchaser with a record interest in real property over someone who has an unrecorded interest in the same property.

The current version of the act provides, in pertinent part:

> "All deeds, powers of attorney, agreements, or other instruments in writing conveying, encumbering, or affecting the title to real property, certificates, and certified copies of orders, judgments, and decrees of courts of record may be recorded in the office of the county clerk and recorder of the county where such real property is situated . No such unrecorded instrument or document shall be valid against any person with any kind of rights in or to such real property who first records and those holding rights under such person, except between the parties thereto and against those having notice thereof prior to acquisition of such rights. This is a race notice recording statute." *Section 38-35-109(1), C.R.S. 2004.*

This act protects purchasers by giving them notice of real estate ownership and providing an accessible history of title.

## B. Parties' Arguments

The parties recognize an apparent tension between the *stolen property* statute and the *recording act.*

Under the *stolen property* statute, Strekal appears to have the superior right: the statute expressly allows an owner to recover against good faith purchasers. And the 1967 amendment -- allowing recovery for property obtained by "theft" -- suggests that an owner may be able to recover even when the property was obtained by fraud or deception. Strekal contends that the 1967 amendment implicitly repealed protections accorded to good faith purchasers of real property under the recording act, and he urges us to resolve this case by simple reliance on the plain language of § 18-4-405.

Under the *recording act*, the Espes appear to have the superior right: they have a recorded interest in the house, while Strekal does not. And Colorado courts have recognized that a prior recorded interest is superior to the rights of an owner who was the victim of fraudulent or deceptive conduct. The Espes contend that the stolen property statute did not abrogate any part of the *recording act*. They argue that the house -- voluntarily conveyed by Strekal under fraudulent circumstances, and subsequently conveyed to a good faith purchaser -- is not "property obtained by theft," within the meaning of § 18-4-405.

We agree with the Espes.

## C. Analysis

In *Keybank v. Mascarenas, (Colo. App. 2000)*, a division of this court confronted an apparent conflict between the stolen property statute and a provision of the Uniform Commercial Code (UCC), § 4-2-403. In that case, owners entrusted their cars to a dealer so that he could sell them on consignment. The dealer sold the cars to good faith buyers, but he fraudulently kept the money instead of remitting it to the owners. When the county clerk and recorder learned of the fraudulent activity, she refused to transfer record title to the cars. This prompted a suit between a lender that wanted to record liens on the titles and the former owners, who wanted their cars back.

In resolving this dispute, the division first noted that the buyers were protected under § 4-2-403. That statute provides, in effect, that if an owner entrusts property to a merchant who customarily sells that kind of goods, the merchant has authority to transfer all of the owner's rights to a buyer in the ordinary course of business.

The division next concluded that the stolen property statute does not defeat the protections of § 4-2-403. The division observed that § 4-2-403 maintains the traditional distinction between ordinary theft, in which the owner is unaware of a physical taking, and fraud or larceny by trick. Thus, within the meaning of § 4-2-403, entrustment cannot occur through ordinary theft, but it does occur if an owner voluntarily surrenders property under fraudulent circumstances. And if an entrustment occurs, the merchant can transfer good title to a buyer in the ordinary course of business.

Accordingly, held the division, the stolen property statute was inapplicable:

> "We therefore conclude that 'theft' as used in § 18-4-405 does not encompass a larceny by trick or fraud, even if punishable under the criminal law, in which a person voluntarily delivers possession of his or her property under an agreement, giving the perpetrator authority to sell it under the UCC."

Strekal argues that *Keybank* is inapposite because the real property at issue in this case stands outside the scope of § 4-2-403. Although Strekal is right about the applicability of *Keybank's* narrow holding, he is wrong about the value of its underlying observations. *Keybank* is instructive because it addresses an apparent conflict between the stolen property statute and a provision in the UCC, and resolves that conflict by recognizing an implicit limitation in the stolen property statute. We are persuaded that the apparent conflict between the *stolen property statute* and the *recording act* should be resolved in a similar manner.

We begin by stating the obvious: the security and marketability of real estate titles is an "essential state interest." This interest is best served by a bright line rule that enables potential buyers to determine the validity of a title and its potential encumbrances. The *recording act* is an essential part of a scheme "intended to ensure titles to real property are secure and marketable."

Accordingly, we will give full effect to the *recording act* absent the clearest expression of contrary legislative intent. We will not presume that the legislature intended to eliminate longstanding and substantial features of real estate law merely by changing provisions located in the criminal code.

We see no indication that, when the legislature amended the *stolen property statute* in 1967, it intended to abrogate the provisions and principles that have served to ensure the basic marketability of real estate titles. Thus, in our view, Colorado law still recognizes the distinction between title obtained by force or forgery, which will not trigger protections of the *recording act*, and title obtained by trick or fraud, which will.

Generally, a bona fide purchaser will acquire title over a prior owner. However, when the initial deed is void, as in the case of a forged deed, title cannot pass to the subsequent purchaser, and, as a result, the defrauded owner prevails.

We therefore conclude that the *stolen property statute* does not authorize recovery against a good faith purchaser who holds record title to real property earlier conveyed under fraudulent circumstances.

## D. Application Here

We now address whether the Espes are good faith purchasers protected by the *recording act.*

To be a good faith purchaser of real property, one must give value for the property, act in good faith, and lack notice of any defect in the title to the property. Whether a party is a good faith purchaser is a question of fact.

Here, the parties do not dispute the pertinent facts. Rather, they dispute the legal significance of one uncontested fact: the Espes acquired their interest after Strekal filed the notice of lis pendens. Under these circumstances, we may conduct the applicable legal inquiry to determine whether the Espes are good faith purchasers.

Strekal contends that the notice of lis pendens bars the Espes from gaining the status of good faith purchasers. The Espes contend that the notice of lis pendens does not matter because they gained the status of good faith purchasers under the "shelter rule." We agree with the Espes.

The "Shelter Rule" provides that one who is not a bona fide purchaser, but who takes an interest in property from a bona fide purchaser, may be sheltered in the latter's protective status. The rule is a venerable principle of Colorado property law. The rule exists to protect the marketability of title.

There are two exceptions to the shelter rule. First, when a good faith purchaser obtains the property from a grantor who had notice of an outstanding interest in the property, the shelter rule does not apply if the property is reconveyed to the grantor. Second, the shelter rule does not apply if the property is reconveyed from a good faith purchaser to a person who is guilty of violating a trust or duty with respect to the property. Neither of these exceptions applies here.

Therefore, the Espes will prevail if they acquired their interest from a good faith purchaser who took without notice of a potential defect in the title. And it is clear that the Espes acquired their rights under a chain of title that included a good faith purchaser without notice.

After acquiring the property from Strekal, Lee Crow conveyed the property to David Masters by deed. At the same time, Masters gave his lender, Pacific Rim

Financial Service, a deed of trust on the property. Strekal has never suggested that Pacific Rim had notice of any potential defect in title before it acquired or recorded its deed of trust. (Although Strekal named Pacific Rim as a defendant in this action, his claims were dismissed for failure to state a claim.) Therefore, Pacific Rim was a good faith purchaser who took without notice.

Pacific Rim was subsequently dissolved, and its assets, including the deed of trust from Masters, were acquired by Utah Mortgage Center, Inc. Because Pacific Rim was a good faith purchaser without notice, Utah Mortgage acquired the status of a good faith purchaser without notice under the shelter rule.

Thus, when the Espes bought the property from Utah Mortgage, following foreclosure of the Masters deed of trust, they acquired the status of good faith purchasers without notice under the shelter rule, even though they took with notice of the lis pendens.

For this reason, we conclude that Strekal cannot recover under § 18-4-405 against the Espes' recorded interest.

The judgment is affirmed.

Note: **Caveat:** Remember, there are at least two very important matters about land ownership and use that will never show up in the public records – no matter how carefully the records are searched. One of these matters is the possibility of adverse possession, which was covered in Chapter 1. Regardless of who appears to own the land, based on the documents that have been properly recorded, the actual legal title may be in someone entirely different, who has secured ownership of the land by adverse possession. Usually there will be absolutely nothing in the public records to indicate that the record title has in fact been lost to an adverse possessor, whose name appears nowhere in the public records.

Another very important matter that will not appear of record is restrictions on the use of land that are the result of an *implied reciprocal negative easement*, which will be described in Chapter 6.

## D. Equitable Conversion

At the beginning of this chapter there was discussion of the time interval that usually exists between the time a contract of sale is signed by the parties, and the actual closing – when the buyer pays the money and the seller conveys the deed to the land. This interval of time is frequently referred to either as the *gap*, or as the *executory period*. Sometimes there is serious damage to the property during the executory period. Then who takes the loss – the buyer or the seller?

Different states have different rules on this, but the following case illustrates the problem.

### SUPREME COURT OF COLORADO
### PETITIONER: BRUSH GROCERY KART, INC.,
### V.
### RESPONDENT: SURE FINE MARKET, INC.,

JUNE 3, 2002

**JUSTICE COATS delivered the Opinion of the Court.**

Brush Grocery Kart, Inc. sought review of the court of appeals' judgment affirming the district court's determination of Brush's obligation on an option contract to purchase a building from Sure Fine Market, Inc. The district court found that Brush was not entitled to a price abatement for damages caused by a hail storm that occurred during litigation between the parties over the purchase price of the property. The court of appeals affirmed on the grounds that equitable title to the property vested in Brush when it exercised its option to purchase, whether or not it also had a right of possession, and therefore Brush bore the risk of any casualty loss after that time. Because we hold that Brush was entitled to specific performance of the contract with an abatement of the purchase price reflecting the casualty loss, the judgment of the court of appeals is reversed.

## FACTUAL AND PROCEDURAL HISTORY

In October 1992 Brush Grocery Kart, Inc. and Sure Fine Market, Inc. entered into a five-year "Lease with Renewal Provisions and Option to Purchase" for real property, including a building to be operated by Brush as a grocery store. Under the contract's purchase option provision, any time during the last six months of the lease, Brush could elect to purchase the property at a price equal to the average of the appraisals of an expert designated by each party.

Shortly before expiration of the lease, Brush notified Sure Fine of its desire to purchase the property and begin the process of determining a sale price. Although each party offered an appraisal, the parties were unable to agree on a final price by the time the lease expired. Brush then vacated the premises, returned all keys to Sure

Fine, and advised Sure Fine that it would discontinue its casualty insurance covering the property during the lease. Brush also filed suit, alleging that Sure Fine failed to negotiate the price term in good faith and asking for the appointment of a special master to determine the purchase price. Sure Fine agreed to the appointment of a special master and counterclaimed, alleging that Brush negotiated the price term in bad faith and was therefore the breaching party.

During litigation over the price term, the property was substantially damaged during a hail storm. With neither party carrying casualty insurance, each asserted that the other was liable for the damage. The issue was added to the litigation at a stipulated amount of $ 60,000. The court appointed a special master pursuant to C.R.C.P. 53 and accepted his appraised value of $ 375,000. The court then found that under the doctrine of equitable conversion, Brush was the equitable owner of the property and bore the risk of loss. It therefore declined to abate the purchase price or award damages to Brush for the loss.

Brush appealed the loss allocation, and the court of appeals affirmed on similar grounds. It considered the prior holdings of this court acknowledging the doctrine of equitable conversion and found that in *Wiley v. Lininger, (1949)*, that doctrine was applied to allocate the risk of casualty loss occurring during the executory period of a contract for the purchase of real property. Relying heavily on language from the opinion purporting to adopt the "majority rule," the court of appeals found that our characterization of the rule as placing the risk of casualty loss on a vendee who "is in possession," reflected merely the facts of that case rather than any intent to limit the rule to vendees who are actually in possession. Noting that allocation of the risk of loss in circumstances where the vendee is not in possession had not previously been addressed by an appellate court in this jurisdiction, the court of appeals went on to conclude that a "bright line rule" allocating the risk of loss to the vendee, without regard to possession, would best inform the parties of their rights and obligations under a contract for the sale of land.

Brush petitioned for a writ of certiorari to determine the proper allocation of the risk of loss and the appropriate remedy under these circumstances. Where no statute controls, interests in real property must be determined by reference to the common law.

## THE RISK OF CASUALTY LOSS IN THE ABSENCE OF STATUTORY AUTHORITY

In the absence of statutory authority, the rights, powers, duties, and liabilities arising out of a contract for the sale of land have frequently been derived by reference to the theory of equitable conversion. This theory or doctrine, which has been described as a legal fiction, is based on equitable principles that permit the vendee to be considered the equitable owner of the land and debtor for the purchase money and the vendor to be regarded as a secured creditor. The changes in rights and liabilities that occur upon the making of the contract result from the equitable right to specific performance. Even with regard to third parties, the theory has been relied on to determine, for example, the devolution, upon death, of the rights and liabilities of each party with respect to the land, and to ascertain the powers of creditors of each party to reach the land in payment of their claims.

The assignment of the risk of casualty loss in the executory period of contracts for the sale of real property varies greatly throughout the jurisdictions of this country. What appears to yet be a slim majority of states, places the risk of loss on the vendee from the moment of contracting, on the rationale that once an equitable conversion takes place, the vendee must be treated as owner for all purposes. Once the vendee becomes the equitable owner, he therefore becomes responsible for the condition of the property, despite not having a present right of occupancy or control. In sharp contrast, a handful of other states reject the allocation of casualty loss risk as a consequence of the theory of equitable conversion and follow the equally rigid "Massachusetts Rule," under which the seller continues to bear the risk until actual transfer of the title, absent an express agreement to the contrary. A substantial and growing number of jurisdictions, however, base the legal consequences of no-fault casualty loss on the right to possession of the property at the time the loss occurs. This view has found expression in the Uniform Vendor and Purchaser Risk Act, and while a number of states have adopted some variation of the Uniform Act, others have arrived at a similar position through the interpretations of their courts.

This court has applied the theory of equitable conversion in limited circumstances affecting title, and refused to apply it in some circumstances. It has also characterized the theory as affording significant protections to purchasers of realty in Colorado. It has never before, however, expressly relied on the theory of equitable conversion alone as allocating the risk of casualty loss to a vendee.

In *Wiley v. Lininger*, where fire destroyed improvements on land occupied by the vendee during the multi-year executory period of an installment land contract, we held, according to the generally accepted rule, that neither the buyer nor the seller, each of whom had an insurable interest in the property, had an obligation to insure the property for the benefit of the other. We also adopted a rule, which we characterized as "the majority rule" that the vendee under a contract for the sale of land, being regarded as the equitable owner, assumes the risk of destruction of or injury to the property *where he is in possession*, and the destruction or loss is not proximately caused by the negligence of the vendor." The vendee in possession was therefore not relieved of his obligation to continue making payments according to the terms of the contract, despite material loss by fire to some of the improvements on the property.

Largely because we included a citation, preceded by the introductory signal, "see," to an A.L.R. annotation, describing a "majority rule" without reference to possession, the court of appeals found our characterization of the rule, as imposing the risk on vendees who are in possession, to be uncontrolling. While it may have been unnecessary to determine more than the obligations of a vendee in possession in that case, rather than limit the holding to that situation, this court pointedly announced a broader rule. The rule expressly articulated by this court limited the transfer of the risk of loss to vendees who are already in possession. Had this not been the court's deliberate intention, there would have been no need to mention possession at all *→ Blue* because a rule governing all vendees would necessarily include vendees in possession. Whether or not a majority of jurisdictions would actually limit the transfer of risk in precisely the same way, the rule as clearly stated and adopted by this court was supported by strong policy and theoretical considerations at the time, and those considerations apply equally today.

Those jurisdictions that indiscriminately include the risk of casualty loss among the incidents or "attributes" of equitable ownership do so largely in reliance on ancient authority or by considering it necessary for consistent application of the theory of equitable conversion. Under virtually any accepted understanding of the theory, however, equitable conversion is not viewed as entitling the purchaser to every significant right of ownership, and particularly not the right of possession. As *→ Blue* a matter of both logic and equity, the obligation to maintain property in its physical condition follows the right to have actual possession and control rather than a legal right to force conveyance of the property through specific performance at some future date.

The equitable conversion theory is literally stood on its head by imposing on a vendee, solely because of his right to specific performance, the risk that the vendor will be unable to specifically perform when the time comes because of an accidental casualty loss. It is counterintuitive, at the very least, that merely contracting for the sale of real property should not only relieve the vendor of his responsibility to main- *→ Maybe black* tain the property until execution but also impose a duty on the vendee to perform despite the intervention of a material, no-fault casualty loss preventing him from ever receiving the benefit of his bargain. Such an extension of the theory of equitable conversion to casualty loss has never been recognized by this jurisdiction, and it is neither necessary nor justified solely for the sake of consistency.

By contrast, there is substantial justification, both as a matter of law and policy, for not relieving a vendee who is entitled to possession before transfer of title, like the vendee in *Wiley*, of his duty to pay the full contract price, notwithstanding an accidental loss. In addition to having control over the property and being entitled to the benefits of its use, an equitable owner who also has the right of possession has already acquired virtually all of the rights of ownership and almost invariably will have already paid at least some portion of the contract price to exercise those rights. By expressly including in the contract for sale the right of possession, which otherwise generally accompanies transfer of title, the vendor has for all practical purposes already transferred the property as promised, and the parties have in effect expressed their joint intention that the vendee pay the purchase price as promised.

*not black*

In *Wiley*, rather than adopting a rule to the effect that a vendee assumes the risk of casualty loss as an incident of equitable ownership, our holding stands for virtually the opposite proposition. Despite being the equitable owner, the vendee in that case was prohibited from rescinding only because he was already rightfully in possession at the time of the loss. While *Wiley* could be read to have merely resolved the situation under an installment contract for the sale of land that gave the vendee a right of immediate possession, the rule we adopted foreshadowed the resolution of this case as well. In the absence of a right of possession, a vendee of real property that suffers a material casualty loss during the executory period of the contract, through no fault of his own, must be permitted to rescind and recover any payments he had already made.

Furthermore, where a vendee is entitled to rescind as a result of casualty loss, the vendee should generally also be entitled to partial specific performance of the contract with an abatement in the purchase price reflecting the loss. Where the damage is ascertainable, permitting partial specific performance with a price abatement allows courts as nearly as possible to fulfill the expectations of the parties expressed in the contract, while leaving each in a position that is equitable relative to the other. Partial specific performance with a price abatement has long been recognized in this jurisdiction as an alternative to rescission in the analogous situation in which a vendor of real property is unable to convey marketable title to all of the land described in the contract.

Here, Brush was clearly not in possession of the property as the equitable owner. Even if the doctrine of equitable conversion applies to the option contract between Brush and Sure Fine and could be said to have converted Brush's interest to an equitable ownership of the property at the time Brush exercised its option to purchase, neither party considered the contract for sale to entitle Brush to possession. Brush was, in fact, not in possession of the property, and the record indicates that Sure Fine considered itself to hold the right of use and occupancy and gave notice that it would consider Brush a holdover tenant if it continued to occupy the premises other than by continuing to lease the property. The casualty loss was ascertainable and in fact stipulated by the parties, and neither party challenged the district court's enforcement of the contract except with regard to its allocation of the casualty loss. Both the court of appeals and the district court therefore erred in finding that the doctrine of equitable conversion required Brush to bear the loss caused by hail damage.

## IV. CONCLUSION

Where Brush was not an equitable owner in possession at the time of the casualty loss, it was entitled to rescind its contract with Sure Fine. At least under the circumstances of this case, where Brush chose to go forward with the contract under a stipulation as to loss from the hail damage, it was also entitled to specific performance with an abatement of the purchase price equal to the casualty loss. The judgment of the court of appeals is therefore reversed and the case is remanded for further proceedings consistent with this opinion.

### E. Mechanic's Liens

Another important thing that may be found in the land records is a *mechanic's lien.* When a contractor does work on a building, and does not get paid, the contractor is in a tough position. Unlike the seller of a car, for example, the contractor cannot easily just take back the new bedroom that has been added to the house, or take back the new shingles nailed onto the roof. Non-payment by the owner of the building may be especially harmful to someone like a carpenter – who really does not have the assets to be able to sue over a bill for $1,000. So state laws provide for mechanic's liens. These are liens that can be recorded as charges on the land – just like mortgages.

If the owner of the building does not pay the contractor for work done, the contractor may file a mechanic's lien. And if the owner still doesn't pay, then the contractor may foreclose on the mechanic's lien – just as a bank might foreclose on a mortgage. Then the land will be sold at a foreclosure sale, and as much of the proceeds of the sale as are necessary will be used to pay the debt.

In the following small segment from a mechanic's lien statute, notice how many different people come under the protections of the mechanic's lien statute.

C.R.S.§ 38-22-101. Liens in favor of whom--when filed--definition of person

(1) Every person who furnishes or supplies laborers, machinery, tools, or equipment in the prosecution of the work, and mechanics, materialmen, contractors, subcontractors, builders, and all persons of every class performing labor upon or furnishing directly to the owner or persons furnishing labor, laborers, or materials to be used in construction, alteration, improvement, addition to, or repair, either in whole or in part, of any building, mill, bridge, ditch, flume, aqueduct, reservoir, tunnel, fence, railroad, wagon road, tramway, or any other structure or improvement upon land, including adjacent curb, gutter, and sidewalk, and also architects, engineers, draftsmen, and artisans who have furnished designs, plans, plats, maps, specifications, drawings, estimates of cost, surveys, or superintendence, or who have rendered other professional or skilled service, or bestowed labor in whole or in part, describing or illustrating, or superintending such structure, or work done or to be done, or any part connected therewith, shall have a lien upon the property upon which they have furnished laborers or supplied machinery, tools, or equipment or rendered service or bestowed labor or for which they have furnished materials or mining or milling machinery or other fixtures, for the value of such laborers, machinery, tools, or equipment supplied, or services rendered or labor done or laborers or materials furnished, whether at the instance of the owner, or of any other person acting by the owner's authority or under the owner, as agent, contractor, or otherwise for the laborers, machinery, tools, or equipment supplied, or work or labor done or services rendered or laborers or materials furnished by each, respectively, whether supplied or done or furnished or rendered at the instance of the owner of the building or other improvement, or the owner's agent; and every contractor, architect, engineer, subcontractor, builder, agent, or other person having charge of the construction, alteration, addition to, or repair, either in whole or in part, of said building or other improvement shall be held to be the agent of the owner for the purposes of this article.

The following case illustrates how a mechanic's lien works.

DECEMBER 5, 2017


Opinion


<u>ROBERT M. CLAYTON III</u>, Judge


## I. BACKGROUND

This case concerns the enforceability of a mechanic's lien for labor and materials allegedly furnished by Plaintiff at real property located at 6169 Westminster Place in the City of St. Louis ("the Property"). Plaintiff, a general contractor, alleges in his petition that on December 1, 2008, he entered into a contract with the owners of the Property to provide the labor and materials necessary for the renovation of the Property, and the owners agreed to pay him $178,000 upon completion of his work. Plaintiff also alleges he completed the renovation work on or before April 27, 2015 and he made a demand for payment of $178,000, but the owners failed and refused to pay. Accordingly, on July 27, 2015, Plaintiff filed a mechanic's lien against the Property in the Office of the Clerk of the Circuit Court of the City of St. Louis.

On January 27, 2016, which was exactly six months after his mechanic's lien was filed, Plaintiff filed a petition to enforce his mechanic's lien in the Circuit Court of the City of St. Louis. The petition was filed against several underlying defendants including the purported owners of the Property and Wells Fargo, which has an interest in the Property pursuant to a deed of trust. The docket sheets indicate that although Plaintiff paid the requisite filing fee for his petition and the petition was accepted and deemed filed on January 27, there was an insufficient filing fee for the issuance of summonses in the amount of $43.00, and the summonses were not issued on January 27. Plaintiff paid the additional $43.00 filing fee on January 28, and the circuit clerk issued the summonses on February 4.

Subsequently, Wells Fargo filed a motion to dismiss Plaintiff's petition to enforce his mechanic's lien, arguing Plaintiff failed to commence his action within the six-month statute of limitations set forth in <u>section 429.170</u>. In its motion to dismiss, Wells Fargo conceded Plaintiff's petition was filed within the applicable six-month period but argued the action was not timely commenced because the summons for Wells Fargo was not issued within that timeframe. Plaintiff filed a response contending his action was timely filed because an action is commenced upon the filing of a petition alone and his petition to enforce was filed within six months of the filing of his mechanic's lien.

The trial court ruled against plaintiff.

## II. DISCUSSION

In Plaintiff's sole point on appeal, he asserts the trial court erred in dismissing his petition as to Wells Fargo on the grounds Plaintiff's action was not commenced within the six-month statute of limitations set forth in <u>section 429.170</u>. For the reasons discussed below, we agree.

### A. The Standard of Review and the Statute of Limitations

<u>Section 429.170</u>, which is the statute of limitations for mechanic's lien cases, provides that an action to enforce a mechanic's lien:

> ... shall be commenced within six months after filing the lien, and prosecuted without unnecessary delay to final judgment; and no lien shall continue to exist by virtue of the provisions of said sections, for more than six months after the lien shall be filed, unless within that time an action shall be instituted thereon, as herein prescribed.

### B. Relevant Law and Analysis

In this case, it is undisputed Plaintiff's petition to enforce his mechanic's lien, which was filed on January 27, 2016, was filed within six months after Plaintiff filed his mechanic's lien on July 27, 2015. It is also undisputed the summons for Wells Fargo issued by the circuit clerk on February 4, 2016 was not issued within six months after Plaintiff filed his mechanic's lien. The issue in this case is whether, for purposes of the six-month statute of limitations set forth in <u>section 429.170</u>, an action to enforce a mechanic's lien is commenced by, (1) the filing of a petition alone; or (2) the filing of a petition and the issuance of a summons.

First, we look to the statutes in Chapter 429 discussing the practice associated with mechanic's liens. While <u>section 429.170</u> specifies there is a six-month statute of limitations for mechanic's lien cases, there is no other provision in that chapter defining the "commencement" of a mechanic's lien action filed by a claimant. Without guidance from Chapter 429, we look to the general rule on the commencement of a civil action set forth in Rule 53.01.

Rule 53.01 provides: "A civil action is commenced by filing a petition with the court." The current and applicable version of the Rule makes no reference to "suing out of process" or "issuance of a summons."

The Missouri Supreme Court has directly addressed the requirements of the post-1972 version of Rule 53.01 and the question of what steps are required under the Rule for the commencement of a general civil action. The Supreme Court has held that Rule 53.01, in its current and applicable form, "only requires the filing of a petition with the court to commence an action." The purpose of the 1972 amendment to Rule 53.01 and the elimination of the issuance of the summons requirement from the definition of commencement was "to create certainty as to when a lawsuit is commenced" and to put the timing of commencement in the party's hands rather than it being subject to the hands of the circuit clerk. As explained by this Court:

> When a party files a petition, the party has done all the party can do. The issuing of the summons is not in the party's hands, but in the hands of the clerk. Delay may occur due to matters even beyond the clerk's control, such as insufficient staff, staff who are out sick or on vacation, or a heavy volume of cases. Thus, the old version of Rule 53.01 would appear unfair to penalize the party for any delay in the clerk's office in issuing the summons.

Based upon the plain language of the post-1972 version of Rule 53.01 and controlling decisions from the Missouri Supreme Court we hold a plaintiff's mechanic's lien action is commenced by the filing of a petition alone.

It is undisputed Plaintiff's petition to enforce his mechanic's lien, filed on January 27, 2016, was filed within six months after Plaintiff filed his mechanic's lien on July 27, 2015. Therefore, Plaintiff's action was commenced within the six-month statute of limitations set forth in section 429.170, and the trial court erred in dismissing Plaintiff's petition as to Wells Fargo on the grounds Plaintiff's action was barred by the statute of limitations. Point granted.

## III. CONCLUSION

The trial court's judgment dismissing Plaintiff's petition as to Wells Fargo is reversed, and the cause is remanded for further proceedings in accordance with this opinion.

## F. Mortgages – Foreclosures

Most people are not able to pay cash for the purchase of a house. So they get a loan from the bank. As part of the loan process the borrower signs a *note*, which is basically a one page document, like an I.O.U., by which the borrower promises to repay the money, at the stated rate of interest. But no bank is likely to lend someone $200,000 just based on the borrower's promise to repay. The bank needs more security than that. So the borrower also gives the bank a mortgage, giving the bank the right to foreclose the mortgage, have the house sold at a foreclosure sale, and use the proceeds of the sale to pay off the balance of the loan, if the buyer does not make the mortgage payments as agreed to in the mortgage. [The borrower is the *mortgagor*, the bank is the *mortgagee*.] Any mortgage is usually a very detailed document, running for 20 pages or more.

Different states have different rules on mortgages, and on the complex process required for foreclosure. In some states the document used to secure the loan is called a mortgage. In other states, the document usually used to secure the loan is called a *Deed of Trust*. Both serve the same purpose, and both are subject to very detailed statutory provisions involving foreclosure.

Some of the basics are illustrated by the following three cases.

### SUPREME COURT OF COLORADO
### LIBERTY MORTGAGE CORPORATION, A GEORGIA CORPORATION; BB&T CORPORATION, A NORTH CAROLINA CORPORATION; AND BRANCH BANKING AND TRUST COMPANY, A NORTH CAROLINA CORPORATION, PETITIONERS;
### V.
### RAYMOND L. FISCUS, A/K/A RAY FISCUS, RESPONDENT.

MAY 16, 2016

Opinion

JUSTICE EID delivered the Opinion of the Court.

Petitioner Branch Banking and Trust Company asks us to decide whether a deed of trust securing a promissory note is a negotiable instrument under Article 3 of

Colorado's Uniform Commercial Code ("UCC"). The court of appeals held that deeds of trust are not negotiable instruments within the meaning of Article 3, and therefore the bank was not a holder in due course with respect to the deed at issue here.

We affirm the judgment of the court of appeals, but on different grounds. In this case, the deed and other documents were forged. [We hold that, even assuming a deed of trust qualifies as a negotiable instrument, holder-in-due-course status does not preclude a purported maker from asserting a forgery defense.] Here, the purported maker possesses a valid forgery defense, his negligence did not contribute to the forgery, and he did not ratify the forged documents. As such, we need not and do not reach the issue of the negotiability of deeds of trust under Article 3.

## I.

Respondent Ray Fiscus ("Husband") married Vickie Casper–Fiscus ("Wife") in 1985. In 1987, he purchased property in Grand Junction, Colorado, and titled it solely in his name. He financed the purchase with a mortgage loan, and the couple used the property as their marital home. Throughout their marriage, Wife managed their finances, which included the payment of household bills as well as mortgage and credit card debts. Husband neither confirmed these payments nor reviewed the couple's bank statements or tax returns, and so he had little knowledge of their precise finances.

In June 2008, without his knowledge or authorization, Wife signed Husband's name on a General Power of Attorney, a Limited Power of Attorney, and a Power of Attorney (Real Estate) (collectively, the "forged POAs"), which together purported to appoint her as Husband's lawful attorney. Her daughter from a previous marriage notarized the documents. Using the forged POAs, Wife closed on a promissory note for approximately $220,000 with Liberty Mortgage Corporation and secured it with a deed of trust (the "2008 deed") purporting to encumber the property. She signed the 2008 deed as "Raymond Fiscus by Vickie L. Casper–Fiscus as Attorney in Fact." The couple's 2008 tax return, signed by both spouses, included a mortgage interest deduction in the amount of $1,722. This was consistent with the amount Husband would have expected to have paid on the original 1987 mortgage loan. At no time in 2008 did Husband become aware of the note Wife executed.

In early 2009, Wife began making inquiries about refinancing the 2008 note. While doing so, she sent an email to a mortgage broker informing him that Husband "is out of town a lot so I have power of attorney" and asking if proceeding with the refinancing by power of attorney would be a problem. In February and March, she signed Husband's name to several loan application documents, and, on March 30, she executed another note in the amount of $220,000 with Liberty Mortgage, once again using the forged POAs, securing the note with a deed of trust purporting to encumber the property (the "2009 deed"), and signing both documents as "Raymond Fiscus by Vickie L. Casper–Fiscus as Attorney in Fact." Husband never authorized her to execute the 2009 note or deed in his name and had no knowledge of them at the time. Wife paid off the 2008 note with the proceeds from the 2009 note, and the 2008 note was released. Liberty Mortgage subsequently assigned the 2009 note and deed to BB&T Corporation, which, in turn, assigned them to petitioner Branch Banking and Trust.

The mortgage interest deduction on the couple's 2009 tax return was $12,323, an amount much higher than Husband would have expected to claim on the original mortgage loan from 1987. Wife signed his name on the tax return without his knowledge, and, when he asked about it, she told him he did not need to sign it because he had authorized electronic filing. Husband never saw the tax return.

Wife hid all the documents evidencing the 2008 and 2009 transactions in the crawl space of their home. Husband did not learn of the transactions until 2011 when his broker contacted him to authorize an attempted withdrawal from his IRA account in the amount of $5,000. During that conversation, Husband learned that Wife had made an unauthorized withdrawal from his account earlier for $10,000 with the help of her son-in-law, who had impersonated Husband on the phone. Husband then performed a credit check and discovered the 2009 note. After discovering the note, he checked the county property records and uncovered the 2008 and 2009 deeds as well as the forged POAs. He filed an identity theft report with the sheriff's office and an identity theft statement with Branch Banking and Trust. He also sued Liberty Mortgage, BB&T, and Branch Banking and Trust under the spurious lien statute, §§ 38–35–201 to –204, C.R.S. (2015), seeking to have the 2009 deed invalidated.

The district court held a show cause hearing in August 2012 at which Husband, Wife, Wife's daughter, and a BB&T representative, among others, testified. In a detailed order, the district court held that the 2009 deed was spurious because it was not created, suffered, assumed, or agreed to by Husband, the property's sole owner, and contained a material misstatement, that is, Husband's signature.

The court also rejected Branch Banking and Trust's defenses. As relevant here, the bank argued that, under Article 3 of the UCC, it qualified as a holder in due course and took the 2009 deed free from any forgery defense. In the alternative, it contended that Husband's negligence contributed to the making of the forged deed and that he ratified the deed. The trial court, however, held that the 2009 deed was not a "negotiable instrument" but a "security instrument," and therefore the bank could not assert a holder-in-due-course or negligent-contribution defense under Article 3. It also rejected Branch Banking and Trust's ratification argument, concluding instead that Husband lacked knowledge of the facts relating to the documents' creation until December 2011 and took no action at that time to approve them. Consequently, the court invalidated the 2009 deed and ordered its release.

The court of appeals affirmed.

Branch Banking and Trust petitioned this court to review the court of appeals' holding, and we granted certiorari to determine whether a lender in possession of a promissory note secured by a deed of trust on real property may assert a holder-in-due-course defense under section 4–3–305, C.R.S. (2015), to a claim that the deed of trust was forged. We conclude, however, that Husband has a valid forgery defense, not barred by negligence or ratification, and thus decline to address this issue. We therefore affirm the judgment of the court of appeals, but on other grounds.

## II.

Branch Banking and Trust argues that the 2009 deed is a negotiable instrument under Article 3 because it secures the promise to pay contained in the 2009 note, which plainly qualifies as a negotiable instrument. But even assuming (without deciding) that Branch Banking and Trust is correct, we conclude that, on these facts, Husband has a valid forgery defense to any claim the bank might assert as a holder in due course, and that this defense is not precluded by any negligence or ratification on Husband's part. As such, we need not and do not address the negotiability of a deed of trust under Article 3.

Article 3 of the UCC governs the issuance, transfer, enforcement, and discharge of negotiable instruments. Under Article 3, a holder in due course of a negotiable instrument takes it free of most defenses. Nevertheless, some defenses, such as infancy, duress, lack of legal capacity, and "fraud that induced the obligor to sign the instrument with neither knowledge nor reasonable opportunity to learn of its character or its essential terms," still apply to holders in due course.

By its plain terms, the statute only identifies the defenses that apply to the right of a holder in due course to *enforce the obligation* of a party to pay the instrument. *See also* § 4–3–305(a) (listing the defenses to which the right to *enforce the obligation* of a party to pay an instrument is subject.) This language presupposes that an obligation exists and that the holder in due course has a right to enforce it.

When a purported maker raises a forgery defense, however, he is challenging the very existence of the obligation itself, not its enforcement. For an instrument to bind a person under Article 3, that person must either personally sign the instrument or be represented by an agent who signs it on his behalf. § 4–3–401, C.R.S. (2015); *see also* § 4–3–401 cmt. 1 ("Obligation on an instrument depends on a signature that is binding on the obligor. The signature may be made by the obligor personally or by an agent authorized to act for the obligor."). This requirement is plainly not satisfied where his name is signed without authorization. Indeed, section 4–3–403(a), C.R.S. (2015), specifically provides that an "unauthorized signature" does not bind the person whose name is signed absent ratification, and section 4–1–201(b)(41), C.R.S. (2015), specifies that the term "unauthorized signature" includes a forgery.

It follows that a party may still assert forgery against a holder in due course. See *Real Defense, Black's Law Dictionary* (10th ed. 2014) (listing "forgery of a necessary signature" as a "defense that is good against any possible claimant, so that the maker or drawer of a negotiable instrument can raise it even against a holder in due course").

Article 3's requirements for proving the validity of signatures on a negotiable instrument bolster this conclusion. In general, when a party files suit to enforce an instrument, the court presumes that signatures are valid unless specifically contested by the purported maker. Holder-in-due-course status becomes relevant *only after* the validity of the signatures has been established.

Therefore, consistent with other jurisdictions interpreting their versions of Article 3, we hold that a purported maker may raise forgery as a defense to an obligation on an instrument held by a party claiming holder-in-due-course status.

On the facts as found by the district court, Husband has a valid forgery defense. The district court found that he never appointed Wife as his attorney or authorized her to sign his name on the forged POAs, any of the notes or deeds, or the loan applications. She thus was not an "an agent or representative" of Husband within the meaning of section 4–3–401. Yet she fraudulently signed his name on all of these documents, had her daughter from a prior marriage notarize them, and represented herself as his attorney. Husband therefore has a valid forgery defense.

Furthermore, although Article 3 bars a person whose signature was forged from asserting forgery as a defense if his own negligence contributed to the forgery, § 4–3–406(a), C.R.S. (2015), the district court's detailed factual findings preclude any finding of negligence on Husband's part here. Given that the interest deduction on the 2008 tax return was in the amount he expected, the district court concluded that the earliest Husband could or should have discovered the 2009 deed by the exercise of reasonable diligence was in April 2010, when he could have reviewed the 2009 tax returns. But when he asked Wife about the returns, she deliberately misled him, telling him that he did not need to sign them. We decline to declare him negligent for trusting his wife. And the next time he detected suspicious activity—in December 2011—he exercised "ordinary care" under section 4–3–406 by performing a credit check and filing identity theft reports with the police and the bank.

This was not a case where a purported maker failed to exercise reasonable control over his checks or signing devices. Rather, it was an active effort on Wife's part to encumber the property without Husband's knowledge. She forged his signature on three powers of attorney by signing his name without his permission; had her daughter from a previous marriage fraudulently notarize them; encumbered the property without his consent using the forged POAs; falsely advised the mortgage broker that he was unavailable and that they therefore had to proceed using powers of attorney; hid the documents evidencing the transactions in the crawl space of their home; and lied when he asked her about the 2009 tax returns. In short, Wife went to great lengths to defraud Husband, and he was not negligent for falling victim to her elaborate scheme.

We also agree with the court of appeals that the record supported the district court's finding on ratification. While a purported holder may ratify an unauthorized signature, and thus make it binding on him, ratification can never exist unless it is clearly shown that the party charged with ratification has full knowledge of all material facts, and thereafter knowingly accepts and approves the contract. The party alleging ratification—here, Branch Banking and Trust—carries the burden of proof. Husband testified, however, that he never knew of the 2008 or 2009 loan transactions or their resulting deeds of trust, and the district court credited that testimony. The record therefore supports the district court's conclusion that he lacked "full knowledge of all material facts" about the transactions required for ratification.

Overall, then, the facts as found by the district court indicate that Husband has a valid forgery defense, did not negligently contribute to the forgery, and never ratified the notes or the deeds of trust securing them. On these facts, even assuming without deciding that Article 3 applies to the 2009 deed of trust, Husband prevails.

Because Husband has a valid forgery defense, not precluded by any negligence or ratification on his part, we need not and do not reach the question of whether a deed of trust is a negotiable instrument under Article 3. Correspondingly, we hold that it was unnecessary for the court of appeals to address this issue, and we affirm its judgment on other grounds.

III.

We affirm the judgment of the court of appeals on other grounds.

# SUPREME COURT OF NEW HAMPSHIRE
## PREMIER CAPITAL, LLC
### V.
## NICKOLAS SKALTSIS AND ANOTHER

MARCH 30, 2007

BRODERICK, C.J.

The defendants, Nickolas and Lorraine Skaltsis, appeal an order of the Superior Court entering judgment for the plaintiff, Premier Capital, LLC, on a promissory note in the amount of $703,504.99. They argue that the trial court erred in ruling that: (1) the applicable statute of limitations on the note was twenty years; (2) the plaintiff had standing to bring this action; (3) there was sufficient evidence of the amount due under the note; and (4) the plaintiff's claim was not barred by laches. Following oral argument before this court, the parties were allowed to file supplemental memoranda further addressing the statute of limitations issue. We affirm.

## I

On March 12, 1990, the defendants executed a promissory note in the amount of $565,000 in favor of First NH Banks, Exeter Banking Company. The note provided for a variable interest rate equal to the Bank of Boston base rate plus 1.50% adjusted daily, and provided for amortization over twenty-five years. The note was secured by first mortgages on 3A Rose Street and 124 Broadway in Dover, together with an assignment of leases and rents on those properties. In 1992, the promissory note and mortgages were assigned to Hilco Realty Corp., and in 1993 they were further assigned to AMRESCO New Hampshire, Inc.

The defendants defaulted on the note in 1992 and filed unsuccessfully for bankruptcy protection. In December 1993, AMRESCO New Hampshire, Inc. made a demand upon the defendants for the balance then due on the note, which was $659,632.79. Subsequently, AMRESCO New Hampshire, Inc. advertised and conducted a mortgage foreclosure sale in June 1994 on both properties. In March 1996 AMRESCO New Hampshire, Inc. assigned the original promissory note to AMRESCO New Hampshire, L.P. On September 23, 1997, AMRESCO New Hampshire, L.P. assigned the note to Premier Capital, *Inc.* On September 10, 2003, the plaintiff commenced this action, alleging that it had been assigned the promissory note originally given by the defendants to Exeter Banking Company in March 1990. Following a bench trial, the court entered judgment for the plaintiff in the amount of $703,504.99. This appeal followed.

## II

The defendants first argue that the trial court erred in applying the twenty-year statute of limitations under RSA 508:6 rather than the three-year statute of limitations under RSA 508:4. They contend that our decision in *Cross v. Gannett*, (1859), "squarely holds that once the mortgage has been foreclosed, even if no discharge is recorded, the mortgage is no longer enforceable and no action may be brought on it within the meaning of the statute."

In the case before us, the defendants both made the note and gave the mortgages to secure it. Thus, under an unwavering line of decisions from this court, "although the mortgagee no longer has recourse to the property once it has been sold free and clear at a foreclosure sale, he may still assert, in an action against his debtor (the mortgagor), that where the covenants of the mortgage given to secure the note remain undischarged, the debtor waived the right to plead the statute of limitations for twenty years." Accordingly, we hold that ...the trial court correctly concluded that the "action was clearly brought within 20 years of the defendants' default, and is therefore not barred by the statute of limitations."

→ Really important

## III

The defendants next argue that the trial court's ruling that the plaintiff had standing to bring this action on the note was not supported by the evidence. No particular phraseology is required to effect an assignment. The ultimate test is the intention of the assignor to give and the assignee to receive present ownership of the claim. A valid assignment may be made by any words or acts which fairly indicate an intention to make the assignee the owner of a claim. The important thing is the act and the evidence of intent; formalities are not material. Thus, whether or not an assignment occurred is a question of fact for the trial court.

John Cummings, an account manager at plaintiff Premier Capital *LLC*, testified that the defendants' file was given to him by an authorized representative of Premier Capital, *Inc.* with the intent that it be transferred to Premier Capital, *LLC*. The trial court found:

Cummings credibly testified that a representative from Premier *Inc.* gave him the defendants' file and told him to enforce it on behalf of Premier *LLC.* The physical transfer was conducted with the intent to give Cummings, as an agent of Premier *LLC,* the right to enforce the note. As such, the transfer from Premier *Inc.* to Premier *LLC* was a valid transfer and vested Premier *LLC* with Premier Inc.'s right to enforce the note. Therefore, Premier *LLC* has standing to bring this action.

We affirm the trial court's factual findings as they are supported by the record before us.

The defendants also contend that the plaintiff does not have standing because the note was not a negotiable instrument and, thus, it could only be conveyed by an assignment for value for which there was no evidence. We reject this argument, however, because it is not necessary that there should be any consideration where the question arises between the assignee and the debtor.

## IV

The defendants next argue that the trial court erred by ruling that there was sufficient evidence of the amount due under the note and that insufficient funds were generated from the foreclosure sale. They also contend that the evidence submitted to prove the amount of the deficiency owed was insufficient.

On review, we consider the evidence in the light most favorable to the prevailing party below and will overturn a damage award only if we find it to be clearly erroneous. As to the foreclosure sale, a mortgagee must exert every reasonable effort to obtain a fair and reasonable price under the circumstances. What constitutes a fair price, or whether the mortgagee must establish an upset price, adjourn the sale, or make other reasonable efforts to assure a fair price, depends upon the circumstances of each case. Inadequacy of price alone is not sufficient to demonstrate bad faith unless the price is so low as to shock the judicial conscience.

The 1994 tax assessments for the properties were $154,600 for the Rose Street property and $313,200 for the Broadway property. Cummings testified that he believed the fair value on the properties was $80,000 for Rose Street and $170,000 for Broadway. The foreclosure sale brought $51,000 for Rose Street and $190,000 for Broadway. The trial court found that although the prices realized at auction were significantly below the tax assessment values of the properties, the properties carried significant tax burdens for the years the defendants did not pay their taxes, thus making them less valuable to potential buyers. In addition, the court found that there was evidence that " there may have been a glut in the property market at the time of the foreclosure sale."

Finally, the court found that the defendants had approximately one year between the withdrawal of their bankruptcy petition and the foreclosure, during which time they made no payments and no effort to sell the property. As the court stated in its order:

> Being relatively sophisticated real estate investors, the defendants surely would have sold the properties had they been able to secure a high enough price on the properties to satisfy a large portion of the outstanding mortgage. No steps to find a buyer were taken until after Ameresco [sic] foreclosed on the property. The court can reasonably infer that the defendants did not sell the properties because they could not obtain as high a selling price as they would need to satisfy their mortgage obligations.

We hold that the record supports the trial court's finding that the foreclosure sale obtained a reasonable price under the circumstances and that the price was not so low as to support a finding of bad faith.

As to the amount of the deficiency owed, the record likewise supports the trial court's findings. Although Cummings did not use the Bank of Boston interest rate specified in the note to calculate the amount owed, he testified "that the Federal Reserve prime rate was equal to the Bank of Boston base rate at times when the Bank of Boston base rate was available and that the Federal Reserve prime rate is a reliable and accurate measure to use for the time period the Bank of Boston rate was unavailable that is, when Bank of Boston was ultimately consumed by another bank." *Cf. F.D.I.C. v. Cage,* (where the interest rate on a note is determined by reference to the prime rate of a failed institution, it is reasonable to compute interest based on an alternative prime rate selected by FDIC). Furthermore, as the trial court noted, the plaintiff's evidence of the defendants' payment history was "essentially uncontroverted by the defendants."

## V

The defendants' final argument is that the trial court erred by ruling that the plaintiff was not guilty of laches. The defendants assert that they destroyed all of their records relating to the note at issue based upon their belief that any actions under the note would be barred by the statute of limitations. They argue that they have been prejudiced by the plaintiff's delay in bringing this action and should therefore not be obligated to pay the debt.

Laches is an equitable doctrine that bars litigation when a potential plaintiff has slept on his rights. Laches is not a mere matter of time, but is principally a question of the inequity of permitting the claim to be enforced-an inequity founded on some change in the conditions or relations of the property or the parties involved. When the delay in bringing the suit is less than the applicable statute of limitations period, laches will constitute a bar to suit only if the delay was unreasonable and prejudicial. In determining whether the doctrine should apply to bar a suit, the court should consider the knowledge of the plaintiffs, the conduct of the defendants, the interests to be vindicated, and the resulting prejudice. The trial court has broad discretion in deciding whether the circumstances justify its application, and unless we find that the trial court's decision is unsupported by the evidence or erroneous as a matter of law, we will not overturn it.

The trial court stated in its ruling:

> The defendants' destruction of their financial records relating to this note between the foreclosure and the commencement of this action was not reasonable because it was based upon an inaccurate interpretation of the law and does not amount to sufficient prejudice. The defendants are not unsophisticated, they were savvy real estate purchasers and sellers, and operated their business running considerable lines of credit and transferring large amounts of real estate. Additionally, Skaltsis testified he and his wife ceased making payments on this note because they no longer wanted to maintain control of the properties. The defendants consciously defaulted on the note, hoping the foreclosure would absolve them of their responsibilities under the note. As such, any prejudice resulting from the defendants' destruction of the records relating to this note is purely the defendants' own fault and the court will not impose the equitable doctrine of laches to discharge their obligation to pay on this note.

We find no error. *Affirmed.*

Note: Once a mortgage has been foreclosed, the mortgagor will usually be given one more chance to pay the debt, (and the foreclosure expenses), and get the land back. This is sometimes called the *equity of redemption*, or the *right to redeem.* The specific rules for foreclosure vary widely from state to state.

If, after a foreclosure sale there is some money left after the various liens on the land have been paid, and the expenses of the foreclosure process have been paid, then the excess money goes back to the mortgagor. The following case illustrates some of the important technicalities of a foreclosure sale.

## SUPREME COURT OF KANSAS
## FIDELITY BANK, F/K/A FIDELITY SAVINGS ASSOCIATION OF KANSAS, FSB, PLAINTIFF,
## V.
## JAMES M. KING, ET AL., DEFENDANTS AND U.S. BANK, N.A., DEFENDANT/APPELLANT. RIVER CITY ENTERPRISES, L.L.C., APPELLEE.

JUNE 16, 2006

## OPINION

BEIER, J.: This foreclosure appeal requires us to determine whether a junior mortgage holder waives its claim to excess sheriff's sale proceeds if it fails to appear and assert its position in a senior mortgage holder's action. We hold that it does.

Defendants James and Carolyn King assumed the debt on certain real property in Wichita in 1997. Fidelity Bank, f/k/a Fidelity Savings Associations of Kansas, FSB (Fidelity), was the mortgage holder on this first mortgage. In 2000, the Kings executed a second mortgage on the property with U.S. Bank, N.A. (U.S. Bank), for $32,000. The Kings defaulted, and Fidelity sued to foreclose its mortgage on the property, which was the senior lien..

In its petition, Fidelity named the Kings as defendants, as well as U.S. Bank, (which held a junior lien), and Commercial Federal Bank, (which held a judgment lien against the Kings). The defendants were properly served. Commercial Federal Bank filed a notice disclaiming any interest. U.S. Bank did not appear or file an answer or otherwise participate in the foreclosure.

The district court entered a decree of foreclosure, ruling that Fidelity held a first and prior lien upon the property. It entered judgment in favor of Fidelity and against the Kings for $65,321.25 plus interest, costs, taxes, and fees. The district court did not recognize any interest in any other party and stated that the defendants and all persons claiming by, through, or under Fidelity would be forever barred and excluded from asserting any title, interest, estate in, lien upon, or claim against the property. The court set a redemption period of 3 months from the date of the sale and ordered that proceeds derived from the sale would be applied: (1) to pay costs of the action and sale; (2) to pay real estate and special assessment taxes; and (3) to pay Fidelity's judgment, including interest. The court ordered "the balance, if any, to be held by the Clerk of the Court, subject to further order of the Court."

The sale was held on January 28, 2004. U.S. Bank was the high bidder at the sale, purchasing the property for $93,500. The district court confirmed the sale on February 13, 2004, and paid Fidelity $73,092.71 in full satisfaction of its judgment. The clerk of the court held the remaining proceeds of $20,407.29.

On February 25, 2004, River City Enterprises, LLC (RCE), filed a motion in the district court, seeking distribution of the excess sale proceeds. RCE had acquired all of the rights and interest of the Kings just before the sale. Standing in the Kings' shoes, RCE moved the court to distribute the $ 20,407.29 held by the clerk to RCE.

The next day, the court granted the motion and ordered that the excess proceeds be distributed to RCE as the owner of all the Kings' rights and interest in the property. The court noted that no notice was necessary; Fidelity was the only party that had appeared in the foreclosure action and its judgment had been paid in full.

On March 5, 2004, U.S. Bank filed a motion requesting that the court set aside its February order, deny RCE's motion, and instead distribute the excess proceeds to U.S. Bank. U.S. Bank alleged that it was still owed $29,680.67 on its mortgage on the property, that it had an interest superior to RCE's because of its status as a junior lienholder, and that it was entitled to receive the surplus proceeds from the sale in satisfaction of its lien. RCE filed a response, arguing U.S. Bank had lost any interest it had in the property, including any right to recover surplus proceeds, when it failed to adjudicate its lien in Fidelity's foreclosure.

At the hearing on U.S. Bank's motion before the district court, U.S. Bank argued that there was no clear Kansas authority on the issue of whether a junior lienholder is required to appear and adjudicate its lien in a senior lienholder's foreclosure action to preserve a claim to surplus proceeds. Although it had not appeared in the foreclosure, U.S. Bank asserted that it had bid up the price on the property roughly $20,500 at the sale. Further, it argued it had priority in the surplus proceeds over RCE because RCE purchased only the Kings' right of redemption. It conceded that it no longer had any rights tied to the property, including a right to redeem, because it had not adjudicated its interest. However, it advanced cases from other jurisdictions and language from the Restatement (Third) of Property in support of the idea that its right to surplus proceeds survived its failure to appear and protect its interest in the foreclosure.

For its part, RCE agreed that proceeds from a sheriff's sale must be distributed to lienholders in order of priority before any excess goes to the debtor, but it argued that U.S. Bank's failure to appear or adjudicate its lien in the foreclosure meant it lost its right in the property and forfeited its status as a junior lienholder. Rather, U.S. Bank had become a mere unsecured creditor of the Kings and had no right to surplus proceeds from the foreclosure sale.

The district court denied U.S. Bank's motion, and the Court of Appeals affirmed the district court's decision.

Our review in this appeal is unlimited, as it raises only questions of law.

The proceeds of a foreclosure sale are generally applied to costs and taxes and then to the judgment owed to the foreclosing party, as set forth in the district court's foreclosure decree. Although statutes govern procedures for foreclosure sales, there is no statute governing distribution of excess proceeds from such a sale. In this statutory vacuum, we look to the Restatement (Third) of Property: Mortgages §7.4 (1996), which lays out the following guiding principles: "When the foreclosure sale price exceeds the amount of the mortgage obligation, the surplus is applied to liens and other interests terminated by the foreclosure in order of their priority and the remaining balance if any, is distributed to the holder of the equity of redemption." These principles are consistent with long-standing Kansas law.

Neither party to this appeal urges us to depart from these principles. The question here is whether U.S. Bank must have appeared in the Fidelity foreclosure and adjudicated its junior rights tied to the property to preserve its lienholder status and thus its priority entitlement to surplus proceeds. It insists that its participation in the foreclosure was not necessary. RCE insists that it was.

U.S. Bank's arguments are the following: (1) It is accepted practice in Kansas for a junior lienholder to protect its interest in surplus proceeds merely by bidding at a foreclosure sale; (2) the lower courts' holdings are ambiguous and rely upon faulty analysis; (3) as a policy matter, the Court of Appeals' decision will have a negative impact on Kansas citizens; and (4) the distribution of surplus proceeds in Kansas is governed purely by equity, which favors its position.

We can quickly dispose of U.S. Bank's second and third arguments. Our review of the holdings of the lower courts, as set forth above, is unlimited. In such expansive review, if any "fault" or "ambiguity" exists, it will be addressed and corrected. With regard to the third argument, we will not reach a decision in a case based on public policy when we have legal authority that guides us to appropriate resolution. The courts will not pass on the propriety, wisdom, necessity, and expedience of existing law, otherwise constitutional, even if the court does not consider it to be in the public interest of the state.

U.S. Bank's first argument -- that bidding by a junior lienholder, as opposed to participating in the foreclosure suit, is common practice and sufficient to preserve a priority right to surplus proceeds -- assumes that surplus proceeds are not bound to an interest in the land subjected to sale. This necessary premise is incorrect.

U.S. Bank relies on *McFall*, for the proposition that proceeds from a foreclosure sale are cash separate from the land. On the contrary, *McFall* says:

Since inferior judgment liens are cut off by the sale, *surplus takes the place of the land,* and the lienholders may apply for distribution of proceeds of sale .... Whenever surplus, *standing for the land to which the lien attached,* ought in equity to be distributed to lienholders, it may be distributed to them, on application to the court having control of the surplus. This is the very purpose and object of reserving, in judgment and order of sale, power to dispose of surplus. (Emphasis added.)

Because surplus proceeds remain tied to the land that is the subject of the foreclosure, those with preserved interests in the land are paid first. Under Kansas law, payment to lienholders in order of priority comes directly after payment of costs. Thereafter, any surplus belongs to the debtor in execution. In this case, RCE has acquired the debtors' remaining interest in the land. This includes the debtor's right to surplus. Unless U.S. Bank is a lienholder, *i.e.,* a holder of an interest in the subject land, it does not, as a matter of law, come before RCE in the surplus proceeds payment queue.

The problem for U.S. Bank is that it did absolutely nothing to preserve and ensure its lienholder status when Fidelity's first mortgage was foreclosed. It ignored its chance to protect its priority for surplus proceeds. In Kansas, as the Court of Appeals stated, "a mortgage foreclosure merges all junior liens on the land." When the foreclosure decree was issued, it was silent on any continuing role or right for U.S. Bank. At that point, U.S. Bank was still the holder of a promissory note that could be sued upon, but the mortgage that had secured that note by providing it a lien on the land no longer had legal effect. Again, as our Court of Appeals noted correctly, the Kings' debt to U.S. Bank was thereafter unsecured.

U.S. Bank's fourth argument -- that equity rather than law controls and commands a different result -- also fails.

To the extent equity should be *a* factor in the outcome rather than *the only* factor, it favors RCE rather than U.S. Bank. We agree with the Court of Appeals' assessment:

U.S. Bank explains that junior mortgage holders often choose to protect their interest by bidding at the foreclosure sale in order to make sure the property brings a price sufficient to satisfy the junior lien in case the property is subsequently redeemed. Otherwise, the holder of the redemption right might be able to redeem for an amount exclusive of junior liens. U.S. Bank argues that if River City receives the surplus, U.S. Bank's debt remains unsatisfied, the Kings remain owing on the debt, and River City, a stranger to the original note and mortgage, gets away with the Kings' equity and U.S. Bank's additional funds it paid to protect itself at the sheriff's sale.

U.S. Bank also argues that not allowing recovery of surplus proceeds by a foreclosed second mortgage holder over the holder of the equity of redemption will result in the chilling of bids at Kansas foreclosure sales and of lending to property owners for second mortgages. U.S. Bank asserts that if it is forced to appear in every foreclosure action, great expense would be incurred by junior lienholders, who would, to avoid excessive legal expenses, be required to spend excessive time and money specifically finding the value of foreclosed real property, determining whether it is financially prudent to answer foreclosure petitions, and then considering bidding at a foreclosure sale.

We are not persuaded by U.S. Bank's claims of equity. First and foremost, U.S. Bank is the owner of the Kings' property by virtue of its high bid at the sheriff's sale and theoretically can recoup any amount paid through subsequent sale of the property. Second, U.S. Bank has an enforceable note for approximately $30,000 due from the Kings. U.S. Bank can reduce the note to judgment and pursue collections remedies against the Kings. In its reply brief, U.S. Bank argues that River City is awarded a windfall by receiving the surplus proceeds. How River City came into ownership of the Kings' property rights and for what purchase price is irrelevant for our determination. River City purchased all the incidents of ownership, including the right to redemption and the right to any surplus proceeds after payment of the foreclosed interest. The Kings apparently benefitted from the exchange.

Third, we doubt our decision will have a chilling effect on bids at sheriff's sales and on the ability of individuals to obtain a second mortgage loan. The consequence we foresee will be an enforcement of the understanding that in order to protect a junior lien, a financial institution must appear in the foreclosure action brought by the senior mortgage holder, assert the junior lienholder's position, have the court adjudicate the junior lien, and then make sure the junior lien is recognized in the journal entry of foreclosure.

To this discussion, we add only that today's holding furthers the simple and straightforward equitable principle that a party that chooses to sleep on its rights loses them. U.S. Bank took a long nap during Fidelity's foreclosure. This awakening may be rude, but it has the virtue of advancing future clarity and predictability in Kansas law governing surplus proceeds.

The judgment of the Court of Appeals affirming the district court is affirmed.

## G. The Fair Housing Act

Over the years, racial discrimination has occurred far too often in the sale of residential property. So the federal Fair Housing Act was enacted in 1968 to try to put an end to such discrimination. It is a very carefully drafted statute, designed to cover a wide spectrum of housing discrimination – including sale of vacant land that is intended to be used for housing - for example. Most states also have parallel state Fair Housing acts.

The following recent U.S. Supreme Court cases illustrate some of the components of the federal Fair Housing Act.

### SUPREME COURT OF THE UNITED STATES
### BANK OF AMERICA CORP. ET AL., PETITIONERS
### V.
### CITY OF MIAMI, FLORIDA
### WELLS FARGO & CO., ET AL., PETITIONERS
### V.
### CITY OF MIAMI, FLORIDA

MAY 1, 2017

BREYER, J., delivered the opinion of the Court, in which ROBERTS, C.J., and GINSBURG, SOTOMAYOR, and KAGAN, JJ., joined. THOMAS, J., filed an opinion concurring in part and dissenting in part, in which KENNEDY and ALITO, JJ., joined. GORSUCH, J., took no part in the consideration or decision of the cases.

Opinion
Justice BREYER delivered the opinion of the Court.

The Fair Housing Act (FHA or Act) forbids
"discriminating against any person in the terms, conditions, or privileges of sale or rental of a dwelling, or in the provision of services or facilities in connection therewith, because of race...." 42 U.S.C. § 3604(b).

It further makes it unlawful for
"any person or other entity whose business includes engaging in residential real estate-related transactions to discriminate against any person in making available such a transaction, or in the terms or conditions of such a transaction, because of race...." § 3605(a).

The statute allows any "aggrieved person" to file a civil action seeking damages for a violation of the statute. §§ 3613(a)(1)(A), 3613(c)(1). And it defines an "aggrieved person" to include "any person who ... claims to have been injured by a discriminatory housing practice." § 3602(i).

The City of Miami claims that two banks, Bank of America and Wells Fargo, intentionally issued riskier mortgages on less favorable terms to African–American and Latino customers than they issued to similarly situated white, non-Latino customers, in violation of §§ 3604(b) and 3605(a). The City, in amended complaints, alleges that these discriminatory practices have (1) "adversely impacted the racial composition of the City;" (2) "impaired the City's goals to assure racial integration and desegregation; (3) "frustrated the City's longstanding and active interest in promoting fair housing and securing the benefits of an integrated community; and (4) disproportionately "caused foreclosures and vacancies in minority communities in Miami." Those foreclosures and vacancies have harmed the City by decreasing "the property value of the foreclosed home as well as the values of other homes in the neighborhood," thereby (a) "reducing property tax revenues to the City," and (b) forcing the City to spend more on municipal services that it provided and still must provide to remedy blight and unsafe and dangerous conditions which exist at properties that were foreclosed as a result of the Banks' illegal lending practices. The City claims that those practices violate the FHA and that it is entitled to damages for the listed injuries.

The Banks respond that the complaints do not set forth a cause of action for two basic reasons. First, they contend that the City's claimed harms do not "arguably" fall within the "zone of interests" that the statute seeks to protect, hence, the City is not an "aggrieved person" entitled to sue under the Act, § 3602(i). Second, they say that the complaint fails to draw a "proximate-cause" connection between the violation claimed and the harm allegedly suffered. In their view, even if the City proves the violations it charges, the distance between those violations and the harms the City claims to have suffered is simply too great to entitle the City to collect damages.

We hold that the City's claimed injuries fall within the zone of interests that the FHA arguably protects. Hence, the City is an "aggrieved person" able to bring suit under the statute. We also hold that, to establish proximate cause under the FHA, a plaintiff must do more than show that its injuries foreseeably flowed from the alleged statutory violation. The lower court decided these cases on the theory that foreseeability is all that the statute requires, so we vacate and remand for further proceedings.

I

In 2013, the City of Miami brought lawsuits in federal court against two banks, Bank of America and Wells Fargo. The City's complaints charge that the Banks discriminatorily imposed more onerous, and indeed "predatory," conditions on loans made to minority borrowers than to similarly situated nonminority borrowers. Those "predatory" practices included, among others, excessively high interest rates, unjustified fees, teaser low-rate loans that overstated refinancing opportunities, large prepayment penalties, and—when default loomed—unjustified refusals to refinance or modify the loans. Due to the discriminatory nature of the Banks' practices, default and foreclosure rates among minority borrowers were higher than among otherwise similar white borrowers and were concentrated in minority neighborhoods. Higher foreclosure rates lowered property values and diminished property-tax revenue. Higher foreclosure rates—especially when accompanied by vacancies—also increased demand for municipal services, such as police, fire, and building and code enforcement services, all needed "to remedy blight and unsafe and dangerous conditions" that the foreclosures and vacancies generate. The complaints describe statistical analyses that trace the City's financial losses to the Banks' discriminatory practices.

The District Court dismissed the complaints on the grounds that (1) the harms alleged, being economic and not discriminatory, fell outside the zone of interests the FHA protects; (2) the complaints fail to show a sufficient causal connection between the City's injuries and the Banks' discriminatory conduct; and (3) the complaints fail to allege unlawful activity occurring within the Act's 2–year statute of limitations. The City then filed amended complaints (the complaints now before us) and sought reconsideration. The District Court held that the amended complaints could solve only the statute of limitations problem. It consequently declined to reconsider the dismissals.

The Court of Appeals reversed.

The Banks filed petitions for certiorari, asking us to decide whether, as the Court of Appeals had in effect held, the amended complaints satisfied the FHA's zone-of-interests and proximate-cause requirements. We agreed to do so.

## II

To satisfy the Constitution's restriction of this Court's jurisdiction to "Cases" and "Controversies," Art. III, § 2, a plaintiff must demonstrate constitutional standing. To do so, the plaintiff must show an "injury in fact" that is "fairly traceable" to the defendant's conduct and "that is likely to be redressed by a favorable judicial decision." This Court has also referred to a plaintiff's need to satisfy "prudential" or "statutory" standing requirements. The requirement at issue is in reality tied to a particular statute. The question is whether the statute grants the plaintiff the cause of action that he asserts. In answering that question, we presume that a statute ordinarily provides a cause of action "only to plaintiffs whose interests fall within the zone of interests protected by the law invoked." We have added that "whether a plaintiff comes within 'the zone of interests' is an issue that requires us to determine, using traditional tools of statutory interpretation, whether a legislatively conferred cause of action encompasses a particular plaintiff's claim."

Here, we conclude that the City's claims of financial injury in their amended complaints—specifically, lost tax revenue and extra municipal expenses—satisfy the "cause-of-action" (or "prudential standing") requirement. To use the language of *Data Processing*, the City's claims of injury it suffered as a result of the statutory violations are, at the least, "*arguably* within the zone of interests" that the FHA protects.

The FHA permits any "aggrieved person" to bring a housing-discrimination lawsuit. 42 U.S.C. § 3613(a). The statute defines "aggrieved person" as "any person who" either "claims to have been injured by a discriminatory housing practice" or believes that such an injury "is about to occur." § 3602(i).

This Court has repeatedly written that the FHA's definition of person "aggrieved" reflects a congressional intent to confer standing broadly. We have said that the definition of "person aggrieved" in the original version of the FHA, § 810(a), 82 Stat. 85, "showed a congressional intention to define standing as broadly as is permitted by Article III of the Constitution."

Thus, we have held that the Act allows suits by white tenants claiming that they were deprived benefits from interracial associations when discriminatory rental practices kept minorities out of their apartment complex, *Trafficante*; a village alleging that it lost tax revenue and had the racial balance of its community undermined by racial-steering practices, *Gladstone*; and a nonprofit organization that spent money to combat housing discrimination, *Havens Realty*. Contrary to the dissent's view, those cases did more than "suggest" that plaintiffs similarly situated to the City have a cause of action under the FHA. They held as much. And the dissent is wrong to say that we characterized those cases as resting on "ill-considered dictum." The "dictum" we cast doubt on in *Thompson* addressed who may sue under Title VII, the employment discrimination statute, not under the FHA.

Finally, in 1988, when Congress amended the FHA, it retained without significant change the definition of "person aggrieved" that this Court had broadly construed. Indeed, Congress "was aware of" our precedent and "made a considered judgment to retain the relevant statutory text."

The Banks do not deny the broad reach of the words "aggrieved person" as defined in the FHA. But they do contend that those words nonetheless set boundaries that fall short of those the Constitution sets. The Court's language in *Trafficante, Gladstone,* and *Havens Realty,* they argue, was exaggerated and unnecessary to decide the cases then before the Court. Moreover, they warn that taking the Court's words literally—providing everyone with constitutional standing a cause of action under the FHA—would produce a legal anomaly. The Banks say it would be similarly farfetched if restaurants, plumbers, utility companies, or any other participant in the local economy could sue the Banks to recover business they lost when people had to give up their homes and leave the neighborhood as a result of the Banks' discriminatory lending practices. That, they believe, cannot have been the intent of the Congress that enacted or amended the FHA.

We need not discuss the Banks' argument at length, for even if we assume for argument's sake that some form of it is valid, we nonetheless conclude that the City's financial injuries fall within the zone of interests that the FHA protects. Our case law with respect to the FHA drives that conclusion. The City's complaints allege that the Banks "intentionally targeted predatory practices at African–American and Latino neighborhoods and residents." That unlawful conduct led to a "concentration" of "foreclosures and vacancies" in those neighborhoods. Those concentrated "foreclosures and vacancies" caused "stagnation and decline in African–American and Latino neighborhoods." They hindered the City's efforts to create integrated, stable neighborhoods. And, highly relevant here, they reduced property values, diminishing the City's property-tax revenue and increasing demand for municipal services.

Those claims are similar in kind to the claims the Village of Bellwood raised in *Gladstone*. There, the plaintiff village had alleged that it was "injured by having its housing market wrongfully and illegally manipulated to the economic and social detriment of the citizens of the village." We held that the village could bring suit. We wrote that the complaint in effect alleged that the defendant-realtors' racial steering "affected the village's racial composition," "reduced the total number of buyers in the Bellwood housing market," "precipitated an exodus of white residents," and caused "prices to be deflected downward." Those circumstances adversely affected the village by, among other things, *producing* a "significant reduction in property values that directly injures a municipality by diminishing its tax base, thus threatening its ability to bear the costs of local government and to provide services."

The upshot is that the City alleges economic injuries that arguably fall within the FHA's zone of interests, as we have previously interpreted that statute. Principles of *stare decisis* compel our adherence to those precedents in this context. And principles of statutory interpretation require us to respect Congress' decision to ratify those precedents when it reenacted the relevant statutory text.

# III

The remaining question is one of causation: Did the Banks' allegedly discriminatory lending practices proximately cause the City to lose property-tax revenue and spend more on municipal services? The Eleventh Circuit concluded that the answer is "yes" because the City plausibly alleged that its financial injuries were foreseeable results of the Banks' misconduct. We conclude that foreseeability alone is not sufficient to establish proximate cause under the FHA, and therefore vacate the judgment below.

It is a "well established principle of the common law that in all cases of loss, we are to attribute it to the proximate cause, and not to any remote cause." We assume Congress "is familiar with the common-law rule and does not mean to displace it *sub silentio*" in federal causes of action. A claim for damages under the FHA—which is akin to a "tort action," is no exception to this traditional requirement. "Proximate-cause analysis is controlled by the nature of the statutory cause of action. The question it presents is whether the harm alleged has a sufficiently close connection to the conduct the statute prohibits."

In these cases, the "conduct the statute prohibits" consists of intentionally lending to minority borrowers on worse terms than equally creditworthy nonminority borrowers and inducing defaults by failing to extend refinancing and loan modifications to minority borrowers on fair terms. The City alleges that the Banks' misconduct led to a disproportionate number of foreclosures and vacancies in specific Miami neighborhoods. These foreclosures and vacancies purportedly harmed the City, which lost property-tax revenue when the value of the properties in those neighborhoods fell and the city was forced to spend more on municipal services in the affected areas.

The Eleventh Circuit concluded that the City adequately pleaded that the Banks' misconduct proximately caused these financial injuries. The court held that in the context of the FHA "the proper standard" for proximate cause "is based on foreseeability." The City, it continued, satisfied that element: Although there are "several links in the causal chain" between the charged discriminatory lending practices and the claimed losses, the City plausibly alleged that "none are unforeseeable."

We conclude that the Eleventh Circuit erred in holding that foreseeability is sufficient to establish proximate cause under the FHA. As we have explained, proximate cause "generally bars suits for alleged harm that is 'too remote' from the defendant's unlawful conduct." In the context of the FHA, foreseeability alone does not ensure the close connection that proximate cause requires. The housing market is interconnected with economic and social life. A violation of the FHA may, therefore, "be expected to cause ripples of harm to flow" far beyond the defendant's misconduct. Nothing in the statute suggests that Congress intended to provide a remedy wherever those ripples travel. And entertaining suits to recover damages for any foreseeable result of an FHA violation would risk "massive and complex damages litigation."

Rather, proximate cause under the FHA requires some direct relation between the injury asserted and the injurious conduct alleged. A damages claim under the statute is analogous to a number of tort actions recognized at common law, and we have repeatedly applied directness principles to statutes with common-law foundations. The general tendency in these cases, in regard to damages at least, is not to go beyond the first step. What falls within that "first step" depends in part on the nature of the statutory cause of action, and an assessment of what is administratively possible and convenient.

The parties have asked us to draw the precise boundaries of proximate cause under the FHA and to determine on which side of the line the City's financial injuries fall. We decline to do so. The Eleventh Circuit grounded its decision on the theory that proximate cause under the FHA is "based on foreseeability" alone. We therefore lack the benefit of its judgment on how the contrary principles we have just stated apply to the FHA. Nor has any other court of appeals weighed in on the issue. The lower courts should define, in the first instance, the contours of proximate cause under the FHA and decide how that standard applies to the City's claims for lost property-tax revenue and increased municipal expenses.

## IV

The judgments of the Court of Appeals for the Eleventh Circuit are vacated, and the cases are remanded for further proceedings consistent with this opinion.

*It is so ordered.*

Note: Another aspect of the Fair Housing Act, (the issue of disparate impact), is discussed in the recent U.S. Supreme Court case below.

# SUPREME COURT OF THE UNITED STATES
## TEXAS DEPARTMENT OF HOUSING AND COMMUNITY AFFAIRS, ET AL., PETITIONERS
### V.
## THE INCLUSIVE COMMUNITIES PROJECT, INC., ET AL.

JUNE 25, 2015

KENNEDY, J., delivered the opinion of the Court, in which GINSBURG, BREYER, SOTOMAYOR, and KAGAN, JJ., joined. THOMAS, J., filed a dissenting opinion. ALITO, J., filed a dissenting opinion, in which ROBERTS, C.J., and SCALIA and THOMAS, JJ., joined.

Opinion

Justice KENNEDY delivered the opinion of the Court.

The underlying dispute in this case concerns where housing for low-income persons should be constructed in Dallas, Texas—that is, whether the housing should be built in the inner city or in the suburbs. This dispute comes to the Court on a disparate-impact theory of liability. In contrast to a disparate-treatment case, where a "plaintiff must establish that the defendant had a discriminatory intent or motive," a plaintiff bringing a disparate-impact claim challenges practices that have a "disproportionately adverse effect on minorities" and are otherwise unjustified by a legitimate rationale. The question presented for the Court's determination is whether disparate-impact claims are cognizable under the Fair Housing Act (or FHA), 82 Stat. 81, as amended, 42 U.S.C. § 3601 *et seq.*

## I

### A

Before turning to the question presented, it is necessary to discuss a different federal statute that gives rise to this dispute. The Federal Government provides low-income housing tax credits that are distributed to developers through designated state agencies. 26 U.S.C. § 42. Congress has directed States to develop plans identifying selection criteria for distributing the credits. Those plans must include certain criteria, such as public housing waiting lists, as well as certain preferences, including that low-income housing units "contribute to a concerted community revitalization plan" and be built in census tracts populated predominantly by low-income residents.

Federal law thus favors the distribution of these tax credits for the development of housing units in low-income areas.

In the State of Texas these federal credits are distributed by the Texas Department of Housing and Community Affairs (Department). Under Texas law, a developer's application for the tax credits is scored under a point system that gives priority to statutory criteria, such as the financial feasibility of the development project and the income level of tenants. The Texas Attorney General has interpreted state law to permit the consideration of additional criteria, such as whether the housing units will be built in a neighborhood with good schools. Those criteria cannot be awarded more points than statutorily mandated criteria.

The Inclusive Communities Project, Inc. (ICP), is a Texas-based nonprofit corporation that assists low-income families in obtaining affordable housing. In 2008, the ICP brought this suit against the Department and its officers in the United States District Court for the Northern District of Texas. As relevant here, it brought a disparate-impact claim under §§ 804(a) and 805(a) of the FHA. The ICP alleged the Department has caused continued segregated housing patterns by its disproportionate allocation of the tax credits, granting too many credits for housing in predominantly black inner-city areas and too few in predominantly white suburban neighborhoods. The ICP contended that the Department must modify its selection criteria in order to encourage the construction of low-income housing in suburban communities.

The District Court concluded that the ICP had established a prima facie case of disparate impact. It relied on two pieces of statistical evidence. First, it found "from 1999–2008, the Department approved tax credits for 49.7% of proposed non-elderly units in 0% to 9.9% Caucasian areas, but only approved 37.4% of proposed non-elderly units in 90% to 100% Caucasian areas." Second, it found "92.29% of low-income housing tax credit units in the city of Dallas were located in census tracts with less than 50% Caucasian residents."

The District Court then placed the burden on the Department to rebut the ICP's prima facie showing of disparate impact.

The District Court's remedial order required the addition of new selection criteria for the tax credits. For instance, it awarded points for units built in neighborhoods with good schools and disqualified sites that are located adjacent to or near hazardous conditions, such as high crime areas or landfills. The remedial order contained no explicit racial targets or quotas.

While the Department's appeal was pending, the Secretary of Housing and Urban Development (HUD) issued a regulation interpreting the FHA to encompass disparate-impact liability. The regulation also established a burden-shifting framework for adjudicating disparate-impact claims. Under the regulation, a plaintiff first must make a prima facie showing of disparate impact. That is, the plaintiff "has the burden of proving that a challenged practice caused or predictably will cause a discriminatory effect." If a statistical discrepancy is caused by factors other than the defendant's policy, a plaintiff cannot establish a prima facie case, and there is no liability. After a plaintiff does establish a prima facie showing of disparate impact, the burden shifts to the defendant to "prove that the challenged practice is necessary to achieve one or more substantial, legitimate, nondiscriminatory interests."

The Court of Appeals for the Fifth Circuit held, consistent with its precedent, that disparate-impact claims are cognizable under the FHA. On the merits, however, the Court of Appeals reversed and remanded.

The Department filed a petition for a writ of certiorari on the question whether disparate-impact claims are cognizable under the FHA. The question was one of first impression, and certiorari followed. It is now appropriate to provide a brief history of the FHA's enactment and its later amendment.

B

*De jure* residential segregation by race was declared unconstitutional almost a century ago, *Buchanan v. Warley*, (1917), but its vestiges remain today, intertwined with the country's economic and social life. Some segregated housing patterns can be traced to conditions that arose in the mid–20th century. Rapid urbanization, concomitant with the rise of suburban developments accessible by car, led many white families to leave the inner cities. This often left minority families concentrated in the center of the Nation's cities. During this time, various practices were followed, sometimes with governmental support, to encourage and maintain the separation of the races: Racially restrictive covenants prevented the conveyance of property to minorities, see *Shelley v. Kraemer*, (1948); steering by real-estate agents led potential buyers to consider homes in racially homogenous areas; and discriminatory lending practices, often referred to as redlining, precluded minority families from purchasing homes in affluent areas. By the 1960's, these policies, practices, and prejudices had created many predominantly black inner cities surrounded by mostly white suburbs.

The mid–1960's was a period of considerable social unrest; and, in response, President Lyndon Johnson established the National Advisory Commission on Civil Disorders, commonly known as the Kerner Commission. After extensive factfinding the Commission identified residential segregation and unequal housing and economic conditions in the inner cities as significant, underlying causes of the social unrest. The Commission found that "nearly two-thirds of all nonwhite families living in the central cities today live in neighborhoods marked by substandard housing and general urban blight." The Commission further found that both open and covert racial discrimination prevented black families from obtaining better housing and moving to integrated communities. The Commission concluded that "our Nation is moving toward two societies, one black, one white—separate and unequal." To reverse "this deepening racial division," it recommended enactment of "a comprehensive and enforceable open-occupancy law making it an offense to discriminate in the sale or rental of any housing ... on the basis of race, creed, color, or national origin."

In April 1968, Dr. Martin Luther King, Jr., was assassinated in Memphis, Tennessee, and the Nation faced a new urgency to resolve the social unrest in the inner cities. Congress responded by adopting the Kerner Commission's recommendation and passing the Fair Housing Act. The statute addressed the denial of housing opportunities on the basis of "race, color, religion, or national origin." Then, in 1988, Congress amended the FHA. Among other provisions, it created certain exemptions from liability and added "familial status" as a protected characteristic.

## II

The issue here is whether, under a proper interpretation of the FHA, housing decisions with a disparate impact are prohibited. Before turning to the FHA, however, it is necessary to consider two other antidiscrimination statutes that preceded it.

The first relevant statute is § 703(a) of Title VII of the Civil Rights Act of 1964. The Court addressed the concept of disparate impact under this statute in *Griggs v. Duke Power Co.*, (1971). There, the employer had a policy requiring its manual laborers to possess a high school diploma and to obtain satisfactory scores on two intelligence tests. The Court of Appeals held the employer had not adopted these job requirements for a racially discriminatory purpose, and the plaintiffs did not challenge that holding in this Court. Instead, the plaintiffs argued § 703(a)(2) covers the discriminatory effect of a practice as well as the motivation behind the practice.

In interpreting § 703(a)(2), the Court reasoned that disparate-impact liability furthered the purpose and design of the statute. The Court explained that, in § 703(a)(2), Congress "proscribed not only overt discrimination but also practices that are fair in form, but discriminatory in operation.

The second relevant statute that bears on the proper interpretation of the FHA is the Age Discrimination in Employment Act of 1967. The Court first addressed whether this provision allows disparate-impact claims in *Smith v. City of Jackson*, (2005). There, a group of older employees challenged their employer's decision to give proportionately greater raises to employees with less than five years of experience.

Explaining that *Griggs* "represented the better reading of Title VII's statutory text," a plurality of the Court concluded that the same reasoning pertained to § 4(a)(2) of the ADEA.

Together, *Griggs* holds and the plurality in *Smith* instructs that antidiscrimination laws must be construed to encompass disparate-impact claims when their text refers to the consequences of actions and not just to the mindset of actors, and where that interpretation is consistent with statutory purpose. These cases also teach that disparate-impact liability must be limited so employers and other regulated entities are able to make the practical business choices and profit-related decisions that sustain a vibrant and dynamic free-enterprise system. And before rejecting a business justification—or, in the case of a governmental entity, an analogous public interest—a court must determine that a plaintiff has shown that there is "an available alternative practice that has less disparate impact and serves the entity's legitimate needs.

Turning to the FHA, the ICP relies on two provisions. Section 804(a) provides that it shall be unlawful:

> "To refuse to sell or rent after the making of a bona fide offer, or to refuse to negotiate for the sale or rental of, or otherwise make unavailable or deny, a dwelling to any person because of race, color, religion, sex, familial status, or national origin." 42 U.S.C. § 3604(a).

Here, the phrase "otherwise make unavailable" is of central importance to the analysis that follows.

Section 805(a), in turn, provides:

> "It shall be unlawful for any person or other entity whose business includes engaging in real estate-related transactions to discriminate against any person in making available such a transaction, or in the terms or conditions of such a transaction, because of race, color, religion, sex, handicap, familial status, or national origin." § 3605(a).

Applied here, the logic of *Griggs* and *Smith* provides strong support for the conclusion that the FHA encompasses disparate-impact claims.

In addition, it is of crucial importance that the existence of disparate-impact liability is supported by amendments to the FHA that Congress enacted in 1988. By that time, all nine Courts of Appeals to have addressed the question had concluded the Fair Housing Act encompassed disparate-impact claims.

When it amended the FHA, Congress was aware of this unanimous precedent. And with that understanding, it made a considered judgment to retain the relevant statutory text.

Against this background understanding in the legal and regulatory system, Congress' decision in 1988 to amend the FHA while still adhering to the operative language in §§ 804(a) and 805(a) is convincing support for the conclusion that Congress accepted and ratified the unanimous holdings of the Courts of Appeals finding disparate-impact liability.

Further and convincing confirmation of Congress' understanding that disparate-impact liability exists under the FHA is revealed by the substance of the 1988 amendments. The amendments included three exemptions from liability that assume the existence of disparate-impact claims.

The relevant 1988 amendments were as follows. First, Congress added a clarifying provision: "Nothing in the FHA prohibits a person engaged in the business of furnishing appraisals of real property to take into consideration factors other than race, color, religion, national origin, sex, handicap, or familial status." Second, Congress provided: "Nothing in the FHA prohibits conduct against a person because such person has been convicted by any court of competent jurisdiction of the illegal manufacture or distribution of a controlled substance." And finally, Congress specified: "Nothing in the FHA limits the applicability of any reasonable ... restrictions regarding the maximum number of occupants permitted to occupy a dwelling."

Recognition of disparate-impact claims is consistent with the FHA's central purpose. The FHA, like Title VII and the ADEA, was enacted to eradicate discriminatory practices within a sector of our Nation's economy. "It is the policy of the United States to provide, within constitutional limitations, for fair housing throughout the United States."

Unlawful practices include zoning laws and other housing restrictions that function unfairly to exclude minorities from certain neighborhoods without any sufficient justification. Suits targeting such practices reside at the heartland of disparate-impact liability. See, *e.g., Huntington,* (invalidating zoning law preventing construction of multifamily rental units); *Black Jack,* (invalidating ordinance prohibiting construction of new multifamily dwellings); *Greater New Orleans Fair Housing Action Center v. St. Bernard Parish,* (invalidating post-Hurricane Katrina ordinance restricting the rental of housing units to only " blood relatives " in an area of the city that was 88.3% white and 7.6% black). The availability of disparate-impact liability, furthermore, has allowed private developers to vindicate the FHA's objectives and to protect their property rights by stopping municipalities from enforcing arbitrary and, in practice, discriminatory ordinances barring the construction of certain types of housing units.

Recognition of disparate-impact liability under the FHA also plays a role in uncovering discriminatory intent: It permits plaintiffs to counteract unconscious prejudices and disguised animus that escape easy classification as disparate treatment. In this way disparate-impact liability may prevent segregated housing patterns that might otherwise result from covert and illicit stereotyping.

But disparate-impact liability has always been properly limited in key respects that avoid the serious constitutional questions that might arise under the FHA, for instance, if such liability were imposed based solely on a showing of a statistical disparity. Disparate-impact liability mandates the "removal of artificial, arbitrary, and unnecessary barriers," not the displacement of valid governmental policies. The FHA is not an instrument to force housing authorities to reorder their priorities. Rather, the FHA aims to ensure that those priorities can be achieved without arbitrarily creating discriminatory effects or perpetuating segregation.

The underlying dispute in this case involves a novel theory of liability. This case, on remand, may be seen simply as an attempt to second-guess which of two reasonable approaches a housing authority should follow in the sound exercise of its discretion in allocating tax credits for low-income housing.

An important and appropriate means of ensuring that disparate-impact liability is properly limited is to give housing authorities and private developers leeway to state and explain the valid interest served by their policies. This step of the analysis is analogous to the business necessity standard under Title VII and provides a defense against disparate-impact liability.

It would be paradoxical to construe the FHA to impose onerous costs on actors who encourage revitalizing dilapidated housing in our Nation's cities merely because some other priority might seem preferable. Entrepreneurs must be given latitude to consider market factors. Zoning officials, moreover, must often make decisions based on a mix of factors, both objective (such as cost and traffic patterns) and, at least to some extent, subjective (such as preserving historic architecture). These factors contribute to a community's quality of life and are legitimate concerns for housing authorities. The FHA does not decree a particular vision of urban development; and it does not put housing authorities and private developers in a double bind of liability, subject to suit whether they choose to rejuvenate a city core or to promote new low-income housing in suburban communities. As HUD itself recognized in its recent rulemaking, disparate-impact liability "does not mandate that affordable housing be located in neighborhoods with any particular characteristic."

In a similar vein, a disparate-impact claim that relies on a statistical disparity must fail if the plaintiff cannot point to a defendant's policy or policies causing that disparity. A robust causality requirement ensures that "racial imbalance does not, without more, establish a prima facie case of disparate impact" and thus protects defendants from being held liable for racial disparities they did not create.

The litigation at issue here provides an example. From the standpoint of determining advantage or disadvantage to racial minorities, it seems difficult to say as a general matter that a decision to build low-income housing in a blighted inner-city neighborhood instead of a suburb is discriminatory, or vice versa. If those sorts of judgments are subject to challenge without adequate safeguards, then there is a danger that potential defendants may adopt racial quotas—a circumstance that itself raises serious constitutional concerns.

Courts must therefore examine with care whether a plaintiff has made out a prima facie case of disparate impact and prompt resolution of these cases is important. A plaintiff who fails to allege facts at the pleading stage or produce statistical evidence demonstrating a causal connection cannot make out a prima facie case of disparate impact. For instance, a plaintiff challenging the decision of a private developer to construct a new building in one location rather than another will not easily be able to show this is a policy causing a disparate impact because such a one-time decision may not be a policy at all. It may also be difficult to establish causation because of the multiple factors that go into investment decisions about where to construct or renovate housing units.

The FHA imposes a command with respect to disparate-impact liability. Here, that command goes to a state entity. In other cases, the command will go to a private person or entity. Governmental or private policies are not contrary to the disparate-impact requirement unless they are "artificial, arbitrary, and unnecessary barriers." Difficult questions might arise if disparate-impact liability under the FHA caused race to be used and considered in a pervasive and explicit manner to justify governmental or private actions that, in fact, tend to perpetuate race-based considerations rather than move beyond them. Courts should avoid interpreting disparate-impact liability to be so expansive as to inject racial considerations into every housing decision.

The limitations on disparate-impact liability discussed here are also necessary to protect potential defendants against abusive disparate-impact claims. If the specter of disparate-impact litigation causes private developers to no longer construct or renovate housing units for low-income individuals, then the FHA would have undermined its own purpose as well as the free-market system. And as to governmental entities, they must not be prevented from achieving legitimate objectives, such as ensuring compliance with health and safety codes.

Were standards for proceeding with disparate-impact suits not to incorporate at least the safeguards discussed here, then disparate-impact liability might displace valid governmental and private priorities, rather than solely "removing artificial, arbitrary, and unnecessary barriers." And that, in turn, would set our Nation back in its quest to reduce the salience of race in our social and economic system.

It must be noted further that, even when courts do find liability under a disparate-impact theory, their remedial orders must be consistent with the Constitution. Remedial orders in disparate-impact cases should concentrate on the elimination of the offending practice that "arbitrarily operates invidiously to discriminate on the basis of race." If additional measures are adopted, courts should strive to design them to eliminate racial disparities through race-neutral means.

While the automatic or pervasive injection of race into public and private transactions covered by the FHA has special dangers, it is also true that race may be considered in certain circumstances and in a proper fashion.

⌐The Court holds that disparate-impact claims are cognizable under the Fair Housing Act upon considering its results-oriented language ⌐

## III

In light of the longstanding judicial interpretation of the FHA to encompass disparate-impact claims and congressional reaffirmation of that result, residents and policymakers have come to rely on the availability of disparate-impact claims. Indeed, many of our Nation's largest cities—entities that are potential defendants in disparate-impact suits—have submitted an *amicus* brief in this case supporting disparate-impact liability under the FHA. The existence of disparate-impact liability in the substantial majority of the Courts of Appeals for the last several decades "has not given rise to dire consequences."

Much progress remains to be made in our Nation's continuing struggle against racial isolation. In striving to achieve our "historic commitment to creating an integrated society," we must remain wary of policies that reduce homeowners to nothing more than their race. But since the passage of the Fair Housing Act in 1968 and against the backdrop of disparate-impact liability in nearly every jurisdiction, many cities have become more diverse. The FHA must play an important part in avoiding the Kerner Commission's grim prophecy that "our Nation is moving toward two societies, one black, one white—separate and unequal." The Court acknowledges the Fair Housing Act's continuing role in moving the Nation toward a more integrated society.

⌐The judgment of the Court of Appeals for the Fifth Circuit is affirmed, and the case is remanded for further proceedings consistent with this opinion. ⌐

*It is so ordered.*

# CHAPTER SIX

# EASEMENTS, COVENANTS AND EQUITABLE SERVITUDES

## INTRODUCTION

Many times individual landowners agree to special rights or restrictions with regard to use of their land. These private restrictions usually come in the form of easements, covenants, or equitable servitudes. For the most part these restrictions are put into writing, and are recorded in the land records, so that any future purchaser of the land will be on notice of the existing private restrictions.

## A. Easements

Easements are the most frequently used private land use restrictions. When landowner Sam gives adjacent landowner Debby, (and her successors in interest), a right to drive across Sam's land, as a shorter way to reach the highway, then Debby has an easement across Sam's land. Debby is the dominant owner, because it is her land that benefits from the easement. Sam is the servient owner, because it is his land that is subject to the easement. This would be an easement appurtenant, because Sam's land is adjacent to Debby's land, and the easement is of benefit to Debby, and anyone to whom she later sells the land.

Virtually all urban land is also subject to various easements in gross, to allow the electric company, for example, a right to run the wires for electricity across virtually all of the parcels in the city – so that everyone has access to electricity. These easements owned by entities such as the electric company are called easements in gross, since they do not benefit any specific piece of land. They are nearly always commercial easements in gross, and may be sold by one electric company to its successor. Most utilities have the legal right to condemn the necessary easements, but that usually is not necessary. When a developer develops a piece of urban land the developer will automatically donate the necessary utility easements.

All easements are considered to be an ownership interest in land. When Sam grants Debby (and her successors) a right of way to go across Sam's land, Debby (and then her successors) have an interest in Sam's land. Because easements are interests in land, they are not subject to changed conditions, and they cannot be extinguished except by agreement between the dominant and servient owners, release by the dominant owner, or abandonment by the dominant owner.

When the dominant and servient owner agree to create an easement, they will usually specify just which part of the servient owner's land is subject to the easement – where the road or right of way is to be located.

The following very old, and very famous case makes that point clear.

## SUPREME COURT OF NEW HAMPSHIRE
### SAKANSKY ET AL.
### v.
### WEIN ET AL.

NOVEMBER 7, 1933

Petition for injunction. The facts were found by a master.

At the time of the filing of the petition, the plaintiff Sakansky was the owner of a certain parcel of land with the buildings thereon, situated on the westerly side of Main street in Laconia. The deed by means of which he took title also conveyed to him a right of way, eighteen feet in width, over land which for the purposes of this case may be regarded as belonging to the defendants. Before trial Sakansky conveyed this property, together with the right of way, to the plaintiff J. J. Newberry Company. This right of way, with no expressed limitation as to mode of use, originated in a deed to the plaintiff's ancestor in title in 1849. This deed gave the right of way definite location upon the ground.

The defendants wish to develop their servient estate by erecting a building over the land subjected to the plaintiff's easement. They proposed to leave an opening in their new building at the place where it crosses the way; this opening to allow headroom of eight feet for the way where it passes under the defendant's building. They also propose to lay out a new way over level ground around the westerly end of the new building, which new way will give access to the same point on the dominant estate as the old way. This new way is free from obstruction and affords an easy means of access for vehicles whose height would prevent them from continuing to use the old way. The plaintiff objected and excepted to the introduction of evidence concerning the proposed new way.

The master ruled that neither party had any absolute or unlimited rights in the old right of way, but that the rights of each were to be determined by the rule of reasonableness. He further ruled that what was reasonable was a question of fact, to be determined by considering all the circumstances of all of the property, including the advantages accruing to the defendants and the disadvantages to be suffered by the plaintiff.

Applying the above principles he found that, considering the proposed additional right of way, the defendants' proposed reduction in height of the old right of way was not an unreasonable interference with the plaintiff's rights. But he found further that if it was not proper for him to take into consideration the proposed new way, then a reduction in height of the old way, as proposed, would be an unreasonable interference with the plaintiff's rights. On the basis of the above rulings of law and findings of fact, and giving consideration to the proposed new way, he recommended a decree permitting the defendants to build over the old way upon condition that they provide the plaintiff with the new way as proposed by them.

The plaintiff's exception to the admission of evidence concerning the new right of way, and the question of whether the plaintiff is entitled to an injunction, were transferred without ruling by Burque, J.

WOODBURY, Justice.

In this state the respective rights of dominant and servient owners are not determined by reference to some technical and more or less arbitrary rule of property law as expressed in some ancient maxim, but are determined by reference to the rule of reason. The application of this rule raises a question of fact to be determined by consideration of all the surrounding circumstances, including the location and uses of both dominant and servient estates, and taking into consideration the advantage to be derived by one and the disadvantage to be suffered by the other owner. The same rule has been applied to easements other than rights of way; for example, to aqueduct rights and to rights of flowage, both as to surface water and as to water in a stream. In the somewhat analogous cases involving the reciprocal rights of adjoining owners the same principle has been applied. The master's general rulings of law are in accordance with the foregoing and are therefore correct.

The error arises in the application of the above principle to the situation presented in the case at bar.

Implicit in the master's findings of fact is the finding that it is reasonable for the plaintiff to have access to the rear of its premises for vehicles over eight feet high. The master has applied the rule of reason to deflect this reasonable use over the new way which the defendants propose to create. This may not be done under the circumstances of this case.

The rule of reason is a rule of interpretation. Its office is either to give a meaning to words which the parties or their ancestors in title have actually used, as was done in <u>Farmington, etc., Ass'n v. Trafton,</u> in which the word "necessary" was held to mean "reasonably necessary," or else to give a detailed definition to rights created by general words either actually used, or whose existence is implied by law. This rule of reason does not prevent the parties from making any contract regarding their respective rights which they may wish, regardless of the reasonableness of their wishes on the subject. The rule merely refuses to give unreasonable rights, or to impose unreasonable burdens, when the parties, either actually or by legal implication, have spoken generally.

In the case at bar the parties are bound by a contract which not only gave the dominant owner a way across the servient estate for the purpose of access to the rear of its premises, but also gave that way definite location upon the ground. The use which the plaintiff may make of the way is limited by the bounds of reason, but within those bounds it has the unlimited right to travel over the land set apart for a way. It has no right to insist upon the use of any other land of the defendants for a way, regardless of how necessary such other land may be to it, and regardless of how little damage or inconvenience such use of the defendants' land might occasion to them. No more may the defendants compel the plaintiff to detour over other land of theirs.

The rule of reason is to be applied to determine whether or not the plaintiff has the right to approach the rear of its building with vehicles over eight feet high. This question having been answered in the affirmative, the plaintiff, by virtue of the grant, has the right to use that land, and only that land, which was set apart for the purpose of a way, and it may insist upon that right regardless of whether such insistence on its part be reasonable or not.

This does not mean that the defendants may not build over the old way at all. The plaintiff has no absolute right to have the way remain open to the sky. What, if any, structure the defendants may build over the way depends upon what is reasonable. The master has already found that a height of only eight feet for the old way is not reasonable. The defendants must provide more headroom. How much more is a question of fact, which may be determined later in further proceedings before the master if the defendants wish for a definition of the extent of this right.

In view of the fact that the rule of reason may not be invoked to deflect the plaintiff's reasonable travel over the new way, evidence concerning that way becomes immaterial and irrelevant, and hence it was error for the master to have admitted it. Had the rule of reason been applicable, it would not have been error to have admitted evidence regarding this other means of access, since it was one of the surrounding circumstances affecting the situation and the fact that the defendants proposed to lay it out over their own land for the plaintiff's benefit does not render it any the less one of the surrounding circumstances.

The argument advanced that what is reasonable must be considered in the light of the situation as it was at the time the way was granted in 1849 is without merit. What is or is not a reasonable use of a way does not become crystallized at any particular moment of time. Changing needs of either owner may operate to make unreasonable a use of the way previously reasonable, or to make reasonable a use previously unreasonable. There is an element of time as well as of space in this question of reasonableness. In the absence of contract on the subject, the owner of the dominant estate is not limited in his use of the way to such vehicles only as were known at the time the way was created, but he may use the way for any vehicle which his reasonable needs may require in the development of his estate. In this respect the use of the way is analogous to the use of a highway.

Case discharged. All concurred.

Note: Most easements are created by grant, by a specific writing. But they may also be created in two other ways – by prescription or by implication.

1. Prescriptive Easements.

If Debby just drives across Sam's land long enough, without Sam's permission, then Debby will gain a prescriptive easement appurtenant. This is very much like adverse possession. The difference is that Debby just has a right to use Sam's land for the easement – she does not actually have full title to Sam's land – just title to that easement. Sam can still do anything he likes with the land, as long as he does not interfere with Debby's right to use of the easement.

When Debby gains a prescriptive easement across Sam's land that is a *private prescriptive easement*, and will continue to be an easement appurtenant to Debby's land when she sells the land to another person.

If all the kids in the neighborhood cut across Sam's land on the way to school, without Sam's permission, then that may well turn into a *public prescriptive easement*

– for the benefit of the public as a whole. Sam will not be allowed to stop the public from using that path, once a prescriptive easement has been established.

Prescriptive easements are one of many reasons the buyer of land, or the lawyer for the buyer, really has to take a look at the land itself. Prescriptive easements, like adverse possession, will not show up in the land records. They are simply not recorded. But if a buyer notices roads or paths across the land, the buyer is on inquiry notice to find out who has been using those roads or paths, and for how long. Once a prescriptive easement has been established, it has a definite location, and any use of the servient estate cannot interfere with the prescriptive easement.

Remember: If an owner just gives others *permission* to cross the land, then no prescriptive easement will be established, and the owner has a right to revoke that permission at any time.

The following case is an entertaining case about a prescriptive easement, and points out that the dominant owner has a right to do whatever is necessary to maintain the easement.

## COURT OF APPEALS OF COLORADO
## HELEN MARY SHRULL
## V.
## MIKE RAPASARDI AND ROBERT WENZEL, A/K/A ROBERT RAPASARDI

### NOVEMBER 20, 1973

OPINION BY: COYTE

This case involves the right of a landowner to clean and maintain a drainage ditch across the property of an adjoining landowner. The trial court held that defendant Rapasardi had an easement which permitted him to clean and maintain a ditch across plaintiff's property. Plaintiff appeals and we affirm.

The case was initiated by Shrull's filing a complaint alleging that defendants committed a trespass in September 1969 when they entered her property and excavated a ditch by means of explosives. In their answer, defendants admitted entering the property and opening a ditch, but raised various defenses including existence of an easement, estoppel, and consent.

The record discloses that plaintiff and defendant Mike Rapasardi own adjoining ranches in Garfield County, Colorado. Portions of the defendant's ranch lie to the north and to the south of a triangular-shaped portion of plaintiff's ranch. The land in the area of the ranches generally slopes in a southerly direction. Surface water and irrigation waste water drain from the northern portion of defendant's ranch across the triangular-shaped portion of plaintiff's ranch to the southern portion of defendant's ranch. There is a spring that develops some water on the contested portion of plaintiff's property. This property consists of a low, swampy area of several acres. The swampy area extends onto the northern portion of defendant's property. Drainage from this swampy area is intercepted by a ditch near the southerly line of plaintiff's property and the water is used for irrigation of the southern portion of defendant's ranch.

Defendants admitted entering plaintiff's property and opening a ditch across it by means of blasting powder. Defendants testified that they had maintained a ditch across the property since 1929. They further testified that because of the swampy nature of the area it was necessary to reopen the ditch periodically. The nature of the ground made it impossible to use machinery and in prior years the ditch had been opened by hand, but in 1952, 1962, and again in 1969, blasting powder was used for that purpose. Defendants testified that the ditch across plaintiff's property served a two-fold purpose: To minimize damage from water backing up and thereby causing expansion of the swamp; and to assure a constant flow of water for irrigating the southern portion of the ranch.

Plaintiff purchased her property in 1957. There was considerable testimony about the events which occurred in connection with the use of blasting powder by defendants in 1962. Plaintiff and her husband were nearby when defendants excavated the ditch. They testified that they immediately objected to any blasting. On the other hand, there was testimony that when the reason for the blasting was explained to plaintiff, she said that since defendants had started the excavation they could continue with it.

The trial court found that both surface and subsurface water had drained through the swampy area on plaintiff's property for many years. However, the court found that there was no man-made ditch across the area when plaintiff purchased the property, and accordingly, it held that she had purchased the property without notice and free from any easement for a ditch. The trial court further found, however, that the excavation conducted in 1962 was carried out with the knowledge of plaintiff and without any interference by her at the time or during the subsequent period until this suit was filed some seven years later.

Relying upon *Leonard v. Buerger*, the trial court concluded that defendants have a right-of-way for a ditch across plaintiff's property. Accordingly, the court entered judgment for defendants and ruled that defendants could maintain a ditch across plaintiff's property subject to certain conditions, including a requirement that they give plaintiff twenty-four hours advance notice of any blasting, limit the dimensions of the ditch, and clean up the debris. On appeal, plaintiff challenges the trial court's ruling with respect to the ditch right-of-way and the extent of defendants' right to enter upon her property to maintain the ditch.

The trial court correctly applied the law. As stated in *Leonard v. Buerger, supra*:

> "There is no law which forbids one to grant permission to his neighbor to dig an irrigation ditch across his land without first purchasing a right of way and getting a deed to it. When, under such circumstances, the ditch actually is excavated and put into use without objection, or by approval, the owner of land traversed thereby may not thereafter withdraw his consent, deny the right of maintenance or destroy the ditch. Such consent need not even be in writing. Where the ditch has been in existence for any appreciable time, consent to its original construction is presumed."

Accordingly, the judgment of the trial court granting an easement must be affirmed.

The remaining question is the nature and extent of defendant's right to go upon plaintiff's property to excavate and maintain the ditch.

If the owner of the dominant estate does not unnecessarily inconvenience the owner of the servient estate and use of the easement is not expanded, the owner of the dominant estate may do whatever is reasonably necessary for the enjoyment of the easement, including repairs, ingress and egress, with space therefor as exigency may show. The right of an owner with respect to a ditch excavated over the private land of another extends to the bed of the ditch and sufficient ground on either side to operate it properly, depending necessarily, in each case, upon the particular circumstances and conditions.

We conclude that the trial court's order allowing defendants, under the conditions imposed, to excavate and maintain a ditch through the swampy area of plaintiff's property was a reasonable and proper incident of the easement for a drainage ditch.

Judgment affirmed.

## 2. Implied Easement by Necessity

In virtually all states there is a strong public policy against allowing any piece of land to become "landlocked" – to have no access to a public road. So the doctrine of *implied easement by necessity* allows a court to determine that there *is* an *implied* easement, allowing access to a public road. This implied easement by necessity will always be over "the last brick in the wall" – the land which finally cuts the landlocked piece of land off from access to a public road. It is always over land which was once owned by a common owner - the same person owned the land that has become land-locked, and the land that was "the last brick in the wall."

The following case will make that clearer. It also describes the difference between a *lien theory* state and a *title theory* state.

### UNITED STATES DISTRICT COURT
### DISTRICT OF MONTANA
### ESSEX VENTURES, LLP, DAVID A. TRIPP, THE WEEKS AT ALASKA COMMUNITY PROPERTY TRUST, KTM, LLC, FLOYD C. BOSSARD, MARGARET J. BOSSARD, J&MC, L.L.P., WILLIAM BOUCHEE, AS PERSONAL REPRESENTATIVE OF THE ESTATE OF GRACE M. BROOKS, AND THE RICHARD C. BOSSARD AND MARGARET B. BOSSARD REVOCABLE TRUST, PLAINTIFFS,
### V.
### ROBERT C. SAMUEL, DEFENDANT

### DECEMBER 15, 2015

ORDER

Dana L. Christensen, Chief Judge, United States District Court

BACKGROUND

This case arises from a single property owner offering two separate but abutting portions of her real property as security for two separate loans. The material facts surrounding these transactions are not in dispute. Plaintiffs are the current owners of the so-called "Riverside Lot," a triangular piece of real property situated along the

Clark Fork River west of Missoula, Montana. The Riverside Lot is landlocked to the extent it lacks legal access to a public road. Apart from its boundary with the Clark Fork River, the Riverside Lot borders private property, including Defendant Robert C. Samuel's (Samuel) so-called "Exhibit C Properties," in all directions.

The Riverside Lot and Exhibit C Properties were once under single ownership. Bonnie G. Snavely (Snavely), whose family historically owned much of the land in this immediate part of Missoula County, mortgaged the Exhibit C Properties, among others, to secure a loan from American West Bank in 2003. In 2005, American West assigned its mortgage interest to Samuel. Both the Snavely mortgage and the assignment were properly recorded. In 2006, Snavely mortgaged the Riverside Lot to secure a loan from Plaintiffs. This mortgage was also properly recorded.

Snavely ultimately defaulted on both loans—first the loan held by Samuel, then the loan held by Plaintiffs. Samuel obtained a judgment and decree of foreclosure on the Exhibit C Properties on December 14, 2006 and, following a sheriffs sale on November 18, 2008 and expiration of the one year redemption period, procured a sheriffs deed to the Exhibit C Properties on November 20, 2009. Likewise, Plaintiffs obtained a judgment and decree of foreclosure on the Riverside Lot on September 28, 2010 and, following a sheriff's sale on November 18, 2010 and expiration of the redemption period, procured a sheriff's deed to the Riverside Lot on January 3, 2014. To date, the Riverside Lot remains landlocked without legal access to a public road.

Plaintiffs filed this declaratory judgment action in the Montana Fourth Judicial District Court in September 2014. They seek to establish legal access by implication, and urge the Court to declare both their entitlement to, and the form of, such access. Samuel removed the case to federal court, citing this Court's diversity jurisdiction, in October 2014. This matter is set to be tried to a jury on January 11, 2016.

## ANALYSIS

A federal court sitting in diversity applies the substantive law of the forum state to state law claims. Thus, the Court decides this matter pursuant to well-developed Montana law on easements.

I. Plaintiffs' motion for summary judgment.

Plaintiffs move for summary judgment as to the their entitlement to an implied easement by necessity across Samuel's land. Because the undisputed facts establish Plaintiffs' right to the easement, and because none of Samuel's arguments are supported by Montana law, the Court will grant Plaintiffs' motion for summary judgment, reserving for trial the scope of the easement.

Montana law recognizes the existence of easements by necessity as a species of implied easements. Easements by necessity arise from a legal fiction that the owner of a tract of land would not sell parts of the land so as to isolate and landlock a remaining portion of it without having intended to reserve a way of access to the parcel over the lands being severed. The law implies intent by the landowner to provide an easement by necessity in favor of the landlocked parcel across the landowner's other lands when necessary to reach a public road. In easement terms, the landlocked parcel is the dominant estate, and the landowner's other sold property that must be crossed to reach the landlocked parcel is the servient estate.

An easement by necessity can arise only within the context of land held in common ownership at the time a severance creates a landlocked parcel, and cannot exist over the land of a third person whose land was not part of the common ownership. Implied easements by necessity have never been intended to provide access across the land of others to benefit any and all landlocked property.

The party seeking an implied easement by necessity must prove two essential elements by clear and convincing evidence: (1) unity of ownership, and (2) strict necessity. If the easement is established, the servient property owner then suffers permanent loss of some of his property rights without any compensation. Therefore, easements by necessity are considered with extreme caution because they deprive the servient tenement owner of property rights through mere implication.

The unity of ownership element is met where the owner of a tract of land severs part of the tract so as to create a landlocked parcel without expressly providing an outlet to a public road. A single owner must at one time have owned both the landlocked tract to be benefited by the easement (the dominant tenement) and the tract across which the easement would pass (the servient tenement). This element also requires that the dominant and servient parcels were owned by one person or entity *immediately prior* to the severance that gives rise to necessity.

The element of strict necessity requires that there be no practical access to a public road from the landlocked parcel except across lands that were formerly in common ownership. Strict necessity must exist at the time the tracts are severed from the original ownership and at the time the easement is exercised. A developed way of access to the landlocked parcel need not actually exist at the time of severance, and an easement by necessity is distinguished from other implied easements on the simple ground that a developed way need not be in existence at the time of conveyance. The requisite necessity is the necessity to cross land formerly in common ownership for access to a public road.

Plaintiffs meet both elements of an implied easement by necessity. First, Snavely owned, subject to the parties' respective mortgages, both the Riverside Lot and the Exhibit C Properties immediately prior to the severance that gave rise to necessity. In this case, the severance of the Exhibit C Properties from Snavely's larger holdings took place at the time Samuel obtained a sheriff's deed to the parcels on November 20, 2009. Involuntary severance may occur in several ways, such as when part of a common owner's land is sold at a mortgage foreclosure sale or other judicial proceeding. If either the parcel sold or the parcel retained is deprived of access by virtue of the sale, an implied easement of necessity may result. Second, when Samuel obtained the sheriff's deed, the Riverside Lot remained in Snavely's possession, yet was almost entirely surrounded by the Exhibit C Properties. Thus, there was no practical access to a public road from the Riverside Lot except across the Exhibit C Properties, that were formerly in common ownership with the Riverside Lot. This condition persists, meaning that necessity existed at the time the tracts were severed from the original ownership and at the time the easement is exercised.

None of Samuel's arguments negate the above analysis. First, while Samuel is correct that courts view implied easements with a measure of skepticism, he does not, and cannot, argue that they are unrecognized in Montana. *See Yellowstone River, LLC v. Meriwether Land Fund I,* (Mont. 2011). Because recognition of implied easements rests upon exceptions to the rule that written instruments speak for themselves such implications are limited to narrow situations, including necessity.

Second, Samuel is incorrect that Plaintiffs bear the burden of proving lack of contrary intent as a third element to an implied easement by necessity claim. In any event, the Court finds no contrary intent here. Samuel cites *Yellowstone River, LLC* for the proposition that to establish an easement by necessity, a plaintiff must overcome any circumstances surrounding the operative severance that negate the inference that the mortgagor intended to reserve an easement. There is an aspect of truth to this statement, in that a court may not uphold the legal fiction underlying an implied easement by necessity where the facts indicate the parties did not intend that an easement be created. However, this prohibition against *a court* finding an implied easement in the face of contrary facts does not translate to an affirmative duty on the part of a plaintiff seeking the easement. If anything, the responsibility might fall on Samuel to bring forth any information highlighting contrary intent, and on the Court to evaluate it.

In this case, none of Samuel's allegations regarding contrary intent prohibit the Court from implying an easement over the Exhibit C Properties in Plaintiffs' favor. Samuel contends that Plaintiffs intended to take ownership of the Riverside Lot without legal access, because they were on actual notice that the property lacked access,[1] they accepted a security interest nonetheless, and they opted not to insure legal access through their title insurance policy. To believe that these allegations represent issues of material fact, the Court must believe another scenario—that Plaintiffs made a bet in 2006 that Snavely would default on both their loan and Samuel's loan, separately severing the Exhibit C Properties and the Riverside Lot and laying the foundation for this implied easement claim. While not outside the realm of possibility, it is equally likely that Plaintiffs took a security interest on the Riverside Lot because it was part of a proposed luxury home subdivision, western Montana was in the throws of a housing boom, and a loan to Snavely seemed like a good investment.

Regardless, *Plaintiffs'* intent is not at issue here. The severance that created the necessity occurred when Samuel took ownership of the Exhibit C Properties and Snavely continued to own the Riverside Lot, over four years before Plaintiffs took ownership of the Riverside Lot. Thus, the question is whether the record contains any information indicating that Snavely and Samuel did not intend to create an easement across the Exhibit C Properties for Snavely's benefit. The Court finds no such information in the parties' various submissions.

Third, Samuel's argument that Plaintiffs fail to carry their burden as to the scope of the implied easement is without merit. In *Leisz*, the Montana Supreme Court's discussion of easement scope was limited to one of the district court's factual findings, and appears in a section of the opinion pertaining to prescriptive easements. Prescriptive easement analysis focuses on actual, historical use, making the scope of the easement an important part of the equation. Ultimately, the fact that the scope of the easement Plaintiffs seek remains in question is in no way fatal to their motion for summary judgment.

Based on the foregoing, the Court finds that Plaintiffs are entitled to an implied easement by necessity benefitting the Riverside Lot and encumbering Samuel's Exhibit C Properties, and will grant Plaintiffs' motion for summary judgment accordingly.

## II. Samuel's cross-motion for summary judgment.

In addition to other arguments, Samuel contends in his brief that because Snavely mortgaged the Exhibit C Properties prior to her acquisition of the Riverside Lot, she

---

[1]  Samuel suggests that Plaintiffs were on actual notice of the lack of legal access because it was readily apparent on the ground that the Riverside Lot lacked a physical access. However, absence of a road, two-track, or other sign of a travelway cannot serve to put Plaintiffs on notice as Samuel urges. *See Frame*, 231 P.3d at 592 ("an easement by necessity is distinguished from other implied easements on the simple ground that a developed way need not be in existence at the time of conveyance").

did not own the Exhibit C Properties at that time and therefore there was no unity of ownership at the time of severance.

Samuel bases this argument on *Leonard v. Bailwitz,* (Conn. 1960), in which the Supreme Court of Connecticut ruled that the severance of ownership germane to the implied easement scenario in the case occurred at the time certain parcels were mortgaged. The *Leonard* court noted that, in Connecticut, a "decree of foreclosure merely cuts off the mortgagor's outstanding right of redemption," meaning that a mortgagee holds title as a result of the mortgage itself and "the extent of the interest or title of the mortgagee is not increased or enlarged by the foreclosure." This is because Connecticut "follows the 'title theory' of mortgages, which provides that on the execution of a mortgage on real property, the mortgagee holds legal title and the mortgagor holds equitable title to the property." "In a title theory state such as Connecticut, a mortgage is a vested fee simple interest subject to complete defeasance by the timely payment of the mortgage debt, and the mortgagor has the right to redeem the legal title previously conveyed by performing the conditions specified in the mortgage document."

On the contrary, Montana is a "lien theory" state, meaning that a mortgagee's interest in mortgaged real property is akin to a lien on that property, and the mortgagor retains title. *See* Mont. Code Ann. § 71-1-202 (2015) ("A mortgage of real property shall not be deemed a conveyance.")

Because of these differences in state real property law, Samuel's reliance on *Leonard* is misplaced and his contention that Snavely severed her interest in the Exhibit C Properties prior to obtaining the Riverside Lot is simply incorrect. Snavely retained title in the Exhibit C Properties until her right of redemption expired post-foreclosure in November 2009, and it is undisputed that she had acquired the Riverside Lot by that time. Thus, *Leonard* does not alter the Court's unity of ownership analysis above, and Samuel's cross-motion for summary judgment will be denied.

## CONCLUSION

Plaintiffs are entitled to an implied easement by necessity benefitting the landlocked Riverside Lot and encumbering Samuel's Exhibit C Properties. Both properties were held in common ownership prior to the severance that gave rise to the necessity—the foreclosure and subsequent expiration of Snavely's one-year statutory redemption period on November 20, 2009. There is strict necessity for the easement in that the Riverside Lot lacks legal access to a public road, except to travel over the Exhibit C Properties. Neither public policy against implied easements, contrary intent on Plaintiffs' part, lack of evidence regarding the easement's scope, nor questions regarding the timing of Snavely's acquisition of the Riverside Lot compel a different result. The scope of Plaintiffs' implied easement remains at issue in this case.

Accordingly, IT IS ORDERED that Plaintiffs' motion for summary judgment is GRANTED and Defendant Samuel's motion for summary judgment is DENIED.

Note: What is considered to be necessary access in Florida may differ from what is considered to be necessary access in Montana, as illustrated by the following rather amusing case.

## DISTRICT COURT OF APPEAL OF FLORIDA
## WAYNE GOLDMAN, MARIANNE GOLDMAN AND SEAN ACOSTA, APPELLANTS,
## V.
## STEPHEN LUSTIG, APPELLEE.

JANUARY 24, 2018

**Opinion**

Forst, J.

In a case of "what's up, dock?," both Appellants Marianne Goldman, Wayne Goldman, and Sean Acosta ("Unit Owners") and Appellee/Cross-appellant Stephen Lustig seek a declaration of their rights to a dock located behind Lustig's property.

**Background**

This case involves a multi-year dispute over the right to use and access a wooden dock located behind Lustig's waterfront property. In 2007, Unit Owners filed a complaint seeking a declaration of their right to use a portion of that dock, as well as a permanent injunction to prevent Lustig from prohibiting their continued use of the dock. Unit Owners and Lustig lived in a community called 900 Hillsboro Mile, located in Broward County. It is comprised of four separate townhouse units, common areas, and a dock located behind the first unit. The Declaration of Covenants and Restrictions ("Declaration") for 900 Hillsboro Mile established a homeowner's association ("Association"). In their complaint, Unit Owners explained that the

Association and Lustig entered into a quitclaim assignment ("Assignment") in which Lustig expressly severed his riparian rights to a portion of the dock.

Lustig sought a declaratory judgment that would detail his rights to the dock behind his unit, and requested a permanent injunction to enjoin Unit Owners from using any portion of the dock as well as accessing it from his property.

After years of litigation, the parties attended a bench trial in 2014. After trial, the trial court entered its written final judgment, dismissing both Unit Owners' complaint and Lustig's counterclaim, and concluding that "no party prevailed." Both parties appeal that final judgment.

## Analysis

### A. Dockage Rights

The parties agree that the trial court erred by failing to determine the parties' rights to the dock, and that this Court can adjudicate the matter on appeal. The Unit Owners maintain that Lustig clearly and unambiguously severed his riparian rights and agreed not to impede or interfere with the riparian rights of the Unit Owners when he executed the Assignment, as the Assignment contemplated that Lustig could only use a forty-four-foot strip of that dock, and that the Unit Owners had a right to use the remaining portion. Lustig argues that only he has any rights to the dock and the Assignment was invalid as a matter of law because the Association could not assign any rights. Moreover, Lustig contends that the Florida Department of Environmental Protection, (DEP) already decided the instant matter when it denied the original developer's application for a permit to construct a marginal dock due to there being insufficient evidence of upland interest.

We find that Unit Owners are entitled to use a portion of the dock. As an initial matter, and as both parties assert, the trial court's final judgment is inadequate. The trial court, pursuant to Florida's Declaratory Judgment Act, should have provided both parties with a declaration of their rights to the dock as they had requested.

Here, Unit Owners have a right to use a certain portion of the dock given that they and Lustig executed the Assignment. Riparian interests may be severed only by an "express bilateral agreement to do so." First, the title of the Assignment is telling: "Nonrecourse Quitclaim *Assignment of Dockage Rights.*" Next, in the text of the Assignment itself, Lustig agreed to the fact that the dock was "constructed for the benefit of the owners of townhouses at the Association for the dockage of vessels adjacent thereto," and then agreed that he was acquiring "the right to the use of a portion of the Dock described as the Forty Four (44) feet of dock located at the outside northwest corner of the Dock." He also "agreed not to impede or interfere with any other party's rights at the dock." Three pages later, he signed the plat map which designated the portion of the dock that only he could use. In light of the title of the Assignment, as well as its specific provisions, Lustig unequivocally severed his riparian rights.

Lustig conceded at trial that Unit Owners had a right to use a portion of the dock. He stated during cross-examination that "I'm contending that I own the vertical piece, and the horizontal piece to a certain point." Then, he agreed that Unit Owners "have the rest of the dock," but that "they just can't get to it." He further explained he would have no problem with Unit Owners using a portion of the dock, as long as they built their own access pier to it. His main concern was evident: he no longer wanted to see his neighbors accessing the dock by encroaching on his land and pier.

## B. Easement by Necessity

Lustig's main concern brings us to our next issue on appeal: whether Unit Owners, who have a right to use the dock, have the right to access that dock by way of an easement by necessity. We find that they do not have the right to access Lustig's pier by way of such an easement.

A party who seeks to establish a way of necessity, whether in regard to an implied grant or statutory way, has the burden of proof to establish that he or she has no practicable route of ingress or egress. Section 704.01(1), Florida Statutes (2017), codifies the requirements for obtaining an implied easement by necessity:

> Such an implied grant exists where a person has heretofore granted or hereafter grants lands to which there is no accessible right-of-way except over her or his land, or has heretofore retained or hereafter retains land which is inaccessible except over the land which the person conveys. In such instances a right-of-way is presumed to have been granted or reserved. Such an implied grant or easement in lands or estates exists where there is no other reasonable and practicable way of egress, or ingress and same is reasonably necessary for the beneficial use or enjoyment of the part granted or reserved.

In the instant case, there is no dispute that the only way for Unit Owners to currently access the dock by land is by first crossing into Lustig's backyard and then walking on his pier.

However, just because Unit Owners cannot currently access the dock by land does not mean that they have a need for an easement. As stated by the Florida Supreme Court in *Tortoise Island Communities, Inc. v. Moorings Association, Inc.*, (1986), an easement by necessity requires a showing of an "*absolute necessity.*" Given that Unit

Owners live on waterfront property, they can reach the dock by constructing their own access pier, which would be a "reasonable and practicable way of egress, or ingress." Or, they can find an alternate means of accessing the dock, such as using a canoe or kayak departing from their own property.

## Conclusion

We reverse and remand for the trial court to amend its final judgment and find that Unit Owners are entitled to use a portion of the dock, but are not entitled to an easement by necessity in order to access it. Lustig expressly severed some of his riparian rights to the dock in the Assignment, and conceded as much at trial. However, Unit Owners do not merit an easement by necessity because they have failed to demonstrate an absolute need for such an easement.

*Reversed and remanded.*

## B. Covenants and Equitable Servitudes

The easy way to distinguish between a covenant and an equitable servitude is that a covenant is a promise between two landowners. An equitable servitude is simply a restriction on the use of land that is put on the land, unilaterally, by the owner of the land. So a covenant requires two people. An equitable servitude requires only one person. Both are tools that may be used to restrict the use of land – to single-family residences only, or to buildings that are no more than 40 feet in height, for example.

## 1. Covenants

A *real covenant* is one that is intended to *run with the land* – to be binding on future owners of the land. To create a real covenant at common law three things are required: there must be *privity of estate* between the parties; and the covenant must *touch and concern* the land, and the covenant must be *intended to run with the land*. To have *privity of estate* the two parties to the covenant must both *simultaneously* have a legal interest in the land. This can occur in only three situations: Grantor/Grantee; Dominant and Servient Owner; or Landlord/Tenant. The Grantor/Grantee privity of estate exists only in the deed itself. A later document between the same two parties would be too late to create a real covenant, because the parties would no long have a simultaneous interest in the land, once title had passed to the buyer.

Dominant and servient owners of an easement have sufficient privity of estate during the whole time that the easement is in existence – for a covenant that involves the easement. Landlord and tenant have sufficient privity of estate during the term of the lease – for something that involves the lease.]

For example, the grantor and grantee could agree in the deed that the land being sold would never be used for anything except residential purposes. The dominant and servient owner could agree that the servient owner would be the one to plow the snow off the easement. The landlord and tenant could agree that the tenant would repaint the premises once a year during the term of the lease. In cases where privity of estate is lacking, courts hold that a real covenant has not been created, so the covenant is not binding on any successors in interest. It is just a contract between the parties – not a real covenant that runs with the land.

[The *touch and concern* requirement for a real covenant is pretty easy. The covenant must have something to do with the use of the land]– it cannot just be a promise to pay money, for example.

[Similarly, the *intent to run with the land* is a requirement that is easily met. The parties simply must state in the covenant that the covenant is intended to run with the land, and to be binding on successive owners of the land.]

## 2. Equitable Servitudes

[The most frequent use of *equitable servitudes* is when the owner of land, a developer, for example, unilaterally imposes restrictions on the entire tract of land, before dividing it into smaller parcels to be sold to individual owners.]Such restrictions might include, for example, a requirement that the land could be used only for single-family houses, which must be set back at least 40 feet from the road, and must include an attached garage for not more than two cars.

[An equitable servitude is binding on any future buyer who buys with notice of the equitable servitude.]So as a standard practice, a developer will simply record the equitable servitude that sets forth the various restrictions. That way, anyone who later buys any part of the land will be on record notice of the equitable servitude.

## 3. Changed Conditions

Both covenants and equitable servitudes are subject to changed conditions. If the entire surrounding area becomes heavily commercial, for example, then either a covenant or an equitable servitude requiring single-family homes may become unenforceable, because of the changed conditions.[Only a court has the authority to decide when a covenant or an equitable servitude has become unenforceable because of changed conditions. So there is always a bit of uncertainty as to whether or not a covenant or equitable servitude is still in force.

An easement, however, will *never* become unenforceable because of changed conditions. Because an easement is considered to be an ownership interest in land – not just a restriction on the use of land – an easement will continue, no matter how great the change in the surrounding area.

## C. Reciprocal Negative Easements

A *reciprocal negative easement* is an important restriction on the use of land that is not an easement, not a covenant, and not an equitable servitude. In fact, it is not even in writing! You would never be able to ascertain the existence of a reciprocal negative easement just by checking the chain of title for the parcel of land being purchased. A reciprocal negative easement is simply a land use restriction that is *made up* by a court, in certain circumstances, when the court feels that justice requires it to do so. Yikes! Try explaining that to a client who asks you to ascertain what restrictions there are on land that the client is considering buying! The only real way to find out whether or not there is a reciprocal negative easement restricting the use of the land is to litigate – and see what the court decides.

The following case, *Sanborn v. McLean,* created the concept of a reciprocal negative easement in 1925. Courts are still struggling to define the set of circumstances under which a court should create a reciprocal negative easement by implication. *Sanborn v. McLean* has had a long life.

### SUPREME COURT OF MICHIGAN
### SANBORN V. MCLEAN

DECEMBER 22, 1925

**OPINION BY: WIEST**

Defendant Christina McLean owns the west 35 feet of lot 86 of Green Lawn subdivision, at the northeast corner of Collingwood avenue and Second boulevard, in the city of Detroit, upon which there is a dwelling house, occupied by herself and her husband, defendant John A. McLean. The house fronts Collingwood avenue. At the rear of the lot is an alley. Mrs. McLean derived title from her husband and, in the course of the opinion, we will speak of both as defendants. Mr. and Mrs. McLean started to erect a gasoline filling station at the rear end of their lot, and they were enjoined by decree from doing so and bring the issues before us by appeal.

Collingwood avenue is a high-grade residence street between Woodward avenue and Hamilton boulevard, with single, double and apartment houses, and plaintiffs who are owners of land adjoining, and in the vicinity of defendants' land, and who trace title, as do defendants, to the proprietors of the subdivision, [claim that the proposed gasoline station will be a nuisance *per se,* is in violation of the general plan fixed for use of all lots on the street for residence purposes only, as evidenced by restrictions upon 53 of the 91 lots fronting on Collingwood avenue, and that defendants' lot is subject to a reciprocal negative easement barring a use so detrimental to the enjoyment and value of its neighbors.]Defendants insist that no restrictions appear in their chain of title and they purchased without notice of any reciprocal negative easement, and deny that a gasoline station is a nuisance *per se.*]We find no occasion to pass upon the question of nuisance, as the case can be decided under the rule of reciprocal negative easement.

This subdivision was planned strictly for residence purposes, except lots fronting Woodward avenue and Hamilton boulevard. The 91 lots on Collingwood avenue were platted in 1891, designed for and each one sold solely for residence purposes, and residences have been erected upon all of the lots. Is defendants' lot subject to a reciprocal negative easement?

[If the owner of two or more lots, so situated as to bear the relation, sells one with restrictions of benefit to the land retained, the servitude becomes mutual, and, during the period of restraint, the owner of the lot or lots retained can do nothing forbidden to the owner of the lot sold. For want of a better descriptive term this is styled a reciprocal negative easement. It runs with the land sold by virtue of express fastening and abides with the land retained until loosened by expiration of its period of service or by events working its destruction. It is not personal to owners but operative upon use of the land by any owner having actual or constructive notice thereof. It is an easement passing its benefits and carrying its obligations to all purchasers of land subject to its affirmative or negative mandates. It originates for mutual benefit and exists with vigor sufficient to work its ends. It must start with a common owner. Reciprocal negative easements are never retroactive; the very nature of their origin forbids. They arise, if at all, out of a benefit accorded land retained, by restrictions upon neighboring land sold by a common owner. Such a scheme of restrictions must start with a common owner; it cannot arise and fasten upon one lot by reason of other lot owners conforming to a general plan. If a reciprocal negative easement attached to defendants' lot it was fastened thereto while in the hands of the common owner of it and neighboring lots by way of sale of other lots with restrictions beneficial at that time to it. This leads to inquiry as to what lots, if any, were sold with restrictions by the common owner before the sale of defendants' lot. While the proofs cover another avenue we need consider sales only on Collingwood.

December 28, 1892, Robert J. and Joseph R. McLaughlin, who were then evidently owners of the lots on Collingwood avenue, deeded lots 37 to 41 and 58 to 62, inclusive, with the following restrictions:

"No residence shall be erected upon said premises, which shall cost less than $2,500 and nothing but residences shall be erected upon said premises. Said residences shall front on Helene (now Collingwood) avenue and be placed no nearer than 20 feet from the front street line."

July 24, 1893, the McLaughlins conveyed lots 17 to 21 and 78 to 82, both inclusive, and lot 98 with the same restrictions. Such restrictions were imposed for the benefit of the lands held by the grantors to carry out the scheme of a residential district, and a restrictive negative easement attached to the lots retained, and title to lot 86 was then in the McLaughlins. Defendants' title, through mesne conveyances, runs back to a deed by the McLaughlins dated September 7, 1893, without restrictions mentioned therein. Subsequent deeds to other lots were executed by the McLaughlins, some with restrictions and some without. Previous to September 7, 1893, a reciprocal negative easement had attached to lot 86 by acts of the owners, as before mentioned, and such easement is still attached and may now be enforced by plaintiffs, provided defendants, at the time of their purchase, had knowledge, actual or constructive, thereof. The plaintiffs run back with their title, as do defendants, to a common owner. This common owner, as before stated, by restrictions upon lots sold, had burdened all the lots retained with reciprocal restrictions. Defendants' lot and plaintiff Sanborn's lot, next thereto, were held by such common owner, burdened with a reciprocal negative easement and, when later sold to separate parties, remained burdened therewith and right to demand observance thereof passed to each purchaser with notice of the easement. The restrictions were upon defendants' lot while it was in the hands of the common owners, and abstract of title to defendants' lot showed the common owners and the record showed deeds of lots in the plat restricted to perfect and carry out the general plan and resulting in a reciprocal negative easement upon defendants' lot and all lots within its scope, and defendants and their predecessors in title were bound by constructive notice under our recording acts. The original plan was repeatedly declared in subsequent sales of lots by restrictions in the deeds, and while some lots sold were not so restricted the purchasers thereof, in every instance, observed the general plan and purpose of the restrictions in building residences. For upward of 30 years the united efforts of all persons interested have carried out the common purpose of making and keeping all the lots strictly for residences, and defendants are the first to depart therefrom.

When Mr. McLean purchased on contract in 1910 or 1911, there was a partly built dwelling house on lot 86, which he completed and now occupies. He had an abstract of title which he examined and claims he was told by the grantor that the lot was unrestricted. Considering the character of use made of all the lots open to a view of Mr. McLean when he purchased, we think he was put thereby to inquiry, beyond asking his grantor whether there were restrictions. He had an abstract showing the subdivision and that lot 86 had 97 companions; he could not avoid noticing the strictly uniform residence character given the lots by the expensive dwellings thereon, and the least inquiry would have quickly developed the fact that lot 86 was subjected to a reciprocal negative easement, and he could finish his house and, like the others, enjoy the benefits of the easement. We do not say Mr. McLean should have asked his neighbors about restrictions, but we do say that with the notice he had from a view of the premises on the street, clearly indicating the residences were built and the lots occupied in strict accordance with a general plan, he was put to inquiry, and had he inquired he would have found of record the reason for such general conformation, and the benefits thereof serving the owners of lot 86 and the obligations running with such service and available to adjacent lot owners to prevent a departure from the general plan by an owner of lot 86.

We notice the decree in the circuit directed that the work done on the building be torn down. If the portion of the building constructed can be utilized for any purpose within the restrictions it need not be destroyed.

With this modification the decree in the circuit is affirmed, with costs to plaintiffs.

Note: In 2017 the concept established by *Sanborn v. McLean* is still of significant concern to landowners, attorneys and courts. In the following case, decided in 2017, the court decides to use a slightly different label, (implied reciprocal negative servitude), but the Nebraska Supreme Court is clearly talking about the concept established by *Sanborn v. McLean*.

JULY 28, 2017

Wright, J.

[At issue in this case is whether the property owned by Steven W. Colford and Sara J. Colford is subject to the neighboring subdivision's restrictive covenants by virtue of the doctrine of implied reciprocal negative servitudes. The district court concluded that it was not and granted summary judgment to the appellees, the Colfords. We affirm.

## PROCEDURAL BACKGROUND

The plaintiffs, Gary J. Walters and Denise R. Walters, brought suit against the Colfords seeking a mandatory injunction for violation of the neighboring subdivision's restrictive covenants.

## FACTUAL BACKGROUND

The plaintiffs are neighbors to the Colfords. The plaintiffs live in a platted subdivision known as the Adamy subdivision. The Adamy subdivision was platted and dedicated in 1976, and the founding documents were filed with the Butler County register of deeds. The plat and dedication included restrictive covenants, which, among other things, limited the structures on the lots to one single-family, two-story house and one two- or three-car garage. The subdivision contains 14 lots created from a piece of property consisting of around 16.5 acres. The Adamy family, which created the Adamy subdivision, also owned much of the property adjacent to the subdivision, including the entire quarter-section (approximately 160 acres) of land in which the subdivision was located.

The Colfords purchased 5 acres of property from a member of the Adamy family in 2013 for $25,000. When Adamy sold the property to the Colfords, the property was not subject to any restrictive covenants. The Colfords were aware that there were restrictive covenants in place on the adjacent Adamy subdivision, but did not know their details.

After purchasing the property, the Colfords constructed a large metal building, approximately 30 by 50 feet, which the plaintiffs alleged was in violation of the Adamy subdivision covenants. The Colfords used the building to store building material to build a house on the property.

ANALYSIS

There is no evidence that the Colford Property is expressly subject to the Adamy subdivision restrictive covenants. The Colford Property is not a part of the Adamy subdivision. The Adamy subdivision restrictive covenants expressly apply only to the lots within the subdivision. The plaintiffs may prevail only if they can establish that the Colford Property is restricted through the doctrine of implied reciprocal negative servitudes.

The plaintiffs argue that the Colford Property is subject to the Adamy subdivision restrictions through the doctrine of implied reciprocal negative servitudes.

(a) Overview of Doctrine

Restrictive covenants on property use are often utilized in developments to maintain the character of the neighborhood in accord with the development plan and to protect property values. When restrictive covenants are created for the mutual benefit of all of the properties within a development, they may be enforced by each of the property owners against the other. While at common law, restrictive covenants on land use were categorized as either "real covenants" or "equitable servitudes" depending on whether they were enforced in law or equity, the distinction between these two has blurred over time. The modern trend is to refer to both real covenants and equitable servitudes simply as servitudes.

The doctrine of implied reciprocal negative servitudes[10] allows—under very limited circumstances—a servitude to be created by implication, even where no express servitude applies to the property at issue. The requirements for the application of this doctrine are as follows: (1) There is a common grantor of property who has a general plan or scheme of development for the property; (2) the common grantor conveys a significant number of parcels or lots in the development subject to servitudes (restrictive covenants) designed to mutually benefit the properties in the development and advance the plan of development; (3) it can be reasonably inferred, based on the common grantor's

---

10   See, generally, Krueger v. Oberto, (Illinois, 1999); Schovee v. Mikolasko,(Maryland 1999); Evans v. Pollock.(Texas 1990); Sharts v. Walters,(New Mexico 1988); Mid-State Equipment Co. v. Bell (Virginia 1976); Williams v. Waldrop (Georgia 1961); Nashua Hospital v. Gage,(New Hampshire 1932); Sanborn v. McLean,(Michigan 1925).

conduct, representations, and implied representations, that the grantor intended the property against which the servitude is implied to be subject to the same servitudes imposed on all of the properties within the plan of development; (4) the property owner against whom the restriction is enforced has actual or constructive notice of the implied servitude; (5) the party seeking to enforce the restriction possesses an interest in property in the development that is subject to the servitude and has reasonably relied upon the representations or implied representations of the common grantor that other properties within the general scheme of development will be subject to the servitude; and (6) injustice can be avoided only by implying the servitude.

While the doctrine of implied reciprocal negative servitudes has a long pedigree and is well established,[17] courts tend to use it only with great trepidation. We have said that the law disfavors restrictions on the use of land. As one court reasoned, "Logically, if express restrictive covenants are disfavored under the law, implied restrictive covenants are to be viewed with even less favor." We have also said that because implied restrictive covenants mandate relaxation of the writing requirement, courts are generally reluctant and cautious to conclude implied restrictive covenants exist. As another court said, "the doctrine of implied reciprocal negative servitudes should be applied with extreme caution because in effect it lodges discretionary power in a court to deprive a person of his or her property by imposing a servitude through implication." Some courts require clear and convincing evidence to establish that a property is subject to the restrictions of an implied reciprocal negative servitude.

Whether a general plan or scheme of development exists and the scope and boundary of that plan are questions of fact.

> Representations by the developer normally provide the basis for finding that land was conveyed pursuant to a general plan of development. The representations may take the form of direct expressions that the project is a planned development, a restricted community, a quality residential subdivision, or the like. Representations may be found in advertisements, brochures, or statements made by sales personnel. Indirect representations may be found in maps, or pictures displayed to prospective purchasers. Representations may also be found in the language or nature of the servitudes imposed on the lots conveyed.

We said in *Skyline Woods Homeowners Assn. v. Broekemeier* that a grantor's intent to create a plan of development may be proved "from the conduct of parties or from the language used in deeds, plats, maps, or general building development plans" and

---

17  E.g., Evans v. Pollock, supra note 10, ("implied reciprocal negative easement doctrine has long been recognized in many jurisdictions").

by looking "to matters extrinsic to related written documents, including conduct, conversation, and correspondence."

[Determining which properties are included within a plan of development is relatively easy where land is platted or subdivided, because "in the absence of other evidence, the inference is normally justified that all of the land within a platted subdivision is subject to the general plan, and that land outside the subdivision is not included."]Thus, where property is subdivided or platted pursuant to a plan of development, a presumption arises that the plan of development includes only those properties in the plat or subdivision.

The property included within a plan of development, for purposes of the doctrine, does not necessarily include all of the developer's land, but can be limited to "certain well-defined similarly situated lots." And where a development is subdivided or platted in separate phases, each phase constitutes its own separate plan of development.

In addition to the aforementioned limitations on the scope of this doctrine, there is another limitation on its application that is key to the resolution of the case at bar.

### (b) Gap-Filling Function of Doctrine

The doctrine of implied reciprocal negative servitudes functions as a gap-filler. It is an equitable doctrine created to protect property owners. [Where a property owner purchases a lot from a developer that is subject to a restrictive covenant in the individual lot deed, but where the developer subsequently conveys a lot within the development without a restriction in the deed, the doctrine steps in to fill the gap.] It fills the gap in order to protect the other property owners' reasonable expectations that all of the lots within the plan of development will be similarly restricted.

The doctrine arose in the historical context of a time in which developers typically restricted properties within a plan of development by placing restrictive covenants in each individual property deed. As one court explained:

> The implied negative reciprocal easement or servitude doctrine arose before the advent
> of comprehensive zoning in order to provide a measure of protection for those who
> bought lots in what they reasonably expected was a general development in which
> all of the lots would be equally burdened and benefited. In those early days, it was
> unusual for the developer to evidence the development or impose uniform restric-
> tions through a recorded Declaration that would later be incorporated in individual
> deeds. They often filed subdivision plats of one kind or another but did not take the
> extra step of using one instrument to impose the restrictions. The common, almost
> universal, practice, instead, was for the developer to place the restrictions in the deeds

to individual lots and, sometimes, to represent to the purchasers of those lots that the same restrictions would be placed in subsequent deeds to the other lots. Litigation arose most frequently when the developer then neglected to include the restrictions in one or more of the subsequent deeds and those buyers proceeded or proposed to use their property in a manner that would not be allowed by the restrictions.

Because developers historically restricted properties as part of their plan of development on a deed-by-deed basis, the doctrine was created to fill the gap where a property was conveyed without restrictions in the deed.

But a common practice today is for developers to place restrictions on an entire development all at once through executing and recording a declaration of restrictions. Where this occurs, there is no need for the doctrine's gap-filling function. The drafters of the Restatement took the position that the doctrine has no application where a development's restrictions are created through a declaration of restrictions rather than through restrictive covenants placed in individual lot deeds.

The idea underlying the implied-reciprocal-servitude doctrine is that when a purchaser buys land subject to restrictions imposed to carry out a general plan of development, the purchaser is entitled to assume that all the land in the development is, or will be, similarly restricted to carry out the general plan. By selling land with restrictions designed to put into effect a general plan of development, the developer impliedly represents to the purchasers that the rest of the land included in the plan is, or will be, similarly restricted. That representation is enforced, on the grounds of estoppel, by imposing an implied reciprocal servitude on the developer's remaining land included in the plan. Because the implied-reciprocal-servitude doctrine undercuts the Statute of Frauds and creates uncertainty in land titles, it should be applied only when the existence of a general plan is clear and establishment of the servitude is necessary to avoid injustice.

We agree that the doctrine of implied reciprocal negative servitudes has no application where a developer follows the practice of creating restrictions on a development through a declaration of restrictions. We agree with this approach because it furthers the interests of protecting the reasonable expectations of property purchasers and promoting reliance on our property recording system.

A buyer of property has no reasonable expectation that neighboring property will be restricted as part of a plan of development where the entire development has been restricted through a declaration of restrictions that does not include that neighboring property. Such a buyer knows, or should know, that the neighboring property is not a part of the development and not necessarily subject to the same restrictions as the buyer's property.

The purpose of the doctrine is to protect the reasonable expectations of purchasers of property who reasonably rely on the representations or implied representations of a developer that the other properties within a development will be restricted. But the need for implied restrictions is obviated when the entire plan of development is restricted at once with a declaration of restrictions. A purchaser of property within such a development knows precisely what properties are—and what properties are *not*—subject to the same restrictions. The buyer can look at the records. The declaration tells the buyer what the restrictions are and to what properties they apply. Where the restrictions of a development are imposed all at once through a declaration of restrictions, the doctrine of implied reciprocal negative servitudes is not necessary to protect reasonable expectations of property buyers, because the buyer knows exactly what he or she is getting.

Limiting the scope of the implied reciprocal servitudes doctrine to situations where restrictive covenants are placed in individual deeds also serves the interest of promoting reliance on our property recording system. By definition, an *implied* servitude is not written and recorded. A prospective property purchaser cannot trek down to the local register of deeds and see if there are any *implied* servitudes on a particular piece of property. The potential for unwritten, unrecorded, implied servitudes creates uncertainty. This uncertainty is at odds with our recording system, which aims to yield clear answers about the ownership of property. Where a purchaser of property can find a recorded declaration of restrictions, showing the scope of a development's restrictions, the purchaser should be able to rely on that information.

[The doctrine of implied reciprocal negative servitudes does not apply where the grantor restricts all of the properties within a planned development through a declaration of restrictions] Where the grantor uses a declaration, the express restrictions within the declaration will control within the plan of development. The doctrine does not apply to property outside the planned development.]

Here, the restrictive covenants placed on the Adamy subdivision were created through a plat and declaration in 1976. The restrictions were put in place as to all of the lots within the planned development. At the time the plaintiffs purchased their lots within the subdivision, the plat and declaration document was on file with the Butler County register of deeds. [All of the plaintiffs had the opportunity to look at that record. Had they done so, they would have seen that the Colford Property was not a part of their subdivision and not subject to the same restrictions.] With this information available, the plaintiffs had no reasonable expectation that the Colford Property would be subject to the Adamy subdivision restrictions, regardless of what any real estate sales brochures may have implied.

We affirm the district court's grant of summary judgment.

# CHAPTER SEVEN

# PRIVATE NUISANCE

## INTRODUCTION

Private nuisance is an interesting concept. It is based on the idea that no matter what specific zoning requirements may be, or what specific restrictions there may be on the land because of easements, covenants, or equitable servitudes, no landowner is allowed to use his or her own land in a way that is unreasonably annoying to another landowner. This concept is frequently expressed in Latin – "Sic utero tuo ut alienum non laedas." [Use your property so as not to cause injury to another.]

The prohibition is against *unreasonable* use. So, what is reasonable, or unreasonable, varies with the circumstances. Usually the courts will balance the harm to the plaintiff compared to the utility of the use by the defendant. Courts also take into consideration the benefits conferred on the community by the use defendant is making of the land. Another factor will probably be how difficult or expensive it would be for the defendant to modify the use, so that it would not be so annoying to the plaintiff.

Sometimes the same use – a strongly smelling feedlot, full of cattle waiting to be shipped off to a processing plant, for example – might be both a public and a private nuisance. The basic distinction is that if the use is annoying to many people, it is probably a public nuisance. If it is annoying just to nearby neighbors, then it will probably be a private nuisance. As a practical matter, some governmental entity, such as the District Attorney's Office, will bring the action to close down a public nuisance. A private landowner will bring the action to close down a private nuisance. In this chapter we are concerned only with private nuisance.

The following case is somewhat complex from a procedural point of view, but it is nevertheless a dramatic and memorable illustration of the fact that even though an activity complies with all public and private land use restrictions, it may still be enjoined as a private nuisance at the request of an unhappy neighbor.

# SUPREME COURT OF COLORADO
## ARLENE HOBBS, PETITIONER,
### V.
## M. P. SMITH ET AL., RESPONDENTS.

FEBRUARY 22, 1972

HODGES, Justice.

We granted certiorari in this case to consider petitioner's argument that the decision of the Court of Appeals is contrary to the decision of this court in Robinson Brick Co. v. Luthi.

The Court of Appeals affirmed a trial court judgment which granted an injunction prohibiting the continuation of circumstances which constituted a private nuisance. The petitioner interprets the Robinson case to stand for the proposition that when legislative authorities, by zoning ordinances, permit an act or a particular use of land, a court has no authority to enjoin a public or private nuisance naturally resulting therefrom.

The trial court found that the petitioner kept one to two horses in the backyard of her home, which was located in a residential section of Jefferson County. A Jefferson County Zoning Ordinance permitted the keeping of two horses on petitioner's property. The trial court found that petitioner was exercising all reasonable skill and care in maintaining the property where the animals were kept and that no health regulations were being violated. However, the trial court also found that flies were attracted to the general area by the horses and that noxious odors therefrom permeated the area. It was found that the respondents suffered a substantial interference with the use and enjoyment of their property which adjoined petitioner's property. The trial court ruled that while the keeping of horses did not violate the zoning ordinance, it did constitute a nuisance in fact (per accidens) and therefore, there was a proper basis for granting an injunction prohibiting the keeping of horses on the petitioner's property. It has been held that a lawful use may become a nuisance in fact or per accidens by reason of locality, surroundings, or other circumstances.

In its opinion, affirming the trial court's judgment, the Court of Appeals held that even though zoning regulations permit an act to be done, and the act is being done with reasonable care and skill, the courts may grant relief where it is found that the acts complained of constitute a nuisance per accidens, and that to hold otherwise would be to state that the legislative body may license a nuisance.

*Robinson Brick Co. v. Luthi*, is anything but a model of judicial clarity. Whether the circumstances therein were primarily treated as a public or a private nuisance is difficult to determine. The nuisance complained of in that case was a clay mining operation which resulted in substantial amounts of dust being blown onto adjoining property including the plaintiff's. The plaintiff was engaged in the greenhouse business and the dust had damaged and was adversely affecting the growth of some plants. In *Robinson*, at the time the action was brought, the clay mine was a nonconforming use under the applicable zoning ordinance, [meaning that because of a change in zoning, the use was no longer permitted by the new zoning, but would be allowed to continue for a specified time]. The trial court issued an injunction prohibiting any further excavations and ordering that the existing excavation be filled in. The plaintiff also received $10 in nominal damages.

On writ of error, this court in Robinson upheld the award of damages but reversed the trial court on the injunctions, stating:

> "Where the legislative arm of the government has declared by statute and zoning
> resolution what activities may or may not be conducted in a prescribed zone, it has in
> effect declared what is or is not a public nuisance. What might have been a proper field
> for judicial action prior to such legislation becomes improper when the law-making
> branch of government has entered the field. None of the numerous cases cited appears
> to go so far as to approve the enjoining of a business operating under valid legislative
> zoning authority."

Robinson is a 1946 case. An examination of many more current cases in numerous jurisdictions reveals a contrary situation to that expressed in the last sentence of the above quotation. It is now the generally accepted rule that regardless of compliance with zoning ordinances or regulations, both business and residential uses may be enjoined if they constitute a nuisance to an adjoining property owner or resident. Robinson has been construed to mean that in the situation where a lawful use constitutes a nuisance, the proper remedy is damages and not an injunction. In 58 Am.Jur.2d Nuisances s 230, the authors cite the Robinson case for just such a proposition and then state:

> "According to the weight of authority, however, while what is authorized by law
> cannot be a public nuisance, it may nevertheless be a private nuisance, and the legisla-
> tive authorization does not affect any claim of a private citizen for damages for any
> special inconvenience and discomfort caused by the authorized act not experienced by
> the public at large, or for an injunction."

In our analysis, the holding in the Robinson case is far narrower than that ascribed to it by the above cited authorities.

The court in Robinson also stated:

"In the instant case, it will be noted that the trial court by its decree held that clay mining on the premises of the brick company was both a public and a private nuisance. * * * We are of the opinion that the state of Colorado and the county of Arapahoe already have preempted the field of public nuisance as it relates to this case, not only for the reasons already mentioned, but also because of the provision in section 19 of the County Planning Act which reads in part: 'The board of county commissioners may in any zoning resolution provide for the termination of non-conforming uses, either by specifying the period or periods in which non-conforming uses shall be required to cease, or by providing a formula or formulae whereby the compulsory termination of a non-conforming use may be so fixed as to allow for the recovery or amortization of the investment in the non-conformance.' In the case before us the zoning resolution contains no provision for termination of a nonconforming use; but even if it had, the two methods suggested for so terminating in the quoted statutory provision are much less harsh and are contrary in spirit to the prohibitory and mandatory injunctions of the trial court which make no provision or allowance whatever whereby the defendant may recover his investment in his property."

"It is evident that the two injunctions * * * which were granted by the trial court can not be justified on the ground that the defendant's clay mining operations constituted a public nuisance. Neither do they have legal sanction if defendant's operations are deemed to be merely a private nuisance."

Our analysis of the statements and holding of the Robinson case causes us to believe that the theory of that case rests on the often repeated rule of equity that where there is an adequate legal remedy, equity will not substitute an injunction for that legal remedy. It is our view that Robinson does, in effect, hold that where there is an adequate legal remedy which provides for the orderly termination of a non-conforming use, an injunction which is unduly harsh in its application will not be allowed to be used as a substitute for those legal means of phasing out the non-conforming use. The holding of the Robinson case should be so limited.

Judgment affirmed.

Note: So, as attorney for the owner of the horses, what would you suggest that she do now? If the plaintiff bought her land after it had already been zoned for horses, why is it not the plaintiff who is required to find another place to live?

*Hobbs v. Smith* is a dramatic case. But it is consistent with the basic rules of private nuisance. Even compliance with all applicable zoning and land use regulations will not automatically protect a landowner against a claim of private nuisance.

The next case illustrates the point that even if a plaintiff "moves to the nuisance" – even if the unpleasant use was there first, (and probably affected the price of the land), an unhappy neighbor can successfully sue the landowner who is causing the nuisance.

In some jurisdictions "moving to the nuisance" would bar the new landowner from bringing suit. But in many jurisdictions, as illustrated by the case below, "moving to the nuisance" would not be a bar to successful litigation.

## COLORADO COURT OF APPEALS
## H. J. MILLER AND SONDRA MILLER, PLAINTIFFS-APPELLEES,
## V.
## CARNATION COMPANY, A DELAWARE CORPORATION, AND ALBERS MILLING COMPANY, A DELAWARE CORPORATION, A DIVISION THEREOF, D/B/A BRIGHTON EGG COMPANY, DEFENDANTS-APPELLANTS.

### FEBRUARY 3, 1977
### (CERTIORARI DENIED MAY 16, 1977)

KELLY, Judge.

The Carnation Company appeals from an adverse judgment entered on a verdict in favor of the plaintiffs, Harry and Sondra Miller, for damages for trespass and nuisance arising out of the operation of the Brighton Egg Company, a poultry ranch owned by Carnation. The jury returned a special verdict awarding $101,748 in compensatory damages, which the trial court later remitted to $85,748. The jury also awarded $300,000 in exemplary damages. Carnation does not contest its liability on the claim, but asserts that both verdicts are excessive and that both are the result of passion and prejudice of the jury. The Millers cross-appeal, claiming pre-judgment interest on a portion of the award. We affirm the judgment against Carnation and reverse as to the denial of interest on the judgment.

In June 1966, the Millers purchased and moved into a home on property abutting Carnation's egg ranch. Shortly thereafter, the plaintiffs were besieged and their property was invaded by inordinate numbers of flies and rodents. The Millers' evidence demonstrated that Carnation's failure to remove chicken manure frequently and regularly from beneath its chicken houses provided these pests with ideal conditions for breeding. The flies existed in such numbers that the plaintiffs were deprived of the use and enjoyment of their property, and their influx damaged the Miller home and required increased maintenance. Persistent complaints to the egg ranch management proved unavailing. Although Carnation began a program of extensive insecticide spraying of both its ranch and the Miller property, the spraying proved ineffective and no less an inconvenience than the flies. It was uncontroverted that the most effective method of abatement was regular and frequent removal of the manure. Nevertheless, Carnation did not intensify its cleaning efforts, and the Millers were continually harassed by flies and rodents.

The case has been twice tried. At the conclusion of the second trial, the jury returned the verdicts above noted, and the plaintiffs agreed to a remittitur of $16,000 as ordered by the court.

I.

Regarding the compensatory damages, Carnation contends that submission of the case on the theories of trespass and nuisance impermissibly allowed the jury to award double damages, and that the compensatory damages were excessive because they were the product of passion and prejudice. We disagree.

In its special verdict, the jury apportioned the damages, awarding $28,000 for deprivation of use and enjoyment of the property, evenly divided between Mr. and Mrs. Miller, and $72,000 for 'annoyance, discomfort, inconvenience, and loss of ability to enjoy their lives,' attributing $18,000 to Mr. Miller and $54,000 to Mrs. Miller.

Contrary to Carnation's contention, damages for loss of use and enjoyment of property, on the one hand, and for annoyance and discomfort, on the other hand, are not duplicative. The use and enjoyment of land is a proprietary interest, while annoyance and discomfort are personal, not proprietary, interests. In its remittitur the trial court correctly limited recovery for loss of use and enjoyment to the loss of rental value occasioned by the invasion. This distinction between the elements of damage leads to the rule that the owner of land who is not an occupant may recover only for the impaired value of his property, while an occupant-owner may recover both his proprietary and personal loss.]

[Carnation also maintains that the compensatory damages were excessive in that they were the result of the passion and prejudice of the jury, and further, that the jury could not award damages based on annual loss, since flies were a problem only during warm months.]The first point is without merit, and the second misconstrues the nature of the damages awarded.

Carnation's argument that the unremitted[damages for annoyance and discomfort] were improperly predicated on an annual basis when they should have been limited to those months when flies were at their most numerous is not well taken.[These damages, unlike those sustained in the loss of use and enjoyment of the property, are not suffered on a weekly, monthly, or seasonal basis. They are absolute. It was within the discretion of the jury to determine when and how extensively the Millers suffered,]and there is no indication in the record that their determination is without foundation.

## II.

Carnation argues that the exemplary damage award was excessive and that the trial court would have, and should have, remitted the award or ordered a new trial. According to Carnation, the trial court refrained from striking the exemplary damage award because it failed to properly interpret our opinion in *Miller v. Carnation, I.* In its order denying the motion for a new trial, the trial court noted its disagreement with the exemplary damage award. This alone, however, does not warrant a reversal of the verdict.

In overseeing the functions of the jury, it is not the place of the trial judge to sit as a thirteenth juror.[Although the court may disagree with the verdict, the granting of a motion for a new trial is improper where the evidence palpably supports the verdict. In the face of conflicting evidence, the trial court may not substitute its view for that of the jury.]The plaintiffs were entitled to an instruction on exemplary damages, since there was evidence to support it. The trial court's action in not setting aside the exemplary damage award, despite its disagreement with the verdict is, therefore, consistent with established principles, and the record does not justify reversal of its denial of a new trial.

Carnation further contends that the trial court failed to consider whether the damages were excessive, but we do not agree. This court is not warranted in assuming that the trial court ignored the question of excessiveness simply because it noted its disagreement with the jury but did not reduce the award. On the contrary, the trial court is presumed to have considered all properly raised objections.

We also reject Carnation's position that the amount of exemplary damages was excessive as a matter of law. While exemplary damages must bear a reasonable relationship to compensatory damages, no fixed mathematical formula exists to determine reasonableness. The relationship between exemplary and compensatory damages is but one test to be applied in assessing the excessiveness of the award. Of equal importance, the verdict must be sufficient to punish the defendant and effectively deter others in similar circumstances.

Here, there was sufficient evidence of Carnation's wanton and reckless disregard for the Millers' rights to justify submission of the question to the jury. The award was not so large in relation to the purposes underlying s 13-21-102, C.R.S.1973, and in relation to Carnation's financial resources as to require reversal by this court.

## III.

We need not reach the merits of Carnation's additional assignments.

## IV.

Section 13-21-101, C.R.S.1973, provides that interest on personal injury damage awards may be recovered from the date the complaint is filed. The Millers contend that they are entitled to the benefits of this provision on that portion of the award relating to annoyance and discomfort. The trial court's denial of interest on this portion of the award from the date of the complaint is error.

An injury is personal when it impairs the well-being or the mental or physical health of the victim. In contrast, an injury is not personal when inflicted on property. Therefore, interest on the award for annoyance and discomfort is recoverable from the date of the filing of the Millers' complaint.

The judgment is affirmed with respect to Carnation's liability and the damages awarded in the jury's verdict, as remitted. The order denying interest requested by the plaintiffs is reversed, and the cause is remanded with directions to the trial court to enter judgment on the award for annoyance and discomfort, together with interest thereon at the rate of six per cent per annum from the date of the filing of the original complaint in this action to the date of the entry of judgment pursuant to this remand.

Note: So now the Millers should be able to afford to buy a new house, in a much better location. Correct?

In the following recent case, involving Kentucky bourbon, the court must deal with far more complex issues regarding a claim for private nuisance which involves both state property law and the federal Clean Air Act.

## SUPREME COURT OF KENTUCKY
## BROWN-FORMAN CORPORATION AND HEAVEN HILL DISTILLERIES, INC., APPELLANTS
## V.
## GEORGE MILLER, APPELLEE

SEPTEMBER 28, 2017

OPINION OF THE COURT BY JUSTICE WRIGHT

I. BACKGROUND

Appellee, George Miller owns properly in Jefferson County near warehouses owned by Appellants, Brown-Forman Corporation and Heaven Hill Distilleries, Inc. (referred to collectively as Brown-Forman). Brown-Forman's warehouses contain barrels of aging bourbon.

Bourbon is a uniquely Kentucky liquor. The confluence of geology, geography, fertile soil, and availability of land helped birth the bourbon industry in Kentucky. The Commonwealth's easily accessible limestone water, abundance of oak trees, and expansive land—combined with a four-season climate conducive to growing corn and aging liquor in barrels—enabled Kentucky's nascent bourbon industry to grow and prosper. According to Brown-Forman, as of 2014, Kentucky distillers produce 95% of bourbon worldwide.

Bourbon's enticing characteristics come from distilling a unique combination of ingredients and the use of a distinct aging process. Before being labelled bourbon, the distilled spirit must be aged a minimum of two-years in new charred-oak barrels. This distinct aging process is at the epicenter of this dispute.

During the aging process, Brown-Forman uses warehouses in Jefferson County to store its barrels of bourbon. As it ages, the bourbon interacts with the barrel as the liquid expands and contracts based on ambient temperature and air-flow. Warmer temperatures cause the bourbon to expand and seep further into the barrel, while colder temperatures cause contraction and less contact with the barrel. Movement into and out of the wood over time gives bourbon its color and taste.

Miller's complaint centers around fugitive ethanol emissions (the so-called "angels' share") that escape from the barrels during this aging process. These fugitive emissions promote the growth of the *Baudoinia compniacensis* fungus (colloquially referred to as "whiskey fungus"). Miller alleges the whiskey fungus causes a black film-like substance to proliferate on his property, covering virtually all outdoor surfaces—including wood, vinyl, metal, and concrete.

Miller filed suit in Jefferson County seeking damages based on several state tort theories, and injunctive relief. Brown- Forman filed a motion to dismiss for failure to state a claim upon which relief could be granted. The trial court granted Brown-Forman's motion to dismiss, as it determined the federal Clean Air Act preempted Miller's claims. Miller appealed and the Court of Appeals reversed and remanded, holding that the Act did not preempt Miller's claims. This Court granted Brown-Forman's motion for discretionary review.

## ANALYSIS

### A. Clean Air Act

We will first look to the federal act on which this litigation hinges. In passing the Clean Air Act, Congress delegated its implementation and administration to the federal Environmental Protection Agency (EPA). However, Congress also specifically designated a role for states.

Under the Act, each state may adopt a State Implementation Plan setting out emission limitations, emission standards, and other requirements to meet the National Ambient Air Quality Standards established by the EPA. States submit their individual plans to the EPA Administrator for approval. The Act sets out the contents and the authority states must possess before the Administrator may approve a State Plan.

After significant amendments to the Clean Air Act in 1990, Congress allowed the Administrator to authorize state and local governments (called permitting authorities) to issue operating permits. The Act defines the requisite legal authority each permitting authority must possess, prescribes the process for judicial review of permitting decisions, and allows the EPA to promulgate other requirements. Once a permitting authority's plan satisfies those requirements, then the Administrator may authorize it to issue permits under the Act.

In Jefferson County, the Administrator specifically authorized the Louisville Metro Air Pollution Control District (Metro District) to issue operating permits. The

Administrator also approved Kentucky's State Plan, which includes Metro District's regulations. Brown-Forman and Heaven Hill both maintain permits, and Miller does not allege either distiller is in violation of its operating permit; therefore, we proceed under the premise that the companies are in full compliance with the requisite permits mandated by the Act.

### 1. Federal Preemption

The Supremacy Clause makes the laws of the United States the supreme "Law of the Land any Thing in the Constitution or Laws of any State to the Contrary notwithstanding." Put simply, federal law preempts contrary state law.

With that in mind, we turn back to the federal Clean Air Act, which seeks to strike a balance between encouraging economic development and protecting the environment—a task here entrusted to both the Metro District and EPA. Specifically, in taking a cost-benefit approach, the Act directs the Administrator to consider all of the economic, public health, and environmental benefits of efforts to comply with such standard, as well as the effects of such standard on employment, productivity, cost of living, economic growth, and the overall economy.

After this careful balancing was taken into account, Brown-Forman and Heaven Hill were issued separate kinds of permits based on the amount of air pollutants each releases.

### 2. Savings Clauses

In determining whether the Act preempts any or all of Miller's claims, we must construe the Act as a whole and give effect to two separate savings clauses. These savings clauses allow states to retain power in spite of the Act's other provisions. In these clauses, Congress declared that certain types of conflicts between the Act and state law that might otherwise be preempted should, instead, be tolerated.

Specifically, 42 U.S.C. § 7416 reserves to the states the power to adopt and enforce more stringent standards than those established by the Act. That clause reads:

> "Nothing in this chapter shall preclude or deny the right of any State or political sub-
> division thereof to adopt or enforce (1) any standard or limitation respecting emissions
> of air pollutants or (2) any requirement respecting control or abatement of air pollu-
> tion; except that if an emission standard or limitation is in effect under an applicable
> implementation plan, such State or political subdivision may not adopt or enforce any

emission standard or limitation which is less stringent than the standard or limitation under such plan or section."]

[The second savings clause appears in 42 U.S.C. § 7604 and grants individuals the power to commence citizen suits to enforce the Act.] While we acknowledge that Miller did not bring a citizen suit, § 7604 also covers other actions. In particular, the subsection titled "Nonrestriction of other rights" states: ["Nothing in this section shall restrict *any right* which any person (or class of persons) may have under *any statute or common law* to seek enforcement of any emission standard or limitation or to seek any other relief."]

## B. State Tort Claims

Again, this case is before us on the trial court's order to dismiss Miller's, case for failure to state a claim upon which relief can be granted. At the trial court, Miller sought damages under state tort theories of negligence, trespass, and nuisance.

The text of the Clean Air Act and its legislative history, Supreme Court precedent construing the virtually identical provisions of the Clean Water Act, persuasive opinions from other federal courts and a state court, and the strong presumption against preemption in the field of environmental regulation, all persuade us to affirm the Court of Appeals insofar as it held that the Clean Air Act did not preempt Wilson's state tort causes of action.

### 3. Monetary Damages

[We further hold that the Act does not preempt a trial court from awarding monetary damages on state tort causes of action.] Awarding damages for a particular harm to specific property in no way retards, impedes, burdens, or in any manner controls, the operations of the Act. Nor does it stand as an obstacle to the accomplishment and execution of the full purposes and objectives of Congress.

An award of monetary damages to an aggrieved party fundamentally differs from supplanting a permitting decision of an expert agency. This is primarily so because the Act does not provide damage remedies to harmed individuals. Monetary damages also withstand scrutiny in part because personalized remedies are not a first priority of the Act.

To be sure, the Supreme Court in *American Electric Power Co. v. Connecticut*, (2011), held that a public nuisance claim was preempted because the Act displaced *federal* common law. But in doing so, the Court made clear that its analysis of federal common law differed from that of state law. Specifically, it stated: Legislative displacement of federal common law does not require the same sort of evidence of a clear and manifest congressional purpose demanded for preemption of state law.

Furthermore, that case rests upon the premise that under the Act, the duty to prevent and abate public nuisances is vested in the EPA and permitting authorities. The regulatory regime created by the Act supplants federal public nuisance claims because the Act incorporates those same types of protections against generalized harm. However, the case at bar differs from *American Electric Power*.

The nuisance at issue here is a private nuisance claim under state tort law, rather than a public nuisance claim under federal common law. It is a claim for damages caused by specific harm to specific property rather than general harm.

The Act does not provide a mechanism for awarding monetary compensation to an injured party suffering from a particularized harm. Thus, a property owner seeking full compensation for harm related to the use and enjoyment of property at a specific location must resort to common law or state law theories to obtain a full recovery.

We agree with the Iowa Supreme Court that state common law and nuisance actions have a different purpose than the regulatory regime established by the Act. The purpose of state nuisance and common law actions is to protect the use and enjoyment of specific property, not to achieve a general regulatory purpose. Miller here seeks damages related to specific properties at specific locations allegedly caused by a specific source. The purpose and function of the Act differs sufficiently from the purpose and function of a private lawsuit seeking damages anchored in ownership of real property.

The Act does not state that Congress intended to prevent injured property owners suffering particularized harm from recovering monetary damages under state law. Absent such language or a vividly demonstrable obstacle to the Act's operation, we cannot conclude it preempts state trial courts from awarding monetary damages in tort actions for negligence, private nuisance, or trespass.

## C. Injunction

The injunction Miller sought from the trial court would have required Brown-Forman to implement pollution-control technology not required by its permit issued under the Clean Air Act.

We must first determine if the Act preempts this type of injunctive relief. In doing so, we must construe the Act as a whole. We will first turn to the second of the Act's savings clauses (the citizen-suit clause discussed above) to determine if the Act saved the powers in question for the states.

First, Congress's creation of the citizen suit as a statutory remedy does not limit remedies otherwise available. Nothing in the section authorizing citizen suits, revokes other available remedies, including injunctive relief linked to state tort law. In other words, Congress did not intend citizen suits to be an exclusive remedy. Therefore, the Clean Air Act does not preempt state injunctive relief.

However, even though injunctive relief is not preempted by the Act, it is still unavailable in this case. The Act and Kentucky regulations provide for citizen input in the permitting process. The permit is issued only after careful balancing of the economic and environmental impact. So long as companies operate within the bounds of their permits concerning air pollutants (which is not contested in the case at bar), injunctive relief for an alleged nuisance is not an appropriate remedy. Here, by seeking an injunction demanding a particular pollution-control technology, Miller asked the trial court to second-guess the reasonableness of a decision the Act undeniably entrusted to Metro District and the EPA. In making the decision to issue the permits, citizens have the opportunity for input. The agency made a specific determination which balanced the risks to the environment with the economic impact of any pollution-control measures. For the trial court to issue the injunction Miller seeks would impose higher standards than the Clean Air Act requires.

Furthermore, while the Act's states' rights savings clause, specifically reserves to the states the power to adopt and enforce more stringent standards than those established by the Act, the Kentucky General Assembly has restricted the Energy and Environment Cabinet from exercising that saved power. Specifically, the General Assembly has charged the Energy and Environment Cabinet with adopting clean air regulations that are no more stringent than federal requirements. Even though the Act would allow Kentucky to enact more stringent standards under this savings clause, Kentucky statutes expressly prohibit the Cabinet from issuing more stringent regulations. We find the fact that Kentucky has explicitly chosen not to allow its regulatory body to utilize more stringent regulations persuasive as to the Legislature's intent.

We hold that the requested injunction, which would require implementation of a particular type of pollution-control technology not required under Brown-Forman's and Heaven Hill's permits, conflicts with the Act by invading EPA and Metro District's "regulatory turf," in a manner that the Kentucky General Assembly has spoken against. Therefore, an injunction to control an alleged nuisance when the state has already specifically balanced those factors is inappropriate. To conclude otherwise would produce the untenable situation where courts act on limited records on an *ad-hoc* basis in an arena where they do not possess the necessary scientific, economic and technological expertise. We cannot have the circuit courts of this Commonwealth imposing pollution control technologies on distillers that might differ from circuit to circuit. The impact on the bourbon industry would be far too dire. Our holding is limited to injunctive relief in nuisance cases where the regulatory authority (in this case, both federal and state) has issued a permit after carefully balancing environmental and economic factors. Issuing an injunction to require different technology to prevent a nuisance is markedly different from issuing an injunction for other purposes, such as when public health or the environment are endangered or there is a violation of law.

Therefore, we reverse the Court of Appeals insofar as it would allow this type of injunctive relief. The trial court properly dismissed the plea for injunctive relief as it indeed failed to state a claim upon which relief could be granted.

## CONCLUSION

For the foregoing reasons, we affirm the Court of Appeals as to Miller's state-law damages claims; however, we reverse the Court of Appeals insofar as it held that Miller's claim for injunctive relief could go forward. Therefore, we remand this case to Jefferson Circuit Court for further proceedings consistent with this opinion.

# CHAPTER EIGHT

# CONDOMINIUMS

When buying a home, many people purchase a unit in a condominium, for a number of reasons. First, condominiums are usually well designed and attractive. From a practical standpoint, it may be handy to be able to leave the basic maintenance of the building to the condominium association – so that the individual unit owner does not have to worry about maintaining the grounds, shoveling the snow, or making sure that the swimming pool and various other common areas are properly managed. Frequently, it is also the case that a buyer will be able to get more floor-space, per dollar, in a condominium, rather than in a detached single family home.

But there are certain standard features of condominium ownership that differ significantly from ownership of single family homes. It is important that lawyers be aware of these differences, so that they can explain them to their clients. Some of the basic provisions involving condominium ownership are found in the condominium *Declarations*. The Declarations for each condominium project will be a bit different from the provisions for other condominium projects, but the fundamentals are all about the same. Specific state statutes may also be applicable.

Perhaps the easiest way to understand the basics of condominium ownership may be just to look at a small sample from the actual Declarations of a condominium. The following excerpt is a very condensed version - usually Declarations go on for many pages. But this sample will give you an idea of some of the special provisions that will be applicable to almost any condominium.

The developer of a condominium project will record the Declarations for that project in the land records, so that every subsequent purchaser will have notice of the various provisions, and will take ownership subject to the provisions of the Declarations. Condominium Declarations really are a form of equitable servitude imposed on the land, unilaterally, by the developer. Thus, they are binding on every subsequent purchaser who takes the land, with notice. And everyone will be deemed to have notice, because the Declarations are recorded.

In the following sample, important provisions have been underlined, to make them stand out. In the actual Declarations, there would not be this sort of underlining. When provisions are especially important, and unique to condominiums, some comments have been added, in brackets. As you read these Declarations watch particularly for the right of first refusal, the "obsolescence clause" and the provisions on pets and gardening.

## A. SAMPLE CONDOMINIUM DECLARATIONS WITH COMMENTS

KNOW ALL MEN BY THESE PRESENTS:

THAT WHEREAS, THREE FOUNTAINS, A JOINT VENTURE HEREINAFTER CALLED THE "DECLARANT", IS THE OWNER OF THE REAL PROPERTY SITUATE IN THE CITY AND COUNTY OF DENVER, STATE OF COLORADO, DESCRIBED AS FOLLOWS, TO-WIT:

A tract of land in the Southeast one-quarter of Section 33, Township 4 south, Range 67 west of the 6th P.M., City and County of Denver, Colorado, described as follows: ... [Rest of legal description omitted] and;

WHEREAS, Declarant desires to establish a condominium project under the Condominium Ownership Act of the State of Colorado, and;

WHEREAS, by this Declaration a plan is established for the separate ownership of the condominium units and for submitting the above described property to condominium use, and;

WHEREAS, the DECLARANT contemplates that additional property shall be set aside and improved as a recreation area for the use of all of the owners of interest in the real property hereinabove described, and for the owners of additional property which Declarant may, but need not, commit to condominium usage, and; *[Note: Would it make a difference if the swimming pool is shared by 240 units, instead of 48 units?]*

big difference

WHEREAS, there will be constructed on the above described property not more than 48 units, together with other improvements, the construction of which shall be accomplished in stages, each stage to be evidenced by a condominium map to be filed for record subsequent to substantial completion of the improvement as is provided hereafter;

NOW THEREFORE, Declarant does hereby <u>publish and declare</u> that the following terms, covenants, conditions, easements, reservations, restrictions, uses, limitations and obligations shall be deemed to <u>run with the land</u>, shall be a burden and a benefit to Declarant, its transferees, assigns, and successors, and <u>any person</u> acquiring or owning an interest in the real property and improvements, their <u>grantees, successors, heirs, executors, administrators, devisees or assigns.</u> *[Technically, only real covenants should be said to "run with the land," and this is a unilateral declaration, not a covenant between two parties. In any case, it is clear that these Declarations will be binding on anyone who may subsequently become the owner of the condo.]*

## 1. DEFINITIONS

a. "Unit" means an individual <u>air space</u> which is contained within the perimeter walls, floors, and ceilings of each unit in a building as shown on the condominium map, together with all improvements and fixtures contained therein, but <u>not including any of the structural components</u> of the building within which such air space is located.

b. "Building" means one of the building improvements containing units as shown on the map.

c. "Condominium Unit" means the fee simple interest and title in and to the unit and the appurtenant <u>undivided interest</u> in and to the general and limited common elements.

d. "Owner" means a person, firm, corporation, partnership association or other legal entity, or any combination thereof, who owns one or more condominium units.

e. <u>"General Common Elements"</u> means that portion of the land first hereinabove described allocated to one or more buildings as is shown and described on the map; the structural components of the buildings thereon; the patios thereon as shown on the map; and all other parts of such land and the improvements thereon necessary or convenient to its existence, maintenance and safety which are <u>normally and reasonably in common usage</u> including the air space above such land, except those in air spaces identified on the map as units all of which shall be owned, as <u>tenants in common</u>, by the owners of the separate units each owner of a unit having an <u>equal undivided one-forty eighth (1/48<sup>th</sup>) interest in such general common elements.</u>

f. "Limited Common Elements" means those parts of the general common elements which are either limited to and reserved for the exclusive use of an owner of a condominium unit or are limited to and reserved for the common use of more than one but fewer than all of the condominium unit owners, all as shown on the map or as may be subsequently determined by the association of unit owners.

g. "Entire Premises of Property" means and includes the land, the buildings, all improvements and structures thereon and all rights, easements and appurtenances belonging thereto.

h. "Common Expenses" means and includes expenses for maintenance, repair, operation, management and administration; expenses declared common expenses by the provisions of this Declaration and by the By-Laws of Three Fountains Association; and all sums lawfully assessed against the general common elements by the Association. *[Note: The individual unit owner may not have to worry about shoveling the snow, but he or she will have to chip in on the expenses of having it done – plus some management and administrative fees. The monthly assessments for such expenses often may amount to as much as about one-third of the payments due under the provisions of a first mortgage. And unlike mortgage payments, the monthly assessments may usually be raised at any time by a vote of the unit owners – with those who voted against the increased assessments nevertheless being legally obligated to pay the increased assessments.]*

i. "Association of Unit Owners" or "Association" means Three Fountains Association, a Colorado Corporation, not for profit, the By-Laws of which shall govern the administration of this and other condominium property, the members of which shall be all of the owners of the condominium units in the entire premises and all of the Owners in other property which Declarant may commit to condominium purposes all as is hereafter provided.

j. "Map of Plans" means and includes the engineering survey of the land, locating thereon all of the improvements, the floor and elevation plans and any other drawing or diagrammatic plan depicting a part or all of the improvements in land.

## 2. CONDOMINIUM MAP:

The map may be filed for record in whole or in sections from time to time as the stages of construction of units and other improvements are substantially completed.

## 3. LIMITED COMMON ELEMENTS:

A portion of the general common elements is set aside and reserved for the use of the individual owners of units as follows: Exclusive Use - patio, porches and storage area. Each patio, porch and storage area adjoining and associated with a unit as shown on the map shall be used exclusively by the owner of such unit and his guests, notwithstanding any other provisions of this Declaration. Each owner shall be responsible for keeping his patio, porch and storage area in good condition, free from snow or debris of any kind.

## 4. DIVISION OF PROPERTY INTO CONDOMINIUM UNITS:

The property is hereby divided into separate fee simple estates, each such estate consisting of the following:

The unit, each such unit to be identified and located on the condominium map.
An appurtenant and undivided one-forty eighth (1/48th) interest in and to the general common elements as shown on the map.
The limited common elements allocable to each unit as described above.

## 5. INSEPARABILITY OF A CONDOMINIUM UNIT:

Each unit and the undivided interest in the general and limited common elements appurtenant thereto shall be <u>inseparable and may be conveyed, leased, rented or encumbered only as a condominium unit.</u>

## 6. NON-PARTITIONABILITY OF GENERAL COMMON ELEMENTS:

The general common elements shall remain undivided and <u>no owner shall bring any action for partition or division thereof.</u> Nothing contained herein shall be construed as a limitation of the right of partition of a condominium unit between the owners thereof, but such partition shall not affect any other condominium unit.

## 7. DESCRIPTION OF CONDOMINIUM UNIT:

Every contract for the sale of a condominium unit written prior to the substantial completion of the building in which it is to be located and prior to the filing of the map may legally describe a condominium unit by its identifying unit and building designation followed by the words "Three Fountains Filing No. 1", with further reference to the map thereof to be filed for record and the recorded Declaration.

## 8. OWNERSHIP TITLE:

A condominium unit may be held and owned by more than one person <u>as joint tenants, or as tenants in common,</u> or in any real property tenancy relationship recognized under the laws of the State of Colorado.

## 9. SEPARATE ASSESSMENT AND TAXATION - NOTICE TO ASSESSOR:

Declarant shall give written notice to the assessor of the City and County of Denver, State of Colorado, of the creation of condominium ownership of this property as provided by law, so that <u>each unit and the undivided interest in the general common elements appurtenant thereto shall be deemed a separate parcel and subject to separate assessment and taxation.</u>

## 10. USE OF GENERAL AND LIMITED COMMON ELEMENTS:

Each owner may use the general common elements in common with the other condominium unit owners, and the limited common elements in accordance with the purpose for which they are intended. The Association may adopt rules and regulations governing the use of general and limited common elements, and pursuant to which general common elements are allocated to the exclusive use of the owners of particular units as limited common elements, provided such rules and regulations shall be uniform and non-discriminatory.

## 11. USE AND OCCUPANCY

Each unit shall be occupied and used <u>only as and for a single family residential dwelling for the owner, his family or his guests</u>, provided Declarant and its employees, representatives, agents and contractors may maintain business and sales offices, construction facilities and yards, model units and other facilities on the property during the period of construction and sales.

## 12. EASEMENTS FOR ENCROACHMENTS:

If any portion of the general common elements encroaches upon a unit, a valid easement for the encroachment and for the maintenance of same as long as it stands shall and does exist. If any portion of a unit encroaches upon the general common area or upon an adjoining unit, a valid easement for the encroachment and for the maintenance of same so long as it stands shall and does exist. It is expressly understood that there are appurtenant to some units fireplaces located in walls common to two units. As easement is hereby reserved in favor of each such unit for the purpose of maintenance, utilization, repair or replacement of the said fireplaces by the respective owners of such units. For title or other purposes, such encroachments and easements shall not be considered or determined to be encumbrances either on the general common elements or on the unit.

## 13. MECHANIC'S LIEN RIGHTS AND INDEMNIFICATION:

Subsequent to the completion of the improvements described on the map, <u>no labor performed or materials furnished and incorporated in a unit with the consent of or at the request of the owner thereof</u>, or his agent, or his contractor or subcontractor <u>shall be the basis for filing of a lien against the condominium unit of any other owner</u> not expressly consenting to or requesting the same. Each owner shall indemnify and hold harmless each of the owners from and against all liability arising from the claim of any lien against the condominium unit of any other owner for construction performed, or for labor, materials, service or products incorporated in the owner's unit at such owner's express or implied request. The provisions herein contained are subject to the rights of the Association as set forth later in this document.

## 14. ADMINISTRATION AND MANAGEMENT:

The administration of this condominium property shall be governed by the By-Laws of Three Fountains Association, a Colorado corporation, not for profit, hereinafter referred to as the "Association." An owner of a condominium unit shall become a member of the Association upon conveyance to him of his condominium unit and shall remain a member for the period of his ownership. As shown and reserved to Declarant in the Articles of Incorporation and By-Laws for Three Fountains Association, until a date five years from the date of the recording of this Declaration, the designation and appointment of a Board of Managers for the Association may, at Declarant's option, be exercised by the Declarant. *[Note: So for a new condominium* project, [*if the units are not selling well the developer could unilaterally add some nice amenities, and increase the monthly assessments of people who had already bought into the project, when the monthly assessments were lower?*]

## 15. OWNERS' MAINTENANCE RESPONSIBILITY OF UNIT:

For purposes of maintenance, repair, alteration and remodeling, an owner shall be deemed to own the interior nonsupporting walls, the material (such as, but not limited to, plaster, gypsum, dry wall, paneling, wall-paper, paint, wall and floor tile, and floorings, but not including the sub-flooring) making up the finished surfaces of the perimeter walls, ceilings and floors within the unit and the unit doors and windows. The owner shall not be deemed to own lines, pipes, wires, conduits, or systems (which for brevity are hereafter referred to as utilities) running through his unit which serve one or more other units except as a tenant in common with the other owners. Such utilities shall not be disturbed or relocated by any owner without the written consent and approval of the Association. Any right to repair, alter and remodel shall carry the obligation to replace any finishing or other materials removed with similar or other types or kind of materials. An owner shall maintain and keep in repair the interior of his unit, including the fixtures thereof.

All fixtures and equipment installed within the unit commencing at a point where the utilities enter the unit shall be maintained and kept in repair by the owner thereof. An owner shall do no act or work that will impair the structural soundness or integrity of the building or impair any easement or hereditament. The Association shall not be liable for any failure of water supply, or other service to be obtained and paid for by the Association hereunder, or by another owner or person or property caused by the elements, or by another owner or person in the project, or resulting from electricity, water, rain, dust or sand which may leak or flow from outside or from any parts of the buildings or from any of its pipes, drains, conduits, appliances or equipment or from any other place unless caused by gross negligence of the Association or its agents.

[*Note: This means that the owner of a condo unit may actually have fewer rights than a tenant in an apartment building when the utilities fail, because of the simple negligence of the Association.*]

## 16. REVOCATION OR AMENDMENT TO DECLARATION:

Except as is otherwise stated herein, this Declaration shall not be revoked nor shall any of the provisions herein be amended unless: (A) The consent and permission of the <u>Association</u> be first obtained, and (B<u>) the consent of 85 per cent</u>, or more, of the owners representing an aggregate ownership interest in the general common elements be first obtained, <u>and (C) the consent of all of the holders of any recorded instruments;</u> provided, however, that the fraction of the undivided interest in the general common elements appurtenant to each unit shall have a permanent character and <u>shall not</u> be altered without the consent of all of the condominium unit owners as expressed in a duly recorded amendment to this Declaration.

## 17. ASSESSMENT FOR COMMON EXPENSES:

All owners shall be obligated to pay the estimated assessments imposed by the Association to meet the common expenses attributable to the property included in this Declaration. The assessment shall be made pro rata, one-forty eighth ($1/48^{th}$) part assessable to the owner of each unit, except that assessments for insurance premiums shall be based upon the proportion of the total premiums that the insurance carried on an individual condominium unit bears to total coverage. The limited common elements shall be maintained as general common elements and owners having exclusive use thereof shall not be subjected to any special charges or assessments. Assessments for the estimated common expenses, including insurance, shall be due monthly, in advance, on the first day of each month. The Association shall prepare and deliver by mail to each owner a monthly statement for the estimated actual expenses.

## 18. INSURANCE:

The Association shall obtain and maintain at all times insurance of the type and kind provided hereinabove, and including such other risks of a similar or dissimilar nature as are or shall hereafter customarily be covered with respect to other condominium buildings, fixtures, equipment and personal property, similar in construction design, all issued by responsible insurance companies authorized to do business in the State of Colorado.

Insurance coverage on the furnishings and other items of personal property belonging to an owner, and casualty and public liability insurance coverage within each individual unit, shall be the responsibility of the owner thereof.

## 19. LIEN FOR NON-PAYMENT OF ASSESSMENTS:

All sums assessed by the Association but unpaid by the owner of any condominium unit, including <u>interest thereon at eight per cent per annum</u>, shall constitute a lien on such unit superior (prior) to all other liens and encumbrances, except only for tax and special assessment liens in favor of a governmental assessing entity, and all sums unpaid on a first mortgage or first trust deed of record, including all unpaid obligatory sums as may be provided by such encumbrance, and including additional advances made thereon prior to the arising of such lien.

20. OWNERS' OBLIGATION FOR PAYMENT OF ASSESSMENTS:

The amount of the expenses assessed by the Association against each condominium unit shall be the personal and individual debt of the owner thereof at the time the assessment is made. Suit to recover a money judgment for unpaid common expenses shall be maintainable without foreclosing or waiving the lien securing same. No owner may exempt himself from liability for his contribution toward the common expenses by a waiver of the use or enjoyment of any of the common elements or by abandonment of his unit.

[Note: Even though the unit owner has no intention of using the swimming pool, the clubhouse, or the state-of-the-art fitness room, the unit owner is still obligated to pay for all of those amenities. Note also that even though the unit owner simply walks away from his or her unit, as sometimes happens in a bad economy, the unit owner is still liable for the monthly assessments. If a number of unit owners simply abandon their units during hard times, and cannot be found, then of course the assessments on the remaining unit owners will need to be increased dramatically.]

21. MORTGAGING A CONDOMINIUM UNIT – PRIORITY:

Any owner shall have the right from time to time to mortgage or encumber his interest by deed of trust, mortgage or other security instrument. A first mortgage shall be one which has first and paramount priority under applicable law. The owner of a condominium unit may create junior mortgages on the following conditions: (1) that any such junior mortgages shall always be subordinate to all terms, conditions, expenses, and other obligations created by this Declaration and by the By-Laws; (2) that the mortgagee under any junior mortgage shall release, for the purpose of restoration or any improvement upon the mortgaged premises, all of his right, title and interest in and to the proceeds under all insurance policies upon such premises, which insurance policies were affected and placed upon the mortgaged premises by the Association. Such release shall be furnished forthwith by a junior mortgagee upon written request of the Association and, if not granted, be executed by the Association as attorney in fact for such junior mortgagee.

## 22. RIGHT OF FIRST REFUSAL BY OWNERS:

In the event any owner of a condominium unit other than the Declarant shall wish to sell, lease or rent the same, and shall have received a bona fide offer therefor from a prospective purchaser, lessee or tenant, the remaining owners shall be given written notice thereof together with an executed copy of such offer and terms thereof. Such notice and copy shall be given to the Association for all of the owners. The remaining owners through the Association, or a person named by it, shall have the right to purchase, lease or rent the subject unit upon the same terms and conditions as set forth in the offer therefor; provided, however, that written notice of such election to purchase, lease or rent is given to the selling, leasing or renting owner and a matching down payment or deposit is provided to the selling, leasing or renting owner during the five-day period immediately following the delivery to the Association of the notice of the bona fide offer and copy thereof to purchase, lease or rent.

In the event any owner other than the Declarant shall attempt to sell, lease or rent his condominium unit without affording to the other owners the right of first refusal herein provided, such sale, lease, or rental shall be wholly null and void and shall confer no possessory rights, title or interest whatsoever upon the intended purchaser, lessee or tenant who shall be subject to eviction and removal, forcible or otherwise, with or without process of law.

The subleasing or sub renting of said interest shall be subject to the same limitations as are applicable to the leasing or renting thereof. The liability of the owner under these covenants shall continue, notwithstanding the fact that he may have leased or rented such interest as provided herein.

*[Note: In other words, the unit owner remains liable for the assessments, even during a sublease.]*

In no case shall the right of first refusal reserved herein affect the right of an owner to subject his interest to a bona fide trust deed, mortgage or other security instrument. The right of first refusal shall <u>not</u> apply to leases or subleases having a term of less than sixty-one days; provided, however, that any renewal or extension of such lease shall be subject to the provisions contained in this paragraph. The failure of or refusal by the Association to exercise the right to so purchase, lease or rent shall not constitute or be deemed to be a waiver of such right to purchase, lease or rent when an owner receives any subsequent bona fide offer from the same or a different prospective purchaser, lessee or tenant.

*[Note: The lawyer for anyone buying a condominium unit should be sure to check that these obligations of notice have been complied with exactly. Why do you suppose that nearly all condo Declarations have provisions like these for a right of first refusal? Could it be that condo owners want to have the right to keep certain people out of the condo development – because of race? Or because lawyers or law students have too much of an interest in enforcing rules as written? Or because someone with purple hair really just wouldn't fit in with the other people using the swimming pool? Are there some possible Constitutional problems here?]*

The right of first refusal, as provided herein, shall extend and run for the period of the lives of Brad Wolff, Frank Perkins, and Thomas Grimshaw, the Incorporators of Three Fountains Association, and the survivor of them, plus twenty-one years. *[Note: "lives in being plus 21 years!" Were these developers, or their lawyer, actually remembering about the Rule Against Perpetuities?!]*

## 23. EXEMPTION FROM RIGHT OF FIRST REFUSAL:

In the event of any default on the part of any owner under any first mortgage which entitles the holder thereof to foreclose same, any sale under such foreclosure, including delivery of a deed to the first mortgagee in lieu of such foreclosure, shall be made free and clear of the provisions above, and the purchaser (or grantee under such deed in lieu of foreclosure) of such condominium unit shall thereupon and thereafter be subject to the provisions of this Declaration and By-Laws.

*[Note: So the person with purple hair can join the other unit owners using the swimming pool without any problems if the purple-haired person buys at a foreclosure sale initiated by the bank that held the first mortgage on the unit? Interesting.]*

## 24. ASSOCIATION – ATTORNEY IN FACT:

This Declaration does hereby make mandatory the irrevocable appointment of any attorney in fact to deal with the property upon its damage, destruction or obsolescence. Title to any condominium unit is declared and expressly made subject to the terms and conditions hereof, and acceptance by any grantee of a deed from the Declarant or from any owner shall constitute appointment of the attorney in fact herein provided. All of the owners irrevocably constitute and appoint Three Fountains Association, a Colorado Corporation, not for profit, their true and lawful attorney in their name, place and stead for the purpose of dealing with their property upon its damage, destruction or obsolescence as is hereinafter provided.

In the event of damage or destruction due to fire or other disaster, the insurance proceeds, if sufficient to reconstruct the improvements, shall be applied by the Association, as attorney in fact, to such reconstruction, and the improvements shall be promptly repaired and reconstructed.

Very → Important

[The owners representing an aggregate ownership interest of <u>eighty-five per cent,</u> or more, of the general common elements may <u>agree</u> that the condominium units are <u>obsolete</u> and that the same should be <u>sold</u>. Such plan (agreement) must have the approval of the Association and the <u>unanimous approval of every first mortgagee of record at the time of the adoption of such plan</u>. In such instance, the Association shall forthwith record a notice setting forth such fact or facts, and upon the recording of such notice by the Association <u>the entire premises shall be sold by the Association,</u> as attorney in fact for <u>all</u> of the owners, free and clear of the provisions contained in the Declaration, the map and the By-Laws.]

*[Wait! So a unit owner's fee simple interest in her unit could be <u>sold</u>, without her consent, just because 85% of the other unit owners want to sell the whole place to a big developer? Yes! That is exactly what might happen. This would be really tough on a unit owner who had just put lots of time and money into remodeling her unit so that it was just perfect for her. Without a provision such as this obsolescence clause the problem would be, of course, that one unit owner would have a right to hold onto her one unit; her 1/48<sup>th</sup> corner of the swimming pool, etc. If the entire condominium project is to be sold, there has to be some way of preventing a few people from vetoing the sale. But this "obsolescence clause" does come as a great surprise to most buyers of condominium units. Notice that the Declarations do not require that the condominium actually be obsolete – only that 85 % of the unit owners, (and all the holders of the first mortgages) <u>declare</u> that the whole condominium project is obsolete. Sometimes the percentage of unit owners required is as low as 65%!]*

The sales proceeds shall be apportioned between the owners on the basis of one-forty eighth (1/48<sup>th</sup>) part to each, and such apportioned proceeds shall be paid into separate accounts, each such account representing one condominium unit. Each such account shall be in the name of the Association, and shall be further identified by the number of the unit, building symbol, and the name of the owner. From each separate account, the Association, as attorney in fact, shall use and disburse the total amount of each of such accounts, without contribution from one account to another.

## 25. RESTRICTIVE COVENANTS:

The property is hereby restricted to residential dwellings for residential use and uses related to the convenience and enjoyment of such residential use. All buildings or structures erected upon the property shall be of new construction and no buildings or structures shall be moved from other locations onto said premises, and no subsequent building other than a building shown on the map shall be built on the property except where the builder thereof has properly programmed and constructed such building. No structure of temporary character, trailer, basement, tent, shack, garage, barn, or other outbuilding shall be used or permitted to be kept or stored on any portion of the premises at any time either temporarily or permanently.

*[Note: So kids can't camp out in the backyard in a tent on a summer's night?]*

No animals, livestock or poultry of any kind shall be raised, bred or kept on the property except that dogs, cats or other household pets may be kept, subject to the rules and regulations from time to time adopted and amended by the Association.

*[Note: Sometimes these pet provisions are a great deal more restrictive. Best to warn any potential buyer about these provisions – and the fact that they might be changed at any time by "rules and regulations" adopted by the Association.]*

No advertising signs (except one of not more than one square foot "For Rent" or "For Sale" sign per unit), billboards, unsightly objects, or nuisances shall be erected, placed or permitted to remain on the premises; nor shall the premises be used in any way or for any purpose which may endanger the health or unreasonably disturb the owner of any condominium unit or an resident thereof. Further, no business activities of any kind whatever shall be conducted in any building or in any portion of the property. Provided further, however, the foregoing covenants shall not apply to the business activities, signs and billboard or the construction and maintenance of buildings and improvements, if any, of the Declarant, its agents, contractors, and assigns during the construction and sale period and of the Association, its successors and assigns, in furtherance of the powers and purposes as hereinafter set forth.

*[Note: Would this prohibition on signs prevent any political signs? Would that raise Constitutional issues? Or not? Would it be legal to use the second bedroom for a home office – for a lawyer, or a teacher grading exams at night?]*

All clotheslines, equipment, garbage cans, service yards, wood piles, or storage piles shall be kept screened by adequate planting or fencing so as to conceal them from view of neighboring units and streets. All rubbish, trash, or garbage shall be regularly removed from the property, and shall not be allowed to accumulate thereon.

Except in the individual patio areas, no planting or gardening shall be done, and no fences, hedges or walls shall be erected or maintained upon said property, except such as are installed in accordance with the initial construction of the buildings located thereon or as approved by the Association.

No exterior additions, alterations or decorating of any buildings, nor changes in fences, hedges, walls, gates and other structures shall be commenced, erected or maintained until the plans and specifications showing the nature, kind, shape, height, materials, location and approximate cost of same shall have been submitted to and approved in writing as to conformity and harmony or external design and location with existing structures in the property by the Association, or by a representative designated by it.

## B. TIME-SHARE AND INTERVAL ESTATES

In resort areas there may be a different form of ownership, which may be some variety of time share estate. This is a form of fee ownership, but instead of the ownership lasting for the full year, the owner just owns the unit for a week or two, at the same time each year. For example, a buyer might purchase the ownership of Unit 14 in a specific condominium project in Vail, for the first week of January. Another person might purchase the ownership of the same unit for the second week of January, and so on.

For time-share estates it is very important to read the specific documents, and the relevant statutory provisions. In Colorado, for example, a "Time-span" estate would give the buyer the ownership of Unit 14 for the first week of January – forever.

In contrast, the buyer of an "Interval" estate would have ownership of Unit 14 for the first week of January for a definite period of time, for example, 20 years. At the end of the twenty years the ownership of the specific unit would end, and the buyer would have an undivided remainder interest in the entire building, OR the developer would have that undivided remainder interest in the entire building. Obviously there should be a significant price difference between a *time-span* estate that would last forever, and an *interval estate*, which is scheduled to end after one more year, with the remainder then going to the developer.

Another issue with time-share or interval estates is that when there might be as many as fifty-two people who each have a one week ownership interest in Unit 14, collection of taxes and assessments might prove difficult. So in Colorado there is a special statutory provision, C.R.S. 38-33-111, which provides that:

> "With respect to each time share unit, <u>each</u> owner of a time share estate therein shall be individually liable to the unit owners' association or corporation for <u>all</u> assessments, property taxes and charges levied against that unit. ...However, with respect to each other, each time share owner shall be responsible only for a fraction of such assessments, property taxes, and charges proportionate to the magnitude of his undivided interest in the fee to the unit." (Emphasis added.)

In other words, any one of the 52 different owners of Unit 14 may be required to pay the taxes due on that unit for the <u>full year</u>. Then that unit owner has the right to bring suit against 51 other people, to force them to chip in the $500 or so that they may owe for taxes.

The lawyer for any purchaser of a time share or interval estate should be certain to warn the buyer of possible consequences such as these.

CHAPTER NINE

# WATER LAW

## INTRODUCTION

Water is increasingly valuable, in all parts of the country, but the need for water is especially important in the more arid parts of the country. Within the United States there are two different patterns of water law. On the east coast, and in the Midwest, the doctrine of *Riparian rights* generally prevails. Anyone who owns land next to a river has a right to use the water in the river, as long as that use does not interfere with the rights of any other riparian owner. Usually, there is enough for everyone, if riparian landowners make reasonable use of the water. In dry years, all riparian owners must cut back on water use as necessary.

In more arid parts of the United States, particularly in the west, a different pattern of water law prevails – the doctrine of *Prior Appropriation*. Basically the doctrine of prior appropriation allows the first person who puts the water to a beneficial use to continue using that same amount of water – regardless of whether or not that person owns any land next to the river. Thus in a prior appropriation state water may be transported, by means of ditches and canals, to the place where it is put to beneficial use.

In a prior appropriation state, the first person to put water from a river to a beneficial use has priority #1. The second person to put water from the same river to beneficial use will have priority #2. It does not matter who is upstream from whom, and it does not matter that neither owner of a water right has land adjacent to the river. The person with priority number one is entitled to use the full quantity of water to which #1 is entitled, before #2 is entitled to take a drop of water from the river. And a person who owns land next to the river, but does not have any water rights under the prior appropriation system, may not have the right to take one drop of water from the river flowing by his or her land. In a prior appropriation state, land and water rights are sold separately. So it is vital, when buying land, to be sure that there will also be available water rights.

The following case is one of the earliest prior appropriate cases, and sets forth the need for the doctrine of prior appropriation. Notice how far the water is transported, by means of various ditches and natural streams.

## SUPREME COURT OF COLORADO
## COFFIN ET AL.
## V.
## THE LEFT HAND DITCH COMPANY.

### DECEMBER 1, 1882

**Appeal from District Court of Boulder County.**

HELM, J.

Appellee, who was plaintiff below, claimed to be the owner of certain water by virtue of an appropriation thereof from the south fork of the St. Vrain creek. It appears that such water, after its diversion, is carried by means of a ditch to the James creek, and thence along the bed of the same to Left Hand creek, where it is again diverted by lateral ditches and used to irrigate lands adjacent to the last named stream. Appellants are the owners of lands lying on the margin and in the neighborhood of the St. Vrain below the mouth of said south fork thereof, and naturally irrigated therefrom.

In 1879 there was not a sufficient quantity of water in the St. Vrain to supply the ditch of appellee and also irrigate the said lands of appellant. A portion of appellee's dam was torn out, and its diversion of water thereby seriously interfered with by appellants. The action is brought for damages arising from the trespass, and for injunctive relief to prevent repetitions thereof in the future.

[Plaintiff, Appellee, was awarded judgment below.]

Two important questions upon the subject of water rights are fairly presented by the record, and we cannot well avoid resting our decision upon them.

It is contended by counsel for appellants that the common law principles of riparian proprietorship prevailed in Colorado until 1876, and that the doctrine of priority of right to water by priority of appropriation thereof was first recognized and adopted in the constitution. But we think the latter doctrine has existed from the date of the earliest appropriations of water within the boundaries of the state. The climate is dry, and the soil, when moistened only by the usual rainfall, is arid and unproductive; except in a few favored sections, artificial irrigation for agriculture is an absolute necessity. Water in the various streams thus acquires a value unknown in moister climates. Instead of being a mere incident to the soil, it rises, when appropriated, to the dignity of a distinct usufructuary estate, or right of property. It has always been the policy of the national, as well as the territorial and state governments, to encourage the diversion and use of water in this country for agriculture; and vast expenditures of time and money have been made in reclaiming and fertilizing by irrigation portions of our unproductive territory. Houses have been built, and permanent improvements made; the soil has been cultivated, and thousands of acres have been rendered immensely valuable, with the understanding that appropriations of water would be protected. Deny the doctrine of priority or superiority of right by priority of appropriation, and a great part of the value of all this property is at once destroyed.

The right to water in this country, by priority of appropriation thereof, we think it is, and has always been, the duty of the national and state governments to protect. The right itself, and the obligation to protect it, existed prior to legislation on the subject of irrigation.

We conclude, then, that the common law doctrine giving the riparian owner a right to the flow of water in its natural channel upon and over his lands, even though he makes no beneficial use thereof, is inapplicable to Colorado. Imperative necessity, unknown to the countries which gave it birth, compels the recognition of another doctrine in conflict therewith. And we hold that, in the absence of express statutes to the contrary, the first appropriator of water from a natural stream for a beneficial purpose has, with the qualifications contained in the constitution, a prior right thereto, to the extent of such appropriation.

It is urged, however, that even if the doctrine of priority or superiority of right by priority of appropriation be conceded, appellee in this case is not benefited thereby. Appellants claim that they have a better right to the water because their lands lie along the margin and in the neighborhood of the St. Vrain. They assert that, as against them, appellee's diversion of said water to irrigate lands adjacent to Left Hand creek, though prior in time, is unlawful.

In the absence of legislation to the contrary, we think that the right to water acquired by priority of appropriation thereof is not in any way dependent upon the locus of its application to the beneficial use designed. And the disastrous consequences of our adoption of the rule contended for, forbid our giving such a construction to the statutes as will concede the same, if they will properly bear a more reasonable and equitable one.

The doctrine of priority of right by priority of appropriation for agriculture is evoked, as we have seen, by the imperative necessity for artificial irrigation of the soil. And it would be an ungenerous and inequitable rule that would deprive one of its benefit simply because he has, by large expenditure of time and money, carried the water from one stream over an intervening watershed and cultivated land in the valley of another. It might be utterly impossible, owing to the topography of the country, to get water upon his farm from the adjacent stream; or if possible, it might be impracticable on account of the distance from the point where the diversion must take place and the attendant expense; or the quantity of water in such stream might be entirely insufficient to supply his wants. It sometimes happens that the most fertile soil is found along the margin or in the neighborhood of the small rivulet, and sandy and barren land beside the larger stream. To apply the rule contended for would prevent the useful and profitable cultivation of the productive soil, and sanction the waste of water upon the more sterile lands. It would have enabled a party to locate upon a stream in 1875, and destroy the value of thousands of acres, and the improvements thereon, in adjoining valleys, possessed and cultivated for the preceding decade. Under the principle contended for, a party owning land ten miles from the stream, but in the valley thereof, might deprive a prior appropriator of the water diverted therefrom whose lands are within a thousand yards, but just beyond an intervening divide.

The judgment of the court below will be affirmed.

Affirmed.

Note: Sometimes in states where rainfall is plentiful, the problem is what to do with the excess water that may fall on a parcel of land. Can the landowner do whatever is necessary to get rid of the excess water? Or must the landowner take steps necessary to make sure that the discharge of excess water does not cause unreasonable damage to the land farther down the hill?

# SUPREME COURT OF NEW JERSEY

DAVID K. ARMSTRONG AND MARY JANE ARMSTRONG, HIS WIFE,
PLAINTIFFS-RESPONDENTS,

V.

THE FRANCIS CORPORATION, A CORPORATION OF THE STATE OF NEW JERSEY,
DEFENDANT-APPELLANT,

AND

GEORGE O. KLEMP AND C. KLEMP, HIS WIFE, DEFENDANTS-RESPONDENTS.

JANUARY 16, 1956

The opinion of the court was delivered by
WILLIAM J. BRENNAN, Jr., J.

The Chancery Division, after trial, entered a final judgment against the defendant, the Francis Corporation. Francis appealed to the Appellate Division, and we certified the appeal here on our own motion.

A small natural stream rose in Francis' 42-acre tract, which lies immediately south of Lake Avenue in Rahway. The stream flowed in a northerly direction 1200 feet across the Francis lands through a seven-foot box culvert under Lake Avenue and emptied into Milton Lake, 900 feet north of the avenue. It was the natural drainway for the larger 85-acre area south of Lake Avenue which includes the Francis tract.

Francis stripped its tract and erected 186 small homes thereon in a development known as Duke Estates, Section 2. It also built some 14 houses on an adjacent small tract known as Duke Estates, Section 1, lying in another drainage area. It constructed a drainage system of streets, pavements, gutters, ditches, culverts and catch basins to serve both developments. The system emptied into a corrugated iron pipe laid by Francis below the level of the natural stream bed on its lands. The pipe followed the course of the stream bed to the box culvert under Lake Avenue, although deviating from the course at some places. The pipe was covered with fill on Francis' tract and all evidence of the natural stream there has disappeared.

The drainage of the original 85 acres was thus augmented not only by the drainage of some 2 1/2 acres of the Duke Estates, Section 1, but also by waters percolating into the joints of the pipe where it lay below the level of the water table of the Francis tract. The pipe joints were expressly designed to receive such percolating waters, and, to the extent that the percolation lowered the level of the water table, the result was to provide a drier terrain more suitable to housing development.

Where the stream passes north of Lake Avenue en route to Milton Lake after leaving the box culvert it remains largely in its natural state and forms the boundary line between the residential tracts of the plaintiffs Armstrong and the defendants Klemp. [The Klemps were made parties defendant by Francis' cross-claim but prevailed thereon and were allowed the same relief as the Armstrongs.] The stream passes through a 36-inch culvert under the Klemp driveway and thence, across lands of the Union County Park Commission, to the Lake.

The Francis improvement resulted in consequences for the Armstrongs and the Klemps fully described by Judge Sullivan in his oral opinion as follows:

"Now the stream as it emerges from the underground pipe goes under Lake Avenue and then flows past and through the Armstrong and Klemp properties is no longer the 'babbling brook' that Mr. Klemp described. Now there is a constant and materially increased flow in it. The stream is never dry. The water is now discolored and evil smelling and no longer has any fish in it. A heavy deposit of silt or muck up to eighteen inches in depth now covers the bottom of the stream. After a heavy rainstorm the stream undergoes a remarkable change for several hours. All of the upstream rain water that used to be absorbed or held back is now channeled in undiminished volume and at great speed into this stream. This causes a flash rise or crest in the stream, with a tremendous volume of water rushing through at an accelerated speed. As a result, the stream has flooded on several occasions within the last year, although this was unheard of previously. More distressing, however, is the fact that during these flash situations the body of water moving at the speed it does tears into the banks of the brook particularly where the bed may turn or twist. At a point even with the plaintiff's (Armstrong) house the stream makes a sharp bend. [Here the effect of the increased flow of water is most apparent since the bank on plaintiff's side of the stream has been eaten away to the extent of about ten feet. This erosion is now within fifteen feet of the Armstrong septic tank system. It is difficult to say where it will stop, where the erosion will stop. The silting has, of course, raised the bed of the stream up to eighteen inches in places and the raising of the stream results in water action against different areas of the bank so that the erosion problem while unpredictable is ominous. The eating away of the banks in several places has loosened rocks or boulders which have been rolled downstream by the force of the water. Those stones, however, as they rolled through the Klemp culvert cracked and broke the sides and bottom of the culvert and the water is now threatening to undermine the entire masonry. There is no doubt but that the defendant's activities have caused all of the conditions just related.

A matter of some concern is that defendant's housing development occupies only about one-half of the area which drains into this brook. At the present time there is a forty acre undeveloped section to the south of the defendant and it is reasonable to assume that it, too, will be improved and built upon at some future time. Defendant's underground trunk sewer was built to accommodate any possible runoff from this tract. If and when that section is developed, Armstrong and Klemp will have that much more erosion, silting and flooding to deal with."

Judge Sullivan concluded that the Armstrongs and the Klemps were plainly entitled to relief in these circumstances and 'that the only sensible and permanent solution to the problem is to pipe the rest of the brook,' that is, from the culvert outlet at Lake Avenue the entire distance to Milton Lake. A plan for that purpose had been prepared by Francis' engineer and approved by the Armstrongs and the Klemps at a time when efforts were being made to compromise the dispute before the trial. The final judgment orders Francis, at its expense, forthwith to proceed with and complete within 60 days the work detailed on that plan. The Union County Park Commission has given its formal consent to the doing of the work called for by the plan on its lands.

The important legal question raised by the appeal is whether the damage suffered by the Armstrongs and the Klemps is Damnum absque injuria, namely, merely the non-actionable consequences of the privileged expulsion by Francis of waters from its tract as an incident to the improvement thereof.

Turning, then, to the basic question for decision, appellant grounds its argument upon the following statement of the Appellate Division in *Yonadi v. Homestead Country Homes,* (1955):

"While the New Jersey cases do not deal with the matter explicitly, we conclude that where surface water is concentrated through a drain or other artificial means and is conducted to some place substantially where it otherwise would have flowed, the defendant will not be liable even though by reason of improvements he has made in the land, the water is brought there in larger quantities and with greater force than would have occurred prior to the improvements. The policies underlying the general rule come to bear here. What reasonably could the upland proprietor or occupant do in the present case with this excess water? Rather than require him to dispose of it-and so perhaps require him to secure the cooperation of a number of lowland properties through which the water must eventually be brought-the burden is cast on each low-land proprietor to protect his own land."

We might summarily dispose of this point against the appellant upon the ground that more than the surface water drained from the 85-acre tract is involved here. Appellant has augmented the volume of water passing through the Lake Avenue culvert with water from another drainage area and with water percolating into its pipe where the level of the natural water table on its tract is higher, and so the cited proposition would not in any event apply. But, because we do not agree that the quoted proposition, in the form stated, which makes no allowance for differences in factual situations, is or should be the law governing the liability of the landowner who alters the flow of surface waters with resulting material harm to other landowners, we shall treat the case as if only the disposal of surface water from the 85-acre tract was involved and determine appellant's point upon that premise.

In their article 'Interferences with Surface Waters', 24 Minn.L.Rev. 891, 899, (1940), Professor Kinyon and Mr. McClure have convincingly demonstrated that there was no true common law of surface waters and that the law in that respect has been largely developed since 1850, both in England and in the United States.

The casting of surface waters from one's own land upon the land of another, in circumstances where the resultant material harm to the other was foreseen or foreseeable, would appear on the face of it to be tortious conduct, as actionable where the consequences of an unreasonable use of the possessor's land, as in the case of the abstraction or diversion of water from a stream which unreasonably interferes with the use of the stream below, Prosser, Torts (1951), p. 586, and as in the case of the unreasonable use of percolating or subterranean waters, and as in the case of artificial construction on one's land which unreasonably speeds the waters of a stream past one's property onto that of an owner below, causing harm. Yet only the courts of the states of New Hampshire and Minnesota have expressly classified the possessor's liability, where imposed, for harm by the expulsion of surface waters to be a tort liability. [Those courts have evolved the 'reasonable use' rule laying down the test that each possessor is legally privileged to make a reasonable use of his land, even though the flow of surface waters is altered thereby and causes some harm to others, but incurs liability when his harmful interference with the flow of surface waters is unreasonable.]

All other states have treated the legal relations of the parties as a branch of property law-that is, have done so, if we emphasize only the language of the decisions and ignore the actual results reached. Two rules have been evolved which, in their statement, are directly opposed, for under one the possessor would not be liable in any case and under the other he would be liable in every case. But an analysis of the results reached under both rules shows that neither is anywhere strictly applied. The first rule, purportedly applicable in our own State, stems from the view that surface waters are the common enemy. The "common enemy" rule emphasizes the possessor's privilege to rid his lands of surface waters as he will. That rule "is, in substance, that a possessor of land has an unlimited and unrestricted legal privilege to deal with the surface water on his land as he pleases, regardless of the harm which he may thereby cause others."

The other rule, borrowed from the civil law of foreign nations and called the "civil law" rule, emphasizes not the privileges of the possessor but the duties of the possessor to other landowners who are affected by his expulsion of surface waters from his lands. That rule is to the effect that "a person who interferes with the Natural flow of surface waters so as to cause an invasion of another's interests in the use and enjoyment of his land is subject to liability to the other."

The quoted statement describing the common enemy rule implies that what Francis did here was absolutely privileged, which is the clear import of the common enemy rule. But our decisions have invariably refused to apply the rule according to its letter where it works injustice.

Nor have states which are said to follow the civil law rule held that the possessor may not under any circumstances rid his lands of surface water without incurring liability if harm is caused to another. In sum, the courts here and elsewhere, in terms of results, have actually come out at the "reasonable use" doctrine.

We therefore think it appropriate that this court declare, as we now do, our adherence in terms to the reasonable use rule and thus accord our expressions in cases of this character to the actual practice of our courts. Indeed, Judge Sullivan did so in his oral opinion below when he pronounced his judgment as based upon his finding that what Francis did was not "done in the reasonable use of his (its) land," relying for authority upon the decision of the former Court of Chancery in *Smith v. Orben*. And it is significant of the true state of the law that the Restatement on Torts, sec. 833, has adopted the reasonable use test as the rule actually prevailing.

The rule of reasonableness has the particular virtue of flexibility. The issue of reasonableness or unreasonableness becomes a question of fact to be determined in each case upon a consideration of all the relevant circumstances, including such factors as the amount of harm caused, the foreseeability of the harm which results, the purpose or motive with which the possessor acted, and all other relevant matters. It is, of course, true that society has a great interest that land shall be developed for the greater good. It is therefore properly a consideration in these cases whether the utility of the possessor's use of his land outweighs the gravity of the harm which results from his alteration of the flow of surface waters⟩ But while today's mass home building projects, of which the Francis development is typical, are assuredly in the social good, no reason suggests itself why, in justice, the economic costs incident to the expulsion of surface waters in the transformation of the rural or semi-rural areas of our State into urban or suburban communities should be borne in every case by adjoining landowners rather than by those who engage in such projects for profit. Social progress and the common wellbeing are in actuality better served by a just and right balancing of the competing interests according to the general principles of fairness and common sense which attend the application of the rule of reason.

Affirmed.

Note: The two prior cases are the easy cases. As water has become more and more precious, more complexities have arisen with regard to the use of water. In the following case, for example, the Arizona Supreme Court is faced with the issue of how the water rights of the Native American tribes fit in with the doctrine of prior appropriation adopted by state law. The case also covers the relationship between the preemptive power of the federal government, and the general federal recognition that individual states should be permitted to enact their own rules regarding the ownership of property, including water, within the limits set by the U.S. Constitution.

As you read the following case, notice what impact Indian water rights will have on a state's rules of prior appropriation. And notice the distinction between federal water rights for a National Monument, for example, and Indian water rights.


## SUPREME COURT OF ARIZONA
## IN RE THE GENERAL ADJUDICATION OF ALL RIGHTS TO USE WATER IN THE GILA RIVER SYSTEM AND SOURCE.

NOVEMBER 26, 2001


OPINION

ZLAKET, Chief Justice.

We are presented with another issue in the Gila River general stream adjudication. The facts and procedural history of this matter are well documented.

On December 11, 1990, we granted interlocutory review of six issues decided by the trial court. Four of these have been resolved. Today the court addresses issue 3:

"What is the appropriate standard to be applied in determining the amount of water reserved for federal lands?"

## PROCEDURAL HISTORY

In its September 1988 decision, the trial court stated that each Indian reservation was entitled to:

> "such water as is necessary to effectuate the purpose of that reservation. While as to other types of federal lands courts have allowed controversy about what the purpose of the land is and how much water will satisfy that purpose, as to Indian reservations the courts have drawn a clear and distinct line. It is that the amount is measured by the amount of water necessary to irrigate all of the *practically irrigable acreage* (PIA) on that reservation.

We review this determination utilizing a de novo standard.

## DISCUSSION

### A. Prior Appropriation and the Winters Doctrine

In Arizona, surface water is subject to the doctrine of prior appropriation. An appropriator acquires a legal right to water by putting it to a beneficial use, which is "the basis, measure and limit" of any such entitlement. So long as utilization continues, the right remains secure. However, when an owner "ceases or fails to use the water appropriated for five successive years, the right to the use shall cease, and the water shall revert to the public and shall again be subject to appropriation."

Prior appropriation adheres to a seniority system determined by the date on which the user initially puts water to a beneficial use. According to state law, the person "first appropriating the water shall have the better right." This chronological staging becomes important in times of shortage because preference is given according to the appropriation date, allowing senior holders to take their entire allotments of water before junior appropriators receive any at all. In short, "the oldest titles shall have precedence."

Federal water rights are different from those acquired under state law. Beginning with *Winters v. United States,* 207 U.S. 564 (1908), the Supreme Court has consistently held that "when the Federal Government withdraws its land from the public domain and reserves it for a federal purpose, the Government, by implication, reserves appurtenant water then unappropriated to the extent needed to accomplish the purpose of the reservation."

According to *Winters* and its progeny, a federal right vests on the date a reservation is created, not when water is put to a beneficial use. Although this entitlement remains subordinate to rights acquired under state law prior to creation of the reservation, it is senior to the claims of all future state appropriators, even those who use the water before the federal holders. In this sense, a federally reserved water right is preemptive. Its creation is not dependent on beneficial use, and it retains priority despite non-use.

Our task is to determine the manner in which water rights on Indian lands are to be quantified. Consideration of this subject necessarily begins with the *Winters* case. The Fort Belknap Indian reservation in Montana was created by Congress on May 1, 1888 as a "permanent home and abiding place" for the Gros Ventre and Assiniboine tribes. According to treaty, the government reserved 600,000 acres of land for Indian use, which was a small fraction of the tribes' original holdings. The agreement, however, was silent as to tribal water rights. Within a short period of time, white settlers began to dam or otherwise divert water from the Milk River, which bordered the reservation. In 1905, a federal reservation superintendent wrote to the Commissioner of Indian Affairs protesting these diversions and imploring the government to take "radical action" on the tribes' behalf. Relief came in a lawsuit filed by the government to enjoin Winters and other homesteaders, who claimed senior rights under the doctrine of prior appropriation, from "interfering in any manner with the use by the reservation of 5,000 inches of the water of the river."

The Supreme Court, recognizing the "lands were arid, and, without irrigation, were practically valueless," held that Congress, by creating the Indian reservation, impliedly reserved "all of the waters of the river necessary for the purposes for which the reservation was created." As noted by the Court, the purpose for creating the Fort Belknap reservation was to establish a permanent homeland for the Gros Ventre and Assiniboine Indians. The Court further declared that this reservation of water was not only for the present needs of the tribes, but "for a use which would be necessarily continued through years."

Granted, *Winters* was not a general stream adjudication. Moreover, congressional intent to reserve water was not expressed in the Fort Belknap treaty; it was found by the Court to be implied. The principle outlined in *Winters,* however, is now well-established in our nation's jurisprudence: the government, in establishing Indian or other federal reservations, impliedly reserves enough water to fulfill the purpose of each such reservation. "In so doing the United States acquires a reserved right in unappropriated water which vests on the date of the reservation and is superior to the rights of future appropriators."

Since *Winters*, the Supreme Court has strengthened the reserved rights doctrine. In *Arizona I*, the government asserted rights to Colorado River water on behalf of five Indian reservations in Arizona, California, and Nevada. Arizona claimed that because each of the reservations was created or expanded by Executive Order, rather than by treaty, water rights were not retained. This argument was expressly rejected by the Court. It noted that when these reservations were established, the federal government was aware "that most of the lands were of the desert kind—hot, scorching sands—and that water from the river would be essential to the life of the Indian people and to the animals they hunted and the crops they raised." As such, the Court found that the United States reserved water rights "to make the reservations livable." This allocation was intended to "satisfy the future as well as the present needs of the Indian Reservations."

The Supreme Court has further clarified the reserved rights doctrine in two non-Indian cases. In *Cappaert*, the government brought a lawsuit to declare its rights to an underground pool of water appurtenant to Devil's Hole in the Death Valley National Monument. The Cappaerts, by pumping groundwater, were threatening the amount of water available to an endangered species of desert fish. Nevada argued that the *Winters* doctrine was an equitable one which called for a "balancing of competing interests." The Court disagreed, stating that the central issue was "whether the Government intended to reserve unappropriated and thus available water. Intent is inferred if the previously unappropriated waters are necessary to accomplish the purposes for which the reservation was created." Because the Devil's Hole Monument had been established in part to conserve natural and historical objects and the wildlife therein, the Court found a reserved water right to fulfill this purpose. In an important caveat, however, the Court stated that this right "reserves only that amount of water necessary to fulfill the purpose of the reservation, no more." Thus, the allocation must be tailored to the "minimal need" of the reservation.

In *United States v. New Mexico*, the issue before the Court was whether the New Mexico Supreme Court, in an adjudication concerning the Rio Mimbres, properly quantified the federally reserved water right associated with the Gila National Forest. After reiterating *Cappaert's* limiting principle, that the "implied-reservation-of-water doctrine" applies only to that amount of water necessary to fulfill a reservation's purpose, the Court emphasized that "both the asserted water right and the specific purposes for which the land was reserved" must be examined to ascertain "that without the water the purposes of the reservation would be entirely defeated." Because federally reserved water rights are implied, the Court also determined that

"Where water is necessary to fulfill the very purposes for which a federal reservation was created, it is reasonable to conclude, even in the face of Congress' express deference to state water law in other areas, that the United States intended to reserve the necessary water. Where water is only valuable for a secondary use of the reservation, however, there arises the contrary inference that Congress intended that the United States would acquire water in the same manner as any other public or private appropriator."

This is now known as the "primary-secondary purposes test," and its application to federal Indian reservations is one of the issues before us today.

## B. Purpose

Generally, the "purpose of a federal reservation of land defines the scope and nature of impliedly reserved water rights." However, when applying the *Winters* doctrine, it is necessary to distinguish between Indian and non-Indian reservations.

The government may exercise total dominion over water rights on federal non-Indian lands. "The United States can lease, sell, quitclaim, release, encumber or convey its own federal reserved water rights." But unlike those attached to Indian lands, which have reserved water rights for "future needs and changes in use," non-Indian reserved rights are narrowly quantified to meet the original, primary purpose of the reservation; water for secondary purposes must be acquired under state law. Thus, the primary purpose for which the federal government reserves non-Indian land is strictly construed after careful examination. The test for determining such a right is clear.

For each federal claim of a reserved water right, the trier of fact must examine the documents reserving the land from the public domain and the underlying legislation authorizing the reservation; determine the precise federal purposes to be served by such legislation; determine whether water is essential for the primary purposes of the reservation; and finally determine the precise quantity of water—the minimal need as set forth in *Cappaert* and *New Mexico*—required for such purposes.

Indian reservations, however, are different. In its role as trustee of such lands, the government must act for the Indians' benefit. This fiduciary relationship is referred to as "one of the primary cornerstones of Indian law." Felix S. Cohen, *Handbook of Federal Indian Law* (1982). Thus, treaties, statutes, and executive orders are construed liberally in the Indians' favor. Such an approach is equally applicable to the federal government's actions with regard to water for Indian reservations. "The purposes of Indian reserved rights are given broader interpretation in order to further the federal goal of Indian self-sufficiency."

The parties dispute the purposes of the several Indian reservations involved in this case. The United States and the tribal litigants argue that federal case law has preemptively determined that every Indian reservation was established as a permanent tribal homeland. The state litigants disagree, contending instead that the trial court must analyze each tribe's treaty or enabling documentation to determine that reservation's individual purpose. We need not decide whether federal case law has preemptively determined the issue. We agree with the Supreme Court that the essential purpose of Indian reservations is to provide Native American people with a "permanent home and abiding place," that is, a "livable" environment.

While courts may choose to examine historical documents in determining the purpose and reason for creating a federal reservation on non-Indian lands, the utility of such an exercise with respect to Indian reservations is highly questionable. This is so for a variety of reasons.

First, as pointed out by the state litigants, many Indian reservations were pieced together over time. For example, the boundaries of the Gila River Indian Community changed ten times from its creation in 1859 until 1915, resulting in overall growth from 64,000 to 371,422 acres. But some of the changes along the way actually decreased the size of the reservation or limited the scope of previous additions. If these alterations had different purposes, as the state litigants suggest, it might be argued that water reserved to a specific parcel could not be utilized elsewhere on the same reservation, or that water once available could no longer be accessed. Such an arbitrary patchwork of water rights would be unworkable and inconsistent with the concept of a permanent, unified homeland.

A second problem lies in the fact that congressional intent to reserve water for tribal land is not express, but implied. As Franks points out, "because the intent is merely imputed—that is, its historical reality is irrelevant for purposes of establishing reserved rights—it seems strained to impute an historical definition to that imputed intent for the purpose of quantifying an extremely valuable right to a scarce resource."

Courts construe Indian treaties according to the way in which the Indians themselves would have understood them. But the historical search for a reservation's purpose tends to focus only on the motives of Congress—tribal intent is easily and often left out of the equation. It is doubtful that any tribe would have agreed to surrender its freedom and be confined on a reservation without some assurance that sufficient water would be provided for its well-being.

The most recognizable difficulty with the historical approach is that many documents do not accurately represent the true reasons for which Indian reservations were created. It is well known that in the nineteenth century, the federal government made conflicting promises. On one hand, it offered white settlers free land, an abundance of resources, and safety if they would travel to and inhabit the West. The government also assured Indians that they would be able to live on their lands in peace. The promises to the tribes were not kept.

General William T. Sherman made clear that "if the Indians wander outside [the boundaries of the reservation] they at once become objects of suspicion, liable to be attacked by the troops as hostile." In a November 9, 1871 letter to the Secretary of War, Sherman closed by stating that General Crook, head of the Army in Arizona, "may feel assured that whatever measures of severity he may adopt to reduce these Apaches to a peaceful and subordinate condition will be approved by the War Department and the President."

Despite what may be set forth in official documents, the fact is that Indians were forced onto reservations so that white settlement of the West could occur unimpeded. "Cynical motives aside, the goals of the reservation system were to move Indian tribes out of the path of white settlement, provide them a homeland, and 'civilize' individual tribal members, often by attempting to transform them into yeoman farmers." As recognized by former Arizona Congressman Morris K. Udall, the federal government "can be kindly described as having been less than diligent in its efforts to secure sufficient water supplies for the Indian community to develop its arable lands and achieve meaningful economic self-sufficiency and self-determination."

The trial court here failed to recognize any particular purpose for these Indian reservations, only finding that the PIA [Practicably Irrigable Acreage] standard should be applied when quantifying tribes' water rights. It is apparent that the judge was leery of being "drawn into a potential racial controversy" based on historical documentation. But it seems clear to us that each of the Indian reservations in question was created as a "permanent home and abiding place" for the Indian people, as explained in *Winters*. This conclusion comports with the belief that "the general purpose, to provide a home for the Indians, is a broad one and must be liberally construed." Such a construction is necessary for tribes to achieve the twin goals of Indian self-determination and economic self-sufficiency.

Limiting an Indian reservation's purpose to agriculture, as the PIA standard implicitly does, assumes that the Indian peoples will not enjoy the same style of evolution as other people, nor are they to have the benefits of modern civilization. The homeland concept assumes that the homeland will not be a static place frozen in an instant of time but that the homeland will evolve and will be used in different ways as the Indian society develops.

Other right holders are not constrained in this, the twenty-first century, to use water in the same manner as their ancestors in the 1800s. Although over 40% of the nation's population lived and worked on farms in 1880, less than 5% do today.

Likewise, agriculture has steadily decreased as a percentage of our gross domestic product. *See* U.S. Census Bureau, *Statistical Abstract of the United States,* demonstrating that agricultural output as a percentage of GDP has declined from 10.7% in 1930 to 2.84% in 1997. Just as the nation's economy has evolved, nothing should prevent tribes from diversifying their economies if they so choose and are reasonably able to do so. The permanent homeland concept allows for this flexibility and practicality. We therefore hold that the purpose of a federal Indian reservation is to serve as a "permanent home and abiding place" to the Native American people living there.

### C. Primary–Secondary Purpose Test

Next arises the question of whether the primary-secondary purpose test applies to Indian reservations. In *New Mexico,* a case dealing with a national forest, the Supreme Court reaffirmed that "where water is necessary to fulfill the very purposes for which a federal reservation was created," it is implied that the United States reserved water for it. However, where the "water is only valuable for a secondary use of the reservation," any right must be acquired according to state law. All parties agree that this distinction applies to non-Indian federal reservations. The trial court here rejected the primary-secondary test, finding that the "rule is a little different for entrusted lands, Indian reservations." We agree.

It is true that some courts have utilized the primary-secondary purpose test or looked to it for guidance when dealing with Indian lands. Nevertheless, we believe the significant differences between Indian and non-Indian reservations preclude application of the test to the former. As Judge Canby has noted, "while the purpose for which the federal government reserves other types of lands may be strictly construed, the purposes of Indian reservations are necessarily entitled to broader interpretation if the goal of Indian self-sufficiency is to be attained." W. Canby, *American Indian Law* (1981). Parenthetically, even if the *New Mexico* test were to apply, tribes would be entitled to the full measure of their reserved rights because water use necessary to the establishment of a permanent homeland is a primary, not secondary, purpose.

### D. Quantifying Winters Rights

The *Winters* doctrine retains the concept of "minimal need" by reserving "only that amount of water necessary to fulfill the purpose of the reservation, no more." The method utilized in arriving at such an amount, however, must satisfy both present and future needs of the reservation as a livable homeland.

## E. The PIA Standard

(The trial court in this matter held that each Indian reservation was entitled to "the amount of water necessary to irrigate all of the *practicably irrigable acreage* (P.I.A.) on that reservation." The PIA standard was developed by Special Master Rifkind in *Arizona I,* That case dealt with the water rights of similarly-situated tribes in Arizona, California, and Nevada. Without much amplification, the Supreme Court declared:

> "We also agree with the Master's conclusion as to the quantity of water intended to
> be reserved. He found that the water was intended to satisfy the future as well as the
> present needs of the Indian Reservations and ruled that enough water was reserved to
> irrigate all the practicably irrigable acreage on the reservations."

Other courts have since adopted the PIA standard in quantifying reserved water rights for Indian tribes.

PIA constitutes "those acres susceptible to sustained irrigation at reasonable costs." This implies a two-step process. First, it must be shown that crops can be grown on the land, considering arability and the engineering practicality of irrigation. Second, the economic feasibility of irrigation must be demonstrated.

This is accomplished by subjecting proposed irrigation projects to a cost-benefit analysis, "comparing the likely costs of the project to the likely financial returns. If the latter outweighs the former, the project can be found economically feasible, and the underlying land 'practicably irrigable.'"

On its face, PIA appears to be an objective method of determining water rights. But while there may be some "value of the certainty inherent in the practicably irrigable acreage standard," its flaws become apparent on closer examination.

The first objection to an across-the-board application of PIA lies in its potential for inequitable treatment of tribes based solely on geographical location. Arizona's topography is such that some tribes inhabit flat alluvial plains while others dwell in steep, mountainous areas. This diversity creates a dilemma that PIA cannot solve. As stated by two commentators:

> "There can be little doubt that the PIA standard works to the advantage of tribes inhab-
> iting alluvial plains or other relatively flat lands adjacent to stream courses. In contrast,
> tribes inhabiting mountainous or other agriculturally marginal terrains are at a severe
> disadvantage when it comes to demonstrating that their lands are practicably irrigable."

Tribes who fail to show either the engineering or economic feasibility of proposed irrigation projects run the risk of not receiving any reserved water under the PIA, for example water rights might be denied to the Mescalero Apache Tribe, situated in a mountainous region of southern New Mexico, for failure to prove irrigation projects were economically feasible. This inequity is unacceptable and inconsistent with the idea of a permanent homeland.

Another concern with PIA is that it forces tribes to pretend to be farmers in an era when "large agricultural projects are risky, marginal enterprises. This is demonstrated by the fact that no federal project planned in accordance with the Principles and Guidelines adopted by the Water Resources Council of the Federal Government has been able to show a positive benefit/cost ratio in the last decade [1981 to 1991]." A permanent homeland requires water for multiple uses, which may or may not include agriculture. The PIA standard, however, forces tribes to prove economic feasibility for a kind of enterprise that, judging from the evidence of both federal and private willingness to invest money, is simply no longer economically feasible in the West.

Limiting the applicable inquiry to a PIA analysis not only creates a temptation for tribes to concoct inflated, unrealistic irrigation projects, but deters consideration of actual water needs based on realistic economic choices. We again agree with the analysis of Justice Richard V. Thomas in *Big Horn I*:

> "I would be appalled if the Congress began expending money to develop water projects for irrigating these Wyoming lands when far more fertile lands in the midwestern states now are being removed from production due to poor market conditions. I am convinced that those lands which were included as practicably irrigable acreage, based upon the assumption of the construction of a future irrigation project, should not be included for the purpose of quantification of the Indian peoples' water rights. They may be irrigable academically, but not as a matter of practicality."

The PIA standard also potentially frustrates the requirement that federally reserved water rights be tailored to minimal need. Rather than focusing on what is necessary to fulfill a reservation's overall design, PIA awards what may be an overabundance of water by including every irrigable acre of land in the equation.

For the foregoing reasons, we decline to approve the use of PIA as the exclusive quantification measure for determining water rights on Indian lands.

## F. Proper Factors for Consideration

Recognizing that the most likely reason for PIA's endurance is that "no satisfactory substitute has emerged," Dan A. Tarlock, *One River, Three Sovereigns: Indian and Interstate Water Rights*, (1987), we now enter essentially uncharted territory. In *Gila III*, this court stated that determining the amount of water necessary to accomplish a reservation's purpose is a "fact-intensive inquiry that must be made on a reservation-by-reservation basis." We still adhere to the belief that this is the only way federally reserved rights can be tailored to meet each reservation's minimal need.

When *Big Horn I* went before the Supreme Court, one of the present state litigants, in an amicus brief, argued that there should be a "balancing of a myriad of factors" in quantifying reserved water rights. During oral argument in the present case, counsel for the Apache tribes made a similar argument. Considering the objective that tribal reservations be allocated water necessary to achieve their purpose as permanent homelands, such a multi-faceted approach appears best-suited to produce a proper outcome.

Tribes have already used this methodology in settling water rights claims with the federal government. One feature of such settlements has been the development of master land use plans specifying the quantity of water necessary for different purposes on the reservation. (Fort McDowell Indian Community utilized a land use plan in conjunction with its water rights settlement based on agricultural production, commercial development, industrial use, residential use, recreational use, and wilderness).

While we commend the creation of master land use plans as an effective means of demonstrating water requirements, tribes may choose to present evidence to the trial court in a different manner. The important thing is that the lower court should have before it actual and proposed uses, accompanied by the parties' recommendations regarding feasibility and the amount of water necessary to accomplish the homeland purpose. In viewing this evidence, the lower court should consider the following factors, which are not intended to be exclusive.

A tribe's history will likely be significant. Deference should be given to practices requiring water use that are embedded in Native American traditions. Some rituals may date back hundreds of years, and tribes should be granted water rights necessary to continue such practices into the future. An Indian reservation could not be a true homeland otherwise.

In addition to history, the court should consider tribal culture when quantifying federally reserved rights. Preservation of culture benefits both Indians and non-Indians; for this reason, Congress has recognized the "unique values of Indian culture" in our society. Water uses that have particular cultural significance should be respected, where possible. The length of time a practice has been engaged in, its nature (e.g., religious or otherwise), and its importance in a tribe's daily affairs may all be relevant.

The court should also consider the tribal land's geography, topography, and natural resources, including groundwater availability. As mentioned earlier, one of the biggest problems with PIA is that it does not allow for flexibility in this regard. It has also been observed that "irrigation is one of the most inefficient and ecologically damaging ways to use water. Increasing the use of water for irrigation runs counter to a historic trend in western water use—the transition from agricultural to less consumptive and higher-valued municipal and industrial uses." This does not mean that tribes are prohibited from including agriculture/irrigation as part of their development plans. However, future irrigation projects are subject to a PIA-type analysis: irrigation must be both practically and economically feasible. Tribes should be free to develop their reservations based on the surroundings they inhabit. We anticipate that any development plan will carefully consider natural resources (including potential water uses), so that the water actually granted will be put to its best use on the reservation.

In conjunction with natural resources, the court should look to a tribe's economic base in determining its water rights. Tribal development plans or other evidence should address, and the court should consider, the optimal manner of creating jobs and income for the tribes and the most efficient use of the water. Economic development and its attendant water use must be tied, in some manner, to a tribe's current economic station. Physical infrastructure, human resources, including the present and potential employment base, technology, raw materials, financial resources, and capital are all relevant in viewing a reservation's economic infrastructure.

Past water use on a reservation should also be considered when quantifying a tribe's rights. The historic use of water may indicate how a tribe has valued it. Logically, tribal prioritization of past water use will affect its future development. For example, a tribe that has never used water to irrigate is less likely to successfully and economically develop irrigation projects in the future. This does not mean that Indians may not use their water allocations for new purposes on a reservation. However, any proposed projects should be scrutinized to insure that they are practical and economical. Such projects should also be examined to determine that they are, in fact, appropriate to a particular homeland.

While it should never be the only factor, a tribe's present and projected future population may be considered in determining water rights. We recognize that the Supreme Court has rejected any quantification standard based solely on the "number of Indians." However, if a federally reserved water right is to be tailored to a reservation's "minimal need," as we believe it must, then population necessarily must be part of the equation. To act without regard to population would ignore the fact that water will always be used, most importantly, for human needs. Therefore, the number of humans is a necessary element in quantifying water rights. Such consideration is not at odds with the need to satisfy tribes' "future as well as present needs." Population forecasts are common in today's society and are recognized and relied upon by the legal system. It is therefore proper to use population evidence in conjunction with other factors in quantifying a tribe's *Winters* rights.

The state litigants argue that courts should act with sensitivity toward existing state water users when quantifying tribal water rights. They claim that this is necessary because when a water source is fully appropriated, there will be a gallon-for-gallon decrease in state users' water rights due to the tribes' federally reserved rights. When an Indian reservation is created, the government impliedly reserves water to carry out its purpose as a permanent homeland. The court's function is to determine the amount of water necessary to effectuate this purpose, tailored to the reservation's minimal need. We believe that such a minimalist approach demonstrates appropriate sensitivity and consideration of existing users' water rights, and at the same time provides a realistic basis for measuring tribal entitlements.

Again, the foregoing list of factors is not exclusive. The lower court must be given the latitude to consider other information it deems relevant to determining tribal water rights. We require only that proposed uses be reasonably feasible. As with PIA, this entails a two-part analysis. First, development projects need to be achievable from a practical standpoint—they must not be pie-in-the-sky ideas that will likely never reach fruition. Second, projects must be economically sound. When water, a scarce resource, is put to efficient uses on the reservation, tribal economies and members are the beneficiaries.

## CONCLUSION

We wish it were possible to dispose of this matter by establishing a bright line standard, easily applied, in order to relieve the lower court and the parties of having to engage in the difficult, time-consuming process that certainly lies ahead. Unfortunately, we cannot.

In a quote attributed to Mark Twain, it is said that "in the west, whiskey is for drinkin' and water is for fightin'." While this remains true in parts of Arizona, it is our hope that interested parties will work together in a spirit of cooperation, not antagonism. Water is far too ecologically valuable to be used as a political pawn in the effort to resolve the centuries-old conflict between Native Americans and those who followed them in settling the West. This is especially so now, when the welfare and progress of our indigenous population is inextricably tied to and inseparable from the welfare and progress of the entire state.

The relevant portion of the September 9, 1988 order is vacated and the trial court is directed to proceed in a manner consistent with this opinion.

Note: The next case goes into some detail on the hydrologic cycle – the fact that water in streams, underground water, and rainfall are all interrelated. The basic issue is whether or not a landowner is entitled to demand payment from some third person – or prevent the third person from storing water in a natural aquifer under the landowner's land. Does the cujus doctrine, which was discussed in Chapter One, in *Edwards v. Sims,* (the cave case), give a landowner control of the natural water storage space under his or her land?

**SUPREME COURT OF COLORADO**
**THE BOARD OF COUNTY COMMISSIONERS OF THE**
**COUNTY OF PARK AND JAMES B. GARDNER AND AMANDA**
**WOODBURY, PLAINTIFFS–APPELLANTS,**
**V.**
**PARK COUNTY SPORTSMEN'S RANCH, LLP, A LIMITED**
**LIABILITY PARTNERSHIP, DEFENDANT–APPELLEE**

APRIL 8, 2002

Opinion

Justice HOBBS delivered the Opinion of the Court.

In this appeal from a judgment of the District Court for Water Division No. 1 (Water Court), Plaintiffs–Appellants, the Park County Board of County Commissioners, James B. Gardner, and Amanda Woodbury (Landowners) claimed in a declaratory judgment action that Park County Sportsmen's Ranch, LLP (PCSR) has "no right to occupy the space beneath the lands of the Plaintiffs to store water or other substances on or below the surface of the lands. Any such placement or storage of water on or below the surface constitutes a trespass for which the Defendant may be liable for damages." For this proposition, the Landowners rely upon the common-law property doctrine "Cujus est solum ejus est usque ad coelum et ad inferos" (cujus doctrine). [This phrase translates to mean: "To whomsoever the soil belongs, he owns also to the sky and to the depths."]

The Water Court determined that artificial recharge activities involving the movement of underground water into, from, or through aquifers underlying surface lands of the Landowners would not constitute a trespass because the project did not involve the construction of any facilities on or in the Landowners' properties. We agree with the Water Court and uphold its judgment.

## FACTS

The Landowners and PCSR own property in South Park, Colorado, a high mountain valley approximately seventy-five miles southwest of Denver. The South Park formation is a natural geological structure containing aquifers PCSR intends to utilize in connection with its project.

PCSR owns 2,307 acres of land in South Park. PCSR claimed the right to occupy saturated and unsaturated portions of the South Park aquifer formation for water extraction, augmentation, and storage as part of a water project intended to provide water for the City of Aurora for municipal use. Project features would include twenty-six wells to withdraw water from the South Park formation and six surface reservoirs for artificially recharging the aquifers. PCSR's application did not propose to locate any of the project's recharge and extraction features on the Landowners' properties.

We have previously determined that the aquifers of the South Platte formation, extending under approximately 115 square miles of land, are tributary to a natural stream and projects affecting them are subject to Colorado's prior appropriation law.

The Landowners objected to PCSR's Water Court application. They filed a complaint for declaratory relief, seeking a determination that the placement or storage of water above or below the surface of their lands, absent their consent, would constitute a trespass.

The Water Court found that PCSR's project did not include the construction of any facilities on or in the Landowners' properties and the Landowners had not alleged that the use, benefit, and enjoyment of their properties would be invaded or compromised in any way. The Water Court determined as a matter of law that PCSR's project did not require the Landowners' consent or condemnation and payment of just compensation.

# LANDOWNERS' TRESPASS CLAIM

The Landowners claimed that the movement of artificially recharged water into, from, and through portions of an aquifer extending under the surface of their lands as a result of PCSR's proposed project would constitute a trespass. The Water Court held it would not.

To support their theory, the Landowners invoke our decision in *Walpole v. State Board of Land Commissioners*, (1917) where we said:

> Land has an indefinite extent upward and downward from the surface of earth, and therefore includes whatever may be erected upon it, and whatever may lie in a direct line between the surface and the center of the earth. At common law a grant of land carries with it all that lies beneath the surface down to the center of the earth.

# TRIBUTARY AQUIFER HYDROLOGY

Legislators, administrators, and judges generally have a better understanding of surface water systems than ground water systems. Some states that allocate their surface water by the principles of prior appropriation nevertheless allocate ground water by a rule of capture that permits overlying landowners to possess the ground water appearing under their land without regard to the effect of its extraction upon other ground water and surface water users. However, such a rule of capture defies hydrologic reality and impairs the security and reliability of senior water use rights that depend on an interconnected ground and surface water system. Colorado law contains a presumption that all ground water is tributary to the surface stream unless proved or provided by statute otherwise.

An aquifer is a subsurface water bearing formation. Hydrologic continuity exists if there is a hydrologic connection between a surface stream and the water table of an aquifer. The water moves through a shared, permeable layer. Ground water, in an interconnected hydrologic system, provides a base flow for surface streams through the saturated layer of the water bearing formation. Water added to a ground water system can increase the flow of the surface stream; conversely, well pumping that results in lowering the water table can deplete the surface stream.

Aquifers consist of unsaturated and saturated zones. The unsaturated zone contains both air and water in the spaces between the grains of sand, gravel, silt, clay, and cracks within the rock. The movement of water in the unsaturated zone above the water table is controlled by gravity and capillary forces. In the saturated zone, these voids are completely filled with water. The upper surface of the saturated zone is the water table. Water that infiltrates the land surface moves downward through unsaturated areas to the water table to become ground water. Once the water has infiltrated the soil, its passage downward to join the ground water depends on the geologic structures and rock composition. The ground water typically moves laterally within the ground water system. Well pumping creates a cone of depression. This causes surrounding water in the aquifer to flow into the cone from all sides.

The interaction between streams and tributary aquifers occurs in three basic ways: streams gain water from inflow of ground water into the surface stream, streams lose water to the aquifer from outflow from the stream, or do both by gaining water from aquifers in some reaches and losing it to aquifers in other reaches. Without human intervention, the surface/ground water interconnected system exists in a state of approximate equilibrium which implies a long-term balance between natural recharge and discharge processes in a groundwater basin.

"Recharge," whether natural or artificial, is "the addition of water to the upper surface of the saturated zone." "Discharge" is the contribution of aquifer water that migrates to the surface. "Storage" is the retention of ground water in the aquifer for a temporal period. The length of the retention time depends upon the specific characteristics of the aquifer:

> "Aquifers have two main functions in the underground phase of the water cycle. They store water for varying periods in the underground reservoir, and they act as pathways or conduits to pass water along through the reservoir. Although some are more efficient as pipelines (e.g., cavernous limestones) and some are more effective as storage reservoirs (e.g., sandstones), most aquifers perform both functions continuously."

Hydrologists and commentators refer to the entire zone of saturation as a "groundwater reservoir":

> "While the entire zone of saturation is referred to as the *groundwater reservoir,* it is seldom a single, homogeneous geologic formation. Usually a variety of rock types are present at any given location, and even though they may all be saturated, they often have widely varying hydrologic properties. Some would be called aquifers and others would not. The term aquifer comes from two Latin words *aqua,* meaning water, and *ferre,* to bear.
> To be called an aquifer, a geologic formation must be porous and permeable. It must store, transmit, and yield significant amounts of water to springs and wells."

The extent of underground storage available for artificial recharge without interfering with the aquifer's natural recharge capacity or injuring senior ground or surface water rights is a central issue in any proposal to use an aquifer for artificial recharge and storage.

Resolution of the Landowners' trespass claim against PCSR's proposed use of the aquifers underneath the surface of their properties is before us. The aquifers PCSR proposes to utilize extend under approximately 115 square miles of land in South Park.

## STATUTORY AUTHORIZATION

When parties have use rights to water they have captured, possessed, and controlled, they may place that water into an aquifer by artificial recharge and enjoy the benefit of that water as part of their decreed water use rights, if the aquifer can accommodate the recharged water without injury to decreed senior water rights.

C.R.S. 37–87–101(1) provides that the right to store water of a natural stream is a right of appropriation in order of priority, and section 37–87–101(2) provides that underground aquifers can be used for storage of water that the applicant artificially recharges into the aquifer pursuant to a decreed right.

The legislature has clearly enunciated: (1) a natural stream consists of all underflow and tributary waters; (2) all waters of the natural stream are subject to appropriation, adjudication, and administration in the order of their decreed priority; (3) the policy of the state is to integrate the appropriation, use, and administration of underground water tributary to a stream with the use of surface water in such a way as to maximize the beneficial use of all of the waters of the state.

## WATER USE RIGHTS AND LAND OWNERSHIP RIGHTS UNDER COLORADO LAW

Colorado law differs fundamentally from the English common law it replaced. The English case of *Acton v. Blundell*, (1843) set forth the common-law rule of surface streams and ground water, based on Roman precedent. Enjoyment of the flowing surface stream was a riparian right of property owners whose land abutted the stream:

> "Each proprietor of the land has a right to the advantage of the stream flowing in
> its natural course over his land, to use the same as he pleases, for any purposes of
> his own, not inconsistent with a similar right in the proprietors of the land above or
> below; so that, neither can any proprietor above diminish the quantity or injure the

quality of the water which would otherwise naturally descend, nor can any proprietor below throw back the water without the license for the grant of the proprietor above."

In contrast to the surface stream, so the court declared, ground water moves "through the hidden veins of the earth beneath its surface; no man can tell what changes these underground sources have undergone in the progress of time." The court then held that ground water was not governed by the law that applies to rivers and flowing streams; rather, it was subject to the cujus doctrine. The court asserted that ground water:

> "Falls within that principle, which gives to the owner of the soil all that lies beneath his surface; that the land immediately below is his property, whether it is solid rock, or porous ground, or venous earth, or part soil, part water; that the person who owns the surface may dig therein, and apply all that is there found to his own purposes at his free will and pleasure; and that if, in the exercise of such right, he intercepts or drains off the water collected from underground springs in his neighbour's well, this inconvenience to his neighbor falls within the description of damnum absque injuria, which cannot become the ground of an action."

In the United States, advancing the national agenda of settling the public domain in the west required abandonment of the pre-existing common-law rules of property ownership in regard to water and water use rights. Reducing the public land and water to possession and ownership was a preoccupation of territorial and state law from the outset. A new law of custom and usage in regard to water use rights and land ownership rights arose from "imperative necessity" in the western region. This new doctrine established that: (1) water is a public resource, dedicated to the beneficial use of public agencies and private persons wherever they might make beneficial use of the water under use rights established as prescribed by law; (2) the right of water use includes the right to cross the lands of others to place water into, occupy and convey water through, and withdraw water from the natural water bearing formations within the state in the exercise of a water use right; and (3) the natural water bearing formations may be used for the transport and retention of appropriated water. This new common law established a property-rights-based allocation and administration system which promotes multiple use of a finite resource for beneficial purposes.

As stated in *Yunker v. Nichols,*(1872):

"Rules respecting the tenure of private property must yield to the physical laws of nature, whenever such laws exert a controlling influence.

When the lands of this territory were derived from the general government, they were subject to the law of nature, which holds them barren until awakened to fertility by nourishing streams of water, and the purchasers could have no benefit from the grant without the right to irrigate them. It may be said, that all lands are held in subordination to the dominant right of others, who must necessarily pass over them to obtain a supply of water to irrigate their own lands, and this servitude arises, not by grant, but by operation of law."

In *Coffin v. Left Hand Ditch Co.*, (1882), we held that an appropriator could capture water from a stream and transport it to another watershed, using streams in both watersheds to convey the appropriated water to its place of beneficial use.

Accordingly, by reason of Colorado's constitution, statutes, and case precedent, neither surface water, nor ground water, nor the use rights thereto, nor the water-bearing capacity of natural formations belong to a landowner as a stick in the property rights bundle.

## ACCOMMODATION OF WATER USE RIGHTS AND LAND OWNERSHIP RIGHTS

Upon adoption of Colorado's constitution, the state struck an accommodation between two kinds of property interests—water use rights and land rights—by requiring the owners of water use rights to obtain the consent of, or pay just compensation to, owners of land in, upon, or across which the water right holders constructed dams, reservoirs, ditches, canals, flumes, or other manmade facilities for the diversion, conveyance, or storage of water.

But, this requirement does not extend to vesting in landowners the right to prevent access to the water source or require compensation for the water use right holder's employment of the natural water bearing surface and subsurface formations on or within the landowners' properties for the movement of its appropriated water.

Of particular significance to the case before us, we held in *Southwestern* that: (1) federal patents to land did not include water; (2) ground water is not a mineral under the federal mining laws or Colorado law; (3) federal statutes as interpreted by the United States Supreme Court recognize Colorado's authority to adopt its own system for the use of all waters within the state in accordance with the needs of its citizens, subject to the prohibitions against interference with federal reserved rights, with interstate commerce, and with the navigability of any navigable waters; (4) the right of prior appropriation applies under Colorado law to waters of the natural stream, including surface water and tributary ground water; (5) the property rights of land-owners do not include the right to control the use of water in the ground, whatever the character of that water; and (6) the General Assembly has plenary control over the use and disposition of ground water that is not part of the natural stream. *See also Andrus v. Charlestone Stone Prods.,* (1978) (stating that "under the appropriation doctrine prevailing in most of the Western States, the mere fact that a person controls land adjacent to a body of water means relatively little").

Despite our holding in *Southwestern,* the Landowners claim a common-law prop-erty right to require consent or just compensation for an easement to use the subsur-face estate for artificial recharge and storage of water in aquifers extending through their properties, asserting that "fee ownership includes the space underneath the land" which the water occupies. The Landowners rely on *Walpole* and *Wolfley* for this proposition, but these are mineral cases which are clearly distinguishable from water cases, as we held in *Southwestern.*

In deference to the laws of nature, which we held to be foundational in *Yunker v. Nichols,* Colorado law does not recognize a land ownership right by which the Landowners can claim control of the aquifers as part of their bundle of sticks. To the contrary, as knowledge of the science of hydrology advanced, it became clear that natural streams are surface manifestations of extensive tributary systems, including underground water in stream basins, and passage of appropriated water through the natural streams is part of the Colorado law of water use rights.

However, Colo. Const. art. XVI, § 7 does subject the construction of artificial water facilities on another's land to the payment of just compensation and grants a right of private condemnation for the construction of such waterworks:

> "All persons and corporations shall have the right of way across public, private and
> corporate lands for the construction of ditches, canals and flumes for the purpose of
> conveying water for domestic purposes, for the irrigation of agricultural lands, and
> for mining and manufacturing purposes, and for drainage, upon payment of just
> compensation."

Contrary to the Landowners' argument that use of their subsurface estate is differ-ent from use of their surface estate—over which appropriators may transport water in natural stream channels without payment of compensation—Colorado holds no distinction between surface water and ground water, tributary or non-tributary, in regard to the right and ability of the holders of decreed water rights to employ the natural water bearing formations in the exercise of those rights. Colorado's common law and statutory law in this regard rests on the bedrock of: (1) the plenary authority Congress recognized in the states and territories for the establishment and exercise of water use rights; (2) the election of Congress to patent land separately from water, so that the states and territories could legislate in regard to water and water rights as they deemed fit; and (3) Colorado's choice to include all water wherever it resides or travels through the natural formations as a public resource held open and available for the establishment of use rights as prescribed by law.

In sum, [the holders of water use rights may employ underground as well as surface water bearing formations in the state for the placement of water into, occupation of water in, conveyance of water through, and withdrawal of water from the natural water bearing formations in the exercise of water use rights] *See Coffin v. Left Hand Ditch.*

We reject the Landowners' claim that the cujus doctrine provides them with a property right to require consent for artificial recharge and storage of water in aquifers that extend through their land. Water is not a mineral. The law of minerals and property ownership we relied on in *Walpole* and *Wolfley* is inapplicable to water and water use rights.

## CONDEMNATION FOR CONSTRUCTED WATERWORKS

We now address the [Landowners' contention that certain statutory provisions, in combination with Article II, sections 14 and 15 of the Colorado Constitution, evidence legislative intent to require consent or the payment of just compensation for the right of storage occupancy in aquifers extending through the Landowners' properties. )

The Colorado Constitution prohibits the taking of private property for public or private use without the property owner's consent, but provides five exceptions to this prohibition, four of which pertain to constructed water facilities. Article XVI, section 7: (1) provides for access to the water source across the lands of others, embodying the common-law right-of-way rule for artificial water structures we first articulated in *Yunker v. Nichols;* and (2) requires compensation for the construction of water project features on the land of those who do not consent. Article II, section 14 further recognizes and addresses the private right of condemnation for the construction of waterworks:

> "Private property shall not be taken for private use unless by consent of the owner, except for private ways of necessity, and except for reservoirs, drains, flumes, or ditches on or across the lands of others for agricultural, mining, milling, domestic or sanitary purposes."

In the case before us, the proposed project facilities include constructed wells, dams, recharge reservoirs, and other water works, but the project does not include the location of any artificial features on or in the Landowners' properties. Thus, PCSR would not need the consent of the Landowners or an easement, nor would it have to pay just compensation to them, and no trespass occurs simply as the result of water moving into an aquifer and being contained or migrating in the course of the aquifer's functioning underneath the lands of another.

Allowing property owners to control who may store water in natural formations, or charging water right use holders for easements to occupy the natural water bearing surface or underground formations with their appropriated water, would revert to common-law ownership principles that are antithetical to Colorado water law and the public's interest in a secure, reliable, and flexible water supply made available through the exercise of decreed water use rights. It would disharmonize Colorado's historical balance between water use rights and land ownership rights. It would inflate and protract litigation by adding condemnation actions to procedures for obtaining water use decrees. It would counter the state's goals of optimum use, efficient water management, and priority administration.

We agree with the Water Court's holding that artificially recharging an aquifer "is analogous to the use of an unconfined aquifer or natural stream for transport." This comports with longstanding principles of Colorado water law that have allowed passage of the appropriator's water across the lands of another. Section 37–87–102(4), 10 C.R.S. (2001) provides, for example:

> "The owners of any reservoir may conduct the waters legally stored therein *into and along any of the natural streams of the state* but not so as to raise the waters thereof above the ordinary high watermark, and may take the same out again at any point desired if no material injury results to the prior or subsequent rights of others to other waters in said natural streams."

Artificial recharge in the course of implementing either an augmentation or storage plan utilizing an aquifer is practically indistinguishable from the conveyance of appropriated water in the natural surface channel across the property of others. Only the rate of the water's movement differs significantly; water in the ground generally migrates much more slowly.

Augmentation plans include filling subsurface porous spaces with water by injection or artificial water spreading structures, such as unlined ditches and recharge ponds that utilize water appropriated for that purpose, and then re-extracting the stored water or taking credit for the appropriated water's return to the natural river system through underground formations extending through the lands of others.

The Landowners assert that their property rights claims do not affect recharge or augmentation plans, only water storage utilizing the aquifer extending through their properties. This distinction ignores both nature's course and the law's course in Colorado. Artificial recharge, augmentation, storage and the occupancy of porous spaces by water in aquifers are intertwined. We agree with the Water Court that the common-law rule that the Landowners advocate would contravene longstanding Colorado law, injecting nearly unfathomable factual issues into the exercise of water use rights.

The Water Court did not err in concluding that PCSR's recharge, augmentation, and storage activities in aquifers pursuant to a decreed water use right would not constitute a trespass or require condemnation and the payment of just compensation, unless project features are constructed on or in the Landowners' properties. Accordingly, we affirm the Water Court's judgment.

# CHAPTER TEN

# OIL AND GAS

Not surprisingly, the property rights in oil and gas, and various minerals, are different from the property rights in water. Basically, the rules for minerals such as coal, copper and the like, are very much the same as the rules for oil and gas. In all such cases, the cujus doctrine does apply – the owner of the land owns everything below the land to the center of the earth – until there has been a severance – giving the surface rights to one person and the mineral rights to another.

At the time the following case was decided Bob Magness was said to be one of the richest men in the world. Presumably, he could have afforded to buy the mineral rights when he bought the surface. Or did his lawyers simply not advise him of the potential consequences of owning the surface, but not the minerals? Or did Bob Magness simply not listen to his lawyers? Might there be security concerns for a very wealthy person if a constantly changing group of oil workers had broad access to the land on which the wealthy person resided?

What about a non-wealthy person? Might there also be problems if an oil company decided to drill 100 feet from the family home?

### SUPREME COURT OF COLORADO,
### GERRITY OIL & GAS CORPORATION, PETITIONER,
### V.
### BOB MAGNESS, RESPONDENT.

OCTOBER 20, 1997

Justice MARTINEZ delivered the Opinion of the Court.

In 1983, Bob Magness purchased a surface estate encompassing approximately 1,270 acres of land in Weld County, Colorado. Magness began using a portion of the land to raise Arabian horses and Limousin cattle. Magness also conducted farming operations to provide pasture land for the livestock. Magness acquired the surface estate in fee simple subject to a reservation of the underlying mineral estate. That estate had been severed prior to Magness's acquisition of the surface estate.

In 1970, the owners of the mineral estate, who are not parties to this litigation, executed an oil and gas lease naming T.S. Pace as lessee. Pace later assigned rights acquired under the lease to Pan American Petroleum Corporation, now doing business as Amoco Production Company (Amoco). On June 30, 1992, Amoco and Gerrity Oil and Gas Corporation (Gerrity) signed an agreement which made Gerrity the lessee of record under the lease.

In October, 1992, Gerrity notified Magness of its intent to drill four oil wells on the parcel. The parties commenced negotiations to determine locations of the wells that would minimize crop damage and disruption of livestock operations. In response to various concerns expressed by Magness's representatives, Gerrity agreed to move the drill sites from their initial proposed locations.

On November 11, 1992, the parties agreed on the location of one of the four wells, the "No. 6" well. The same day, Gerrity began work on this site. However, on November 18, 1992, after Gerrity had expressed a desire to begin work on a second well, the "2-D" well, an agent of Magness informed Gerrity that it did not have authority to commence operations on any additional wells.

By the end of November, negotiations between the parties had broken down and Magness had not consented to Gerrity's entry on the property to drill additional wells. On November 27, 1992, Gerrity filed a motion for a temporary restraining order and preliminary injunction with the District Court of Weld County and requested that the court enjoin Magness from preventing access onto the 2-D well site and order Magness to remove equipment and other materials. The district court granted the motion.

Gerrity later filed a motion to convert the temporary restraining order and preliminary injunction into a permanent injunction. By this time, Gerrity had completed all four wells on the Magness property. In response to this motion, Magness asserted several counterclaims, including a request for a declaratory judgment. Magness claimed that Gerrity acted negligently by failing to properly and completely restore and remediate the drill sites to a condition as close as practical as existed before Gerrity's operation, by leaving drilling mud and other foreign substances in the excavated pits, by failing to timely restore and remediate the drill sites, by depositing hazardous and toxic substances on Magness's property, by contaminating the property with hazardous, toxic and controlled substances, and by contaminating Magness's property.

Magness also asserted a claim of trespass based on the same alleged acts.

At the conclusion of the trial, the trial court denied Gerrity's request for a permanent injunction, noting that Gerrity had been on the Magness property for over a year and that there had been "no problems between the parties regarding Gerrity's right to reasonable access to the property." The trial court also denied Magness's request for a declaratory judgment, finding that the dispute was essentially factual and not amenable to declaratory judgment.

The court of appeals reversed the judgment of the trial court and remanded the case for a new trial.

We granted Gerrity's petition for writ of certiorari to review the decision of the court of appeals.

Severed mineral rights lack value unless they can be developed. For this reason, the owner of a severed mineral estate or lessee is privileged to access the surface and use that portion of the surface estate that is reasonably necessary to develop the severed mineral interest. See *Rocky Mountain Fuel Co. v. Heflin*, (1961) ("the severed mineral owner's right of access includes the "rights of ingress, egress, exploration, and surface usage as are reasonably necessary to the successful exploitation of the mineral interest.") The right to use the surface as is reasonably necessary, known as the rule of reasonable surface use, does not include the right to destroy, interfere with or damage the surface owner's correlative rights to the surface.

In the absence of statutes, regulations, or lease provisions to the contrary, unless the conduct of an operator in accessing, exploring, drilling, and using the surface is reasonable and necessary to the development of the mineral interest, the conduct is a trespass. In this sense, the right of access to the mineral estate is in the nature of an implied easement, since it entitles the holder to a limited right to use the land in order to reach and extract the minerals. (In the absence of relevant lease provisions, "it has been held that such surface easements are implied as will permit the lessee or mineral owner to enjoy the interest conveyed."). As the owner of property subject to the easement, the surface owner continues to enjoy all the rights and benefits of proprietorship *consistent with the burden of the easement.* The surface owner thus continues to enjoy the right to use the entire surface of the land as long as such use does not preclude exercise of the lessee's privilege.

The fact that neither the surface owner nor the severed mineral rights holder has any absolute right to exclude the other from the surface may create tension between competing surface uses. The broad principle by which these tensions are to be resolved is that each owner must have due regard for the rights of the other in making use of the estate in question. This "due regard" concept requires mineral rights holders to accommodate surface owners to the fullest extent possible consistent with their right to develop the mineral estate. How much accommodation is necessary will, of course, vary depending on surface uses and on the alternatives available to the mineral rights holder for exploitation of the underlying mineral estate. However, when the operations of a lessee or other holder of mineral rights would preclude or impair uses by the surface owner, and when reasonable alternatives are available to the lessee, the doctrine of reasonable surface use requires the lessee to adopt an alternative means. *See* 6 *American Law of Mining* (Rocky Mountain Mineral Law Foundation e*d,* 1996).

Because a mineral rights holder is legally privileged to make such use of the surface as is reasonable and necessary to develop underlying minerals, a trespass occurs at the point when the holder exceeds the scope of that implied easement and thereby exceeds the legal authorization permitting mineral development activities. *Visintainer Sheep Co. v. Centennial Gold* (1987) (because mineral claimant was legally authorized to enter land owned by another to prospect for minerals, its entry and staking of mining claims could not be a trespass). (Any intentional use of another's real property without authorization *and without a privilege by law to do so* is actionable as a trespass without regard to harm.) In determining whether the scope of an easement or privilege has been exceeded, a court must look to its nature and purpose. Because the scope of a mineral rights holder's implied easement is defined in terms of reasonableness and necessity, the reasonableness of the holder's conduct is not only relevant, but is essential to any resolution of a trespass claim. Until it is found that the lessee's conduct was not reasonable and necessary for the exploration or extraction of the minerals, a cause of action for trespass must fail.

Given these principles, the trial court did not err in concluding that a claim of trespass against a lessee based on the lessee's alleged excessive surface use requires the court to consider the reasonableness, as well as the necessity, of the lessee's actions. If a privilege to enter the property of another is defined in terms of reasonableness, trespass may only occur when the holder of the privilege acts unreasonably or unnecessarily. *See Magliocco v. Olson,*(1987) (where landlord-tenant lease permitted landlord to enter tenant's premises at reasonable times, no trespass could occur without showing that landlord's entry was unreasonable). Or, stated conversely, in its necessary use of the surface the lessee has a responsibility to exercise its privilege reasonably, in a manner designed to minimize intrusion and surface damages. When it fails in such responsibility, it commits a trespass.

Our precedent is consistent with this analysis. In *Grynberg,* we held that the City of Northglenn committed a geophysical trespass after it drilled test holes on land for the purpose of ascertaining whether the land contained commercial deposits of coal. Although Northglenn had obtained permission from the severed surface owner to conduct the testing, it had failed to obtain permission from either the record owner of the mineral estate, the State of Colorado, or its lessee, Grynberg. We held that the permission actually obtained by Northglenn was ineffectual because its exploration activities constituted a trespass against the mineral estate, not the surface estate. Consequently, Northglenn's testing was unauthorized because the surface owner could not validly consent to the invasion of a property interest which the surface owner did not hold.

Our decision in *Grynberg* thus stands for the broad principle that unauthorized intrusions on the property interests of another may subject the intruder to liability for trespass. In the present case, the rule of reasonable surface use makes clear that Gerrity's conduct is "unauthorized" when it is not reasonable and necessary to the development of its mineral interest.

In *Walker v. City of Denver*, (1986), the plaintiff, Walker, filed trespass and conversion claims against Denver for alleged damage done to Walker's bar by city police officers executing a search warrant. According to Walker, the officers "exceeded the boundaries and scope of the warrant" by destroying or removing various fixtures on the premises. After concluding that the officers were neither authorized by statute nor by the search warrant to sever fixtures from the property, the court concluded that the officers were liable as trespassers.

We conclude that an operator's use of the surface is limited to that which is reasonable and necessary to the development of the mineral estate. We therefore hold that the appropriate inquiry on a trespass claim based on an operator's excessive surface use is whether the operator's surface use exceeded that which was reasonable and necessary to access the mineral estate.

We conclude that violations of commission rules are valid, but not conclusive, evidence that a lessee breached a duty owed to the surface owner.

At trial, Magness alleged that Gerrity violated commission rules by failing to remove all plastic, bentonite, and other waste in the water and reserve pits, and by burying such material without Magness's prior, written consent. In addition, Magness alleged that Gerrity failed to give Magness notice before commencing reclamation operations, and neglected to consult with Magness and the local district of the state soil conservation service with respect to the proposed reclamation operations.

We conclude that the trial court erred in refusing to consider, based on Magness's failure to present expert testimony, whether Gerrity committed a trespass. Thus, Magness is entitled to a new trial on the trespass claim.

We therefore affirm the court of appeals judgment granting a new trial on all issues.

Note: What about adverse possession of mineral interests. What are the rules that apply in that situation?

# COURT OF APPEALS OF ARKANSAS
## SEECO, INC.; JOYCE WALLS; AND JACK G. WALLS AND JOYCE J. WALLS AS CO-TRUSTEES OF THE JACK G. WALLS AND JOYCE J. WALLS REVOCABLE TRUST, APPELLANTS
### V.
## CARVER L. HOLDEN; CHESAPEAKE OPERATING, INC.; CHESAPEAKE EXPLORATION, LIMITED PARTNERSHIP; CHESAPEAKE EXPLORATION, LLC; CHESAPEAKE INVESTMENTS; BP AMERICA PRODUCTION COMPANY; BHP BILLITON PETROLEUM (FAYETTEVILLE), LLC; AND RIVERBEND EXPLORATION AND PRODUCTION, LLC, APPELLEES.

OCTOBER 7, 2015

Opinion

DAVID M. GLOVER, Judge

In this oil-and-gas case, appellant Joyce Walls and her lessee, SEECO, Inc., appeal from an order vesting ownership of certain minerals in appellee Carver L. Holden. We reverse and remand for further proceedings.

## I. Background

The minerals in question are subsurface to approximately 95 acres in Section 18, Township 9 North, Range 7 West in White County. In 1912, appellant Joyce Walls's grandfather, W.M. Howell, acquired the acreage and its minerals. Howell later sold the property to Clotene and Raymond Cox in 1948, but he retained an undivided one-half mineral interest in himself.

In 1952, Mr. and Mrs. Cox deeded the 95 acres to Ola and Carver Ray Holden, the parents of appellee Carver L. Holden. The deed granted Mr. and Mrs. Holden the entire interest in the property, save and except the undivided one-half mineral interest previously reserved by W.M. Howell.

Howell died in 1953. His one-half mineral interest then passed to his daughter, Grace Marshall. Ms. Marshall did not pay the taxes on the minerals, and a tax-delinquency sale was conducted in 1958. At the sale, Carver Ray Holden purchased Ms. Marshall's one-half mineral interest. This purchase, when combined with Carver

Ray's ownership of the surface and the other one-half mineral interest, appeared to unify the property's ownership in him.

In 1983, Grace Marshall died, leaving a son, Duane Marshall, and a daughter, appellant Joyce Walls. Duane died in 2000, after which Walls considered herself the sole owner of the undivided one-half mineral interest that had been retained by her grandfather many years earlier. In November 2005, Walls executed an oil-and-gas lease of the 95 acres to the T.S. Dudley Land Company. The lease was subsequently assigned to SEECO. However, Walls conducted no drilling on the property.

In September 2006, Carver Ray Holden deeded the 95 acres and all of its minerals to his son, appellee Carver L. Holden. Thereafter, Carver L. Holden executed a mineral lease to Chesapeake Exploration Limited Partnership. Chesapeake began drilling operations on May 21, 2007, and, as of January 2008, three wells were producing natural gas.

Joyce Walls would later testify that she became aware of Holden's wells in April 2009. On September 4, 2009, she filed a quiet-title action to protect her interest in the minerals. Her complaint alleged that the 1958 tax sale, by which Holden's predecessor obtained a deed to her family's one-half mineral interest, was void. She therefore claimed that she retained ownership of that half interest and that she was entitled to an accounting for the production and income from the wells. Holden responded that Walls's suit was time-barred because it was filed more than two years after his drilling operations had begun.

A bench trial was held, and the court heard the evidence described above. In addition, Sherry Williams, an employee of the White County Tax Collector's Office, testified that the county's 1957 assessments, from which the 1958 tax sale arose, did not subjoin the mineral interests to surface interests. Instead, she said, the mineral interests were located in a separate part of the assessment book. Another witness, Chesapeake land man Jim Kelly, acknowledged that Walls's mineral interest in the 95 acres was listed in Chesapeake's Declaration of Pooling in the subject area in White County. Kelly said, however, that Walls's interest was listed out of an abundance of caution, on the chance that she did have a legitimate mineral interest.

Following the trial, the circuit court ruled that Walls did not own the mineral rights she purported to lease; that she did not have possession of the mineral rights within two years before she commenced her lawsuit; that Holden took possession of the minerals on May 21, 2007, upon drilling the first well; and that Walls's September 2009 suit was therefore barred by the two-year statute of limitations in Arkansas Code Annotated section 18–61–106(a). The court quieted title to the disputed one-half mineral interest in Holden and declared that his lessees had the rights afforded them by lease or assignment. Walls filed this appeal.

## II. Standard of Review [omitted]

## III. Walls's Ownership of Mineral Interest

Walls first argues that the circuit court erred in declaring that she did not own the mineral interests that she leased to Dudley/SEECO in 2005. She contends that, to the contrary, her family maintained good title to an undivided one-half mineral interest because the 1958 tax sale, by which Holden's predecessors purported to buy her half interest, was void. We agree.

The undisputed testimony of White County tax official Sherry Williams was that, at the time the tax sale in this case took place, the severed mineral assessments in White County were located in a separate part of the county assessment book from surface interests. The mineral assessments therefore were not subjoined to the surface assessments as required by the law at that time. As a result, the power to sell for delinquent taxes was lacking. Thus, the 1958 tax sale of the one-half mineral interest and the accompanying tax deed to Holden's predecessor were void. The Walls family therefore maintained their ownership of an undivided one-half mineral interest and, consequently, Walls and Holden each now hold legal title to an undivided one-half mineral interest in the 95 acres.

Nevertheless, a defective mineral deed such as Holden's can ripen into good title. As explained in the next section, for that to occur, the holder of the defective deed must disseize the legal owner by adversely possessing the minerals for two years before the legal owner files suit.

## IV. The Two–Year Statute of Limitations

The two-year adverse-possession requirement arises from the statute of limitations found in Arkansas Code Annotated section 18–61–106(a)

> No action for the recovery of any lands or for the possession thereof against any
> person or persons, their heirs and assigns, who may hold such lands by virtue of a
> purchase thereof at a sale by the collector, or the Commissioner of State Lands, for the
> nonpayment of taxes ... shall be maintained, unless it appears that the plaintiff, his or
> her ancestors, predecessors, or grantors, was seized or possessed of the lands in ques-
> tion within (2) two years next before the commencement of the suit or action.

This statute has been interpreted to mean that a person holding land (or a mineral estate) by virtue of an invalid tax deed may nevertheless dispossess the legal owner and gain good title if he possesses the property adversely and continuously for two years before the legal owner files suit⌡

Citing the above statute, the circuit court ruled that Holden possessed the disputed one-half mineral interest and disseized Walls by drilling for minerals on the property continuously for two years before Walls filed suit in September 2009. Walls argues that the court erred in its ruling. We agree.

The parties initially argue over what point marks the beginning of the two-year limitations period. Walls insists that Holden's January 2008 onset of gas production is the starting point, thus making her September 2009 lawsuit timely. Holden claims (and the circuit court agreed) that the statute of limitations commenced with his drilling activities in May 2007 and continued for two years thereafter, thus barring Walls's September 2009 suit. Our court has stated that, to be in possession of a constructively severed mineral interest, "actual production" is required.

We need not decide the point, however. As Walls also argues, regardless of when the statute of limitations began to run, neither Holden's mineral exploration nor his production was shown to be adverse to Wall's undivided one-half interest in the minerals.

⌈The adverse possession required by section 18–61–106(a) must be of such character as to put the legal owner on notice that his rights are being challenged.⌋ As mentioned, Walls and Holden each hold an undivided one-half interest in the minerals. ⌈As co-owners of the mineral interests, they each have an equal right to go onto the 95 acres and drill for minerals, subject only to the duty to account to their co-owner.⌋ ⌈Thus, whatever infringement occurred when Holden went onto the land and drilled for minerals without Walls's consent it was not sufficient to constitute notice to Walls of his exclusive possession of the minerals or an intent to oust her of her undivided one-half interest.⌋ We therefore agree with Walls that Holden's possession was not adverse, as required for his defective tax deed to ripen into good title. Accordingly, Walls's quiet-title action is not barred by the statute of limitations, and we reverse and remand for further proceedings.⌋

Reversed and remanded.

# CHAPTER ELEVEN

# ZONING

## INTRODUCTION

We now come to a study of some of the most frequent public land use restrictions. Federal, state, and local governments frequently put a number of restrictions on the use of private land. Generally, these restrictions are upheld. Courts only strike down restrictions imposed by a governmental body if the courts decide that the restrictions are "arbitrary and capricious," in violation of the constitution, or if the restrictions are so severe that the courts decide that the restrictions constitute a taking.

As you will see from the following cases, usually when a landowner is contesting land use restrictions imposed by a governmental entity, the landowner will claim both that the restrictions are unconstitutional, and that the restrictions constitute a taking. If the restrictions are held to be unconstitutional, they are void. If the restrictions are held to constitute a taking, then the governmental entity must pay for the land taken - or back off from the restrictions.

Zoning is the most common form of land use restriction imposed by a governmental entity. It is usually imposed by the municipality in which the land is located, for the benefit of the community as a whole. The landowner does not have any veto power to avoid the restriction, even though the restriction may impose severe financial hardship on the individual landowner involved.

The following case, *Village of Euclid v. Ambler Reality,* is a very famous case because it was the first time that the U.S. Supreme Court specifically upheld the validity of zoning. The case gives a detailed description of how the zoning process still works in most municipalities. It is this case from which the term "Euclidian zoning" is derived.

Note the financial consequences to the landowner, who alleges that the zoning restrictions have taken away up to 75% of the value of his land. If the zoning is held to be valid, the individual landowner will not be entitled to any reimbursement for this very large loss in the value of his investment. The individual landowner will be required to suffer the very serious financial loss − "for the good of the community."

## SUPREME COURT OF THE UNITED STATES
## VILLAGE OF EUCLID, OHIO, ET AL.
## V.
## AMBLER REALTY CO.

NOVEMBER 22, 1926

**Opinion**

Mr. Justice SUTHERLAND delivered the opinion of the Court.

The village of Euclid is an Ohio municipal corporation. It adjoins and practically is a suburb of the city of Cleveland. Its estimated population is between 5,000 and 10,000, and its area from 12 to 14 square miles, the greater part of which is farm lands or unimproved acreage. It lies, roughly, in the form of a parallelogram measuring approximately 3 1/2 miles each way. East and west it is traversed by three principal highways: Euclid avenue, through the southerly border, St. Clair avenue, through the central portion, and Lake Shore boulevard, through the northerly border, in close proximity to the shore of Lake Erie. The Nickel Plate Railroad lies from 1,500 to 1,800 feet north of Euclid avenue, and the Lake Shore Railroad 1,600 feet farther to the north. The three highways and the two railroads are substantially parallel.

Appellee is the owner of a tract of land containing 68 acres, situated in the westerly end of the village, abutting on Euclid avenue to the south and the Nickel Plate Railroad to the north. Adjoining this tract, both on the east and on the west, there have been laid out restricted residential plats upon which residences have been erected.

On November 13, 1922, an ordinance was adopted by the village council, establishing a comprehensive zoning plan for regulating and restricting the location of trades, industries, apartment houses, two-family houses, single family houses, etc., the lot area to be built upon, the size and height of buildings, etc.

The entire area of the village is divided by the ordinance into six classes of use districts, denominated U-1 to U-6, inclusive; three classes of height districts, denominated H-1 to H-3, inclusive; and four classes of area districts, denominated A-1 to A-4, inclusive. The use districts are classified in respect of the buildings which may be erected within their respective limits, as follows: U-1 is restricted to single family dwellings, public parks, water towers and reservoirs, suburban and interurban electric railway passenger stations and rights of way, and farming, non-commercial greenhouse nurseries, and truck gardening; U-2 is extended to include two-family dwellings; U-3 is further extended to include apartment houses, hotels, churches, schools, public libraries, museums, private clubs, community center buildings, hospitals, sanitariums, public playgrounds, and recreation buildings, and a city hall and courthouse; U-4 is further extended to include banks, offices, studios, telephone exchanges, fire and police stations, restaurants, theaters and moving picture shows, retail stores and shops, sales offices, sample rooms, wholesale stores for hardware, drugs, and groceries, stations for gasoline and oil (not exceeding 1,000 gallons storage) and for ice delivery, skating rinks and dance halls, electric substations, job and newspaper printing, public garages for motor vehicles, stables and wagon sheds (not exceeding five horses, wagons or motor trucks), and distributing stations for central store and commercial enterprises; U-5 is further extended to include billboards and advertising signs (if permitted), warehouses, ice and ice cream manufacturing and cold storage plants, bottling works, milk bottling and central distribution stations, laundries, carpet cleaning, dry cleaning, and dyeing establishments, blacksmith, horseshoeing, wagon and motor vehicle repair shops, freight stations, street car barns, stables and wagon sheds (for more than five horses, wagons or motor trucks), and wholesale produce markets and salesroom; U-6 is further extended to include plants for sewage disposal and for producing gas, garbage and refuse incineration, scrap iron, junk, scrap paper, and rag storage, aviation fields, cemeteries, crematories, penal and correctional institutions, insane and feeble-minded institutions, storage of oil and gasoline (not to exceed 25,000 gallons), and manufacturing and industrial operations of any kind other than, and any public utility not included in a class U-1, U-2, U-3, U-4, or U-5 use. There is a seventh class of uses which is prohibited altogether.

Class U-1 is the only district in which buildings are restricted to those enumerated. In the other classes the uses are cumulative-that is to say, uses in class U-2 include those enumerated in the preceding class U-1; class U-3 includes uses enumerated in the preceding classes, U-2, and U-1; and so on. In addition to the enumerated uses, the ordinance provides for accessory uses; that is, for uses customarily incident to the principal use, such as private garages. Many regulations are provided in respect of such accessory uses.

The height districts are classified as follows: In class H-1, buildings are limited to a height of 2 1/2 stories, or 35 feet; in class H-2, to 4 stories, or 50 feet; in class H-3, to 80 feet. To all of these, certain exceptions are made, as in the case of church spires, water tanks, etc.

The classification of area districts is: In A-1 districts, dwellings or apartment houses to accommodate more than one family must have at least 5,000 square feet for interior lots and at least 4,000 square feet for corner lots; in A-2 districts, the area must be at least 2,500 square feet for interior lots, and 2,000 square feet for corner lots; in A-3 districts, the limits are 1,250 and 1,000 square feet, respectively; in A-4 districts, the limits are 900 and 700 square feet, respectively. The ordinance contains, in great variety and detail, provisions in respect of width of lots, front, side, and rear yards, and other matters, including restrictions and regulations as to the use of billboards, signboards, and advertising signs.

A single family dwelling consists of a basement and not less than three rooms and a bathroom. A two-family dwelling consists of a basement and not less than four living rooms and a bathroom for each family, and is further described as a detached dwelling for the occupation of two families, one having its principal living rooms on the first floor and the other on the second floor.

Appellee's tract of land comes under U-2, U-3 and U-6. The first strip of 620 feet immediately north of Euclid avenue falls in class U-2, the next 130 feet to the north, in U-3, and the remainder in U-6. The uses of the first 620 feet, therefore, do not include apartment houses, hotels, churches, schools, or other public and semipublic buildings, or other uses enumerated in respect of U-3 to U-6, inclusive. The uses of the next 130 feet include all of these, but exclude industries, theaters, banks, shops, and the various other uses set forth in respect of U-4 to U-6, inclusive.

Annexed to the ordinance, and made a part of it, is a zone map, showing the location and limits of the various use, height, and area districts, from which it appears that the three classes overlap one another; that is to say, for example, both U-5 and U-6 use districts are in A-4 area district, but the former is in H-2 and the latter in H-3 height districts. The plan is a complicated one, and can be better understood by an inspection of the map, though it does not seem necessary to reproduce it for present purposes.

The lands lying between the two railroads for the entire length of the village area and extending some distance on either side to the north and south, having an average width of about 1,600 feet, are left open, with slight exceptions, for industrial and all other uses. This includes the larger part of appellee's tract. Approximately one-sixth of the area of the entire village is included in U-5 and U-6 use districts. That part of the village lying south of Euclid avenue is principally in U-1 districts. The lands lying north of Euclid avenue and bordering on the long strip just described are included in U-1, U-2, U-3, and U-4 districts, principally in U-2.

The enforcement of the ordinance is intrusted to the inspector of buildings, under rules and regulations of the board of zoning appeals. Meetings of the board are public, and minutes of its proceedings are kept. It is authorized to adopt rules and regulations to carry into effect provisions of the ordinance. Decisions of the inspector of buildings may be appealed to the board by any person claiming to be adversely affected by any such decision. The board is given power in specific cases of practical difficulty or unnecessary hardship to interpret the ordinance in harmony with its general purpose and intent, so that the public health, safety and general welfare may be secure and substantial justice done. Penalties are prescribed for violations, and it is provided that the various provisions are to be regarded as independent and the holding of any provision to be unconstitutional, void or ineffective shall not affect any of the others.

The ordinance is assailed on the grounds that it is in derogation of section 1 of the Fourteenth Amendment to the federal Constitution in that it deprives appellee of liberty and property without due process of law and denies it the equal protection of the law, and that it offends against certain provisions of the Constitution of the state of Ohio. The prayer of the bill is for an injunction restraining the enforcement of the ordinance and all attempts to impose or maintain as to appellee's property any of the restrictions, limitations or conditions.

The court below held the ordinance to be unconstitutional and void, and enjoined its enforcement.

Before proceeding to a consideration of the case, it is necessary to determine the scope of the inquiry. The bill alleges that the tract of land in question is vacant and has been held for years for the purpose of selling and developing it for industrial uses, for which it is especially adapted, being immediately in the path for progressive industrial development; that for such uses it has a market value of about $10,000 per acre, but if the use be limited to residential purposes the market value is not in excess of $2,500 per acre; that the first 200 feet of the parcel back from Euclid avenue, if unrestricted in respect of use, has a value of $150 per front foot, but if limited to residential uses, and ordinary mercantile business be excluded therefrom, its value is not in excess of $50 per front foot.

It is specifically averred that the ordinance attempts to restrict and control the lawful uses of appellee's land, so as to confiscate and destroy a great part of its value; that it is being enforced in accordance with its terms; that prospective buyers of land for industrial, commercial, and residential uses in the metropolitan district of Cleveland are deterred from buying any part of this land because of the existence of the ordinance and the necessity thereby entailed of conducting burdensome and expensive litigation in order to vindicate the right to use the land for lawful and legitimate purposes; that the ordinance constitutes a cloud upon the land, reduces and destroys its value, and has the effect of diverting the normal industrial, commercial, and residential development thereof to other and less favorable locations.

The record goes no farther than to show, as the lower court found, that the normal and reasonably to be expected use and development of that part of appellee's land adjoining Euclid avenue is for general trade and commercial purposes, particularly retail stores and like establishments, and that the normal and reasonably to be expected use and development of the residue of the land is for industrial and trade purposes. Whatever injury is inflicted by the mere existence and threatened enforcement of the ordinance is due to restrictions in respect of these and similar uses.

We proceed, then, to a consideration of those provisions of the ordinance to which the case as it is made relates, first disposing of a preliminary matter.

A motion was made in the court below to dismiss the bill on the ground that, because complainant (appellee) had made no effort to obtain a building permit or apply to the zoning board of appeals for relief, as it might have done under the terms of the ordinance, the suit was premature. The motion was properly overruled, the effect of the allegations of the bill is that the ordinance of its own force operates greatly to reduce the value of appellee's lands and destroy their marketability for industrial, commercial and residential uses, and the attack is directed, not against any specific provision or provisions, but against the ordinance as an entirety. Assuming the premises, the existence and maintenance of the ordinance in effect constitutes a present invasion of appellee's property rights and a threat to continue it. Under these circumstances, the equitable jurisdiction is clear.

It is not necessary to set forth the provisions of the Ohio Constitution which are thought to be infringed. The question is the same under both Constitutions, namely, as stated by appellee: Is the ordinance invalid, in that it violates the constitutional protection "to the right of property in the appellee by attempted regulations under the guise of the police power, which are unreasonable and confiscatory?"

Building zone laws are of modern origin. They began in this country about 25 years ago. Until recent years, urban life was comparatively simple; but, with the great increase and concentration of population, problems have developed, and constantly are developing, which require, and will continue to require, additional restrictions in respect of the use and occupation of private lands in urban communities. Regulations, the wisdom, necessity, and validity of which, as applied to existing conditions, are so apparent that they are now uniformly sustained, a century ago, or even half a century ago, probably would have been rejected as arbitrary and oppressive. Such regulations are sustained, under the complex conditions of our day, for reasons analogous to those which justify traffic regulations, which, before the advent of automobiles and rapid transit street railways, would have been condemned as fatally arbitrary and unreasonable. And in this there is no inconsistency, for, while the meaning of constitutional guaranties never varies, the scope of their application must expand or contract to meet the new and different conditions which are constantly coming within the field of their operation. In a changing world it is impossible that it should be otherwise. But although a degree of elasticity is thus imparted, not to the meaning, but to the application of constitutional principles, statutes and ordinances, which, after giving due weight to the new conditions, are found clearly not to conform to the Constitution, of course, must fall.

The ordinance now under review, and all similar laws and regulations, must find their justification in some aspect of the police power, asserted for the public welfare. The line which in this field separates the legitimate from the illegitimate assumption of power is not capable of precise delimitation. It varies with circumstances and conditions. A regulatory zoning ordinance, which would be clearly valid as applied to the great cities, might be clearly invalid as applied to rural communities. In solving doubts, the maxim 'sic utere tuo ut alienum non laedas,' which lies at the foundation of so much of the common law of nuisances, ordinarily will furnish a fairly helpful clew. And the law of nuisances, likewise, may be consulted, not for the purpose of controlling, but for the helpful aid of its analogies in the process of ascertaining the scope of, the power. Thus the question whether the power exists to forbid the erection of a building of a particular kind or for a particular use, like the question whether a particular thing is a nuisance, is to be determined, not by an abstract consideration of the building or of the thing considered apart, but by considering it in connection with the circumstances and the locality. A nuisance may be merely a right thing in the wrong place, like a pig in the parlor instead of the barnyard. If the validity of the legislative classification for zoning purposes be fairly debatable, the legislative judgment must be allowed to control.

There is no serious difference of opinion in respect of the validity of laws and regulations fixing the height of buildings within reasonable limits, the character of materials and methods of construction, and the adjoining area which must be left open, in order to minimize the danger of fire or collapse, the evils of overcrowding and the like, and excluding from residential sections offensive trades, industries and structures likely to create nuisances.

Here, however, the exclusion is in general terms of all industrial establishments, and it may thereby happen that not only offensive or dangerous industries will be excluded, but those which are neither offensive nor dangerous will share the same fate. But this is no more than happens in respect of many practice-forbidding laws which this court has upheld, although drawn in general terms so as to include individual cases that may turn out to be innocuous in themselves. The inclusion of a reasonable margin, to insure effective enforcement, will not put upon a law, otherwise valid, the stamp of invalidity. Such laws may also find their justification in the fact that, in some fields, the bad fades into the good by such insensible degrees that the two are not capable of being readily distinguished and separated in terms of legislation. In the light of these considerations, we are not prepared to say that the end in view was not sufficient to justify the general rule of the ordinance, although some industries of an innocent character might fall within the proscribed class. It cannot be said that the ordinance in this respect "passes the bounds of reason and assumes the character of a merely arbitrary fiat." Moreover, the restrictive provisions of the ordinance in this particular may be sustained upon the principles applicable to the broader exclusion from residential districts of all business and trade structures, presently to be discussed.

It is said that the village of Euclid is a mere suburb of the city of Cleveland; that the industrial development of that city has now reached and in some degree extended into the village, and in the obvious course of things will soon absorb the entire area for industrial enterprises; that the effect of the ordinance is to divert this natural development elsewhere, with the consequent loss of increased values to the owners of the lands within the village borders. But the village, though physically a suburb of Cleveland, is politically a separate municipality, with powers of its own and authority to govern itself as it sees fit, within the limits of the organic law of its creation and the state and federal Constitutions. Its governing authorities, presumably representing a majority of its inhabitants and voicing their will, have determined, not that industrial development shall cease at its boundaries, but that the course of such development shall proceed within definitely fixed lines. If it be a proper exercise of the police power to relegate industrial establishments to localities separated from residential sections, it is not easy to find a sufficient reason for denying the power because the effect of its exercise is to divert an industrial flow from the course which it would follow, to the injury of the residential public, if left alone, to another course where such injury will be obviated. It is not meant by this, however, to exclude the possibility of cases where the general public interest would so far outweigh the interest of the municipality that the municipality would not be allowed to stand in the way.

We find no difficulty in sustaining restrictions of the kind thus far reviewed. The serious question in the case arises over the provisions of the ordinance excluding from residential districts apartment houses, business houses, retail stores and shops, and other like establishments. This question involves the validity of what is really the crux of the more recent zoning legislation, namely, the creation and maintenance of residential districts, from which business and trade of every sort, including hotels and apartment houses, are excluded. Upon that question this court has not thus far spoken. The decisions of the state courts are numerous and conflicting; but those which broadly sustain the power greatly outnumber those which deny it altogether or narrowly limit it, and it is very apparent that there is a constantly increasing tendency in the direction of the broader view.

The matter of zoning has received much attention at the hands of commissions and experts, and the results of their investigations have been set forth in comprehensive reports. These reports which bear every evidence of painstaking consideration, concur in the view that the segregation of residential, business and industrial buildings will make it easier to provide fire apparatus suitable for the character and intensity of the development in each section; that it will increase the safety and security of home life, greatly tend to prevent street accidents, especially to children, by reducing the traffic and resulting confusion in residential sections, decrease noise and other conditions which produce or intensify nervous disorders, preserve a more favorable environment in which to rear children, etc. With particular reference to apartment houses, it is pointed out that the development of detached house sections is greatly retarded by the coming of apartment houses, which has sometimes resulted in destroying the entire section for private house purposes; that in such sections very often the apartment house is a mere parasite, constructed in order to take advantage of the open spaces and attractive surroundings created by the residential character of the district. Moreover, the coming of one apartment house is followed by others, interfering by their height and bulk with the free circulation of air and monopolizing the rays of the sun which otherwise would fall upon the smaller homes, and bringing, as their necessary accompaniments, the disturbing noises incident to increased traffic and business, and the occupation, by means of moving and parked automobiles, of larger portions of the streets, thus detracting from their safety and depriving children of the privilege of quiet and open spaces for play, enjoyed by those in more favored localities-until, finally, the residential character of the neighborhood and its desirability as a place of detached residences are utterly destroyed. Under these circumstances, apartment houses, which in a different environment would be not only entirely unobjectionable but highly desirable, come very near to being nuisances.

If these reasons, thus summarized, do not demonstrate the wisdom or sound policy in all respects of those restrictions which we have indicated as pertinent to the inquiry, at least, the reasons are sufficiently cogent to preclude us from saying, as it must be said before the ordinance can be declared unconstitutional, that such provisions are clearly arbitrary and unreasonable, having no substantial relation to the public health, safety, morals, or general welfare.

It is true that when, if ever, the provisions set forth in the ordinance in tedious and minute detail, come to be concretely applied to particular premises, including those of the appellee, or to particular conditions, or to be considered in connection with specific complaints, some of them, or even many of them, may be found to be clearly arbitrary and unreasonable. But where the equitable remedy of injunction is sought, as it is here, not upon the ground of a present infringement or denial of a specific right, or of a particular injury in process of actual execution, but upon the broad ground that the mere existence and threatened enforcement of the ordinance, by materially and adversely affecting values and curtailing the opportunities of the market, constitute a present and irreparable injury, the court will not scrutinize its provisions, sentence by sentence, to ascertain by a process of piecemeal dissection whether there may be, here and there, provisions of a minor character, or relating to matters of administration, or not shown to contribute to the injury complained of, which, if attacked separately, might not withstand the test of constitutionality. In respect of such provisions, of which specific complaint is not made, it cannot be said that the landowner has suffered or is threatened with an injury which entitles him to challenge their constitutionality.

The relief sought here is an injunction against the enforcement of any of the restrictions, limitations, or conditions of the ordinance. And the gravamen of the complaint is that a portion of the land of the appellee cannot be sold for certain enumerated uses because of the general and broad restraints of the ordinance. What would be the effect of a restraint imposed by one or more of the innumerable provisions of the ordinance, considered apart, upon the value or marketability of the lands, is neither disclosed by the bill nor by the evidence, and we are afforded no basis, apart from mere speculation, upon which to rest a conclusion that it or they would have any appreciable effect upon those matters. Under these circumstances, therefore, it is enough for us to determine, as we do, that the ordinance in its general scope and dominant features, so far as its provisions are here involved, is a valid exercise of authority, leaving other provisions to be dealt with as cases arise directly involving them.

And this is in accordance with the traditional policy of this court. In the realm of constitutional law, especially, this court has perceived the embarrassment which is likely to result from an attempt to formulate rules or decide questions beyond the necessities of the immediate issue. It has preferred to follow the method of a gradual approach to the general by a systematically guarded application and extension of constitutional principles to particular cases as they arise, rather than by out of hand attempts to establish general rules to which future cases must be fitted. This process applies with peculiar force to the solution of questions arising under the due process clause of the Constitution as applied to the exercise of the flexible powers of police, with which we are here concerned.

Decree reversed.

Note: The type of zoning described here, in which all of the uses in the most restrictive zone, U-1, are also permitted in the next, less restrictive zone, U-2, is a form of *cumulative* zoning. It is also called *Euclidian zoning*, based on this case – from the village of Euclid, Ohio. *Euclidian zoning* has nothing to do with algebra.

Today, pure Euclidian zoning has fallen out of favor in many municipalities. It has turned out that it is not convenient for homeowners to be surrounded by a very large number of other houses – with a long drive necessary to reach a grocery store, or a coffee shop. So the increasingly popular form of land use restriction for a municipality is something in the nature of a PUD, a *planned unit development*. A developer, owning a large tract of land, will work with the municipality to determine what is the best way to develop the land – with a *mix* of different uses. For example, small grocery stores, coffee shops and the like might be located along the major streets bordering the new development. There might be a small buffer of two-story apartment buildings or townhomes, and then a collection of single family homes, with larger yards, in the center. Ideally, nearly everyone would be able to walk the short distance to the stores, the young children would be protected from areas of heavy traffic, and the whole development would have more of a sense of community.

Note that in relatively large developments the developer would also be expected to donate some land to the municipality, to be used for school or park purposes. That seems to be a standard aspect of the negotiations that take place between a municipality and a developer with regard to a planned unit development.

The next case, *Belle Terre v. Borass,* illustrates how detailed the restrictions may become with standard zoning. Is this result constitutional?

## SUPREME COURT OF THE UNITED STATES
## VILLAGE OF BELLE TERRE ET AL., APPELLANTS,
## V.
## BRUCE BORAAS ET AL.

APRIL 1, 1974

Mr. Justice DOUGLAS delivered the opinion of the Court.

Belle Terre is a village on Long Island's north shore of about 220 homes inhabited by 700 people. Its total land area is less than one square mile. It has restricted land use to one-family dwellings excluding lodging houses, boarding houses, fraternity houses, or multiple-dwelling houses. The word "family" as used in the ordinance means, "one or more persons related by blood, adoption, or marriage, living and cooking together as a single housekeeping unit, exclusive of household servants. A number of persons but not exceeding two (2) living and cooking together as a single housekeeping unit though not related by blood, adoption, or marriage shall be deemed to constitute a family."

Appellees, the Dickmans, are owners of a house in the village and leased it in December 1971 for a term of 18 months to Michael Truman. Later Bruce Boraas became a colessee. Then Anne Parish moved into the house along with three others. These six are students at nearby State University at Stony Brook and none is related to the other by blood, adoption, or marriage. When the village served the Dickmans with an "Order to Remedy Violations" of the ordinance, the owners plus three tenants thereupon brought this action under 42 U.S.C. s 1983 for an injunction and a judgment declaring the ordinance unconstitutional. The District Court held the ordinance constitutional, and the Court of Appeals reversed, one judge dissenting. The case is here by appeal, and we noted probable jurisdiction.

This case brings to this Court a different phase of local zoning regulations from those we have previously reviewed.

In *Village of Euclid v. Ambler Realty* the Court sustained the zoning ordinance under the police power of the State, saying that the line "which in this field separates the legitimate from the illegitimate assumption of power is not capable of precise delimitation. It varies with circumstances and conditions." And the Court added: "A nuisance may be merely a right thing in the wrong place, like a pig in the parlor instead of the barnyard. If the validity of the legislative classification for zoning purposes be fairly debatable, the legislative judgment must be allowed to control." The Court listed as considerations bearing on the constitutionality of zoning ordinances the danger of fire or collapse of buildings, the evils of overcrowding people, and the possibility that "offensive trades, industries, and structures might create nuisance to residential sections." But even those historic police power problems need not loom large or actually be existent in a given case. For the exclusion of "all industrial establishments" does not mean that "only offensive or dangerous industries will be excluded." That fact does not invalidate the ordinance; the Court held:

> "The inclusion of a reasonable margin to insure effective enforcement, will not put upon a law, otherwise valid, the stamp of invalidity. Such laws may also find their justification in the fact that, in some fields, the bad fades into the good by such insensible degrees that the two are not capable of being readily distinguished and separated in terms of legislation."

The main thrust of the case in the mind of the Court was in the exclusion of industries and apartments, and as respects that it commented on the desire to keep residential areas free of "disturbing noises; increased traffic; the hazard of moving and parked automobiles; the depriving children of the privilege of quiet and open spaces for play, enjoyed by those in more favored localities." The ordinance was sanctioned because the validity of the legislative classification was "fairly debatable" and therefore could not be said to be wholly arbitrary.

Our decision in Berman v. Parker, sustained a land use project in the District of Columbia against a landowner's claim that the taking violated the Due Process Clause and the Just Compensation Clause of the Fifth Amendment. The essence of the argument against the law was, while taking property for ridding an area of slums was permissible, taking it "merely to develop a better balanced, more attractive community" was not. We refused to limit the concept of public welfare that may be enhanced by zoning regulations. We said:

> "Miserable and disreputable housing conditions may do more than spread disease and crime and immorality. They may also suffocate the spirit by reducing the people who live there to the status of cattle. They may indeed make living an almost insufferable burden. They may also be an ugly sore, a blight on the community which robs it of charm, which makes it a place from which men turn. The misery of housing may despoil a community as an open sewer may ruin a river.

> "We do not sit to determine whether a particular housing project is or is not desirable. The concept of the public welfare is broad and inclusive. The values it represents are spiritual as well as physical, aesthetic as well as monetary. It is within the power of the legislature to determine that the community should be beautiful as well as healthy, spacious as well as clean, well-balanced as well as carefully patrolled."

If the ordinance segregated one area only for one race, it would immediately be suspect under the reasoning of Buchanan v. Warley, where the Court invalidated a city ordinance barring a black person from acquiring real property in a white residential area by reason of an 1866 Act of Congress, now 42 U.S.C. s 1982, and an 1870 Act, now 42 U.S.C. s 1981, both enforcing the Fourteenth Amendment.

In Seattle Title Trust Co. v. Roberge, Seattle had a zoning ordinance that permitted a "philanthropic home for children or for old people" in a particular district "when the written consent shall have been obtained of the owners of two-thirds of the property within four hundred (400) feet of the proposed building." The Court held that provision of the ordinance unconstitutional, saying that the existing owners could "withhold consent for selfish reasons or arbitrarily and may subject the trustee (owner) to their will or caprice." The Court concluded that the Seattle ordinance was invalid since the proposed home for the aged poor was not shown by its maintenance and construction "to work any injury, inconvenience or annoyance to the community, the district or any person."

The present ordinance is challenged on several grounds: that it interferes with a person's right to travel; that it interferes with the right to migrate to and settle within a State; that it bars people who are uncongenial to the present residents; that it expresses the social preferences of the residents for groups that will be congenial to them; that social homogeneity is not a legitimate interest of government; that the restriction of those whom the neighbors do not like trenches on the newcomers' rights of privacy; that it is of no rightful concern to villagers whether the residents are married or unmarried; that the ordinance is antithetical to the Nation's experience, ideology, and self-perception as an open, egalitarian, and integrated society.

We find none of these reasons in the record before us. It is not aimed at transients. Cf. Shapiro v. Thompson, It involves no procedural disparity inflicted on some but not on others such as was presented by Griffin v. Illinois, It involves no "fundamental" right guaranteed by the Constitution, such as voting, Harper v. Virginia State Board, the right of association, NAACP v. Alabama ex rel. Patterson, the right of access to the courts, NAACP v. Button, or any rights of privacy, cf.Griswold v. Connecticut. We deal with economic and social legislation where legislatures have historically drawn lines which we respect against the charge of violation of the Equal Protection Clause if the law be "reasonable, not arbitrary" and bears "a rational relationship to a permissible state objective."

It is said, however, that if two unmarried people can constitute a "family," there is no reason why three or four may not. But every line drawn by a legislature leaves some out that might well have been included. That exercise of discretion, however, is a legislative, not a judicial, function.

It is said that the Belle Terre ordinance reeks with an animosity to unmarried couples who live together. There is no evidence to support it; and the provision of the ordinance bringing within the definition of a "family" two unmarried people belies the charge.

The ordinance places no ban on other forms of association, for a "family" may, so far as the ordinance is concerned, entertain whomever it likes.

The regimes of boarding houses, fraternity houses, and the like present urban problems. More people occupy a given space; more cars rather continuously pass by; more cars are parked; noise travels with crowds.

[A quiet place where yards are wide, people few, and motor vehicles restricted are legitimate guidelines in a land-use project addressed to family needs. This goal is a permissible one within *Berman v. Parker, supra*. The police power is not confined to elimination of filth, stench, and unhealthy places. It is ample to lay out zones where family values, youth values, and the blessings of quiet seclusion and clean air make the area a sanctuary for people.]

The suggestion that the case may be moot need not detain us. A zoning ordinance usually has an impact on the value of the property which it regulates. But in spite of the fact that the precise impact of the ordinance sustained in *Euclid* on a given piece of property was not known, the Court, considering the matter a controversy in the realm of city planning, sustained the ordinance. Here we are a step closer to the impact of the ordinance on the value of the lessor's property. He has not only lost six tenants and acquired only two in their place; it is obvious that the scale of rental values rides on what we decide today. When *Berman* reached us it was not certain whether an entire tract would be taken or only the buildings on it and a scenic easement. But that did not make the case any the less a controversy in the constitutional sense. [When Mr. Justice Holmes said for the Court in Block v. Hirsh, "property rights may be cut down, and to that extent taken, without pay," he stated the issue here. As is true in most zoning cases, the precise impact on value may, at the threshold of litigation over validity, not yet be known.]

Reversed.


Mr. Justice MARSHALL, dissenting.

This case draws into question the constitutionality of a zoning ordinance of the incorporated village of Belle Terre, New York, which prohibits groups of more than two unrelated persons, as distinguished from groups consisting of any number of persons related by blood, adoption, or marriage, from occupying a residence within the confines of the township. Lessor-appellees, the two owners of a Belle Terre residence, and three unrelated student tenants challenged the ordinance on the ground that it establishes a classification between households of related and unrelated individuals, which deprives them of equal protection of the laws. In my view, the disputed classification burdens the students' fundamental rights of association and privacy guaranteed by the First and Fourteenth Amendments. Because the application of strict equal protection scrutiny is therefore required, I am at odds with my Brethren's conclusion that the ordinance may be sustained on a showing that it bears a rational relationship to the accomplishment of legitimate governmental objectives.

I am in full agreement with the majority that zoning is a complex and important function of the State. It may indeed be the most essential function performed by local government, for it is one of the primary means by which we protect that sometimes difficult to define concept of quality of life. I therefore continue to adhere to the principle of Village of Euclid v. Ambler Realty Co., that deference should be given to governmental judgments concerning proper land-use allocation. That deference is a principle which has served this Court well and which is necessary for the continued development of effective zoning and land-use control mechanisms. Had the owners alone brought this suit alleging that the restrictive ordinance deprived them of their property or was an irrational legislative classification, I would agree that the ordinance would have to be sustained. Our role is not and should not be to sit as a zoning board of appeals.

I would also agree with the majority that local zoning authorities may properly act in furtherance of the objectives asserted to be served by the ordinance at issue here: restricting uncontrolled growth, solving traffic problems, keeping rental costs at a reasonable level, and making the community attractive to families. The police power which provides the justification for zoning is not narrowly confined. See Berman v. Parker, (1954). And, it is appropriate that we afford zoning authorities considerable latitude in choosing the means by which to implement such purposes. But deference does not mean abdication. This Court has an obligation to ensure that zoning ordinances, even when adopted in furtherance of such legitimate aims, do not infringe upon fundamental constitutional rights.

When separate but equal was still accepted constitutional dogma, this Court struck down a racially restrictive zoning ordinance. Buchanan v. Warley, (1917). I am sure the Court would not be hesitant to invalidate that ordinance today. The lower federal courts have considered procedural aspects of zoning, and acted to insure that land-use controls are not used as means of confining minorities and the poor to the ghettos of our central cities. These are limited but necessary intrusions on the discretion of zoning authorities. By the same token, I think it clear that the First Amendment provides some limitation on zoning laws. It is inconceivable to me that we would allow the exercise of the zoning power to burden First Amendment freedoms, as by ordinances that restrict occupancy to individuals adhering to particular religious, political, or scientific beliefs. Zoning officials properly concern themselves with the uses of land-with, for example, the number and kind of dwellings to be constructed in a certain neighborhood or the number of persons who can reside in those dwellings. But zoning authorities cannot validly consider who those persons are, what they believe, or how they choose to live, whether they are Negro or white, Catholic or Jew, Republican or Democrat, married or unmarried.

My disagreement with the Court today is based upon my view that the ordinance in this case unnecessarily burdens appellees' First Amendment freedom of association and their constitutionally guaranteed right to privacy. Our decisions establish that the First and Fourteenth Amendments protect the freedom to choose one's associates. Constitutional protection is extended, not only to modes of association that are political in the usual sense, but also to those that pertain to the social and economic benefit of the members. The selection of one's living companions involves similar choices as to the emotional, social, or economic benefits to be derived from alternative living arrangements.

The freedom of association is often inextricably entwined with the constitutionally guaranteed right of privacy. The right to "establish a home" is an essential part of the liberty guaranteed by the Fourteenth Amendment. And the Constitution secures to an individual a freedom "to satisfy his intellectual and emotional needs in the privacy of his own home." Constitutionally protected privacy is, in Mr. Justice Brandeis' words, "as against the Government, the right to be let alone . . . the right most valued by civilized man." The choice of household companions - of whether a person's 'intellectual and emotional needs' are best met by living with family, friends, professional associates, or others - involves deeply personal considerations as to the kind and quality of intimate relationships within the home. That decision surely falls within the ambit of the right to privacy protected by the Constitution.

The instant ordinance discriminates on the basis of just such a personal lifestyle choice as to household companions. It permits any number of persons related by blood or marriage, be it two or twenty, to live in a single household, but it limits to two the number of unrelated persons bound by profession, love, friendship, religious or political affiliation, or mere economics who can occupy a single home. Belle Terre imposes upon those who deviate from the community norm in their choice of living companions significantly greater restrictions than are applied to residential groups who are related by blood or marriage, and compose the established order within the community. The village has, in effect, acted to fence out those individuals whose choice of lifestyle differs from that of its current residents.

[This is not a case where the Court is being asked to nullify a township's sincere efforts to maintain its residential character by preventing the operation of rooming houses, fraternity houses, or other commercial or high-density residential uses.] Unquestionably, a town is free to restrict such uses. Moreover, as a general proposition, I see no constitutional infirmity in a town's limiting the density of use in residential areas by zoning regulations which do not discriminate on the basis of constitutionally suspect criteria. This ordinance, however, limits the density of occupancy of only those homes occupied by unrelated persons. It thus reaches beyond control of the use of land or the density of population, and undertakes to regulate the way people choose to associate with each other within the privacy of their own homes.

It is no answer to say, as does the majority that associational interests are not infringed because Belle Terre residents may entertain whomever they choose. Only last Term Mr. Justice Douglas indicated in concurrence that he saw the right of association protected by the First Amendment as involving far more than the right to entertain visitors. He found that right infringed by a restriction on food stamp assistance, penalizing households of "unrelated persons." As Mr. Justice Douglas there said, freedom of association encompasses the "right to invite the stranger into one's home not only for entertainment but to join the household as well." I am still persuaded that the choice of those who will form one's household implicates constitutionally protected rights.

Because I believe that this zoning ordinance creates a classification which impinges upon fundamental personal rights, it can withstand constitutional scrutiny only upon a clear showing that the burden imposed is necessary to protect a compelling and substantial governmental interest. And, once it be determined that a burden has been placed upon a constitutional right, the onus of demonstrating that no less intrusive means will adequately protect the compelling state interest and that the challenged statute is sufficiently narrowly drawn, is upon the party seeking to justify the burden.

A variety of justifications have been proffered in support of the village's ordinance. It is claimed that the ordinance controls population density, prevents noise, traffic and parking problems, and preserves the rent structure of the community and its attractiveness to families. As I noted earlier, these are all legitimate and substantial interests of government. But I think it clear that the means chosen to accomplish these purposes are both overinclusive and underinclusive, and that the asserted goals could be as effectively achieved by means of an ordinance that did not discriminate on the basis of constitutionally protected choices of lifestyle. The ordinance imposes no restriction whatsoever on the number of persons who may live in a house, as long as they are related by marital or sanguinary bonds - presumably no matter how distant their relationship. Nor does the ordinance restrict the number of income earners who may contribute to rent in such a household, or the number of automobiles that may be maintained by its occupants. In that sense the ordinance is underinclusive. On the other hand, the statute restricts the number of unrelated persons who may live in a home to no more than two. It would therefore prevent three unrelated people from occupying a dwelling even if among them they had but one income and no vehicles. While an extended family of a dozen or more might live in a small bungalow, three elderly and retired persons could not occupy the large manor house next door. Thus the statute is also grossly overinclusive to accomplish its intended purposes.

There are some 220 residences in Belle Terre occupied by about 700 persons. The density is therefore just above three per household. The village is justifiably concerned with density of population and the related problems of noise, traffic, and the like. It could deal with those problems by limiting each household to a specified number of adults, two or three perhaps, without limitation on the number of dependent children. By providing an exception for dependent children, the village would avoid any doubts that might otherwise be posed by the constitutional protection afforded the choice of whether to bear a child.

The burden of such an ordinance would fall equally upon all segments of the community. It would surely be better tailored to the goals asserted by the village than the ordinance before us today, for it would more realistically restrict population density and growth and their attendant environmental costs. Various other statutory mechanisms also suggest themselves as solutions to Belle Terre's problems - rent control, limits on the number of vehicles per household, and so forth, but, of course, such schemes are matters of legislative judgment and not for this Court. Appellants also refer to the necessity of maintaining the family character of the village. There is not a shred of evidence in the record indicating that if Belle Terre permitted a limited number of unrelated persons to live together, the residential, familial character of the community would be fundamentally affected.

By limiting unrelated households to two persons while placing no limitation on households of related individuals, the village has embarked upon its commendable course in a constitutionally faulty vessel. I would find the challenged ordinance unconstitutional. But I would not ask the village to abandon its goal of providing quiet streets, little traffic, and a pleasant and reasonably priced environment in which families might raise their children. Rather, I would commend the village to continue to pursue those purposes but by means of more carefully drawn and even-handed legislation.

I respectfully dissent.


Note: In the next case, the Narragansett Indian Tribe seemed to have found a skillful way around having to comply with building or zoning restrictions imposed by the town of Charlestown, Rhode Island.

# SUPREME COURT OF THE UNITED STATES
## DONALD L. CARCIERI, GOVERNOR OF RHODE ISLAND, ET AL., PETITIONERS,
## V.
## KEN L. SALAZAR, SECRETARY OF THE INTERIOR, ET AL.

FEBRUARY 24, 2009

Justice THOMAS delivered the opinion of the Court.

The Indian Reorganization Act of 1934, (IRA or Act) authorizes the Secretary of the Interior, a respondent in this case, to acquire land and hold it in trust "for the purpose of providing land for Indians." The IRA defines the term "Indian" to "include all persons of Indian descent who are members of any recognized Indian tribe now under Federal jurisdiction." § 479. The Secretary notified petitioners - the State of Rhode Island, its Governor, and the town of Charlestown, Rhode Island - that he intended to accept in trust a parcel of land for use by the Narragansett Indian Tribe in accordance with his claimed authority under the statute. In proceedings before the Interior Board of Indian Appeals (IBIA), the District Court, and the Court of Appeals for the First Circuit, petitioners unsuccessfully challenged the Secretary's authority to take the parcel into trust.

In reviewing the determination of the Court of Appeals, we are asked to interpret the statutory phrase "now under Federal jurisdiction" in § 479.

We agree with petitioners and hold that, for purposes of § 479, the phrase "now under Federal jurisdiction" refers to a tribe that was under federal jurisdiction at the time of the statute's enactment. As a result, § 479 limits the Secretary's authority to taking land into trust for the purpose of providing land to members of a tribe that was under federal jurisdiction when the IRA was enacted in June 1934. Because the record in this case establishes that the Narragansett Tribe was not under federal jurisdiction when the IRA was enacted, the Secretary does not have the authority to take the parcel at issue into trust. We reverse the judgment of the Court of Appeals.

At the time of colonial settlement, the Narragansett Indian Tribe was the indigenous occupant of much of what is now the State of Rhode Island. Initial relations between colonial settlers, the Narragansett Tribe, and the other Indian tribes in the region were peaceful, but relations deteriorated in the late 17th century. The hostilities peaked in 1675 and 1676 during the 2-year armed conflict known as King Philip's War. Hundreds of colonists and thousands of Indians died. The Narragansett Tribe, having been decimated, was placed under formal guardianship by the Colony of Rhode Island in 1709. The Narragansett Tribe recognized today is the successor to two tribes, the Narragansett and the Niantic Tribes. The two predecessor Tribes shared territory and cultural traditions at the time of European settlement and effectively merged in the aftermath of King Philip's War.

Not quite two centuries later, in 1880, the State of Rhode Island convinced the Narragansett Tribe to relinquish its tribal authority as part of an effort to assimilate tribal members into the local population. The Tribe also agreed to sell all but two acres of its remaining reservation land for $5,000. Almost immediately, the Tribe regretted its decisions and embarked on a campaign to regain its land and tribal status. In the early 20th century, members of the Tribe sought economic support and other assistance from the Federal Government. But, in correspondence spanning a 10-year period from 1927 to 1937, federal officials declined their request, noting that the Tribe was, and always had been, under the jurisdiction of the New England States, rather than the Federal Government.

Having failed to gain recognition or assistance from the United States or from the State of Rhode Island, the Tribe filed suit in the 1970's to recover its ancestral land, claiming that the State had misappropriated its territory in violation of the Indian Non-Intercourse Act, 25 U.S.C. § 177, which provides that: "No purchase, grant, lease, or other conveyance of lands, or of any title or claim thereto, from any Indian nation or tribe of Indians, shall be of any validity in law or equity, unless the same be made by treaty or convention entered into pursuant to the Constitution."

The claims were resolved in 1978 by enactment of the Rhode Island Indian Claims Settlement Act. Under the agreement codified by the Settlement Act, the Tribe received title to 1,800 acres of land in Charlestown, Rhode Island, in exchange for relinquishing its past and future claims to land based on aboriginal title. The Tribe also agreed that the 1,800 acres of land received under the Settlement Act "shall be subject to the civil and criminal laws and jurisdiction of the State of Rhode Island."

The Narragansett Tribe's ongoing efforts to gain recognition from the United States Government finally succeeded in 1983. In granting formal recognition, the Bureau of Indian Affairs (BIA) determined that "the Narragansett community and its predecessors have existed autonomously since first contact, despite undergoing many modifications." The BIA referred to the Tribe's "documented history dating from 1614" and noted that "all of the current membership are believed to be able to trace to at least one ancestor on the membership lists of the Narragansett community prepared after the 1880 Rhode Island "detribalization act." After obtaining federal recognition, the Tribe began urging the Secretary to accept a deed of trust to the 1,800 acres conveyed to it under the Rhode Island Indian Claims Settlement Act.

In 1991, the Tribe's housing authority purchased an additional 31 acres of land in the town of Charlestown adjacent to the Tribe's 1,800 acres of settlement lands.

Soon thereafter, a dispute arose about whether the Tribe's planned construction of housing on that parcel had to comply with local regulations. The Tribe's primary argument for noncompliance - that its ownership of the parcel made it a "dependent Indian community" and thus "Indian country" under 18 U.S.C. § 1151 - ultimately failed. But, while the litigation was pending, the Tribe sought an alternative solution to free itself from compliance with local regulations: It asked the Secretary to accept the 31-acre parcel into trust for the Tribe pursuant to 25 U.S.C. § 465. By letter dated March 6, 1998, the Secretary notified petitioners of his acceptance of the Tribe's land into trust. Petitioners appealed the Secretary's decision to the IBIA, which upheld the Secretary's decision.

Petitioners sought review of the IBIA decision pursuant to the Administrative Procedure Act. The Court of Appeals for the First Circuit affirmed.

We granted certiorari, and now reverse.

This case requires us to apply settled principles of statutory construction under which we must first determine whether the statutory text is plain and unambiguous.

The Secretary may accept land into trust only for "the purpose of providing land for Indians." 25 U.S.C. § 465. "Indian" is defined by statute as follows:

> "The term 'Indian' as used in this Act shall include all persons of Indian descent who are *members of any recognized Indian tribe now under Federal jurisdiction*, and all persons who are descendants of such members who were, on June 1, 1934, residing within the present boundaries of any Indian reservation, and shall further include all other persons of one-half or more Indian blood. The term 'tribe' wherever used in this Act shall be construed to refer to any Indian tribe, organized band, pueblo, or the Indians residing on one reservation." § 479

The parties are in agreement, as are we, that the Secretary's authority to take the parcel in question into trust depends on whether the Narragansetts are members of a "recognized Indian Tribe now under Federal jurisdiction." That question, in turn, requires us to decide whether the word "now under Federal jurisdiction" refers to 1998, when the Secretary accepted the 31-acre parcel into trust, or 1934, when Congress enacted the IRA.

We hold that the term "now under Federal jurisdiction" in § 479 unambiguously refers to those tribes that were under the federal jurisdiction of the United States when the IRA was enacted in 1934. None of the parties or *amici*, including the Narragansett Tribe itself, has argued that the Tribe was under federal jurisdiction in 1934. And the evidence in the record is to the contrary. Moreover, the petition for writ of certiorari filed in this case specifically represented that "in 1934, the Narragansett Indian Tribe was neither federally recognized nor under the jurisdiction of the federal government." The respondents' brief in opposition declined to contest this assertion. Under our rules, that alone is reason to accept this as fact for purposes of our decision in this case. We therefore reverse the judgment of the Court of Appeals.

*It is so ordered.*

Note: Some of you may have seen the popular movie, *Field of Dreams,* or may be able to get it on Netflix. The following case involves the specific land involved in that movie. It is also a very good illustration of the politics involved in a great many zoning decisions, and a description of an interesting technique for insuring that the people most affected by the new zoning will not be able to mount an effective protest – short of voting out the city council.

When dealing with zoning issues in any municipality, it may be well to remember how important politics may be to any particular decision.

## SUPREME COURT OF IOWA

### RESIDENTIAL AND AGRICULTURAL ADVISORY COMMITTEE, LLC, AN IOWA LIMITED LIABILITY COMPANY; MATT MESCHER; ALLAN R. DEMMER; CATHERINE DEMMER; WAYNE AMESKAMP; SHARON AMESKAMP; VERNON BOGE; DONALD BOGE; MARY ANN RUBLY; JOHN R. RUBLY; DOLORES THIER; LARRY THIER; GARY BURKLE; CINDY BURKLE; WAYNE VORWALD; LINDA VORWALD; JEFF PAPE; GERALD WOLF; AND JOANNE WOLF, APPELLANTS,

### V.

### DYERSVILLE CITY COUNCIL, MAYOR JAMES A. HEAVENS, MIKE ENGLISH, MARK BREITBACH, ROBERT PLATZ, MOLLY EVERS, AND DAN WILLENBORG, APPELLEES.

DECEMBER 9, 2016

Opinion

ZAGER, Justice.

The Dyersville City Council voted to rezone the area containing the *Field of Dreams* movie site from A-1 Agricultural to C-2 Commercial in order to facilitate the development of a baseball and softball complex. Community members filed suit, challenging the rezoning.

## I. Background Facts and Proceedings.

The 1989 *Field of Dreams* movie was filmed primarily at the Lansing farm now located in Dyersville, in rural Dubuque County. At the time the movie was filmed, the Lansing farm was not yet annexed into the City of Dyersville.

Due to the popularity of the film, Donald and Rebecca Lansing kept the baseball field and their white farmhouse intact for visitors and tourists. The house and baseball diamond were a popular destination, and thousands of tourists visited the Lansing property each year. In recent years, however, tourist numbers have been declining.

The City of Dyersville has a comprehensive plan for the city that has been in place for many years. In the early 1960s, the city enacted a plan, Zoning Ordinance No. 285, that sets forth some of the purposes for rezoning, including:

> "to lessen congestion in the streets; to secure safety from fire, panic and other dangers; to promote health and the general welfare; to provide adequate light and air; to prevent the overcrowding of land; to avoid undue concentration of population; to facilitate the adequate provision of transportation, water, sewerage, schools, parks, and other public requirements; to conserve the value of buildings and property; and to encourage the most appropriate use of land throughout the City with reasonable consideration, in accordance with a comprehensive plan."

In 1974, Dyersville enacted a comprehensive development plan that included goals for future land use. The development plan included key policy goals and recommendations specific to commercial and business development. One of the goals was to "discourage proliferation of scattered commercial development throughout the residential community." Another recommendation was to encourage the expansion of the already-existing central business district through a coordinated design scheme. The plan also noted that the city should encourage businesses to be located only in those areas that were easily accessible for water and sewage services. In 1975, the city supplemented the plan with a requirement for a detailed evaluation of water, sewage, and waste systems.

In 1991, the city drafted a community builder plan. This plan expressly addressed the impact of the *Field of Dreams* movie on the city's tourism and concluded that the main concern was that "Dyersville must become much more aggressive in guiding and encouraging its own growth." The 1991 plan listed twelve opportunities for growth in the city, one of which was "continued (national/international) attention for Field of Dreams and other tourist attractions." It also identified eleven threats to the city's growth, one of which was "loss of Field of Dreams or other major tourist attraction."

In 2003, the City of Dyersville drafted a future annexation plan that identified areas of nearby land that were likely to be annexed into the city in the future. The annexation plan grouped areas of land into those likely to be annexed within five years, five to ten years, or ten to twenty years. At that time, the *Field of Dreams* property was not included in any of these annexation estimates.

In 2010, the Lansings listed their property for sale. Their property included the baseball diamond and white farmhouse, and an additional 193 acres that are used as farmland. Ultimately, the Lansings signed a purchase agreement with Mike and Denise Stillman. The sale was contingent upon the property being rezoned for commercial use, among other things. The Stillmans intended to create All-Star Ballpark Heaven on the land, a baseball and softball complex with up to twenty-four fields to be used for youth baseball and softball. They intended to continue to maintain the farmhouse and original baseball diamond as a tourist attraction.

The Dyersville City Council met on November 21, 2011. In December, the Stillmans organized a bus trip to Des Moines for the purpose of meeting with legislators and other state officials to discuss financing the All-Star Ballpark Heaven project. The mayor and two city council members joined the Stillmans on the bus trip to Des Moines, and they also attended a group dinner. A member of the planning and zoning commission also participated in the bus trip to Des Moines. The Stillmans presumably funded both the bus trip and the dinner. The purpose of the trip and the dinner was to begin lobbying state officials for financial assistance in developing the project.

In early 2012, a Strategic Economics Group from Des Moines completed an economic and fiscal impact study report regarding the proposed project.

The city council met on February 20, 2012, and one of the agenda items was the "Field of Dreams Extension." A number of the petitioners and other community members attended the meeting and were able to speak about the proposed All-Star Ballpark Heaven complex. Petitioner Wayne Vorwald expressed concerns about having open-range cattle in the area if the project were completed because of the juxtaposition of urban and farming areas. Petitioners Jeff Pape and Wayne Ameskamp mentioned concerns with runoff into the nearby creek and flooding. Ron Oberbroeckling was worried about the project interfering with deer hunting in the area. A number of community members talked about growing up on family farms and wanting to maintain those farms and values for their own families. Petitioner Matt Mescher discussed traffic concerns because one of the most dangerous intersections in the state is located in Dyersville. He also stated that his "neighbors do not want ball fields in the middle of their cornfields."

On July 2, the council met to discuss the resolution regarding the voluntary annexation of property into the City of Dyersville. The mayor and all five city council members were present, in addition to the city attorney. A number of community members were present. A few community members, some of whom are petitioners in this case, appeared at the meeting with their attorney, Susan Hess. A television crew from KCRG Channel 9 news was present at the meeting.

Stillman spoke first in support of the project. She then introduced Ron Kittle, a former professional baseball player. He spoke about the impact of baseball in his life and the benefits the project could bring to Dyersville. The council then opened the meeting up to community members who spoke against the proposed project. Petitioner Mescher spoke about funding concerns and the impact on taxpayers. He also spoke about growing division in the small community and how the council should be taking noise and pollution into account in addition to economic benefits.

The city council unanimously voted to send the resolution to the zoning commission. On July 3, the zoning commission sent a notice to interested property owners about the public hearing it would hold regarding the proposed rezoning.

The zoning commission met to discuss rezoning the *Field of Dreams* property from agricultural to commercial. The city administrator began by providing an overview to the zoning commission about the proposed rezoning. He described the area to be rezoned, which included a 200-foot buffer zone on three sides of the area that would remain agricultural. He explained that the buffer zone was "created to protect adjoining property owners" and would prevent concerns about children playing baseball right up against the adjoining property lines. He also described how the buffer zone would allow the adjacent farms to continue to spread manure and engage in other farming activities without interrupting the baseball and softball facilities. He informed the zoning commission that the city council had looked into the impact on property values, storm water and drainage issues, and crime.

At the August 6 city council meeting, attorney Hess spoke first. She urged the council to remain impartial and stated it was acting in a quasi-judicial manner and therefore was required to remain impartial. She noted concerns with the planning and zoning commission and opined that it had failed to remain impartial because the members attended a work session presentation put on by the developer. She asked the council not to vote on the rezoning at the meeting and to table the topic for a later meeting.

The city council voted to approve the first reading of the ordinance, and the motion passed in a vote of 4–1, with council member Evers voting no. Evers then read a written statement and expressed community concerns about the project. She stated that more members of the community opposed the project than favored it. The council moved to waive the second and third readings of the ordinance. The motions passed with votes of 4–1. Evers was the sole council member voting no.

On September 4, 2012, the Residential and Agricultural Advisory Committee, L.L.C. and twenty-three other individuals (petitioners) filed suit.

## II. Analysis.

On appeal, the petitioners raise a number of issues. They argue the district court applied the incorrect standard of review to the city council's rezoning of the land. They argue the council's actions were quasi-judicial in nature rather than legislative, triggering a different standard of review.

**Correct Standard of Review of the City Council's Actions.** We must first address the proper standard of review in this action. The petitioners argue that the council's actions were quasi-judicial in nature rather than legislative. The district court order concluded that, for purposes of determining whether certiorari was available, the council was acting in a quasi-judicial manner. However, the underlying decision to rezone was a legislative function and the council was therefore not required to make findings of fact or provide for a more formal proceeding similar to a judicial proceeding.

Iowa Code section 414.4 provides that the city council "shall provide for the manner in which the regulations and restrictions and the boundaries of the districts shall be determined, established, and enforced, and from time to time amended, supplemented, or changed." To do so, the city council must also follow proper procedure. The council must give the community members published notice of the time and place of a public hearing with at least seven days' notice. The council must hold a public hearing during which community members are offered the opportunity to offer opinions regarding the proposed zoning or rezoning. Iowa Code section 414.5 provides specific voting rules for situations where an ordinance would change land from one zoning district to another. In this situation, if twenty percent or more of the owners of property located within 200 feet of the proposed rezoning area file a written protest, the council is required to approve the rezoning ordinance by a vote of at least three-fourths of the members.

The statutory scheme set forth in the Iowa Code mirrors the general rule that zoning determinations are a legislative function of a city council or board of supervisors. Likewise, we have long recognized that "zoning decisions are an exercise of the police power to promote the health, safety, order and morals of society." A city council or board of supervisors exercises its delegated police power through zoning decisions so long as the decisions are "made in accordance with a comprehensive plan and designed to encourage efficient urban development patterns and to promote health and the general welfare." A zoning decision or regulation is an exercise of delegated police powers so long as it is made with reasonable consideration, among other things, as to the character of the area of the district and the peculiar suitability of such area for particular uses, and with a view to conserving the value of buildings and encouraging the most appropriate use of land throughout the city.

However, we have also recognized that there are some situations in which a zoning decision can take on a quasi-judicial nature that may necessitate a different standard of review than the normally limited standard of review we utilize when reviewing zoning decisions.

Some historical perspective helps in our analysis. In *Buechele v. Ray*, we laid out the test to determine whether an action is judicial or quasi-judicial, which we noted is a difficult determination.

In this case, the city council was acting in a legislative function in furtherance of its delegated police powers. The council was not sitting to "determine adjudicative facts to decide the legal rights, privileges or duties of a particular party based on that party's particular circumstances." The city council decision to rezone was not undertaken to weigh the legal rights of one party (the All-Star Ballpark Heaven) versus another party (the petitioners). The council weighed all of the information, reports, and comments available to it in order to determine whether rezoning was in the best interest of the city as a whole. We therefore hold that the proper standard of review in this case is "the generally limited scope of review" we utilize in order "to determine whether the decision by the Board to rezone is fairly debatable."

Zoning regulations carry a strong presumption of validity. A zoning regulation "is valid if it has any real, substantial relation to the public health, comfort, safety, and welfare, including the maintenance of property values." If the reasonableness of a zoning ordinance is "fairly debatable," then we decline to substitute our judgment for that of the city council or board of supervisors. The reasonableness of a zoning ordinance is "fairly debatable" when for any reason it is open to dispute or controversy on grounds that make sense or point to a logical deduction, and where reasonable minds may differ; or where the evidence provides a basis for a fair difference of opinion as to its application to a particular property.

Spot zoning. _— OK when it's rational_

["Spot zoning is the creation of a small island of property with restrictions on its use different from those imposed on surrounding property." Not all spot zoning is illegal, however, and we have created a three-prong test for determining whether spot zoning is valid. Under this test, we consider:

> "(1)whether the new zoning is germane to an object within the police power; (2) whether there is a reasonable basis for making a distinction between the spot zoned land and the surrounding property; and (3) whether the rezoning is consistent with the comprehensive plan."]

[When there is spot zoning, "there must be substantial and reasonable grounds or basis for the discrimination when one lot or tract is singled out."]

As a preliminary matter, we acknowledge that the rezoning appears to constitute spot zoning. The property surrounding the new commercial area is agricultural land. The rezoning created a commercial "island" of property amidst land zoned as agricultural. However, that does not end our inquiry. The next step is to determine whether the spot zoning was valid.

First, we have already determined that the rezoning was made within the scope of the city council's general police power. The decision to rezone the area for the project was made in consideration of the general health and welfare of the community. Second, the council had a reasonable basis for its decision to rezone the land despite the surrounding property. The *Field of Dreams* property has been a unique site for years. The baseball field on the Lansing farm has been used in the community for baseball and softball games, in addition to local and national tourism. Part of the location's charm is simply that it is a baseball field surrounded by farmland. The council made the decision to rezone and allow for more baseball fields to capitalize on this unique site and increase tourism for the City of Dyersville. Last, as we already concluded, the spot zoning is consistent with the overall comprehensive plan. The city's community builder plan expressly mentions the necessity of maintaining the *Field of Dreams* site and increasing tourism for the city. We agree with the decision of the district court and hold that this was not illegal spot zoning.]

Use of 200-Foot Buffer Zone.

The ordinance that rezoned the *Field of Dreams* property included a 200-foot buffer zone of agricultural land that surrounded the property that was rezoned to commercial.

The petitioners challenge the use of this 200-foot buffer zone. They argue that the buffer zone was put in place in order to prevent the nearby property owners from objecting to the project under the procedure outlined in Iowa Code section 414.5. The council asserts that the purpose of the 200-foot buffer zone was to address some of the concerns raised about manure spreading, farming activities, and children playing baseball up against the property line of adjoining owners.

At first blush, the 200-foot buffer zone can appear to be unfair, as it limits the number of adjacent landowners who can object to the rezoning. However, it does provide a benefit to adjacent landowners by addressing their expressed concerns with the rezoning. A number of petitioners raised concerns about hunting, spreading of manure, and grazing if their farming property was directly adjacent to the new ballfields. The buffer zone provides a solution to those concerns.

Additionally, a number of other courts have held that a council may avoid a supermajority vote requirement by creating a buffer zone between the property to be rezoned and the land of adjacent property owners.

Nevertheless, even if the petitioners had established the requirement of a supermajority vote under Iowa Code section 414.5, the requirement was met. The statute requires the pertinent ordinance to pass by a vote of three-fourths of all members of the council, or seventy-five percent. Iowa Code § 414.5. The rezoning of the *Field of Dreams* site passed by a vote of 4–1, or eighty percent.

The rezoning decision here clearly meets the rational-basis test. The council made the decision to rezone the *Field of Dreams* site in consideration of the best interests of Dyersville. It considered the economic impact of increased tourism and investigated any water, sewage, traffic, and crime issues the rezoning could create. The decision was made with the overall zoning scheme of the city in mind, as one of the main goals of the comprehensive plan is to expand tourism to Dyersville via the *Field of Dreams* site. There was a "realistically conceivable" purpose for the rezoning that served a legitimate government interest, because the council believed the rezoning could increase tourism to the city. The council's determination that the ballpark could increase tourism to the city and could lead to more jobs and to an increased tax base for the city was based on facts presented to and considered by the council. The council ordered studies done regarding the financial impact on the city and listened to the opinions of multiple community members. Additionally, the use of the 200-foot buffer zone was a reasonable solution to the concerns of the community members and was not arbitrary or capricious. Last, as we determined above, the reason for the rezoning was not arbitrary.

### III. Conclusion.

We conclude that the district court was correct in upholding the rezoning.

We note that neither the Lansings nor the Stillmans were ever a party to the proceedings. By the time the district court issued this order, the closing had occurred and the Stillmans owned the *Field of Dreams* site.

# CHAPTER TWELVE

# CONDEMNATION

## INTRODUCTION

Governmental entities have the power of eminent domain. They have the power to condemn private property for public use. For example, the state highway department has the power to condemn the land that it needs to build a highway across the state. The location of the highway simply cannot be left to the vagaries of which landowners are willing to sell their land to the highway department, and which landowners are not willing to sell – or would sell only at an exorbant price.

Normally, it is the governmental entity that begins the process of condemnation. And the landowner is paid for the land taken.

However, if the government just starts using the land, without initiating the process of condemnation, then the landowner may bring a suit in *inverse condemnation* – to make the government pay. Basically, if the governmental entity starts the action it is called condemnation. If the individual landowner starts the suit it is called *inverse condemnation.*

The case which follows is one of the leading cases in the area of inverse condemnation.

# SUPREME COURT OF THE UNITED STATES
## UNITED STATES
## V.
## CAUSBY ET UX.

MAY 27, 1946

Mr. Justice DOUGLAS delivered the opinion of the Court.

This is a case of first impression. The problem presented is whether respondents' property was taken within the meaning of the Fifth Amendment by frequent and regular flights of army and navy aircraft over respondents' land at low altitudes. The Court of Claims held that there was a taking and entered judgment for respondent, one judge dissenting. The case is here on a petition for a writ of certiorari which we granted because of the importance of the question presented.

Respondents own 2.8 acres near an airport outside of Greensboro, North Carolina. It has on it a dwelling house, and also various outbuildings which were mainly used for raising chickens. The end of the airport's northwest-southeast runway is 2,220 feet from respondents' barn and 2,275 feet from their house. The path of glide to this runway passes directly over the property-which is 100 feet wide and 1,200 feet long. The 30 to 1 safe glide angle approved by the Civil Aeronautics Authority passes over this property at 83 feet, which is 67 feet above the house, 63 feet above the barn and 18 feet above the highest tree. The use by the United States of this airport is pursuant to a lease executed in May, 1942, for a term commencing June 1, 1942 and ending June 30, 1942, with a provision for renewals until June 30, 1967, or six months after the end of the national emergency, whichever is the earlier.

Various aircraft of the United States use this airport - bombers, transports and fighters. The direction of the prevailing wind determines when a particular runway is used. The northwest-southeast runway in question is used about four per cent of the time in taking off and about seven per cent of the time in landing. Since the United States began operations in May, 1942, its four-motored heavy bombers, other planes of the heavier type, and its fighter planes have frequently passed over respondents' land and buildings in considerable numbers and rather close together. They come close enough at times to appear barely to miss the tops of the trees and at times so close to the tops of the trees as to blow the old leaves off. The noise is startling. And at night the glare from the planes brightly lights up the place. As a result of the noise, respondents had to give up their chicken business. As many as six to ten of their chickens were killed in one day by flying into the walls from fright. The total chickens lost in that manner was about 150. Production also fell off. The result was the destruction of the use of the property as a commercial chicken farm. Respondents are frequently deprived of their sleep and the family has become nervous and frightened. Although there have been no airplane accidents on respondents' property, there have been several accidents near the airport and close to respondents' place. These are the essential facts found by the Court of Claims. On the basis of these facts, it found that respondents' property had depreciated in value. It held that the United States had taken an easement over the property on June 1, 1942, and that the value of the property destroyed and the easement taken was $2,000.

## I.

The United States relies on the Air Commerce Act of 1926. Under those statutes the United States has 'complete and exclusive national sovereignty in the air space' over this country. They grant any citizen of the United States "a public right of freedom of transit in air commerce through the navigable air space of the United States." And "navigable air space" is defined as "airspace above the minimum safe altitudes of flight prescribed by the Civil Aeronautics Authority." And it is provided that "such navigable airspace shall be subject to a public right of freedom of interstate and foreign air navigation." It is, therefore, argued that since these flights were within the minimum safe altitudes of flight which had been prescribed, they were an exercise of the declared right of travel through the airspace. The United States concludes that when flights are made within the navigable airspace without any physical invasion of the property of the landowners, there has been no taking of property. It says that at most there was merely incidental damage occurring as a consequence of authorized air navigation. It also argues that the landowner does not own superadjacent airspace which he has not subjected to possession by the erection of structures or other occupancy. Moreover, it is argued that even if the United States took airspace owned by respondents, no compensable damage was shown. Any damages are said to be merely consequential for which no compensation may be obtained under the Fifth Amendment.

It is ancient doctrine that at common law ownership of the land extended to the periphery of the universe - Cujus est solum ejus est usque ad coelum. But that doctrine has no place in the modern world. The air is a public highway, as Congress has declared. Were that not true, every transcontinental flight would subject the operator to countless trespass suits. Common sense revolts at the idea. To recognize such private claims to the airspace would clog these highways, seriously interfere with their control and development in the public interest, and transfer into private ownership that to which only the public has a just claim.

But that general principle does not control the present case. For the United States conceded on oral argument that if the flights over respondents' property rendered it uninhabitable, there would be a taking compensable under the Fifth Amendment. It is the owner's loss, not the taker's gain, which is the measure of the value of the property taken. Market value fairly determined is the normal measure of the recovery. And that value may reflect the use to which the land could readily be converted, as well as the existing use. If, by reason of the frequency and altitude of the flights, respondents could not use this land for any purpose, their loss would be complete. It would be as complete as if the United States had entered upon the surface of the land and taken exclusive possession of it.

We agree that in those circumstances there would be a taking. Though it would be only an easement of flight which was taken, that easement, if permanent and not merely temporary, normally would be the equivalent of a fee interest. It would be a definite exercise of complete dominion and control over the surface of the land. The fact that the planes never touched the surface would be as irrelevant as the absence in this day of the feudal livery of seisin on the transfer of real estate. The owner's right to possess and exploit the land - that is to say, his beneficial ownership of it - would be destroyed.

It would not be a case of incidental damages arising from a legalized nuisance such as was involved in Richards v. Washington Terminal Co. In that case property owners whose lands adjoined a railroad line were denied recovery for damages resulting from the noise, vibrations, smoke and the like, incidental to the operations of the trains. In the supposed case the line of flight is over the land. And the land is appropriated as directly and completely as if it were used for the runways themselves.

There is no material difference between the supposed case and the present one, except that here enjoyment and use of the land are not completely destroyed. But that does not seem to us to be controlling. The path of glide for airplanes might reduce a valuable factory site to grazing land, an orchard to a vegetable patch, a residential section to a wheat field. Some value would remain. But the use of the airspace immediately above the land would limit the utility of the land and cause a diminution in its value. That was the philosophy of Portsmouth Harbor Land & Hotel Co. v. United States. In that case the petition alleged that the United States erected a fort on nearby land, established a battery and a fire control station there, and fired guns over petitioner's land. The Court, speaking through Mr. Justice Holmes, held that "the specific facts set forth would warrant a finding that a servitude has been imposed."

The fact that the path of glide taken by the planes was that approved by the Civil Aeronautics Authority does not change the result. The navigable airspace which

Congress has placed in the public domain is "airspace above the minimum safe altitudes of flight prescribed by the Civil Aeronautics Authority." If that agency prescribed 83 feet as the minimum safe altitude, then we would have presented the question of the validity of the regulation. But nothing of the sort has been done. The path of glide governs the method of operating - of landing or taking off. The altitude required for that operation is not the minimum safe altitude of flight which is the downward reach of the navigable airspace. The minimum prescribed by the authority is 500 feet during the day and 1000 feet at night for air carriers and from 300 to 1000 feet for other aircraft depending on the type of plane and the character of the terrain. Hence, the flights in question were not within the navigable airspace which Congress placed within the public domain. If any airspace needed for landing or taking off were included, flights which were so close to the land as to render it uninhabitable would be immune. But the United States concedes, as we have said, that in that event there would be a taking. Thus, it is apparent that the path of glide is not the minimum safe altitude of flight within the meaning of the statute. The Civil Aeronautics Authority has, of course, the power to prescribe air traffic rules. But Congress has defined navigable airspace only in terms of one of them - the minimum safe altitudes of flight.

We have said that the airspace is a public highway. Yet it is obvious that if the landowner is to have full enjoyment of the land, he must have exclusive control of the immediate reaches of the enveloping atmosphere. Otherwise buildings could not be erected, trees could not be planted, and even fences could not be run. The principle is recognized when the law gives a remedy in case overhanging structures are erected on adjoining land. The landowner owns at least as much of the space above the ground as he can occupy or use in connection with the land. The fact that he does not occupy it in a physical sense - by the erection of buildings and the like - is not material. As we have said, the flight of airplanes, which skim the surface but do not touch it, is as much an appropriation of the use of the land as a more conventional entry upon it. We would not doubt that if the United States erected an elevated railway over respondents' land at the precise altitude where its planes now fly, there would be a partial taking, even though none of the supports of the structure rested on the land. The reason is that there would be an intrusion so immediate and direct as to subtract from the owner's full enjoyment of the property and to limit his exploitation of it. While the owner does not in any physical manner occupy that stratum of airspace or make use of it in the conventional sense, he does use it in somewhat the same sense that space left between buildings for the purpose of light and air is used. The superadjacent airspace at this low altitude is so close to the land that continuous invasions of it affect the use of the surface of the land itself. We think that the landowner, as an incident to his ownership, has a claim to it and that invasions of it are in the same category as invasions of the surface.

In this case the damages were the product of a direct invasion of respondents' domain. As stated in United States v. Cress, "it is the character of the invasion, not the amount of damage resulting from it, so long as the damage is substantial, that determines the question whether it is a taking."

We said in United States v. Powelson, that while the meaning of "property" as used in the Fifth Amendment was a federal question, "it will normally obtain its content by reference to local law." If we look to North Carolina law, we reach the same result. Sovereignty in the airspace rests in the State "except where granted to and assumed by the United States." Gen.Stats. 1943, s 63-11. The flight of aircraft is lawful "unless at such a low altitude as to interfere with the then existing use to which the land or water, or the space over the land or water, is put by the owner, or unless so conducted as to be imminently dangerous to persons or property lawfully on the land or water beneath." Subject to that right of flight, "ownership of the space above the lands and waters of this State is declared to be vested in the several owners of the surface beneath." Our holding that there was an invasion of respondents' property is thus not inconsistent with the local law governing a landowner's claim to the immediate reaches of the superadjacent airspace.

The airplane is part of the modern environment of life, and the inconveniences which it causes are normally not compensable under the Fifth Amendment. The airspace, apart from the immediate reaches above the land, is part of the public domain. We need not determine at this time what those precise limits are. Flights over private land are not a taking, unless they are so low and so frequent as to be a direct and immediate interference with the enjoyment and use of the land. We need not speculate on that phase of the present case. For the findings of the Court of Claims plainly establish that there was a diminution in value of the property and that the frequent, low-level flights were the direct and immediate cause. We agree with the Court of Claims that a servitude has been imposed upon the land.

II.

We need not decide whether repeated trespasses might give rise to an implied contract. If there is a taking, the claim is "founded upon the Constitution" and within the jurisdiction of the Court of Claims to hear and determine. Thus, the jurisdiction of the Court of Claims in this case is clear.

## III.

The Court of Claims held, as we have noted, that an easement was taken. But the findings of fact contain no precise description as to its nature. It is not described in terms of frequency of flight, permissible altitude, or type of airplane. Nor is there a finding as to whether the easement taken was temporary or permanent. Yet an accurate description of the property taken is essential, since that interest vests in the United States. It is true that the Court of Claims stated in its opinion that the easement taken was permanent. But the deficiency in findings cannot be rectified by statements in the opinion. Findings of fact on every "material issue" are a statutory requirement. The importance of findings of fact based on evidence is emphasized here by the Court of Claims' treatment of the nature of the easement. It stated in its opinion that the easement was permanent because the United States "no doubt intended to make some sort of arrangement whereby it could use the airport for its military planes whenever it had occasion to do so." That sounds more like conjecture rather than a conclusion from evidence; and if so, it would not be a proper foundation for liability of the United States. We do not stop to examine the evidence to determine whether it would support such a finding, if made. For that is not our function.

Since on this record it is not clear whether the easement taken is a permanent or a temporary one, it would be premature for us to consider whether the amount of the award made by the Court of Claims was proper.

The judgment is reversed and the cause is remanded to the Court of Claims so that it may make the necessary findings in conformity with this opinion.

Reversed.

Note: How does the actual process of condemnation work? Who determines the value of the land taken, and thus the amount of money that must be paid by the government to the landowner? The following case, involving Vail Ski Resort, illustrates the process.

# SUPREME COURT OF COLORADO
## BOARD OF COUNTY COMMISSIONERS OF EAGLE COUNTY, AND THE DEPARTMENT OF HIGHWAYS, STATE OF COLORADO, PLAINTIFFS IN ERROR,
### V.
## VAIL ASSOCIATES, LTD., WESTERN FEDERAL SAVINGS AND LOAN ASSOCIATION, DENVER U.S. NATIONAL BANK, H. A. D. ENTERPRISES, INC., VIRGIL H. WILLIAMS AS TREASURER AND PUBLIC TRUSTEE OF EAGLE COUNTY, DEFENDANTS IN ERROR.

APRIL 6, 1970

LEE, Justice.

This writ of error is directed to an eminent domain proceeding in the District Court of Eagle County, Colorado. The Board of County Commissioners of Eagle County and the Department of Highways, State of Colorado, petitioned to acquire by the exercise of the power of eminent domain a strip of land containing approximately 129 acres owned by respondent Vail Associates, Ltd. We herein refer to petitioners as the "State" and to the respondent as "Vail."

The right-of-way being acquired was for the purpose of constructing a portion of U.S. Interstate 70 in the Gore Creek Valley which runs westerly from the west side of Vail Pass to Dowd Junction at the intersection of U.S. Highways Nos. 6 and 24. I-70 was to replace U.S. No. 6. Vail's lands in Gore Valley, which consisted of approximately 1,125 acres, were bisected by U.S. 6. The portion lying south of U.S. 6 had been developed into a ski resort known as Vail Village. The core of the Village development consisted of approximately eighty acres from which the ski lifts ascended southward into the Mill Creek area of the White River National Forest. The initial development of Vail Village and the adjoining ski area commenced during the early part of 1962. By the time of the trial in November of 1967, the development was a thriving ski resort. A variety of ski slopes had been created and were serviced by 9 ski lifts installed at a cost of approximately two million dollars. It was anticipated that when the ski area was fully developed a total of 20 ski lifts would have been installed.

Vail Village is a municipal corporation. It consists of numerous commercial enterprises, including shops, restaurants, hotels, motels, lodges, condominiums and individual residences, the construction cost of which was estimated to be from

$27,000,000 to $29,000,000. Utility services for water, sewer, electricity and gas were available, as were fire and police protection. To the end that the area would develop into a year-round recreation resort, the Vail Metropolitan Recreation District was formed and had commenced construction of an 18-hole golf course, tennis courts and other summer recreation facilities. In sum total, the evidence showed a vital, thriving and growing community with great promise of significant additional expansion in the future. The State expert appraiser, in describing the successful manner in which the Vail ski area had been developed, characterized the management and general procedures followed by Vail Associates in the operation of the ski area and in planning for the future as outstanding. It is in this setting that the State, in the interest of constructing another segment of I-70 across the State of Colorado, exercised its power of eminent domain.

The property of Vail lying north of U.S. 6 was undeveloped, raw land; and it was through this area that I-70 was to be constructed. An arrangement had been worked out between the State and Vail that the portion of U.S. 6 lying outside of the I-70 right-of-way no longer needed for highway purposes would revert to Vail upon completion of I-70 through the Gore Valley area. This reversion consisted of approximately sixteen acres.

Although the condemnation proceedings were conducted before a commission of three freeholders, the court presided throughout the entire trial, ruling upon all issues and reducing the role of the commissioners to that of a jury.

Witnesses for both Vail and the State agreed that the highest and best use of the property being condemned was for an extension of the Vail ski area resort. Vail's evidence showed plans for the future development of a new ski area to be known as Lion's Head, which lay to the west of the existing Mill Creek area. Included in the development plans were the installation of additional ski lifts from the base of the Lion's Head area upward to new ski trails which eventually would be interconnected with the older development lying to the south and east. The plan envisioned a new commercial development radiating from the base of the new ski lifts, which would include uses similar to those existing in the Vail Village area. These plans were preliminary projections of the thinking of Vail as to the best utilization of the Lion's Head area; but in no sense of the word could they be considered finalized. No platting of this area had been accomplished, nor had streets been laid out or dedicated, nor had final engineering been undertaken or completed. Vail contended that there was an agreement with the State that Vail would deliberately postpone final planning, subdividing, and engineering until such time as the State definitely determined the route of I-70. The State disputed any such agreement. In any event the land over which I-70 was to cross was undeveloped and unplatted land.

The expert appraisers for both the State and Vail used the comparable sales approach, or market data approach. The appraisers disagreed sharply in their valuations. Vail's most generous appraiser placed the fair market value of the land taken at $1,508,000, or approximately $11,600 per acre, and the value of the U.S. 6 reversion at $363,600, or approximately $22,700 per acre; whereas the State expert was of the opinion that the taking was worth only $332,000, or approximately $2,570 per acre, and the reversion was worth $35,195, or approximately $2,000 per acre. The award of the commission was $1,378,096 for the taking, at the rate of about $10,930 per acre, and $335,694 for the reversion, at the rate of approximately $20,970 per acre.

The State contends prejudicial error was committed in several respects relating to the admission of evidence and, therefore, the commission's certificate of ascertainment and assessment should be set aside and the cause remanded for a new hearing. We agree, and discuss the specifications which we deem significant.

I.

The first contention relates to evidence consisting of two exhibits. The first, exhibit 17, depicted a hypothetical division of Vail's raw, undeveloped land into small areas or plots divided by hypothetical roads or streets. This exhibit was designated as 'Vail Village Lion's Head Land Use Plan.' It has been prepared by Vail's land planning consultant and represented the contemplated Lion's Head development heretofore discussed. It graphically depicted the highest and best use of this area, according to the testimony of Vail's witnesses. To each hypothetical plot was ascribed a certain land use, including such uses as for a shopping center, motels, lodges and apartments, highway services, condominiums, parking, medium-high density residential and hillside residential, etc.

The second exhibit, No. 18, captioned 'Vail Village Land Take and Reversion-Summary by Land Use and Location,' showed the right-of-way being condemned. On it were the hypothetical land uses as depicted on exhibit 17, traversed by the right-of-way. The amount of acreage being taken from each hypothetical use plot was set forth. For example, of the proposed shopping center use, exhibit 18 indicated the right-of-way took 3.186 acres; of the motel and highway services use, the right-of-way took 9.681 acres; etc. In addition, exhibit 18 showed land uses and acreages taken from each use in the eastern part of Gore Creek Valley, which were not shown on the Lion's Head Land Use Plan.

Vail's appraiser, Bresnahan, testified that in his opinion, considering the highest and best use as shown by exhibits 17 and 18, the total taking was worth $1,508,000. On cross-examination he indicated that he arrived at this figure by assigning a present market value per acre to each type of hypothetical use. He then determined how many acres of the particular use were being taken and multiplied the acreage by the hypothetical value assigned to that use. This figure was added together with those determined by this method for all other hypothetical use acreages taken, in order to arrive at the total market value of the right-of-way being condemned.

The State contends that the use of exhibits 17 and 18 and the testimony of Vail's appraiser, which assigned hypothetical use values to the use areas designated on the exhibits in order to arrive at the total value, is prohibited by the rule announced in *Schulhoff*. It is fundamental that evidence of the highest and best use to which the property may reasonably be applied in the future by men of ordinary prudence and judgment is admissible to assist the commission or jury in arriving at the present cash market value of the property being taken. Concerning the admission of the exhibits, we do not find any abuse of discretion in permitting the use of such exhibits to graphically illustrate and demonstrate the expert's opinion of the highest and best uses of the condemned property. We do not consider such to be forbidden by *Schulhoff*. The admission of such exhibits should be governed by the general rules relating to the use of demonstrative evidence.

However, *Schulhoff* expressly forbids the use of the method of valuation employed by Vail's appraiser:

> "Each of the appraisers agreed in the trial court that the highest and best use of Parcel No. 320 was for subdivision into residential building sites. The Schulhoffs' appraisers, however, were permitted to arrive at their opinions of the fair market value of Parcel No. 320 by hypothetically carving it up into residential building sites, estimating the value of each site, and then adding the estimated values of all the sites together. The State contends that this method of evaluation was improper and highly speculative. We agree and hold that the error in admitting such evidence was prejudicial."

We find no substantial difference in adding the individual values of Building sites to arrive at a total value, than, as was done here, in adding together individual values of Use areas as shown on exhibits 17 and 18 to arrive at a total value. The measure of compensation is not the aggregate of values of individual plots into which the tract taken could best be divided, but rather the value of the Whole tract as it exists at the time of the condemnation, taking into consideration its highest and best future use. A departure from the rule of *Schulhoff* would permit undue consideration by a commission or jury of speculative or prospective values based upon assumed future uses of the property being condemned. We hold that the opinion evidence of Vail's appraiser was rendered incompetent by reason of the method by which he arrived at his total valuation of the taking.

## II.

We further find that prejudicial error was committed in permitting the commission to hear and consider evidence of the sales of subdivided sites in Vail Village. It is quite apparent from the record that Vail's experts relied on these sales to bolster their estimate of value placed upon the respective use areas shown on exhibits 17 an 18, the total of which constituted their opinion of the value of the taking. One of Vail's appraisers, Mr. Bresnahan, stated, "I relied very much on a composite of the commercial sales, with the projection that a person, typical buyer that would buy the land that is in question here in this case, would know what he could eventually realize from the purchase of this land."

It is entirely permissible to show prices paid for other lands, provided the lands are similar in locality and character, and the sales are not too remote in point of time. It follows that when other so-called comparable sales are so dissimilar in respect to either locality, character of the lands involved, or remoteness in time, such other sales may not be shown and evidence thereof is incompetent and inadmissible. Whether such sales are sufficiently similar to be of probative value in aiding the fact finder in fixing the value of lands being taken is for the trial court to determine in the exercise of its sound discretion.

Vail's appraiser, Bresnahan, testified to 13 comparable sales of undeveloped, raw land in the Gore Creek Valley, all occurring within five years of the condemnation, and varying in size from 7.84 acres to 135 acres. All of these sales met the tests of comparability as to locality, character, and proximity in time. The price ranged from $700 per acre for the 135-acre tract to a high of $5,000 per acre for a 20-acre tract. However, the appraiser was then allowed, over objection, to testify concerning 23 sales of subdivided commercial, motel, lodge and condominium sites within Vail Village, which varied in size from a minimum of 294 square feet to a maximum of 99,273 square feet (2.279 acres). These sites sold for prices ranging from a low of $1.50 per square foot ($65,340 per acre) to a high of $5 per square foot ($217,800 per acre). In our view these sales of subdivided sites were clearly not comparable to the land being taken, because of the obvious differences in size, character, and development, and evidence as to such sales under the circumstances of this case was incompetent and inadmissible.

There may be situations where resort to the use of sales of subdivided sites is necessitated by a lack of comparable sales of undeveloped raw lands. However, such rule of necessity is not applicable here where there were available for comparison purposes thirteen comparable sales of undeveloped raw lands in the Gore Creek Valley.

## III.

The State further contends that prejudicial error occurred when the trial court permitted the use of a sale the price of which was enhanced by reason of the improvement being undertaken by the State, here the construction of an interchange on I-70. The particular sale was of a 3.22-acre parcel located at the southwest corner of one of the I-70 interchanges. This parcel was purchased by Vail HI (Holiday Inn) after the project had been announced and the plans for this improvement had been finalized. We agree that this sale included an enhancement of land value as a direct result of the highway improvement and, therefore, it becomes dissimilar for comparison purposes. A landowner is not entitled to recover an increase or enhancement in value of his land caused by the proposed improvement for which his land is being taken. Nor should a landowner be entitled to indirectly increase the value of his land being taken by comparing it with a sale of other land the value of which has been enhanced by the public improvement contemplated.

## IV.

As heretofore noted, the proceedings were conducted before a commission of three freeholders. The trial judge presided over the entire hearing, treating the commission in effect as a jury. Our statutes contemplate that in the absence of a request for a jury trial, eminent domain proceedings shall be conducted by a commission of three freeholders appointed by the court. It is not required that the trial judge preside at all of the meetings of the commission. Specifically, the duties of the court, in the absence of a jury, are initially to appoint the commissioners, administer the oath of office to them, fix the time and place of their first meeting, instruct them in writing as to their duties and, at the conclusion of the testimony, instruct them in writing as to the applicable and proper law to be followed by them in arriving at their ascertainment. The court shall upon request make rulings upon the propriety of the proofs and objections of the parties. It was not the intent of the statute that the judge of the court should preside over the commission proceedings in the same manner as he is required to do in a jury trial. Although this matter was not raised as error by either of the parties, we deem it advisable to direct attention to the specific duties enumerated in the statute in order that trial judges, faced with a series of eminent domain proceedings arising out of a continuing public works project such as the construction of I-70 across the state of Colorado, will not feel compelled to devote their entire time and attention to such proceedings to the exclusion of the ordinary business of the courts.

In view of our discussion hereinabove, we deem it unnecessary to consider any further alleged errors asserted by the State.

The certificate of ascertainment and assessment of the commission is hereby set aside and the cause remanded for a new trial consonant with the views expressed herein.

Note: Building an interstate highway is clearly an appropriate use for condemnation. Sometimes, however, there is a real issue as to whether the powers of condemnation have been used appropriately. Compare the results in the two following cases from the U.S. Supreme Court – one decided in 1954 and the other decided in 2005. What are the major factual differences between the two situations?

## SUPREME COURT OF THE UNITED STATES
## SAMUEL BERMAN AND SOLOMON H. FELDMAN, EXECUTORS OF THE ESTATE OF MAX R. MORRIS, DECEASED, APPELLANTS,
## V.
## ANDREW PARKER, JOHN A. REMON, JAMES E. COLLIFLOWER, ET AL.

### NOVEMBER 22, 1954

**Opinion**

Mr. Justice DOUGLAS delivered the opinion of the Court.

This is an appeal from the judgment of the District Court which dismissed a complaint seeking to enjoin the condemnation of appellants' property under the District of Columbia Redevelopment Act of 1945. The challenge was to the constitutionality of the Act, particularly as applied to the taking of appellants' property. The District Court sustained the constitutionality of the Act.

By Sec. 2 of the Act, Congress made a "legislative determination" that "owing to technological and sociological changes, obsolete lay-out, and other factors, conditions existing in the District of Columbia with respect to substandard housing and blighted areas, including the use of buildings in alleys as dwellings for human habitation, are injurious to the public health, safety, morals, and welfare, and it is hereby declared to be the policy of the United States to protect and promote the welfare of the inhabitants of the seat of the Government by eliminating all such injurious conditions by employing all means necessary and appropriate for the purpose."

Section 2 goes on to declare that acquisition of property is necessary to eliminate these housing conditions.

Section 4 creates the District of Columbia Redevelopment Land Agency (hereinafter called the Agency), composed of five members, which is granted power by Sec. 5(a) to acquire and assemble, by eminent domain and otherwise, real property for "the redevelopment of blighted territory in the District of Columbia and the prevention, reduction, or elimination of blighting factors or causes of blight."

After the real estate has been assembled, the Agency is authorized to transfer to public agencies the land to be devoted to such public purposes as streets, utilities, recreational facilities, and schools, Sec. 7(a), and to lease or sell the remainder as an entirety or in parts to a redevelopment company, individual, or partnership. Sec. 7(b), (f). The leases or sales must provide that the lessees or purchasers will carry out the redevelopment plan and that 'no use shall be made of any land or real property included in the lease or sale nor any building or structure erected thereon' which does not conform to the plan. Preference is to be given to private enterprise over public agencies in executing the redevelopment plan.

The first project undertaken under the Act relates to Project Area B in Southwest Washington, D.C. In 1950 the Planning Commission prepared and published a comprehensive plan for the District. Surveys revealed that in Area B, 64.3% of the dwellings were beyond repair, 18.4% needed major repairs, only 17.3% were satisfactory; 57.8% of the dwellings had outside toilets, 60.3% had no baths, 29.3% lacked electricity, 82.2% had no wash basins or laundry tubs, 83.8% lacked central heating. In the judgment of the District's Director of Health it was necessary to redevelop Area B in the interests of public health. The population of Area B amounted to 5,012 persons, of whom 97.5% were Negroes.

The plan for Area B specifies the boundaries and allocates the use of the land for various purposes. It makes detailed provisions for types of dwelling units and provides that at least one-third of them are to be low-rent housing with a maximum rental of $17 per room per month.

After a public hearing, the Commissioners approved the plan and the Planning Commission certified it to the Agency for execution. The Agency undertook the preliminary steps for redevelopment of the area when this suit was brought.

Appellants own property in Area B at 712 Fourth Street, S.W. It is not used as a dwelling or place of habitation. A department store is located on it. Appellants object to the appropriation of this property for the purposes of the project. They claim that their property may not to taken constitutionally for this project. It is commercial, not residential property; it is not slum housing; it will be put into the project under the management of a private, not a public, agency and redeveloped for private, not public, use. That is the argument; and the contention is that appellants' private property is being taken contrary to two mandates of the Fifth Amendment—(1) "No person shall be deprived of property, without due process of law"; (2) "nor shall private property be taken for public use, without just compensation." To take for the purpose of ridding the area of slums is one thing; it is quite another, the argument goes, to take a man's property merely to develop a better balanced, more attractive community. The District Court, while agreeing in general with that argument, saved the Act by construing it to mean that the Agency could condemn property only for the reasonable necessities of slum clearance and prevention, its concept of "slum" being the existence of conditions "injurious to the public health, safety, morals and welfare."

The power of Congress over the District of Columbia includes all the legislative powers which a state may exercise over its affairs. We deal, in other words, with what traditionally has been known as the police power. An attempt to define its reach or trace its outer limits is fruitless, for each case must turn on its own facts. The definition is essentially the product of legislative determinations addressed to the purposes of government, purposes neither abstractly nor historically capable of complete definition. Subject to specific constitutional limitations, when the legislature has spoken, the public interest has been declared in terms well-nigh conclusive. In such cases the legislature, not the judiciary, is the main guardian of the public needs to be served by social legislation, whether it be Congress legislating concerning the District of Columbia, or the States legislating concerning local affairs. This principle admits of no exception merely because the power of eminent domain is involved. The role of the judiciary in determining whether that power is being exercised for a public purpose is an extremely narrow one.

Public safety, public health, morality, peace and quiet, law and order—these are some of the more conspicuous examples of the traditional application of the police power to municipal affairs. Yet they merely illustrate the scope of the power and do not delimit it. Miserable and disreputable housing conditions may do more than spread disease and crime and immorality. They may also suffocate the spirit by reducing the people who live there to the status of cattle. They may indeed make living an almost insufferable burden. They may also be an ugly sore, a blight on the community which robs it of charm, which makes it a place from which men turn. The misery of housing may despoil a community as an open sewer may ruin a river.

We do not sit to determine whether a particular housing project is or is not desirable. The concept of the public welfare is broad and inclusive. The values it represents are spiritual as well as physical, aesthetic as well as monetary. It is within the power of the legislature to determine that the community should be beautiful as well as healthy, spacious as well as clean, well-balanced as well as carefully patrolled. In the present case, the Congress and its authorized agencies have made determinations that take into account a wide variety of values. It is not for us to reappraise them. If those who govern the District of Columbia decide that the Nation's Capital should be beautiful as well as sanitary, there is nothing in the Fifth Amendment that stands in the way.

Once the object is within the authority of Congress, the right to realize it through the exercise of eminent domain is clear. For the power of eminent domain is merely the means to the end. Once the object is within the authority of Congress, the means by which it will be attained is also for Congress to determine. Here one of the means chosen is the use of private enterprise for redevelopment of the area. Appellants argue that this makes the project a taking from one businessman for the benefit of another businessman. But the means of executing the project are for Congress and Congress alone to determine, once the public purpose has been established. The public end may be as well or better served through an agency of private enterprise than through a department of government—or so the Congress might conclude. We cannot say that public ownership is the sole method of promoting the public purposes of community redevelopment projects. What we have said also disposes of any contention concerning the fact that certain property owners in the area may be permitted to repurchase their properties for redevelopment in harmony with the overall plan. That, too, is a legitimate means which Congress and its agencies may adopt, if they choose.

In the present case, Congress and its authorized agencies attack the problem of the blighted parts of the community on an area rather than on a structure-by-structure basis. That, too, is opposed by appellants. They maintain that since their building does not imperil health or safety nor contribute to the making of a slum or a blighted area, it cannot be swept into a redevelopment plan by the mere dictum of the Planning Commission or the Commissioners. The particular uses to be made of the land in the project were determined with regard to the needs of the particular community. The experts concluded that if the community were to be healthy, if it were not to revert again to a blighted or slum area, as though possessed of a congenital disease, the area must be planned as a whole. It was not enough, they believed, to remove existing buildings that were insanitary or unsightly. It was important to redesign the whole area so as to eliminate the conditions that cause slums—the overcrowding of dwellings, the lack of parks, the lack of adequate streets and alleys, the absence of recreational areas, the lack of light and air, the presence of outmoded street patterns. It was believed that the piecemeal approach, the removal of individual structures that were offensive, would be only a palliative. The entire area needed redesigning so that a balanced, integrated plan could be developed for the region, including not only new homes but also schools, churches, parks, streets, and shopping centers. In this way it was hoped that the cycle of decay of the area could be controlled and the birth of future slums prevented. Such diversification in future use is plainly relevant to the maintenance of the desired housing standards and therefore within congressional power.

The District Court below suggested that, if such a broad scope were intended for the statute, the standards contained in the Act would not be sufficiently definite to sustain the delegation of authority. We do not agree. We think the standards prescribed were adequate for executing the plan to eliminate not only slums as narrowly defined by the District Court but also the blighted areas that tend to produce slums. Property may of course be taken for this redevelopment which, standing by itself, is innocuous and unoffending. But we have said enough to indicate that it is the need of the area as a whole which Congress and its agencies are evaluating. If owner after owner were permitted to resist these redevelopment programs on the ground that his particular property was not being used against the public interest, integrated plans for redevelopment would suffer greatly. The argument pressed on us is, indeed, a plea to substitute the landowner's standard of the public need for the standard prescribed by Congress. But as we have already stated, community redevelopment programs need not, by force of the Constitution, be on a piecemeal basis—lot by lot, building by building.

It is not for the courts to oversee the choice of the boundary line nor to sit in review on the size of a particular project area. Once the question of the public purpose has been decided, the amount and character of land to be taken for the project and the need for a particular tract to complete the integrated plan rests in the discretion of the legislative branch.

The District Court indicated grave doubts concerning the Agency's right to take full title to the land as distinguished from the objectionable buildings located on it. We do not share those doubts. If the Agency considers it necessary in carrying out the redevelopment project to take full title to the real property involved, it may do so. It is not for the courts to determine whether it is necessary for successful consummation of the project that unsafe, unsightly, or insanitary buildings alone be taken or whether title to the land be included, any more than it is the function of the courts to sort and choose among the various parcels selected for condemnation.

The rights of these property owners are satisfied when they receive that just compensation which the Fifth Amendment exacts as the price of the taking.

The judgment of the District Court, as modified by this opinion, is affirmed.

Affirmed.

The following U.S. Supreme Court case was the subject of a very good book, called "The Little Pink House," and a documentary film in 2018 based on the book, and having the same title. Both show the human cost of condemnations. One interesting aspect of the book was the description of how the plaintiffs, (Kelo and friends), obtained some valuable information for the litigation by "dumpster diving." Entities defending the actions of the city put some important documents into black trash bags, without shredding the documents, and then tossed the trash bags into a dumpster. The trash bags, and valuable information, were later retrieved by people on Kelo's side.

## SUPREME COURT OF THE UNITED STATES
## SUSETTE KELO, ET AL., PETITIONERS,
## V.
## CITY OF NEW LONDON, CONNECTICUT, ET AL.

### JUNE 23, 2005

**Opinion**

Justice STEVENS delivered the opinion of the Court.

In 2000, the city of New London approved a development plan that, in the words of the Supreme Court of Connecticut, was "projected to create in excess of 1,000 jobs, to increase tax and other revenues, and to revitalize an economically distressed city, including its downtown and waterfront areas." In assembling the land needed for this project, the city's development agent has purchased property from willing sellers and proposes to use the power of eminent domain to acquire the remainder of the property from unwilling owners in exchange for just compensation. The question presented is whether the city's proposed disposition of this property qualifies as a "public use" within the meaning of the Takings Clause of the Fifth Amendment to the Constitution.

The city of New London (hereinafter City) sits at the junction of the Thames River and the Long Island Sound in southeastern Connecticut. Decades of economic decline led a state agency in 1990 to designate the City a "distressed municipality." In 1996, the Federal Government closed the Naval Undersea Warfare Center, which had been located in the Fort Trumbull area of the City and had employed over 1,500 people. In 1998, the City's unemployment rate was nearly double that of the State, and its population of just under 24,000 residents was at its lowest since 1920.

These conditions prompted state and local officials to target New London, and particularly its Fort Trumbull area, for economic revitalization. To this end, respondent New London Development Corporation (NLDC), a private nonprofit entity established some years earlier to assist the City in planning economic development, was reactivated. In January 1998, the State authorized a $5.35 million bond issue to support the NLDC's planning activities and a $10 million bond issue toward the creation of a Fort Trumbull State Park. In February, the pharmaceutical company Pfizer Inc. announced that it would build a $300 million research facility on a site immediately adjacent to Fort Trumbull; local planners hoped that Pfizer would draw new business to the area, thereby serving as a catalyst to the area's rejuvenation. After receiving initial approval from the city council, the NLDC continued its planning activities and held a series of neighborhood meetings to educate the public about the process.

The Fort Trumbull area is situated on a peninsula that juts into the Thames River. The area comprises approximately 115 privately owned properties, as well as the 32 acres of land formerly occupied by the naval facility (Trumbull State Park now occupies 18 of those 32 acres). The development plan encompasses seven parcels. Parcel 1 is designated for a waterfront conference hotel at the center of a "small urban village" that will include restaurants and shopping. This parcel will also have marinas for both recreational and commercial uses. A pedestrian "riverwalk" will originate here and continue down the coast, connecting the waterfront areas of the development. Parcel 2 will be the site of approximately 80 new residences organized into an urban neighborhood and linked by a public walkway to the remainder of the development, including the state park. This parcel also includes space reserved for a new U.S. Coast Guard Museum. Parcel 3, which is located immediately north of the Pfizer facility, will contain at least 90,000 square feet of research and development office space. Parcel 4A is a 2.4–acre site that will be used either to support the adjacent state park, by providing parking or retail services for visitors, or to support the nearby marina. Parcel 4B will include a renovated marina, as well as the final stretch of the riverwalk. Parcels 5, 6, and 7 will provide land for office and retail space, parking, and water-dependent commercial uses.

The NLDC intended the development plan to capitalize on the arrival of the Pfizer facility and the new commerce it was expected to attract. In addition to creating jobs, generating tax revenue, and helping to "build momentum for the revitalization of downtown New London," the plan was also designed to make the City more attractive and to create leisure and recreational opportunities on the waterfront and in the park.

The city council approved the plan in January 2000, and designated the NLDC as its development agent in charge of implementation. The city council also authorized the NLDC to purchase property or to acquire property by exercising eminent domain in the City's name. The NLDC successfully negotiated the purchase of most of the real estate in the 90–acre area, but its negotiations with petitioners failed. As a consequence, in November 2000, the NLDC initiated the condemnation proceedings that gave rise to this case.

## II

Petitioner Susette Kelo has lived in the Fort Trumbull area since 1997. She has made extensive improvements to her house, which she prizes for its water view. Petitioner Wilhelmina Dery was born in her Fort Trumbull house in 1918 and has lived there her entire life. Her husband Charles (also a petitioner) has lived in the house since they married some 60 years ago. In all, the nine petitioners own 15 properties in Fort Trumbull—4 in parcel 3 of the development plan and 11 in parcel 4A. Ten of the parcels are occupied by the owner or a family member; the other five are held as investment properties. There is no allegation that any of these properties is blighted or otherwise in poor condition; rather, they were condemned only because they happen to be located in the development area.

In December 2000, petitioners brought this action in the New London Superior Court. The Superior Court granted a permanent restraining order prohibiting the taking of the properties located in parcel 4A (park or marina support). It, however, denied petitioners relief as to the properties located in parcel 3 (office space).

Both sides took appeals to the Supreme Court of Connecticut. That court held that all of the City's proposed takings were valid.

We granted certiorari to determine whether a city's decision to take property for the purpose of economic development satisfies the "public use" requirement of the Fifth Amendment.

## III

Two polar propositions are perfectly clear. On the one hand, it has long been accepted that the sovereign may not take the property of *A* for the sole purpose of transferring it to another private party *B*, even though *A* is paid just compensation. On the other hand, it is equally clear that a State may transfer property from one private party to another if future "use by the public" is the purpose of the taking. The condemnation of land for a railroad with common-carrier duties is a familiar example. Neither of these propositions, however, determines the disposition of this case.

As for the first proposition, the City would no doubt be forbidden from taking petitioners' land for the purpose of conferring a private benefit on a particular private party. Nor would the City be allowed to take property under the mere pretext of a public purpose, when its actual purpose was to bestow a private benefit. The takings before us, however, would be executed pursuant to a "carefully considered" development plan.

On the other hand, this is not a case in which the City is planning to open the condemned land—at least not in its entirety—to use by the general public. This Court long ago rejected any literal requirement that condemned property be put into use for the general public. Indeed, while many state courts in the mid-19th century endorsed "use by the public" as the proper definition of public use, that narrow view steadily eroded over time. Not only was the "use by the public" test difficult to administer (e.g., what proportion of the public need have access to the property? at what price?), but it proved to be impractical given the diverse and always evolving needs of society. Accordingly, when this Court began applying the Fifth Amendment to the States at the close of the 19th century, it embraced the broader and more natural interpretation of public use as "public purpose." Thus, in a case upholding a mining company's use of an aerial bucket line to transport ore over property it did not own, Justice Holmes' opinion for the Court stressed "the inadequacy of use by the general public as a universal test." We have repeatedly and consistently rejected that narrow test ever since.

The disposition of this case therefore turns on the question whether the City's development plan serves a "public purpose." Without exception, our cases have defined that concept broadly, reflecting our longstanding policy of deference to legislative judgments in this field.

In *Hawaii Housing Authority v. Midkiff,* (1984), the Court considered a Hawaii statute whereby fee title was taken from lessors and transferred to lessees (for just compensation) in order to reduce the concentration of land ownership. We unanimously upheld the statute and rejected the Ninth Circuit's view that it was "a naked attempt on the part of the state of Hawaii to take the property of A and transfer it to B solely for B's private use and benefit." Reaffirming *Berman's* deferential approach to legislative judgments in this field, we concluded that the State's purpose of eliminating the "social and economic evils of a land oligopoly" qualified as a valid public use. Our opinion also rejected the contention that the mere fact that the State immediately transferred the properties to private individuals upon condemnation somehow diminished the public character of the taking. "It is only the taking's purpose, and not its mechanics," we explained, that matters in determining public use.

Viewed as a whole, our jurisprudence has recognized that the needs of society have varied between different parts of the Nation, just as they have evolved over time in response to changed circumstances. Our earliest cases in particular embodied a strong theme of federalism, emphasizing the "great respect" that we owe to state legislatures and state courts in discerning local public needs. For more than a century, our public use jurisprudence has wisely eschewed rigid formulas and intrusive scrutiny in favor of affording legislatures broad latitude in determining what public needs justify the use of the takings power.

## IV

Those who govern the City were not confronted with the need to remove blight in the Fort Trumbull area, but their determination that the area was sufficiently distressed to justify a program of economic rejuvenation is entitled to our deference. The City has carefully formulated an economic development plan that it believes will provide appreciable benefits to the community, including—but by no means limited to—new jobs and increased tax revenue. As with other exercises in urban planning and development, the City is endeavoring to coordinate a variety of commercial, residential, and recreational uses of land, with the hope that they will form a whole greater than the sum of its parts. To effectuate this plan, the City has invoked a state statute that specifically authorizes the use of eminent domain to promote economic development. Given the comprehensive character of the plan, the thorough deliberation that preceded its adoption, and the limited scope of our review, it is appropriate for us, as it was in *Berman,* to resolve the challenges of the individual owners, not on a piecemeal basis, but rather in light of the entire plan. Because that plan unquestionably serves a public purpose, the takings challenged here satisfy the public use requirement of the Fifth Amendment.

To avoid this result, petitioners urge us to adopt a new bright-line rule that economic development does not qualify as a public use. Putting aside the unpersuasive suggestion that the City's plan will provide only purely economic benefits, neither precedent nor logic supports petitioners' proposal. Promoting economic development is a traditional and long-accepted function of government. There is, moreover, no principled way of distinguishing economic development from the other public purposes that we have recognized. In our cases upholding takings that facilitated agriculture and mining, for example, we emphasized the importance of those industries to the welfare of the States in question. It would be incongruous to hold that the City's interest in the economic benefits to be derived from the development of the Fort Trumbull area has less of a public character than any of those other interests. Clearly, there is no basis for exempting economic development from our traditionally broad understanding of public purpose.

Petitioners contend that using eminent domain for economic development imper-missibly blurs the boundary between public and private takings. Again, our cases foreclose this objection. Quite simply, the government's pursuit of a public purpose will often benefit individual private parties. For example, in *Midkiff,* the forced trans-fer of property conferred a direct and significant benefit on those lessees who were previously unable to purchase their homes

It is further argued that without a bright-line rule nothing would stop a city from transferring citizen *A*'s property to citizen *B* for the sole reason that citizen *B* will put the property to a more productive use and thus pay more taxes. Such a one-to-one transfer of property, executed outside the confines of an integrated development plan, is not presented in this case. While such an unusual exercise of government power would certainly raise a suspicion that a private purpose was afoot, the hypo-thetical cases posited by petitioners can be confronted if and when they arise. They do not warrant the crafting of an artificial restriction on the concept of public use.

Alternatively, petitioners maintain that for takings of this kind we should require a "reasonable certainty" that the expected public benefits will actually accrue. Such a rule, however, would represent an even greater departure from our precedent. "When the legislature's purpose is legitimate and its means are not irrational, our cases make clear that empirical debates over the wisdom of takings—no less than debates over the wisdom of other kinds of socioeconomic legislation—are not to be carried out in the federal courts."

Just as we decline to second-guess the City's considered judgments about the efficacy of its development plan, we also decline to second-guess the City's deter-minations as to what lands it needs to acquire in order to effectuate the project. "It is not for the courts to oversee the choice of the boundary line nor to sit in review on the size of a particular project area. Once the question of the public purpose has been decided, the amount and character of land to be taken for the project and the need for a particular tract to complete the integrated plan rests in the discretion of the legislative branch." *Berman.*

In affirming the City's authority to take petitioners' properties, we do not mini-mize the hardship that condemnations may entail, notwithstanding the payment of just compensation. We emphasize that nothing in our opinion precludes any State from placing further restrictions on its exercise of the takings power. Indeed, many States already impose "public use" requirements that are stricter than the federal baseline. Some of these requirements have been established as a matter of state con-stitutional law, while others are expressed in state eminent domain statutes that care-fully limit the grounds upon which takings may be exercised. As the submissions of the parties and their *amici* make clear, the necessity and wisdom of using eminent domain to promote economic development are certainly matters of legitimate public debate. This Court's authority, however, extends only to determining whether the City's proposed condemnations are for a "public use" within the meaning of the Fifth Amendment to the Federal Constitution. Because over a century of our case law interpreting that provision dictates an affirmative answer to that question, we may not grant petitioners the relief that they seek.

The judgment of the Supreme Court of Connecticut is affirmed.

*It is so ordered.*

Note: After the Kelo case, there was such widespread reaction against this use of condemnation that a number of states enacted laws to prohibit such things. Within a few years, Pfizer, for whom the redevelopment had been expected to be attractive, moved out of New London.

# CHAPTER THIRTEEN

# REGULATORY TAKINGS

## INTRODUCTION

Sometimes land use regulations imposed by a federal, state, or local government go so far as to constitute a taking – even though title to the land does not actually pass to the governmental entity. The governmental regulations just make the land virtually worthless to the landowner – so that all the landowner has left is legal title to the land – and the obligation to pay taxes.

There is no bright line as to when a regulation crosses the line, and becomes a taking – except when the regulation constitutes a permanent physical invasion.

This chapter includes a sample of the most-well known *regulatory takings* cases – in chronological order, (except for the first case). Each case is still good law, and in each case the U.S. Supreme Court declines to make any bright-line rules. Each individual case must be decided on its own merits – when the landowner has sufficient financial resources to take the matter to the U.S. Supreme Court.

As you read the cases in this chapter, the following case, *Loretto v. Teleprompter,* will probably become your favorite case, though every case in the chapter presents interesting issues.

# SUPREME COURT OF THE UNITED STATES
## JEAN LORETTO, FOR HERSELF AND ALL OTHERS SIMILARLY SITUATED, APPELLANT
### V.
## TELEPROMPTER MANHATTAN CATV CORP. ET AL.

JUNE 30, 1982

Justice MARSHALL delivered the opinion of the Court. ⌐ *Issue*

This case presents the question (whether a minor but permanent physical occupation of an owner's property authorized by government constitutes a "taking" of property for which just compensation is due under the Fifth and Fourteenth Amendments of the Constitution.) New York law provides that a landlord must permit a cable television company to install its cable facilities upon his property. [In this case, the cable installation occupied portions of appellant's roof and the side of her building.] (The New York Court of Appeals ruled that this appropriation does not amount to a taking. Because we conclude that such a physical occupation of property is a taking, we reverse.]

## I

Appellant Jean Loretto purchased a five-story apartment building located at 303 West 105th Street, New York City, in 1971. The previous owner had granted appellees Teleprompter Corp. and Teleprompter Manhattan CATV (collectively Teleprompter) permission to install a cable on the building and the exclusive privilege of furnishing cable television (CATV) services to the tenants. The New York Court of Appeals described the installation as follows:

> "On June 1, 1970 TelePrompter installed a cable slightly less than one-half inch in diameter and of approximately 30 feet in length along the length of the building about 18 inches above the roof top, and directional taps, approximately 4 inches by 4 inches by 4 inches, on the front and rear of the roof. By June 8, 1970 the cable had been extended another 4 to 6 feet and cable had been run from the directional taps to the adjoining building at 305 West 105th Street."

Teleprompter also installed two large silver boxes, [each about the size of a bread box], along the roof cables. The cables are attached by screws or nails penetrating the masonry at approximately two-foot intervals, and other equipment is installed by bolts.

Initially, Teleprompter's roof cables did not service appellant's building. They were part of what could be described as a cable "highway" circumnavigating the city block, with service cables periodically dropped over the front or back of a building in which a tenant desired service. Crucial to such a network is the use of so-called "crossovers" - cable lines extending from one building to another in order to reach a new group of tenants. Two years after appellant purchased the building, Teleprompter connected a "noncrossover" line-*i.e.*, one that provided CATV service to appellant's own tenants - by dropping a line to the first floor down the front of appellant's building.

Prior to 1973, Teleprompter routinely obtained authorization for its installations from property owners along the cable's route, compensating the owners at the standard rate of 5% of the gross revenues that Teleprompter realized from the particular property. To facilitate tenant access to CATV, the State of New York enacted § 828 of the Executive Law, effective January 1, 1973. Section 828 provides that a landlord may not "interfere with the installation of cable television facilities upon his property or premises," and may not demand payment from any tenant for permitting CATV, or *Blue* → demand payment from any CATV company "in excess of any amount which the State Commission on Cable Television shall, by regulation, determine to be reasonable." The landlord may, however, require the CATV company or the tenant to bear the cost of installation and indemnify the landlord for any damage caused by the installation. Pursuant to § 828(1)(b), the State Commission has ruled that a one-time $1 payment is the normal fee to which a landlord is entitled.

The Commission ruled that this nominal fee, which the Commission concluded was equivalent to what the landlord would receive if the property were condemned pursuant to New York's Transportation Corporations Law, satisfied constitutional requirements "in the absence of a special showing of greater damages attributable to the taking."

Appellant did not discover the existence of the cable until after she had purchased the building. She brought a class action against Teleprompter in 1976 on behalf of all owners of real property in the State on which Teleprompter has placed CATV components, alleging that Teleprompter's installation was a trespass and, insofar as it relied on § 828, a taking without just compensation. She requested damages and injunctive relief.

Appellee City of New York, which has granted Teleprompter an exclusive franchise to provide CATV within certain areas of Manhattan, intervened. The Supreme Court, Special Term, granted summary judgment to Teleprompter and the city, upholding the constitutionality of § 828 in both crossover and noncrossover situations. The

Appellate Division affirmed without opinion. On appeal, the Court of Appeals, over dissent, upheld the statute.

We noted probable jurisdiction.

## II

When faced with a constitutional challenge to a permanent physical occupation of real property, this Court has invariably found a taking. As early as 1872, in *Pumpelly v. Green Bay Co.* this Court held that the defendant's construction, pursuant to state authority, of a dam which permanently flooded plaintiff's property constituted a taking. A unanimous Court stated, without qualification, that "where real estate is actually invaded by additions of water, earth, sand, or other material, or by having any artificial structure placed on it, so as to effectually destroy or impair its usefulness, it is a taking, within the meaning of the Constitution." Seven years later, the Court reemphasized the importance of a physical occupation by distinguishing a regulation that merely restricted the use of private property. In *Northern Transportation Co. v. Chicago*, (1879), the Court held that the city's construction of a temporary dam in a river to permit construction of a tunnel was not a taking, even though the plaintiffs were thereby denied access to their premises, because the obstruction only impaired the use of plaintiffs' property. The Court distinguished earlier cases in which permanent flooding of private property was regarded as a taking, *e.g., Pumpelly*, as involving "a physical invasion of the real estate of the private owner, and a practical ouster of his possession."

Since these early cases, this Court has consistently distinguished between flooding cases involving a permanent physical occupation, on the one hand, and cases involving a more temporary invasion, or government action outside the owner's property that causes consequential damages within, on the other. A taking has always been found only in the former situation.

Two wartime takings cases are also instructive. In *United States v. Pewee Coal Co.*, the Court unanimously held that the Government's seizure and direction of operation of a coal mine to prevent a national strike of coal miners constituted a taking, though members of the Court differed over which losses suffered during the period of Government control were compensable. The plurality had little difficulty concluding that because there had been an "actual taking of possession and control," the taking was as clear as if the Government held full title and ownership. In *United States v. Central Eureka Mining Co.* by contrast, the Court found no taking where the Government had issued a wartime order requiring nonessential gold mines to cease operations for the purpose of conserving equipment and manpower for use in mines more essential to the war effort. Over dissenting Justice Harlan's complaint that "as a practical matter the Order led to consequences no different from those that would have followed the temporary acquisition of physical possession of these mines by the United States," the Court reasoned that "the Government did not occupy, use, or in any manner take physical possession of the gold mines or of the equipment connected with them." The Court concluded that the temporary though severe restriction on *use* of the mines was justified by the exigency of war.

In *Kaiser Aetna* the Court held that the Government's imposition of a navigational servitude requiring public access to a pond was a taking where the landowner had reasonably relied on Government consent in connecting the pond to navigable water. The Court emphasized that the servitude took the landowner's right to exclude, "one of the most essential sticks in the bundle of rights that are commonly characterized as property."

Although the easement of passage, not being a permanent occupation of land, was not considered a taking *per se, Kaiser Aetna* reemphasizes that a physical invasion is a government intrusion of an unusually serious character.

In short, when the "character of the governmental action," is a permanent physical occupation of property, our cases uniformly have found a taking to the extent of the occupation, without regard to whether the action achieves an important public benefit or has only minimal economic impact on the owner.

### B

The historical rule that a permanent physical occupation of another's property is a taking has more than tradition to commend it. Such an appropriation is perhaps the most serious form of invasion of an owner's property interests. To borrow a metaphor, the government does not simply take a single "strand" from the "bundle" of property rights: it chops through the bundle, taking a slice of every strand.

Property rights in a physical thing have been described as the rights "to possess, use and dispose of it." To the extent that the government permanently occupies physical property, it effectively destroys *each* of these rights. First, the owner has no right to possess the occupied space himself, and also has no power to exclude the occupier from possession and use of the space. The power to exclude has traditionally been considered one of the most treasured strands in an owner's bundle of property rights. Second, the permanent physical occupation of property forever denies the owner any power to control the use of the property; he not only cannot exclude others, but can make no nonpossessory use of the property. Although deprivation of the right to use and obtain a profit from property is not, in every case, independently sufficient to establish a taking, it is clearly relevant. Finally, even though the owner may retain the bare legal right to dispose of the occupied space by transfer or sale, the permanent occupation of that space by a stranger will ordinarily empty the right of any value, since the purchaser will also be unable to make any use of the property. ] ]

Our holding today in no way alters the analysis governing the State's power to require landlords to comply with building codes and provide utility connections, mailboxes, smoke detectors, fire extinguishers, and the like in the common area of a building. So long as these regulations do not require the landlord to suffer the physical occupation of a portion of his building by a third party, they will be analyzed under the multifactor inquiry generally applicable to nonpossessory governmental activity.

## III

Our holding today is very narrow. We affirm the traditional rule that a permanent physical occupation of property is a taking. In such a case, the property owner entertains a historically rooted expectation of compensation, and the character of the invasion is qualitatively more intrusive than perhaps any other category of property regulation. We do not, however, question the equally substantial authority upholding a State's broad power to impose appropriate restrictions upon an owner's *use* of his property.

Furthermore, our conclusion that § 828 works a taking of a portion of appellant's property does not presuppose that the fee which many landlords had obtained from Teleprompter prior to the law's enactment is a proper measure of the value of the property taken. The issue of the amount of compensation that is due, on which we express no opinion, is a matter for the state courts to consider on remand.

The judgment of the New York Court of Appeals is reversed, and the case is remanded for further proceedings not inconsistent with this opinion. ]

*It is so ordered.*

Note: The following case, *Penn Central*, is the case which is considered to have set the standard for contemporary issues regarding regulatory takings. The case describes a number of prior U.S. Supreme Court cases in which the court *upheld* regulations of private property which actually destroyed all financially beneficial uses of the property – without giving the owner any right to payment for the damages inflicted by the regulations. The court admits that there is no bright line distinguishing between when a regulation is constitutional, and when the regulation has simply gone too far. The case sets forth various factors which should be considered when making a decision – as each case is decided on an individual basis.

When *Penn Central* was decided, the discussion of TDRs (transferrable development rights), was what caught the most attention. Now the most enduring concept is that the property must be considered on the basis of the "parcel as a whole." The final case in this chapter, *Murr v. Wisconsin* (2017), adds some complexity to that concept of the "parcel as a whole."

As you read this case, notice what the process is for designating a building, or area, as one that should be preserved because of the benefits of historic preservation. How many people decide whether or not a building should be given "landmark" designation? Are those people elected?

## SUPREME COURT OF THE UNITED STATES
## PENN CENTRAL TRANSPORTATION COMPANY ET AL., APPELLANTS,
## V.
## CITY OF NEW YORK ET AL.

JUNE 26, 1978

### Opinion

Mr. Justice BRENNAN delivered the opinion of the Court.

The question presented is whether a city may, as part of a comprehensive program to preserve historic landmarks and historic districts, place restrictions on the development of individual historic landmarks—in addition to those imposed by applicable zoning ordinances—without effecting a "taking" requiring the payment of "just compensation." Specifically, we must decide whether the application of New York City's Landmarks Preservation Law to the parcel of land occupied by Grand Central Terminal has "taken" its owners' property in violation of the Fifth and Fourteenth Amendments.

Over the past 50 years, all 50 States and over 500 municipalities have enacted laws to encourage or require the preservation of buildings and areas with historic or aesthetic importance. These nationwide legislative efforts have been precipitated by two concerns. The first is recognition that, in recent years, large numbers of historic structures, landmarks, and areas have been destroyed without adequate consideration of either the values represented therein or the possibility of preserving the destroyed properties for use in economically productive ways. The second is a widely shared belief that structures with special historic, cultural, or architectural significance enhance the quality of life for all.] Not only do these buildings and their workmanship represent the lessons of the past and embody precious features of our heritage, they serve as examples of quality for today. "Historic conservation is but one aspect of the much larger problem, basically an environmental one, of enhancing—or perhaps developing for the first time—the quality of life for people."

New York City, responding to similar concerns and acting pursuant to a New York State enabling Act, adopted its Landmarks Preservation Law in 1965. The city acted from the conviction that "the standing of New York City as a world-wide tourist center and world capital of business, culture and government" would be threatened if legislation were not enacted to protect historic landmarks and neighborhoods from precipitate decisions to destroy or fundamentally alter their character. The city believed that comprehensive measures to safeguard desirable features of the existing urban fabric would benefit its citizens in a variety of ways: e. g., "fostering civic pride in the beauty and noble accomplishments of the past; protecting and enhancing the city's attractions to tourists and visitors; supporting and stimulating business and industry; strengthening the economy of the city; and promoting the use of historic districts, landmarks, interior landmarks and scenic landmarks for the education, pleasure and welfare of the people of the city."

[The New York City law is typical of many urban landmark laws in that its primary method of achieving its goals is not by acquisitions of historic properties, but rather by involving public entities in land-use decisions affecting these properties and providing services, standards, controls, and incentives that will encourage preservation by private owners and users. While the law does place special restrictions on landmark properties as a necessary feature to the attainment of its larger objectives, the major theme of the law is to ensure the owners of any such properties both a "reasonable return" on their investments and maximum latitude to use their parcels for purposes not inconsistent with the preservation goals.]

→ maybe blue?

The operation of the law can be briefly summarized. The primary responsibility for administering the law is vested in the Landmarks Preservation Commission (Commission), a broad based, 11-member agency assisted by a technical staff. The Commission first performs the function of identifying properties and areas that have "a special character or special historical or aesthetic interest or value as part of the development, heritage or cultural characteristics of the city, state or nation." If the Commission determines, after giving all interested parties an opportunity to be heard, that a building or area satisfies the ordinance's criteria, it will designate a building to be a "landmark," or will designate an area to be a "historic district."

Thus far, 31 historic districts and over 400 individual landmarks have been finally designated, and the process is a continuing one.

Final designation as a landmark results in restrictions upon the property owner's options concerning use of the landmark site. First, the law imposes a duty upon the owner to keep the exterior features of the building "in good repair" to assure that the law's objectives not be defeated by the landmark's falling into a state of irremediable disrepair. Second, the Commission must approve in advance any proposal to alter the exterior architectural features of the landmark or to construct any exterior improvement on the landmark site, thus ensuring that decisions concerning construction on the landmark site are made with due consideration of both the public interest in the maintenance of the structure and the landowner's interest in use of the property.

Although the designation of a landmark and landmark site restricts the owner's control over the parcel, designation also enhances the economic position of the landmark owner in one significant respect. Under New York City's zoning laws, owners of real property who have not developed their property to the full extent permitted by the applicable zoning laws are allowed to transfer development rights to contiguous parcels on the same city block - to include lots "across a street and opposite to another lot or lots which, except for the intervention of streets or street intersections, form a series extending to the lot occupied by the landmark building , provided that all lots are in the same ownership."

This case involves the application of New York City's Landmarks Preservation Law to Grand Central Terminal (Terminal). The Terminal, which is owned by the Penn Central Transportation Co. and its affiliates (Penn Central), is one of New York City's most famous buildings. Opened in 1913, it is regarded not only as providing an ingenious engineering solution to the problems presented by urban railroad stations, but also as a magnificent example of the French beaux-arts style.

The Terminal is located in midtown Manhattan. Its south facade faces 42nd Street and that street's intersection with Park Avenue. At street level, the Terminal is bounded on the west by Vanderbilt Avenue, on the east by the Commodore Hotel, and on the north by the Pan-American Building. Although a 20-story office tower, to have been located above the Terminal, was part of the original design, the planned tower was never constructed. The Terminal itself is an eight-story structure which Penn Central uses as a railroad station and in which it rents space not needed for railroad purposes to a variety of commercial interests. The Terminal is one of a number of properties owned by appellant Penn Central in this area of midtown Manhattan. The others include the Barclay, Biltmore, Commodore, Roosevelt, and Waldorf-Astoria Hotels, the Pan-American Building and other office buildings along Park Avenue, and the Yale Club. At least eight of these are eligible to be recipients of development rights afforded the Terminal by virtue of landmark designation.

[On August 2, 1967, following a public hearing, the Commission designated the Terminal a "landmark" and designated the site it occupies a "landmark site." The Board of Estimate confirmed this action on September 21, 1967. On January 22, 1968, appellant Penn Central, to increase its income, entered into a renewable 50-year lease and sublease agreement with appellant UGP Properties, Inc. (UGP), a wholly owned subsidiary of Union General Properties, Ltd., a United Kingdom corporation. Under the terms of the agreement, UGP was to construct a multistory office building above the Terminal. UGP promised to pay Penn Central $1 million annually during construction and at least $3 million annually thereafter. The rentals would be offset in part by a loss of some $700,000 to $1 million in net rentals presently received from concessionaires displaced by the new building. Appellants UGP and Penn Central then applied to the Commission for permission to construct an office building atop the Terminal.]

Two separate plans, both designed by architect Marcel Breuer and both apparently satisfying the terms of the applicable zoning ordinance, were submitted to the Commission for approval. The first, Breuer I, provided for the construction of a 55-story office building, to be cantilevered above the existing facade and to rest on the roof of the Terminal. The second, Breuer II Revised, called for tearing down a portion of the Terminal that included the 42nd Street facade, stripping off some of the remaining features of the Terminal's facade, and constructing a 53-story office building. The Commission denied a certificate of no exterior effect. The Commission's reasons for rejecting certificates respecting Breuer II Revised are summarized in the following statement: "To protect a Landmark, one does not tear it down. To perpetuate its architectural features, one does not strip them off."

Quite simply, the tower would overwhelm the Terminal by its sheer mass. The "addition" would be four times as high as the existing structure and would reduce the Landmark itself to the status of a curiosity.

"Landmarks cannot be divorced from their settings—particularly when the setting is a dramatic and integral part of the original concept. The Terminal, in its setting, is a great example of urban design. Such examples are not so plentiful in New York City that we can afford to lose any of the few we have."

Appellants filed suit in New York Supreme Court, Trial Term, claiming, *inter alia*, that the application of the Landmarks Preservation Law had "taken" their property without just compensation in violation of the Fifth and Fourteenth Amendments and arbitrarily deprived them of their property without due process of law in violation of the Fourteenth Amendment. Appellants sought a declaratory judgment, injunctive relief barring the city from using the Landmarks Law to impede the construction of any structure that might otherwise lawfully be constructed on the Terminal site, and damages for the "temporary taking" that occurred between August 2, 1967, the designation date, and the date when the restrictions arising from the Landmarks Law would be lifted. The trial court granted the injunctive and declaratory relief, but severed the question of damages for a "temporary taking."

Appellees appealed, and the New York Supreme Court, Appellate Division, reversed. The New York Court of Appeals affirmed. Appellants filed a notice of appeal in this Court. We noted probable jurisdiction. We affirm.

The issues presented by appellants are (1) whether the restrictions imposed by New York City's law upon appellants' exploitation of the Terminal site effect a "taking" of appellants' property for a public use within the meaning of the Fifth Amendment, which of course is made applicable to the States through the Fourteenth Amendment, and, (2), if so, whether the transferable development rights afforded appellants constitute "just compensation" within the meaning of the Fifth Amendment. We need only address the question whether a "taking" has occurred.

The question of what constitutes a "taking" for purposes of the Fifth Amendment has proved to be a problem of considerable difficulty. While this Court has recognized that the "Fifth Amendment's guarantee is designed to bar Government from forcing some people alone to bear public burdens which, in all fairness and justice, should be borne by the public as a whole," this Court, quite simply, has been unable to develop any "set formula" for determining when "justice and fairness" require that economic injuries caused by public action be compensated by the government, rather than remain disproportionately concentrated on a few persons. Indeed, we have frequently observed that whether a particular restriction will be rendered invalid by the government's failure to pay for any losses proximately caused by it depends largely "upon the particular circumstances in that case."

In engaging in these essentially ad hoc, factual inquiries, the Court's decisions have identified several factors that have particular significance. The economic impact of the regulation on the claimant and, particularly, the extent to which the regulation has interfered with distinct investment-backed expectations are, of course, relevant considerations. So, too, is the character of the governmental action. A "taking" may more readily be found when the interference with property can be characterized as a physical invasion by government, than when interference arises from some public program adjusting the benefits and burdens of economic life to promote the common good.

"Government hardly could go on if to some extent values incident to property could not be diminished without paying for every such change in the general law," and this Court has accordingly recognized, in a wide variety of contexts, that government may execute laws or programs that adversely affect recognized economic values.

[More importantly for the present case, in instances in which a state tribunal reasonably concluded that "the health, safety, morals, or general welfare" would be promoted by prohibiting particular contemplated uses of land, this Court has upheld land-use regulations that destroyed or adversely affected recognized real property interests.] "Taking" challenges have been held to be without merit in a wide variety of situations when the challenged governmental actions prohibited a beneficial use to which individual parcels had previously been devoted and thus caused substantial individualized harm. *Miller v. Schoene*, (1928), is illustrative. In that case, a state entomologist, acting pursuant to a state statute, ordered the claimants to cut down a large number of ornamental red cedar trees because they produced cedar rust fatal to apple trees cultivated nearby. Although the statute provided for recovery of any expense incurred in removing the cedars, and permitted claimants to use the felled *Blue* trees, it did not provide compensation for the value of the standing trees or for the resulting decrease in market value of the properties as a whole. A unanimous Court held that this latter omission did not render the statute invalid. The Court held that the State might properly make "a choice between the preservation of one class of property and that of the other" and since the apple industry was important in the State involved, concluded that the State had not exceeded "its constitutional powers by deciding upon the destruction of one class of property without compensation in order to save another which, in the judgment of the legislature, is of greater value to the public."

See also *United States v. Central Eureka Mining Co.* (Government order closing gold mines so that skilled miners would be available for other mining work held not a taking.)

*Pennsylvania Coal Co. v. Mahon*, (1922), is the leading case for the proposition that a state statute that substantially furthers important public policies may nevertheless so frustrate distinct investment-backed expectations as to amount to a "taking." There the claimant had sold the surface rights to particular parcels of property, but expressly reserved the right to remove the coal thereunder. A Pennsylvania statute, enacted after the transactions, forbade any mining of coal that caused the subsidence of any house, unless the house was the property of the owner of the underlying coal and was more than 150 feet from the improved property of another. Because the statute made it commercially impracticable to mine the coal, and thus had nearly the same effect as the complete destruction of rights claimant had reserved from the owners of the surface land, the Court held that the statute was invalid as effecting a "taking" without just compensation.

Finally, government actions that may be characterized as acquisitions of resources to permit or facilitate uniquely public functions have often been held to constitute "takings." *United States v. Causby; Portsmouth Co. v. United States,* (1922) (United States military installations' repeated firing of guns over claimant's land is a taking).

Before considering appellants' arguments, we emphasize what is not in dispute. Because this Court has recognized, in a number of settings, that States and cities may enact land-use restrictions or controls to enhance the quality of life by preserving the character and desirable aesthetic features of a city, see *Village of Belle Terre v. Boraas* and *Berman v. Parker,* appellants do not contest that New York City's objective of preserving structures and areas with special historic, architectural, or cultural significance is an entirely permissible governmental goal. They also do not dispute that the restrictions imposed on its parcel are appropriate means of securing the purposes of the New York City law. Finally, appellants do not challenge any of the specific factual premises of the decision below. They accept for present purposes both that the parcel of land occupied by Grand Central Terminal must, in its present state, be regarded as capable of earning a reasonable return, and that the transferable development rights afforded appellants by virtue of the Terminal's designation as a landmark are valuable, even if not as valuable as the rights to construct above the Terminal.

In deciding whether a particular governmental action has effected a taking, this Court focuses both on the character of the action and on the nature and extent of the interference with rights in the parcel as a whole—here, the city tax block designated as the "landmark site."

Stated baldly, appellants' position appears to be that the only means of ensuring that selected owners are not singled out to endure financial hardship for no reason is to hold that any restriction imposed on individual landmarks pursuant to the New York City scheme is a "taking" requiring the payment of "just compensation." Agreement with this argument would, of course, invalidate not just New York City's law, but all comparable landmark legislation in the Nation. We find no merit in it.

It is true, as appellants emphasize, that both historic-district legislation and zoning laws regulate all properties within given physical communities whereas landmark laws apply only to selected parcels. But, contrary to appellants' suggestions, landmark laws are not like discriminatory, or "reverse spot," zoning: that is, a land-use decision which arbitrarily singles out a particular parcel for different, less favorable treatment than the neighboring ones In contrast to discriminatory zoning, which is the antithesis of land-use control as part of some comprehensive plan, the New York City law embodies a comprehensive plan to preserve structures of historic or aesthetic interest wherever they might be found in the city, and as noted, over 400 landmarks and 31 historic districts have been designated pursuant to this plan.

Next, appellants observe that New York City's law differs from zoning laws and historic-district ordinances in that the Landmarks Law does not impose identical or similar restrictions on all structures located in particular physical communities. It is, of course, true that the Landmarks Law has a more severe impact on some landowners than on others, but that in itself does not mean that the law effects a "taking."

The Landmarks Law's effect is simply to prohibit appellants or anyone else from occupying portions of the airspace above the Terminal, while permitting appellants to use the remainder of the parcel in a gainful fashion.

Rejection of appellants' broad arguments is not, however, the end of our inquiry, for all we thus far have established is that the New York City law is not rendered invalid by its failure to provide "just compensation" whenever a landmark owner is restricted in the exploitation of property interests, such as air rights, to a greater extent than provided for under applicable zoning laws. We now must consider whether the interference with appellants' property is of such a magnitude that "there must be an exercise of eminent domain and compensation to sustain it."

The New York City law does not interfere in any way with the present uses of the Terminal. Its designation as a landmark not only permits but contemplates that appellants may continue to use the property precisely as it has been used for the past 65 years: as a railroad terminal containing office space and concessions. So the law does not interfere with what must be regarded as Penn Central's primary expectation concerning the use of the parcel. More importantly, on this record, we must regard the New York City law as permitting Penn Central not only to profit from the Terminal but also to obtain a "reasonable return" on its investment.

To the extent appellants have been denied the right to build above the Terminal, it is not literally accurate to say that they have been denied *all* use of even those pre-existing air rights. Their ability to use these rights has not been abrogated; they are made transferable to at least eight parcels in the vicinity of the Terminal, one or two of which have been found suitable for the construction of new office buildings. Although appellants and others have argued that New York City's transferable development-rights program is far from ideal, the New York courts here supportably found that, at least in the case of the Terminal, the rights afforded are valuable. While these rights may well not have constituted "just compensation" if a "taking" had occurred, the rights nevertheless undoubtedly mitigate whatever financial burdens the law has imposed on appellants and, for that reason, are to be taken into account in considering the impact of regulation.

On this record, we conclude that the application of New York City's Landmarks Law has not effected a "taking" of appellants' property. The restrictions imposed are substantially related to the promotion of the general welfare and not only permit reasonable beneficial use of the landmark site but also afford appellants opportunities further to enhance not only the Terminal site proper but also other properties.

*Affirmed.*

Note: The next case is an illustration of a situation in which the U.S. Supreme Court decided that the land restrictions simply had gone too far, and would be unconstitutional if applied as written.

## SUPREME COURT OF THE UNITED STATES
### JAMES PATRICK NOLLAN, ET UX., APPELLANT
### V.
### CALIFORNIA COASTAL COMMISSION.

JUNE 26, 1987

**Opinion**

Justice SCALIA delivered the opinion of the Court.

James and Marilyn Nollan appeal from a decision of the California Court of Appeal ruling that the California Coastal Commission could condition its grant of permission to rebuild their house on their transfer to the public of an easement across their beachfront property. [The California court rejected their claim that imposition of that condition violates the Takings Clause of the Fifth Amendment, as incorporated against the States by the Fourteenth Amendment.] We noted probable jurisdiction.

The Nollans own a beachfront lot in Ventura County, California. A quarter-mile north of their property is Faria County Park, an oceanside public park with a public beach and recreation area. Another public beach area, known locally as "the Cove," lies 1,800 feet south of their lot. A concrete seawall approximately eight feet high separates the beach portion of the Nollans' property from the rest of the lot. The historic mean high tide line determines the lot's oceanside boundary.

The Nollans originally leased their property with an option to buy. The building on the lot was a small bungalow, totaling 504 square feet, which for a time they rented to summer vacationers. After years of rental use, however, the building had fallen into disrepair, and could no longer be rented out.

The Nollans' option to purchase was conditioned on their promise to demolish the bungalow and replace it. In order to do so, under Cal.Pub.Res. Code Ann. they were required to obtain a coastal development permit from the California Coastal Commission. On February 25, 1982, they submitted a permit application to the

Commission in which they proposed to demolish the existing structure and replace it with a three-bedroom house in keeping with the rest of the neighborhood.

The Nollans were informed that their application had been placed on the administrative calendar, and that the Commission staff had recommended that the permit be granted subject to the condition that they allow the public an easement to pass across a portion of their property bounded by the mean high tide line on one side, and their seawall on the other side. This would make it easier for the public to get to Faria County Park and the Cove. The Nollans protested imposition of the condition, but the Commission overruled their objections and granted the permit subject to their recordation of a deed restriction granting the easement.

The Commission found that the new house would increase blockage of the view of the ocean, thus contributing to the development of "a wall of residential structures" that would prevent the public "psychologically from realizing a stretch of coastline exists nearby that they have every right to visit." The new house would also increase private use of the shorefront. These effects of construction of the house, along with other area development, would cumulatively "burden the public's ability to traverse to and along the shorefront." Therefore the Commission could properly require the Nollans to offset that burden by providing additional lateral access to the public beaches in the form of an easement across their property. The Commission also noted that it had similarly conditioned 43 out of 60 coastal development permits along the same tract of land, and that of the 17 not so conditioned, 14 had been approved when the Commission did not have administrative regulations in place allowing imposition of the condition, and the remaining 3 had not involved shorefront property.

The Superior Court granted the writ of mandamus and directed that the permit condition be struck. The Commission appealed to the California Court of Appeal. While that appeal was pending, the Nollans satisfied the condition on their option to purchase by tearing down the bungalow and building the new house, and bought the property. They did not notify the Commission that they were taking that action.

The Court of Appeal reversed the Superior Court. The Nollans appealed to this Court, raising only the constitutional question.

Had California simply required the Nollans to make an easement across their beachfront available to the public on a permanent basis in order to increase public access to the beach, rather than conditioning their permit to rebuild their house on their agreeing to do so, we have no doubt there would have been a taking.

Given, then, that requiring uncompensated conveyance of the easement outright would violate the Fourteenth Amendment, the question becomes whether requiring it to be conveyed as a condition for issuing a land-use permit alters the outcome. We have long recognized that land-use regulation does not effect a taking if it "substantially advances legitimate state interests" and does not "deny an owner economically viable use of his land."

. The Commission argues that a permit condition that serves the same legitimate police-power purpose as a refusal to issue the permit should not be found to be a taking if the refusal to issue the permit would not constitute a taking. We agree. Thus, if the Commission attached to the permit some condition that would have protected the public's ability to see the beach notwithstanding construction of the new house - for example, a height limitation, a width restriction, or a ban on fences - so long as the Commission could have exercised its police power (as we have assumed it could) to forbid construction of the house altogether, imposition of the condition would also be constitutional. Moreover (and here we come closer to the facts of the present case), the condition would be constitutional even if it consisted of the requirement that the Nollans provide a viewing spot on their property for passersby with whose sighting of the ocean their new house would interfere. Although such a require-ment, constituting a permanent grant of continuous access to the property, would have to be considered a taking if it were not attached to a development permit, the Commission's assumed power to forbid construction of the house in order to protect the public's view of the beach must surely include the power to condition construc-tion upon some concession by the owner, even a concession of property rights, that serves the same end. If a prohibition designed to accomplish that purpose would be a legitimate exercise of the police power rather than a taking, it would be strange to conclude that providing the owner an alternative to that prohibition which accom-plishes the same purpose is not.

The evident constitutional propriety disappears, however, if the condition substi-tuted for the prohibition utterly fails to further the end advanced as the justification for the prohibition. When that essential nexus is eliminated, the situation becomes the same as if California law forbade shouting fire in a crowded theater, but granted dispensations to those willing to contribute $100 to the state treasury. While a ban on shouting fire can be a core exercise of the State's police power to protect the public safety, and can thus meet even our stringent standards for regulation of speech, adding the unrelated condition alters the purpose to one which, while it may be legitimate, is inadequate to sustain the ban. Therefore, even though, in a sense, requiring a $100 tax contribution in order to shout fire is a lesser restriction on speech than an out-right ban, it would not pass constitutional muster. Similarly here, the lack of nexus between the condition and the original purpose of the building restriction converts that purpose to something other than what it was. The purpose then becomes, quite simply, the obtaining of an easement to serve some valid governmental purpose, but without payment of compensation. In short, unless the permit condition serves the same governmental purpose as the development ban, the building restriction is not a valid regulation of land use but "an out-and-out plan of extortion."

The Commission claims that it concedes as much, and that we may sustain the condition at issue here by finding that it is reasonably related to the public need or burden that the Nollans' new house creates or to which it contributes. We can accept, for purposes of discussion, the Commission's proposed test as to how close a "fit" between the condition and the burden is required, because we find that this case does not meet even the most untailored standards. The Commission's principal contention to the contrary essentially turns on a play on the word "access." The Nollans' new house, the Commission found, will interfere with "visual access" to the beach. That in turn (along with other shorefront development) will interfere with the desire of people who drive past the Nollans' house to use the beach, thus creating a "psychological barrier" to "access." The Nollans' new house will also, by a process not altogether clear from the Commission's opinion but presumably potent enough to more than offset the effects of the psychological barrier, increase the use of the public beaches, thus creating the need for more "access." These burdens on "access" would be alleviated by a requirement that the Nollans provide "lateral access" to the beach.

Rewriting the argument to eliminate the play on words makes clear that there is nothing to it. It is quite impossible to understand how a requirement that people already on the public beaches be able to walk across the Nollans' property reduces any obstacles to viewing the beach created by the new house. It is also impossible to understand how it lowers any "psychological barrier" to using the public beaches, or how it helps to remedy any additional congestion on them caused by construction of the Nollans' new house. We therefore find that the Commission's imposition of the permit condition cannot be treated as an exercise of its land-use power for any of these purposes.

We do not share Justice BRENNAN's confidence that the Commission "should have little difficulty in the future in utilizing its expertise to demonstrate a specific connection between provisions for access and burdens on access," that will avoid the effect of today's decision. We view the Fifth Amendment's Property Clause to be more than a pleading requirement, and compliance with it to be more than an exercise in cleverness and imagination. As indicated earlier, our cases describe the condition for abridgement of property rights through the police power as a "*substantial* advancing" of a legitimate state interest. We are inclined to be particularly careful about the adjective where the actual conveyance of property is made a condition to the lifting of a land-use restriction, since in that context there is heightened risk that the purpose is avoidance of the compensation requirement, rather than the stated police-power objective.

California is free to advance its "comprehensive program," if it wishes, by using its power of eminent domain for this "public purpose," but if it wants an easement across the Nollans' property, it must pay for it.

*Reversed.*

Note: The following case, *Lucas v. South Carolina Coastal Commission,* would perhaps seem unremarkable – except for the discussion of "background principles of state nuisance law," which might be found to "inhere in the title itself," but which might not have been "discovered" until very recently. Would this now become a defense that should be raised in every regulatory taking case? What are the guidelines as to when that defense might be effective?

As always, try to imagine how such regulations must seem to the individual landowner who is denied all, or virtually all of the reasonable use of the land individually owned – "for the benefit of the community."

## SUPREME COURT OF THE UNITED STATES
## DAVID H. LUCAS, PETITIONER,
## V.
## SOUTH CAROLINA COASTAL COUNCIL.

JUNE 29, 1992

**Opinion**

Justice SCALIA delivered the opinion of the Court.

In 1986, petitioner David H. Lucas paid $975,000 for two residential lots on the Isle of Palms in Charleston County, South Carolina, on which he intended to build single-family homes. In 1988, however, the South Carolina Legislature enacted the Beachfront Management Act, which had the direct effect of barring petitioner from erecting any permanent habitable structures on his two parcels. A state trial court found that this prohibition rendered Lucas's parcels "valueless." This case requires us to decide whether the Act's dramatic effect on the economic value of Lucas's lots accomplished a taking of private property under the Fifth and Fourteenth Amendments requiring the payment of "just compensation."

South Carolina's expressed interest in intensively managing development activities in the so-called "coastal zone" dates from 1977 when, in the aftermath of Congress's passage of the federal Coastal Zone Management Act of 1972, the legislature enacted a Coastal Zone Management Act of its own. In its original form, the South Carolina Act required owners of coastal zone land that qualified as a "critical area" (defined in the legislation to include beaches and immediately adjacent sand dunes, to obtain a permit from the newly created South Carolina Coastal Council (Council) (respondent here) prior to committing the land to a "use other than the use the critical area was devoted to on September 28, 1977."

In the late 1970's, Lucas and others began extensive residential development of the Isle of Palms, a barrier island situated eastward of the city of Charleston. Toward the close of the development cycle for one residential subdivision known as "Beachwood East," Lucas in 1986 purchased the two lots at issue in this litigation for his own account. No portion of the lots, which were located approximately 300 feet from the beach, qualified as a "critical area" under the 1977 Act; accordingly, at the time Lucas acquired these parcels, he was not legally obliged to obtain a permit from the Council in advance of any development activity. His intention with respect to the lots was to do what the owners of the immediately adjacent parcels had already done: erect single-family residences. He commissioned architectural drawings for this purpose.

The Beachfront Management Act brought Lucas's plans to an abrupt end. Under that 1988 legislation, the Council was directed to establish a "baseline" connecting the landward-most "points of erosion during the past forty years" in the region of the Isle of Palms that includes Lucas's lots. In an action not challenged here, the Council fixed this baseline landward of Lucas's parcels. That was significant, for under the Act construction of occupiable improvements was flatly prohibited seaward of a line drawn 20 feet landward of, and parallel to, the baseline. The Act provided no exceptions.

Lucas promptly filed suit in the South Carolina Court of Common Pleas, contending that the Beachfront Management Act's construction bar effected a taking of his property without just compensation.

The trial court found that the Beachfront Management Act decreed a permanent ban on construction insofar as Lucas's lots were concerned, and that this prohibition "deprived Lucas of any reasonable economic use of the lots, and rendered them valueless." The court thus concluded that Lucas's properties had been "taken" by operation of the Act, and it ordered respondent to pay "just compensation" in the amount of $1,232,387.50.

The Supreme Court of South Carolina reversed. We granted certiorari.

Prior to Justice Holmes's exposition in *Pennsylvania Coal Co. v. Mahon*, (1922), it was generally thought that the Takings Clause reached only a "direct appropriation" of property, or the functional equivalent of a "practical ouster of the owner's possession." In 70–odd years of succeeding "regulatory takings" jurisprudence, we have generally eschewed any" 'set formula' "for determining how far is too far, preferring to "engage in essentially ad hoc, factual inquiries." *Penn Central.* We have, however, described at least two discrete categories of regulatory action as compensable without case-specific inquiry into the public interest advanced in support of the restraint. The first encompasses regulations that compel the property owner to suffer a physical "invasion" of his property. In general (at least with regard to permanent invasions), no matter how minute the intrusion, and no matter how weighty the public purpose behind it, we have required compensation.

The second situation in which we have found categorical treatment appropriate is where regulation denies all economically beneficial or productive use of land. As we have said on numerous occasions, the Fifth Amendment is violated when land-use regulation "does not substantially advance legitimate state interests *or denies an owner economically viable use of his land.*"

We have never set forth the justification for this rule. Perhaps it is simply, as Justice Brennan suggested, that total deprivation of beneficial use is, from the land-owner's point of view, the equivalent of a physical appropriation. Surely, at least, in the extraordinary circumstance when *no* productive or economically beneficial use of land is permitted, it is less realistic to indulge our usual assumption that the legislature is simply "adjusting the benefits and burdens of economic life," in a manner that secures an "average reciprocity of advantage" to everyone concerned.

On the other side of the balance, affirmatively supporting a compensation requirement, is the fact that regulations that leave the owner of land without economically beneficial or productive options for its use—typically, as here, by requiring land to be left substantially in its natural state—carry with them a heightened risk that private property is being pressed into some form of public service under the guise of mitigating serious public harm.

We think, in short, that there are good reasons for our frequently expressed belief that when the owner of real property has been called upon to sacrifice *all* economically beneficial uses in the name of the common good, that is, to leave his property economically idle, he has suffered a taking.

The trial court found Lucas's two beachfront lots to have been rendered valueless by respondent's enforcement of the coastal-zone construction ban.

Petitioner "conceded that the beach/dune area of South Carolina's shores is an extremely valuable public resource; that the erection of new construction, *inter alia,* contributes to the erosion and destruction of this public resource; and that discouraging new construction in close proximity to the beach/dune area is necessary to prevent a great public harm.

It is correct that many of our prior opinions have suggested that "harmful or noxious uses" of property may be proscribed by government regulation without the requirement of compensation. For a number of reasons, however, we think the South Carolina Supreme Court was too quick to conclude that that principle decides the present case. The "harmful or noxious uses" principle was the Court's early attempt to describe in theoretical terms why government may, consistent with the Takings Clause, affect property values by regulation without incurring an obligation to compensate—a reality we nowadays acknowledge explicitly with respect to the full scope of the State's police power.

The transition from our early focus on control of "noxious" uses to our contemporary understanding of the broad realm within which government may regulate without compensation was an easy one, since the distinction between "harm-preventing" and "benefit-conferring" regulation is often in the eye of the beholder. It is quite possible, for example, to describe in *either* fashion the ecological, economic, and esthetic concerns that inspired the South Carolina Legislature in the present case. One could say that imposing a servitude on Lucas's land is necessary in order to prevent his use of it from "harming" South Carolina's ecological resources; or, instead, in order to achieve the "benefits" of an ecological preserve.

Where the State seeks to sustain regulation that deprives land of all economically beneficial use, we think it may resist compensation only if the logically antecedent  inquiry into the nature of the owner's estate shows that the proscribed use interests were not part of his title to begin with. This accords, we think, with our "takings" jurisprudence, which has traditionally been guided by the understandings of our citizens regarding the content of, and the State's power over, the "bundle of rights" that they acquire when they obtain title to property. It seems to us that the property owner necessarily expects the uses of his property to be restricted, from time to time, by various measures newly enacted by the State in legitimate exercise of its police powers; "as long recognized, some values are enjoyed under an implied limitation and must yield to the police power." And in the case of personal property, by reason of the State's traditionally high degree of control over commercial dealings, he ought to be aware of the possibility that new regulation might even render his property economically worthless (at least if the property's only economically productive use is sale or manufacture for sale). See *Andrus v. Allard,* (prohibition on sale of eagle feathers).

In the case of land, however, we think the notion pressed by the Council that title is somehow held subject to the "implied limitation" that the State may subsequently eliminate all economically valuable use is inconsistent with the historical compact recorded in the Takings Clause that has become part of our constitutional culture.

Where "permanent physical occupation" of land is concerned, we have refused to allow the government to decree it anew (without compensation), no matter how weighty the asserted "public interests" involved, though we assuredly *would* permit the government to assert a permanent easement that was a pre-existing limitation upon the land owner's title.

We believe similar treatment must be accorded confiscatory regulations, *i.e.*, regulations that prohibit all economically beneficial use of land: [Any limitation so severe cannot be newly legislated or decreed (without compensation), but must inhere in the title itself, in the restrictions that background principles of the State's law of property and nuisance already place upon land ownership.] A law or decree with such an effect must, in other words, do no more than duplicate the result that could have been achieved in the courts—by adjacent landowners (or other uniquely affected persons) under the State's law of private nuisance, or by the State under its complementary power to abate nuisances that affect the public generally, or otherwise.

On this analysis, the owner of a lake-bed, for example, would not be entitled to compensation when he is denied the requisite permit to engage in a landfilling operation that would have the effect of flooding others' land. Nor the corporate owner of a nuclear generating plant, when it is directed to remove all improvements from its land upon discovery that the plant sits astride an earthquake fault. Such regulatory action may well have the effect of eliminating the land's only economically productive use, but it does not proscribe a productive use that was previously permissible under relevant property and nuisance principles. The use of these properties for what are now expressly prohibited purposes was *always* unlawful, and (subject to other constitutional limitations) it was open to the State at any point to make the implication of those background principles of nuisance and property law explicit. In light of our traditional resort to "existing rules or understandings that stem from an independent source such as state law" to define the range of interests that qualify for protection as "property" under the Fifth and Fourteenth Amendments, [this recognition that the Takings Clause does not require compensation when an owner is barred from putting land to a use that is proscribed by those "existing rules or understandings" is surely unexceptional. When, however, a regulation that declares "off-limits" all economically productive or beneficial uses of land goes beyond what the relevant background principles would dictate, compensation must be paid to sustain it.]

[The "total taking" inquiry we require today will ordinarily entail (as the application of state nuisance law ordinarily entails) analysis of, among other things, the degree of harm to public lands and resources, or adjacent private property, posed by the claimant's proposed activities, the social value of the claimant's activities and their suitability to the locality in question, and the relative ease with which the alleged harm can be avoided through measures taken by the claimant and the government (or adjacent private landowners). The fact that a particular use has long been engaged in by similarly situated owners ordinarily imports a lack of any common-law prohibition (though changed circumstances or new knowledge may make what was previously permissible no longer so). So also does the fact that other landowners, similarly situated, are permitted to continue the use denied to the claimant.

It seems unlikely that common-law principles would have prevented the erection of any habitable or productive improvements on petitioner's land; they rarely support prohibition of the "essential use" of land. The question, however, is one of state law to be dealt with on remand. We emphasize that to win its case South Carolina must do more than proffer the legislature's declaration that the uses Lucas desires are inconsistent with the public interest, or the conclusory assertion that they violate a common-law maxim such as *sic utere tuo ut alienum non laedas.* As we have said, a "State, by *ipse dixit,* may not transform private property into public property without compensation." Instead, as it would be required to do if it sought to restrain Lucas in a common-law action for public nuisance, South Carolina must identify background principles of nuisance and property law that prohibit the uses he now intends in the circumstances in which the property is presently found. Only on this showing can the State fairly claim that, in proscribing all such beneficial uses, the Beachfront Management Act is taking nothing.

The judgment is reversed, and the case is remanded for proceedings not inconsistent with this opinion.

*So ordered.*

Note: How much can the value of land be decreased by regulation before it becomes a taking? Ninety percent? Nintey-four percent? At what point should the community as a whole have to pay for land use regulations which benefit the whole community, but which fall almost entirely on one individual owner?

## SUPREME COURT OF THE UNITED STATES
## ANTHONY PALAZZOLO, PETITIONER,
### V.
## RHODE ISLAND ET AL.

JUNE 28, 2001

Justice KENNEDY delivered the opinion of the Court.

Petitioner Anthony Palazzolo owns a waterfront parcel of land in the town of Westerly, Rhode Island. Almost all of the property is designated as coastal wetlands under Rhode Island law. After petitioner's development proposals were rejected by respondent Rhode Island Coastal Resources Management Council (Council), he sued in state court, asserting the Council's application of its wetlands regulations took the property without compensation in violation of the Takings Clause of the Fifth Amendment, binding upon the State through the Due Process Clause of the Fourteenth Amendment. Petitioner sought review in this Court, contending the Supreme Court of Rhode Island erred in rejecting his takings claim. We granted certiorari.

I

The town of Westerly is on an edge of the Rhode Island coastline. The town's western border is the Pawcatuck River, which at that point is the boundary between Rhode Island and Connecticut. Situated on land purchased from the Narragansett Indian Tribe, the town was incorporated in 1669 and had a precarious, though colorful, early history. Both Connecticut and Massachusetts contested the boundaries - and indeed the validity - of Rhode Island's royal charter; and Westerly's proximity to Connecticut invited encroachments during these jurisdictional squabbles. When the borders of the Rhode Island Colony were settled by compact in 1728, the town's development was more orderly, and with some historical distinction. For instance, Watch Hill Point, the peninsula at the southwestern tip of the town, was of strategic importance in the Revolutionary War and the War of 1812.

In later times Westerly's coastal location had a new significance: It became a popular vacation and seaside destination. One of the town's historians gave this happy account:

> "After the Civil War the rapid growth of manufacture and expansion of trade had created a spending class on pleasure bent, and Westerly had superior attractions to offer, surf bathing on ocean beaches, quieter bathing in salt and fresh water ponds, fishing, annual sail and later motor boat races. The broad beaches of clean white sand dip gently toward the sea; there are no odorous marshes at low tide, no railroad belches smoke, and the climate is unrivalled on the coast, that of Newport only excepted. In the phenomenal heat wave of 1881 ocean resorts from northern New England to southern New Jersey sweltered as the thermometer climbed to 95 and 104 degrees, while Watch Hill enjoyed a comfortable 80. When Providence to the north runs a temperature of 90, the mercury in this favored spot remains at 77."

Westerly today has about 20,000 year-round residents, and thousands of summer visitors come to enjoy its beaches and coastal advantages.

One of the more popular attractions is Misquamicut State Beach, a lengthy expanse of coastline facing Block Island Sound and beyond to the Atlantic Ocean. The primary point of access to the beach is Atlantic Avenue, a well-traveled 3-mile stretch of road running along the coastline within the town's limits. At its western end, Atlantic Avenue is something of a commercial strip, with restaurants, hotels, arcades, and other typical seashore businesses. The pattern of development becomes more residential as the road winds eastward onto a narrow spine of land bordered to the south by the beach and the ocean, and to the north by Winnapaug Pond, an intertidal inlet often used by residents for boating, fishing, and shellfishing.

In 1959 petitioner, a lifelong Westerly resident, decided to invest in three undeveloped, adjoining parcels along this eastern stretch of Atlantic Avenue. To the north, the property faces, and borders upon, Winnapaug Pond; the south of the property faces Atlantic Avenue and the beachfront homes abutting it on the other side, and beyond that the dunes and the beach. To purchase and hold the property, petitioner and associates formed Shore Gardens, Inc. (SGI). After SGI purchased the property petitioner bought out his associates and became the sole shareholder. In the first decade of SGI's ownership of the property the corporation submitted a plat to the town subdividing the property into 80 lots; and it engaged in various transactions that left it with 74 lots, which together encompassed about 20 acres. During the same period SGI also made initial attempts to develop the property and submitted intermittent applications to state agencies to fill substantial portions of the parcel. Most of the property was then, as it is now, salt marsh subject to tidal flooding. The wet ground and permeable soil would require considerable fill - as much as six feet in some places - before significant structures could be built. SGI's proposal, submitted in 1962 to the Rhode Island Division of Harbors and Rivers (DHR), sought to dredge from Winnapaug Pond and fill the entire property. The application was denied for lack of essential information. A second, similar proposal followed a year later. A third application, submitted in 1966 while the second application was pending, proposed more limited filling of the land for use as a private beach club. These latter two applications were referred to the Rhode Island Department of Natural Resources, which indicated initial assent. The agency later withdrew approval, however, citing adverse environmental impacts. SGI did not contest the ruling.

No further attempts to develop the property were made for over a decade. Two intervening events, however, become important to the issues presented. First, in 1971, Rhode Island enacted legislation creating the Council, an agency charged with the duty of protecting the State's coastal properties. Regulations promulgated by the Council designated salt marshes like those on SGI's property as protected "coastal wetlands," on which development is limited to a great extent. Second, in 1978, SGI's corporate charter was revoked for failure to pay corporate income taxes; and title to the property passed, by operation of state law, to petitioner as the corporation's sole shareholder.

In 1983, petitioner, now the owner, renewed the efforts to develop the property. An application to the Council, resembling the 1962 submission, requested permission to construct a wooden bulkhead along the shore of Winnapaug Pond and to fill the entire marshland area. The Council rejected the application, noting it was "vague and inadequate for a project of this size and nature." The agency also found that "the proposed activities will have significant impacts upon the waters and wetlands of Winnapaug Pond," and concluded that "the proposed alteration will conflict with the Coastal Resources Management Plan presently in effect." Petitioner did not appeal the agency's determination.

Petitioner went back to the drawing board, this time hiring counsel and preparing a more specific and limited proposal for use of the property. The new application, submitted to the Council in 1985, echoed the 1966 request to build a private beach club. The details do not tend to inspire the reader with an idyllic coastal image, for the proposal was to fill 11 acres of the property with gravel to accommodate "50 cars with boat trailers, a dumpster, port-a-johns, picnic tables, barbecue pits of concrete, and other trash receptacles."

The application fared no better with the Council than previous ones. Under the agency's regulations, a landowner wishing to fill salt marsh on Winnapaug Pond needed a "special exception" from the Council. In a short opinion the Council said the beach club proposal conflicted with the regulatory standard for a special exception. To secure a special exception the proposed activity must serve "a compelling public purpose which provides benefits to the public as a whole as opposed to individual or private interests." This time petitioner appealed the decision to the Rhode Island courts, challenging the Council's conclusion as contrary to principles of state administrative law. The Council's decision was affirmed.

Petitioner filed an inverse condemnation action in Rhode Island Superior Court, asserting that the State's wetlands regulations, as applied by the Council to his parcel, had taken the property without compensation in violation of the Fifth and Fourteenth Amendments. The suit alleged the Council's action deprived him of "economically, beneficial use" of his property, resulting in a total taking requiring compensation under *Lucas v. South Carolina Coastal Council.* He sought damages in the amount of $3,150,000, a figure derived from an appraiser's estimate as to the value of a 74-lot residential subdivision. The State countered with a host of defenses. After a bench trial, a justice of the Superior Court ruled against petitioner, accepting some of the State's theories.

The Rhode Island Supreme Court affirmed.

We disagree with the Supreme Court of Rhode Island. We remand for further consideration of the claim under the principles set forth in *Penn Central.*

## II

The Takings Clause of the Fifth Amendment, applicable to the States through the Fourteenth Amendment, prohibits the government from taking private property for public use without just compensation. The clearest sort of taking occurs when the government encroaches upon or occupies private land for its own proposed use. Our cases establish that even a minimal "permanent physical occupation of real property" requires compensation under the Clause. *Loretto v. Teleprompter.* In *Pennsylvania Coal Co. v. Mahon,* the Court recognized that there will be instances when government actions do not encroach upon or occupy the property yet still affect and limit its use to such an extent that a taking occurs. In Justice Holmes' well-known, if less than self-defining, formulation, "while property may be regulated to a certain extent, if a regulation goes too far it will be recognized as a taking."

Since *Mahon,* we have given some, but not too specific, guidance to courts confronted with deciding whether a particular government action goes too far and effects a regulatory taking. First, we have observed, with certain qualifications, that a regulation which "denies all economically beneficial or productive use of land" will require compensation under the Takings Clause. Where a regulation places limitations on land that fall short of eliminating all economically beneficial use, a taking nonetheless may have occurred, depending on a complex of factors including the regulation's economic effect on the landowner, the extent to which the regulation interferes with reasonable investment-backed expectations, and the character of the government action. *Penn Central.* These inquiries are informed by the purpose of the Takings Clause, which is to prevent the government from "forcing some people alone to bear public burdens which, in all fairness and justice, should be borne by the public as a whole."

Petitioner seeks compensation under these principles. At the outset, however, we face the two threshold considerations invoked by the state court to bar the claim: ripeness, and acquisition which postdates the regulation.

## A

In *Williamson County Regional Planning Comm'n*, the Court explained the require-ment that a takings claim must be ripe. The Court held that a takings claim challeng-ing the application of land-use regulations is not ripe unless "the government entity charged with implementing the regulations has reached a final decision regarding the application of the regulations to the property at issue." A final decision by the respon-sible state agency informs the constitutional determination whether a regulation has deprived a landowner of "all economically beneficial use" of the property, see *Lucas*, or defeated the reasonable investment-backed expectations of the landowner to the extent that a taking has occurred, see *Penn Central*. These matters cannot be resolved in definitive terms until a court knows "the extent of permitted development" on the land in question. Drawing on these principles, the Rhode Island Supreme Court held that petitioner had not taken the necessary steps to ripen his takings claim.

The central question in resolving the ripeness issue, under *Williamson County* and other relevant decisions, is whether petitioner obtained a final decision from the Council determining the permitted use for the land. As we have noted, SGI's early applications to fill had been granted at one point, though that assent was later revoked. Petitioner then submitted two proposals: the 1983 proposal to fill the entire parcel, and the 1985 proposal to fill 11 of the property's 18 wetland acres for construc-tion of the beach club. The court reasoned that, notwithstanding the Council's deni-als of the applications, doubt remained as to the extent of development the Council would allow on petitioner's parcel. We cannot agree.

The court based its holding in part upon petitioner's failure to explore "any other use for the property that would involve filling substantially less wetlands." It relied upon this Court's observations that the final decision requirement is not satisfied when a developer submits, and a land-use authority denies, a grandiose develop-ment proposal, leaving open the possibility that lesser uses of the property might be permitted. The suggestion is that while the Council rejected petitioner's effort to fill all of the wetlands, and then rejected his proposal to fill 11 of the wetland acres, perhaps an application to fill (for instance) 5 acres would have been approved. Thus, the reasoning goes, we cannot know for sure the extent of permitted development on petitioner's wetlands.

This is belied by the unequivocal nature of the wetland regulations at issue and by the Council's application of the regulations to the subject property. Winnapaug Pond is classified under the CRMP as a Type 2 body of water. A landowner, as a general rule, is prohibited from filling or building residential structures on wetlands adjacent to Type 2 waters, but may seek a special exception from the Council to engage in a prohibited use. The Council is permitted to allow the exception, however, only where a "compelling public purpose" is served. The proposal to fill the entire property was not accepted under Council regulations and did not qualify for the special exception. The Council determined the use proposed in the second application (the beach club) did not satisfy the "compelling public purpose" standard. There is no indication the Council would have accepted the application had petitioner's proposed beach club occupied a smaller surface area. To the contrary, it ruled that the proposed activity was not a "compelling public purpose."

*Williamson County*'s final decision requirement "responds to the high degree of discretion characteristically possessed by land-use boards in softening the strictures of the general regulations they administer." While a landowner must give a land-use authority an opportunity to exercise its discretion, once it becomes clear that the agency lacks the discretion to permit any development, or the permissible uses of the property are known to a reasonable degree of certainty, a takings claim is likely to have ripened. The case is quite unlike those upon which respondents place principal reliance, which arose when an owner challenged a land-use authority's denial of a substantial project, leaving doubt whether a more modest submission or an application for a variance would be accepted.

These cases stand for the important principle that a landowner may not establish a taking before a land-use authority has the opportunity, using its own reasonable procedures, to decide and explain the reach of a challenged regulation. Under our ripeness rules a takings claim based on a law or regulation which is alleged to go too far in burdening property depends upon the landowner's first having followed reasonable and necessary steps to allow regulatory agencies to exercise their full discretion in considering development plans for the property, including the opportunity to grant any variances or waivers allowed by law. As a general rule, until these ordinary processes have been followed the extent of the restriction on property is not known and a regulatory taking has not yet been established. Government authorities, of course, may not burden property by imposition of repetitive or unfair land-use procedures in order to avoid a final decision.

With respect to the wetlands on petitioner's property, the Council's decisions make plain that the agency interpreted its regulations to bar petitioner from engaging in any filling or development activity on the wetlands, a fact reinforced by the Attorney General's forthright responses to our questioning during oral argument in this case. The rulings of the Council interpreting the regulations at issue, and the briefs, arguments, and candid statements by counsel for both sides, leave no doubt on this point: On the wetlands there can be no fill for any ordinary land use. There can be no fill for its own sake; no fill for a beach club, either rustic or upscale; no fill for a subdivision; no fill for any likely or foreseeable use. And with no fill there can be no structures and no development on the wetlands. Further permit applications were not necessary to establish this point.

As noted above, however, not all of petitioner's parcel constitutes protected wetlands. The trial court accepted uncontested testimony that an upland site located at the eastern end of the property would have an estimated value of $200,000 if developed. While Council approval is required to develop upland property which lies within 200 feet of protected waters, the strict "compelling public purpose" test does not govern proposed land uses on property in this classification. Council officials testified at trial, moreover, that they would have allowed petitioner to build a residence on the upland parcel. The State Supreme Court found petitioner's claim unripe for the further reason that he "has not sought permission for any use of the property that would involve development only of the upland portion of the parcel."

In assessing the significance of petitioner's failure to submit applications to develop the upland area it is important to bear in mind the purpose that the final decision requirement serves. Our ripeness jurisprudence imposes obligations on landowners because "a court cannot determine whether a regulation goes 'too far' unless it knows how far the regulation goes." Ripeness doctrine does not require a landowner to submit applications for their own sake. Petitioner is required to explore development opportunities on his upland parcel only if there is uncertainty as to the land's permitted use.

The State asserts the value of the uplands is in doubt. It relies in part on a comment in the opinion of the Rhode Island Supreme Court that "it would be possible to build at least one single-family home on the upland portion of the parcel." It argues that the qualification "at least" indicates that additional development beyond the single dwelling was possible. The attempt to interject ambiguity as to the value or use of the uplands, however, comes too late in the day for purposes of litigation before this Court. It was stated in the petition for certiorari that the uplands on petitioner's property had an estimated worth of $200,000. The figure not only was uncontested but also was cited as fact in the State's brief in opposition. In this circumstance ripeness cannot be contested by saying that the value of the nonwetland parcels is unknown.

The State's prior willingness to accept the $200,000 figure, furthermore, is well founded. The only reference to upland property in the trial court's opinion is to a single parcel worth an estimated $200,000. There was, it must be acknowledged, testimony at trial suggesting the existence of an additional upland parcel elsewhere on the property. The testimony indicated, however, that the potential, second upland parcel was on an "island" which required construction of a road across wetlands, and, as discussed above, the filling of wetlands for such a purpose would not justify a special exception under Council regulations. Perhaps for this reason, the State did not maintain in the trial court that additional uplands could have been developed. To the contrary, its post-trial memorandum identified only the single parcel that petitioner concedes retains a development value of $200,000. The trial court accepted the figure. So there is no genuine ambiguity in the record as to the extent of permitted development on petitioner's property, either on the wetlands or the uplands.

A final ripeness issue remains. In concluding that *Williamson County*'s final decision requirement was not satisfied, the State Supreme Court placed emphasis on petitioner's failure to "apply for permission to develop the seventy-four-lot subdivision" that was the basis for the damages sought in his inverse condemnation suit. The court did not explain why it thought this fact significant, but respondents and *amici* defend the ruling. The Council's practice, they assert, is to consider a proposal only if the applicant has satisfied all other regulatory preconditions for the use envisioned in the application. The subdivision proposal that was the basis for petitioner's takings claim, they add, could not have proceeded before the Council without, at minimum, zoning approval from the town of Westerly and a permit from the Rhode Island Department of Environmental Management allowing the installation of individual sewage disposal systems on the property. Petitioner is accused of employing a hide the ball strategy of submitting applications for more modest uses to the Council, only to assert later a takings action predicated on the purported inability to build a much larger project.

It is difficult to see how this concern is relevant to the inquiry at issue here. Petitioner was informed by the Council that he could not fill the wetlands; it follows of necessity that he could not fill and then build 74 single-family dwellings upon it. Petitioner's submission of this proposal would not have clarified the extent of development permitted by the wetlands regulations, which is the inquiry required under our ripeness decisions. The State's concern may be that landowners could demand damages for a taking based on a project that could not have been constructed under other, valid zoning restrictions quite apart from the regulation being challenged. This, of course, is a valid concern in inverse condemnation cases alleging injury from wrongful refusal to permit development. The instant case does not require us to pass upon the authority of a State to insist in such cases that landowners follow normal planning procedures or to enact rules to control damages awards based on hypothetical uses that should have been reviewed in the normal course, and we do not intend to cast doubt upon such rules here. The mere allegation of entitlement to the value of an intensive use will not avail the landowner if the project would not have been allowed under other existing, legitimate land-use limitations. When a taking has occurred, under accepted condemnation principles the owner's damages will be based upon the property's fair market value, an inquiry which will turn, in part, on restrictions on use imposed by legitimate zoning or other regulatory limitations.]

The state court, however, did not rely upon state-law ripeness or exhaustion principles in holding that petitioner's takings claim was barred by virtue of his failure to apply for a 74-lot subdivision; it relied on *Williamson County.* As we have explained, *Williamson County* and our other ripeness decisions do not impose further obligations on petitioner, for the limitations the wetland regulations imposed were clear from the Council's denial of his applications, and there is no indication that any use involving any substantial structures or improvements would have been allowed. [Where the state agency charged with enforcing a challenged land-use regulation entertains an application from an owner and its denial of the application makes clear the extent of development permitted, and neither the agency nor a reviewing state court has cited noncompliance with reasonable state-law exhaustion or pre-permit processes, federal ripeness rules do not require the submission of further and futile applications with other agencies.]

B

We turn to the second asserted basis for declining to address petitioner's takings claim on the merits. [When the Council promulgated its wetlands regulations, the disputed parcel was owned not by petitioner but by the corporation of which he was sole shareholder. When title was transferred to petitioner by operation of law, the wetlands regulations were in force.] The state court held the postregulation acquisition of title was fatal to the claim for deprivation of all economic use, and to the *Penn Central* claim. While the first holding was couched in terms of background principles of state property law, see *Lucas,* and the second in terms of petitioner's reasonable investment-backed expectations, see *Penn Central,* the two holdings together amount to a single, sweeping, rule: A purchaser or a successive title holder like petitioner is deemed to have notice of an earlier-enacted restriction and is barred from claiming that it effects a taking.

The theory underlying the argument that postenactment purchasers cannot challenge a regulation under the Takings Clause seems to run on these lines: Property rights are created by the State. So, the argument goes, by prospective legislation the State can shape and define property rights and reasonable investment-backed expectations, and subsequent owners cannot claim any injury from lost value. After all, they purchased or took title with notice of the limitation.

The State may not put so potent a Hobbesian stick into the Lockean bundle. [The right to improve property, of course, is subject to the reasonable exercise of state authority, including the enforcement of valid zoning and land-use restrictions.] See

*Pennsylvania Coal.* "Government hardly could go on if to some extent values incident to property could not be diminished without paying for every such change in the general law"). The Takings Clause, however, in certain circumstances allows a landowner to assert that a particular exercise of the State's regulatory power is so unreasonable or onerous as to compel compensation. Just as a prospective enactment, such as a new zoning ordinance, can limit the value of land without effecting a taking because it can be understood as reasonable by all concerned, other enactments are unreasonable and do not become less so through passage of time or title. Were we to accept the State's rule, the postenactment transfer of title would absolve the State of its obligation to defend any action restricting land use, no matter how extreme or unreasonable. A State would be allowed, in effect, to put an expiration date on the Takings Clause. This ought not to be the rule. Future generations, too, have a right to challenge unreasonable limitations on the use and value of land.

Nor does the justification of notice take into account the effect on owners at the time of enactment, who are prejudiced as well. Should an owner attempt to challenge a new regulation, but not survive the process of ripening his or her claim (which, as this case demonstrates, will often take years), under the proposed rule the right to compensation may not be asserted by an heir or successor, and so may not be asserted at all. The State's rule would work a critical alteration to the nature of property, as the newly regulated landowner is stripped of the ability to transfer the interest which was possessed prior to the regulation. The State may not by this means secure a windfall for itself. (A State, by *ipse dixit,* may not transform private property into public property without compensation.) The proposed rule is, furthermore, capricious in effect. The young owner contrasted with the older owner, the owner with the resources to hold contrasted with the owner with the need to sell, would be in different positions. The Takings Clause is not so quixotic. A blanket rule that purchasers with notice have no compensation right when a claim becomes ripe is too blunt an instrument to accord with the duty to compensate for what is taken.

Direct condemnation, by invocation of the State's power of eminent domain, presents different considerations from cases alleging a taking based on a burdensome regulation. In a direct condemnation action, or when a State has physically invaded the property without filing suit, the fact and extent of the taking are known. In such an instance, it is a general rule of the law of eminent domain that any award goes to the owner at the time of the taking, and that the right to compensation is not passed to a subsequent purchaser. ("It is well settled that when there is a taking of property by eminent domain in compliance with the law, it is the owner of the property *at the time of the taking* who is entitled to compensation"). A challenge to the application of a land-use regulation, by contrast, does not mature until ripeness requirements have been satisfied, under principles we have discussed; until this point an inverse condemnation claim alleging a regulatory taking cannot be maintained. It would be illogical, and unfair, to bar a regulatory takings claim because of the post-enactment transfer of ownership where the steps necessary to make the claim ripe were not taken, or could not have been taken, by a previous owner.

There is controlling precedent for our conclusion. *Nollan* presented the question whether it was consistent with the Takings Clause for a state regulatory agency to require oceanfront landowners to provide lateral beach access to the public as the condition for a development permit. The principal dissenting opinion observed it was a policy of the California Coastal Commission to require the condition, and that the Nollans, who purchased their home after the policy went into effect, were "on notice that new developments would be approved only if provisions were made for lateral beach access." A majority of the Court rejected the proposition. "So long as the Commission could not have deprived the prior owners of the easement without compensating them," the Court reasoned, "the prior owners must be understood to have transferred their full property rights in conveying the lot."

It is argued that *Nollan* 's holding was limited by the later decision in *Lucas*. In *Lucas* the Court observed that a landowner's ability to recover for a government deprivation of all economically beneficial use of property is not absolute but instead is confined by limitations on the use of land which "inhere in the title itself." This is so, the Court reasoned, because the landowner is constrained by those "restrictions that background principles of the State's law of property and nuisance already place upon land ownership." It is asserted here that *Lucas* stands for the proposition that any new regulation, once enacted, becomes a background principle of property law which cannot be challenged by those who acquire title after the enactment.

We have no occasion to consider the precise circumstances when a legislative enactment can be deemed a background principle of state law or whether those circumstances are present here. It suffices to say that a regulation that otherwise would be unconstitutional absent compensation is not transformed into a background principle of the State's law by mere virtue of the passage of title. This relative standard would be incompatible with our description of the concept in *Lucas,* which is explained in terms of those common, shared understandings of permissible limitations derived from a State's legal tradition. A regulation or common-law rule cannot be a background principle for some owners but not for others. The determination whether an existing, general law can limit all economic use of property must turn on objective factors, such as the nature of the land use proscribed. The 'total taking' inquiry we require today will ordinarily entail analysis of, among other things, the degree of harm to public lands and resources, or adjacent private property, posed by the claimant's proposed activities". A law does not become a background principle for subsequent owners by enactment itself. *Lucas* did not overrule our holding in *Nollan,* which, as we have noted, is based on essential Takings Clause principles.

For reasons we discuss next, the state court will not find it necessary to explore these matters on remand in connection with the claim that all economic use was deprived; it must address, however, the merits of petitioner's claim under *Penn Central.* That claim is not barred by the mere fact that title was acquired after the effective date of the state-imposed restriction.

## III

As the case is ripe, and as the date of transfer of title does not bar petitioner's takings claim, we have before us the alternative ground relied upon by the Rhode Island Supreme Court in ruling upon the merits of the takings claims. It held that all economically beneficial use was not deprived because the uplands portion of the property can still be improved. On this point, we agree with the court's decision. Petitioner accepts the Council's contention and the state trial court's finding that his parcel retains $200,000 in development value under the State's wetlands regulations. He asserts, nonetheless, that he has suffered a total taking and contends the Council cannot sidestep the holding in *Lucas* "by the simple expedient of leaving a landowner a few crumbs of value."

Assuming a taking is otherwise established, a State may not evade the duty to compensate on the premise that the landowner is left with a token interest. This is not the situation of the landowner in this case, however. A regulation permitting a landowner to build a substantial residence on an 18-acre parcel does not leave the property "economically idle."

> → this is below 50% in this case

In his brief submitted to us petitioner attempts to revive this part of his claim by reframing it. He argues, for the first time, that the upland parcel is distinct from the wetlands portions, so he should be permitted to assert a deprivation limited to the latter. This contention asks us to examine the difficult, persisting question of what is the proper denominator in the takings fraction. Some of our cases indicate that the extent of deprivation effected by a regulatory action is measured against the value of the parcel as a whole, but we have at times expressed discomfort with the logic of this rule, see *Lucas,* a sentiment echoed by some commentators. Whatever the merits of these criticisms, we will not explore the point here. Petitioner did not press the argument in the state courts, and the issue was not presented in the petition for certiorari. The case comes to us on the premise that petitioner's entire parcel serves as the basis for his takings claim, and, so framed, the total deprivation argument fails.

For the reasons we have discussed, the State Supreme Court erred in finding petitioner's claims were unripe and in ruling that acquisition of title after the effective date of the regulations barred the takings claims. The court did not err in finding that petitioner failed to establish a deprivation of all economic value, for it is undisputed that the parcel retains significant worth for construction of a residence. The claims under the *Penn Central* analysis were not examined, and for this purpose the case should be remanded.

The judgment of the Rhode Island Supreme Court is affirmed in part and reversed in part, and the case is remanded for further proceedings not inconsistent with this opinion.

Note: In 2017 the U.S. Supreme Court is still working with *Penn Central* as the basis for decision. But notice the new concern about defining just what is "the parcel as a whole." Does this add another interesting layer of complexity to a field which already had very few clear lines of demarcation between an acceptable regulation and a "taking" for which compensation must be paid?

## SUPREME COURT OF THE UNITED STATES
## JOSEPH P. MURR, ET AL., PETITIONERS
## V.
## WISCONSIN, ET AL.

DECIDED JUNE 23, 2017

**Opinion**

Justice KENNEDY delivered the opinion of the Court.

The classic example of a property taking by the government is when the property has been occupied or otherwise seized. In the case now before the Court, petitioners contend that governmental entities took their real property—an undeveloped residential lot—not by some physical occupation but instead by enacting burdensome regulations that forbid its improvement or separate sale because it is classified as substandard in size. The relevant governmental entities are the respondents.

Against the background justifications for the challenged restrictions, respondents contend there is no regulatory taking because petitioners own an adjacent lot. The regulations, in effecting a merger of the property, permit the continued residential use of the property including for a single improvement to extend over both lots. This retained right of the landowner, respondents urge, is of sufficient offsetting value that the regulation is not severe enough to be a regulatory taking. To resolve the issue whether the landowners can insist on confining the analysis just to the lot in question, without regard to their ownership of the adjacent lot, it is necessary to discuss the background principles that define regulatory takings.

The St. Croix River originates in northwest Wisconsin and flows approximately 170 miles until it joins the Mississippi River, forming the boundary between Minnesota and Wisconsin for much of its length. The lower portion of the river slows and widens to create a natural water area known as Lake St. Croix. Tourists and residents of the region have long extolled the picturesque grandeur of the river and surrounding area. *E.g.,* E. Ellett, Summer Rambles in the West (1853).

[Under the Wild and Scenic Rivers Act, the river was designated, by 1972, for federal protection. In compliance, Wisconsin authorized the State Department of Natural Resources to promulgate rules limiting development in order to "guarantee the protection of the wild, scenic and recreational qualities of the river for present and future generations."]

[Petitioners are two sisters and two brothers in the Murr family. Petitioners' parents arranged for them to receive ownership of two lots the family used for recreation along the Lower St. Croix River in the town of Troy, Wisconsin. The lots are adjacent, but the parents purchased them separately, put the title of one in the name of the family business, and later arranged for transfer of the two lots, on different dates, to petitioners. The lots, which are referred to in this litigation as Lots E and F, are described in more detail below.]

For the area where petitioners' property is located, the Wisconsin rules prevent the use of lots as separate building sites unless they have at least one acre of land suitable for development. A grandfather clause relaxes this restriction for substandard lots which were "in separate ownership from abutting lands" on January 1, 1976, the effective date of the regulation. The clause permits the use of qualifying lots as separate building sites. The rules also include a merger provision, however, which provides that adjacent lots under common ownership may not be "sold or developed as separate lots" if they do not meet the size requirement. The Wisconsin rules require localities to adopt parallel provisions, so the St. Croix County zoning ordinance contains identical restrictions. The Wisconsin rules also authorize the local zoning authority to grant variances from the regulations where enforcement would create "unnecessary hardship."

Petitioners' parents purchased Lot F in 1960 and built a small recreational cabin on it. In 1961, they transferred title to Lot F to the family plumbing company. In 1963, they purchased neighboring Lot E, which they held in their own names.

The lots have the same topography. A steep bluff cuts through the middle of each, with level land suitable for development above the bluff and next to the water below it. The line dividing Lot E from Lot F runs from the riverfront to the far end of the property, crossing the blufftop along the way. Lot E has approximately 60 feet of river frontage, and Lot F has approximately 100 feet. Though each lot is approximately 1.25 acres in size, because of the waterline and the steep bank they each have less than one acre of land suitable for development. Even when combined, the lots' buildable land area is only 0.98 acres due to the steep terrain.

The lots remained under separate ownership, with Lot F owned by the plumbing company and Lot E owned by petitioners' parents, until transfers to petitioners. Lot F was conveyed to them in 1994, and Lot E was conveyed to them in 1995.

A decade later, petitioners became interested in moving the cabin on Lot F to a different portion of the lot and selling Lot E to fund the project. The unification of the lots under common ownership, however, had implicated the state and local rules barring their separate sale or development. Petitioners then sought variances from the St. Croix County Board of Adjustment to enable their building and improvement plan, including a variance to allow the separate sale or use of the lots. The Board denied the requests, and the state courts affirmed in relevant part. In particular, the Wisconsin Court of Appeals agreed with the Board's interpretation that the local ordinance "effectively merged" Lots E and F, so petitioners "could only sell or build on the single larger lot."

Petitioners filed the present action in state court, alleging that the state and county regulations worked a regulatory taking by depriving them of "all, or practically all, of the use of Lot E because the lot cannot be sold or developed as a separate lot." The parties each submitted appraisal numbers to the trial court. Respondents' appraisal included values of $698,300 for the lots together as regulated; $771,000 for the lots as two distinct buildable properties; and $373,000 for Lot F as a single lot with improvements. Petitioners' appraisal included an unrebutted, estimated value of $40,000 for Lot E as an undevelopable lot, based on the counterfactual assumption that it could be sold as a separate property.

The Circuit Court of St. Croix County granted summary judgment to the State.

The Wisconsin Court of Appeals affirmed. The Supreme Court of Wisconsin denied discretionary review. This Court granted certiorari.

The Takings Clause of the Fifth Amendment provides that private property shall not "be taken for public use, without just compensation." The Clause is made applicable to the States through the Fourteenth Amendment. As this Court has recognized, the plain language of the Takings Clause "requires the payment of compensation whenever the government acquires private property for a public purpose," but it does not address in specific terms the imposition of regulatory burdens on private property]

[*Mahon* initiated this Court's regulatory takings jurisprudence, declaring that "while property may be regulated to a certain extent, if regulation goes too far it will be recognized as a taking." A regulation, then, can be so burdensome as to become a taking, yet the *Mahon* Court did not formulate more detailed guidance for determining when this limit is reached.]

In the near century since *Mahon,* the Court for the most part has refrained from elaborating this principle through definitive rules. This area of the law has been characterized by "ad hoc, factual inquiries, designed to allow careful examination and weighing of all the relevant circumstances."[The Court has, however, stated two guidelines relevant here for determining when government regulation is so onerous that it constitutes a taking. First, "with certain qualifications, a regulation which 'denies all economically beneficial or productive use of land' will require compensation under the Takings Clause." *Palazzolo.* Second, when a regulation impedes the use of property without depriving the owner of all economically beneficial use, a taking still may be found based on "a complex of factors," including (1) the economic impact of the regulation on the claimant; (2) the extent to which the regulation has interfered with distinct investment-backed expectations; and (3) the character of the governmental action. *Palazzolo,* (citing *Penn Central*).]

→) Blue

By declaring that the denial of all economically beneficial use of land constitutes a regulatory taking, *Lucas* stated what it called a "categorical" rule. Even in *Lucas,* however, the Court included a caveat recognizing the relevance of state law and land-use customs:[The complete deprivation of use will not require compensation if the challenged limitations "inhere ... in the restrictions that background principles of the State's law of property and nuisance already placed upon land ownership."]

A central dynamic of the Court's regulatory takings jurisprudence, then, is its flexibility. This has been and remains a means to reconcile two competing objectives central to regulatory takings doctrine. One is the individual's right to retain the interests and exercise the freedoms at the core of private property ownership. Property rights are necessary to preserve freedom, for property ownership empowers persons to shape and to plan their own destiny in a world where governments are always eager to do so for them.

The other persisting interest is the government's well-established power to "adjust rights for the public good." As Justice Holmes declared, "Government hardly could go on if to some extent values incident to property could not be diminished without paying for every such change in the general law." In adjudicating regulatory takings cases a proper balancing of these principles requires a careful inquiry informed by the specifics of the case. In all instances, the analysis must be driven "by the purpose of the Takings Clause, which is to prevent the government from 'forcing some people alone to bear public burdens which, in all fairness and justice, should be borne by the public as a whole.' " *Palazzolo.*

This case presents a question that is linked to the ultimate determination whether a regulatory taking has occurred: What is the proper unit of property against which to assess the effect of the challenged governmental action? Put another way, "because our test for regulatory taking requires us to compare the value that has been taken from the property with the value that remains in the property, one of the critical questions is determining how to define the unit of property whose value is to furnish the denominator of the fraction.

As commentators have noted, the answer to this question may be outcome determinative. Defining the property at the outset, however, should not necessarily preordain the outcome in every case. In some, though not all, cases the effect of the challenged regulation must be assessed and understood by the effect on the entire property held by the owner, rather than just some part of the property that, considered just on its own, has been diminished in value. This demonstrates the contrast between regulatory takings, where the goal is usually to determine how the challenged regulation affects the property's value to the owner, and physical takings, where the impact of physical appropriation or occupation of the property will be evident.

While the Court has not set forth specific guidance on how to identify the relevant parcel for the regulatory taking inquiry, there are two concepts which the Court has indicated can be unduly narrow.

First, the Court has declined to limit the parcel in an artificial manner to the portion of property targeted by the challenged regulation.

The second concept about which the Court has expressed caution is the view that property rights under the Takings Clause should be coextensive with those under state law. Although property interests have their foundations in state law, the *Palazzolo* Court reversed a state-court decision that rejected a takings challenge to regulations that predated the landowner's acquisition of title. The Court explained that States do not have the unfettered authority to "shape and define property rights and reasonable investment-backed expectations," leaving landowners without recourse against unreasonable regulations. *Could be blue*

By the same measure, defining the parcel by reference to state law could defeat a challenge even to a state enactment that alters permitted uses of property in ways inconsistent with reasonable investment-backed expectations. For example, a State might enact a law that consolidates nonadjacent property owned by a single person or entity in different parts of the State and then imposes development limits on the aggregate set. If a court defined the parcel according to the state law requiring consolidation, this improperly would fortify the state law against a takings claim, because the court would look to the retained value in the property as a whole rather than considering whether individual holdings had lost all value.

As the foregoing discussion makes clear, no single consideration can supply the exclusive test for determining the denominator. Instead, courts must consider a number of factors. These include the treatment of the land under state and local law; the physical characteristics of the land; and the prospective value of the regulated land. The endeavor should determine whether reasonable expectations about property ownership would lead a landowner to anticipate that his holdings would be treated as one parcel, or, instead, as separate tracts. The inquiry is objective, and the reasonable expectations at issue derive from background customs and the whole of our legal tradition.

First, courts should give substantial weight to the treatment of the land, in particular how it is bounded or divided, under state and local law. The reasonable expectations of an acquirer of land must acknowledge legitimate restrictions affecting his or her subsequent use and dispensation of the property. A reasonable restriction that predates a landowner's acquisition, however, can be one of the objective factors that most landowners would reasonably consider in forming fair expectations about their property. A prospective enactment, such as a new zoning ordinance, can limit the value of land without effecting a taking because it can be understood as reasonable by all concerned. In a similar manner, a use restriction which is triggered only after, or because of, a change in ownership should also guide a court's assessment of reasonable private expectations.

*Local lawyer would be aware of a prospective law*

Second, courts must look to the physical characteristics of the landowner's property. These include the physical relationship of any distinguishable tracts, the parcel's topography, and the surrounding human and ecological environment. In particular, it may be relevant that the property is located in an area that is subject to, or likely to become subject to, environmental or other regulation. Coastal property may present such unique concerns for a fragile land system that the State can go further in regulating its development and use than the common law of nuisance might otherwise permit.

Third, courts should assess the value of the property under the challenged regulation, with special attention to the effect of burdened land on the value of other holdings. Though a use restriction may decrease the market value of the property, the effect may be tempered if the regulated land adds value to the remaining property, such as by increasing privacy, expanding recreational space, or preserving surrounding natural beauty. A law that limits use of a landowner's small lot in one part of the city by reason of the landowner's nonadjacent holdings elsewhere may decrease the market value of the small lot in an unmitigated fashion. The absence of a special relationship between the holdings may counsel against consideration of all the holdings as a single parcel, making the restrictive law susceptible to a takings challenge. On the other hand, if the landowner's other property is adjacent to the small lot, the market value of the properties may well increase if their combination enables the expansion of a structure, or if development restraints for one part of the parcel protect the unobstructed skyline views of another part. That, in turn, may counsel in favor of treatment as a single parcel and may reveal the weakness of a regulatory takings challenge to the law.

State and federal courts have considerable experience in adjudicating regulatory takings claims that depart from these examples in various ways. The Court anticipates that in applying the test above they will continue to exercise care in this complex area.

The State of Wisconsin and petitioners each ask this Court to adopt a formalistic rule to guide the parcel inquiry. Neither proposal suffices to capture the central legal and factual principles that inform reasonable expectations about property interests.

The merger provision here is likewise a legitimate exercise of government power, as reflected by its consistency with a long history of state and local merger regulations that originated nearly a century ago.

When States or localities first set a minimum lot size, there often are existing lots that do not meet the new requirements, and so local governments will strive to reduce substandard lots in a gradual manner. The regulations here represent a classic way of doing this: by implementing a merger provision, which combines contiguous substandard lots under common ownership, alongside a grandfather clause, which preserves adjacent substandard lots that are in separate ownership. Also, as here, the harshness of a merger provision may be ameliorated by the availability of a variance from the local zoning authority for landowners in special circumstances.

Under the appropriate multifactor standard, it follows that for purposes of determining whether a regulatory taking has occurred here, petitioners' property should be evaluated as a single parcel consisting of Lots E and F together.

First, the treatment of the property under state and local law indicates petitioners' property should be treated as one when considering the effects of the restrictions. As the Wisconsin courts held, the state and local regulations merged Lots E and F. The decision to adopt the merger provision at issue here was for a specific and legitimate purpose, consistent with the widespread understanding that lot lines are not dominant or controlling in every case. Petitioners' land was subject to this regulatory burden, moreover, only because of voluntary conduct in bringing the lots under common ownership after the regulations were enacted. As a result, the valid merger of the lots under state law informs the reasonable expectation they will be treated as a single property.

Second, the physical characteristics of the property support its treatment as a unified parcel. The lots are contiguous along their longest edge. Their rough terrain and narrow shape make it reasonable to expect their range of potential uses might be limited. The land's location along the river is also significant. Petitioners could have anticipated public regulation might affect their enjoyment of their property, as the Lower St. Croix was a regulated area under federal, state, and local law long before petitioners possessed the land.

Third, the prospective value that Lot E brings to Lot F supports considering the two as one parcel for purposes of determining if there is a regulatory taking. Petitioners are prohibited from selling Lots E and F separately or from building separate residential structures on each. Yet this restriction is mitigated by the benefits of using the property as an integrated whole, allowing increased privacy and recreational space, plus the optimal location of any improvements.

The special relationship of the lots is further shown by their combined valuation. The point that is useful for these purposes is that the combined lots are valued at $698,300, which is far greater than the summed value of the separate regulated lots (Lot F with its cabin at $373,000, according to respondents' appraiser, and Lot E as an undevelopable plot at $40,000, according to petitioners' appraiser). The value added by the lots' combination shows their complementarity and supports their treatment as one parcel.

Considering petitioners' property as a whole, the state court was correct to conclude that petitioners cannot establish a compensable taking in these circumstances. Petitioners have not suffered a taking under *Lucas*, as they have not been deprived of all economically beneficial use of their property. They can use the property for residential purposes, including an enhanced, larger residential improvement.

Petitioners furthermore have not suffered a taking under the more general test of *Penn Central*. The expert appraisal relied upon by the state courts refutes any claim that the economic impact of the regulation is severe. Petitioners cannot claim that they reasonably expected to sell or develop their lots separately given the regulations which predated their acquisition of both lots. Finally, the governmental action was a reasonable land-use regulation, enacted as part of a coordinated federal, state, and local effort to preserve the river and surrounding land.

Like the ultimate question whether a regulation has gone too far, the question of the proper parcel in regulatory takings cases cannot be solved by any simple test. Courts must instead define the parcel in a manner that reflects reasonable expectations about the property. Courts must strive for consistency with the central purpose of the

Takings Clause: to "bar Government from forcing some people alone to bear public burdens which, in all fairness and justice, should be borne by the public as a whole."] Treating the lots in question as a single parcel is legitimate for purposes of this takings inquiry, and this supports the conclusion that no regulatory taking occurred here.

The judgment of the Wisconsin Court of Appeals is affirmed.

*It is so ordered.*

# CHAPTER FOURTEEN

# GIFTS, GIFTS CAUSA MORTIS AND BAILMENTS

## PART A. GIFTS

## INTRODUCTION

Gifts, of course, may be made of either land or personal property. Personal property includes anything that is not land. Gifts of land are made by deed or will. Gifts of personal property are frequently made in a much less formal manner – simply by handing the gift to the donee. The gifts involved in this chapter are gifts of personal property.

When there is no written documentation of the gift, conflicts may arise. Did the donor actually intend to make a gift? Or was the transaction really a *bailment* – like asking your friend to hold your Property book while you lock your bike? Or was it an *agency* relationship – like giving a friend the keys to your car so that the friend can act as your *agent* to go pick up a pizza?

The following cases illustrate some of the basic rules of law used to determine whether an actual gift was made. A valid inter vivos gift is irrevocable – the donor cannot take the item back. An agency relationship, however, is always subject to being terminated by the *principal* - the person who appointed the agent.

OCTOBER 3, 2017

MEMORANDUM OPINION AND JUDGMENT ON APPEAL

Bishop, Judge.

## INTRODUCTION

Following the death of Robert Eugene Howard (Robert), his nephew, John Howard (John), objected to the personal representative's inclusion of $25,228.03 derived from two of Robert's bank accounts into the estate inventory. John claimed Robert gifted to him all the funds within these accounts prior to his death. John appeals from the decision of the county court for Douglas County which concluded Robert did not gift the funds to John, John had no entitlement to the accounts, and the bank accounts were estate assets. We affirm.

## BACKGROUND

Robert died intestate on May 21, 2011. He was unmarried, without issue, and was preceded in death by six siblings. He was survived by two sisters, Judy and Annabelle, and a number of nieces and nephews and their children. Judy became personal representative of Robert's estate in September 2011 and filed an accounting showing that the assets in the estate totaled $28,408.03, of which $25,228.03 was "Cash from Bank Account." After deductions for obligations of the estate, the remaining balance for proposed distribution was $25,045.99. The Proposed Schedule of Distribution" reflects 22 distributees standing to inherit between 1/7 and 1/84 of the estate. The distributee list includes John. The dispute is over how much, if anything, should be distributed to John.

On February 26, 2015, a hearing took place on the petition and John's objection to closing the estate. A summary of the testimony follows.

John testified that, growing up, he remembered Robert visiting and helping with projects like pouring sidewalks or fixing the roof. John said, as an adult, "I suppose, really, after my father passed away, I really had no true family role model so Robert was it." John acknowledged he had a felony conviction on a drug charge in 2001 for which he did jail time. When asked if he had other convictions, John responded, "Oh, probably many," and he noted two felonies, which included another drug-related charge. John believed his involvement with Robert helped him behave himself.

For the two years prior to Robert's death, John said he visited Robert at home and the two often went out to eat at a café or another restaurant. Robert and John met for breakfast at the café every Sunday, and they would only contact each other during the week if one of them had to cancel the breakfast.

One Sunday in May 2011, Robert was not at the café and he had not canceled. John asked café employees if Robert had arrived and left before John's arrival. Upon learning Robert had not been to the café, John called Robert's house, but no one answered the phone. John then drove to Robert's home and knocked on the door. John noticed three days of newspapers remained on the porch and said "that's when I started getting a bad feeling."

John left and continued with plans to celebrate Mother's Day with his sister, Jeanne. Later in the day, John discussed his concerns about Robert with Jeanne. After speaking with Jeanne, John went to O'Rourke Apartments, where Robert worked as a maintenance engineer, and confirmed Robert had been to his last scheduled shift on the preceding Friday. Jeanne called Peggy, who in turn called area hospitals and learned Robert had been admitted to the Nebraska Medical Center. Peggy recalled this being "at least a week" before Robert's death.

John said he went to visit Robert every day after learning about his hospitalization, spending at least 2–1/2 hours there each day. Several days after Robert was admitted, John's brother-in-law, Murray, called and told John that Robert wanted to see him. John went to the hospital after the phone call. During this visit, [John stated Robert gave him two plastic debit cards and two paper bank cards displaying account numbers. These cards provided access to Robert's money market and checking accounts at Bank of the West. John also claimed Robert provided the PIN numbers for each card.]

With the cards and the PIN numbers, John could withdraw funds from Robert's respective bank accounts using an "ATM machine." Robert died on May 21, 2011. Between May 23 and June 6, John withdrew $4,803.00 from Robert's checking account in 16 separate withdrawals. Each withdrawal during this period was approximately $300, the maximum withdrawal allowed "at any given time." John withdrew $900 on May 23; $300 on May 24; $300 on May 25; $300 on May 26; $303 on May 27; $1,200 on May 31; $300 on June 1; $300 on June 2; $300 on June 3; and $600 on June 6.

John said he made the first $300 withdrawal with Jeanne and gave the money to Judy for funeral expenses. John testified he believed he was entitled to withdraw money from the accounts, but did not provide an explanation for the remaining withdrawals. From the time of Robert's death (May 2011) until Judy was appointed as personal representative (September 2011), John maintained control of the bank cards. Eventually, John gave the cards to other people, one to Judy and the other to his sister, Jeanne. John did not believe giving the cards to his family members relinquished his right to the money in the accounts, but Judy and Jeanne never returned the cards. Judy included the value of the bank accounts associated with the two cards in the value of the estate.

Judy testified that, as personal representative, she closed Robert's personal accounts at Bank of the West and transferred the funds into an estate account. Judy said when she closed Robert's accounts at Bank of the West, the only name on Robert's personal accounts was his own; there was no other beneficiary listed. She also collected and sold Robert's personal property, and filed a final accounting and a proposed distribution with the court.

On March 4, 2015, the county court entered a "Formal Order for Complete Settlement after Formal Intestate Proceeding." In relevant part, the court approved the final accounting and schedule of distribution, and overruled John's objection to including the bank account funds in the estate. The court found the bank accounts were estate assets, Robert did not gift the funds to John, and John had no right to any portion of the funds. John timely appealed.

ANALYSIS

*Gift of Cash in Bank Accounts.*

John claims Robert gifted his bank accounts to him as evidenced by Robert giving him the debit cards and their PIN numbers. John argues that Robert's actions met the requirements for a valid gift: "Robert physically delivered the plastic debit cards. He physically or verbally furnished the personal identification numbers. At that point, he had given John unfettered access to funds, not dependent upon any further human action or approval." John also suggests that there was "nothing more that Robert could have done to effect such a gift from his bed." Further, John asserts that "the donor Robert retained nothing."

To make a valid and effective gift inter vivos, there must be an intention to transfer title to the property, and a delivery by the donor and acceptance by the donee. The person asserting the gift must prove all the essential elements by clear, direct, positive, express, and unambiguous evidence. Dominion over and title to the gift must pass to the donee by the voluntary, intentional act of the donor. It must be such a delivery as will wholly pass title to the property which is the subject-matter of the gift and place it entirely beyond the control and dominion of the donor.

Judy argues the ATM cards only represented a means of access to the funds within the accounts, not title to or ownership of the funds within the accounts. She asserts that because Robert maintained title and dominion over the bank accounts after John gained access through the debit cards, Robert did not gift the accounts to John. Judy claims, "At best, John had a limited agency during his uncle's life, which terminated at his uncle's death." We agree.

Any statements made by Robert allegedly giving John the money in his bank accounts are irrelevant insofar as such statements would not affect Robert's ownership of his accounts or his ability to access or restrict access to the funds in those accounts. To the extent Robert's alleged action of giving John the debit cards and PIN numbers to his bank accounts could be construed to give John some kind of temporary agency authority over the accounts, the death of the sole party or last surviving party of a bank account terminates the authority of an agent.

There was no evidence presented that Robert's accounts were anything other than single-party accounts, nor was there any evidence that John, or anyone else, was named as a beneficiary payable upon death or otherwise. All such personal bank accounts are subject to statutes governing nonprobate transfers of accounts.

An "agent means a person authorized to make account transactions for a party." § 30–2716(2). The amount on deposit in a single-party account without a payable on death designation is transferred as part of the decedent's estate. § 30–2723(c). The type of account held by the decedent may be altered by written notice by a party to the financial institution, and the "notice must be signed by a party and received by the financial institution during the party's lifetime." § 30–2724(a).

There was no evidence received to indicate Robert's bank accounts were anything other than single-party accounts as set forth in § 30–2719(a). Therefore, any alteration to such an account, including making a payable upon death designation, must be made by written notice to the financial institution during the party's lifetime. See § 30–2724(a). That was not done here.

Accordingly, John's mere possession of Robert's debit cards and PIN numbers does not qualify as a valid and effective inter vivos gift, as such possession did not constitute a delivery that wholly passed title to the bank accounts, nor placed those accounts entirely beyond the control and dominion of Robert. John's lack of control over those bank accounts following Robert's death was evidenced by his own testimony that he eventually turned the debit cards over to Judy and Jeanne. Since the accounts remained solely titled in Robert's name, the accounts were transferred to Robert's estate upon his death as required by law. John failed to prove all the essential elements of an inter vivos gift by clear, direct, positive, express, and unambiguous evidence.

*Excluded Evidence.*

John claims the trial court improperly excluded certain testimony. As to the excluded testimony, John's trial counsel made an offer of proof that Peggy "would testify that the decedent explained to her that he would like her husband to receive his home and that he would like her brother, the plaintiff here, John, and herself to receive the money in his bank accounts." Finally, an offer of proof was made that if John was "allowed to testify, he would testify his uncle gave him the PIN numbers because he wanted him to have all the money in the accounts." Hearsay objections were sustained as to this evidence.

The admission or exclusion of evidence is not reversible error unless it unfairly prejudiced a substantial right of the complaining party. The exclusion of the noted evidence in this case cannot be said to have prejudiced any substantial right belonging to John because any evidence of Robert's intent to gift his bank accounts is irrelevant in light of statutory restrictions on how such accounts must be transferred upon the account owner's death. As previously discussed, Robert's personal bank accounts were subject to statutes governing nonprobate transfers of such accounts. Therefore, regardless of Robert's intent to gift the money in his bank accounts (as allegedly expressed verbally by Robert), when John took possession of the debit cards, any temporary agency authority over the accounts John may have had to access Robert's bank accounts while Robert was alive would have terminated upon Robert's death. As set forth above, the death of the sole party or last surviving party of a bank account terminates the authority of an agent. The balances remaining in Robert's accounts were transferred as part of the decedent's estate by operation of law. Robert's intent with regard to his bank accounts is irrelevant since the law specifically states how any balance remaining in such accounts upon death must be transferred. The exclusion did not unfairly prejudice a substantial right of the complaining party (John) in that admission of the evidence would not have changed the outcome.

## CONCLUSION

For the reasons set forth above, the decision of the county court is affirmed.
    AFFIRMED.

Note: There is much litigation over ownership of the money in bank accounts – especially when an elderly person adds a younger person as a joint tenant on the account. The issue then arises, was the younger person added to the account just for the *convenience* of the elderly person, making it a *convenience account*? Or was the younger person intended to be a joint tenant with right of survivorship?

When the elderly person dies, if it was a *convenience account* the money remaining in the account goes to the elderly person's estate. If it was a true *joint tenancy* account the money remaining goes to the younger person as the surviving joint tenant. It all depends on the intent of the elderly person when the elderly person added the younger person to the account. Without written documentation by the elderly person, it may be very difficult to prove which type of account the elderly person intended to create.

Is there such a thing as a conditional gift? One that only becomes irrevocable after certain conditions have been met?

## COURT OF APPEALS OF MISSISSIPPI.
### EMILY F. COOLEY, APPELLANT
### V.
### LAWRENCE J. TUCKER JR., APPELLEE

SEPTEMBER 6, 2016

**Opinion**

ISHEE, J., FOR THE COURT:

In December 2011, Lawrence J. Tucker Jr. proposed marriage to Emily F. Cooley, and presented her with a diamond engagement ring. In November 2014, Tucker broke off the engagement. Thereafter, Cooley maintained possession of the ring despite Tucker's requests to have the ring returned. Tucker filed a replevin action in the Lafayette County Chancery Court in February 2015 seeking return of the ring. After a trial on the merits, the chancery court ruled in favor of Tucker. In August 2015, the chancery court ordered Cooley to return the ring. Aggrieved, Cooley appeals. Finding no error, we affirm.

## STATEMENT OF FACTS

Tucker and Cooley began dating in April 2009. In the summer of 2010, Cooley relocated from Hattiesburg, Mississippi, to Oxford, Mississippi, and began cohabiting with Tucker in Tucker's home. Tucker averred that the relationship was tumultuous. Tucker testified that after consistent requests from Cooley to become engaged, he believed an engagement would improve the relationship. Accordingly, Tucker proposed marriage to Cooley in December 2011.

Tucker presented Cooley with a ring upon asking her to marry him. The ring appraised at approximately $40,000. Cooley accepted the proposal, and wore the ring continuously thereafter. Tucker immediately acquired insurance on the ring. He listed himself as the sole insured on the policy. Cooley was not referenced anywhere in the policy.

Tucker and Cooley could not agree, among other things, on the type of wedding they desired. A wedding date was never chosen, nor were any wedding plans pursued. Tucker testified that the relationship remained troubled and without improvement following the engagement. Tucker also stated that he attempted to end the relationship numerous times in person, but that Cooley's adverse reactions and threats to harm herself dissuaded him from pushing the issue. Tucker ultimately ended the relationship through an email in November 2014.

Cooley moved out of Tucker's house within a few days of receiving the email. Thereafter, Tucker requested that Cooley return the engagement ring. Cooley refused. After numerous failed attempts to recoup the ring from Cooley, Tucker ultimately filed a replevin action in the chancery court seeking return of the ring.

A trial took place before the chancellor on May 21, 2015. Tucker and Cooley both testified. Cooley asserted that the ring was an inter vivos gift to her from Tucker. Tucker countered that the ring was a conditional gift, premised on the condition that he and Cooley would marry. On July 29, 2015, the chancellor entered an order awarding Tucker possession of the ring. The chancellor determined that the ring was a conditional gift, and since Tucker and Cooley did not fulfill the condition of marriage, Cooley was not entitled to keep it. Cooley now appeals the chancery court's judgment.

## DISCUSSION

Cooley asserts that the chancery court erred in its determination that the ring was a conditional gift rather than an inter vivos gift. The elements of a valid inter vivos gift are as follows: (1) a donor competent to make a gift; (2) a voluntary act of the donor with donative intent; (3) the gift must be complete with nothing else to be done; (4) there must be delivery to the donee; and (5) the gift must be irrevocable.

The cases relied upon by Cooley, *Lomax v. Lomax*, (2015), and *Neville v. Neville*, (1999), are divorce cases that question which party should be awarded the engagement ring post-divorce. In both cases, we determined that the wife should keep the engagement ring because "it was not a marital asset subject to equitable division."

The engagement ring is to be considered an inter vivos gift conditioned upon the parties getting married—a condition that, obviously, occurred in the cases cited by Cooley. Hence, in those cases, the requirements for an *inter vivos* gift were met, including the element mandating that the gift be completed with nothing more to be done.

Here, the chancellor ultimately determined that "the engagement ring was a conditional gift presented in contemplation of a marriage that did not occur." It is from this determination that the chancellor awarded Tucker the ring. This conclusion is supported by Mississippi case law and by fact.

THE JUDGMENT OF THE LAFAYETTE COUNTY CHANCERY COURT IS AFFIRMED. ALL COSTS OF THIS APPEAL ARE ASSESSED TO THE APPELLANT.

Note: Who would own the ring if the facts had been a bit different? Suppose that Cooley and Tucker had been in a boat out on a lake when Cooley, instead of Tucker, decided to end the engagement. To make it clear that she was doing so, she took off the ring and handed it back to Tucker. That was so upsetting to Tucker that he immediately threw the ring into the lake. The next day a young child found the ring, and brought it to shore. Tucker then demanded that the child give the ring to Tucker. Would the child be legally obligated to do so? The answer to that question will be discussed in Chapter 15, Lost and Found Personal Property.

From the two preceding cases it is clear that there must be a complete, unconditional delivery for a traditional inter vivos gift to be valid and irrevocable. There must also be acceptance by the donee, or by someone on behalf of the donee. But if the gift is beneficial to the done courts are not reluctant to imply that there was the necessary acceptance.

Another, special form of gift, a *gift causa mortis*, is always considered to be both revocable and conditional. A *gift causa mortis* may be made only when the donor is in fear of imminent death, *mortis* being the Latin word for death.

The following case explains the basic differences between a traditional inter vivos gift and a *gift causa mortis*.

## COURT OF APPEALS OF INDIANA
### JAY GARRISON, APPELLANT-RESPONDENT,
### V.
### PAMELA GARRISON, APPELLEE-PLAINTIFF.

MARCH 9, 2017

**Opinion**

Shepard, Senior Judge

When someone on his deathbed transfers his property under circumstances where competence may be in question, how should the burden of proof concerning the transfer be applied?

**Facts and Procedural History**

While on his deathbed, Thomas R. Garrison transferred title on two cars to one of his sons, Jay Garrison. After Thomas' death, his widow Pamela Garrison as the personal representative of the estate, filed a petition to recover assets. She contested what she deemed *inter vivos* gifts of the cars to Jay and sought to have them returned to the estate, explicitly disputing Thomas' competency. Jay intervened, challenging Pamela's petition. The trial court ordered the return of the vehicles to the estate, finding that they were gifts *causa mortis* for which Thomas was not competent to form donative intent. The trial court certified its order for interlocutory appeal. Agreeing with the trial court's conclusion that the evidence of Thomas' competence was in equipoise, and, thus, the assets should be recovered by the estate, we affirm, albeit on other grounds.

Pamela and Thomas were married for twenty-eight years before Thomas' death, and while no children were born of the marriage, they each had children from prior relationships. Thomas was diagnosed with terminal lung cancer on July 27, 2015, ultimately passing away on August 9, 2015. On August 11, 2015, two days prior to Thomas' funeral, Jay, who was accompanied by police officers, came to Pamela and Thomas' house to take possession of a 2013 Chevrolet Corvette Z06 and a 2006 Ford Explorer XLT. Those vehicles had been titled in Thomas' name, but as of July 30, 2015, were titled in Jay's name.

An unsupervised estate was opened on August 18, 2015. Pamela filed a petition to recover assets, seeking to nullify the *inter vivos* gifts of the vehicles to Jay.

Those who testified at the contested hearing agreed that Thomas frequently smoked cigarettes, especially prior to his death, and that he consumed whiskey and beer in increasingly large quantities before his death. Most witnesses acknowledged that after his diagnosis, Thomas was sad and in considerable physical pain.

According to some, including Jay, Thomas' sister Janet Baller, and Janet's husband David Lee Baller, Thomas' behavior in the period leading up to his death remained fairly consistent with behavior they had observed over the years. Thomas was an alcoholic, who smoked a great deal, and had an unusual sense of humor.

In contrast, Pamela testified that beginning in June 2015, Thomas exhibited drastically changed behavior.

The trial judge concluded that the evidence of Thomas' competency to make a gift *causa mortis* was evenly split, and that the vehicles must therefore be returned to the estate. Jay now appeals.

## Discussion and Decision

Jay argues that 1) the trial court erroneously concluded it was a gift *causa mortis* as opposed to a gift *inter vivos*, 2) applied the wrong standard of review, and 3) based its decision on insufficient evidence.

Pamela raised a straight claim of incompetence in her petition to recover assets.

There are two different kinds of gifts—*inter vivos* gifts and gifts *causa mortis*. An *inter vivos* gift is one where the donee becomes the absolute owner of a thing given in the lifetime of the donor. An *inter vivos* gift is made when: (1) the donor is competent to contract; (2) the donor has freedom of will; (3) the donor intends to make a gift; (4) the gift is completed with nothing left undone; (5) the property is delivered by the donor and accepted by the donee; and (6) the gift is immediate and absolute.

A gift *causa mortis*, on the other hand, is accomplished when: (1) the gift was the donor's property; (2) the gift was given when the donor was in peril of death or while under the apprehension of impending death from an existing malady; (3) the donor dies as a result of the disorder without intervening recovery; and, (4) there was actual or constructive delivery of the thing given to the donee with the intention that the title vest conditionally upon the death of the donor.

Delivery of the gift—*inter vivos* or *causa mortis*—is an indispensable requirement without which the gift fails. Still, manual transfer is not always necessary. It is sufficient if the delivery is as complete as the thing and the circumstances of the parties will permit, because delivery may be actual, constructive or symbolic.

The mental capacity required to make a valid *inter vivos* gift is the same as the capacity required to execute a will. The same is true of the donor of a gift *causa mortis*, who "must possess sufficient mental capacity to make the gift, that is, must be mentally competent or of sound mind." Indeed, "generally, the same degree of mental capacity is required to make a gift causa mortis as is required to make a will." The determination of mental capacity is tested at the moment the gift is made.

The parties to this case contest the burden of establishing the type of gift versus the presumptions of competency for each kind of gift, the burden imposed on the challenger, and the burden of going forward with corresponding rebuttal evidence. Resolution of the appeal turns on whether the parties have met their respective burdens on the issue of competency.

For an *inter vivos* gift, when determining whether a transfer qualified as such, the burden of proof is a preponderance of the evidence. For a gift *causa mortis*, because of the opportunity for the perpetration of fraud on the decedent, the evidence establishing such a gift must be clear and convincing, and must be accompanied by a delivery of the subject matter. The burden cannot be met by the sole uncorroborated testimony of the donee.

Certain transfers are viewed differently based on the relationship of the donor and donee. In *Lucas v. Frazee*, (1984), we examined whether a deed should be rescinded because it was procured through constructive fraud or upheld as a gift. We acknowledged that establishment of the existence of certain relationships, such as parent and child, lead to a presumption that the questioned transaction was the result of undue influence exerted by the dominant party, constructively fraudulent, and, therefore, void. In that situation, the burden of proof shifts to the dominant party to demonstrate that the transaction was conducted at arm's length, and thus was valid. The dominant party must rebut the presumption of fraud by clear and unequivocal proof. Evidence of the donor/subordinate party's competence is relevant to consideration of the validity of such gift.

Inasmuch as Thomas and Jay were father and son, the presumption of undue influence arose with respect to the transfer. Jay presented testimony that Thomas was competent at the time of the transfer, and that Jay possessed certificates of title to the two vehicles dated July 30, 2015. Pamela, however, presented testimonial evidence of Thomas' incompetency before and at the time of transfer. The trial court found the evidence of competency was evenly split. Jay, therefore, has not rebutted the presumption of undue influence, and the estate is entitled to recovery of the vehicles.

Conclusion

For the foregoing reasons, we affirm the decision of the trial court.

Affirmed.

## PART B. BAILMENTS

## INTRODUCTION

What happens if the owner of personal property gives possession and control of the property to another person – with no intention of relinquishing title? Then a *bailment* is created, with the owner of the property being the *bailor* and the person who has temporary possession and control of the property being the *bailee*.

A bailment is always created, for example, when you use valet parking at a hotel or restaurant. In other situations it may not always be so clear. One of the interesting aspects of the law of bailments is that the bailee has an absolute obligation to return the property to the bailor. If the bailee cannot do so, there is a presumption of negligence against the bailee, and the bailee pays the damages.

### SUPREME COURT OF TENNESSEE
### BETTY J. ALLEN, PLAINTIFF-APPELLEE
### V.
### HYATT REGENCY--NASHVILLE HOTEL,
### DEFENDANT -APPELLANT

#### MARCH 26, 1984

**OPINION BY: HARBISON**

In this case the Court is asked to consider the nature and extent of the liability of the operator of a commercial parking garage for theft of a vehicle during the absence of the owner. Both courts below, on the basis of prior decisions from this state, held that a bailment was created when the owner parked and locked his vehicle in a modern, indoor, multi-story garage operated by appellant in conjunction with a large hotel in downtown Nashville. We affirm.

There is almost no dispute as to the relevant facts. Appellant is the owner and operator of a modern high-rise hotel in Nashville fronting on the south side of Union Street. Immediately to the rear, or south, of the main hotel building there is a multi-story parking garage with a single entrance and a single exit to the west, on Seventh Avenue, North. As one enters the parking garage at the street level, there is a large sign reading "Welcome to Hyatt Regency-Nashville." There is another Hyatt Regency sign inside the garage at street level, together with a sign marked "Parking." The garage is available for parking by members of the general public as well as guests of the hotel, and the public are invited to utilize it.

On the morning of February 12, 1981, appellee's husband, Edwin Allen, accompanied by two passengers, drove appellee's new 1981 automobile into the parking garage. Neither Mr. Allen nor his passengers intended to register at the hotel as a guest. Mr. Allen had parked in this particular garage on several occasions, however, testifying that he felt that the vehicle would be safer in an attended garage than in an unattended outside lot on the street. The single entrance was controlled by a ticket machine. The single exit was controlled by an attendant in a booth just opposite to the entrance and in full view thereof.

Appellee's husband entered the garage at the street level and took a ticket which was automatically dispensed by the machine. The machine activated a barrier gate which rose and permitted Mr. Allen to enter the garage. He drove to the fourth floor level, parked the vehicle, locked it, retained the ignition key, descended by elevator to the street level and left the garage. When he returned several hours later, the car was gone, and it has never been recovered. Mr. Allen reported the theft to the attendant at the exit booth, who stated, "Well, it didn't come out here." The attendant did not testify at the trial.

Mr. Allen then reported the theft to security personnel employed by appellant, and subsequently reported the loss to the police. Appellant regularly employed a number of security guards, who were dressed in a distinctive uniform, two of whom were on duty most of the time. These guards patrolled the hotel grounds and building as well as the garage and were instructed to make rounds through the garage, although not necessarily at specified intervals. One of the security guards told appellee's husband that earlier in the day he had received the following report:

> "He said, 'It's a funny thing here. On my report here a lady called me somewhere around nine-thirty or after and said that there was someone messing with a car.'"

The guard told Mr. Allen that he closed his office and went up into the garage to investigate, but reported that he did not find anything unusual or out of the ordinary.

Customers such as Mr. Allen, upon entering the garage, received a ticket from the dispensing machine. On one side of this ticket are instructions to overnight guests to present the ticket to the front desk of the hotel. The other side contains instructions to the parker to keep the ticket and that the ticket must be presented to the cashier upon leaving the parking area. The ticket states that charges are made for the use of parking space only and that appellant assumes no responsibility for loss through fire, theft, collision or otherwise to the car or its contents. The ticket states that cars are parked at the risk of the owner, and parkers are instructed to lock their vehicles. The record indicates that these tickets are given solely for the purpose of measuring the time during which a vehicle is parked in order that the attendant may collect the proper charge, and that they are not given for the purpose of identifying particular vehicles. It is not insisted that the language of the ticket is sufficient to exonerate appellant, since the customer is not shown to have read it or to have had it called to his attention.

The question of the legal relationship between the operator of a vehicle which is being parked and the operator of parking establishments has been the subject of frequent litigation in this state and elsewhere. The authorities are in conflict, and the results of the cases are varied.

It is legally and theoretically possible, of course, for various legal relationships to be created by the parties, ranging from the traditional concepts of lessor-lessee, licensor-licensee, bailor-bailee, to that described in some jurisdictions as a "deposit." Several courts have found difficulty with the traditional criteria of bailment in analyzing park-and-lock cases. One of the leading cases is *McGlynn v. Parking Authority of City of Newark, (1981).* There the Supreme Court of New Jersey reviewed numerous decisions from within its own state and from other jurisdictions, and it concluded that it was more "useful and straightforward" to consider the possession and control elements in defining the duty of care of a garage operator to its customers than to consider them in the context of bailment. That Court concluded that the "realities" of the relationship between the parties gave rise to a duty of reasonable care on the part of operators of parking garages and parking lots. It further found that a garage owner is usually better situated to protect a parked car and to distribute the cost of protection through parking fees. It also emphasized that owners usually expect to receive their vehicles back in the same condition in which they left them and that the imposition of a duty to protect parked vehicles and their contents was consistent with that expectation. The Court went further and stated that since the owner is ordinarily absent when theft or damage occurs, the obligation to come forward with affirmative evidence of negligence could impose a difficult, if not insurmountable, burden upon him. After considering various policy considerations, which it acknowledged to be the same as those recognized by courts holding that a bailment is created, the New Jersey Court indulged or authorized a presumption of negligence from proof of damage to a car parked in an enclosed garage.

Although the New Jersey Court concluded that a more flexible and comprehensive approach could be achieved outside of traditional property concepts, Tennessee courts generally have analyzed cases such as this in terms of sufficiency of the evidence to create a bailment for hire by implication. We believe that this continues to be the majority view and the most satisfactory and realistic approach to the problem, unless the parties clearly by their conduct or by express contract create some other relationship.

The subject has been discussed in numerous previous decisions in this state. One of the leading cases is *Dispeker v. New Southern Hotel.* In that case the guest at a hotel delivered his vehicle to a bellboy who took possession of it and parked it in a lot adjoining the hotel building. The owner kept the keys, but the car apparently was capable of being started without the ignition key. The owner apparently had told the attendant how to so operate it. Later the employee took the vehicle for his own purposes and damaged it. Under these circumstances the Court held that a bailment for hire had been created and that upon proof of misdelivery of the vehicle the bailee was liable to the customer.

In the subsequent case of *Scruggs v. Dennis,* upon facts practically identical to those of the instant case, the Court again held that an implied bailment contract had been created between a customer who parked and locked his vehicle in a garage. Upon entry he received a ticket dispensed by a machine, drove his automobile to the underground third level of the garage and parked. He retained his ignition key, but when he returned to retrieve the automobile in the afternoon it had disappeared. It was recovered more than two weeks later and returned to the owner in a damaged condition.

In that case the operator of the garage had several attendants on duty, but the attendants did not ordinarily operate the parked vehicles, as in the instant case. (Appellant's employees occasionally parked the vehicles of patrons who were handicapped and under other unusual circumstances.)

Although the Court recognized that there were some factual differences between the *Scruggs* case and that of *Dispeker v. New Southern Hotel Co.,* it concluded that a bailment had been created when the owner parked his vehicle for custody and safe keeping in the parking garage, where there was limited access and where the patron had to present a ticket to an attendant upon leaving the premises.

A bailment relationship was also found in *Jackson v. Metropolitan Government of Nashville,* when faculty members of a high school conducted an automobile parking operation for profit upon the high school campus. A customer who parked his vehicle there was allowed recovery for theft, even though he had parked the vehicle himself after paying a fee, had locked the vehicle and had kept the keys.

On the contrary, in the case of *Rhodes v. Pioneer Parking Lot,* a bailment was found not to exist when the owner left his vehicle in an open parking lot which was wholly unattended and where he simply inserted coins into a meter, received a ticket, then parked the vehicle himself and locked it. Denying recovery, the Court said:

"In the case at bar, however, we find no evidence to justify a finding that the plaintiff delivered his car into the custody of the defendant, nor do we find any act or conduct upon the defendant's part which would justify a reasonable person believing that an obligation of bailment had been assumed by the defendant."

In the instant case, appellee's vehicle was not driven into an unattended or open parking area. Rather it was driven into an enclosed, indoor, attended commercial garage which not only had an attendant controlling the exit but regular security personnel to patrol the premises for safety.

Under these facts we are of the opinion that the courts below correctly concluded that a bailment for hire had been created, and that upon proof of nondelivery appellee was entitled to the statutory presumption of negligence.

We recognize that there is always a question as to whether there has been sufficient delivery of possession and control to create a bailment when the owner locks a vehicle and keeps the keys. Nevertheless, the realities of the situation are that the operator of the garage is, in circumstances like those shown in this record, expected to provide attendants and protection. In practicality the operator does assume control and custody of the vehicles parked, limiting access thereto and requiring the presentation of a ticket upon exit. As stated previously, the attendant employed by appellant did not testify, but he told appellee's husband that the vehicle did not come out of the garage through the exit which he controlled. This testimony was not amplified, but the attendant obviously must have been in error or else must have been inattentive or away from his station. The record clearly shows that there was no other exit from which the vehicle could have been driven.

Appellant made no effort to rebut the presumption created by statute in this state (which is similar to presumptions indulged by courts in some other jurisdictions not having such statutes). While the plaintiff did not prove positive acts of negligence on the part of appellant, the record does show that some improper activity or tampering with vehicles had been called to the attention of security personnel earlier in the day of the theft in question, and that appellee's new vehicle had been removed from the garage by some person or persons unknown, either driving past an inattentive attendant or one who had absented himself from his post, there being simply no other way in which the vehicle could have been driven out of the garage.

Under the facts and circumstances of this case, we are not inclined to depart from prior decisions or to place the risk of loss upon the consuming public as against the operators of commercial parking establishments such as that conducted by appellant. We recognize that park-and-lock situations arise under many and varied factual circumstances. It is difficult to lay down one rule of law which will apply to all cases.

The expectations of the parties and their conduct can cause differing legal relationships to arise, with consequent different legal results. We do not find the facts of the present case, however, to be at variance with the legal requirements of the traditional concept of a bailment for hire. In our opinion it amounted to more than a mere license or hiring of a space to park a vehicle, unaccompanied by any expectation of protection or other obligation upon the operator of the establishment.

The judgment of the courts below is affirmed at the cost of appellant. The cause will be remanded to the trial court for any further proceedings which may be necessary.

Note: In the following case, considering the surrounding facts and circumstances, is there anything that the plaintiff's lawyer could have done better? What would be an appropriate solution for this situation?

## UNITED STATES COURT OF FEDERAL CLAIMS
## MAJD KAM-ALMAZ, PLAINTIFF,
### V.
## THE UNITED STATES OF AMERICA, DEFENDANT.

JANUARY 7, 2011

ORDER/OPINION

BASKIR, Judge.

Plaintiff seeks compensation for losses occasioned by the seizure of his laptop computer by U.S. Customs agents.

## I. Introduction

According to an editorial in The New York Times of November 15, 2010, during an 18-month period between 2008 and 2010, some 3,000 returning Americans had their laptop computers seized and their contents examined by U.S. Customs. Moreover, as was the case with Mr. Kam Almaz, U.S. Customs agents may freely share the data from those computers-personal and business records, web-site visits, email-again without a warrant or even reasonable suspicion. Challenges in District Court to these Fourth Amendment exceptions have not been successful. The New York Times calls for legislative limits on the Government's right to access and share computer data. Such legislation would presumably not help Mr. Kam Almaz, who has a more prosaic complaint-he seeks compensation for losses he suffered from damage to the computer and its data while in the possession of U.S. Customs.

## II. Background

The following facts are taken from Plaintiff's Complaint and Amended Complaint, as well as from the parties' briefs. Plaintiff alleges the Government breached an implied-in-fact bailment contract or effected an uncompensated taking when it seized Plaintiff's business laptop computer and flash disks.

On April 7, 2006, Agent Craig Moldowan, of the U.S. Immigration and Customs Enforcement Division (ICE) of the U.S. Department of Homeland Security, seized Plaintiff's Hewlett-Packard Pavilion laptop computer and flash disks at the Dulles International Airport in Loudoun County, Virginia. Plaintiff alleges that Agent Moldowan stated the laptop would be seized for "no more than seven days." Plaintiff also alleges that he received a document receipt on a Customs Form 6051D that stated "shipments may be detained for up to thirty (30) days, unless statutory authority of interagency agreement mandates that a longer period of time is required or the imports/exporter/subject requests a longer detention period through the Port Director."

Plaintiff requested that he be permitted to make a full copy of the files on his computer, but Agent Moldowan denied this request. Plaintiff did not have any other backup copies of the files on his computer.

The Government withheld the laptop until June 21, 2006, some ten weeks. During this time, Plaintiff on several occasions repeated his request to copy the files on the computer. These requests were also denied. While in ICE custody, the computer crashed. This resulted in permanent damage to the Plaintiff's operating software, his data files, and the software warranty. Plaintiff claims damages for equipment and warranty costs; replacement hardware, software, and warranty; and lost contract costs totaling $469,480.00.

Plaintiff filed his Complaint on January 5, 2009, and an Amended Complaint on January 25, 2010. Defendant filed a Motion to Dismiss on June 30, 2010, that argued Plaintiff's claims should be dismissed for lack of jurisdiction and for failure to state a claim upon which relief can be granted.

## III. Discussion

### A. Standard of Review

The Rules of the U.S. Court of Federal Claims state that the Court may dismiss a complaint for failure to state a claim upon which relief can be granted. To survive a 12(b)(6) motion to dismiss, a complaint must "state a claim to relief that is plausible on its face," thus containing sufficient factual content on which a court may "draw the reasonable inference that the defendant is liable for the misconduct alleged." The plausibility standard "asks for more than a sheer possibility that the defendant has acted unlawfully." Though the Court must accept the alleged factual allegations to be true, the trial court is "not bound to accept as true a legal conclusion couched as a factual allegation." A complaint must also state a "plausible claim for relief," meaning that the factual allegations "plausibly suggest an entitlement to relief."

RCFC Rule 12(b)(1) states that the Court may dismiss a complaint for lack of subject matter jurisdiction. Generally, this Court possesses jurisdiction to entertain monetary claims founded upon the Takings Clause of the United States Constitution, statutes, regulations, or contracts. The statutory or constitutional claims a plaintiff asserts must be "money-mandating" to come within the jurisdiction of this Court. The plaintiff bears the burden of establishing jurisdiction by a preponderance of the evidence.

### B. Breach of Contract Claim

Plaintiff's claim for breach of contract must be dismissed for failure to state a claim because Plaintiff fails to plead facts in his Complaint that establish an implied-in-fact bailment contract. To prove an implied-in-fact contract, Plaintiff must establish (1) mutuality of intent, (2) consideration, (3) an unambiguous offer and acceptance, and (4) actual authority on the part of the government's representative to bind the government in contract. A bailment is a type of contract whereby "an owner, while retaining title, delivers personalty to another for some particular purpose. The relationship includes a return of the goods to the owner or a subsequent disposition in accordance with his instructions."

The Complaint fails to allege sufficient facts to find a bailment in a number of aspects. Plaintiff contends that both the oral promise to return the computer within seven days and the signed Customs Form 6051D stating that the computer would be returned within thirty days gave rise to an implied promise to use due care during the alleged bailment. However, these Government promises do not give rise to a bailment. First, the Complaint does not allege that Plaintiff "delivered personalty" to the Government. Rather, the property was seized. Second, the Complaint does not allege that the computer would be returned "in accordance with Plaintiff's instructions." Moreover, there are no facts in the Complaint demonstrating an explicit promise that the goods would be guarded or carefully handled. *See Hatzlachh Supply Co. v. United States,* (holding no implied bailment created when plaintiff could not point to any "promise, representation or statement that plaintiff's goods would be guarded or carefully handled pending resolution of the forfeitures incurred").

Furthermore, the Complaint fails to allege facts demonstrating the parties' mutual intent. The "purely unilateral act" of seizing a person's personal property does not evidence intent to enter into a bailment contract. Moreover, the Complaint describes the Government's actions as a "seizure." The oral promise to return the computer in seven days and the Customs Form 6051D are not enough to overcome the unilateral nature of the transaction. *See Husband v. United States,* (no bailment despite a government receipt given to Plaintiff at the time of seizure). Plaintiff involuntarily gave up his property because he did not have any choice but to accept the Government's actions; the Court cannot find the mutual intent necessary to form a contract.

In addition to these several deficiencies, any one of which is fatal to Plaintiff's cause, the Complaint also lacks the necessary allegations of Agent Moldowan's authority to enter into a bailment contract. A government officer must have actual authority to enter into a contract, and this authority either explicitly arises through a provision in the Constitution, a statute, or a regulation, or implicitly arises when such authority is an integral part of the officer's duties. The Complaint does not cite any provisions demonstrating an authority to contract, nor does it cite facts showing that the authority to contract was integral to Agent Moldowan's duties as a Custom's Agent.

## C. Takings Claim

Plaintiff's takings claim must be dismissed for failure to state a claim because property seized and retained pursuant to the police power is not taken for a "public use" within the context of the takings clause.

The police power encompasses Customs' ability to seize and retain property if the officer has "reasonable cause to believe that any law or regulation enforced by Customs and Border Protection or Immigration and Customs Enforcement has been violated."

Plaintiff argues that the laptop was not seized according to the police power but rather according to an "administrative border search for security purposes." However, agents do not have authority to seize property without having "reasonable cause to suspect a violation of law," and thus, agents cannot randomly seize property for general security purposes as Plaintiff argues occurred in this case. If property could be randomly seized without reasonable cause, Plaintiff might argue that such a seizure was for a "public use"-to protect the general welfare. However, this argument must fail given the limit on seizure authority granted in 19 C.F.R. § 162 .21 and the lack of any facts in Plaintiff's Complaint demonstrating an administrative search and seizure.

If Agent Moldowan did not have "reasonable cause" to believe a violation of the law occurred, the seizure would have been unlawful and unauthorized. First, this Court does not have jurisdiction to hear claims contesting the lawfulness of a search and seizure because due process and Fourth Amendment claims are reserved to the District Court. Second, this Court only possesses jurisdiction to consider takings claims that arise "as the direct, natural, or probable result of an *authorized* activity" by Government officials.

Finally, even if the Government's action was authorized and the taking was based on an "unreasonable delay" in returning the property, Plaintiff's claim must still fail for lack of jurisdiction. Though an owner of property has a due process right to have the government either return seized property or initiate forfeiture proceedings, a claim of damages for delay in returning seized property is again a due process claim that must be heard in District Court.

In *Arcadia*, Plaintiffs argued that a seizure of its goods for four years was a compensable taking based on unreasonable delay. The Court disagreed. The Plaintiff could bring a due process claim for delay in District Court, but the Due Process Clause is not a money-mandating provision conferring jurisdiction on this Court.

## IV. Conclusion

For the foregoing reasons, Defendant's Motion to Dismiss is GRANTED. The Clerk is directed to enter judgment for the Defendant and DISMISS the Complaint. Parties are to bear their own costs.

IT IS SO ORDERED.

Note: In the following case, what, specifically, did the landlord personally do that was wrong? Why did the court mention that the defendant had a winter home in Argentina? What was the legal significance of that fact? What were the written documents involved?

# UNITED STATES BANKRUPTCY COURT, N.D. ILLINOIS
## SCOTT B. ALLEY, DEBTOR
## CHARLES J. MYLER, TRUSTEE, PLAINTIFF
## V.
## ELIS GIANNINI, DEFENDANT.

DECEMBER 2, 2010.

MANUEL BARBOSA, Judge.

For the reasons set forth below, judgment in the amount of $600 in damages and $571.25 in attorneys' fees is granted against Elis Giannini and in favor of the Trustee. Mr. Giannini's request for the payment of Chapter 7 administrative expense is DENIED.

The Trustee has filed an adversary complaint against the landlord of the building where the Debtor operated a retail furniture store, Elis Giannini, alleging that he damaged inventory that the Debtor had left there and also seeking sanctions against the landlord for refusing to allow the Trustee access to the inventory. The landlord, in turn, has filed a request that the Court authorize payment of rent to him as an administrative expense for the time that the inventory was stored on his property post-petition. The Court held an evidentiary hearing on both matters on November 5, 2010, and sets forth the following findings of fact and conclusions of law.

## A. Factual Background

Prior to filing bankruptcy, the Debtor, Scott Alley, owned and operated a log furniture store and rustic art gallery, named Nature's Gallery, in Geneva, Illinois. The store mostly sold handcrafted aspen log furniture but also sold rustic art. Mr. Alley purchased his log furniture from Colorado, which was handmade and which he specially ordered to his own specifications. He personally transported the furniture to the store, driving back and forth from Colorado. The store had an ordinary door, so at least some of the furniture, such as bunk beds, had to be disassembled and reassembled to be moved into or out of the store.

His store was located on property that he rented from Elis Giannini, and his store was at that location for ten years. Mr. Alley's clientele were mostly wealthy, and he characterized the furniture as 'high-end.' Often his customers were buying furniture for second houses. Because of this, his business suffered with the recent crash in the housing and construction market, and he ultimately closed the business in March 2009. He originally wanted to close in December 2008, but Mr. Giannini was out of the country at that time. Mr. Giannini has a winter home in Argentina, and convinced Mr. Alley to stay at the location until he returned to the U.S. in March. To persuade Mr. Alley to stay, Mr. Giannini agreed to a reduced rent of $5,000 for the three-month period of January through March, which Mr. Alley paid.

Mr. Alley vacated the building on March 15, 2009. He spoke with Mr. Giannini before he left the building, and mentioned that he was leaving some furniture and other inventory behind temporarily. When Mr. Alley left, he moved the inventory to the back of the space, but knew he was going to file for bankruptcy, and "assumed that the Bankruptcy Court would take care of the inventory since there's no way I could move it." Mr. Giannini rented the space to a bicycle shop beginning April 7, 2009, for $2,400 per month. The new tenants agreed to work around the inventory until May 1, but wanted it out by then because they planned to open for business May 1st. At some point before May 1st, the inventory had not been removed and the new tenant wanted it moved out. Mr. Giannini had a bad arm and a bad leg, so some of the employees for the new tenant agreed to disassemble and move the inventory. Mr. Giannini gave the bicycle shop a discount on the first month's rent because they had to work around the inventory, and gave them a discount of between $500 and $1,000 on the second month's rent because they had disassembled and moved the furniture for him. They moved the majority of the inventory to the downstairs boiler room, and the remainder was moved to Mr. Giannini's garage down the street and his upstairs loft area. Unfortunately, the bicycle shop employees also threw away at least some of the artwork in the dumpster without Mr. Giannini's knowledge.

The parties dispute the value of the inventory both as of the petition date and as of today's date. The pieces of furniture were handmade by individuals who cut their own wood, and were made to Mr. Alley's specifications. Mr. Alley testified that he took stock of the furniture when he vacated the premises a few days before filing his petition, and valued it at $41,900. This was what he considered to be the 'retail' value, and he arrived at it by doubling his own purchase cost plus his cost in transporting the items from Colorado. ...However, Mr. Alley also testified that, towards the end of his business, he put the furniture on sale for 60% off retail, and then 80% off, and was still unable to sell the inventory that remained when he vacated the building.

Mr. Alley filed his bankruptcy petition on March 23, 2009. The Trustee reviewed the file, contacted Mr. Alley around April 2nd, and learned of the furniture, which he believed was still in the rental space. The Trustee attempted to reach Mr. Giannini by phone to ask him about the furniture inventory. He called Mr. Giannini numerous times, but could only reach his son. Finally, in mid- to late April, the Trustee was able to get in contact with Mr. Giannini by phone. The Trustee explained that he was the bankruptcy trustee for Mr. Alley's estate, that he had a duty to sell and liquidate the inventory, and that Mr. Giannini would be entitled to an administrative expense claim for the actual rental of the space until the inventory could be sold. However, Mr. Giannini refused to grant the Trustee access to the inventory and demanded payment of rent before he would provide access. Mr. Giannini also stated that the inventory had been moved to three different locations, but would not disclose where the locations were. The Trustee filed a motion for rule to show cause and holding of contempt against Mr. Giannini on May 5, 2009, with a hearing set for May 14, 2009. Sometime before May 14th, Mr. Giannini spoke with an attorney named Michael Dimand, and learned that he had no right to deny access to the Trustee. Mr. Dimand called the Trustee on Mr. Giannini's behalf sometime before the 14th, and explained that Mr. Giannini had realized that he was in the wrong and would cooperate fully with the Trustee. Based on that discussion, and the representation that Mr. Giannini would cooperate, the Trustee agreed to withdraw the motion for contempt. Thereafter, Mr. Giannini provided full access to the furniture.

Mr. Alley viewed the inventory sometime in late May with a potential bidder from Highland Furniture. He noticed that the furniture had been moved and mostly disassembled, and that the artwork had been thrown in the dumpster and was broken and no longer salable. ...When pressed by the Trustee, Highland made an offer for around $1,500 for all of the furniture, which the Trustee rejected.

In September 2009, Mr. Giannini had Mr. Dimand call the Trustee to warn him that the current storage areas were not weather-tight or safe for storage in the winter. The boiler room could get up to 120 degrees in the winter and became full of soot when the furnace was running, and the garage tended to flood in the winter. At least some of the inventory was damaged during the winter of 2009. One item of inventory that was permanently destroyed was an eight-foot tall teddy bear. Mr. Alley had purchased the bear for $2,500, and therefore gave it a retail value of $5,000. The teddy bear got moved to Mr. Giannini's garage, and during the winter of 2009, it got waterlogged and infested with mice, and had to be thrown away.

Other than the artwork and the teddy bear, the inventory has remained in the boiler room and the garage areas.

## B. Discussion

### 1. Request for Administrative Expenses.

Mr. Giannini seeks $3,570 in rent for the use of his storage areas through July 31, 2010, plus an additional $210 per month for every month thereafter during which the inventory remains on his property as an administrative expense of the estate under Section 503(b). Mr. Giannini admitted that he did not typically rent out the storage areas and admitted that his estimate of $210 per month was somewhat "arbitrary," but thought that he "should be compensated somehow" for the use of the boiler room and garage.

Section 507(a)(1) of the Bankruptcy Code grants first priority in the distribution of the assets of a bankruptcy estate to administrative expenses allowed under 11 U.S.C. § 503(b). Administrative expense claims are governed by section 503(b) of the Bankruptcy Code, which provides, in pertinent part, "(b) After notice and a hearing, there shall be allowed administrative expenses, other than claims allowed under section 502(f) of this title, including-(1)(A) the actual, necessary costs and expenses of preserving the estate." To be entitled to priority, the claim must arise from a transaction with the Trustee post-petition which was beneficial to the estate. ("A claim will be afforded priority under § 503 if the debt both (1) arises from a transaction with the debtor-in-possession and (2) is beneficial to the debtor-in-possession in the operation of the business.")

To qualify as actual and necessary expenses, expenditures must benefit the estate as a whole. Accordingly, claims pursuant to section 503(b)(1)(A) shall be measured by the benefit received by the estate, rather than the costs incurred by a claimant. Thus, the focus for purposes of determining a benefit to the estate turns on actual benefits conferred upon the estate, not losses sustained by the creditor.

The Court is sympathetic to the imposition that was placed on Mr. Giannini in storing the furniture for over a year and a half, but Mr. Giannini has not demonstrated by the preponderance of the evidence that the estate gained anything by storing the furniture in the way it was stored. At the very least, the storage during the winter months seems to have *diminished* the value, particularly with respect to the teddy bear that became infested with mice.

Even if the Court were willing to grant administrative expense priority, it would want to limit such claim to a percentage of the *actual* proceeds that the estate received from the disposition of the property. However, the furniture has still not been sold, yet, and the Court is not convinced that, after 18 months without success, a sale to *any* buyer is likely in the future. The highest bid that the Trustee has received was for $1,500, but that was over a year ago, and before the teddy bear was destroyed and the remainder of the inventory suffered through a winter of flooding or excessive heat and soot. Instead, it seems that no one wants to have anything to do with the furniture. While the furniture theoretically could have value to the right buyer, no one seems to want to risk incurring the cost or effort of preparing, moving and reassembling the furniture, when there might be missing parts, hidden damage, or no buyers in this poor market. The Debtor abandoned the inventory for the bankruptcy trustee to deal with. Mr. Giannini pushed it off into the corners of his property. The bankruptcy trustee laments the current state of the furniture, but is unwilling to incur the costs of moving the furniture to better storage areas and reassembling it, and can't find an auctioneer or other third party who would be willing to do so. Even the one potential buyer, Highland Furniture, expressed doubt about how it would get the furniture "out of there" and reassembled, even if it were interested. Mr. Giannini ended up paying as much as $1,000 to move the furniture *into* storage and to *disassemble* it. One would imagine that reassembling it and moving it long-distance would be even more expensive and more daunting a task.

Given that no one appears to be doing anything with the furniture, the Court has deep concerns as to why it has sat in storage for over a year and a half. In the context of the bailment claim, the Trustee tried to present evidence that the furniture is currently "worthless," yet the Court wonders why he didn't abandon it long ago if he truly felt so. If the costs of moving and properly preparing the furniture for sale outweigh the risk-adjusted benefits of a successful sale, it would seem of little value to the estate. However, no party has filed a motion to abandon or to compel abandonment under Section 554, and the Court will not raise such a motion sua sponte.

## 2. Bailment and Damage to the Inventory

The Trustee seeks damages against Mr. Giannini under Illinois common law on the theory that Mr. Giannini was a bailee of the inventory and is liable for damage to the property caused by his negligence during his custody. Under Illinois law, a bailment is "a consensual relationship that can be established by express contract or by implication and the agreement of the parties to a bailment may be implied in law or in fact." A constructive bailment, or a bailment implied in law, may be found where the property of one person is voluntarily received by another for some purpose other than that of obtaining ownership. In such cases, the law implies a contract for the keeping of the property until it shall be restored to the owner or his agent, and the holder is bound to take care of, keep, and preserve the property, not for the sake of any benefit to himself or upon any expectation of compensation for his services, but solely for the convenience and accommodation of the owner.

To recover under a bailment theory, the plaintiff must allege: (1) an express or implied agreement to create a bailment; (2) delivery of the property in good condition; (3) the bailee's acceptance of the property; and (4) the bailee's failure to return the property or the bailee's redelivery of the property in a damaged condition. When a *prima facie* case of bailment is established, there is a presumption of the defendant's negligence. The defendant must then present sufficient evidence to support a finding that the presumed fact did not exist and that the defendant was free from fault.

Here, the Court finds that Mr. Giannini entered into two implied agreements creating a bailment. First, he entered into a bailment for the sole benefit of the bailor when he agreed to allow Mr. Alley to leave the inventory on the premises for a limited time. Second, the bailment became a bailment for mutual benefit or a bailment for hire when Mr. Giannini demanded rent of the Trustee and was promised a potential administrative expense claim for rent. When Mr. Alley vacated the rental space and left behind the inventory with Mr. Giannini's consent, the property was delivered into Mr. Giannini's control and was accepted by him. The Trustee has stated a *prima facie* case with respect to the teddy bear and the artwork, since these were either destroyed or never returned. However, the Trustee has failed to prove that the remainder of the inventory was redelivered in a damaged condition. The Trustee's only witness as to the condition of the furniture testified that, although it had been disassembled, the furniture, other than the artwork, "appeared to be alright." The Trustee presented no evidence that the remaining furniture could not be easily reassembled or any evidence that it had been permanently damaged.

The Court finds, however, that Mr. Giannini has rebutted the presumption of negligence with respect to the teddy bear. Mr. Giannini warned the Trustee in advance that the garage and boiler room were not safe places for storage during the winter months. The Trustee also had access to the furniture if he had so desired, and the Trustee's attorney, Mr. Larsen, had viewed the areas where the items were being stored. Yet, despite the warnings and the Trustee's knowledge of the conditions of the storage areas, the Trustee took no action. He did not take repossession of any of the inventory or ask that it be moved. In light of these circumstances, the Court cannot find that Mr. Giannini was to blame for the damage to the bear. Although it is true that Mr. Giannini originally moved the furniture into the storage areas, and that he did so without Mr. Alley's or the Trustee's knowledge or consent, there was no suggestion that the storage areas were unsafe when he moved them in the spring, or in the summer or fall. Furthermore, at the time he moved the items, he had a reasonable expectation that the items would be sold within weeks, not months or years. By the time winter came, the original rental space had been rented to and occupied by the bicycle shop for half a year, and the furniture could not be moved back to that area.

Moreover, in light of the somewhat involuntary way that Mr. Giannini became a bailee, the Court cannot fault Mr. Giannini where he alerted the Trustee of the risks well in advance. The Trustee had previously made clear to Mr. Giannini that he was not to move the inventory without the Trustee's consent, and the Trustee offered him no alternative but to leave the items where they were in the storage areas. Therefore, the Court finds that the damage to the bear was not caused by the negligence of Mr. Giannini for purposes of a bailment claim.

In contrast, the Court finds that Mr. Giannini has failed to rebut the presumption of negligence with respect to the artwork. Although the artwork was thrown out by employees of the new tenant bicycle shop, not by or at the express direction of Mr. Giannini, Mr. Giannini had asked the bicycle shop employees to take care of moving and disassembling the furniture, and he provided consideration for them to do so, through the rent discount. Under Illinois law, a bailee may be liable for losses resulting from the acts or negligence of his employees or servants. Mr. Giannini chose to have the bicycle shop employees take care of the furniture, and did so without the knowledge or consent of either Mr. Alley or the Trustee. Furthermore, it appears that the bicycle shop employees threw out the artwork while within the scope of the duties for which he had hired them. The Trustee has therefore demonstrated that Mr. Giannini was liable for the damage to the artwork.

The final question is damages. In Illinois, the ordinary measure of damages for personal property is the fair market value at the time of the loss. The Seventh Circuit has noted that an "asset's value depends on the price that could be agreed by willing buyers and sellers negotiating for a replacement." However, the parties did not provide evidence of any offers to purchase the artwork or list any sales of comparable property. Mr. Alley placed a retail price for the artwork of $3,000 with little to no explanation about how he came to that value. In contrast, Mr. Giannini argued that the artwork must have had no value, since it could not even be sold when offered for 80% off the retail price. The artwork had already been destroyed by the time Highland Furniture viewed the inventory and made its offer, so the artwork was not included in its $1,500 offer. The Court is skeptical that Mr. Alley's retail price is an accurate estimate of the fair market value at the time the artwork was destroyed, yet, the Court does not believe it had no value, either. With very little details to make its own determination, the Court will take the value offered by the parties that is closest to what the Court feels is the true value. The Court therefore finds that the artwork was worth $600, or 20% of Mr. Alley's 'retail' price. The Court recognizes that liquidation sales are not always an accurate indicator of 'true' market value, and that the artwork at issue did not sell even at the liquidation sale. However, the fact that Mr. Alley offered to sell the artwork for $600 indicates that, at least at the time, that was the value that he placed on it. In the absence of any other evidence, the Court finds it was worth $600 at the time it was destroyed, and will set the damages at $600.

3. Sanctions for Non-cooperation.

Section 542(a) of the Bankruptcy Code directs that, with limited exceptions, anyone "in possession, custody, or control" of property of the estate "shall deliver to the trustee, and account for, such property or the value of such property, unless such property is of inconsequential value or benefit to the estate." Therefore, even in the absence of a court order, upon the filing of Mr. Alley's bankruptcy case, Mr. Giannini had an obligation to deliver to the trustee the furniture inventory, which was in his possession and which had a value of at least $1,500. There is no requirement in the Code that the trustee make demand, obtain a court order, or take any further action in order to obtain a turnover of the estate's property. Inherent in this obligation to "deliver" property of the estate is at minimum an obligation to provide the trustee reasonable access to the property so that he or she can determine whether it has value to the estate and how it can or should be delivered to or otherwise administered by the trustee. In this case, when the Trustee called Mr. Giannini, Mr. Giannini flatly refused to allow him access to the furniture or to even disclose where it had been moved to unless the Trustee first paid him money. Mr. Giannini was aware of Mr. Alley's bankruptcy, and knew that the furniture was undisputedly the property of Mr. Alley or his bankruptcy estate, and yet willfully refused to provide access. He has offered no justification other than his mistake of law, and has subsequently admitted that his initial refusal and noncompliance was not warranted and "was wrong."

Other courts have held that where a debtor's landlord refuses to grant a trustee access to property of the estate, a bankruptcy court has the power to grant sanctions against the landlord, including the authority for a bankruptcy court to make an award of attorneys' fees and costs in appropriate circumstances.

While Mr. Giannini did quickly correct his course after speaking with legal counsel, he did so only after the Trustee had to file a motion for contempt and incur costs in preparing such motion. Therefore, the Court is willing to award sanctions for Mr. Giannini's initial noncompliance, but only for the actual costs incurred as a result of the noncompliance. There was no dispute that, after his attorney called the Trustee shortly before the May 14th status hearing on the contempt motion, Mr. Giannini complied with the Trustee's every request. Therefore, it is inappropriate to grant the full $7,800 in attorneys' fees that the Trustee seeks, which largely arise out of the Trustee's adversary complaint against Mr. Giannini under the bailment theory. Other than in limited exceptions, U.S. courts follow the "'American Rule,' under which each party bears its own litigation costs. In reviewing the Trustee's itemization of attorneys' fees, the Court finds that the only items which directly resulted from Mr. Giannini's noncompliance were the 1.6 hours spent preparing the motion for contempt, the 1.0 hour telephone conference with Mr. Giannini's attorney shortly before the contempt hearing, and the 1.0 hour the Trustee's attorney spent travelling to the courthouse for the contempt hearing. The Court will additionally reduce each of the last two items from one hour to fifteen minutes. It likely took Mr. Giannini's attorney just a few minutes to explain that his client had realized he was wrong and would comply in the future. Therefore the remainder of the call was not directly related to Mr. Giannini's noncooperation. Similarly, the contempt hearing was part of the Court's regular Geneva call, and since the only thing the Trustee did was to withdraw his motion, the hearing likely took only a few minutes. Furthermore, the Trustee's attorney regularly appears on numerous different matters on the Court's Geneva call, and so it seems inappropriate to attribute the full time he spent in Geneva to this one brief matter. Therefore, the Court will grant the Trustee's actual costs of $571.25 against Mr. Giannini.

## C. Conclusion

For the foregoing reasons, the Court grants the Trustee's actual costs of $571.25 against Mr. Giannini as sanctions for his initial willful noncompliance with the Trustee's request. The Court grants damages of $600.00 against Mr. Giannini and in favor of the Trustee for the damage to the artwork, and denies the remainder of the Adversary Complaint. The Court denies Mr. Giannini's request for administrative expenses.

Note: It is important to be aware of a very important change in bailment law that has been made by the provisions of the Uniform Commercial Code,( UCC), which has been adopted in virtually all states. Under Section 2-403 of the UCC, if you take your watch to be repaired at a shop which also sells used watches, then the UCC gives the repair shop the power to transfer good title to your watch! Even though this entrusting would otherwise have been considered to be a bailment, with all the responsibilities normally imposed on bailees.

U.C.C. Text § 2-403

§ 2-403. Power to Transfer; Good Faith Purchase of Goods; "Entrusting".

(1) A purchaser of goods acquires all title which his transferor had or had power to transfer except that a purchaser of a limited interest acquires rights only to the extent of the interest purchased. A person with voidable title has power to transfer a good title to a good faith purchaser for value. When goods have been delivered under a transaction of purchase the purchaser has such power even though

    (a) the transferor was deceived as to the identity of the purchaser, or

    (b) the delivery was in exchange for a check which is later dishonored, or

    (c) it was agreed that the transaction was to be a "cash sale", or

    (d) the delivery was procured through fraud punishable as larcenous under the criminal law.

(2) Any entrusting of possession of goods to a merchant who deals in goods of that kind gives him power to transfer all rights of the entruster to a buyer in ordinary course of business.

(3) "Entrusting" includes any delivery and any acquiescence in retention of possession regardless of any condition expressed between the parties to the delivery or acquiescence and regardless of whether the procurement of the entrusting or the possessor's disposition of the goods have been such as to be larcenous under the criminal law.

# CHAPTER FIFTEEN

# LOST & FOUND PERSONAL PROPERTY

## INTRODUCTION

What happens when someone finds property which does not appear to be owned by anyone – such as a handful of change on the pavement in a public parking lot? Does the finder then become the owner? Or a bailee?

The following two cases describe the detailed rules regarding "found" property which have existed at common law for hundreds of years. Needless to say, most litigation in this field involves property of significantly more value than a handful of change.

### SUPREME COURT OF IOWA
### HEATH BENJAMIN, APPELLANT,
### V.
### LINDNER AVIATION, INC., APPELLEE,
### AND
### STATE CENTRAL BANK, APPELLEE.

JULY 19, 1995

**Opinion**

TERNUS, Justice.

## Background Facts and Proceedings.

In April of 1992, State Central Bank became the owner of an airplane when the bank repossessed it from its prior owner who had defaulted on a loan. In August of that year, the bank took the plane to Lindner Aviation for a routine annual inspection. Benjamin worked for Lindner Aviation and did the inspection.

As part of the inspection, Benjamin removed panels from the underside of the wings. Although these panels were to be removed annually as part of the routine inspection, a couple of the screws holding the panel on the left wing were so rusty that Benjamin had to use a drill to remove them. Benjamin testified that the panel probably had not been removed for several years.

Inside the left wing Benjamin discovered two packets approximately four inches high and wrapped in aluminum foil. He removed the packets from the wing and took off the foil wrapping. Inside the foil was paper currency, tied in string and wrapped in handkerchiefs. The currency was predominately twenty-dollar bills with mint dates before the 1960s, primarily in the 1950s, and totaling roughly $18,000. The money smelled musty.

Benjamin took one packet to his jeep and then reported what he had found to his supervisor, offering to divide the money with him. However, the supervisor reported the discovery to the owner of Lindner Aviation, William Engle. Engle insisted that they contact the authorities and he called the Department of Criminal Investigation. The money was eventually turned over to the Keokuk police department.

Two days later, Benjamin filed an affidavit with the county auditor claiming that he was the finder of the currency under the provisions of Iowa Code chapter 644 (1991). Lindner Aviation and the bank also filed claims to the money. The notices required by chapter 644 were published and posted. No one came forward within twelve months claiming to be the true owner of the money. (*See id.* § 644.11, if true owner does not claim property within twelve months, the right to the property vests in the finder).

Benjamin filed this declaratory judgment action against Lindner Aviation and the bank to establish his right to the property. The district court held that chapter 644 applies only to "lost" property and the money here was mislaid property. The court awarded the money to the bank, holding that it was entitled to possession of the money to the exclusion of all but the true owner. The court also held that Benjamin was a "finder" within the meaning of chapter 644 and awarded him a ten percent finder's fee. (*See id.* § 644.13, a finder of lost property is entitled to ten percent of the value of the lost property as a reward).

Benjamin appealed.

Whether the money found by Benjamin was treasure trove or was mislaid, abandoned or lost property is a fact question. Therefore, the trial court's finding that the money was mislaid is binding on us if supported by substantial evidence.

### Does Chapter 644 Supersede the Common Law Classifications of Found Property?

Although a few courts have adopted an expansive view of lost property statutes, we think Iowa law is to the contrary. As recently as 1991, we stated that "the rights of →*Black* finders of property vary according to the characterization of the property found." We have continued to use the common law distinctions between classes of found property despite the legislature's enactment of chapter 644 and its predecessors.

In summary, chapter 644 applies only if the property discovered can be catego- ] *Black* rized as "lost" property as that term is defined under the common law

### Classification of Found Property.

Under the common law, there are four categories of found property: (1) abandoned property, (2) lost property, (3) mislaid property, and (4) treasure trove. The rights of a finder of property depend on how the found property is classified.

A. *Abandoned property.* Property is abandoned when the owner no longer wants to possess it. Abandonment is shown by proof that the owner intends to abandon the property and has voluntarily relinquished all right, title and interest in the property. Abandoned property belongs to the finder of the property against all others, including the former owner.

B. *Lost property.* Property is lost when the owner unintentionally and involuntarily parts with its possession and does not know where it is. Stolen property found by someone who did not participate in the theft is lost property. Under chapter 644, lost property becomes the property of the finder once the statutory procedures are followed and the owner makes no claim within twelve months.

C. *Mislaid property.* Mislaid property is voluntarily put in a certain place by the owner who then overlooks or forgets where the property is. It differs from lost property in that the owner voluntarily and intentionally places mislaid property in the location where it is eventually found by another. Property is not considered lost unless the owner parts with it involuntarily.

The finder of mislaid property acquires no rights to the property. The right of possession of mislaid property belongs to the owner of the premises upon which the property is found, as against all persons other than the true owner.

D. *Treasure trove.* Treasure trove consists of coins or currency concealed by the owner. It includes an element of antiquity. To be classified as treasure trove, the property must have been hidden or concealed for such a length of time that the owner is probably dead or undiscoverable. Treasure trove belongs to the finder as against all but the true owner.

### V. Is There Substantial Evidence to Support the Trial Court's Finding That the Money Found by Benjamin Was Mislaid?

We think there was substantial evidence to find that the currency discovered by Benjamin was mislaid property.

Black ←

The place where Benjamin found the money and the manner in which it was hidden are also important here. The bills were carefully tied and wrapped and then concealed in a location that was accessible only by removing screws and a panel. These circumstances support an inference that the money was placed there intentionally. This inference supports the conclusion that the money was mislaid. *Jackson v. Steinberg,* (1948) (fact that $800 in currency was found concealed beneath the paper lining of a dresser indicates that money was intentionally concealed with intention of reclaiming it; therefore, property was mislaid, not lost); *Schley v. Couch,* (1955) (holding that money found buried under garage floor was mislaid property as a matter of law because circumstances showed that money was placed there deliberately and court presumed that owner had either forgotten where he hid the money or had died before retrieving it).

Black ←

The same facts that support the trial court's conclusion that the money was mislaid prevent us from ruling as a matter of law that the property was lost. Property is not considered lost unless considering the place where and the conditions under which the property is found, there is an inference that the property was left there unintentionally. *See Sovern,* (holding that coins found in a jar under a wooden floor of a barn were not lost property because the circumstances showed that the money was hidden there intentionally); *Farrare v. City of Pasco,* (where currency was deliberately concealed, it cannot be characterized as lost property). Contrary to Benjamin's position the circumstances here do not support a conclusion that the money was placed in the wing of the airplane unintentionally. Additionally, as the trial court concluded, there was no evidence suggesting that the money was placed in the wing by someone other than the owner of the money and that its location was unknown to the owner. For these reasons, we reject Benjamin's argument that the trial court was obligated to find that the currency Benjamin discovered was lost property.

We also reject Benjamin's assertion that as a matter of law this money was abandoned property. Both logic and common sense suggest that it is unlikely someone would voluntarily part with over $18,000 with the intention of terminating his ownership. The location where this money was found is much more consistent with the conclusion that the owner of the property was placing the money there for safekeeping. Jackson, (because currency was concealed intentionally and deliberately, the bills ─7 *Black* could not be regarded as abandoned property); 1 Am.Jur.2d *Abandoned Property* § 13, (where property is concealed in such a way that the concealment appears intentional and deliberate, there can be no abandonment). We will not presume that an owner has abandoned his property when his conduct is consistent with a continued claim to the property. Therefore, we cannot rule that the district court erred in failing to find that the currency discovered by Benjamin was abandoned property.

Finally, we also conclude that the trial court was not obligated to decide that this money was treasure trove. Based on the dates of the currency, the money was no older than thirty-five years. The mint dates, the musty odor and the rusty condition of a few of the panel screws indicate that the money may have been hidden for some time. However, there was no evidence of the age of the airplane or the date of its last inspection. These facts may have shown that the money was concealed for a much shorter period of time.

Moreover, it is also significant that the airplane had a well-documented ownership history. The record reveals that there were only two owners of the plane prior to the bank. One was the person from whom the bank repossessed the plane; the other was the original purchaser of the plane when it was manufactured. Nevertheless, there is no indication that Benjamin or any other party attempted to locate and notify the prior owners of the plane, which could very possibly have led to the identification of the true owner of the money. Under these circumstances, we cannot say as a matter of law that the money meets the antiquity requirement or that it is probable that the owner of the money is not discoverable.

We think the district court had substantial evidence to support its finding that the money found by Benjamin was mislaid. The circumstances of its concealment and the location where it was found support inferences that the owner intentionally placed the money there and intended to retain ownership. We are bound by this factual finding.

### Is the Airplane Or the Hangar the "Premises" Where the Money Was Discovered?

Because the money discovered by Benjamin was properly found to be mislaid property, it belongs to the owner of the premises where it was found. Mislaid property is entrusted to the owner of the premises where it is found rather than the finder of the property because it is assumed that the true owner may eventually recall where he has placed his property and return there to reclaim it.

We think that the premises where the money was found is the airplane, not Lindner Aviation's hangar where the airplane happened to be parked when the money was discovered. The policy behind giving ownership of mislaid property to the owner of the premises where the property was mislaid supports this conclusion. If the true owner of the money attempts to locate it, he would initially look for the plane; it is unlikely he would begin his search by contacting businesses where the airplane might have been inspected. Therefore, we affirm the trial court's judgment that the bank, as the owner of the plane, has the right to possession of the property as against all but the true owner.

### Is Benjamin Entitled to a Finder's Fee?

Benjamin claims that if he is not entitled to the money, he should be paid a ten percent finder's fee under section 644.13. The problem with this claim is that only *Black* — the finder of "*lost* goods, money, bank notes, and other things" is rewarded with a finder's fee under chapter 644. Because the property found by Benjamin was mislaid property, not lost property, section 644.13 does not apply here. The trial court erred in awarding Benjamin a finder's fee.

### Summary.

We conclude that the district court's finding that the money discovered by Benjamin was mislaid property is supported by substantial evidence. Therefore, we affirm the district court's judgment that the bank has the right to the money as against all but the true owner. This decision makes it unnecessary to decide whether Benjamin or Lindner Aviation was the finder of the property. We reverse the court's decision awarding a finder's fee to Benjamin.

AFFIRMED IN PART; REVERSED IN PART.

Note: Property which might once have been considered to be mislaid property may later become abandoned property, based on the actions, or lack of actions by the person who "mislaid" the property. Enjoy the following case.

## UNITED STATES DISTRICT COURT, W.D. MISSOURI,
## IN RE SEIZURE OF $82,000 MORE OR LESS.
## JEFFERY CHAPPELL, ET AL., MOVANTS,
## V.
## UNITED STATES OF AMERICA, RESPONDENT.

NOVEMBER 1, 2000

MEMORANDUM AND ORDER

LAUGHREY, District Judge.

These consolidated cases concern the ownership of $82,000 found in a 1995 Volkswagen Golf titled in the name of Helen Chappell. The United States Government asserts that the $82,000 came from illegal drug sales and should be forfeited to the Government. The Chappells contend that the $82,000 belongs to them because it was found in the gas tank of a car which they purchased from the Government, after the car had been forfeited by its owner.

### I. Factual Background

The following facts have been stipulated by the parties. On February 15, 1996, Corporal Jack McMullin of the Missouri State Highway Patrol stopped a 1995 Volkswagen Golf for speeding and following too closely. During the stop, Corporal McMullin interviewed and became suspicious of both passengers in the vehicle, Roberto Lopez–Velez and Guadalupe Cortez–Amezcua. After a consensual search indicated fresh silicone on the undercarriage of the vehicle, Corporal McMullin asked the occupants if they would mind bringing the vehicle to the Missouri State Highway Patrol garage for a more thorough inspection. The occupants agreed to do so.

Once at the garage, Corporal McMullin found that the battery in the vehicle had recently been removed, and he observed plastic baggies in the battery case. He then contacted Special Agent Carl Hicks, of the Drug Enforcement Association ("DEA"), who responded to assist Corporal McMullin. Special Agent Hicks observed that the plastic baggies contained foil-wrapped objects. When he opened the baggies and foil, he found $24,000 in United States Currency and noticed a strong odor of methamphetamine coming from the baggies.

Special Agent Hicks then interviewed Lopez–Velez and Cortez–Amezcua. Both Lopez–Velez and Cortez–Amezcua explained that they had driven the vehicle from Mexico to a Holiday Inn in St. Louis, Missouri; however, they were unable to identify the Holiday Inn. Lopez–Velez stated that he had parked the vehicle in the parking lot. The vehicle was then picked up by unknown persons and returned. Lopez–Velez admitted that he had known that $24,000 was in the battery of the car and that the currency was from the sale of illegal drugs. Lopez–Velez stated that Cortez–Amezcua did not know about the currency. Lopez–Velez refused to name the person who had hired him to make the trip to St. Louis.

At the conclusion of the interview, Special Agent Hicks announced that he was going to seize the $24,000 as drug proceeds, and was going to seize the vehicle as an item used to transport drug proceeds. Hicks advised Lopez–Velez that he was not under arrest and was free to leave. Lopez–Velez and Cortez–Amezcua left the highway patrol garage and have not returned.

Special Agent Hicks sent the plastic baggies and foil for analysis. The substance on the foil was found to be caffeine, an ingredient commonly used as a cutting agent for methamphetamine. The DEA subsequently determined that the 1995 Volkswagen Golf was registered to Miguel Angel Sanchez–Cortez, Punta Del Este, 967 Saltillo, Coah, Mexico.

Following the procedures established by Congress for the disposition of seized property, the DEA initiated an administrative forfeiture action against the $24,000 and the 1995 Volkswagen Golf. The only claimant who came forward to contest the forfeiture of those items was Lopez–Velez, who filed a claim and cost bond on April 30, 1996. On July 10, 1996, an Assistant United States Attorney mailed a stipulation to an attorney for Lopez–Velez, proposing the settlement of the claim prior to the filing of a judicial action. The attorney for Lopez–Velez requested that the stipulation be mailed to him for his client's signature. The stipulation was never returned to the United States Attorney's Office. On April 2, 1998, the United States Attorney's Office, with the concurrence of the attorney for Lopez–Velez, referred the case back to the DEA to have the vehicle and the $24,000 declared abandoned. On June 12, 1998, the DEA declared the 1995 Volkswagen Golf and the $24,000 abandoned.

On September 24, 1998, the DEA referred the 1995 Volkswagen Golf to the General Services Administration ("GSA") for sale because the DEA did not have the capacity to conduct a public auction. The DEA authorized GSA to sell the car but made no mention of the vehicle's contents. The DEA advised GSA that it had no information indicating that the vehicle required repairs, but also advised GSA that it believed the odometer reading was incorrect. The DEA learned of the odometer problem from a May 19, 1998 note contained in the file of the United States Marshal Service. It said that "Laura" drove the 1995 Volkswagen Golf to Innerspace Storage and she noted that the "gages don't work! Gas always shows 'E,' doesn't show speed and odometer never changes. Odometer Discrepancy."

On February 1, 1999, GSA advertised the 1995 Volkswagen Golf for bids. Item No. 030 on the advertisement described the property as follows: "Sedan 1996 Volkswagen Golf 4 cyl Vin: 3VW1931HMSM113340 est 5,955 mile—mileage will not be certi-fied—odometer discrepancy." Helen Chappell was the successful bidder for the 1995 Volkswagen Golf. On April 14, 1999, her son Jeffery Chappell's Discover credit card was used to pay for the vehicle, and Helen Chappell received from GSA a Certificate to Obtain Title to a Vehicle. The vehicle is currently titled in Helen Chappell's name. At the time of this purchase, neither the Chappells, the DEA nor GSA knew that $82,000 was hidden in the fuel tank of the vehicle.

Not surprisingly, the Chappells noticed that the Volkswagen Golf had a fuel prob-lem. Jeffery Chappell took the vehicle to Waldo Imports in Kansas City, Missouri, to have the fuel problem fixed. While working on the car, the Waldo Imports' mechanic found several bundles of currency floating in the fuel tank of the vehicle. He reported his find to the DEA office in Overland Park, Kansas. DEA agents went to Waldo Imports and seized 20 bundles of currency wrapped in plastic, totaling $82,000, more or less. A check of each bill revealed that none of the bills had a printing date later than 1996, when the vehicle was originally seized. On the date of the seizure, Special Agent Melton contacted Jeffery Chappell, who explained that he had recently purchased the vehicle from GSA and had been unaware that the currency was inside the fuel tank.

The Chappells have filed for the return of the currency. The United States has filed for judicial foreclosure claiming the currency as drug proceeds pursuant to 21 U.S.C. § 881.

**Discussion**

It is true that Helen Chappell holds legal title to the car, but Jeffery Chappell paid for the vehicle using his Discover credit card, arguably creating an equitable interest in the Volkswagen Golf *vis a vis* his mother, but not third parties. There is also evidence that Jeffery had possession of the vehicle and paid for its repairs. For purposes of this litigation, therefore, both Helen and Jeffery Chappell have at least a colorable owner-ship interest in the Volkswagen. A definitive ruling on ownership at this juncture will not benefit the Government. Even if the Court dismissed Jeffery Chappell's claim, Helen Chappell's identical claim would go forward.

The Chappells advance two theories to support their claim that they own the $82,000. First, they argue that the contents of a car pass automatically to the purchaser of the car simply because the transferor had the power to transfer the contents. Second, they argue that the $82,000 is mislaid property and the Chappells are entitled to the currency because they own the premises (the vehicle) where the currency was found. Neither argument is viable.

The evidence is insufficient to show that the Government intended to transfer ownership of the $82,000 to the Chappells at the time it sold the Volkswagen to them. There cannot be an agreement to transfer ownership if neither party is aware that the property exists.

Nor can this currency be characterized as mislaid. Property is mislaid if it is voluntarily put down by its owner and its owner forgets where the property is. A purse found on a counter or the seat of a bus will generally be characterized as mislaid because it is logical to assume that the purse was intentionally placed and then forgotten. A wallet found on the floor, however, will be characterized as lost because it is unlikely that someone would put a wallet on the floor intending to return for it. If property is lost, possession of the property is entrusted to the finder of the lost property not the owner of the premises where the property is found. If the property is mislaid, then the owner of the premises where the property is found is entitled to possession, not the finder.

The factual record in this case does not support the Chappells' conclusion that the $82,000 is mislaid property. While the money was almost certainly placed in the gas tank intentionally, it is equally certain that the owners of the currency knew what happened to the money and chose not to claim it. Indeed, at least one district court has concluded that it is "beyond belief" that anyone would hide a large amount of currency and then suddenly forget where it was.

Both cases cited by the Chappells in support of their argument that the currency was mislaid are distinguishable. In *Benjamin v. Lindner Aviation,* a large amount of cash was found in the wing of the airplane. The cash had been in the plane for nearly 30 years and there was no evidence as to why the money was secreted or to whom it belonged. Similarly in *Buzard,* a large amount of cash was secreted in the wall of a building. There was no way to identify how long the money had been in the wall or who might have hidden it. In both cases, the courts characterized the money as mislaid. The courts reasoned that, but for a lapse of memory, the true owners would have returned for such valuable property. The record in this case, however, is not so skeletal. There is a good explanation for why the true owners did not seek to recover the currency even though they knew where it was. The money was owned by drug dealers and if they came to claim it, they might eventually be arrested for participating in a drug conspiracy. Because the Court finds that the owner of the $82,000 knew its location, the second prong of the mislaid property test was not satisfied.

Instead of finding the property lost or mislaid, the Court finds the property abandoned. Abandonment consists of two elements: "(1) an intent to abandon, and (2) the external act by which the intention is carried into effect." Although abandonment should not be presumed lightly, it may be found when the evidence clearly and decisively leads to that conclusion. This is such a case. [Drug traffickers know better *Green* than to stake claims to contraband and drug proceeds. It is far more sensible for such criminals to disclaim any interest in the property and avoid possible prosecution.] In this case, Lopez–Velez originally contested the forfeiture of the vehicle and the $24,000, but he never showed up to pursue his claim. It would stretch credulity to conclude that he knew about the $24,000 in the battery case and that the vehicle was transporting drug proceeds, but he and the owner of the car did not know about the $82,000. Rather, the evidence shows that the original owners of the currency intended to abandon the $82,000 after the 1995 Volkswagen Golf was seized by the DEA, and that they acted on this intent by failing to come forward and claim the funds.

*Black*

Under Missouri law, those who abandon property lose title. Therefore, under Missouri law, no one owned the $82,000 while these funds were hidden in the Volkswagen Golf after it was abandoned. The currency went back into a state of → *Black* nature analogous to wild animals. *See Pierson v. Post,* (1805). The question is who has the right to this currency which was abandoned and for a period of time was owned by no one?

*Black*

[Once property has been abandoned, the first finder who acquires dominion over the property becomes its owner.] The first person to exercise dominion over this $82,000 was the Waldo mechanic. The mechanic, however, was acting as the Chappells' agent at the moment he took possession of the currency. He had been told that there was a fuel problem with the vehicle. It was during his investigation of the fuel problem that he found the $82,000. Under these circumstances should the agent or his principal be entitled to the currency?

*Black*

Missouri has not specifically addressed this question, [but other jurisdictions have held that possession by the agent is in fact possession by the principal.] *South Staffordshire Water Co. v. Sharman,* (1886). In *Ray v. Flower Hosp.* (1981) the Ohio Court of Appeals stated: "In a long line of cases where hotel chambermaids, bank janitors, bank tellers, grocery store bagboys and other employees have found property while in their employ, virtually every case has charged the employee with the duty to turn the found property over to the employer for safekeeping." The reason for such a holding is that[" the possession of the servant is the possession of the employer and that, therefore, the element is wanting which would give the title to the servant as against the master."] Black

Black

[The Court finds the more persuasive position on this question is that abandoned property found by an agent is the property of the principal, so long as the agent is acting within the scope of his agency.]In this case the Chappells told their mechanic to fix the fuel problem in their car and it was during the mechanic's specifically assigned task that the money was located. Finally, and most importantly, this conclusion is consistent with the reasonable expectations of a car owner. [One does not expect that the mechanic to whom a car is entrusted has the right to look through it and keep things which are hidden therein.]For all these reasons, the Court concludes that the Chappells became the owner of the $82,000 when the mechanic first found the money.

The Government, however, contends that it owned the currency prior to it being found in the gas tank. The United States argues that "public policy should not allow anyone to profit from illegal drug trafficking." The question in this case, however, is not whether anyone should profit from drug activity, but rather who should profit from it—the United States or the Chappells. In shielding innocent owners from the forfeiture laws,[Congress has expressed a public policy in favor of allowing innocent people like the Chappells to keep their property even if it consists of drug proceeds.] It should also be noted that the Chappells would never have acquired an interest in this $82,000 if the Government had found the currency during the years that the Volkswagen Golf was in its possession. The reason the car was seized in the first place was the recent work that had been done on the undercarriage. This, plus the fact that the gas gauge always registered empty, might have inspired a search of the gas tank before the car was sold at auction. As early as the 1970s when "Easy Rider" was aired, the Government was on notice that drug dealers use gas tanks to hide their contraband. While the equities do not weigh in the Chappells' favor since the $82,000 is a windfall, neither do the equities weigh in favor of the Government. The common law principles discussed in this Order should, therefore, prevail. Accordingly, it is hereby

ORDERED that the Chappells are innocent owners of the $82,000 at issue in this proceeding, and the Government should release the funds to them.

Note: There is a surprising amount of litigation over the ownership of sunken treasure, to which a special set of laws apply. First, a very brief excerpt from *Cobb Coin v. The Unidentified, Wrecked and Abandoned Sailing Vessel*, 525 F. Supp. 186, just to set the tone.

# COBB COIN
## V.
## THE UNIDENTIFIED, WRECKED AND ABANDONED SAILING VESSEL

OCTOBER 2, 1981

**JAMES LAWRENCE KING, District Judge.**

## HISTORICAL INTRODUCTION

In the early eighteenth century, Spain's dominions extended over one third of the known world. The King of Spain annually sent two fleets of ships to the New World to bring back the wealth of the Americas. One fleet picked up the gold, emeralds, and pearls unearthed from Peruvian mines, at the port of New Granada-present day Cartagena, Colombia; the other boarded delicate pottery and china shipped from the Orient, and Mexican silver, cochineal and indigo dyes, at Veracruz, Mexico. Each year the two fleets met in Havana, Cuba to voyage homeward together across the Atlantic. This afforded the treasure laden galleons some measure of protection from the pirates of the Caribbean who were well aware of the sailing dates of the fleet and the richness of the prize that was theirs if they could but capture one of these vessels.

Normally, the combined fleet sailed by May or June in order to clear the Straits of Florida before the treacherous hurricane season set in, but in the summer of 1715, the fleet of General Don Juan Esteban de Ubilla and General Don Antonio de Echeverz was delayed due to trade problems and the late arrival of four ships from Veracruz.

The Governor General of Havana was painfully aware of the Spanish monarch's critical need for the immense treasure of gold, silver and precious jewels secured in the King's treasure chests awaiting shipment. The Royal Treasury was exhausted by the cost of fighting the war of the Spanish Succession and the failure of the fleet to sail the preceding year. So, notwithstanding that it was the heart of the danger season of the high winds, a treasure fleet of twelve ships departed from Havana Harbor on July 24, 1715.

According to historical accounts, it was an occasion for celebration with brightly colored flags whipping briskly in the breeze and the booming of ceremonial cannon fire ringing in the ears of the throngs of excited citizens crowding the docks. Few of those present, and certainly none of the over two thousand men aboard the ships, had any inkling of what lay ahead on their fateful voyage. Before the week was out, over half their number would be dead and all of their mighty ships, save one, would lie entombed in a watery grave forever.

The galleons sailed northward through the Straits of Florida and past the Florida Keys under a clear and cloudless sky. Their chartered course, and one that they traditionally followed, took them along the east coast of Florida to a point past Cape Canaveral, then following the Gulfstream until it veered eastward to a point north of Bermuda where the fleet would catch the prevailing winds that carried them across the Atlantic to Spain.

By noon on Tuesday, July 30, 1715, a strange calmness had settled in, punctuated by occasional gusts of strong wind that whipped the waves into ever mounting heights of whitecapped water. By mid-afternoon the sky had darkened and the wind was gusting steadily, whipping spray from the breaking waves over the doomed fleet.

In the early morning hours of July 31st, the wind suddenly shifted to the east-northeast, and the hurricane struck with all its fury. The ships, gripped in the incredible force of the crashing waves and mighty winds of nature's most awesome phenomena, were lifted like matchsticks on mountainous crests to be plummeted in the next instant into deep troughs of the ocean. Tons of seawater crashed over the railings of the galleons and, with the shriek of the wind, drowned out the screams of the seamen washed overboard to their death.

Huge anchors were dropped in a desperate attempt to bring the bows of the ships around into the wind and hold them in the deeper waters offshore. As the wind howled and the hurricane increased in intensity, the panic stricken sailors watched the thick anchor lines snap, one by one. Second, and sometimes third, anchors were dropped as the tempestuous sea pounded the ships relentlessly closer and closer to the jagged reefs and shoals. Ultimately, as the oaken hulls of the once proud and mighty Spanish Treasure Fleet were ripped by the cruel coral of the Florida coast, the seawater poured into the smashed ships and they heeled over and sank.

For the wretched survivors, the hurricane had inflicted an incredible measure of death and destruction; one thousand persons perished, eleven galleons sunk, and fourteen million pesos of treasure lost. Only one vessel survived, under the masterful seamanship of its captain, to limp back to Havana with news of the disaster. Destiny brought the ghosts of these Spanish Galleons, that had set sail bravely from Havana Harbor July 24, 1715, to a rendezvous in an Admiralty Court at the United States Courthouse in Key West, Florida, two hundred and sixty-six years later on July 27, 1981. ...

Note: Now for a bit of law, in the following case.


## UNITED STATES DISTRICT COURT, M.D. FLORIDA, ODYSSEY MARINE EXPLORATION, INC., PLAINTIFF, V. UNIDENTIFIED, WRECKED, AND ABANDONED SAILING VESSEL, DEFENDANT.

JULY 30, 2010


**ORDER**

STEVEN D. MERRYDAY, District Judge.

The plaintiff, Odyssey Marine Exploration, Inc., recovers artifacts from sunken wrecks. In this case, the plaintiff seeks title to artifacts recovered from *Le Marquis Tournay,* a French vessel that sank in the English Channel in the late eighteenth century. The plaintiff believes that English privateers owned *Le Marquis Tournay* at the time of the ship's demise. The wreck, which includes cannon and other valuable artifacts, rests on the floor of the English Channel, "beyond the territorial waters or contiguous zone of any sovereign nation."

The plaintiff tendered a brick from the wreck as evidence of "symbolic possession," the clerk issued a warrant of arrest *in rem,* and the plaintiff published notice of the find in The Tampa Tribune and The Times of London. The published notice identifies the wreck as *Le Marquis Tournay* but withholds the location of the wreck.

The plaintiff seeks "title and ownership in the artifacts it has recovered, and those it will recover, from the defendant wreck site

### Discussion

The plaintiff requests, under the law of finds, a default judgment awarding to the plaintiff title to the wreck. Although admiralty law prefers the law of salvage to the law of finds, the law of finds governs the recovery of a long-abandoned wreck. As is typical in admiralty cases, the plaintiff's claim proceeds *in rem* against the wreck.

## I. The Law of Finds and the Law of Salvage

[Both the law of salvage and the law of finds apply to the recovery of property lost at sea. "Under the law of salvage, rescuers take possession of, but not title to, the distressed vessel and its contents" and realize a compensatory salvage award. The law of finds, in contrast, is summed up succinctly as "finders keepers." The law of salvage and the law of finds "serve different purposes and promote different behaviors," and [a claimant cannot "have its cake and eat it too" by invoking both during a single recovery.]       *Black*

### A. The Law of Salvage

Traceable to antiquity, [the law of salvage rewards the voluntary rescue of imperiled property at sea. It functions as a trust on behalf of the true owner and "imposes duties of good faith, honesty, and diligence in protecting the property in the salvors' care." A salvor removes property from a wreck in trust for the owner.]  *Black*

[After recovering lost property, the salvor obtains a maritime lien that allows the salvor to proceed *in rem* to secure a salvage award. The salvor also gains exclusive "possession" over the salvaged property to allow for the uninterrupted delivery of the property to the court-appointed custodian.] [The value of the recovered property governs the salvage award, and, if the salvage award exceeds the value of the salvaged property, the salvor receives title to the property.]   *Black*

### B. The Law of Finds

The law of finds allows a finder to acquire title to abandoned property by "reducing the property to his or her possession." Unlike the law of salvage, the law of finds imposes no trust on the finder, who acquires the property for his own benefit. "To establish a claim under the law of finds, a finder must show (1) intent to reduce property to possession, (2) actual or constructive possession of the property, and (3) that the property is either unowned or abandoned." The finder of abandoned property cannot exclude others from attempting to reduce discovered property to possession. Unlike the law of salvage, an ancient part of the *jus gentium,* the law of finds is a "disfavored common-law doctrine incorporated into admiralty but only rarely applied." Because the law of salvage presumes that property lost at sea is not "abandoned" (and thus the true owner retains title to the lost property), the law of finds traditionally applies only to objects (such as flora and fauna) never owned.

However, the law of finds governs the recovery of an abandoned historical wreck. In *Treasure Salvors I*, the plaintiff asserted title to the discovered wreck of the Spanish frigate *Nuestra Señora de Atocha*, which sank off the Florida Keys in 1622 while carrying precious metals from the new world. *Treasure Salvors I* concludes that "disposition of a wrecked vessel whose very location has been lost for centuries as though its owner were still in existence stretches a fiction to absurd lengths." *see also Klein* (holding that the law of finds rather than the law of salvage applies to the recovery of a two-hundred-year-old wreck privately owned at its sinking). Accordingly, *Treasure Salvors I* holds that the law of finds applies to an abandoned wreck.

## C. The Law of Finds Applies in the Present Case

Under *Treasure Salvors I*, the law of finds governs the plaintiff's claim. The plaintiff believes that the *res* sank more than two hundred years ago, and no owner claims the wreck. If the plaintiff correctly identifies the ship, the original owners were private citizens who passed away more than two centuries ago. Therefore, the plaintiff correctly asserts that the law of finds governs this claim.

## II. Jurisdiction

Generally, in rem jurisdiction "derives entirely from the court's control over the defendant res." By controlling the res, a court declares rights in the res against the world. In this case, jurisdiction extends to the recovered artifacts listed in Exhibit B of the plaintiff's amended motion for default judgment. However, jurisdiction fails to extend to the artifacts on the floor of the English Channel (despite the plaintiff's assurances that those artifacts eventually will arrive in this jurisdiction).

Accordingly, the plaintiff is awarded title under the law of finds only to the specific items listed in Exhibit B.

## B. The Artifacts on the Floor of the English Channel

*In rem* jurisdiction fails to extend to the artifacts that remain in international water, and this want of jurisdiction prevents an adjudication *in rem*. If justice requires a judgment, however, "rigid legalisms" should not defeat jurisdiction. To avoid "rigid legalism," the law of salvage permits the exercise of *in rem* jurisdiction by constructive possession, even if the court possesses only a portion of the total *res*. Relying on the "legal fiction" that the *res* remains undivided, *in rem* jurisdiction by constructive possession derives from the practical impossibility of delivering the entire *res* into the actual possession of the custodian.]Normally, however, [in *rem* jurisdiction by constructive possession attaches only if the entire *res* is located within the territorial jurisdiction of the forum.] Black

In exercising extra-territorial jurisdiction, "a court must be sensitive to the principle of international comity, as the application of international law evokes a sense not only of discretion and courtesy but also of obligation among sovereign states."

Black [To avoid an unreasonable constraint on *in rem* jurisdiction, admiralty law recognizes two exceptions to the requirement that the *res* remain within the territorial jurisdiction]However, because neither exception applies to an attempt to acquire title under the law of finds,(the plaintiff's proposal fails.]
red

### Constructive In Rem Jurisdiction

"Constructive *in rem* jurisdiction" allows the enforcement of an exclusive right to salvage a wreck in international water by expanding the traditional notion of *in rem* jurisdiction by constructive possession. *Titanic I* reasons that the law of salvage, as part of the *jus gentium*, creates a "shared sovereignty" among nations enforcing the *jus gentium*. This "shared sovereignty" allows the declaration of an exclusive right to salvage a wreck outside the territorial jurisdiction.

In stark contrast to the nature and purpose of salvage law, which is an ancient and time-honored part of the maritime *jus gentium*, the law of finds is a disfavored common-law doctrine incorporated into admiralty but only rarely applied. The law of salvage applies only at sea and directly contradicts the common law, which grants no award for the voluntary recovery of another person's property. In contrast, the law of finds in admiralty traditionally reached only natural objects (such as flora and fauna) lacking an owner.(The law of finds applies a doctrine of common law to the seas in narrow, defined circumstances; the law of salvage is exclusively the law of the sea.]Therefore, the law of finds fails to enjoy the universal acceptance necessary to qualify as a part of the *jus gentium*, and the absence of the "shared sovereignty" of the *jus gentium* scuttles any application of the *Titanic I* rationale to a claim governed by the law of finds.

[Under the law of finds, "a finder cannot exclude others from their attempts to obtain first possession of artifacts recovered from an abandoned wreck." In contrast, the law of salvage grants exclusive possession to ensure that the salvor recovers the owner's property intact, and this need supports the exercise of extra-territorial jurisdiction.] In other words, the law of salvage encourages the recovery of property for the benefit of the owner. A declaration granting an exclusive right to salvage the *res* allows the salvor to perform his duty as trustee of the owner's property; competition from other salvors might damage the property and prevent the salvor from fulfilling his duty. On the other hand, the law of finds encourages acquisition for the benefit of the finder. Because a finder acquires title for himself, the finder generally needs no additional incentive to recover lost property. Applying exclusively to the law of salvage in international water, constructive *in rem* jurisdiction fails in this action under the law of finds to support the exercise of jurisdiction over abandoned property on the floor of the English Channel.

The plaintiff's proposal for broad protection of mere finders encourages pillaging the seabed and fails to justify the expansion of extraterritorial jurisdiction.

The plaintiff can secure title under the law of finds only after bringing the artifacts within the territorial jurisdiction.

The plaintiff's motion for issuance of a warrant in *rem* asserts that the plaintiff "invested substantial money and effort in locating, surveying, photographing and researching the history of the Unidentified Shipwrecked Vessel and in planning and conducting the physical recovery of artifacts from the Unidentified Shipwrecked Vessel." However, the record lacks any indication that the plaintiff has exercised control over the wreck beyond discovering the wreck and recovering the few items to which this order adjudicates title. Accordingly, the warrant of arrest is VACATED.

# CHAPTER SIXTEEN

# WILD ANIMALS

## INTRODUCTION

There seems to be an unwritten rule that every law student must read the case of *Pierson v. Post,* not so much for the thrilling results of the case, but for an entertaining look at how scholarly some really bright judges can make a simple case appear to be. The two lawyers who argued the case used the same sort of super-scholarly tone employed by the judges. Why the suit was brought in the first place still remains a mystery. It is interesting to note how many theories may be found as to the fundamental basis for private ownership of property.

One of the challenges of the case has always been to figure out which party was hunting the fox in the first place. Spoiler: Post was the hunter.

### 3 CAI. R. 175
### SUPREME COURT OF NEW YORK.
### PIERSON
### V.
### POST.

#### AUGUST TERM, 1805.

THIS was an action of trespass on the case commenced in a justice's court, by the present defendant against the now plaintiff.

The declaration stated that *Post,* being in possession of certain dogs and hounds under his command, did, "upon a certain wild and uninhabited, unpossessed and waste land, called the beach, find and start one of those noxious beasts called a fox," and whilst there hunting, chasing and pursuing the same with his dogs and hounds, and when in view thereof, *Pierson*, well knowing the fox was so hunted and pursued, did, in the sight of *Post*, to prevent his catching the same, kill and carry it off. A verdict having been rendered for the plaintiff below, the defendant there sued out a *certiorari*, and now assigned for error, that the declaration and the matters therein contained were not sufficient in law to maintain an action.

Opinion

TOMPKINS, J. delivered the opinion of the court.

This cause comes before us on a return to a *certiorari* directed to one of the justices of *Queens* county.

The question submitted by the counsel in this cause for our determination is, whether *Lodowick Post*, by the pursuit with his hounds in the manner alleged in his declaration, acquired such a right to, or property in, the fox, as will sustain an action against *Pierson* for killing and taking him away?

The cause was argued with much ability by the counsel on both sides, and presents for our decision a novel and nice question. It is admitted that a fox is an animal *feræ naturæ*, and that property in such animals is acquired by occupancy only. These admissions narrow the discussion to the simple question of what acts amount to occupancy, applied to acquiring right to wild animals?

If we have recourse to the ancient writers upon general principles of law, the judgment below is obviously erroneous. *Justinian's Institutes*, lib. 2. tit. 1. s. 13. and *Fleta*, lib. 3. c. 2. p. 175. adopt the principle, that pursuit alone vests no property or right in the huntsman; and that even pursuit, accompanied with wounding, is equally ineffectual for that purpose, unless the animal be actually taken. The same principle is recognized by *Bracton*, lib. 2. c. 1. p. 8.

*Puffendorf*, lib. 4. c. 6. s. 2. and 10. defines occupancy of beasts *feræ naturæ*, to be the actual corporal possession of them, and *Bynkershoek* is cited as coinciding in this definition. It is indeed with hesitation that *Puffendorf* affirms that a wild beast mortally wounded, or greatly maimed, cannot be fairly intercepted by another, whilst the pursuit of the person inflicting the wound continues. The foregoing authorities are decisive to show that mere pursuit gave *Post* no legal right to the fox, but that he became the property of *Pierson*, who intercepted and killed him.

It therefore only remains to inquire whether there are any contrary principles, or authorities, to be found in other books, which ought to induce a different decision. Most of the cases which have occurred in *England*, relating to property in wild animals, have either been discussed and decided upon the principles of their positive statute regulations, or have arisen between the huntsman and the owner of the land upon which beasts *feræ naturæ* have been apprehended; the former claiming them by title of occupancy, and the latter *ratione soli.* Little satisfactory aid can, therefore, be derived from the *English* reporters.

*Barbeyrac,* in his notes on *Puffendorf,* does not accede to the definition of occupancy by the latter, but, on the contrary, affirms, [that actual bodily seizure is not, in all cases, necessary to constitute possession of wild animals.] He does not, however, *describe* the acts which, according to his ideas, will amount to an appropriation of such animals to private use, so as to exclude the claims of all other persons, by title of occupancy, to the same animals; and he is far from averring that pursuit alone is sufficient for that purpose. To a certain extent, and as far as *Barbeyrac* appears to me to go, his objections to *Puffendorf's* definition of occupancy are reasonable and correct. [That is to say, that actual bodily seizure is not indispensable to acquire right to, or possession of, wild beasts; but that, on the contrary, the mortal wounding of such beasts, by one not abandoning his pursuit, may, with the utmost propriety, be deemed possession of him; since, thereby, the pursuer manifests an unequivocal intention of appropriating the animal to his individual use, has deprived him of his natural liberty, and brought him within his certain control.] So also, encompassing and securing such animals with nets and toils, or otherwise intercepting them in such a manner as to deprive them of their natural liberty, and render escape impossible, may justly be deemed to give possession of them to those persons who, by their industry and labour, have used such means of apprehending them. *Barbeyrac* seems to have adopted, and had in view in his notes, the more accurate opinion of *Grotius,* with respect to occupancy. That celebrated author, lib. 2. c. 8. s. 3. p. 309. speaking of occupancy, proceeds thus: "*Requiritur autem corporalis quædam possessio ad dominium adipiscendum; atque ideo, vulnerasse non sufficit.*" But in the following section he explains and qualifies this definition of occupancy: "*Sed possessio illa potest non solis manibus, sed instrumentis, ut decipulis, retibus, laqueis dum duo adsint: primum ut ipsa instrumenta sint in nostra potestate, deinde ut fera, ita inclusa sit, ut exire inde nequeat.*" This qualification embraces the full extent of *Barbeyrac's* objection to *Puffendorf's* definition, and allows as great a latitude to acquiring property by occupancy, as can reasonably be inferred from the words or ideas expressed by *Barbeyrac* in his notes. [The case now under consideration is one of mere pursuit, and presents no circumstances or acts which can bring it within the definition of occupancy by *Puffendorf,* or *Grotius,* or the ideas of *Barbeyrac* upon that subject.]

The case cited from 11 *Mod.* 74--130. I think clearly distinguishable from the present; inasmuch as there the action was for maliciously hindering and disturbing the plaintiff in the exercise and enjoyment of a private franchise; and in the report of the same case, 3 *Salk.* 9. *Holt,* Ch. J. states, that the ducks were in the plaintiff's decoy pond, and *so in his possession,* from which it is obvious the court laid much stress in their opinion upon the plaintiff's possession of the ducks, *ratione soli.*

We are the more readily inclined to confine possession or occupancy of beasts *feræ naturæ,* within the limits prescribed by the learned authors above cited, for the sake of certainty, and preserving peace and order in society. If the first seeing, starting, or pursuing such animals, without having so wounded, circumvented or ensnared them, so as to deprive them of their natural liberty, and subject them to the control of their pursuer, should afford the basis of actions against others for intercepting and killing them, it would prove a fertile source of quarrels and litigation.

However uncourteous or unkind the conduct of *Pierson* towards *Post,* in this instance, may have been, yet his act was productive of no injury or damage for which a legal remedy can be applied. We are of opinion the judgment below was erroneous, and ought to be reversed.

LIVINGSTON, J. My opinion differs from that of the court.

Of six exceptions, taken to the proceedings below, all are abandoned except the third, which reduces the controversy to a single question.

Whether a person who, with his own hounds, starts and hunts a fox on waste and uninhabited ground, and is on the point of seizing his prey, acquires such an interest in the animal, as to have a right of action against another, who in view of the huntsman and his dogs in full pursuit, and with knowledge of the chase, shall kill and carry him away?

This is a knotty point, and should have been submitted to the arbitration of sportsmen, without poring over *Justinian, Fleta, Bracton, Puffendorf, Locke, Barbeyrac,* or *Blackstone,* all of whom have been cited; they would have had no difficulty in coming to a prompt and correct conclusion. In a court thus constituted, the skin and carcass of poor *reynard* would have been properly disposed of, and a precedent set, interfering with no usage or custom which the experience of ages has sanctioned, and which must be so well known to every votary of *Diana.* But the parties have referred the question to our judgment, and we must dispose of it as well as we can, from the partial lights we possess, leaving to a higher tribunal, the correction of any mistake which we may be so unfortunate as to make. By the pleadings it is admitted that a fox is a "wild and noxious beast." Both parties have regarded him, as the law of nations does a pirate, "*hostem humani generis,*" and although "*de mortuis nil nisi bonum,*" be a maxim of our profession, the memory of the deceased has not been spared. His depredations on farmers and on barn yards, have not been forgotten; and to put him to death wherever found, is allowed to be meritorious, and of public benefit. Hence it follows, that our decision should have in view the greatest possible encouragement to the destruction of an animal, so cunning and ruthless in his career. But who would keep a pack of hounds; or what gentleman, at the sound of the horn, and at peep of day, would mount his steed, and for hours together, "*sub jove frigido*," or a vertical sun, pursue the windings of this wily quadruped, if, just as night came on, and his stratagems and strength were nearly exhausted, a saucy intruder, who had not shared in the honours or labours of the chase, were permitted to come in at the death, and bear away in triumph the object of pursuit? Whatever *Justinian* may have thought of the matter, it must be recollected that his code was compiled many hundred years ago, and it would be very hard indeed, at the distance of so many centuries, not to have a right to establish a rule for ourselves. In his day, we read of no order of men who made it a business, in the language of the declaration in this cause, "with hounds and dogs to find, start, pursue, hunt, and chase," these animals, and that, too, without any other motive than the preservation of *Roman* poultry; if this diversion had been then in fashion, the lawyers who composed his institutes, would have taken care not to pass it by, without suitable encouragement. If any thing, therefore, in the digests or pandects shall appear to militate against the defendant in error, who, on this occasion, was the foxhunter, we have only to say *tempora mutantur;* and if men themselves change with the times, why should not laws also undergo an alteration?

It may be expected, however, by the learned counsel, that more particular notice be taken of their authorities. I have examined them all, and feel great difficulty in determining, whether to acquire dominion over a thing, before in common, it be sufficient that we barely see it, or know where it is, or wish for it, or make a declaration of our will respecting it; or whether, in the case of wild beasts, setting a trap, or lying in wait, or starting, or pursuing, be enough; or if an actual wounding, or killing, or bodily tact and occupation be necessary. Writers on general law, who have favoured us with their speculations on these points, differ on them all; but, great as is the diversity of sentiment among them, some conclusion must be adopted on the question immediately before us. After mature deliberation, I embrace that of *Barbeyrac,* as the most rational, and least liable to objection. If at liberty, we might imitate the courtesy of a certain emperor, who, to avoid giving offence to the advocates of any of these different doctrines, adopted a middle course, and by ingenious distinctions, rendered it difficult to say (as often happens after a fierce and angry contest) to whom the palm of victory belonged. He ordained, that if a beast be followed with *large dogs and hounds,* he shall belong to the hunter, not to the chance occupant; and in like manner, if he be killed or wounded with a lance or sword; but if chased with *beagles only,* then he passed to the captor, not to the first pursuer. If slain with a dart, a sling, or a bow, he fell to the hunter, if still in chase, and not to him who might afterwards find and seize him.

Now, as we are without any municipal regulations of our own, and the pursuit here, for aught that appears on the case, being with dogs and hounds of *imperial stature,* we are at liberty to adopt one of the provisions just cited, which comports also with the learned conclusion of *Barbeyrac,* that property in animals *feræ naturæ* may be acquired without bodily touch or manucaption, provided the pursuer be within reach, or have a *reasonable* prospect (which certainly existed here) of taking, what he has *thus* discovered an intention of converting to his own use.

When we reflect also that the interest of our husbandmen, the most useful of men in any community, will be advanced by the destruction of a beast so pernicious and incorrigible, we cannot greatly err, in saying, that a pursuit like the present, through waste and unoccupied lands, and which must inevitably and speedily have terminated in corporal possession, or bodily *seisin,* confers such a right to the object of it, as to make any one a wrongdoer, who shall interfere and shoulder the spoil. The *justice's* judgment ought, therefore, in my opinion, to be affirmed.

Judgment of reversal.

Note: Now for a much more recent, and far more important case involving wild animals, which are no longer referred to a "noxious beasts." Note the interaction between various environmental protection statutes, including the Clean Water Act and the Endangered Species Act.

Is chasing an owl with a broom, or subjecting an owl to the cacophony caused by high school students given the same protection today as chasing a fox with hounds of *imperial stature?*

## UNITED STATES COURT OF APPEALS, NINTH CIRCUIT.
## DEFENDERS OF WILDLIFE; SOUTHWEST CENTER FOR BIOLOGICAL DIVERSITY, PLAINTIFFS–APPELLANTS,
## V.
## MIKE BERNAL; ROBERT SMITH, DR., SUPERINTENDENT OF BOARD,
## DEFENDANTS–APPELLEES.

FEBRUARY 28, 2000

OPINION

HUG, Chief Judge

Defenders of Wildlife and the Southwest Center for Biological Diversity (collectively "Defenders") appeal the district court's order lifting a temporary restraining order and denying their motion for a permanent injunction to halt the construction of a new school on property which Defenders contend contains potential habitat for the cactus ferruginous pygmy owl (pygmy-owl), listed as endangered under the Endangered Species Act (ESA). At issue in this case is whether the construction of a critically-needed new high school by the Amphitheater School District (the School District) in northwest Tucson will result in the "take" of the endangered pygmy-owl in violation of section 9 of the ESA.

After a three-day bench trial the district court found that the proposed construction would not result in the take of a pygmy-owl and denied the permanent injunction.

### Factual and Procedural Background

In 1994, the School District paid $1.78 million to purchase a 73 acre site in northwest Tucson, upon which a new high school would be built. The high school complex is intended to accommodate 2,100 students and is composed of several buildings, athletic fields and parking areas for students, faculty and visitors. In December 1994, after the purchase of the school site, the United States Fish and Wildlife Service (FWS) formally published a proposed rule to list the pygmy-owl as an endangered species under the ESA. On March 10, 1997, after the required procedures and commentary period, the FWS listed the pygmy-owl as an endangered species under the ESA.

The pygmy-owl is a small reddish brown owl known for its relatively long tail and monotonous call which is heard primarily at dawn and dusk. The pygmy-owl nests in a cavity of a large tree or large columnar cactus. Its diverse diet includes birds, lizards, insects, and small mammals and frogs. The pygmy-owl occurs from lowland central Arizona south through portions of western Mexico and from southern Texas south through other portions of Mexico on down through portions of Central America. The FWS indicates that there are a total 54,400 acres of suitable pygmy-owl habitat in northwest Tucson, which includes the 73 acre school site. The school site falls within the area designated by the FWS as critical habitat for the pygmy owl.

Within the 73 acre parcel acquired by the School District in 1994, there are three "arroyos," defined as "dry washes" or "ephemeral desert waterways." The U.S. Army Corps of Engineers designated the arroyos as "jurisdictional waters" pursuant to the Clean Water Act. The original design of the School District complex called for some construction within the "jurisdictional waters," thereby requiring the School District to obtain a permit under the Clean Water Act. Because a federal permit was at issue, the FWS informed the Corps that "formal consultation" pursuant to section 7 of the ESA was required to assess the impact of the proposed project on the pygmy-owl. Consultation was initiated, but before completion of the process the School District withdrew its application for the permit because it had redesigned the project so that construction would not affect the jurisdictional waterways. As a result of the redesigned project, no development is planned for the 30 acres containing the arroyos in the western portion of the property. The School District has acquired or will acquire 17 acres to the east of the initially acquired property for utilization in the redesigned school project. Thus, the entire school site is 90 acres, including the 30 acres containing the arroyos. The 30 acre parcel will remain undeveloped and fenced off. For ease in identification in this opinion, the entire 90 acre parcel will be referred to as the "school site." The 60 acres upon which the school complex is designed to be built will be referred to as the "60 acre parcel." The undeveloped 30 acre parcel, which contains the arroyos, will be referred to as the "30 acre parcel."

In March 1998, the School District began plant salvaging operations as a precursor to beginning construction. Defenders immediately filed suit seeking a temporary restraining order and a preliminary injunction against the School District to prevent any action on the school site. Defenders alleged that the proposed construction violated Section 9 of the ESA because it was likely to harm or harass the pygmy-owl, which Defenders assert inhabits or uses the site. Section 9 of the ESA applies to private parties, whereas Section 7 of the ESA, which had earlier been resolved, applies only to actions carried out, funded, or authorized by a federal agency. The district court entered a temporary restraining order. The court later consolidated the hearing on Defenders' request for a preliminary injunction with the trial on the merits. Following a three-day trial, the district court issued its final order, denying the request for a permanent injunction, and lifting the temporary restraining order. We granted Defenders' motion for an injunction pending appeal.

## Statutory Framework

Section 9 of the ESA makes it unlawful to "take" a species listed as endangered or threatened. The term "take" means to harass, harm, pursue, hunt, shoot, wound, kill, trap, capture or collect, or to attempt to engage in any such conduct. The "take" alleged is that the proposed construction will harass or harm the pygmy-owl. The Department of the Interior has promulgated a regulation further defining harm and harass as follows:

> *Harm* in the definition of "take" in the Act means an act which actually kills or injures wildlife. Such act may include significant habitat modification or degradation where it actually kills or injures wildlife by significantly impairing essential behavioral patterns, including breeding, feeding or sheltering.

> *Harass* in the definition of "take" in the Act means an intentional or negligent act or omission which creates the likelihood of injury to wildlife by annoying it to such an extent as to significantly disrupt normal behavioral patterns which include, but are not limited to, breeding, feeding or sheltering.

Harming a species may be indirect, in that the harm may be caused by habitat modification, but habitat modification does not constitute harm unless it "actually kills or injures wildlife."

## Harm and Harassment Claims

In order to prevail in this action Defenders had to prove that the School District's actions would result in an unlawful "take" of a pygmy-owl. An injunction would be appropriate relief.

The district judge explained at some length what evidence he relied on to support his findings. The judge stated that the opinion of scientific experts, the evidence of the habits of the pygmy-owl, and the recent aural detection of the bird, support a logical inference that the bird or birds currently use the areas where they have been detected near the north and west boundaries of the site, and the area between those two points within the arroyo. He noted that because habitat within this arroyo area is suitable for pygmy-owls, provides cover and prey for birds, provides a natural corridor for the owl to travel from the north boundary to the west boundary where it has been frequently sited, an inference can be drawn that the owl uses this area. The judge then contrasted the 30 acre parcel, which he refers to as "the Area", with the rest of the school site:

Contrarily, there have been no sightings of the owl beyond the clusters of detections near the north and west boundaries of the property and extensive surveys of the entire property have failed to produce one single detection of a pygmy-owl. A search of 361 cavities of saguaro cacti on the site, in which pygmy owls prefer to nest, produced no pygmy-owls. There is therefore little factual basis to conclude that the owl uses the rest of the school site, outside of the Area. Because owls display site fidelity and have been seen near the Area but never detected on the school site outside of the Area, in spite of concentrated efforts to find them there, a logical inference can be made that the owl is not using the remainder of the site. Finally, the heaviest concentrations of sitings confirmed by the Arizona Game and Fish Department near the site are in residential areas west of the school site where there is low impact housing (one house on a 3–5 acre plot with minimal disturbance to native vegetation). This supports the inference that the "core" of the owl's activity may not be in the Area but may be west of the school site, and that the 30 acre Area may be the outer fringe of the territory the bird uses.

The Arizona Game and Fish Department had reported that "pygmy-owls are not intimidated by the presence of people or can acclimate to low density urbanization and associated activities." In 1995–96, a K–8 school was constructed and has been operating a short distance north of the proposed school site. One neighbor testified that she had chased an owl shouting at it and waving a broom, but the owl had returned to the residence. At one residence, an owl family was found in a grapefruit tree close to the house and was inspected at close range for weeks on end by the resident and his guests.

### Failure to Apply for an Incidental Take Permit

Defenders contend that the district court should have required the School District to apply for an Incidental Take Permit (ITP). The district court concluded that the permitting provisions found in Section 10 of the ESA are not mandatory.

If a proposed action constitutes a "take" under Section 9 of the ESA, a party may apply for an ITP under Section 10. 16 U.S.C. § 1539(a)(1)(B). If the FWS grants the ITP, the party can proceed with the proposed activity despite the taking of an endangered species. The School District declined to apply for an ITP because its position was that the proposed construction would not result in the "take" of an endangered pygmy-owl. Defenders argue that the district court erred by failing to require the School District to seek an ITP based on the expert scientific testimony presented.

[We have established that pursuing an ITP is not mandatory and a party can choose whether to proceed with the permitting process. However, if a party chooses not to secure a permit and the proposed activity, in fact, "takes" a listed species, the ESA authorizes civil and criminal penalties. Thus a party may proceed without a permit, but it risks civil and criminal penalties if a "take" occurs. The district court did not err in concluding that the School District was not required to seek an ITP.]

### Conclusion

Based on the foregoing, the judgment of the district court is AFFIRMED.

# CHAPTER SEVENTEEN

# LANDLORD/TENANT

## INTRODUCTION

Most people have a basic knowledge of the relationship of landlord/tenant. Now for some important legal rules impacting that relationship.

## A. KINDS OF TENANCIES; SUBLEASE OR ASSIGNMENT

### 1. Four Kinds of Tenancies

There are four basic kinds of tenancies – term for years, periodic tenancy, tenancy at will, and tenancy at sufferance. Each state will have slightly different statutory provisions as to how each of these forms of tenancy may be terminated – by either the landlord or the tenant. The state statutory provisions will specify how much notice one party must give to the other party in order to terminate the tenancy, and what happens if the tenant stays in the premises longer than the tenant is authorized to be there. The basic forms of tenancy are about the same in every jurisdiction.

Term for years: Any lease that has a definite ending date is considered to be a term for years – whether the actual term of the lease is one week or 50 years. The major thing is that both the landlord and the tenant have agreed, in advance, that on a specific date the lease will end, and the tenant must move out. Neither party is required to give the other party notice – the tenancy simply ends.

What happens if the tenant does not move out on the date specified? Then the landlord has several options. Among the options available to the landlord, the landlord may bring legal action to evict the tenant; or the landlord may allow the tenant to stay, while declaring that the lease is thus renewed for a new term, of the same duration, at the same rent. Thus a tenant who is one day late moving out of the premises could find that the tenant is obligated on another five year lease of the same premises – if that is the choice made by the landlord.

Periodic Tenancy: Any tenancy that will automatically renew itself until either the landlord or the tenant decides to terminate the lease, (after proper notice), is called a periodic tenancy. The "period" for the tenancy is usually one month, but may be one week, one year, or ten years – depending on the time specified in the lease. If no period is specified, then the period is usually considered to be the intervals at which rental payments are made. For example, if the rent is paid monthly, it would be a month-to-month periodic tenancy. If rent is paid yearly, it might well be considered to be a year-to-year periodic tenancy. Most apartment leases start out as a term for years, with a definite ending date, and then specify that if the tenant continues in possession the lease will become a month-to-month periodic tenancy.

The practical reason it is important to know whether the lease is a month-to-month periodic tenancy or a year-to-year periodic tenancy is that the state statute is likely to specify how many day's notice must be given to terminate which form of tenancy. If the landlord would have trouble re-renting the apartment, if the tenant doesn't give notice within the time required by the local statute, the landlord may decide to hold the tenant liable for another month's – or year's – rent, if proper notice has not been given to terminate that kind of tenancy.

Tenancy at will: Generally, clients will not be involved in litigation over either a tenancy at will or a tenancy at sufferance. Both are very informal tenancies, which may be ended by either party at any time. When a tenant enters the premises, with the consent of the landlord, without a specific lease term, it is considered a tenancy at will. Perhaps that might occur when someone is selling a house, and gives a friend permission to stay in the house until the house is sold.

Tenancy at sufferance: A tenancy at sufferance occurs when a tenant holds over, after the end of a lease, and the landlord doesn't do anything to evict the tenant, and the tenant doesn't pay any rent. The danger to the tenant at that point is that the landlord may decide to declare that a new term for years or periodic tenancy has begun, making the hold-over tenant legally liable to pay more rent.

2. Sublease or Assignment

During the term of a one year lease, for example, the tenant may wish to leave – as frequently happens at the end of an academic year. If three months still remain on the lease, the tenant may try to get the landlord to accept an early surrender of the lease – which would let the tenant out of the remaining obligations under the lease. Or, if the landlord feels that it might be difficult for the landlord to find a new tenant for just two or three months, the landlord may decide to hold the tenant to the original lease.

In that case, the tenant is likely to try to sublease the premises - to find someone else to live in the apartment, who will pay at least something toward the rent. If the tenant is able to find a sublessee for all or part of the remaining term of the lease, the original tenant will still remain liable to pay the full amount of the rent directly to the landlord, because the landlord and the original tenant always remain in privity of contract.

The benefit to the original tenant in being able to find a sublessee is just that the sublessee will help to pay some part of the rent. The sublessee will make the payments directly to the original tenant. The original tenant remains obligated to send the full amount of the rent to the landlord each month, as specified in the lease.

The following case illustrates some very important rules which apply to assignments.

### SUPREME COURT OF RHODE ISLAND
### JUILLIARD & CO.
### VS.
### AMERICAN WOOLEN COMPANY

#### JUNE 14, 1943

#### OPINION BY: CAPOTOSTO

This is an action to recover installments of rent and taxes in the total amount of $ 2,935.83, allegedly due for the period between September 1940 and March 1941 under a lease of certain premises in the city of Providence. A justice of the superior court, siting without a jury, rendered a decision for the defendant. The case is before us on plaintiff's exception to this decision and also on certain other exceptions to rulings in the case.

On May 12, 1893, the Atlantic Mills leased certain premises in the city of Providence to the Riverside Worsted Mills for the term ending September 1, 1955. In this lease is the specific covenant by which the plaintiff asserts the defendant has agreed to pay rent and certain other charges as therein set forth. This lease contains no restrictions whatever against assignment, nor does it provide that, upon an assignment of the lease, the assignee should assume and be bound for the entire unexpired term by the covenant just mentioned. The plaintiff succeeded to the rights of the lessor in this lease on December 4, 1936.

On April 15, 1899, the lessee, Riverside Worsted Mills, assigned the lease to the American Woolen Company, a New Jersey corporation, which in turn assigned it, on February 15, 1916, to the defendant American Woolen Company, a Massachusetts corporation. Four assignments of the lessee's interests occurred between 1916 and the bringing of this suit on April 14, 1941. The names of the successive assignees and the dates of such assignments are as follows: National & Providence Worsted Mills, a subsidiary of the defendant, December 22, 1931; American Woolen Company, the present defendant, December 26, 1934; Textile Realty Company, also a subsidiary of the defendant, June 1, 1939; and Reo Realty Company, November 21, 1939. The defendant admits that it was virtually the lessee until the lease was assigned to the Reo Realty Company, but denies that in this assignment it retained any beneficial interest in or control of the lease or premises covered thereby. In no one of these assignments did the assignee agree to assume the obligation to pay rent for the unexpired term of the lease.

The law on this point is well settled. As early as 1780, in *Eaton v. Jaques,* Lord Mansfield said "In leases, the lessee being a party to the original contract, continues always liable, notwithstanding any assignment; the assignee is only liable in respect of his possession of the thing. He bears the burden while he enjoys the benefit, and no longer."

Unless fraudulent or colorable, a new assignment of the lease terminates the assignee's liability to the lessor for rent subsequently accruing. If such assignee, by a new assignment, fairly relinquishes not only possession of the leased premises but also all benefits therefrom, it is immaterial that the new assignee may be financially irresponsible, or that he gave no consideration, or even that he received a bonus as an inducement to accept the assignment of the lease.

The case is different, however, where such assignee makes an assignment which, though proper in form, leaves him as a matter of fact in possession of the leased premises or in receipt of benefits therefrom. In such case the assignment is colorable and will not terminate his liability to the lessor for rent, while he, in reality, continues in possession of the premises covered by the lease or enjoys any benefits from the use of such property.

The plaintiff here contends that the assignment by the Textile Realty Company to the Reo Realty Company was colorable. The defendant admits that it created the Textile Realty Company to serve as a medium for the sale of certain properties that it considered either useless or unprofitable, but it vigorously denies that the assignment to the Reo Realty Company was not in good faith.

Among the properties that the defendant desired to sell and which it transferred to the Textile Realty Company for that purpose were the lease under consideration and some vacant land with a railroad siding, which vacant land it had been unable to sell in the open market. In July 1939, one Aaron J. Oster, who was in the scrap metal business, became interested in those properties and bought them the following November for $ 630.30, taking title thereto in the name of the Reo Realty Company, a corporation controlled by him and in which the defendant, according to the record before us, had no interest whatever. Oster, who testified that he purchased the property for "the sole reason of using it and making money with it", then tried to secure from the plaintiff a reduction of the rent payable under the lease but was unsuccessful. There is evidence that the Reo Realty Company paid one installment of rent and expended some money in repairs. We have thus summarized our understanding of the evidence because it is impossible to refer specifically in this opinion to the large amount of correspondence, memoranda and agreements which bear upon this aspect of the case.

The plaintiff claims that the transaction between the defendant, through the Textile Realty Company, and Oster, through the Reo Realty Company, was nothing more than a scheme by the former's officials "to procure a rent reduction and in effect a new lease." It draws this conclusion mainly from the fact that the Reo Realty Company was a new corporation without known assets and that it paid so small a sum for an assignment of the lease and a deed of the vacant land.

The trial justice found that the transaction under consideration was in good faith; that on or about November 29, 1939, the Reo Realty Company "entered into exclusive control and possession of the leased premises", and that since that date "neither the American Woolen Company, the defendant, nor the Textile Realty Company has exercised any control over the leased premises; nor have they or either of them, had possession of such premises." We have found no competent evidence in contradiction of these findings of the trial justice. Unless resort is had to speculation or unwarranted suspicion, there is nothing to show, as the plaintiff states in its brief, that the transaction "envisaged", in the event that Oster failed to obtain a reduction of the rent, "the collapse of the dummy, Reo Realty Company, and the leaving of the property in the same status as if that company had never been formed and no assignment had been attempted." A fair consideration of the record before us shows that each of the parties in interest was assisted by able counsel and dealt with each other at arm's length in effecting a business transaction, which each party considered beneficial to itself.

Granting, as the plaintiff argues, that the amount paid by Oster for the leasehold and the vacant land was relatively small, yet, according to the authorities hereinbefore cited on the point under consideration, this fact was not enough to render the assignment from the Textile Realty Company to the Reo Realty Company colorable, so as to continue the liability, to the plaintiff, of the defendant as an assignee of the lease in constructive possession of the premises. In the absence of collusion, and we find none in the circumstances of this case, the defendant, which was not bound contractually to the contrary, could sell or dispose of its property on such terms as it chose in order to relieve itself of the burden resulting from the possession of property that had become useless or unprofitable, so long as it relinquished all benefits therefrom. For the reasons stated, the trial justice was not in error in finding that the assignment of the lease to the Reo Realty Company terminated defendant's liability for rent under the lease.

The plaintiff's exceptions are all overruled, and the case is remitted to the superior court for the entry of judgment on the decision.

Note: Needless to say, as attorney for the landlord you should *always* put in a provision about assignment. Almost always it is wise to provide that no assignment will be allowed without the written consent of the landlord. Then it is important to add that if the landlord consents to one assignment, no future assignment will be allowed without the written consent of the landlord for each future assignment.

## B. LANDLORD DUTIES

### 1. Warranty of Habitability

At common law, a lease was considered to be a conveyance of an interest in land. Once the term of the lease began, the landlord had virtually no obligation to keep the premises in repair. The tenant was expected to do that. That was the law for centuries. Then the law changed very rapidly beginning in about 1969, so that in nearly all states today there is now an implied warranty of habitability. Two of the leading cases in creating the warranty of habitability follow.

# SUPREME COURT OF HAWAII
## HENRY C. LEMLE
### V.
## MRS. V. E. BREEDEN

NOVEMBER 26, 1969

**OPINION BY: LEVINSON**

This case of first impression in Hawaii involves the doctrine of implied warranty of habitability and fitness for use of a leased dwelling. The plaintiff-lessee (Lemle) sued to recover the deposit and rent payment totaling $1,190.00. Constructive eviction and breach of an implied warranty of habitability and fitness for use were alleged as the basis for recovery. The defendant-lessor (Mrs. Breeden) counterclaimed for damages for breach of the rental agreement. The trial court, sitting without a jury, held for the plaintiff and the case comes to us on appeal from that judgment.

The facts in this case are relatively simple and without substantial conflict. The rented premises involved are owned by the defendant, Mrs. Breeden, and are located in the Diamond Head area of Honolulu. The house fronts on the water with the surrounding grounds attractively landscaped with lauhala trees and other shrubbery. The dwelling consists of several structures containing six bedrooms, six baths, a living room, kitchen, dining room, garage, and salt-water swimming pool. The main dwelling house is constructed in "Tahitian" style with a corrugated metal roof over which coconut leaves have been woven together to give it a "grass shack" effect. The house is relatively open without screening on windows or doorways.

The defendant herself occupied the premises until sometime between September 14 and September 17, 1964, when she returned to the continental United States, having authorized a local realtor to rent the house for her. On September 21, 1964 during the daylight hours, the realtor showed the home to the plaintiff and his wife, newcomers to Hawaii from New York City, and told them that it was available for immediate occupancy. The plaintiff saw no evidence of rodent infestation during the one-half hour inspection.

That evening the rental agreement was executed. It was for the periods September 22, 1964 to March 20, 1965, and April 17, 1965 to June 12, 1965. The rental was $800.00 per month fully furnished. Mrs. Breeden reserved the right to occupy the premises between March 20 and April 17, 1965. The plaintiff tendered a check to the defendant's agent for $1,190.00 at that time.

The very next day, September 22, 1964, the plaintiff, his wife and their four children, who had been staying in a Waikiki hotel, took possession of the premises. That evening it became abundantly evident to the plaintiff that there were rats within the main dwelling and on the corrugated iron roof. It was not clear whether the rats came from within the house or from the rocky area next to the water. During that night and for the next two nights the plaintiff and his family were sufficiently apprehensive of the rats that they slept together in the downstairs living room of the main house, thereby vacating their individual bedrooms. Rats were seen and heard during those three nights.

On September 23, 1964, the day after occupancy, the defendant's agent was informed of the rats' presence and she procured extermination services from a local firm. The plaintiff himself also bought traps to supplement the traps and bait set by the exterminators. These attempts to alleviate the rat problem were only partially successful and the succeeding two nights were equally sleepless and uncomfortable for the family.

On September 25, 1964, three days after occupying the dwelling, the plaintiff and his family vacated the premises after notifying the defendant's agent of his intention to do so and demanding the return of the money which he had previously paid. Subsequently this suit was brought.

The trial judge ruled that there was an implied warranty of habitability and fitness in the lease of a dwelling house, that there was a breach of warranty, that the plaintiff was constructively evicted, and that the plaintiff was entitled to recover $ 1,110.00 plus interest.

We affirm.

## A. THE IMPLIED WARRANTY OF HABITABILITY AND FITNESS OF LEASED PREMISES.

It is important in a case of this type to separate carefully two very distinct doctrines: (1) that of implied warranty of habitability and fitness for the use intended, and (2) that of constructive eviction. The origin, history, and theoretical justification for these legal doctrines are quite different and are not to be confused.

At common law when land was leased to a tenant, the law of property regarded the lease as equivalent to a sale of the premises for a term. The lessee acquired an estate in land and became both owner and occupier for that term subject to the ancient doctrine of *caveat emptor*. Since rules of property law solidified before the development of mutually dependent covenants in contract law, theoretically once an estate was leased, there were no further unexecuted acts to be performed by the landlord and there could be no failure of consideration. Predictably enough, this concept of the lessee's interest has led to many troublesome rules of law which have endured far beyond their historical justifications.

Given the finality of a lease transaction and the legal effect of *caveat emptor* which placed the burden of inspection on the tenant, the actual moment of the conveyance was subject to an untoward amount of legal focus. Only if there were fraud or mistake in the initial transaction would the lessee have a remedy. "Fraud apart, there is no law against letting a tumble-down house." *Robbins* v. *Jones*, 143 Engl. Rep. 768 (1863). In the absence of statute it was generally held that there was no implied warranty of habitability and fitness.

The rule of *caveat emptor* in lease transactions at one time may have had some basis in social practice as well as in historical doctrine. At common law leases were customarily lengthy documents embodying the full expectations of the parties. There was generally equal knowledge of the condition of the land by both landlord and tenant. The land itself would often yield the rents and the buildings were constructed simply, without modern conveniences like wiring or plumbing. Yet in an urban society where the vast majority of tenants do not reap the rent directly from the land but bargain primarily for the right to enjoy the premises for living purposes, often signing standardized leases as in this case, common law conceptions of a lease and the tenant's liability for rent are no longer viable.

American and English courts have attempted to circumvent this historical rigidity by the use of the doctrine of constructive eviction which serves as a substitute for the dependency of covenants in a large class of cases involving the enjoyment of the premises. Furthermore, limited exceptions to the general rule of no implied warranty of habitability and fitness are also widely recognized. The exception raised in this case applies when a furnished dwelling is rented for a short period of time. *Ingalls* v. *Hobbs*, 156 Mass. 348 (1892). This exception has been justified on the ground that there is no opportunity to inspect, therefore the rule of *caveat emptor* does not apply. Nevertheless, some courts have strictly construed this exception limiting it to only "temporary" rentals, defects existing at the time of rental, and defects in furnishings.

While the inability to inspect is the avowed justification for the exception, it is more soundly supported by the obvious fact that the tenant is implicitly or expressly bargaining for immediate possession of the premises in a suitable condition. The fact that a home or apartment is furnished merely demonstrates the desire for immediate inhabitability as does the brevity of the lease. The exception was plainly a method of keeping the rule of *caveat emptor* from working an injustice in those special circumstances.

Yet it is clear that if the expectations of the tenant were the operative test, the exception would soon swallow up the general rule. "It is fair to presume that no individual would voluntarily choose to live in a dwelling that had become unsafe for human habitation." *Bowles* v. *Mahoney*, (D.C. Cir. 1952). We think that the exception itself is artificial and that it is the general rule of *caveat emptor* which must be re-examined.

In the law of sales of chattels, the trend is markedly in favor of implying warranties of fitness and merchantability. The reasoning has been (1) that the public interest in safety and consumer protection requires it, and (2) that the burden ought to be shifted to the manufacturer who, by placing the goods on the market, represents their suitability and fitness. The manufacturer is also the one who knows more about the product and is in a better position to alleviate any problems or bear the brunt of any losses. This reasoning has also been accepted by a growing number of courts in cases involving sales of new homes. *See Carpenter* v. *Donohoe*, 154 Colo. 78, (1964). The same reasoning is equally persuasive in leases of real property.

The application of an implied warranty of habitability in leases gives recognition to the changes in leasing transactions today. It affirms the fact that a lease is, in essence, a sale as well as a transfer of an estate in land and is, more importantly, a contractual relationship. From that contractual relationship an implied warranty of habitability and fitness for the purposes intended is a just and necessary implication. It is a doctrine which has its counterparts in the law of sales and torts and one which when candidly countenanced is impelled by the nature of the transaction and contemporary housing realities. Legal fictions and artificial exceptions to wooden rules of property law aside, we hold that in the lease of a dwelling house, such as in this case, there is an implied warranty of habitability and fitness for the use intended.

Here the facts demonstrate the uninhabitability and unfitness of the premises for residential purposes. For three sleepless nights the plaintiff and his family literally camped in the living room. They were unable to sleep in the proper quarters or make use of the other facilities in the house due to natural apprehension of the rats which made noise scurrying about on the roof and invaded the house through the unscreened openings.

The defendant makes much of the point that the source of the rats was the beach rocks and surrounding foliage. She contends that this exonerated her from the duty to keep the house free of rats. While it is not clear where the rats came from, assuming that they did originate from outside of the premises, the defendant had it within her power to keep them out by proper and timely screening and extermination procedures. Indeed this was done before the next tenant moved in. But to begin such procedures after the plaintiff had occupied the dwelling and to expect that he have the requisite patience and fortitude in the face of trial and error methods of extermination was too much to ask.

We need not consider the ruling of the trial court that the plaintiff was constructively evicted in light of the decision of this court that there was an implied warranty of habitability in this case. The doctrine of constructive eviction, as an admitted
judicial fiction designed to operate as though there were a substantial breach of a
material covenant in a bilateral contract, no longer serves its purpose when the more
flexible concept of implied warranty of habitability is legally available.

## B. CHOICE OF REMEDIES.

It is a decided advantage of the implied warranty doctrine that there are a number of
remedies available. The doctrine of constructive eviction, on the other hand, requires
that the tenant abandon the premises within a reasonable time after giving notice
that the premises are uninhabitable or unfit for his purposes. This is based on the
absurd proposition, contrary to modern urban realities, that "a tenant cannot claim
uninhabitability, and at the same time continue to inhabit." Abandonment is always
at the risk of establishing sufficient facts to constitute constructive eviction or the
tenant will be liable for breach of the rental agreement. Also the tenant is forced
to gamble on the time factor as he must abandon within a "reasonable" time or be
deemed to have "waived" the defects.

Some courts have creatively allowed for alternatives to the abandonment requirement by allowing for a declaration of constructive eviction in equity without forcing
abandonment. Other courts have found *partial* constructive eviction where alternative housing was scarce, thus allowing the tenant to remain in at least part of the
premises. *See Barash v. Penn. Terminal Real Estate Corp.*, (N.Y. App. Div. 1969). In spite
of such imaginative remedies, it appears to us that to search for gaps and exceptions
in a legal doctrine such as constructive eviction which exists only because of the
somnolence of the common law and the courts is to perpetuate further judicial fictions when preferable alternatives exist. We do not agree with Blackstone that "the
law of real property is formed into a fine artificial system, full of unseen connections
and nice dependencies, and he that breaks one link of the chain endangers the dissolution of the whole." The law of landlord-tenant relations cannot be so frail as to
shatter when confronted with modern urban realities and a frank appraisal of the
underlying issues.

By adopting the view that a lease is essentially a contractual relationship with an
implied warranty of habitability and fitness, a more consistent and responsive set of
remedies are available for a tenant. They are the basic contract remedies of damages,
reformation, and rescission. These remedies would give the tenant a wide range of
alternatives in seeking to resolve his alleged grievance.

[In considering the materiality of an alleged breach, both the seriousness of the claimed defect and the length of time for which it persists are relevant factors. Each case must turn on its own facts.] Here there was sufficient evidence for the trier of fact to conclude that the breach was material and that the plaintiff's action in rescinding the rental agreement was justifiable. The plaintiff gave notice of rescission and vacated the premises after the landlord's early attempts to get rid of the rats failed. When the premises were vacated, they were not fit for use as a residence. Nor was there any assurance that the residence would become habitable within a reasonable time.] We affirm the judgment for the plaintiff on the ground that there was a material breach of the implied warranty of habitability and fitness for the use intended which justified the plaintiff's rescinding the rental agreement and vacating the premises.]

Affirmed.

Note: *Lemle* was certainly not decided on behalf of low income tenants. Six bedrooms, six bathrooms, and a salt water swimming pool? Nor is the warranty of habitability tied to any housing code. The court in Hawaii, fully understanding the old common law, simply decides that that law is no longer appropriate in Hawaii.

The next case, *Javins,* was decided after Lemle, but became far more well-known, and is frequently considered to be the case which established the basic concept of a warranty of habitability.

## UNITED STATES COURT OF APPEALS, DISTRICT OF COLUMBIA CIRCUIT
## ETHEL JAVINS, APPELLANT,
## V.
## FIRST NATIONAL REALTY CORPORATION, APPELLEE

MAY 7, 1970

Opinion

J. SKELLY WRIGHT, Circuit Judge:

These cases present the question [whether housing code violations which arise during the term of a lease have any effect upon the tenant's obligation to pay rent.]

Because of the importance of the question presented, we granted appellants' petitions for leave to appeal. [We now reverse and [hold that a warranty of habitability, measured by the standards set out in the Housing Regulations for the District of Columbia, is implied by operation of law into leases of urban dwelling units covered by those Regulations and that breach of this warranty gives rise to the usual remedies for breach of contract.

The facts revealed by the record are simple. By separate written leases, each of the appellants rented an apartment in a three-building apartment complex in Northwest Washington known as Clifton Terrace. The landlord, First National Realty Corporation, filed separate actions in the Landlord and Tenant Branch of the Court of General Sessions on April 8, 1966, seeking possession on the ground that each of the appellants had defaulted in the payment of rent due for the month of April. The tenants, appellants here, admitted that they had not paid the landlord any rent for April. However, they alleged numerous violations of the Housing Regulations as an equitable defense.

Since, in traditional analysis, a lease was the conveyance of an interest in land, courts have usually utilized the special rules governing real property transactions to resolve controversies involving leases. The assumption of landlord-tenant law, derived from feudal property law, that a lease primarily conveyed to the tenant an interest in land may have been reasonable in a rural, agrarian society; it may continue to be reasonable in some leases involving farming or commercial land. In these cases, the value of the lease to the tenant is the land itself. But in the case of the modern apartment dweller, the value of the lease is that it gives him a place to live. When American city dwellers, both rich and poor, seek "shelter" today, they seek a well known package of goods and services — a package which includes not merely walls and ceilings, but also adequate heat, light and ventilation, serviceable plumbing facilities, secure windows and doors, proper sanitation, and proper maintenance. In our judgment the trend toward treating leases as contracts is wise and well considered. Our holding in this case reflects a belief that leases of urban dwelling units should be interpreted and construed like any other contract.

Modern contract law has recognized that the buyer of goods and services in an industrialized society must rely upon the skill and honesty of the supplier to assure that goods and services purchased are of adequate quality. In interpreting most contracts, courts have sought to protect the legitimate expectations of the buyer and have steadily widened the seller's responsibility for the quality of goods and services through implied warranties of fitness and merchantability. Thus without any special agreement a merchant will be held to warrant that his goods are fit for the ordinary purposes for which such goods are used and that they are at least of reasonably average quality. These implied warranties have become widely accepted and well established features of the common law, supported by the overwhelming body of case law.

Today most states, as well as the District of Columbia, have codified and enacted these warranties into statute, as to the sale of goods, in the Uniform Commercial Code.

For example, builders of new homes have recently been held liable to purchasers for improper construction on the ground that the builders had breached an implied warranty of fitness. *Carpenter v. Donohoe* (Colorado 1964) In other cases courts have held builders of new homes liable for breach of an implied warranty that all local building regulations had been complied with.

The Supreme Courts of at least two states, in recent and well reasoned opinions, have held landlords to implied warranties of quality in housing leases. *Lemle v. Breeden*, (Hawaii), and *Reste Realty Corp. v. Cooper*, (New Jersey). In our judgment, the old no-repair rule cannot coexist with the obligations imposed on the landlord by a typical modern housing code, and must be abandoned in favor of an implied warranty of habitability. In the District of Columbia, the standards of this warranty are set out in the Housing Regulations.

The common law rule absolving the lessor of all obligation to repair originated in the early Middle Ages. Such a rule was perhaps well suited to an agrarian economy; the land was more important than whatever small living structure was included in the leasehold, and the tenant farmer was fully capable of making repairs himself.

Court decisions in the late 1800's began to recognize that the factual assumptions of the common law were no longer accurate in some cases. For example, the common law, since it assumed that the land was the most important part of the leasehold, required a tenant to pay rent even if any building on the land was destroyed. Faced with such a rule and the ludicrous results it produced, in 1863 the New York Court of Appeals declined to hold that an upper story tenant was obliged to continue paying rent after his apartment building burned down. The court simply pointed out that the urban tenant had no interest in the land, only in the attached building.

Another line of cases created an exception to the no-repair rule for short term leases of furnished dwellings. (Ingalls v. Hobbs) The Massachusetts Supreme Judicial Court, a court not known for its willingness to depart from the common law, supported this exception, pointing out:

> "(A) different rule should apply to one who hires a furnished room, or a furnished house, for a few days, or a few weeks or months. Its fitness for immediate use of a particular kind, as indicated by its appointments, is a far more important element entering into the contract than when there is a mere lease of real estate. One who lets for a short term a house provided with all furnishings and appointments for immediate residence may be supposed to contract in reference to a well-understood purpose of the hirer to use it as a habitation. It would be unreasonable to hold, under such

circumstances, that the landlord does not impliedly agree that what he is letting is a house suitable for occupation in its condition at the time. "

Since a lease contract specifies a particular period of time during which the tenant has a right to use his apartment for shelter, he may legitimately expect that the apartment will be fit for habitation for the time period for which it is rented. The inequality in bargaining power between landlord and tenant has been well documented. Tenants have very little leverage to enforce demands for better housing. Various impediments to competition in the rental housing market, such as racial and class discrimination and standardized form leases, mean that landlords place tenants in a take it or leave it situation. The increasingly severe shortage of adequate housing further increases the landlord's bargaining power and escalates the need for maintaining and improving the existing stock. Finally, the findings by various studies of the social impact of bad housing has led to the realization that poor housing is detrimental to the whole society, not merely to the unlucky ones who must suffer the daily indignity of living in a slum.

Thus we are led by our inspection of the relevant legal principles and precedents to the conclusion that the old common law rule imposing an obligation upon the lessee to repair during the lease term was really never intended to apply to residential urban leaseholds. Contract principles established in other areas of the law provide a more rational framework for the apportionment of landlord-tenant responsibilities; they strongly suggest that a warranty of habitability be implied into all contracts for urban dwellings.

We believe, in any event, that the District's housing code requires that a warranty of habitability be implied in the leases of all housing that it covers.

We follow the Illinois court in holding that the housing code must be read into housing contracts— a holding also required by the purposes and the structure of the code itself. Yet official enforcement of the housing code has been far from uniformly effective. Innumerable studies have documented the desperate condition of rental housing in the District of Columbia and in the nation. The duties imposed by the Housing Regulations may not be waived or shifted by agreement if the Regulations specifically place the duty upon the lessor.

In the present cases, the landlord sued for possession for nonpayment of rent. Under contract principles, however, the tenant's obligation to pay rent is dependent upon the landlord's performance of his obligations, including his warranty to maintain the premises in habitable condition. In order to determine whether any rent is owed to the landlord, the tenants must be given an opportunity to prove the housing code violations alleged as breach of the landlord's warranty. We agree with the

District of Columbia Court of Appeals that the tenant's private rights do not depend on official inspection or official finding of violation by the city government. At trial, the finder of fact must make two findings: (1) whether the alleged violations existed during the period for which past due rent is claimed, and (2) what portion, if any or all, of the tenant's obligation to pay rent was suspended by the landlord's breach. If no part of the tenant's rental obligation is found to have been suspended, then a judgment for possession may issue forthwith. On the other hand, if the jury determines that the entire rental obligation has been extinguished by the landlord's total breach, then the action for possession on the ground of nonpayment must fail. As soon as the landlord made the necessary repairs rent would again become due. The landlord is free to seek eviction at the terminations of the lease or on any other legal ground.

The jury may find that part of the tenant's rental obligation has been suspended but that part of the unpaid back rent is indeed owed to the landlord. In these circumstances, no judgment for possession should issue if the tenant agrees to pay the partial rent found to be due. If the tenant refuses to pay the partial amount, a judgment for possession may then be entered.

Appellants in the present cases offered to pay rent into the registry of the court during the present action. We think this is an excellent protective procedure. If the tenant defends against an action for possession on the basis of breach of the landlord's warranty of habitability, the trial court may require the tenant to make future rent payments into the registry of the court as they become due; such a procedure would be appropriate only while the tenant remains in possession. The escrowed money will, however, represent rent for the period between the time the landlord files suit and the time the case comes to trial. In the normal course of litigation, the only factual question at trial would be the condition of the apartment during the time the landlord alleged rent was due and not paid.

As a general rule, the escrowed money should be apportioned between the landlord and the tenant after trial on the basis of the finding of rent actually due for the period at issue in the suit. To insure fair apportionment, however, we think either party should be permitted to amend its complaint or answer at any time before trial, to allege a change in the condition of the apartment. In this event, the finder of fact should make a separate finding as to the condition of the apartment at the time at which the amendment was filed. This new finding will have no effect upon the original action; it will only affect the distribution of the escrowed rent paid after the filing of the amendment.

The judgment of the District of Columbia Court of Appeals is reversed and the cases are remanded for further proceedings consistent with this opinion.

So ordered.

## 2. Right to Evict

After a tenant has reported housing code violations, or has tried to make the landlord make necessary repairs, replace burned out light bulbs in the hallways or repair non-working elevators, the landlord might, understandably, be tempted to try to get rid of that tenant. Once that tenant has been evicted, other tenants in the building are less likely to cause problems by trying to make the landlord comply with the landlord's duties of maintenance and repair. Since most urban leases start as month-to-month periodic tenancies, or will have become month-to-month periodic tenancies after the first year, it would not be the least bit difficult for a landlord simply to notify a troublesome tenant that the lease would terminate at the end of the next month – giving whatever notice is required by the applicable local statute.

The following case, *Edwards v. Habib*, decided by Judge Skelly Wright two years before he decided *Javins*, tried to set the standards to prevent such retaliatory evictions.

## UNITED STATES COURT OF APPEALS DISTRICT OF COLUMBIA CIRCUIT
### YVONNE C. EDWARDS, APPELLANT,
### V.
### NATHAN HABIB, APPELLEE.

MAY 17, 1968

**Opinion**

J. SKELLY WRIGHT, Circuit Judge:

In March 1965 the appellant, Mrs. Yvonne Edwards, rented housing property from the appellee, Nathan Habib, on a month-to-month basis. Shortly thereafter she complained to the Department of Licenses and Inspections of sanitary code violations which her landlord had failed to remedy. In the course of the ensuing inspection, more than 40 such violations were discovered which the Department ordered the landlord to correct. Habib then gave Mrs. Edwards a 30-day statutory notice to vacate and obtained a default judgment for possession of the premises. Mrs. Edwards promptly moved to reopen this judgment, alleging as a defense that the notice to quit was given in retaliation for her complaints to the housing authorities. Judge Greene, sitting on motions in the Court of General Sessions, set aside the default judgment and, in a very thoughtful opinion, concluded that a retaliatory motive, if proved, would constitute a defense to the action for possession. At the trial itself, however, a different judge apparently deemed evidence of retaliatory motive irrelevant and directed a verdict for the landlord.

Mrs. Edwards then appealed to this court for a stay pending her appeal to the District of Columbia Court of Appeals, and on December 3, 1965, we granted the stay, provided only that Mrs. Edwards continue to pay her rent. She then appealed to the DCCA, which affirmed the judgment of the trial court. In reaching its decision the DCCA relied on a series of its earlier decisions holding that a private landlord was not required, under the District of Columbia Code, to give a reason for evicting a month-to-month tenant and was free to do so for any reason or for no reason at all. The court acknowledged that the landlord's right to terminate a tenancy is not absolute, but felt that any limitation on his prerogative had to be based on specific statutes or very special circumstances. Here, the court concluded, the tenant's right to report violations of law and to petition for redress of grievances was not protected by specific legislation and any change in the relative rights of tenants and landlords should be undertaken by the legislature, not the courts. We granted appellant leave to appeal that decision to this court. We hold that the promulgation of the housing code by the District of Columbia Commissioners at the direction of Congress impliedly effected just such a change in the relative rights of landlords and tenants and that proof of a retaliatory motive does constitute a defense to an action of eviction. Accordingly, we reverse the decision of the DCCA with directions that it remand to the Court of General Sessions for a new trial where Mrs. Edwards will be permitted to try to prove to a jury that her landlord who seeks to evict her harbors a retaliatory intent.

## I.

Appellant argues first that to evict her because she has reported violations of the law to the housing authorities would abridge her First Amendment rights to report violations of law and to petition the government for redress of grievances. But while it is clear beyond peradventure that the making of such complaints is at the core of protected First Amendment speech, and that punishment, in the form of eviction, if imposed by the state would unconstitutionally abridge First Amendment rights, it is equally clear that these rights are rights against government, not private parties.

There can now be no doubt that the application by the judiciary of the state's common law, even in a lawsuit between private parties, may constitute state action which must conform to the constitutional strictures which constrain the government.

This may be so even where the court is simply enforcing a privately negotiated contract. The central case is, of course, *Shelley v. Kraemer*, where the Court ruled that judicial enforcement of private agreements containing restrictive covenants against selling to Negroes violated the Fourteenth Amendment's command that "no State shall deny to any person within its jurisdiction the equal protection of the laws." But the contours of *Shelley* remain undefined and it is uncertain just how far its reasoning extends.

## II.

Appellant argues that, even if Shelley and the concept of "state action" are interpreted narrowly, and if the judicial implementation of the D.C. Code to effect a retaliatory eviction does not violate her First Amendment rights, her eviction would be unconstitutional nonetheless because the right to petition the government and to report violations of law is constitutionally protected against private as well as governmental interference. There is strong support for this position. In *Crandall v. State of Nevada*, (1868), decided before the Fourteenth Amendment was enacted, the Court struck down Nevada's one-dollar tax on anyone leaving the state in part because the Court felt that such a tax might infringe the individual's right to travel to Washington to participate in, and seek redress from, the government.

## III.

But we need not decide whether judicial recognition of this constitutional defense is constitutionally compelled.

It is true that under specific statutory provisions, in making his affirmative case for possession, a landlord need only show that his tenant has been given the 30-day statutory notice, and he need not assign any reason for evicting a tenant at the end of the lease. But while the landlord may evict for any legal reason or for no reason at all, he is not, we hold, free to evict in retaliation for his tenant's report of housing code violations to the authorities. As a matter of statutory construction and for reasons of public policy, such an eviction cannot be permitted.

The housing and sanitary codes, especially in light of Congress' explicit direction for their enactment, indicate a strong and pervasive congressional concern to secure for the city's slum dwellers decent, or at least safe and sanitary, places to live. Effective implementation and enforcement of the codes obviously depend in part on private initiative in the reporting of violations. For fiscal year 1966 nearly a third of the cases handled by the Department arose from private complaints. To permit retaliatory evictions, then, would clearly frustrate the effectiveness of the housing code as a means of upgrading the quality of housing in Washington.⟩

As judges, "we cannot shut our eyes to matters of public notoriety and general cognizance. When we take our seats on the bench we are not struck with blindness, and forbidden to know as judges what we see as men." *Ho Ah Kow v. Nunan*, (1879). In trying to effect the will of Congress and as a court of equity we have the responsibility to consider the social context in which our decisions will have operational effect. In light of the appalling condition and shortage of housing in Washington, the expense of moving, the inequality of bargaining power between tenant and landlord, and the social and economic importance of assuring at least minimum standards in housing conditions, we do not hesitate to declare that retaliatory eviction cannot be tolerated. There can be no doubt that the slum dweller, even though his home be marred by housing code violations, will pause long before he complains of them if he fears eviction as a consequence. ⌈Hence an eviction under the circumstances of this case would not only punish appellant for making a complaint which she had a constitutional right to make, a result which we would not impute to the will of Congress simply on the basis of an essentially procedural enactment, but also would stand as a warning to others that they dare not be so bold, a result which, from the authorization of the housing code, we think Congress affirmatively sought to avoid.⌉

⌈The notion that the effectiveness of remedial legislation will be inhibited if those reporting violations of it can legally be intimidated is so fundamental that a presumption against the legality of such intimidation can be inferred as inherent in the legislation even if it is not expressed in the statute itself.⌉

The proper balance can only be struck by interpreting 45 D.C. Code §§ 902 and 910 as inapplicable where the court's aid is invoked to effect an eviction in retaliation for reporting housing code violations.

This is not, of course, to say that even if the tenant can prove a retaliatory purpose she is entitled to remain in possession in perpetuity. If this illegal purpose is dissipated, the landlord can, in the absence of legislation or a binding contract, evict his tenants or raise their rents for economic or other legitimate reasons, or even for no reason at all. The question of permissible or impermissible purpose is one of fact for the court or jury, and while such a determination is not easy, it is not significantly different from problems with which the courts must deal in a host of other contexts, such as when they must decide whether the employer who discharges a worker has committed an unfair labor practice because he has done so on account of the employee's union activities. There is no reason why similar factual judgments cannot be made by courts and juries in the context of economic retaliation (against tenants by landlords) for providing information to the government.

Reversed and remanded.

Note: Now for a more recent eviction case, decided by the United States Supreme Court in 2002.

## SUPREME COURT OF THE UNITED STATES
## DEPARTMENT OF HOUSING AND URBAN DEVELOPMENT,
## & OAKLAND HOUSING AUTHORITY, ET AL., PETITIONERS
## V.
## PEARLIE RUCKER ET AL., RESPONDENTS

MARCH 26, 2002

OPINION BY: REHNQUIST

With drug dealers "increasingly imposing a reign of terror on public and other federally assisted low-income housing tenants," Congress passed the Anti-Drug Abuse Act of 1988. The Act, as later amended, provides that each "public housing agency shall utilize leases which provide that any criminal activity that threatens the health, safety, or right to peaceful enjoyment of the premises by other tenants or any drug-related criminal activity on or off such premises, engaged in by a public housing tenant, any member of the tenant's household, or any guest or other person under the tenant's control, shall be cause for termination of tenancy." 42 U.S.C. § 1437d (*l*)(6). Petitioners say that this statute requires lease terms that allow a local public housing authority to evict a tenant when a member of the tenant's household or a guest engages in drug-related criminal activity, regardless of whether the tenant knew, or had reason to know, of that activity. Respondents say it does not. We agree with petitioners.

Respondents are four public housing tenants of the Oakland Housing Authority (OHA). Paragraph 9(m) of respondents' leases, tracking the language of § 1437d(*l*) (6), obligates the tenants to "assure that the tenant, any member of the household, a guest, or another person under the tenant's control, shall not engage in any drug-related criminal activity on or near the premises." Respondents also signed an agreement stating that the tenant "understands that if I or any member of my household or guests should violate this lease provision, my tenancy may be terminated and I may be evicted."

In late 1997 and early 1998, OHA instituted eviction proceedings in state court against respondents, alleging violations of this lease provision. The complaint alleged: (1) that the respective grandsons of respondents William Lee and Barbara Hill, both of whom were listed as residents on the leases, were caught in the apartment complex parking lot smoking marijuana; (2) that the daughter of respondent Pearlie Rucker, who resides with her and is listed on the lease as a resident, was found with cocaine and a crack cocaine pipe three blocks from Rucker's apartment, [in February 1998, OHA dismissed the unlawful detainer action against Rucker, after her daughter was incarcerated, and thus no longer posed a threat to other tenants]; and (3) that on three instances within a 2-month period, respondent Herman Walker's caregiver and two others were found with cocaine in Walker's apartment. OHA had issued Walker notices of a lease violation on the first two occasions, before initiating the eviction action after the third violation.

United States Department of Housing and Urban Development (HUD) regulations administering § 1437d($l$)(6) require lease terms authorizing evictions in these circumstances. The HUD regulations closely track the statutory language, and provide that "in deciding to evict for criminal activity, the public housing authority shall have discretion to consider all of the circumstances of the case." The agency made clear that local public housing authorities' discretion to evict for drug-related activity includes those situations in which "the tenant did not know, could not foresee, or could not control behavior by other occupants of the unit."

After OHA initiated the eviction proceedings in state court, respondents commenced actions against HUD, OHA, and OHA's director in United States District Court. They challenged HUD's interpretation of the statute under the Administrative Procedure Act, arguing that 42 U.S.C. § 1437d($l$)(6) does not require lease terms authorizing the eviction of so-called "innocent" tenants, and, in the alternative, that if it does, then the statute is unconstitutional. The District Court issued a preliminary injunction, enjoining OHA from "terminating the leases of tenants pursuant to paragraph 9(m) of the ' Tenant Lease' for drug-related criminal activity that does not occur within the tenant's apartment unit when the tenant did not know of and had no reason to know of, the drug-related criminal activity."

A panel of the Court of Appeals reversed. An en banc panel of the Court of Appeals reversed and affirmed the District Court's grant of the preliminary injunction.

We granted certiorari, and now reverse, holding that 42 U.S.C. § 1437d($l$)(6) unambiguously requires lease terms that vest local public housing authorities with the discretion to evict tenants for the drug-related activity of household members and guests whether or not the tenant knew, or should have known, about the activity.

That this is so seems evident from the plain language of the statute. It provides that "each public housing authority shall utilize leases which provide that any drug-related criminal activity on or off such premises, engaged in by a public housing tenant, any member of the tenant's household, or any guest or other person under the tenant's control, shall be cause for termination of tenancy." Congress' decision not to impose any qualification in the statute, combined with its use of the term "any" to modify "drug-related criminal activity," precludes any knowledge requirement. As we have explained, "the word 'any' has an expansive meaning, that is, 'one or some indiscriminately of whatever kind.'" Thus, *any* drug-related activity engaged in by the specified persons is grounds for termination, not just drug-related activity that the tenant knew, or should have known, about.

The en banc Court of Appeals also thought it possible that "under the tenant's control" modifies not just "other person," but also "member of the tenant's household" and "guest." The court ultimately adopted this reading, concluding that the statute prohibits eviction where the tenant "for a lack of knowledge or other reason, could not realistically exercise control over the conduct of a household member or guest." But this interpretation runs counter to basic rules of grammar. The disjunctive "or" means that the qualification applies only to "other person." Indeed, the view that "under the tenant's control" modifies everything coming before it in the sentence would result in the nonsensical reading that the statute applies to "a public housing tenant under the tenant's control." HUD offers a convincing explanation for the grammatical imperative that "under the tenant's control" modifies only "other person." According to HUD by "control," the statute means control in the sense that the tenant has permitted access to the premises. Implicit in the terms "household member" or "guest" is that access to the premises has been granted by the tenant. Thus, the plain language of § 1437d(*l*)(6) requires leases that grant public housing authorities the discretion to terminate tenancy without regard to the tenant's knowledge of the drug-related criminal activity.

Comparing § 1437d(*l*)(6) to a related statutory provision reinforces the unambiguous text. The civil forfeiture statute that makes all leasehold interests subject to forfeiture when used to commit drug-related criminal activities expressly exempts tenants who had no knowledge of the activity: "No property shall be forfeited under this paragraph by reason of any act or omission established by that owner to have been committed or omitted without the knowledge or consent of the owner." Because this forfeiture provision was amended in the same Anti-Drug Abuse Act of 1988 that created 42 U.S.C. § 1437d(*l*)(6), the en banc Court of Appeals thought Congress "meant them to be read consistently" so that the knowledge requirement should be read into the eviction provision. But the two sections deal with distinctly different matters. The "innocent owner" defense for drug forfeiture cases was already in existence prior to 1988 as part of 21 U.S.C. § 881(a)(7). All that Congress did in the 1988 Act was to add leasehold interests to the property interests that might be forfeited under the drug statute. And if such a forfeiture action were to be brought against a leasehold interest, it would be subject to the pre-existing "innocent owner" defense. But 42 U.S.C. § 1437(d)(1)(6), with which we deal here, is a quite different measure. It is entirely reasonable to think that the Government, when seeking to transfer private property to itself in a forfeiture proceeding, should be subject to an "innocent owner defense," while it should not be when acting as a landlord in a public housing project. The forfeiture provision shows that Congress knew exactly how to provide an "innocent owner" defense. It did not provide one in § 1437d(*l*)(6).

The en banc Court of Appeals next resorted to legislative history. The Court of Appeals correctly recognized that reference to legislative history is inappropriate when the text of the statute is unambiguous. Given that the en banc Court of Appeals' finding of textual ambiguity is wrong, there is no need to consult legislative history.

Nor was the en banc Court of Appeals correct in concluding that this plain reading of the statute leads to absurd results. The statute does not *require* the eviction of any tenant who violated the lease provision. Instead, it entrusts that decision to the local public housing authorities, who are in the best position to take account of, among other things, the degree to which the housing project suffers from "rampant drug-related or violent crime, the seriousness of the offending action, and the extent to which the leaseholder has taken all reasonable steps to prevent or mitigate the offending action." It is not "absurd" that a local housing authority may sometimes evict a tenant who had no knowledge of the drug-related activity. Such "no-fault" eviction is a common "incident of tenant responsibility under normal landlord-tenant law and practice." Strict liability maximizes deterrence and eases enforcement difficulties.

And, of course, there is an obvious reason why Congress would have permitted local public housing authorities to conduct no-fault evictions: Regardless of knowledge, a tenant who "cannot control drug crime, or other criminal activities by a household member which threaten health or safety of other residents, is a threat to other residents and the project." With drugs leading to "murders, muggings, and other forms of violence against tenants," and to the "deterioration of the physical environment that requires substantial governmental expenditures," it was reasonable for Congress to permit no-fault evictions in order to "provide public and other federally assisted low-income housing that is decent, safe, and free from illegal drugs."

In another effort to avoid the plain meaning of the statute, the en banc Court of Appeals invoked the canon of constitutional avoidance. But that canon "has no application in the absence of statutory ambiguity." "Any other conclusion, while purporting to be an exercise in judicial restraint, would trench upon the legislative powers vested in Congress by Art. I, § 1, of the Constitution." There are, moreover, no "serious constitutional doubts" about Congress' affording local public housing authorities the discretion to conduct no-fault evictions for drug-related crime.

The en banc Court of Appeals held that HUD's interpretation "raises serious questions under the Due Process Clause of the Fourteenth Amendment," because it permits "tenants to be deprived of their property interest without any relationship to individual wrongdoing." But both of these cases deal with the acts of government as sovereign. The situation in the present cases is entirely different. The government is not attempting to criminally punish or civilly regulate respondents as members of the general populace. It is instead acting as a landlord of property that it owns, invoking a clause in a lease to which respondents have agreed and which Congress has expressly required.

The Court of Appeals sought to bolster its discussion of constitutional doubt by pointing to the fact that respondents have a property interest in their leasehold interest, citing *Greene* v. *Lindsey,* (1982). This is undoubtedly true, and *Greene* held that an effort to deprive a tenant of such a right without proper notice violated the Due Process Clause of the Fourteenth Amendment. But, in the present cases, such deprivation will occur in the state court where OHA brought the unlawful detainer action against respondents. There is no indication that notice has not been given by OHA in the past, or that it will not be given in the future. Any individual factual disputes about whether the lease provision was actually violated can, of course, be resolved in these proceedings.

The en banc Court of Appeals cited only the due process constitutional concern. Respondents raise two others: the First Amendment and the Excessive Fines Clause. The statute does not raise substantial First Amendment or Excessive Fines Clause concerns. *Lyng* v. *Automobile Workers,* (1988), forecloses respondents claim that the eviction of unknowing tenants violates the First Amendment guarantee of freedom of association. And termination of tenancy "is neither a cash nor an in-kind payment imposed by and payable to the government" and therefore is "not subject to analysis as an excessive fine."

We hold that Congress has directly spoken to the precise question at issue Section 1437d(*l*)(6) requires lease terms that give local public housing authorities the discretion to terminate the lease of a tenant when a member of the household or a guest engages in drug-related activity, regardless of whether the tenant knew, or should have known, of the drug-related activity.

Accordingly, the judgment of the Court of Appeals is reversed, and the cases are remanded for further proceedings consistent with this opinion.

It is so ordered.

Note: What happens to a tenant who is evicted from public housing? The options in an urban setting may be very grim. The tenant may then join the ranks of the homeless. For a moving description of the importance of public housing to those who live there, read the autobiography of U.S. Supreme Court Justice Sonia Sotomayor, who grew up in public housing, and was appointed to the U.S. Supreme Court on August 8, 2009, roughly nine years after *Department v. Rucker* was decided.

In *Department v. Rucker* no justice filed a dissenting opinion.

Might there be more effective ways of controlling drug use in public housing, rather than evicting Mr. and Mrs. Hill because their grandchildren were caught smoking pot in the parking lot, or evicting a disabled person because his *caregivers*, (not the tenant himself), were found using drugs in the disabled person's apartment? What impact might it have on families, if Mrs. Rucker was allowed to stay in her apartment, once her daughter had been sent to jail for using drugs *off the premises?*

Might Mrs. Hill be evicted if one of the bible study members she had allowed into her apartment was later found using drugs ten miles away?

Perhaps most importantly, does the *discretion* allowed the project manager, as to when a tenant will be evicted, and when a tenant will not be evicted for the same offense, create a serious opportunity for retaliatory eviction, or for other unfair treatment of tenants – when the manager threatens eviction unless the tenant does not cooperate in certain ways?

## 3. Duty of Maintenance

Extensive housing code provisions, and an implied warranty of habitability now make various maintenance duties the obligation of the landlord. But specific lease provisions may have the effect of shifting these duties – as illustrated by the following case. Before reading this case, do you know what an agreement to hold harmless actually means? Is that a common phrase among non-lawyers?

Remember, as attorney for a landlord or tenant it is your obligation to read and understand every word of a proposed lease, and to explain the basic provisions to your client in plain English. A good attorney is very unlikely to accept a proposed lease as written, but will instead make the changes necessary to protect his or her client. Just because it is a standard form is no reason that your client should accept the pre-printed provisions of a proposed lease.

# SUPREME COURT OF COLORADO
## CAROL CONSTABLE, D/B/A FLOWERS N' ROSES, PETITIONER
### V.
## NORTHGLENN, LLC, AND JAYLON INC., RESPONDENTS.

MARCH 21, 2011

Justice COATS delivered the Opinion of the Court.

Constable sought review of the court of appeals' judgment, reversing the district court's order of summary judgment which had been a judgment in her favor.

## I.

Northglenn, LLC, the owner of a shopping center, was named as a defendant in a lawsuit filed by a woman who slipped on ice in the shopping center's parking lot. Northglenn in turn filed a third-party complaint against Carol Constable, who leased commercial space from Northglenn and operated a flower shop in the shopping center, seeking indemnity on the basis of their lease agreement. Constable moved for a determination of law pursuant to C.R.C.P. 56(h), asserting that the indemnity provision of the lease was void as against public policy both because it failed to clearly express the intent of the parties to indemnify Northglenn for its own negligence and because it purported to relieve Northglenn of nondelegable duties, over which Northglenn had exclusive control.

The five-year lease between Constable and Northglenn contained a provision indicating that Constable agreed to indemnify Northglenn from liability for bodily injury or property damage sustained by anyone in "the Premises" or elsewhere in "the Center," as long as that person was present to visit Constable's shop or as a result of her business. The term "Premises" was defined as the floor area comprising Constable's shop, while the "Center" was defined as "that certain shopping center ... currently known as The Washington Center" wherein the Premises are located. An express exception to Constable's indemnity obligation indicated, however, that she would have "no obligation to indemnify Northglenn against harm resulting from Northglenn's own gross negligence or intentional torts."

The precise wording of the provision, in pertinent part, was as follows: "Tenant agrees to exonerate, hold harmless, protect and indemnity [sic] Landlord from and against any and all losses, damages, liability, claims, suits or actions, judgments, costs and expenses which may arise as a result of any bodily injury, personal injury, loss of life or property damage sustained during the term of this lease by any person or entity in the Premises, or elsewhere in the Center if present in order to visit the Premises, or as a result of Tenant's business...."

In a different section altogether, the lease agreement required Northglenn, as landlord, to keep the "Community Areas," defined to include all parking areas and driveways, in "reasonably good order, condition and repair." In that same provision, the lease specified, however, that Constable's "sole right and remedy" for Northglenn's failure to maintain the parking lot would be for Constable to cause the maintenance to be performed herself and to deduct the expenses of that maintenance from her rent.

The district court agreed with Constable that the lease provision was unenforceable, both because it purported to make her responsible for community areas left in the exclusive control of Northglenn and because it failed to clearly define the injuries that would trigger Constable's obligation to indemnify. On direct appeal by Northglenn, the court of appeals reversed. We granted Constable's petition for review.

## II.

An agreement to indemnify another is an agreement by one party to hold another harmless from such loss or damage as may be specified in their contract. While the public policy of this state precludes making an agreement to indemnify an actor for damages resulting from his own "intentional or willful wrongful acts," the same cannot be said of agreements to hold a party harmless for its own negligence.

Quite the contrary, an agreement purporting to indemnify a party against liability for its own negligence *will* be enforced as written as long as it contains a clear and unequivocal expression that the parties intended that result. Although an intent to indemnify another for its own negligence may not be a reasonable inference from less than clear contractual provisions, in a commercial setting involving sophisticated parties of generally equal bargaining power, a category in which we have in the past included lessor-lessee agreements between two businesses, courts justifiably have less concern about either contracts of adhesion or a failure of the parties to appreciate the import of unequivocal contractual terms. In such commercial settings, we have therefore been willing to find broad language of indemnity holding another harmless against liability generally, without any specific reference or limitation to its own negligence, to constitute an adequate expression of intent to indemnify to the extent otherwise permitted by public policy.

There can be no serious question but that the lease agreement at issue here contains a sufficiently clear expression of intent that Constable would indemnify

Northglenn against liability, including even liability for its own negligence. In the lease agreement, Constable "agrees to exonerate, hold harmless, protect and indemnify Northglenn from and against any and all losses, damages, liability, claims, suits or actions, judgments, costs and expenses" which may arise during the lease term due to any bodily injury sustained in the shopping center's community areas by persons present to "visit the Premises" or "as a result of Constable's business." As we have acknowledged in prior holdings, [this kind of "any and all" language obviously encompasses injuries resulting from Northglenn's own negligence.]

Unlike those cases in which the intent of the parties is articulated no more expressly than this, however, it is not necessary here to derive an intent to indemnify against injuries for which Northglenn was itself responsible from this broad language alone. The agreement's additional express exclusion of Northglenn's "own gross negligence or intentional torts" from Constable's indemnity obligation is an even clearer indication that in using broad language of liabilities generally the parties contemplated liability resulting from the fault of Northglenn, as well as anyone else. An exception for Northglenn's gross negligence would otherwise have been wholly unnecessary. And by excluding only injuries resulting from at least *gross* negligence on the part of Northglenn, the agreement plainly left within Constable's obligation to indemnify any harm resulting from Northglenn's own simple negligence. Unlike a number of other contracts we have nevertheless found to be adequately clear and unambiguous, the agreement in this case is expressly tailored to exclude from its broad indemnity obligation only that conduct for which an agreement to indemnify has arguably been held to violate public policy.

[To the extent that an agreement purporting to indemnify another against its own negligence must be declared void as against public policy whenever it lacks a sufficiently clear and unambiguous expression of the parties' intent to do so, the agreement in this case is therefore not void.] And even the district court did not conclude otherwise. Rather than finding ambiguity concerning the parties' intent that Northglenn be indemnified against harm resulting from its own negligence, the district court found only ambiguity concerning the particular patrons to be included within Constable's obligation and ambiguity concerning a possible right of apportionment among Northglenn's tenants. As the court of appeals recognized, however, while ambiguity in the phrases "visit the Premises" or "as a result of Tenant's business" may have significance for an attempt to enforce the indemnity provision against Constable with regard to any particular injured party, it could not affect the clarity of the agreement's expression of intent to indemnify Northglenn against its own negligence, with which public policy is concerned.

## III.

*→ Blue*

Notwithstanding our well-established precedent upholding, as consistent with public policy, agreements containing a clear and unambiguous expression of intent to indemnify a party against its own simple negligence, Constable urges us to hold that an indemnity agreement nevertheless contravenes public policy, and is therefore void, to the extent that it purports to indemnify another against liability for its own breach of a duty of reasonable care that is nondelegable. Constable's theory appears to be that indemnity against liability for violating a duty is tantamount to a delegation of that duty or, at least, that permitting a party to be indemnified against liability for the breach of a nondelegable duty contravenes the policy reasons for imposing the duty on that party in the first place. Constable asserts that, at least under these circumstances, the Premises Liability Act, § 13–21–115, C.R.S. (2010), imposes a nondelegable duty on Northglenn to use reasonable care in maintaining its parking lot for the protection of shopping center patrons, and therefore the indemnity provision of the lease agreement violates public policy.

An agreement to indemnify against liability for the breach of a duty is clearly not the equivalent of delegating that duty to another. An agreement to indemnify in no way purports to relieve the indemnitee of a duty owed to someone else, whether that duty is considered delegable or not. As in this case, an indemnitee remains liable to another for injury resulting from its breach of a duty owed to the injured party, and its indemnitor merely agrees to hold the indemnitee harmless from such loss or damage as may be specified in their contract. Significantly, an agreement to indemnify, by definition, does not (and could not, without becoming something more than an agreement to indemnify) purport to substitute an indemnitor for an indemnitee, or in any way diminish the indemnitee's obligation to a party it has injured, whether the indemnitor ultimately fulfills its agreement or not.

Whether, as a matter of public policy, one should nevertheless be precluded from insuring against its liability for the breach of a nondelegable duty involves virtually the same calculation already resolved with regard to indemnity generally. Since neither case involves shifting or relieving an indemnitee of its duty, the relevant question in both instances is whether the public policy of the jurisdiction reckons it socially beneficial to permit individual arrangements, or contracts, to insure against loss resulting from one's own fault. With regard to intentional torts or wrongs that can be characterized as willful, it is widely accepted, both within and outside this jurisdiction, that public policy does not permit insuring oneself against the ultimate legal consequences of one's conduct. With regard to acts of simple negligence, however, it is widely held to be socially beneficial to permit the allocation of costs and mitigation of risk through indemnity agreements, liability insurance, or otherwise.⌋

Strong policy considerations favoring freedom of contract generally permit business owners to allocate risk amongst themselves as they see fit. ⌈An indemnity agreement in a commercial lessor-lessee setting is a particularly appropriate way of allocating the risk of injury befalling patrons who are present for the benefit of a lessee, rather than the lessor, and of inducing the lessor to enter into the lease in the first place.⌋ It is often the case that such an allocation of the risk of injury, without regard to fault, serves as a constituent component of the consideration demanded for entering into a lease agreement.

The propriety of securing by contract indemnity against the financial burden resulting from breach of even a *nondelegable* duty is also widely acknowledged in other jurisdictions, in a variety of contexts.

Given the express language chosen by the parties in this case, we consider it unnecessary to further determine whether an agreement to indemnify against a risk that is wholly within the control of an indemnitee might alter the public policy calculus or evidence too great a disparity in the bargaining power of the parties. Despite Constable's characterization, we do not understand the lease provision requiring Northglenn to keep community areas, like the parking lot, in "good order, condition and repair" to have precluded Constable from inspecting and performing additional maintenance as she saw fit. This language makes all the more clear that nothing in the contract was intended to relieve Northglenn of its duty involving maintenance of the common areas, but it implies little about Constable's concomitant right, or obligation to invitees, with regard to common areas. Additional language of this provision of the agreement does, however, make clear that, as between the contracting parties, Northglenn would have the primary duty to maintain the common areas but that Constable's "sole right and remedy" for Northglenn's failure to do so would be to cause the maintenance to be performed herself and to deduct the expenses of such maintenance from the rent owed under the lease.

Because the agreement between the parties does not purport to limit Constable's right to ensure that the community areas remained in a safe condition, and in fact appears to contemplate her obligation to do so, we need not consider whether a complete lack of control over affected areas might, under some set of circumstances, also render an indemnity provision void as against public policy.

## IV.

Because the language of the indemnity provision clearly and unequivocally expresses the parties' intent that Constable indemnify Northglenn for injuries or losses suffered by her customers in the shopping center's parking lot, including even injuries resulting from Northglenn's own negligence, and because it does not contravene public policy by purporting to delegate a duty made nondelegable by statute, the judgment of the court of appeals is affirmed.

Affirmed.

## 4. Return of the Security Deposit

Normally, when a tenant signs a lease the tenant will be required to give the landlord about one month's rent as a security deposit – to be sure that the tenant doesn't just skip out without paying the last month's rent, and to give the landlord some financial protection in case the tenant causes damage to the premises. In the past, however, there have been widespread problems when the landlord, without justification, simply refused to return the security deposit to the tenant at the end of the lease. The tenant might be in the midst of moving to a new place, and simply might not have the time or the financial resources to sue the landlord for the return of a $500 security deposit, for example. So most states have enacted some sort of security deposit legislation.

In some states the landlord must put the security deposit into a separate account, and the tenant is entitled to whatever interest may be earned on that account. Other states simply make it much easier for the tenant to sue the landlord for return of the security deposit. It is crucial for the efficacy of any such statutes that there be some sort of provision that the landlord will have to pay the tenant's attorneys fees when a tenant brings successful litigation. Otherwise, it could happen that a tenant pays $7,000 in attorneys fees, to secure return of a $500 security deposit.

Note how the issue of attorneys fees is handled in the following case.

# SUPREME COURT OF COLORADO
## ALVIN MARTINEZ, PLAINTIFF-APPELLANT,
### V.
## JERRY STEINBAUM, D/B/A S.K. MANAGEMENT CO.,
### DEFENDANT-APPELLEE

FEBRUARY 2, 1981

OPINION BY: LOHR

Alvin Martinez (appellant) appeals from a judgment of the district court awarding him $60 on his claims for damages arising out of the alleged eviction of the appellant and his family from their unit in a Denver apartment complex. We affirm in part, reverse in part, and remand for further proceedings.]

The appellant entered into a month-to-month lease with Steinbaum (landlord) in September 1977. The rental was $165 due on the first of each month, and a damage deposit of $165 was required. The lease provided for automatic renewal unless the party desiring termination should give 30 days notice. The appellant and his family began occupancy sometime in September. On Saturday, November 12, the appellant told Robert Smith, one of the resident managers of the apartment complex, that he and his family were going to assist a relative in moving to Montana. He indicated that he would be back by the following Tuesday. The rent for November had been paid.

The appellant did not return to his apartment in November. The rent for December came due but was not paid. On December 6, during the continuing absence of the appellant, the resident manager posted a notice on the appellant's apartment door requiring him either to pay the rent or quit the premises within three days. No payment or other response was forthcoming and on December 14 the landlord filed an action in county court under section 13-40-109, C.R.S. 1973, for unlawful detention in order to gain possession of the premises. Sometime on the morning of December 15 the sheriff served the appellant by posting the summons and complaint on the door of the apartment.

That afternoon Smith received a phone call from the appellant, who explained that he was stranded in Montana and was attempting to obtain funds to return to Denver. Neither party mentioned anything about rent. Smith did not tell the appellant about the proceedings commenced against him.

According to the appellant's testimony, he and his family had started to return to Denver shortly after arriving in Billings, Montana. However, a severe snow storm had forced their return to Billings. At that point the appellant did not have sufficient funds for another trip to Denver. Although the appellant attempted to procure the necessary money by appeal to relief agencies and temporary employment, as of December 15, the date of the call to Smith, the appellant had not yet obtained those funds.

On December 23 judgment for possession was entered by default in Denver county court. However, a writ of restitution was not issued until January 6, 1978. On December 27 Smith changed the lock on the apartment. At that time he noted that the appellant's belongings were undisturbed.

The appellant had left his car, a 1965 Oldsmobile, in the apartment parking lot. On December 15 Smith placed a notice on the car requiring that it be moved within 72 hours. This was not done, so Smith caused the car to be towed away and stored.

The appellant returned to Denver on January 7, 1978. Because the lock had been changed, he could not get into the apartment. Upon inquiring of Smith, the appellant was told that he had to pay in excess of $400, including rent for December and January, attorneys' fees, and other items, before he would be allowed to enter. After contacting one of the landlord's representatives in Denver, the appellant was told he could remove his possessions. The appellant and Smith then entered the apartment and discovered that it had been ransacked. A subsequent investigation revealed that many of the appellant's possessions had been stolen.

When the appellant attempted to obtain his car, he was told by the towing company that he would have to pay $60 storage fees and the towing charge. Lacking the money to pay these charges, he transferred ownership of the car to the towing company.

On January 20 the appellant moved to set aside the default judgment of December 23. The motion was granted and the appellant filed an answer and counterclaims, seeking damages in excess of $1,000. The counterclaims were for wrongful eviction, failure to account for the security deposit, wrongful towing of the appellant's car, damages for the belongings which had been stolen during his absence, and other associated matters. Because the relief sought was in excess of the county court's jurisdiction, the case was transferred to district court and consolidated with a case filed in the district court by the appellant against the landlord. In the district court case, the appellant asserted the same claims made by counterclaims in the county court case.

Prior to trial the appellant filed a motion to declare section 13-40-112, C.R.S. 1973, unconstitutional because it allows service in an unlawful detention action to be effected by the posting of notice on the premises. This motion was denied.

After the presentation of the appellant's case, the landlord moved to dismiss all the claims against him. The motion was granted with respect to the wrongful eviction and related claims, as well as to the claims for loss of belongings.

At the conclusion of the trial, judgment was entered for the appellant on only the wrongful towing claim. The value of the car was not awarded because the court found that the appellant had failed to mitigate his damages. No proof of the towing charge had been offered. Therefore, judgment was entered for the $60 storage charges.

Thereafter, on the appellant's motion, the trial court made written findings of fact and conclusions of law. These findings included (1) that the landlord had a right to conclude that the appellant had abandoned the premises and the Oldsmobile; (2) that the landlord had a right to apply the security deposit to the back rent; (3) that the landlord did not follow the proper procedure for having an abandoned car towed from private property; and (4) that the appellant's car was worth at least $60.

The appellant's motion for new trial was denied. He now appeals to this court.

I

The appellant first asserts as error the trial court's refusal to declare the statutory method of service in unlawful detention actions, section 13-40-112, C.R.S. 1973, unconstitutional on its face or as applied in this case. However, the trial court made a specific finding that the landlord had a right to conclude that the appellant had abandoned the apartment. If this finding is supported, the question of notice need not be reached, for a landlord properly can take possession of an abandoned apartment without resort to legal process.

Such a finding would also be conclusive of the claim for wrongful eviction. Because the appellant had voluntarily relinquished his possessory rights in the premises, even if the landlord's reentry had constituted an eviction, it would not have been wrongful.

Before a finding of abandonment can be made, two elements must be proved, the act of abandonment and an intent to relinquish the premises. The evidence used to prove intent to abandon may be circumstantial. Intent may be determined from the conduct of the parties.

In this case the appellant left his apartment, telling the resident manager that he would return in two or three days. It was almost eight weeks before the appellant actually returned. During that time the rent for December and January became due. The appellant did not pay the rent or give notice of termination. In the phone call of December 15 the appellant did not attempt to negotiate an arrangement for deferred payment of the rent in order to continue the lease in effect. Indeed, the question of rent was not even mentioned. The appellant testified that during the telephone call he inquired about his belongings and Smith told him they were locked up in the apartment. The appellant also testified that he told Smith he was making every effort to obtain money to return to Denver to see about his belongings. Smith could not remember that the subject of belongings was discussed, but did not deny that it was. It can be inferred from the record that the appellant intended to abandon the lease and that his concern was limited to the fate of his possessions.

The question of abandonment is one of fact. Therefore, a finding on that question may not be overturned if there is support for it in the record. We conclude that there is sufficient evidence to support the trial court's finding of abandonment.

## II.

The appellant next contends that the trial court erred in finding that he had failed to mitigate the damages caused by the wrongful towing of his car. We disagree.

The trial court stated in its findings of fact and conclusions of law that the landlord did not follow the proper procedure for having an abandoned car towed from private property. The trial court further concluded that the car was worth at least $60 (the storage charges) and awarded the appellant $60 in compensation for the landlord's wrongful act. No evidence was introduced concerning the towing charges. The appellant estimated the value of his car at $500. He claims that his financial predicament forced him to transfer ownership of the car to the towing company. Although the appellant testified that the towing company refused to extend the time for payment, there is no evidence that it had a right to demand title to the car for nonpayment. Moreover, the appellant testified that his Denver employer owed him $200 in wages. There is nothing in the record to indicate that this sum could not have been used to pay the towing and storage charges.

In *Valley Co. v. Weeks,* we stated: "The rule is well settled that one may not recover damages for an injury which he might by reasonable precautions or exertions have avoided. What constitutes a 'reasonable' precaution is for the trier of facts to determine upon the evidence."

We conclude that the record supports the trial court's conclusion that the appellant failed to mitigate the damages which resulted from the improper procedure employed by the landlord in causing the car to be towed away.

## III.

Finally, the appellant contends that the trial court's finding that the landlord properly could apply the $165 security deposit for rent owed was in error. We agree.

Section 38-12-103(1), C.R.S. 1973, expressly requires that, before a landlord can retain a tenant's security deposit, he must "provide the tenant with a written statement listing the exact reasons for the retention of any portion" of that deposit. Failure to provide such a statement within the statutory time limit works a "forfeiture of all the landlord's rights to withhold any portion of the security deposit." Compliance with section 38-12-103(1) may be achieved by mailing a statement to the tenant's last known address. In this case, however, there is no evidence in the record that such a statement was so mailed. The appellant testified that he received neither his deposit nor a statement of the charges. Although one of the resident managers, Judy Smith, testified that she prepared and sent a statement of the charges to the landlord's California office, there is no evidence in the record that the statement was subsequently sent by the California office to the tenant's last known address. The landlord therefore forfeited the deposit.

The landlord is not precluded from commencing an action for back rent. However, having failed to give the statutorily required statement of the reasons for retention of the security deposit, he simply may not use that deposit to satisfy his claim. No claim for back rent was pled in the instant case.

The appellant also has a right to treble damages for the amount of the forfeited deposit under section 38-12-103(3)(a), C.R.S. 1973.

Section 38-12-103(3)(a), C.R.S. 1973, provides:

> "(3)(a) The willful retention of a security deposit in violation of this section shall render a landlord liable for treble the amount of that portion of the security deposit wrongfully withheld from the tenant, together with reasonable attorneys' fees and court costs; except that the tenant has the obligation to give notice to the landlord of his intention to file legal proceedings a minimum of seven days prior to filing said action."

To support a treble damage award the retention of the appellant's security deposit must have been both "willful" and "wrongful." There is no dispute that the retention was willful, *i.e.*, deliberate. The landlord had the burden of proving that his withholding of the security deposit was not wrongful. Failure to return the deposit, coupled with failure to provide a tenant with the statutorily mandated written statement of reasons for the retention, make the withholding of a deposit wrongful. Having failed to prove that the required statement of reasons was mailed to the appellant, the landlord did not carry his burden of proof that the withholding of the security deposit was not wrongful. (Giving the required statement of reasons and listing the reasons for retention or partial retention will preclude a finding that the retention was wrongful, in the absence of bad faith).

The landlord did not raise any question about compliance with the seven-day notice requirement, and we do not consider that matter.

As an incident to the treble damages claim the appellant has the right to reasonable attorneys' fees. Attorneys' fees allowable include those incurred on appeal. A prevailing treble damage claimant is also entitled to court costs.

Because the trial court erred in holding that the landlord had not forfeited the security deposit, and because the withholding of that deposit was both willful and wrongful, we reverse this part of the judgment and remand the case to the district court for entry of an additional award of $495, (treble the $165 illegally withheld), in favor of the appellant and against the landlord, and for further proceedings to determine and award to the appellant reasonable attorneys' fees and court costs incident to the claim for treble damages. In all other respects the judgment of the district court is affirmed.

# CHAPTER EIGHTEEN

# ENVIRONMENTAL REGULATIONS – CERCLA

## INTRODUCTION

There are many federal statutes that are designed to protect the environment in various ways. Among them are the Clean Water Act and the Endangered Species Act discussed in *Defenders of Wildlife v. Bernal*, in Chapter 16. There are many other similar statutes, such as the Clean Air Act, the Protection of Migratory Game and Insectivorous Birds Act, various Migratory Bird Treaties, the Resource Conservation and Recovery Act, and many other statutes and treaties that would be covered in a course on Environmental Law.

For Property law, one of the environmental statutes that may have the most serious financial impact on a landowner is the Comprehensive Environmental Response, Compensation, and Liability Act of 1980, known as CERCLA, and various amendments thereto. Under CERCLA the current owner of land may be required to pay for removal of hazardous substances from the land, whether or not the current owner had anything to do with the hazardous substances being put on the land. The costs of cleanup under CERCLA may far exceed the original cost of the land, because there are lots of regulations and expenses involved with removal, as well as the basic problem of where to put the polluted soil once it has been removed from the site.

CERCLA is one reason that the purchaser of land, especially rural land, should have an environmental inspection made before purchasing the land. Farm land is no exception, because many chemicals have traditionally been used to increase production on farms. It is for that reason that the house and barn on a farm are sometimes referred to as "the center of death and destruction." When a farmer comes back from spraying some sort of pesticide on the crops, the farmer will usually rinse out his farm equipment near the house or barn – thus greatly increasing the concentration of pesticide on that part of the farm.

There may be other parts of rural land which for one reason or another have had extensive use of various chemicals over the years. Ariel photographs of most land in the US are available since about the 1940s. These photos may be very useful in letting a potential buyer notice that for a ten year period in the 1960s, for example, nothing seemed to be growing in one corner of the land. A more detailed investigation may then reveal that that corner had once been used as an informal dump, which has since been covered over with soil. Yet a wide assortment of chemicals listed on the CERCLA list of hazardous substances may still be present on the land – and may possibly be spreading to other parts of the land via underground plumes. Underground storage tanks are also notorious for eventually springing a leak, allowing pollution to spread, underground, to other parcels of land.

As more knowledge becomes available, more and more substances are added to the list of hazardous substances under 42 USC 9602, (Designation of Additional Hazardous Substances), and various other environmental statutes.

Thus, it may well be that when particular substances were put on the land they were not considered to be hazardous - but then ten or thirty years later they have been designated as hazardous. The person who owns the land when the substances are determined to be hazardous may be required to pay for the very expensive process of cleanup.

Before purchasing any piece of land, particularly rural land, it is important to check the current condition of the land. It is also important to do a title search – to see what sort of entity may have owned the land earlier. Some entities, such as paint factories, various processing plants, or gas stations are known to be particularly likely to have been polluters. And remember that pollution, like water, may move underground from one place to another.

CERCLA applies to "facilities," and the definition of a "facility" may surprise you. 42 USC 9601, (Sec. 101 of CERCLA), specifies that:

> The term "facility" means (A) any building, structure, installation, equipment, pipe or
> pipeline (including any pipe into a sewer or publicly owned treatment works), well,
> pit, pond, lagoon, impoundment, ditch, landfill, storage container, motor vehicle, roll-
> ing stock, or aircraft, or (B) any site or area where a hazardous substance has been
> deposited, stored, disposed of, or placed, or otherwise come to be located; but does not
> include any consumer product in consumer use or any vessel.

The following case, involving urban land, in the City of Chicago, illustrates a few of the issues involved with land ownership under CERCLA.

UNITED STATES COURT OF APPEALS,
SEVENTH CIRCUIT
UNITED STATES OF AMERICA,
PLAINTIFF–APPELLEE,
V.
CAPITAL TAX CORPORATION,
DEFENDANT–APPELLANT.

SEPTEMBER 19, 2008


**Opinion**


CUDAHY, Circuit Judge.

Capital Tax Corporation (Capital Tax) is an Illinois company that purchases distressed real estate properties and resells them for profit. At a Cook County scavenger sale in October 2001, Capital Tax successfully bid on tax certificates to a derelict paint factory on the south side of Chicago. Capital Tax claims that it then entered into an agreement to sell the property to a man named Mervyn Dukatt. Pursuant to this alleged contract, Capital Tax exercised its option on the tax deed and delivered possession of the property to Dukatt. Capital Tax retained legal title to the property, however, as security for the remainder of the purchase price. Dukatt never made another payment, leaving Capital Tax with title to an unwanted property.

Both the Chicago Department of the Environment (CDOE) and the Environmental Protection Agency (EPA) were called to the old paint factory after receiving complaints that toxic paint products were leaking out of the factory into nearby streets and sewers. The inspections revealed thousands of rusty and leaking barrels containing hazardous waste. The EPA ordered Capital Tax to dispose of the waste but Capital Tax refused; the EPA cleaned up the site itself. The Government then brought this suit under Section 107(a) of the Comprehensive Environmental Response, Compensation, and Liability Act of 1980 (CERCLA) for the response costs it incurred. The district court granted summary judgment in favor of the Government on both liability and damages. Capital Tax now appeals, raising two basic arguments. First, it claims that it is not liable under CERCLA because it is not the "owner" of the facility. Second, even if it is liable, Capital Tax claims that it is only responsible for the cleanup of the parcels it owned.

## I.

The hazardous waste site facility at issue in the present case is an old paint manufacturing facility located at 7411–7431 South Green Street in Chicago, Illinois. For many years, this facility was operated by the National Lacquer and Paint Company, Inc., which produced paint products and stored the chemicals and materials used to produce them. This facility, which we call the "National Lacquer site," consists of four two-story buildings, two one-story buildings and two yards; it is situated on one acre of land in a mixed industrial, commercial and residential area of Chicago. Although the site is now divided into seven parcels (Parcels 5, 6, 8, 9, 10, 11 and 12), it was historically operated as a single plant. When viewed on a map, the seven rectangular parcels are stacked neatly on top of one another. Each parcel is connected to the others by a fire door or passageway, and several of the parcels share common yards.

In December 1995, William Lerch and Steven Pedi, through their newly created company, National Lacquer Company (National Lacquer), purchased the assets of the old National Lacquer and Paint Company. From 1995 to 2002, National Lacquer reclaimed paint, manufactured paints and coatings, and performed furniture stripping operations at the site. The company used a number of different hazardous materials, which were stored all over the site. It is undisputed that hazardous materials leaked or were spilled onto the ground throughout this period. In January 1998, for example, the CDOE inspected the site and found "hundreds of rusty, damaged and leaking pails, cans and jars." Not only were these paint products spilling onto the floor, rainwater from a leaky roof mixed with the paint and flowed across the floor into drains and sewers and eventually into the street.

By 2001, National Lacquer had fallen behind on its property taxes, and Cook County made five of the seven parcels available for sale (Pedi retained title to Parcels 8 and 10). At tax scavenger sales, potential buyers bid on the delinquent taxes, and the winning bidder receives a tax certificate for the property. If the original owner fails to redeem the delinquent taxes within a statutory period, the tax sale bidder then has the right to petition for a tax deed to the property. Tax certificates do not pass title; they are similar to an option to later obtain title if the certificate holder chooses to exercise that option. Representatives of Capital Tax visited the National Lacquer site before the scavenger sale and conducted a limited inspection. While they were not able to enter the property, it was apparent to them that the property was a former paint factory. Capital Tax then successfully bid on the tax certificates.

After purchasing the tax certificates but before obtaining the tax deeds, Capital Tax claims that it struck a deal with Dukatt in which Capital Tax agreed to obtain the tax deeds to the property and to convey them to Dukatt in exchange for about

$25,000. No written agreement was ever made. Because Capital Tax did not typically obtain the tax deeds until they had a buyer, Dukatt gave Capital Tax a $15,000 check ostensibly as partial payment for the property. On October 30, 2001, Capital Tax obtained tax deeds for four of the parcels. On February 14, 2002, it obtained a tax deed for the fifth parcel. Capital Tax also obtained an order of eviction to secure possession of the site from its previous owner, Lerch. After that, Capital Tax had very little to do with the property.

Dukatt, however, was frequently at the site. He had the keys to the property and the office. Capital Tax deferred to him on all matters regarding the site. Dukatt hired workers who, over the course of two or three weeks, cut up and removed the paint machines that had been in the garage. They also prepared and replaced an overhead door and knocked down two walls. This work allegedly cost Dukatt $10,000. In April 2002, the CDOE responded to a call concerning a spill of hazardous materials at the site. It discovered that paint containers had recently been moved from parcel to parcel; trails of spilled product traced the movement of these substances. It is unclear whether it was Dukatt, Lerch or perhaps a third party who moved the containers. The CDOE, however, noted that Capital Tax had made little effort to secure the site and it issued Capital Tax a notice of violation for "allowing a spill of hazardous substances due to container movement at the Site." On July 23, 2003, the CDOE officially requested that Capital Tax clean up the site. Capital Tax refused. It later explained that it "didn't care" about the site because it considered it to be Dukatt's problem.

The CDOE referred the matter to the EPA. On July 31, 2003, the EPA conducted its own inspection of the site. The EPA found more than 10,000 containers of various sizes, including gallon drums, storage tanks, cylindrical mixing tanks, vats, buckets, compressed gas cylinders, laboratory jars and bottles—most of which contained hazardous substances. Many of the containers were unsealed, leaking or otherwise deteriorating. The EPA also found evidence of trespassing on the site. [Among other things, the inspectors found alcohol bottles, cans, children's toys, and a hypodermic needle.] On August 15, 2003, the EPA issued a Unilateral Administrative Order (UAO) demanding that Capital Tax clean its five parcels. Capital Tax did not comply. So, on October 6, 2003, the EPA removed the hazardous materials itself. The EPA also cleaned manholes and pits, excavated the top foot of storage yard soil, backfilled and planted the storage yard with grass. It sealed the tanks and pressure washed interior floors and walls to remove potential contamination.

The Government then filed suit against Capital Tax, Pedi and Lerch under CERCLA to recover the costs of the cleanup. The Government also sought civil penalties, and punitive damages, against Capital Tax for failing to comply with the UAOs. Capital Tax denied that it was liable under CERCLA, raising the "security interest" exemption and an "innocent landowner" defense. On April 11, 2006, the Government moved for partial summary judgment on liability, which the district court granted. On August 24, 2006, the Government moved for summary judgment on damages, which the district court also granted, finding Capital Tax jointly and severally liable to the Government for $2,681,337.79 in response costs. It also assessed civil penalties in the amount of $230,250.00.

## II.

[The first major issue here is Capital Tax's liability under § 107(a) of CERCLA for the response costs incurred by the Government in the cleanup of the National Lacquer site.] Under CERCLA the Government may order potentially responsible parties to clean up hazardous waste sites. Further, the Government is authorized to conduct its own cleanups of hazardous waste sites using the Hazardous Waste Superfund. The Government can then bring an action under § 107(a) to recover damages from potentially responsible parties] In either case, the "polluter pays."

[To establish liability under § 107(a), the Government must show that: (1) "the site in question is a 'facility' as defined in § 101(9); (2) the defendant is a responsible party under § 107(a); (3) a release or a threatened release of a hazardous substance has occurred; and (4) the release or threatened release has caused the plaintiff to incur response costs."] Capital Tax concedes three of these elements. The only element in issue here is the second element: [whether Capital Tax is a responsible party under § 107(a). ]

[CERCLA is strict liability statute. Liability is imposed when a party is found to have a statutorily defined "connection" with the facility; that connection makes the party responsible regardless of causation.] Section 107(a) lists four different categories of potentially responsible parties. [The only category at issue here is specified by § 107(a)(1), which makes the current "owner and operator of a facility" liable for cleanup costs.] The Government has not claimed in this court that Capital Tax "operated" the facility in any way. Thus, the Government's argument is that Capital Tax is liable for response costs simply because it is the current "owner" of the facility.

There is very little we can glean from the statute about the meaning of ownership. CERCLA defines "owner" as "any person owning" a facility. The circularity in the statutory language suggests that "the statutory terms have their ordinary meanings rather than unusual or technical meanings." The generality of the term "owner" also suggests that Congress intended us to turn to "common law analogies." Congress did state, however, that the definition of "owner does *not* include a person who, without participating in the management of a facility, holds indicia of ownership primarily to protect his security interest in the vessel or facility." A "security interest" is "a right under a mortgage, deed of trust, assignment, judgment lien, pledge, security agreement, factoring agreement, or lease and any other right accruing to a person to secure the repayment of money, the performance of a duty, or any other obligation by a nonaffiliated person." This has become known as the "security interest" exclusion, and the party seeking to assert it bears the burden of establishing it.

The Government claims that Capital Tax is the "owner" under § 107(a)(1) because it holds legal title to five of the seven parcels at the National Lacquer site. Capital Tax does not dispute that it has legal title to those parcels and thus holds "indicia of ownership." Capital Tax contends, however, that it sold the parcels to Dukatt. According to Capital Tax, it only holds legal title to the property as security for the balance of the purchase price under the contract.

The basic legal principle underlying Capital Tax's argument—that equitable ownership passed from Capital Tax to Dukatt when the land sale contract was executed—has a long history at common law. The rule in the vast majority of jurisdictions is that on entering into a contract for the purchase of land, the purchaser is the owner in equity of the land, and the seller holds legal title as security for payment of the purchase price. Perhaps Capital Tax's constant reference to the "security interest" exception has caused some confusion here, for Capital Tax is not a typical creditor. Capital Tax's argument would be more easily understood if it simply argued that it is the *former* owner of the facility—not the *current* owner—and thus not liable under § 107(a)(1). This, of course, is a classic "equitable conversion" argument.

The central question here is what role, if any, the doctrine of equitable conversion plays in the definition of ownership under CERCLA. As we have already explained, the statute gives little concrete guidance on the issue. Congress intended courts, in defining § 107(a)(1), to draw analogies to common law, and to the ordinary meaning of the term ownership. It is notable that two courts of appeals have held that public or quasi-public companies that hold legal title to property in order to secure the recoupment of development costs are not "owners" under CERCLA. More specifically, a number of district courts have applied the doctrine of equitable conversion in CERCLA cases, both under § 107(a)(1)'s "ownership" provision and under the "security interest" exclusion. Thus, it is difficult to dismiss Capital Tax's argument out of hand.

So we must determine whether, in applying the doctrine of equitable conversion in the CERCLA context, we should attempt to fashion our own federal rule or look to applicable Illinois law as the federal standard. There is no need to escalate the scope of the inquiry by attempting to apply a federal common law here; instead, we merely look to state law for guidance in interpreting the statute. Of course, federal law, as a formal matter, ultimately governs the definition of ownership under § 107(a). But this case presents a particularly strong case for the employment of relevant state law as the proper guide to the federal standard. Property relations have historically been governed by state law. When Congress instructed courts to look to the traditional, common-law meaning of ownership in interpreting CERCLA, it was certainly aware of this history. And Congress gave no indication that it intended to take a new course. The understanding that state law governs property and the expectations built around that understanding strongly suggest that the federal standard should be rooted in an adoption of state property law. This conclusion is bolstered by the fact that there is no practical alternative to this approach. To invent out of whole cloth a distinctly federal law of property would be inappropriate, if not impossible.

The Illinois doctrine of equitable conversion provides that a valid land sale agreement transfers equitable title to the purchaser. Thus, "when the owner enters into a valid and enforceable contract for the sale of realty, the seller continues to hold legal title, but in trust for the buyer; the buyer becomes the equitable owner and holds the purchase money in trust for the seller." But "the doctrine of equitable conversion does not apply where equitable considerations intervene or where the parties intend otherwise." In addition, in order to invoke the doctrine of equitable conversion, the party must show that "a valid and enforceable contract has been entered into." This presents an obstacle for Capital Tax because, under the Illinois Statute of Frauds, a valid contract for the sale of land must generally be in writing. Capital Tax has no such written agreement; it concedes that the contract was oral. Illinois courts, however, have also routinely recognized exceptions to the Statute of Frauds. The relevant exception here is part performance. Under Illinois law, a contract is taken outside the Statute of Frauds if the buyer makes whole or partial payment of the purchase price, takes possession of the property *and* makes substantial and lasting improvements to it. Further, the evidence must be "referable" to the contract—that is, it must actually suggest the existence of a sales agreement. If the actions that purport to show part performance are easily explained without reference to a contract, the Statute of Frauds is not satisfied. Appropriate parol evidence must leave "no reasonable doubt in the mind of the court" that a contract has been formed.

Capital Tax has presented some evidence to support each element of part performance—partial payment, possession and valuable improvements. But the probative value of the evidence is unclear. With respect to partial payment, Capital Tax asserts that Dukatt gave Capital Tax a check for $15,000. The check stated that is was for "taxes," which Capital Tax claims to be a reference to the "taxes" component of the purchase price. Still, there is no evidence that the check specifically refers to the National Lacquer site. Dukatt worked with the principals of Capital Tax on other deals and with other properties; the check could easily have referred to some other deal. Although it may very well display his signature, the check is actually not from Dukatt; it is from an entity called "Snowball's Plaza." Given these uncertainties, we find it perplexing that Capital Tax did not ask Dukatt at his deposition why he had written the check.

Capital Tax also asserts that Dukatt took possession of the property and did work on the garage. It is unclear whether this work would constitute "lasting and valuable" improvements under Illinois law. More importantly, again, we doubt whether this activity was actually "referable" to the contract. Dukatt was loosely affiliated with Capital Tax—a "friend" of the corporation—and, at times, he even represented himself to be "agent" of Capital Tax. Dukatt had frequent conversations with the principals of Capital Tax about the facility. Perhaps Dukatt, when he did work on the garage, was working under Capital Tax's direction. While we do not know the exact nature of the relationship between the parties, Dukatt's presence at the site does not necessarily imply that he was acting *as if* he owned the site.

The district court did not address these issues given its disposition of the case. From this record, it is difficult for us to determine whether Capital Tax had a valid and enforceable contract for the sale of land under Illinois law. If there is no valid contract, then Capital Tax is the "owner" under § 107(a)(1) and is liable under CERCLA. If there is a valid contract and if equitable conversion applies, Capital Tax is not the "owner" under § 107(a)(1) and is not liable under CERCLA. The case will likely turn on whether the facts show that Dukatt was, in fact, a bona fide buyer. Especially given the substantial liability in this case and the uncertainty surrounding many of the issues, it is not for us to resolve them in the first instance. We must remand to the district court to give fresh and full consideration to the question whether Capital Tax had an enforceable land sales contract under Illinois law and whether the doctrine of equitable conversion applies in this case.

## III.

We now consider Capital Tax's alternative argument that it should not be held jointly and severally liable for all the removal costs and instead be found liable for only a portion of those costs. Unlike the first issue, we can answer the divisibility question on the record before us because there are no substantial disagreements about the facts. Once a party is found to be liable under CERCLA, the party is jointly and severally liable for all of the EPA's response costs, "regardless of that party's relative fault." Courts, however, do recognize one judicially created exception to joint and several liability under § 107(a). If a liable party can establish that the harm is divisible—that is, that there is a reasonable means of apportioning the harm among the responsible parties—then that party is not subject to joint and several liability.]

[Divisibility is the exception, however, not the rule. Thus, the burden of establishing divisibility is on the defendant.]

One method of creating a reasonable estimate of damages is to show that the contamination at the facility is geographically divisible. A landowner can establish divisibility by "demonstrating a reasonable basis for concluding that a certain proportion of the contamination did not originate on the portion of the facility that the landowner owned." Typically, this will involve showing that the "site consists of non-contiguous areas of soil contamination." It is difficult to prove divisibility when the facility functioned as a "dynamic, unitary operation" in which materials were moved from location to location during the production process. Further, the "migratory potential" and "actual migration" of the resulting toxic substances can preclude a finding of divisibility. Commingling and cross-contamination will often indicate an indivisible facility.]

Capital Tax's argument that the harm is divisible in this case is based entirely on property lines. Capital Tax argues that it cannot be liable for the two parcels of land that it does not own. But the EPA has broad discretion in defining the boundaries of a particular facility, and the boundaries are normally based on the extent of the contamination. The boundaries of the facility do not necessarily reflect property boundaries, and liability can extend beyond what the defendants actually own. *See Burlington Northern,* (responsible party owned 19% of the facility); *United States v. Rohm & Haas Co.,* (responsible party owned 10% of the facility).

In the present case, contamination was found on almost every parcel of the facility. Further, all of these parcels are contiguous. Capital Tax's parcels are actually interspersed with Lerch's parcels. Parcels 8 and 10, which are owned by Lerch, formed the main mixing room and the pigment room. Parcel 9, which is owned by Capital Tax, contained the roller mill room and was situated right between Parcels 8 and 10. Doors connected the three parcels, and the roller mill room and the pigment room both emptied out onto the storage yard. Further, Capital Tax owned the parcel to the north of Parcels 8 and the parcel to the south of Parcel 10. The EPA's Site Sketch reveals that, while containers were found all over the premises, many were concentrated on these three parcels and in the storage yard shared by Capital Tax and Lerch.

When the factory was in operation, materials passed through all these rooms at some point in the production process—that is, it was a "dynamic, unitary operation." As the district court noted, Capital Tax's mistake is in attempting to apportion liability based on where the hazardous materials were located on the day they were removed. Those hazardous materials could easily have originated in another part of the plant. As in the game of "musical chairs," the fact that the chemicals came to rest in any particular place when production ended was largely happenstance. Thus, Capital Tax cannot show that the hazardous substances found just outside its property lines did not "originate" on its property.

More importantly, there is undisputed evidence that the products and chemicals continued to migrate between parcels after operations at the facility had ceased. Containers were deteriorating and leaking. Indeed, paint and other chemicals mixed with rain water from the leaking roof and were washed to other parts of the building and onto the streets. Chemicals would evaporate into the air, leaving resin that could easily travel to contiguous parcels. Further, it is undisputed that individuals were actually moving containers from parcel to parcel, spilling paint and other substances in the process. It is immaterial whether Capital Tax actually moved any of these containers because it failed to secure the premises from third parties and, in general, turned a blind eye to the property. Because we have commingling, cross-contamination and migration occurring on a site that formerly operated as a single, unitary operation, there is no basis for apportionment.

Finally, Capital Tax believes that the costs can be reasonably apportioned because the EPA tracked and documented all the containers that were removed from the site. We note that the relevant document does not appear to include the costs associated with cleaning the facility, excavating the contaminated ground or sealing off the tanks. Nor does it include travel costs, payroll costs, indirect costs, Department of Justice enforcement costs or interest. More importantly, the fact that containers were actually moved from parcel to parcel raises real doubts about the relevance of where all the containers of waste were on the date of removal. Put simply, a CERCLA owner may not move barrels of hazardous substances across property lines (or allow them to be so moved) in order to reduce its liability under CERCLA.

## IV.

Capital Tax also argues that the district judge erred in assessing costs and penalties based on the removal of waste from parcels 8 and 10. On August 15, 2003, the EPA issued a UAO directing Capital Tax to "perform removal action within the Site which is owned by Respondent or to which Respondent has moved hazardous wastes." Capital Tax failed to comply with this order. CERCLA provides that any person "who, without sufficient cause, willfully violates, or fails or refuses to comply with, any order of the President under subsection (a) of this Section may be fined not more than $27,500 for each day in which such violation occurs or such failure to comply continues." A "sufficient cause" for failing to comply is a reasonable belief that one is not liable under CERCLA. Because we are remanding this case to district court on the issue of liability, we find it appropriate to vacate the award of damages. The district court may reassess the issue of penalties, if it deems that action necessary, after resolving the liability issue.

## V.

For the reasons discussed above, the decision of the district court is VACATED and the case REMANDED for further proceedings in accord with this opinion.

CPSIA information can be obtained
at www.ICGtesting.com
Printed in the USA
FSHW022042221121
86362FS